D1362425

Fifth Edition

PERSUASION AND INFLUENCE IN AMERICAN LIFE

Gary C. Woodward
College of New Jersey

Robert E. Denton, Jr.
Virginia Polytechnic Institute and State University

WAVELAND

PRESS, INC.

Long Grove, Illinois

For information about this book, contact:
Waveland Press, Inc.
4180 IL Route 83, Suite 101
Long Grove, IL 60047-9580
(847) 634-0081
info@waveland.com
www.waveland.com

We dedicate this book to:

Allen and Nellie Woodward, who have always
understood how to mix persuasion with compassion

and

To the memory of Robert Denton's grandparents,
Margie and Bobbie Denton and Walter and Lillie Medlin,
who were always grandteachers,
grandsupporters, and grandpeople.

Contents

Preface to the Fifth Edition   xiii

1   Persuasion and Influence: An Introduction   1
The Necessity of Persuasion   3
Persuasion Defined   4
Four Cases of Persuasion   7
   Doubt and Influence in the Jury Room   7
   Advocating Dangerous Forms of Religion   8
   Persuasion and the Politics of Peace   10
   Persuasion in Everyday Life   12
What These Cases Suggest   13
   Persuasion Is About Sources *and* Messages   13
   Measure Persuasion by Its Effects on Others   15
   Even Minimal Effects Are Important   15
   Personal and Public Forms of Persuasion Are Similar   16
   Persuasion Provokes a Love-Hate Relationship   16
   Persuasion Outcomes Are Unpredictable   17
Three Types of Communication   18
   Pure Information   18
   Pure Expression   18
   Pure Persuasion   19
Summary   20
   Questions and Projects for Further Study   20
   Additional Reading   21
   Notes   22

PART I
ORIGINS OF PERSUASIVE PRACTICE   25
▲

2   The Advocate in an Open Society   **27**

Freedom of Expression and Its Limits   28
   Suppressing Advocacy in a One-Party State   28
   The Value of Public Opinion   32
   Individual Freedom versus Factions   34

The Nature of Open and Closed Societies   36
   The Technological Push toward Openness   37
   The Marketplace Theory   38

How Open Is American Society?   38
   Governmental Controls   38
   Corporate Controls   42
   Free Speech versus True Access   45

Summary   46
   Questions and Projects for Further Study   46
   Additional Reading   47
   Notes   48

3   The Advocate and the Management of Symbols   **51**

The Nature of Language   53
   Signs   54
   Symbols   54
   Meaning   55
   Functions of Language   58

Language, Interaction, and Reality   62
   The Creation of Reality through Interaction   62
   Self as a Product of Interaction with Others   63
   Society as a Product of Interaction with Others   63

Political Uses of Language   64
   Functions of Political Language   65
   Strategic Uses of Political Language   68
   Common Political Language Devices   71

The Changing Nature of Public and Political Discourse   75

Summary   78
   Questions and Projects for Further Study   78
   Additional Reading   79
   Notes   79

PART II
FOUR PERSPECTIVES ON THE NATURE OF PERSUASION 83

▲

4 Persuasion and Reasoning   85

Understanding Practical Arguments   87
  Analytic Arguments and Practical Enthymemes   87
  Demonstration and Argumentation   90
  Factual and Judgmental Claims   91
  Implied and Stated Components of Arguments   92
  Reasoning to Discover and to Defend   94
  Finding Good Reasons for Claims   94
  A False Distinction: Logic or Emotion   95

Common Forms of Defective Reasoning   96
  Ad Hominem   97
  False Cause   98
  Non Sequitur   98
  Circular Argument   99
  Excessive Dependence on Authority   100

How Persuasion and Logical Argumentation Differ   100
  Denial Often Defeats Reasoning   100
  Persuasion's Self-Interest and Argumentation's Public Interest   101

Summary   103
  Questions and Projects for Further Study   104
  Additional Reading   104
  Notes   105

5 Credibility and Authority   107

The Multidimensional Aspects of Authority   109

The Three Meanings of Credibility   110
  Ethos and the Idea of Good Character   110
  The Rational/Legal Ideal of Credibility   112
  Source Credibility as Believability   114
  Credibility Reconsidered   117

Strategic Dimensions of Credibility   118
  Legitimation   118
  Mystification   121
  Source/Placebo Suggestion   121
  Authoritarianism and Acquiescence   122

Summary   125
  Questions and Projects for Further Study   125
  Additional Reading   127
  Notes   127

6   The Psychology of Persuasion   131

Logic and Rationality   132

Components in Attitude Change   133
    Beliefs   133
    Attitudes   135
    Values   140

Behavioral Theories of Persuasion   142
    Stimulus-Response Theory   142
    Reinforcement Theory   144
    Attribution Theory   145
    Consistency Theories   147
    Social Judgment Theory   151
    Long-Term Attitude Change   152
    Elaboration Likelihood Theory   153
    Theory of Reasoned Action   156

Summary   158
    Questions and Projects for Further Study   159
    Additional Reading   159
    Notes   159

7   Persuasion, Audiences, and Social Learning   163

The Idea of an Audience   164

A Conceptual Baseline: Social Learning   167

The Audience Analysis Process   168
    Wiring the Audience: Dial Group Testing   168
    The Principle of Identification   170
    Universal Commonplaces   171
    Audience-Specific Norms   172

Advocates, Messages, and Audiences   174
    Believing in Our Words   175
    High Credibility/High Agreement Persuasion   176
    High Credibility/Low Agreement Persuasion   177
    Low Credibility/High Agreement Persuasion   178
    Low Credibility/Low Agreement Persuasion   179

Unintended Audiences   180

Summary: The Ethics of Adaptation   181
    Questions and Projects for Further Study   182
    Additional Reading   183
    Notes   184

PART III
THE CONTEXTS OF PERSUASION   187

▲

8 Interpersonal Persuasion   189

Dimensions of Interpersonal Communication   191
Variables of Interpersonal Persuasion   192
    Verbal Characteristics   192
    Nonverbal Characteristics   193
    Power and Control   195
    Compliance-Seeking Messages   197
    Conflict   199
    Gender Differences   204
    Culture and Diversity   207
    Leadership   208
Contexts of Interpersonal Persuasion   210
    Organizations   210
    Sales   216
    Interviews   219
Summary   221
    Questions and Projects for Further Study   222
    Additional Reading   223
    Notes   223

9 Public and Mass Persuasion   227

Public Communication and Persuasion   228
    Characteristics of Public Communication   229
    Public Opinion and Persuasion   230
Persuasive Campaigns   232
    Product or Commercial Campaigns   232
    Public Relations Campaigns   233
    Political Campaigns   234
    Issue Campaigns   237
    Social Movements   248
Campaign Implementation   254
Summary   257
    Questions and Projects for Further Study   257
    Additional Reading   258
    Notes   258

10 Advertising as Persuasion   261

What Is Advertising?   264

The Evolution of Advertising from a Communication Perspective   266

The Role of Psychology in Advertising   270

How Advertising Works   273
    High Involvement—Thinking   275
    High Involvement—Feeling   276
    Low Involvement—Thinking   276
    Low Involvement—Feeling   277

Advertising as Myth   280

Common Advertising Appeals   283
    Power   283
    Meaning   283
    Norms   284
    Isolation   285
    Self-Esteem   285
    Guilt   286
    Fear   286
    Sex   287

How to Critique Ads   288

Criticisms of Advertising   290
    Deception   290
    Language   292
    Children   292
    Consumerism   295
    Social Effects   296
    Freedom of Speech   296
    Private versus Public Interests   297

What Can I Do?   298

Summary   298
    Questions and Projects for Further Study   299
    Additional Reading   300
    Notes   300

11 Political Persuasion   303

Four Cases of Political Persuasion   304
    Winning the Vote in 1920   305
    The Campaign for Health Care Reform   306
    The Politics of Religious Doctrine   307
    Selling the City   308

Forms of Political Persuasion   309
    Administrative Persuasion   310
    Legislative Persuasion   312
    Campaign Persuasion   315
    Persuasion through Symbolic and Status Issues   322
    Persuasion in the Context of Entertainment   323

What We Can Learn from Political Persuasion   325
   Limited Effects Model   325
   Significant Effects Model   325
Politics and Trust   326
Summary   327
   Questions and Projects for Further Study   328
   Additional Reading   329
   Notes   330

PART IV
ISSUES AND STRATEGIES OF MESSAGE PREPARATION   335

12 Ethical Considerations of Persuasion   337
Ethics, Values, and Principles   340
Communication, Ethics, and Society   340
   Persuasion and Communication Ethics   342
   Sources of Attitudes and Values   343
   Categories of Communication Ethics   345
Considerations for Ethical Communication   346
   Communicator Considerations   347
   Message Considerations   348
   Medium Considerations   348
   Receiver Considerations   348
   Ethical Values of Communicators   349
Areas of Special Concern   350
   Media and New Technologies   350
   News Journalism   353
   Politics and Political Communication   359
   Public Discourse   363
Summary   364
   Questions and Projects for Further Study   365
   Additional Reading   365
   Notes   366

13 Constructing and Presenting Persuasive Messages   369
Strategic Considerations of a Set Presentation   370
   Know the Audience   370
   Determine Your Objectives   371
   Determine Your Thesis   372
   Develop Main Points   372
   Amplify and Support the Main Points   373
   Write the Introduction   376
   Prepare the Outline   379
   Presenting the Message   382

Strategic Considerations for Discursive Messages   383
  When to Reveal the Thesis   383
  Whether to Recognize Opposing Views   384
  How to Use Persuasive Language   384
Strategic Considerations for Nondiscursive Persuasion   386
  The Visual Image   388
  Honoring Gestalt Values   389
  Set Modest Goals   390
  Keep the Message Simple and Thematically Consistent   392
  Use Effective Aural and Visual Analogues   392
  Position Your Message as Entertainment or Information   395
  Use a Sympathetic Figure or Key Icons   395
  Frame the Discussion in the Imagery of Heroes, Villains, and Victims   396
Summary   396
  Questions and Projects for Further Study   397
  Additional Reading   398
  Notes   398

Index   401

Preface to the Fifth Edition

For a subject that is at least 2500 years old, persuasion remains a remarkably fresh and interesting field of study. Perhaps because it draws from the resources of so many different disciplines—philosophy, art, the history of ideas, and the social sciences—it continually renews itself. The writings and insights of Plato and Aristotle are still relevant, but so are ideas from contemporary political, health, and advertising campaigns. Few subjects for inquiry ask so many interesting questions. And yet—because the study of persuasion sits squarely in the middle of efforts to understand the complex causes of human behavior—it provides few universals and almost never lets itself become an "orderly" study. Popular accounts of the rules and strategies of persuasion often promise easy answers, but the persuasion theorist must have the patience to settle for incomplete answers and contingent conclusions.

When we began work on this book eighteen years ago, we started with several ground rules that we still observe in this edition. A book on this subject, we thought, should place the study of persuasion in the context of its Western intellectual and rhetorical traditions and their pivotal role in the political culture of the United States. It should include the best research but avoid extensive jargon. We also wanted to anchor much of the discussion in specific examples rather than abstract principles. In this field, nothing could be more misleading than the implication that we have theories of influence that apply irrespective of context. Our intention was also to draw conclusions about persuasion primarily from socially significant rather than trivial contexts, redressing the tendency in some quarters to make persuasion just an adjunct of selling.

We have kept our original goal of reviewing the origins of persuasion in ancient Greece and building on that foundation with theories from social influence scholars. Even though most of the book is based on recent studies that use survey research, experimental, and content analysis methodologies, we also explore the timeless philosophical questions regarding the motivations of persuasive acts. Persuasion is—for good or ill—something we *do* with each other. Because it always requests something from others—everything from simple agreement to hard-earned cash—it is not only a field of study but also a form of *conduct* with an inherently moral dimension.

This edition incorporates the sometimes tumultuous political and national events of the new millennium. It also pays more attention to theories and models that track the flow of influence through the filter of the electronic media. For example, the role of the Internet as a vessel of persuasive information is considered in the context of governmental censorship policies, political campaigns, and advertising. There is also greater attention to newer models of media influence, especially refinements of agenda-setting theory. Readers familiar with earlier editions will note that some chapters have been simplified and streamlined, while others have grown to include newer theories and cases.

ORGANIZATION OF THE BOOK

Part I addresses how persuasion serves as a vehicle for social change and the nature of the symbol systems that support all forms of communication. Part II discusses four major approaches to the process of influence: philosophical, source-centered, psychological, and sociological. Part III is an examination of the contexts for persuasion. Two chapters discuss the special features of communication unique to both intimate and large settings. Two others describe the most recognized application of persuasion in modern life: advertising and public policy. Part IV opens with a chapter that reviews ethical issues that confront advocates. The final chapter provides practical guidelines for preparing messages, including traditional face-to-face presentations and shorter messages constructed for various media.

Each chapter concludes with questions for review. Intermixed with the questions are suggestions for putting ideas and strategies to work on specific projects. The projects may be adapted to the reader's or course instructor's needs. Each section also ends with a list of additional resources for readers wishing to explore certain ideas more extensively.

ACKNOWLEDGMENTS

The authors are indebted to many colleagues and students who have contributed ideas and suggestions over the years. Charles Stewart initially encouraged us in this project and helped us by demanding a readable text. Many others have also provided suggestions and guidance, including Tim Clydesdale, Paul Frye, J. Justin Gustainis, Harold Hogstrom, Maryanne Kehoe, John Makay, Jack McCullough, Janette K. Muir, Beth Waggenspack and Paula Wilson. We are especially grateful for the editorial support and friendship of Carol Rowe at Waveland Press. Each new edition reflects her considerable gifts for taming unruly prose and finding visual analogues for key ideas.

We have also received support from our colleagues at The College of New Jersey and Virginia Polytechnic Institute and State University. They have provided the time and resources needed to keep this continuing project afloat. And we recognize the love and patience of our wives, Jan Robbins and Rachel Holloway, who sometimes remind us of the limits of our own powers of persuasion.

Gary C. Woodward
Robert E. Denton Jr.

Persuasion and Influence
An Introduction

Overview

▲ The Necessity of Persuasion

▲ Persuasion Defined

▲ Four Cases of Persuasion
  Doubt and Influence in the Jury Room
  Advocating a Dangerous Form of Religion
  Persuasion and the Politics of Peace
  Persuasion in Everyday Life

▲ What These Cases Suggest
  Persuasion Is about Sources *and* Messages
  Measure Persuasion by Its Effects on Others
  Even Minimal Effects Are Important
  Personal and Public Forms of Persuasion Are Similar
  Persuasion Provokes a Love-Hate Relationship
  Persuasion Outcomes Are Unpredictable

▲ Three Types of Communication
  Pure Information
  Pure Expression
  Pure Persuasion

> *The pursuit of wisdom through discourse is, after all, the characteristic humanistic act. We are all worshipers of* Peitho, *the Goddess of Persuasion.*[1]
>
> —HUGH D. DUNCAN

The tumultuous presidential campaign of 2000 produced a memorable cliff-hanger. A stunned electorate woke up after election day to learn that the presidency hung on a razor-thin vote margin in Florida. The indecisive outcome was further complicated by court battles over how to dispose of poorly punched ballots and their "hanging chads." In the end, a divided Supreme Court gave George W. Bush an electoral edge of 537 votes, enough to give him the state and the nation.

Results around the country were sometimes nearly as close, but the final analysis assured continued Republican control of the White House and the House of Representatives. A 50-50 deadlock in the Senate could be broken in the Republicans' favor by the vice president. In a tight election year, the GOP had miraculously achieved a clean sweep, allowing the new president to pursue his political agenda without the need to deal with a divided Congress. Most significantly, all of the key committee chairs in the House and Senate remained in the hands of the GOP.

Within five months, however, Democrats in the Senate claimed a significant victory, which serves as a reminder of the possibilities and problems of persuasion. Senate Democrats helped engineer the defection of a Republican senator, 67-year-old Jim Jeffords of Vermont. While he could not be persuaded to join the Democrats, the soft-spoken GOP moderate was coaxed to leave his party and to declare himself an independent. The change in affiliation tipped the balance of power against the GOP and forced them to turn over the Senate's committee chairs and political agenda to the Democrats. As Jonathan Alter wrote in *Newsweek*, "rarely has an act of political conscience carried such myriad consequences." The defection was a "one-man mid-term election"[2] that changed the course of American national politics.

Observers of the Senate offered two different narratives about why Jeffords abandoned the GOP. One argues that he was persuaded by Democratic leaders who promised that he could gain more leverage for issues he cared about, including the environment, special education, and pro-choice policies. In this scenario, a handful of Senate Democrats were crucial persuaders. All tried to convince him that he would have greater freedom outside of his party.[3] The same process had happened in reverse a few years earlier when Senators Richard Shelby and Ben Nighthorse Campbell left the Democrats.

A second narrative argues that Jeffords was unintentionally pushed out because of his own party's indifference to the political views of moderates. Jeffords had angered the White House by opposing the President's tax-cut proposal, and by appearing to be out of sync with party orthodoxy. Gloria Borger criticized the heavy-handed tactics of a White House staff that used strong-arm tactics to remind Jeffords who was in charge.

Why not have [White House Chief of Staff Andrew] Card call a Vermont radio station to pressure the senator to vote for the next version of the tax bill? Way to go! And how about planting a leak hinting the White House might deep-six the senator's cherished program aiding state dairy farmers? High-fives! Never mind that Jeffords, who is pro-abortion rights, walked the plank for them on the John Ashcroft nomination. Don't return his phone calls! Leave him off the White House guest list honoring the teacher of the year—who is from Vermont![4]

Inept persuasion always runs the risk of boomeranging. Efforts to cow the independent-minded Jeffords made it easier for him to abandon his ideological roots.

When it dawned on party members that Jeffords was slipping away, his friends within the party lobbied him and the White House to try to prevent his defection. A hurried meeting with President Bush was arranged, but Jeffords had already decided his course of action.[5] When he later met with members of the Republican Party, there was much sadness and disappointment. He was about to force the minority leader and majority leader to change places, redrawing the policymaking map in the nation's capitol. "There were tears from me and tears from them because we'd worked so hard on so many things together." He knew that many of his friends "had dreamed of chairmanships and now they wouldn't keep them."[6]

Rarely does one persuasive event represent so clear a pivot point in an individual's or a nation's life, but this remarkable sequence of events dramatically illustrates the power of persuasion. The process of influence needs a sympathetic audience; it also needs finesse and skill. It should bridge differences rather than emphasize them. Jeffords's case is a sober reminder that outcomes are never guaranteed: that persuasion always carries the risk of alienating those you seek to influence. What could be a more fascinating subject for study?

As will become apparent as you read this book, persuasion is not a subject that yields simple conclusions or easy explanations. One of its early theorists, the Roman philosopher Cicero, noted that "whether it is acquired by art or practice, or the mere powers of nature, it is the most difficult of all attainments."[7] Cicero believed that mastery of the various components of persuasion was beyond the reach of most. Aristotle, who preceded Cicero and wrote one of the first practical persuasion handbooks, was far more certain that its study could be systematized, though he noted that its study belonged to no single science.[8] Both seemed to sense that persuasion was a special subject made all the more interesting by its tendency to put all forms of human genius and frailty conspicuously on display.

THE NECESSITY OF PERSUASION
▲

Communication is the lifeline of our existence. The symbol-using process is unique to humans; it permits us to express the vital, invisible qualities of who we are and what we believe. In contrast to the rest of the living world, we establish a sense of our "place" by the way we define ourselves and the ways others define us. We give language the awesome responsibility of carrying our judgments to others. Words convey praise, blame, guilt, and joy. Persuading others to see a corner of our world as we see it is a basic human need. We are rarely indifferent to the efforts of others to transform what we think and believe, and we are almost never indifferent about our own efforts to have others share our interests, concerns, and values. Persuasion is the process that constantly negotiates this give and take.

The primary goal of this book is to offer a systematic description and vocabulary for the persuasive process, focusing on some of the same questions that drew the attention of its first theorists. How do we change beliefs? What makes us susceptible to or immune from constant attempts to persuade us to accept ideas, products, and people? How do demagogues manipulate people to deny their beliefs and to accept an action that imposes personal hardship or violates their self-interest? The answers to these questions not only equip us to live in our rhetorically saturated world, they also reveal some interesting and surprising characteristics of human nature.

Persuasion occurs in a diverse range of contexts, from simple exchanges of opinions with friends to elaborate debates extended over years. Efforts to manipulate attitudes may grow from one or two persons to encompass vast audiences interconnected by the mass media. Persuaders may be as well-financed as the Microsoft Corporation or as resource-poor as a small band of homeowners fighting the decisions of a local zoning board. The range of human contacts that require skillful persuasion is nearly endless. As citizens in an open society, we cannot escape the responsibility for organizing or participating in public persuasion. As individuals functioning in a web of personal relationships, we must negotiate an enormous range of close contacts within the family, community, and work.

CALVIN AND HOBBES

In the remainder of this chapter we will define persuasion, explore some revealing case studies, and examine characteristic features of the persuasive process. We conclude with a look at the types of communication most commonly encountered.

PERSUASION DEFINED

There are competing beliefs about persuasion. One tradition sees persuasion as an ethically suspect process where advocates firmly anchored in their own beliefs ask others to change. Plato called *rhetoric*—the older term for persuasion—little more than a "knack . . . a part of some business that isn't admirable at all."[9] Others have defined persuaders as "compliance professionals" or "compliance practitioners,"[10] a label that suggests a mastery of deceptive manipulation. It was common to regard some of the messages produced during and after World War II as propaganda. Parts of this tradition remain today in approaches emphasizing that we are potential victims to messages that cleverly muscle out competing points of view.[11] Many in the social sciences have replaced the "vulgar contentiousness and hucksterism" they associate with persuasion with an emphasis on describing and measuring specific conditions that can produce "attitude change."[12]

In the remainder of this book we draw extensively on the research and theory building of the social sciences. We prefer the tradition that is less prejudiced against persuaders and more conscious of the natural and often positive tendency in humans to shape consensus and agreement. Erwin Bettinghaus and Michael Cody reflect this neutrality in their observation that a persuasive situation involves "a conscious attempt by one individual or group to change the attitudes, beliefs, or the behavior of another individual or group of individuals through the transmission of some message."[13] Similarly, Herbert Simons describes persuasion as primarily "a form of attempted influence in the sense that it seeks to alter the way others think, feel or act."[14] Roderick Hart emphasizes what is sometimes missed by persuasion's critics: that it is a cooperative and coactive enterprise. Audiences are more than mere targets or victims. They are often willing participants in their own persuasion. As Hart notes, rhetoric

> is a reciprocal or transactive art, because it brings two or more people together in an atmosphere of potential change. By sharing communication, both speakers and listeners open themselves up to each other's influence. In that sense, communication is not something that is done to others. Rather, it is something that people choose to do to themselves by consenting to communicative contact.[15]

This cooperative feature is important to keep in mind. We often assume that people are objects or victims of persuasion, defenseless against the clever appeals of others. In this view the persuader is sometimes presented as the active agent with selfish motives; the recipient is the vulnerable target. But while this clearly does occur, it often overstates the alleged passivity of those on the receiving end of messages. Successful persuasion usually requires that the concerns and attitudes of audiences must be addressed in ways that satisfy their own critical standards. Suggest to a political candidate that he or she is "sweet-talking" their constituency, and you will probably be corrected. The office-seeker will remind you that the press and public are rarely mollified by simple-minded appeals.[16]

Daniel O'Keefe[17] declines to give a single definition for persuasion, noting that any definition sets up boundaries that are partially arbitrary. He does, however, describe a number of features that are almost always found in typical cases of persuasion. The norm of such messages includes having a specific goal in mind, achieving it through the use of language or symbols, and producing a change in the mental state of the persuadee. O'Keefe also notes that true persuasion implies some free will, free choice, or voluntary action. Forcing someone to act is not the same thing as truly persuading them.

We endorse elements of all the definitions we have cited, but with some modifications. The important qualifier offered by Bettinghaus and Cody that persuasion may affect behavior *as well* as judgments and attitudes is especially relevant. We resist efforts to reduce persuasion to behavioral change only: what people do, rather than what they think.[18] It is important to remember that persuasion may create internal changes that may initially not have any outward form. Or, behavior may hide important conflicting feelings. For example, an individual's behavior in one specific case may indicate only that they have momentarily given in to another's request. If underlying attitudes are not changed, their behavior is likely to revert to its original form. As anyone who has somewhat reluctantly agreed to accompany a friend or spouse to a concert or sports event can tell you, compliant behavior is not necessarily an indicator of a deep level of conviction.

In addition, we would slightly amend the definitions of persuasion above to include the possibility of *strengthening* existing attitudes and actions in addition to modifying or changing them. While persuasion is most apparent when a transformation of some sort occurs within an individual, an exclusive emphasis on change overlooks the pervasive role of communication as a way to prevent the erosion of support. As most advertisers know, the most effective persuasive strategies are essentially defensive. It is easier to reassure a listener's faith in what is already accepted than to urge change to something new. Advertising is often a strategy to protect a product's current share of the market.

Our definition emphasizes that persuasion is an interactive process that takes place between people. It comes with hopes, but no guarantees. One can prepare and present a message and still fail. In true persuasion, as O'Keefe has noted, audiences are autonomous and can easily withhold their consent. Persuasion also holds the possibility of achieving a range of desired outcomes, including the reinforcement or changing of attitudes and affecting the ways people think as well as act.

Persuasion is

1. the interactive process of preparing and presenting
2. verbal or nonverbal messages
3. to autonomous and often receptive individuals
4. in order to alter or strengthen
5. their attitudes, beliefs, and/or behaviors.

The study of a process so fundamental to our social nature can be deceptively complex. In spite of the plethora of self-help books, pop-psychology tracts, and simple "recipes for success" that offer instruction on changing our lives and those around us, the assumption that one individual or group can discover simple nostrums for altering thought and action is largely a myth. The realities of all human encounters are too complex to be reduced to formulas. If it is to be understood at all, the process of persuasion requires an open mind and a capacity to live with conditional rather than certain truths.

FOUR CASES OF PERSUASION

▲

We turn now to some specific examples of individuals with persuasive intentions. These illustrations will be useful when we consider several additional questions of definition in the last part of this chapter.

Doubt and Influence in the Jury Room

Graham Burnett's account of his time spent with eleven other jurors in New York City deciding the fate of a murder suspect illustrates both small and large moments of persuasion.[19] A trial and the private deliberations of a jury are a fascinating microcosm of influence. A jury is chosen for its apparent objectivity in evaluating the pleas of the prosecution and defense; at the same time, they must make a collective and unanimous decision to award the case to one of the sides.

Burnett's trial was at once bizarre and simple. A man dressed as a woman had lured the accused to his apartment in Greenwich Village with the promise of sex. A scuffle ensued, and the tenant of the apartment ended up with multiple and fatal stab wounds. The prosecution argued a simple case of murder. The defense claimed self-defense. They argued that when the defendant realized the seduction was not what it had seemed, he tried to leave. The seducer pulled a knife and a deadly fight began.

In the days of testimony that followed, the basic facts were not in dispute, but there was little evidence supporting a *reason* for the deadly scuffle. Did the victim bait potential lovers and then aggressively pursue them? Had the two men known each other before? The jury was left to decide a verdict of second degree murder or a lesser charge of manslaughter. They could also let the defendant go if they believed his story that he had acted in self-defense.

As an academic historian, Burnett was used to looking at the details of events. Throughout the trial and deliberations at the dreary Criminal Courts building on Centre Street he kept a diary of observations that became the basis of his book. Among his first impressions from the trial was the arrogance of the prosecution. The more the lead attorney for the state spoke, the less Burnett liked him and his message. The defendant—poor and soft spoken—was treated with contempt. Burnett thought the prosecutor used a badgering and sneeringly sarcastic tone in his attempts to get the defendant to change his story. "So egregious did I find the whole performance," notes Burnett, that "I felt a deep desire to see the prosecutor lose the case."[20] By the time Burnett and his colleagues were sent to the jury room, he had privately committed himself to a complete acquittal. The aggressive hostility of the prosecution and the judge had unintentionally boomeranged.

In the first long day of deliberations, the jury was divided and confused. It would now be the task of individual members who had formed a clear position to try to convince others of the defendant's guilt or innocence. People sometimes paired off into groups of two or three, some individuals working to weaken the resistance of others. A few retreated to the lavatory in the jury room to compare notes out of earshot of the others. It was a process that would take four days and test everyone's endurance.

During that period, twelve individuals of considerable diversity engaged in a total of twenty-three hours of sustained conversation in a small, bare room. We ran the gamut of group dynamics: a clutch of strangers yelled, cursed, rolled on the floor, vomited, whispered, embraced, sobbed, and invoked both god and necromancy. . . . (W)e had watched one juror pulled from our midst and rushed to the hospital (a physical collapse, caused by some combination of missing medication and the crucible of deliberations), another make a somewhat half-hearted effort to escape (he was apprehended), and a third insist on her right to contact her own lawyer to extricate her from the whole affair (she was threatened with contempt).[21]

In spite of his quasi-neutral status as foreman, Burnett at times found himself engineering the defeat of some views and pushing others. Weaving his comments around the constant ebb and flow of discussion, he found ways to isolate jurors who he believed were taking the jury down endless black holes. At one point when it appeared that the group edged closer to a not-guilty verdict, Burnett collected ballots in a way that made it easy for others to know the vote of a potential holdout. "I placed it, consciously and more or less conspicuously, at the bottom of the pile. I wanted the full dismay of the room to land on her if she had voted for a conviction."[22]

After three days of deliberations, the stalemate was broken by the sudden eloquence of a man Burnett calls "Dean." He had stereotyped the former bull-riding cowboy who now sold vacuum cleaners as a typical working-class male. But Dean's fluency broke through an impasse that left the jurors wondering how to send a message to the court and the partly culpable defendant, even though their formal charge omitted such subtleties. Dean noted that he believed the defendant "did something very, very wrong in that room. But I also believe that nobody has asked me to play God. I've been asked to apply the law. Justice belongs to God; men only have the law. Justice is perfect, but the law can only be careful."[23]

"To my right I heard Suzy O'Mear whisper something," Burnett recalled. "Looking over, I saw that her eyes brimmed. 'He's convinced me,' she whispered again. It was close to a sob. She said it a third time."[24] The persuasive force of Dean's words broke through the deadlock, and the jury eventually reached a not-guilty verdict.

Advocating Dangerous Forms of Religion

One of the assumptions we make about persuasion is that listeners will weigh messages against their own self-interests. If we buy a car, for example, we are likely to weigh the claims made by the salesperson against our own views of what we need and can afford. We believe that people cannot be easily persuaded to act in harmful or dangerous ways. However, there have been a number of instances of mass suicides committed at the apparent request of a strong cult leader. The 1997 suicides of 39 members of the Heaven's Gate Group in California, and the 1993 fiery immolation of 87 Branch Davidians near Waco, Texas are two examples. The Davidians died in a catastrophic fire after a 51-day standoff with federal agents. The members of Heaven's Gate willingly dosed themselves with poison in the belief that they would leave their "containers" and catch a ride on a spaceship behind the comet Hale-Bopp.[25]

Perhaps the most shocking event occurred in 1978, when over 900 people died in a mass suicide in Guyana in South America. How could so many people willingly agree to their own deaths? What kind of influence did Jim Jones, the leader of a U.S. cult called the People's Temple, possess?

Jones was considered unorthodox in his days as a California evangelist, but he shared more similarities than differences with many other groups that mingled politics with religion and social action with anti-government paranoia. He was especially popular among the poor because his indignation toward "exploiters" and the rich struck a responsive chord. The mission he established attracted members through activities and services designed to make them feel special and different. Like David Koresh, the leader of the Branch Davidians, Jones was a powerful leader. He used his pulpit to preach not only a religious doctrine but also diatribes against secular culture. Also like Koresh, Jones grew increasingly strident and isolated.[26] He began to make every issue a personal one and every member a part of his own private crusade. He cultivated a following by cleverly mixing his gospel of social change with carefully orchestrated demonstrations of support. Members were required to give their money and personal allegiance to "The Father." For Koresh and his Texas followers the price of their isolation and identification with a zealous leader would be the loss of 87 lives in a fiery holocaust. For the residents of Jonestown the losses were even more staggering—912 followers were shot or took their lives in one mass suicide.

The remote Guyana village was an unlikely spot for a U.S. religious commune, but Jones must have realized that a leader's control is enhanced when his followers' dependence is increased though physical isolation. He sold his jungle location as a place free from the persecution and victimage that he preached. "I am preparing a promised land for you in Jonestown," he said. "When you get there all of your tribulations will be over. There will be no need for discipline when you get away from the capitalistic society of America. There you will be able to love and be loved."[27]

According to one member of the People's Temple, for Jones the "only source of pleasure was observing his followers' total devotion to him."[28] He became obsessed with his control over the inhabitants of the new village, and there were ominous signs of his growing paranoia. Members were publicly beaten and humiliated. Bizarre marathon meetings were held in which he revealed his belief that he was the target of assassination plots. He began preaching with a gun at his side and erupting into tirades when a member tried to leave a meeting.

After hearing complaints from members of families that relatives were being held against their wishes, California Congressman Leo Ryan decided to visit the Guyana village with several members of the press. His visit pushed Jones to a deadly state of paranoid rage. In poor health himself, he calmly planned the demise of his commune and everyone in it. After ordering the assassination of Ryan and several reporters, he persuaded and coaxed almost one thousand people to commit the ultimate act of self-destruction. Many willingly gave doses of a fruit drink laced with poison to themselves and to their children, while others were murdered by Jones's bodyguards. A tape recorder that was left running preserved the bizarre final moments:

> So my opinion is that you be kind to children and be kind to seniors and take the potion like they used to take it in ancient Greece, and step over quietly, because we are not committing suicide. It's a revolutionary act. We can't go back, and they won't leave us alone. They're now going back to tell more lies, which means more congressmen. And there's no way, no way, we can survive.[29]

Jones's power to persuade his followers to commit suicide remains a partial mystery. The basic impulse to live should defeat even the most manipulative of persuaders, but we must not overlook the fact that the murder/suicide was only a last step in what had been an incremental process begun years earlier. From its start, the People's Temple had fostered the principle of personal obedience. Members of the church were more than followers of a set of religious beliefs. They were disciples of Jim Jones. Had he been a different person, they might have benefited from their identification with him. The attraction to the idea of the People's Temple—a mission apart from society—became fatally tied to the magnetic personality of Jones. Like David Koresh, he had attracted supporters first to his ideas, then to his isolated mission, and finally to their deaths.

Persuasion and the Politics of Peace

Woodrow Wilson was one of the most eloquent presidential orators in U.S. history. He built much of his long public career around his faith in the power of persuasion, but he overestimated even his considerable skills. His last attempt to shape public opinion eventually cost him his presidency and his life. With enormous reluctance Wilson led America into World War I against Germany in 1917. The United States had been an island of peace preoccupied with its own concerns; European quarrels seemed distant and petty. The 1915 attack and sinking of the liner *Lusitania* near the Irish coast pushed the Western Hemisphere closer to war. Nearly 1,200 passengers perished, victims of new submarine technology and a willingness by the allies to mix civilians with military cargo. Eventually, other German submarine attacks forced Wilson to declare war.

World War I was a brutal and bitter conflict. The machine gun changed the technology of combat, exposing long lines of soldiers to instant death on the desolate northern European plains. Army officers sent to the front to lead battalions of foot soldiers rarely returned alive. The possibility of an armistice began to emerge only after staggering losses developed on all sides. The world had never witnessed such concentrated fighting; 8.5 million soldiers and 28 million civilians were killed.

As early as 1918 Wilson began to grapple with the problem of finding a way to assure peace in Europe. The final form of his proposal was his Fourteen Points, which contained a number of principles to be applied to a negotiated settlement. In a dramatic address before Congress, Wilson announced his plan to save the world from future "selfish aggression." The principles included a call for no secret treaties, absolute freedom of the seas, the removal of Germans from Belgium and other countries, the removal of economic controls between nations, and evacuation of foreign troops from Russia. Wilson's highest goal was Point Fourteen: "a general association of nations must be formed under specific covenants for the purpose of affording natural guarantees of political independence and territorial integrity to great and small states alike."[30] His objective was to establish a world organization devoted to peace to be known as the League of Nations.

Germany was finally defeated, but the bitter fighting had exacted a heavy political cost. The German government soon accepted Wilson's Fourteen Points as a basis for an armistice, but the allies were reluctant to settle for anything less than enormous financial demands. Britain and France did not want to see a prosperous neighbor reemerge to their east. Leaders in both nations felt that the war had forced them to sacrifice the lives of the best and brightest of an entire generation. For his part, Wilson believed—probably naively—that a nonpunitive U.S. solution could be imposed.

Wilson faced two enormous dilemmas, both rooted in his need to change attitudes. One problem was how to win over the allies to accept a peace that did not further humiliate the defeated Germany. The other was how to get the U.S. Senate to ratify the idea of a world organization dedicated to peace. In spite of his best efforts, Wilson failed on both counts. The allies forced Germany to pay a heavy price economically and geographically, and Wilson accepted far less than the original ideals embodied in the Fourteen Points. The ultimate irony, however, is that the resulting Treaty of Versailles probably assured a future war. Germany's resentment made it ripe for a dangerous form of nationalism to develop under Adolph Hitler's Nazi Party.

Wilson's greatest political defeat was his failure to secure Senate ratification of the treaty establishing the League of Nations. He could not convince two-thirds of the Senate to accept his plan and was unwilling to compromise and accept an amended proposal that would satisfy the opposition. Instead, he took his case to the people in a one-man campaign that eventually left him paralyzed and near death. His original plan was a classic presidential ploy. Wilson thought he could persuade the American people that the League was essential and thereby force the Senate to ratify the proposal. His faith in his power to override his opponents by direct appeals to the public was undiminished.

On September 3, 1919, he left Washington on a train that would take him eight thousand miles in twenty-two days and permit him to deliver countless speeches in favor of the League. Radio was still too new to reach a substantial audience. The grueling pace of the trip and Wilson's reluctance to work with the Senate leadership doomed him. After an impassioned speech in Colorado, he suffered a stroke and returned to Washington partially paralyzed.[31] His Republican enemies in the senate—Henry Cabot Lodge and others—remained unmoved by pleas for U.S. participation in the League of Nations. They argued that there could be no participation without compromise. The once energetic Wilson, forever insistent on his vision, spent the last months of his residency in a corner bedroom of the White House, immobile and unable to muster the self-control that had been his trademark. It was a sad end to a supremely proud man.

The United States did not join the League, and a true world organization never developed from the ruinous battles and treaties of World War I. The divisions that had created war remained, and Germany was forced against Wilson's wishes to accept harsh terms of peace. But as Fareed Zakaria noted recently, Wilson's legacy is still intact. "Today, when someone argues in favor of human rights and democracy, advocates self-determination for minority populations or the dismantling of colonial empires, criticizes secret and duplicitous diplomacy, or supports international law and organizations, he is rightly called Wilsonian."[32]

Persuasion in Everyday Life

Not all persuasion settings are nearly so vivid or public as the three examples above. The process of persuasion is equally embedded in the transactions of daily life. Sociologist Erving Goffman had a remarkable ability for seeing subtle recurring patterns of influence and compliance in the smaller moments of communication. He noted that "when an individual appears before others he will have many motives for trying to control the impression they receive of the situation."[33] In routine exchanges with others, we want to be liked and to have our ideas accepted. We want others to respect our feelings and the values that serve as the anchors for our actions. Goffman believed that children, teachers, parents, close friends, employees, employers, spouses, lovers, and coworkers all had strategies for projecting their interests to those with whom they came in contact; he called these strategies *impression management*. Since we perform many of these roles simultaneously, we are constantly faced with the imperatives of impression management: to make our actions and attitudes acceptable to others. Every role we play carries a number of possible strategies for influencing others. In words, gestures, and small signs, we leave a trail of cues that are meant to guide the responses of our audiences. No moment in the routine events of the day is too small to be devoid of persuasion.

Impression management could also be called micro-persuasion. We engineer the terms of daily life to achieve specific effects. Goffman cites George Orwell's account of the routine strategies of restaurant waiters to make this point.

> It is an instructive sight to see a waiter going into a hotel dining room. As he passes the door a sudden change comes over him. The set of his shoulders alters; all the dirt and hurry and irritation have dropped off in an instant. He glides over the carpet, with a solemn priest-like air. I remember our assistant maître d'hôtel, a fiery Italian, pausing at the dining room door to address his apprentice who had broken a bottle of wine. . . . "Do you call yourself a waiter, you young bastard? You a waiter! You're not fit to scrub floors in the brothel your mother came from. . . ." Then he entered the dining room and sailed across it dish in hand, graceful as a swan. Ten seconds later he was bowing reverently to a customer. And you could not help thinking, as you saw him bow and smile, with that benign smile of the trained waiter, that the customer was put to shame by having such an aristocrat to serve him.[34]

Life is full of such moments. Any novel or film could be studied for all of the small but significant cues that are "performed" to elicit acceptance or approval. We "read" such acts so routinely that we tend to forget how essential they are as oil for the machinery of everyday interaction.

Consider, for example, how the following conventional situations invite the use of various persuasive strategies:

- You have agreed to work on a brochure for an organization that promotes literacy and needs to recruit more volunteers who can contribute an evening a week. Should the most important information go on the front or the inside of the brochure? What attention-getting appeal should prospects see first?

- A municipal planning board has allowed a member of your family just five minutes to appeal the decision prohibiting the addition of a room on your existing home.

- A driver has been pulled over by a police officer for going a few miles over the posted speed limit while passing a slow truck.

- A friend has been in a deep depression for days. You would like him to see a counselor, but you don't want to interfere.

- You are broke. The prospect of eating oatmeal for dinner until the next paycheck arrives is too much to bear. Can you persuade some affluent friends to take you to dinner?

- You are an officer in a campus organization that needs new members, and you know some good prospective candidates. How do you convince them to join?

- As a part-time salesperson paid on commission, every sale increases the amount of your monthly paycheck. You attempt to devise a method for identifying serious buyers.

- You have agreed to canvass several neighborhoods on behalf of a candidate for Congress. What do you say to household members when they come to their front doors?

WHAT THESE CASES SUGGEST
▲

These short sketches offer a number of issues that are at the heart of the study of persuasion. They also indicate the range of theories and strategies that inform persuasive analysis and practice. We'll explore many of the key ideas in depth in later chapters, but we will highlight some preliminary conclusions here.

Persuasion Is About Sources *and* Messages

Aristotle noted that good "character may be the most effective means of persuasion" that a person possesses.[35] Messages do not stand alone; consumers weigh the credibility of advocates as well as the quality of their messages. Burnett and presumably some of his jury colleagues were not impressed by the hectoring style of the New York City prosecutor. Wilson felt that his presidential prestige could command a following sufficient to produce a constructive peace. And with terrible efficiency, Jim Jones used his popularity to attract followers to his increasingly demented ideas. In each case, the process of persuasion makes sense only if we specify details about the advocates. Perhaps no politician could have won approval of the League of Nations. However, we assess the failure in terms of Wilson's idealism, as well as what one historian called his "aversion to compromise."[36]

The Ad Council developed this campaign for the National Center for Family Literacy. It effectively promotes the benefits of literacy and invites participation from volunteers.

Measure Persuasion by Its Effects on Others

Since persuasion is always addressed to someone, the audience is always central and never peripheral to the process. Audiences are asked to make financial, personal, or ideological choices all of the time. Hence, Wilson regretfully failed, and Jones perversely succeeded. Burnett's fascinating jury memoir gives us a running account of the arguments and counterarguments that worked or backfired. In the end, justice is whatever a judge or a jury decides.

Even Minimal Effects Are Important

Every student of persuasion needs to keep in mind the theory of minimal effects. In a nutshell, the theory holds that even apparently fluent and effective messages will usually produce only limited effects in their intended receivers. In assessing the most effective selling attempts of Hollywood or Madison Avenue, for example, researchers typically find audience responses that are "selective," "limited," and highly variable from person to person.[37] Think of persuasion as a very steep mountain. The persuader must climb it, while encountering constant and sometimes insurmountable resistance to his or her efforts. Though he tried, Wilson could not move the power-brokers of an independent-minded U.S. Senate to support the League of Nations. The authors of this book—who presumably know a thing or two about effective advocacy—admit to lives filled with noncompliant pets, children, and acquaintances.

In comparison to direct interpersonal contact, the electronic media tend to be weaker in producing persuasive effects than direct contact with other individuals. We often assume that new media technologies reshape or supplant older forms of social interaction, and in some ways they do.[38] But researchers generally find that television and other forms of media have only slight direct effects on the attitudes and behaviors of individuals. As many theoreticians and practical persuaders have noted, face-to-face contact is usually necessary if one's goal is to produce significant changes in attitude. Salespeople know that their job is often about meeting clients rather than calling them. Self-help groups also know that a person sitting and watching a videotaped health message is less likely to change than a person attending a group meeting. Even in the middle of the postindustrial "information age," two people sitting alone in the same space represents perhaps the optimal chance to produce more than minimal change.

We can never be indifferent about even small changes in attitude or behavior. In the fields of politics and marketing, for example, it is useful to think of what we call the "6 percent rule." If only 6 percent of all buyers of a product or voters on election day chose other options, enormous change would result. In 2000, the margin of difference at the presidential level was significantly smaller than 6 percent. In our recent past, a 6 percent change in the popular vote would have denied Bill Clinton, John F. Kennedy, and Richard Nixon the presidency.[39]

CALVIN AND HOBBES

Personal and Public Forms of Persuasion Are Similar

We often dwell on dramatic, headline-making instances of persuasive efforts because they serve as obvious and interesting illustrations. But the persuasive options that presidents, advertisers, and social activists face are not unlike the options the rest of us must also consider. The appeals used by David Koresh to win adherents for the Branch Davidians are probably not very different in form from those used by Wilson to try to forge commitment to the League of Nations or from your own attempts to convince someone to join your group.

All of us respond to arguments based on commonly accepted premises or "truths," and most of us respond to appeals that satisfy unmet needs for membership, self-esteem, and acceptance. Strategies of persuasion can be universalized to many contexts, *if* they are appropriate to the audience, time, and place.

Persuasion Provokes a Love-Hate Relationship

Persuasion both attracts and repels, as the cases we have cited illustrate. Few questions are more intriguing than "What makes people change their minds or alter the ways they act?" We have a natural curiosity about how to influence others and how others do the same to us. Through the ages persuasion has often exposed the darker side of human nature. In fiction and in fact, manipulative "con artists" are villains, whether they are selling cars or misleading potential followers. Villainous persuaders such as Jim Jones remind us that persuasion can succeed for all the wrong reasons. Examine classic or current films and you will find a gallery of characters who cynically exploit the fears and vanities of others. In contrast, some of the New York jurors in our first case were altruistic. As they debated and argued, their personal inconvenience was inconsequential. They were committed to the idea that their deliberations could save each other from making mistakes of reasoning that might cost the freedom of the defendant. Study the leaders of the Civil Rights movement in the 1960s and see the pattern magnified: courageous men and women who risked a great deal to promote a righteous cause.

Persuasion is like that. It may spring from selfish motivations or altruistic ones. We may gain money or prestige from our abilities to influence others; at the other extreme, we may act out of a genuine regard for the welfare of those we seek to influence. Although we may judge much persuasion as propaganda or manipulation, we can also look to personal experience where the communication of influence has been proactive and therapeutic. As we will explore in the next chapter, a society that confronts the realities of persuasive practice—including its sometimes negative aspects—provides its citizens with a valuable service. Analyzing the forms of influence that are common to modern life is the first step in acquiring an effective form of self-defense. Knowing when a good case has been made is as valuable as knowing when it has not. Knowing how to shape events is a critical step in gaining control over our lives. Aristotle wisely emphasized knowledge of persuasive practice as a survival skill:

> It is absurd to hold a man ought to be ashamed of being unable to defend himself with his limbs, but not of being unable to defend himself with speech and reason, when the use of rational speech is more distinctive of a human being than the use of his limbs. And if it be objected that one who uses such power of speech unjustly might do great harm, that is the charge which may be made against the things that are most useful, as strength, health, wealth. . . .[40]

Persuasion Outcomes Are Unpredictable

An entire vocabulary accounts for unusual and dramatic changes in attitudes and behavior: "brainwashing," "indoctrination," "mind control," "conversion," and "subliminal persuasion" are a few examples. From 1946 to 1956, fears about brainwashing drove the House Un-American Activities Committee to investigate alleged Communist infiltration of the entertainment industry. Even a president of the powerful Screen Actor's Guild, Ronald Reagan, believed in the power of propaganda. "The Communist plan for Hollywood," he noted, "was remarkably simple." Part of it would be "to gradually work into the movies the requisite propaganda attitudes . . . to soften the American public's hardening attitude toward Communism."[41]

If only persuasion were so predictable. The dramatic and sudden collapse of the Soviet system after 1986 starkly illustrates that indoctrination and propaganda have limits. Even the society that had allegedly mastered the techniques of political influence—from official Komsomols for teens to nearly complete control of the mass media—could not stifle the desire for political reform and a different kind of society. The rapid unraveling of the Soviet Empire punctured most of the West's assumptions about the efficiency and effectiveness of propaganda.

Despite all of the effort that we have devoted to the subject during the last two thousand years, we are still a long way from creating a science of persuasion. We can recreate and name many appeals, strategies, and effective sequences, but we cannot accurately predict whether they will work in new situations. We have theories that suggest possible cause-and-effect sequences, but we really have no "laws" of human persuasion that can match the predictive power of the laws of physics. Where the biologist can predict accurate timetables of progression and regression in diseases, the student of persuasion deals with a less certain kind of knowledge. The physical world may reveal its laws and secrets willingly, but the origins of human action are far more difficult to pinpoint. Persuasion requires us to look for *subtle* causes with indefinite powers. There are times when the authors reluctantly conclude that they are—at best—custodians to a range of enormously interesting questions about persuasion.[42]

THREE TYPES OF COMMUNICATION

▲

We conclude this introduction with a brief overview of what persuasion is and is not. There is good reason to explore what falls inside and outside the very permeable boundaries of persuasion. Just as one can use a prism to refract ordinary light into the primary colors, we can break down communication into its primary purposes: information-giving, expression, and persuasion. Although virtually every message contains elements of all three, the theoretical differences reveal how we sometimes fool ourselves about our real intentions.

Pure Information

Information-giving involves communicating facts or data. Place a call to directory assistance, and a person (or a machine) will give you the number you seek. If a stranger asks for directions, you respond with specific streets, avenues, or highways. Communicators of pure information have completed their task if we indicate that we have received and understood the information. If we explain to a person how to get from New York City to the center of Philadelphia ("Cross through the Lincoln Tunnel and take the New Jersey Turnpike South. . . ."), they might interject that they dislike the congestion near the tunnel on Ninth Avenue and find the turnpike too crowed and busy. But that is likely to only get a shrug of the shoulder from us. If we have only the intention of communicating information, we may wish them well but do not particularly care how they feel about the information. Reception is the goal of information-giving, not acceptance.

Pure Expression

Pure expression is characterized by a desire to speak one's mind rather than have others agree or disagree, act or not act. We may want to unload our anger, joy, anxieties, or fears merely for the sake of the release it provides. Pure expression gives our feelings an outward form, but it is undertaken more for the pleasure it gives us than for those who overhear it. Many expressions can make us feel better: lecturing the family dog for eating the furniture, cheering on the home team, or delivering a long rant when we ask a patient friend to listen to the injustices inflicted upon us.

Giving our inward feelings outward expression can be its own reward. What we say is not intended to elicit a reaction from someone else but to give vent to a rapid succession of feelings. Former President Harry Truman is famous for having written angry letters to various people that were never actually sent.[43] He declared that the effect of having written them was enough. An unsent letter cleared his head and made it possible to move on to other things.

Pure expression is thus egocentric; it is all about "us." It is intended to be a report of our state of mind. In this mode we ask little of others beyond their considerable patience and silent acceptance. In ordinary life we often take turns with sympathetic others when communicating in the expressive mode. Each person gives the other sufficient time and attention for them to "perform" their feelings.

Pure Persuasion

Pure persuasion differs from and is more complex than either pure information or pure expression. It involves a complex dimension: a concern with how our ideas or actions will affect someone else. The persuasive message is constructed to be believed, not merely understood. In the language of attitude research, it wants *reception* (understanding) as well as *yielding* (acceptance and compliance). If a listener says, "I understand what you are saying, but I do not accept it," the communicator as information giver may still be satisfied. They have achieved their goal. However, the persuader would still be frustrated. She looks for signs of commitment and approval, and perhaps evidence of the persuadee's willingness to use the new facts and ideas as reference points for future thought or conduct.

CALVIN AND HOBBES

In reality, these forms almost always overlap. For example, statistics on automobile seat-belt use indicate that wearing seat belts saves lives. These numbers are—in a simple sense—pieces of information. It is also easy to imagine a persuader using them with the intention of gaining support for increased fines on individuals who still refuse to wear seat belts. If listeners respond by saying that they understand the statistics, the persuader might ask impatiently, "Yes, but do you accept my conclusion?"

It is also apparent from these somewhat artificial distinctions that a good deal of persuasion occurs under the pretext of information-giving. Most of us are far from indifferent to how others accept even simple statements of fact. We want approval and acceptance from others. Information-giving is often an interesting deflection of attention away from deeper persuasive intentions.[44] One thus needs to have a skeptical stance toward news stories, lectures, scientific reports, and entertainment. These are often offered as pure information or diversion. But these benign intentions sometimes mask clear suasory objectives. News and entertainment, for example, depend upon high circulation or ratings figures. Advertisers are attracted by big audiences. So most media forms use content to attract and hold audiences: a clear persuasive intent. Even professors have suasory intentions. Professors hope to impart the wisdom of their disciplines. But professors "profess"; that is, they usually offer data and narratives from their own value-laden experiences. When a course is over, the self-contained world created in the classroom may be abandoned by a student, but not until after the last exam.

Does this mean that all communication is persuasive? Have the authors fallen into the "expert's disease" of describing their subject as the inevitable center of the universe? To both questions we give a qualified "no," but it would not take much effort to engage us in a spirited affirmation of the view that most messages have at least a *latent* persuasive attempt. Persuasion is a far more common process than may at first be evident. We frequently *do* want our messages to change the way others think, act, and feel. It may be the exception rather than the rule when a communicator feels genuine indifference toward whether or not the message is favorably received.

Even so, communication and persuasion are not interchangeable terms. Not all communicators have as their primary goal the listener's acceptance of the legitimacy and importance of their messages. Artists frequently appreciate acceptance of their work by the public, and researchers in the physical sciences often hope their work is recognized. But in both cases it would be wrong to assume that their work is explicitly constructed with an eye on broad public acceptance. This is not the case with persuasion. *Persuasion exists for an audience.* Fail to persuade the audience, and there really aren't many secondary rewards.

SUMMARY

The study of persuasion theory is a journey best taken by the intellectually adventurous. The theorist Kenneth Burke wrote that the effective analyst needs to be prepared to discard what does not work and to search constantly for what does. "So we must keep trying anything and everything," he noted, "improvising, borrowing from others, developing from others, dialectically using one text as comment upon another. . . ."[45] In that spirit this book draws on diverse and sometimes conflicting systems of knowledge: rational and personal forms of logic, universal and culturally specific ways of "knowing," and idealistic values along with pragmatic suggestions. Because human behavior is infinitely complex and varied, individuals do not react in consistent and predictable ways. All individuals have their unique psychological ballast that allows them to weather challenges to their beliefs in unpredictable ways. The best we can usually achieve is a reasonable estimate of an appeal's *probable* effects on an audience. *Peitho*, the Greek Goddess of Persuasion, keeps definitive answers to herself.[46]

Questions and Projects for Further Study

1. Audit your exposure to the many channels of persuasion for one full day. Keep a written log recording the number and types of advertisements you hear or see in newspapers, magazines, and broadcasts. Keep a record of the

news and information sources you see and hear that contain bits and pieces of persuasive messages (for example, a film clip in a newscast in which a doctor warns viewers about the dangers of some product or activity). Note how frequently conversations with others contain requests for your agreement, time, or money.

2. Some analysts have suggested that Jim Jones was a more effective persuader in the remote jungle in Guyana than in the United States. What differences are evident in the two settings that might explain the increased allegiance of his followers in remote Jonestown? How do less dramatic changes in settings (such as moving from home to a college campus) affect individuals?

3. Woodrow Wilson's successors now go to their destinations on Air Force One rather than by train. What other technologies make the "whistle-stop" tour unnecessary or ineffective? Do listeners and viewers who read only printed remarks know as much about a president as those who see the chief executive in the flesh once or twice?

4. In Michael Mann's 2000 docudrama, *The Insider*, we see CBS's Lowell Bergman coax a former tobacco executive into appearing on camera to reveal processes of nicotine manipulation at Brown and Williamson. The film is an extended case study of hard choices made in response to many instances of persuasion and counterpersuasion. Identify a scene in another film where the focus is similarly on private advocacy. Study and discuss it.

5. Look through a magazine, newspaper, or this text for statements that first appear to be informational but argue for a particular point of view. In the examples you find, how is the persuasive intent hidden from the casual reader? How can persuasion be concealed as information?

6. As the Jonestown case suggests, strong leadership may bring misery upon those who succumb to it. Identify other examples of destructive persuasion. Identify positive cases that suggest persuasion can be a constructive process. Compare your examples with a friend.

7. Using examples of your own choice, probe the five features of the authors' definition of persuasion. How adequate are they? Does the definition fail to account for certain kinds of persuasion?

Additional Reading

Aristotle, *The Rhetoric*, trans. by W. R. Roberts in *The Basic Works of Aristotle*, ed. Richard McKeon (New York: Random House, 1941).

Erwin P. Bettinghaus and Michael Cody, *Persuasive Communication*, 5th ed. (New York: Harcourt, 1994).

Robert Cialdini, *Influence: Science and Practice*, 4th ed. (Boston: Allyn & Bacon, 2001).

Erving Goffman, *The Presentation of Self in Everyday Life* (New York: Anchor, 1959).

Rod Hart, *Modern Rhetorical Criticism*, 2nd ed. (Boston: Allyn and Bacon, 1997).

Daniel J. O'Keefe, *Persuasion: Theory and Research*, 2nd ed. (Thousand Oaks, CA: Sage, 2002)

Anthony Pratkanis and Elliot Aronson, *Age of Propaganda* (New York: W. H. Freeman, Revised Edition 2001).

Herbert W. Simons, *Persuasion in Society* (Thousand Oaks, CA: Sage, 2001).

Notes

[1] Hugh D. Duncan, *Language and Literature in Society* (New York: Bedminster Press, 1961), p. x.

[2] Jonathan Alter, "The Odyssey of 'Jeezum Jim,'" *Newsweek*, June 4, 2001, p. 20.

[3] Edward Wals and Helen Dewar, "Daschle, Reid Aided in Decision: Democratic Leaders Courted Jeffords," *Washington Post*, May 25, 2001, p. A1.

[4] Gloria Borger, "A Weak Strong-arm," *U.S. News and World Report*, June 4, 2001, p. 29.

[5] Ibid.

[6] Alter.

[7] Quoted in Lester Thonssen and A. Craig Baird, *Speech Criticism* (New York: Ronald Press, 1948), p. iv.

[8] Aristotle, *The Rhetoric*, Book I, Chapter 1.

[9] Plato, *Gorgias*, trans. by Donald Zeyl (Indianapolis: Hackett, 1987) p. 462e, 463a.

[10] Robert Cialdini, *Influence: Science and Practice*, 4th ed. (Boston: Allyn & Bacon, 2001), p. ix.

[11] See, for example, Anthony Pratkanis and Elliot Aronson, *Age of Propaganda* (New York: W. H. Freeman, 1992), pp. 1–9.

[12] William J. McGuire, "Attitudes and Attitude Change," *Handbook of Social Psychology,* Vol. II, 3rd ed., eds. Gardner Lindzey and Elliot Aronson (Mahwah, NJ: Lawrence Earlbaum, 1985), p. 235.

[13] Erwin B. Bettinghaus and Michael Cody, *Persuasive Communication*, 5th ed. (New York: Holt, Harcourt, 1994), p. 6.

[14] Herbert W. Simons, with Joanne Morreale and Bruce Gronbeck, *Persuasion in Society* (Thousand Oaks, CA: Sage, 2001), p. 7.

[15] Roderick Hart, *Modern Rhetorical Criticism* (Glenview, IL: Scott Foresman, 1990), p. 9.

[16] This perspective is reflected in James Carville's and Mary Matalin's joint memoir on the 1992 presidential campaign, *All's Fair: Love, War and Running for President* (New York: Touchstone, 1994).

[17] Daniel J. O'Keefe, *Persuasion: Theory and Research*, 2nd ed. (Thousand Oaks, CA: Sage, 2002), pp. 1–4.

[18] See, for example, Howard Leventhal and Linda Cameron, "Persuasion and Health Attitudes," in *Persuasion: Psychological Insights and Perspectives*, ed. by Sharon Shavitt and Timothy C. Brock (Boston: Allyn and Bacon, 1994), p. 221.

[19] D. Graham Burnett, *A Trial by Jury* (New York: Knopf, 2001).

[20] Ibid., pp. 72–73.

[21] Ibid., p. 12.

[22] Ibid., p. 166.

[23] Ibid., p. 138.

[24] Ibid., p. 139.

[25] See Barry Bearak, "Odyssey to Suicide," *New York Times*, April 28, 1997, p. A1.

[26] Comparisons between Jones and Koresh abound. See, for example, Melinda Liu and Todd Barrett, "Hard Lessons in the Ashes," *Newsweek*, May 3, 1993, p. 31.

[27] Jones quoted in Jeannie Mills, *Six Years with God* (New York: Times Books, 1979), p. 317.

[28] Ibid., p. 319.

[29] Jones quoted in James Reston, Jr., *Our Father Who Art in Hell* (New York: Times Books, 1981), p. 324.

[30] Wilson Address to Congress, January 8, 1918, in *The Politics of Woodrow Wilson*, ed. by August Heckscher (New York: Harper, 1956), p. 306.

[31] Samuel and Dorthy Rosenman, *Presidential Style: Some Giants and a Pygmy in the White House* (New York: Harper and Row, 1976), pp. 256–59.

[32] Fareed Zakaria, "Our Way," *The New Yorker*, October 14 and 21, 2002, p. 77.

[33] Erving Goffman, *The Presentation of Self in Everyday Life* (New York: Anchor, 1959), p. 15.

[34] Ibid., pp. 121–22.

[35] *The Rhetoric*, Book I, Chapter 2.

[36] Jef Shesol, "A Light That Failed Completely," *New York Times Book Review*, October 14, 2001, p. 12.

[37] See, for example, Melvin L. Defluer and Everette E. Dennis, *Understanding Mass Communication*, 6th ed. (Boston: Houghlin Mifflin, 1998), pp. 438–45.

[38] See, for example, Joshua Meyrowitz, *No Sense of Place* (New York: Oxford, 1985), pp. 1–34.

[39] The 1992 election was made more complex by the presence of Ross Perot, who got 19% of the popular vote.

[40] *The Rhetoric*, Book I, Chapter 1.

41 Ronald Reagan, *Where's the Rest of Me?* (New York: Karz, 1981), p. 163. People named as communist sympathizers were blacklisted; many careers were ruined, and the legacy of this troubled period lives on. At the Academy Awards in 1999, screen director Elia Kazan received the lifetime achievement award to the stony silence of many of his former friends. Kazan had testified before the House Un-American Activities Committee and had named members of the entertainment industry as members of the Communist Party.

42 We are not alone. For two critiques on the unsettled state of persuasion and social influence research see Robert Bostrom, "'Put the Helm Over!' and Steer a New Heading: Communication and 'Social Influence,'" in *Communication: Views from the Helm for the 21st Century*, ed. by Judith Trent (Boston: Allyn and Bacon, 1998), pp. 103–09; and Michael Burgoon, "Social Influence Research: At the Helm, on the Edge, or Over the Abyss?" in Ibid., pp. 88–93.

43 Harry Truman, *Strictly Personal and Confidential: The Letters Harry Truman Never Mailed*, ed. by Monte Poen (Boston: Little, Brown, 1982).

44 Studies in the rhetoric of science sometimes explore the points where knowledge and socially generated values intersect. See, for example, Simons, pp. 307–26, and Alan Gross, "The Origin of Species: Evolution Taxonomy as an Example of the Rhetoric of Science," in *The Rhetorical Turn*, ed. by Herbert Simons (Chicago: University of Chicago Press, 1990), pp. 91–115.

45 Burke quoted in Kermit Lansner, "Burke, Burke, the Lurk," in *Critical Responses to Kenneth Burke*, ed. by William Rueckert (Minneapolis: University of Minnesota Press, 1969), pp. 261–62.

46 Peitho was also known as the goddess of seduction in Greek mythology. Her Roman counterpart was Suadela.

PART I

ORIGINS OF PERSUASIVE PRACTICE

2

The Advocate in an Open Society

Overview

▲ Freedom of Expression and Its Limits
    Suppressing Advocacy in a One-Party State
    The Value of Public Opinion
    Individual Freedom versus Factions

▲ The Nature of Open and Closed Societies
    The Technological Push toward Openness
    The Marketplace Theory

▲ How Open Is American Society?
    Governmental Controls
    Corporate Controls
    Free Speech versus True Access

> *The peculiar evil of silencing the expression of an opinion is that it is robbing the human race. . . . If the opinion is right, they are deprived of the opportunity of exchanging error for truth; if wrong, they lose what is always as great a benefit, the clearer perception and livelier impression of truth, produced by its collision with error.*[1]
> —JOHN STUART MILL

The essence of democracy is that power is shared by a variety of citizens who are, at various times, both the initiators and the recipients of influence. We are nurtured from childhood in the values and attitudes of individualism, tolerance, freedom of thought and speech. We assume that we have the right to influence others, just as they have the right to attempt to persuade us. We routinely believe that everyone has the option to attempt to make claims upon our loyalties: to sell us soap, to encourage us to vote for a candidate for Congress, to speak out against a foreign policy decision of our government. We take these rights of expression—rights to praise, criticize, and seek supporters, as well as the right to resist such appeals—for granted.

FREEDOM OF EXPRESSION AND ITS LIMITS
▲

In this chapter we explore the link between democracy and persuasion. We will briefly trace both of these ideas back to their common roots in the Mediterranean, and we will examine the practical limits of persuasion in open societies in Europe and the United States. We begin with a glance at a society that still struggles to embrace Western ideals of freedom of expression.

Suppressing Advocacy in a One-Party State

It is easier to see the centrality of persuasion in our civil life by looking in places where vigorous social and political advocacy is not yet established. China—with its push toward a modern consumer-oriented economy, its takeover of Hong Kong (a territory that had enjoyed freedom of information and freedom of the press with a noninterventionist government prior to the takeover in 1997), and a repressive Communist government—is an interesting example. The cities of China are dotted with new Starbucks, McDonald's, and shopping centers. The state-run television system broadcasts numerous commercials pitching a broad range of products and services. Yet, the Chinese Communist Party (CCP) is still recognized as the only legitimate national political organization. Its ideology guides the decisions of most governmental agencies. The Legislation Council in Hong Kong is dominated by members who defer to the Chinese government. Nearly all churches, nongovernmental organizations, media outlets, university researchers, and organizations must defer to a web of bureaucracies that interpret the party line. Among many other things, it is a crime to distribute material that "disturbs social order,"

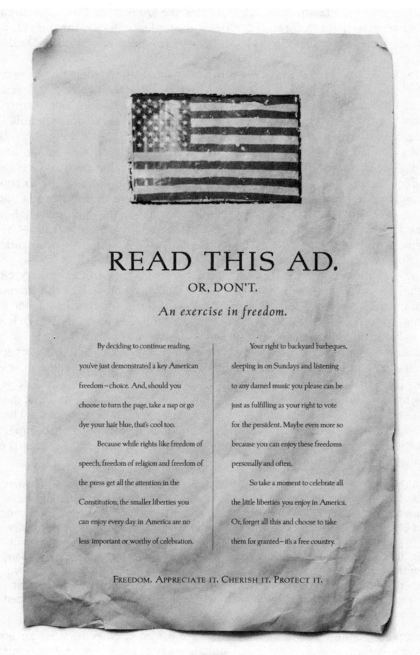

Created pro bono by TBWA/Chiat/Day; this PSA was created on behalf of the Ad Council's Campaign for Freedom.

"preaches the teachings of evil cults," harms the "honor" of China, or communicates state secrets.[2] In October of 2000, for example, writer Qi Yanchen was given a four-year prison sentence for "subversive" articles that were published online and in printed articles.[3]

The Basic Law is the mini-constitution enacted after Hong Kong's return to Chinese rule from the British in 1997. When the handover took place, residents were assured that local freedoms would be preserved under a "one country, two systems" form of government. However, local elections were not scheduled until 2007, and under the terms of Article 23 of the Basic Law, Hong Kong was required to enact a national security law banning treason, sedition, subversion, and the theft of state secrets, with sentences of life imprisonment for many of the offenses. Opponents feared that China's communist leaders would use the law to suppress freedoms and to prevent protests against the government in the name of national security. On July 1, 2003 (the six-year anniversary of the hand-over), 500,000 marched for over six hours to protest the National Security Statute Draft—the largest demonstration since 1989 in Tiananmen Square in Beijing. Demonstrations in Hong Kong normally involve only small groups of activists; the Chinese government was clearly shocked at the outpouring of resistance from ordinary citizens and shelved the statute indefinitely. Joanne Chow, employed in the advertising industry, said, "My daughter asked me why we have to march. I told her it's for freedom, for our future. It's a tragedy if we have to live in a society where we dare not speak our minds and fear persecution."[4]

Some governmental censorship rules seem harmless. The 50,000 advertising firms in China are careful to avoid anything that is sexually suggestive, such as women in short skirts or glimpses of bare shoulders in shampoo ads. The greater problems arise when dissidents, academics, or journalists suggest other political parties should be allowed or that corruption exists in high places. Those who have escaped prison terms often find that they cannot find work in their occupations.[5] The U.S. State Department's recent summary of China's human rights record points to a range of restrictions and rules:

> Although the Government denies that it holds political or religious prisoners and argues that all those in prison are legitimately serving sentences for crimes under the law, an unknown number of persons, estimated at several thousand, are detained in violation of international human rights instruments for peacefully expressing their political, religious, or social views. Persons detained . . . included political activists; leaders of unregistered religious groups; journalists, authors; intellectuals; labor leaders; and members of the Falun Gong movement, among others. Some minority groups, particularly Tibetan Buddhists and Muslim Uighurs, came under increasing pressure as the Government clamped down on dissent and "separatist" activities.[6]

Tempted by the huge market of China's 1.3 billion citizens, Western governments and corporations have tried to keep close economic ties while encouraging the development of more tolerance for peaceful public advocacy. In 1993, for example, the powerful News Corporation tried to get a foothold in Chinese television by taking "offensive" (i.e., impartial and sometimes critical) news reporting off of its Star Television service.[7] Whenever agreements seem near, China's tendency to censor and punish internal dissent triggers heated debates around the world about whether it deserves to be a full economic partner with the West. Even China's bid to host the Summer Olympics was questioned. Many wondered if it was a sufficiently open society to merit such an important prize.

The problem, of course, is that single-party dictatorships are notorious for their intolerance of public discussion and vigorous public debate. They tend to enforce conformity and to suppress information that could endanger their dominant status. Only in 1998, for example, did officials start releasing such basic information as data on air quality in China's packed cities. Many residents knew that pollution was bad in Beijing, Taiyuan, Shanghai, and elsewhere. In fact, 5 of the 10 world's most polluted cities are in China.[8] But acting in the interests of the party, governmental censors had become accustomed to keeping specific readings from the general public. "Releasing the numbers is a revolutionary concept," observed an official of the state Environmental Protection Agency. "We worried that the people would complain that air quality is too serious." Instead, he noted with some relief that the public has been gratified that they could be trusted to know the facts. "So we are gaining points by doing this."[9]

However, when Severe Acute Respiratory Syndrome (SARS) erupted in 2003, China was slow to acknowledge the scope and seriousness of the disease. It reverted to bureaucratic controls on information, the withholding of which could have contributed to the deadly proliferation around the globe. The first cases of SARS appeared in China's Guandong province in November 2002. Although there were 1100 cases and 47 deaths in the province by early February, news about the outbreak was suppressed and neighboring provinces were not warned.[10] SARS spread across China to Vietnam, Hong Kong, and Singapore but China did not cooperate with the World Health Organization until April 2003. The combination of a vast bureaucracy and fears about public panic if information about an epidemic were released plus fears about consequences to potential investments all contributed to China's lack of cooperation and strict control of information.

Perhaps the most anticipated test for China will come as Internet usage increases to the levels that are now common in the West. In many ways the World Wide Web is still an open frontier. Anyone with an opinion can express it and try to find an audience. More troubling for those who want to deny dissenters a forum, it is relatively easy to establish a Web site outside of a nation's political boundaries and use it as a forum for unpopular ideas. The inherent democracy of the Internet no doubt creates sleepless nights for governmental gatekeepers around the world.

Thus far China's leaders have had mixed responses to the growth of the Web. They have encouraged its use among business and management leaders, well aware that no economy can expand without the infrastructure of the digital age. But they have also tried with only limited success to contain Internet usage by blocking many foreign sites, especially the daily news updates of organizations like the *New York Times*, *Washington Post*, and The British Broadcasting Corporation.[11] In 2001, there were about 30,000 sites in China, about one-tenth of which were governmental. There are a number of restrictions placed on Internet content providers, who are warned to block sites that might transmit state secrets or disturb the social order.[12] Presumably, those would include the Web pages of Falun Gong and savetibet.org.

Most citizens in democracies expect social and religious opinions to be unrestricted. An open society is likely to produce ideas that occasionally offend or challenge mainstream beliefs, but liberal democracies believe that a culture is often enriched by such diversity. "What is freedom of expression?" asked Salman Rushdie. The British writer, who was put under a death threat in 1988 by Iranian clerics for writing a novel they considered blasphemous, noted that "without the freedom to challenge, even to satirize all orthodoxies . . . it ceases to exist."[13]

The Value of Public Opinion

Humankind has long struggled with the question of how much conformity should be forced upon individuals within a society. Since humans are by nature social and since living together requires common rules (e.g., whether to drive on the left or the right side of the road, whether criticizing others will be a crime, whether children shall be required to attend school), governments have always sought to impose laws and policies that civilize daily life. In a totalitarian system, the price of citizenship is often enforced silence. In a more open society, institutions and governments rely on public opinion and the legitimacy that it provides. Since the first glimmerings of democracy in Greece about 800 years before the birth of Christ, there have been strong disagreements about the best ways to organize our civil life.

Societies that tolerate a wide range of individual freedoms are the exception rather than the rule. Those who have argued against permitting dissent and vigorous public debate have had powerful allies. The great philosopher Plato is perhaps the most important traditional opponent of democracy and self-government. Several of his key ideas still have credibility today.

Plato spent much of his adult life at his Academy on the edge of Athens arguing that democratic states were bound to fail. He thought ordinary people were incapable of making decisions about their communities because they lacked the intelligence and thorough training necessary for decision making. Plato felt that democracies were governed by mobs unable to separate rhetoric from reason.[14] Few citizens were capable of discriminating between the thoughtful judgments of the well-trained leader—described in *The Republic* as the "philosopher king"—and the irrational pandering of the well-trained persuader. Because the democratic leader owed his power to the people, he would play to their fears and fantasies rather than to the more important needs of the nation. The leader chosen by popular will would substitute flattery of the mob in place of true wisdom. To Plato, leaders guided by public opinion were bound to be as misguided as teachers who let their pupils decide what should be taught.

Plato's view, however, did not go unchallenged. A prolonged debate over the wisdom of democracy developed between him and other teachers who traveled through the city-democracies along the coasts of Greece, Sicily, and Italy. Plato was among the few philosophers of his era to write down what his intellectual adversaries thought. He was deeply troubled and frustrated by the activities of these independent tutors whom affluent parents hired to educate their male children. (The enlightenment of the Hellenic world ended short of including women, slaves, and the impoverished as full citizens—even in democratic Athens.) Among the first tutors was Corax, who taught public-speaking skills to citizens who needed to improve their persuasive abilities in legal and political settings. Plato scorned Corax and other itinerant teachers, who were collectively known as Sophists. He disliked them partly because they worked outside of the prestigious intellectual center of Athens and partly because virtually all of these teachers taught the techniques of persuasion. His dislike of the Sophists was so strong that he named some of the weak-thinking characters in his dialogues after several of them. It is a tribute to Plato's prestige that the term "sophistry" survives as a label for subtly deceptive reasoning.

The case of Gorgias is especially interesting. Plato created a famous dialogue in which the character of his own honored teacher, Socrates, argues with the democratically inclined Gorgias. In the dialogue, Gorgias is portrayed as superficial and illogical; he is no match for Socrates' superior wisdom.[15] The real Gorgias was born in Sicily but taught and gave performances in many cities, including Olympia, Delphi, and Athens.[16] Like all Sophists, he taught many different subjects but always the art of persuasion. According to W. C. Guthrie, "a special feature of his displays was to invite miscellaneous questions from the audience and give impromptu replies." To his credit, "he saw the power of persuasion as paramount in every field, in the study of nature and other philosophical subjects no less than in the law-courts or the political arena."[17] Like many of his contemporaries, Gorgias believed that the freedom to speak in defense of opinions and beliefs required skill in knowing how to hold an audience's attention and how to shape their attitudes.

Plato took issue with Gorgias and other Sophists on several important points. They disagreed about the certainty of truth and the importance of public opinion. Plato believed that most issues that invited persuasion had a single best or "true" answer. Beauty, for example, was not in the eye of the beholder, but closer or farther from the ideal of perfect beauty. Likewise, he felt that large concepts such as justice were not tied to individual values or specific circumstances but to perfect (and perhaps unknowable) forms. We might fall short of actually knowing all that can be discovered about an idea, but better knowledge is always possible. Seriously considering what other people think, he felt, was simply a wasted detour from the path of truth. Since there is perfect truth, perfect justice, and perfect beauty, the best life is spent working toward perfection rather than following the lure of popular approval.

The Sophists believed that many questions of public dispute were not solvable by application of rigorous reasoning; they were better determined by appeals to public opinion. For instance, the question of who would be most qualified to lead a government could not be settled by reference to one single standard. There may be no single true choice, but a range of acceptable options based on the specific interests and priorities of different people. One leader may be better for one group but not for another. On policy issues, good solutions may change as public attitudes change.

If we apply this principle to a contemporary issue, we could argue that a policy of giving out automatic jail terms to convicted drug users is good—whatever its merits in curbing the sale and use of illegal substances—as long as it continues to enjoy public support. Given this view, there is no way that individual facts or truths can substitute for how we collectively feel about an idea. As members of groups, we have values that lead us to certain kinds of preferences. The pluralism of societies composed of mixed racial, religious, and ethnic groups leads us to recognize that others may have their own good reasons for disagreeing with us on topics as diverse as prayer in public schools and the rights of mothers and fetuses under state abortion laws. In democracies, public attitudes are and should be formed by reference to the consensus that emerges (or sometimes fails to emerge) when our values and attitudes are subjected to public debate.

For the Sophists, and for democracies in general, public opinion is everything. Perhaps the clearest statement to that effect came from Protagoras, who offered a convenient declaration which could serve as a seven-word definition of democracy. He said, "*Man is the measure of all things.*"[18] In matters that affect the collective welfare of a society, the people should be left with the power to judge what is just, true, and fair for themselves.

The concept of man as the measure is particularly useful to the persuader. First, it implies that many issues that spark public persuasion and controversy are about preferences rather than truths or ultimate answers. In a decision as trivial as which brand of soap to buy, or as important as a decision to speak against a colleague's proposal, the final choice is personal and unique to our situation. What we think and how we feel determines how we act. The Sophists felt that no quest for absolute truth could remove the responsibility of making choices from a politician, a legislature, or the electorate. Groups and constituencies have different answers and attitudes that may be addressed and changed by outsiders. The Sophists made the common-sense observation that most answers to complex problems cannot be declared totally false or useless for all people at all times.

Second, the idea that man is the measure of all things urges persuaders to have faith in the good sense of an audience to locate both the wisdom and the "puffery" that comes with public debate. Plato's student, Aristotle, seemed to find the right middle ground. He opened his persuasion text by stating a belief in the ultimate soundness of public opinion formed by exposure to various sides of a dispute. Persuasion, he noted, "is useful because things that are true and things that are just have a natural tendency to prevail over their opposites."[19] People, he felt, can judge for themselves. In closed societies where decisions are reserved for the few, there will be hostility to competition from others and the "unofficial" explanation of events. The totalitarian leader can be expected to claim that a variety of viewpoints will confuse and bewilder the ordinary public. The democrat, in contrast, shares the populist's faith that the public can find its own best answers in the give and take of full and vigorous discussion.

Individual Freedom versus Factions

Colonial America inherited a strong intellectual tradition, rooted in the Enlightenment and the ideas of British thinkers such as John Milton and John Locke, in favor of the individual's right to engage in public persuasion. From these European origins, the colonists had acquired a belief in the "natural rights" of humans—freedoms given eloquent expression in the Bill of Rights and the Declaration of Independence. Underpinning these liberties was faith in reason and the freedom necessary to give human logic its rightful reign.

In addition to their philosophical reasons, citizens of the colonies had the more practical goal of establishing local democratic governments to replace the frequently indifferent colonial administrations. They wanted to be able to confront those who were legislating decisions and taxes—an impossibility when the seat of authority was in London. After the War of Independence, they designed independent states and adapted the basic principles and models of the governments which they had known in Europe. They attempted to secure for themselves what England had provided for its own citizens: local governments with direct access to the legislative process and the right to raise and spend their own revenues.

They also had pragmatic reasons for breaking with England. Many families had come to the new world as religious dissidents, most notably Baptists, Quakers, and Catholics. They sought safety in their adopted land by creating governments that recognized the freedom to speak out or to practice a religion different from one's neighbor. By moving to the establishment of a confederation of states to replace rule by a monarchy, the newly independent people attempted to assure that decisions affecting their lives would be subject to public discussion rather than private dictate.

The actual task of inventing a government in the late 1780s was not as easy as it might have seemed. The founders of the United States had to deal with one of the questions that divided Plato and the Sophists: how strong a role should persuasion and public opinion play in setting policy? And could a nation be invented that would not see its civil life devolve into opposing parties?

Among the most eloquent voices heard was Thomas Jefferson's. The unofficial philosopher of American independence expressed enormous faith in the ordinary person and favored local governments with direct ties to its citizens. Jefferson is remembered for his strong opposition to a centralized federal government and his belief in the inherent wisdom of the common citizen. Along with John Adams, whom he eventually defeated for the presidency, he also shared an aversion to formal political parties.[20]

Other founders such as James Madison and Alexander Hamilton had limited faith in how free citizens would ultimately exercise their liberty. They argued for the need to balance the dangers of "factions" against broad individual freedoms. They feared the "turbulence and contention" of pure democracies. Factions—their code word for angry citizens who could rise up and replace a ruling party or group by force or majority rule—had to be checked. "So strong is this propensity of mankind to fall into mutual animosities," noted Madison, "that where no substantial occasion presents itself the most frivolous and fanciful distinctions have been sufficient to kindle unfriendly passions."[21] Madison and other founders wanted to protect land and property owners from mob rule and unchecked public opinion. In the Declaration of Independence Jefferson may have written the words, "all men are created equal," but few of his colleagues were willing to accept the idea that each should have an equal say in the society and its government. They wanted an orderly and stable society, something not necessarily guaranteed in one-person-one-vote democracies.

So the colonists settled on a safer alternative, which provided a layer of insulation between the supposedly unpredictable passions of ordinary citizens and the cooler reasoning of those who would probably run the government. They formed a republic, not strictly a government "of the people," but a government of representatives who would be elected to act for the people. Even after the Constitution was adopted in 1789, only the members of Congress could vote for a president, and citizen voting was restricted to white male landowners. On the whole, the Constitution was intended as much to protect wealth and property as to insure the natural rights of the citizens who waged war against the British.

Speaking for many others, Madison noted that "a pure democracy" was "no cure for the mischiefs of faction."[22] For him, a republic was a safe refuge from rapid changes in public opinion. Even to this day, the Senate of the United States functions as an institution of republican government. Senators are insulated from the public's wrath for six years at a time, and each state has two senators rather than representation based on population. The House of Representatives is more democratic: members represent districts of roughly equal size and face reelection every two years. Even in the hallmark of open societies, there was suspicion of the power of the persuader. The fear that freedom of expression could combine with pure democracy to produce unwanted change was very real among the designers of American government. They believed in popular democracy and public persuasion, but only to a point—unlike Jefferson, who wrote that "government degenerates when trusted to the rulers of the people alone. The people themselves are therefore its only safe depositories."[23] In times of conflict with other nations, even John Adams supported the Alien and Sedition Acts, which curtailed vigorous public debate. The acts made it a crime to utter or write "scandalous" or "malicious" statements against the government.[24]

THE NATURE OF OPEN AND CLOSED SOCIETIES
▲

British philosopher Karl Popper noted that "the open society" is one in which people "base decisions on the authority of their own intelligence."[25] A society is open when the right to make choices is—as much as possible—left to its members. Open societies permit discussion and criticism—and the informed decisions that flow from this give and take. A society is closed when its leaders determine that differing viewpoints are unnecessary or dangerous.

Open societies respond to public opinion. They guarantee the right to debate matters as diverse as religion, politics, and public policy. They sponsor genuine elections, frequently use juries rather than judges to decide cases, encourage competing voices in a variety of mass media, and foster competition among companies and products. Individuals are treated as free agents who may try to enhance their status, improve their education, or alter governmental actions. Most importantly, they may organize into groups and use a wide variety of protected communication forums to seek change.

No society meets all of these standards. Openness is always a matter of degree. Only the most powerful Greek men were legislators. And Popper's own England—

while providing the primary model for parliamentary democracies—was for many years controlled by an upper-class elite. The "old boy" network in government was largely populated by the children of the wealthy, who had attended expensive private schools before going to the universities of Oxford or Cambridge. Even the United States has imposed restrictions on those who seem to favor "dangerous ideas." One human rights organization, for example, has estimated that over 350,000 foreign citizens were barred from visiting the United States between 1980 and 1990, many for espousing the wrong political views.[26]

The Technological Push toward Openness

Freedom of expression is the machine that drives an open society. A totalitarian system sees decentralized public communication as a threat; it attempts to control the flow of information to citizens. Prior to its disintegration in the late 1980s, the Soviet Union regarded photocopy machines and videocassette recorders as potentially dangerous technologies. It is easy to see why. Those devices decentralized the flow of information, making unofficial points of view in print and on tape easy to duplicate without scrutiny for its ideological correctness. Businesspeople who used to work in the Soviet Union remember the periodic appearance of "the hammer man," a worker whose only job was to destroy photocopying machines ready for the junk pile. He always made certain that an old copier was rendered useless.[27] George Orwell's *1984* paints a similar picture of a society that sacrificed personal freedom for rigid certainty, a state that outlawed public debate in favor of centralized control of ideas and conduct. An efficiently run "Ministry of Truth" kept citizens in a form of induced sleep.[28]

Orwell's dark vision was of a society where technology came under the exclusive control of oppressive regimes. But, as we have noted with regard to modern China, the evolution of modern communications methods has the potential to decentralize the control of ideas. In this age of nearly universal phone service, e-mail, faxes, and easy video uplinks to satellites, it is now harder than ever for governmental authorities to insulate citizens from uncensored information. Electronic dissemination of information easily circumvents arbitrary political boundaries—challenging official ideas and approved versions of events. Serbs in the former Yugoslavia had to find alternate means of communication when faced with heavy-handed government censorship of local media. They quickly established sites on the World Wide Web, providing links to each other and to supporters around the world.[29] Similarly, the pro-democracy students who confronted the Chinese leadership in May of 1989 were initially helped in their Tiananmen Square protests by sympathetic journalists who beamed pictures to China's 400 stations.[30] After the protests were crushed, scores of foreign news organizations circumvented the Army and continued to send out stories and pictures via satellite.[31]

The remarkable disintegration of single-party dictatorships in the former Soviet Union offers fascinating examples of changes created through technology that ignores political borders. East Europeans exposed to frequent broadcasts and videotaped programs grew steadily more impatient with the slow pace of political and economic change in their countries. Tides of electronic information eventually swamped efforts by the old regimes to control information. Images of Western materialism planted the seeds of dissatisfaction that later produced popular uprisings in favor of economic reforms.[32]

Despite its undermining of "official voices" at critical moments in the evolution of Eastern Europe, many believe that new media such as the Internet have yet to deliver on promises to redistribute the ability to publicize ideas. Many skeptics in the United States note the increasing commercial presence on the Internet. The merger of Time-Warner and AOL was one sign, as is the growing dissatisfaction of those who first fostered the Internet as a medium of intellectual and scientific exchange. In the words of Robert McChesney, "The digital revolution seems less a process of empowering the less powerful than a process that will further the corporate and commercial penetration of the United States."[33]

The Marketplace Theory

By whatever medium it arrives, persuasion is ultimately the tool that allows a society to renew itself. An open society is marked by a tolerance for differences as well as the desire to see differences translated into constructive and peaceful change. In an open society the verbal battles of all the factions that James Madison worried about can empower individuals. Persuasion and debate can be a basis for countering the power that resides in governments and institutions. In the best of circumstances, the process of public debate gives citizens the chance to be more than cogs in someone else's wheel.[34] New and sometimes unpopular ideas are given the chance to be heard, making government only one of a competing array of voices. Supreme Court Justice Oliver Wendell Holmes clearly summarized the social necessity for freedom of expression in 1919, noting that:

> the ultimate good desired is better reached by free trade in ideas—that the best test of truth is the power of the thought to get itself accepted in the competition of the market.[35]

HOW OPEN IS AMERICAN SOCIETY?

▲

The right to free speech—the right to persuade—is alive and well in the United States. However, it is not an absolute right, nor is it assured by a perfect marketplace for ideas. In this section we briefly review examples from the fields of government and industry that suggest how far we sometimes are from the ideal of free expression.

Governmental Controls

The first and most important amendment to the Constitution states that "Congress shall make no law . . . abridging the freedom of speech or of the press." Recent history, though, is littered with examples of advocates who have been punished for the "crime" of speaking out. Since World War I, thousands of U.S. citizens have been jailed for distributing pamphlets against war, advocating the overthrow of the government, protesting against the military draft, marching against racial segregation, and joining unpopular political causes.[36] To stifle dissent authorities have used laws against libel (uttering false and defamatory accusations), trespassing, spying, disturbing the peace, and marching without a permit. Many government officials make extended claims for the right to keep allegedly sensitive information secret. For example, the *Washington Post's* Meg Greenfield recalled the story of a press officer in the Arms Control and Disarmament Agency who told her that the names of the agency's Advisory Commission were classified. She pointed out that they were already printed in the *public* annual report and went on to note that other classified documents of the agency actually included clippings of *newspaper stories* stamped "secret."[37] Efforts to control as much information as is possible result in censorship even in a relatively free society.

Figure 2.1   The First Amendment

The United States Constitution was written in 1787. Many delegates from the states wanted assurances that the new government would preserve individual liberties. Ten amendments, also known as The Bill of Rights, were finally adopted and took effect in 1791. Even though the wording of the First Amendment is straightforward and unequivocal, Congress, the courts, and public agencies have all placed restrictions on where U.S. citizens may meet, speak, and write.

Amendment 1: Congress shall make no law respecting an establishment of religion, or prohibiting the free exercise thereof; or abridging the freedom of speech, or of the press; or the right of the people peaceably to assemble, and to petition the Government for a redress of grievances.

The right to privacy has been ignored by government and the media, sometimes leading to unwanted publicity and unwarranted attention.[38] Listed below are a few examples of governmentally sanctioned curbs on the flow of ideas or the right to be left alone.

- Soon after the terrorist attacks on the World Trade Center and the Pentagon in 2001, the State Department sought to prohibit the Voice of America from broadcasting an interview with Afghanistan's Taliban leader, Mullah Mohammed Omar. The Voice of America is a government-supported radio service to many nations around the world. State Department spokesperson Richard Boucher said, "We didn't think that the American taxpayer . . . should be broadcasting the voice of the Taliban," which has harbored terrorists groups.[39] But at least one board member disagreed. "I happen to believe that any legitimate news organization in the world would do that interview," said Norman Pattiz. "And if the United States is going to be a proponent of a free press, it has to walk the walk."[40] The interview was eventually broadcast in spite of State Department protests.

- In 1998 two bookstores in Washington, D.C., received subpoenas from Independent Counsel Kenneth Starr asking for information about book purchases made by White House intern Monica Lewinsky. The overzealous prosecutor was apparently interested in determining if Lewinsky had purchased any books as gifts for President Clinton, a link he sought to make in connection with attempts to prove that the president had lied about the alleged affair with the intern. Only after a legal battle in U.S. District Court did Starr and one of the bookstores agree to a compromise of passing the purchase list on to Lewinsky's attorneys.[41]

- The USA Patriot Act passed by Congress in 2001 allows the FBI to examine the lending or sales records of libraries and bookstores, ostensibly to determine if someone is reading something that might jeopardize the safety of the United States. Courts grant warrants for these searches in secret. Librarians and bookstores contacted by the FBI are forbidden from revealing to anyone that a search has been made. Library and bookstore records have long been considered a private matter. That is one reason why secret and open-ended powers are troubling to the president of the American Booksellers Foundation for Free Expression. As he notes, all of this legalized secrecy makes it impossible to monitor abuse of this power by overzealous government officials.[42]

- In 1963 civil rights leader Martin Luther King, Jr. and 3,300 other blacks were arrested in Birmingham, Alabama for parading without a permit. In most urban areas it is illegal to carry out a public protest without a permit from municipal or police officials. In Dr. King's words, "there is nothing wrong in having an ordinance which requires a permit for a parade. But such an ordinance becomes unjust when it is used to maintain segregation and to deny citizens the First Amendment privilege of peaceful assembly and protest."[43]

- In 1998 the Library Board of Loudon County, Virginia, ordered filtering programs to be installed on computers available to patrons. If users attempted to reach a Web site the Board deemed sexually explicit, the program delivered a clear warning: "Violation!! Violation!! Violation!! Access to this site has been blocked." The Board's chairman, John Nicholas, defended the blocking software, noting that he was "not going to be forced by some perceived new right to display pornography in our library." But some patrons complained that the software was clumsy, blocking access to sites ranging from the home page of Yale University's Biology Department to a site sponsored by the Quakers. The library was concerned about minors being able to access indecent material from the World Wide Web. Groups such as the American Library Association have argued that it is not a library's job to function as a censor of information. In their view, patrons have a right to expect that they will see unfiltered information.[44]

- According to one civil rights group, there were 300 documented instances of book banning in the nation's schools in 1996. Objections about the presence of certain books in school libraries usually reach school boards, which agree to ban a particular book 41 percent of the time. The most common books to which students were denied access were John Steinbeck's *Of Mice and Men*, J. D. Salinger's *The Catcher in the Rye*, Maya Angelou's *I Know Why the Caged Bird Sings*, and Mark Twain's *Huckleberry Finn*.[45] A school board in Oklahoma even removed Harper Lee's *To Kill a Mockingbird*, arguing that

ACLU

Protecting America from terrorism is one thing.

Letting the FBI and other police agencies invade the privacy of average Americans is something else altogether.

And it's wrong.

Just days after 9/11, Congress passed Attorney General John Ashcroft's USA PATRIOT Act. In its haste, Congress took away basic civil liberties by allowing the government to secretly:

▶ **SNEAK** into your home when you're not there, and go through your files, your computer, and other personal belongings;

▶ **FORCE** libraries, bookstores, banks, and even your doctor to turn over your personal, medical and financial records;

▶ **EXPAND** the definition of terrorism to include the activities of advocacy groups that have nothing to do with the events of 9/11.

Republicans and Democrats now agree that many provisions of the PATRIOT Act went too far.

That's why more than 150 cities and towns across America have passed resolutions rejecting these government policies that violate our basic constitutional rights.

They know what all Americans know: it's time to fix the PATRIOT Act and restore the civil liberties taken away in the aftermath of 9/11.

America—and Americans—can be both safe *and* free. To learn more, go to www.aclu.org/safeandfree

KEEP AMERICA SAFE AND FREE

Paid for by the American Civil Liberties Union Foundation

some of the comments uttered by its racist antagonists made some students uncomfortable.[46]

- From the outset of the 1991 war in the Persian Gulf, the United States military command set down a series of restrictive rules for news reporters covering the conflict. During both World War II and the Vietnam War, reporters often had wide latitude to move around and visit particular locales and battlefield sites. The rules enforced by the Pentagon were generally much more restrictive, sometimes beyond the understandable need to protect the lives of troops involved in the conflict. Reporters were restricted from many battlefield locations, and they generally had to conduct interviews in the presence of military public-affairs officers. Most ominous of all, stories produced by pool reporters had to be cleared by military censors.[47] To counter criticism about these restrictions, the Pentagon allowed "embedded" reporters to travel with U.S. troops in the invasion of Iraq in 2003.

Issues that involve challenges to freedom of expression frequently require choices between competing values. In many similar instances, courts and legislatures have weighed the ideal of free expression and freedom of the press against the desire for a peaceful and orderly society. Because advocates for causes have often created inconveniences such as traffic jams or angry crowds, careful vigilance is necessary to be sure that such problems do not become a pretext for curtailing the right to persuade. Similarly, we have come to expect that popular government should mean open government. While it may be acceptable and necessary to accept secrecy for activities such as pending military actions against terrorists, most are less inclined to accept a wall of governmental silence that holds back information that is merely embarrassing.

Corporate Controls

Compared to our counterparts in the late 1700s and early 1800s, we receive much less knowledge about the world from neighbors or daily interpersonal contacts. Most of our sources are commercial media outlets. Many of these essentially private sources of information have acquired a power that the first citizens of the United States could not have envisioned. Increasingly, major corporations rather than governments or individuals now play a major role in encouraging and sometimes impeding the flow of information. The much-discussed "power of the media" refers to advertisers, individual media outlets, and the parent corporations that are the major conduits of information to the U.S. public. With some exceptions, advertisers are reluctant to underwrite the kinds of persuasion that may provoke public debate. They pay enormous fees to reach large audiences. In the 2000–2001 television season advertisers on NBC's *ER* and *Friends* paid in excess of $540,000 for just one 30-second spot.[48] For such high stakes, advertisers want to entertain and to reassure audiences rather than to inform and to provoke them. Few corporate sponsors are interested in subsidizing television programs that question or attack the audience's judgments or attitudes; the risk is too great. For their part, the privately held mass media in the United States have increasingly replaced the back fence, the church, and the town meeting as forums in which issues of the day are

CATHY

discussed. But they must also accommodate agendas that are not necessarily the same as the public's. Consider some of the following cases.

- In 2001 CBS decided to cancel its rebroadcast of several episodes of *Family Law* after Procter and Gamble said it would not purchase commercials on the reruns. One episode that was dropped involved a child-custody case where one of the antagonists was shown with a handgun. Other episodes dealt with the death penalty and interfaith marriage. Procter and Gamble refused to discuss their reasons, noting only that the program "has occasionally presented content issues for us."[49]

- In a memo issued by the Chrysler Corporation's ad agency, magazines were asked to notify the company if Chrysler ads were to run in issues that contained content "that encompasses sexual, political, social issues or an editorial that might be construed as provocative or offensive."[50] The company obviously wanted its ads to appear only in magazines where the content was noncontroversial. As *New York* magazine's Milton Glaser noted, this kind of advance restriction has a devastating effect on the idea of a free press and of free inquiry."[51] In essence, the threat of ad cancellations forces magazines to opt for safer content. Other companies that demand what is sometimes called "complementary editorial" content as an environment for their ads include Kmart, Revlon, IBM, AT&T, Ford, and Kimberly-Clark. The latter stipulates that no articles on Down's syndrome or sudden infant death syndrome will appear near their Huggies ads.[52]

- In a 1995 decision to censor itself, CBS decided to alter a segment of its popular *60 Minutes* dealing with the cigarette industry. The segment included an interview with a former Brown and Williamson Tobacco Corporation employee. Lawyers for the network advised cancellation of the interview because they feared that a nondisclosure agreement he had made with his employer might produce a lawsuit against CBS. Brown and Williamson had given no indication it would bring a suit, and attorneys doubted that a media outlet could be successfully prosecuted for interviewing such an employee.[53]

Even so, an earlier suit brought against ABC by another tobacco company apparently made the network cautious. The segment eventually aired in 1996 after CBS was criticized in the press.[54]

- After the terrorist attacks on the United States in 2001 a number of observers noted a new caution from news networks in giving time to anti-war activists. Threatened and actual attacks on Afghanistan and Iraq were usually discussed by the networks without dissenters to American policy. With surprising candor about how commercial concerns can effect news judgment, CNN's Walter Isaacson noted that "If you get on the wrong side of public opinion, you are going to get into trouble."[55] His counterpart at MSNBC boldly asserted that there was no significant dissent: a statement that would have come as a surprise to highly visible doves like Richard Gere, Susan Sarandon, and Phil Donahue.[56]

- *Ms.* magazine is published without advertisements: a precarious way to survive, but a policy that was made necessary after too many advertisers demanded changes in the magazine. Gloria Steinem recalls the frustrating experience of losing advertisers because the politics of feminism was not sufficiently attractive to corporate interests. Philip Morris dropped their ad purchases after readers criticized its Virginia Slims campaign. Clairol also pulled many of its ads after an article appeared discussing skin problems associated with some hair dyes. And food companies avoided the magazine, complaining that it didn't feature recipes and enough articles about food.[57]

- A recent poll conducted by the *Columbia Journalism Review* and the Pew Center for the People and the Press reveals that a quarter of the editors and reporters who responded admitted that they have avoided certain legitimate stories that they felt would be unwanted by their bosses or advertisers.[58] Self-censorship is thought to be a pervasive problem in journalism. It happens when normally curious and skeptical journalists decide not to pursue a story because of the tensions or risks it will pose for their organizations. Is your future secure at ABC if you report critically on the hiring practices at Disney World, which is part of the same conglomerate? Should a reporter at NBC avoid stories about its owner, General Electric? Would it be a good idea for a journalist to write a series of stories about how to get the best price for a new car? A reporter might be cautious and decide against it if his paper has previously experienced anger and the threat of a boycott from car dealers. That was the experience of one California journalist working at the *San Jose Mercury News*, who noted that "the chilling effect can be very subtle. When you start guessing what people will react to, you can find all kinds of reasons not to write a story."[59]

To be sure, the best of the mass media can be remarkably independent of the pressures and views of advertisers, but the constant need for high ratings and large circulation numbers is always a factor in the ways ideas are distributed. The founding fathers could not anticipate that public information would be so heavily tied to information industries dominated by major publishing and broadcasting chains. Their idea of popular government was to disperse rather than to centralize influence.

Free Speech versus True Access

Today when we talk of democracies we mean something vastly different from what the early Greeks and the American colonists had in mind. The first Mediterranean democracies were frequently limited to individual cities. Aristotle said the ideal state is where "the land as well as the inhabitants . . . should be taken in at a single view."[60] He meant that popular government could work only if limited to a group of people that could meet in one place at one time. The designers of the American colonies thought in slightly bigger terms and located colonial legislatures within easy reach of a state's citizens. With these limited spaces and populations in mind, the designers of the First Amendment in 1791 talked about freedom of speech and of the press in a literal way. The standard means of public communication then were simpler. Debate and discussion were largely conducted in local village newspapers, and speeches were delivered in courthouses, churches, and state legislatures. We wonder how the early Americans would react to electronic forums such as ABC's *Nightline* or *Oprah*, which reach millions of viewers spread over an entire continent.

To put the issue another way: the forces of influence that act upon modern Americans are increasingly centered in *national* rather than local institutions. Because of these changes, many critics have asked if the First Amendment itself is in need of an amendment: a new right of access to the mass media which have replaced the town hall and the local newspaper as major opinion-leading sources of news. They argue that freedom of expression is only meaningful to the extent that citizens have access to significant numbers of listeners or readers. As First Amendment scholar Jerome Barron put it:

> In the contemporary life of ideas, the victories and defeats of politics and the fortunes of intensely important issues are resolved in the mass media. . . . Our constitutional guarantee of freedom of press is equipped to deal with direct and crude governmental assaults on freedom of expression, but is incapable of responding to the more subtle challenge of securing admission for ideas to the dominant media.[61]

Barron suggests that the idea of freedom of expression has been rendered impotent. There may be romance in the image of the ordinary citizen standing up for his convictions at a town council meeting, but the real battle ground of public opinion has shifted to the broadcaster and the large daily newspaper. The ideal of freedom of speech, he argues, must now include some sort of means for citizen access to the forums now dominated by the television networks, major newspapers, and corporate advertisers. The Internet, letters to the editor, cable public access channels, and standard news interviews are all vehicles for opening up the mass media to the views of their consumers. But many students of the First Amendment believe that these measures still fall short of giving persuaders genuine opportunities to shape local public opinion. Today, notes George Gerbner, corporations can almost act as "private governments," with the power to buy access to the mass media as the virtual equivalent of the right to operate a private "ministry of culture."[62]

SUMMARY

▲

Throughout history people who have built nations or studied existing societies have disagreed about whether the power of persuasion—left in the care of ordinary people—can result in decisions that will show intelligence and civility. The choices we make as individuals and as citizens of a nation may never satisfy critics who dislike the power of public opinion and distrust its wisdom. But of this we are certain: the greater the diversity of choices within a nation, the more it needs vigorous public discussion. The role of the advocate in U.S. society is basic. Few of us would risk giving up the franchise that allows us to attempt to influence others.

It is also important to note that the freedom to persuade implies responsibilities in addition to privileges. The whole idea of the U.S. marketplace carries obligations for advocates as well as for the society of which they are a part. Persuaders must use their protected rights of freedom of speech and freedom of the press wisely. As we noted in chapter 1, the abuse of an audience's openness can lead to horrible outcomes such as the one in Jonestown, Guyana. For their part, powerful leaders and the mass media should be willing to share their near-monopolies of the channels of communication with less powerful individuals and organizations. The freedom to persuade is rendered meaningless if it does not include the opportunity for ordinary citizens to have access to opinion leaders and audiences.

Questions and Projects for Further Study

1. One of the current battlegrounds over freedom of expression in the United States centers on the Internet. In 1998 the Supreme Court struck down legislation that would have put significant curbs on Internet content. But, as noted in this chapter, other attempts to limit access have come from a range of institutions ranging from foreign governments such as China to local libraries. Develop a position on the question of whether public libraries should employ blocking software that would limit reader access to sensitive sites (i.e., sites that deal with sexual, political, or religious content).

2. The Internet has been called the most democratic of all media, because the requirements to construct messages for it are relatively simple and inexpensive. Anyone with a computer and access to a server or Internet provider can publish their own views. Make a case for or against an individual's ability to use the Internet as a vehicle for public persuasion and influence.

3. The right to freedom of expression is easiest to defend when we consider the cause to be a good one, but free speech issues often develop from more unpopular roots. In 1977, for example, the American Nazi Party decided to hold a parade and make speeches in Skokie, Illinois. The northern suburb of Chicago has a large Jewish population, many of whom were survivors of Hitler's World War II death camps. If you were the judge presented with Skokie's request to issue an injunction against the march, what would you decide? Try to defend your decision to another member of the class. Look at Nat Hentoff's book, *The First Freedom*, to find out what actually happened.

4. In *The Republic, Book VIII*, beginning at section 554, Plato describes the problems in democratic governments. Read the pages of this section, consider his arguments, and prepare a short summary of his complaints against democracy. Use his analysis as the basis of a paper or a short oral summary presented to other members of your class.

5. After the war against Iraq in 1991, many journalists complained about heavy restrictions against the reporting of military actions imposed by all of the governments involved, including the United States. Officials in the Pentagon forcefully argued that reporting restrictions were necessary to avoid passing on valuable information to Iraq about troop movements and damage estimates. Many members of the press argued that controls were much more extensive and designed to minimize the likelihood that Americans would see the horrors of war firsthand. Examining the sources cited on this event in this chapter, defend or attack the general reporting ground rules imposed during this brief war. Compare them to the rules for the war in 2003.

6. Some large cable television companies operate public access channels. Contact a local station and ask if they allow access programming and facilities. Ask them to explain how it works and how it has been used in the past.

7. Students of the First Amendment have argued that some social innovations that eventually find their way into the U.S. mainstream start out as part of a radical movement. Many ideas and policies we now take for granted, such as the progressive income tax, federal regulation of industries, and women's suffrage initially came from fringe groups in the United States. Cite one or two recent examples of ideas or policies that needed First Amendment protections in order to gain acceptance.

8. In this chapter, Thomas Jefferson is described as a democratic hero, a strong believer in liberty and self-determination, yet Jefferson owned slaves. Explain this apparent irony (or hypocrisy). A good place to start is the chapter on Jefferson in Richard Hofstadter's classic book, *The American Political Tradition*.

9. The attacks on the Pentagon and New York's World Trade Center pose serious questions for an open society. How much freedom should we exchange for security? Should we curtail visas for visitors and students? Should we give up some of our privacy for the protection of ourselves and others? How tolerant should we be of airport searches, clandestine government wiretaps, and seizures of property? Write an essay for accepting or denying any one of these forms of curtailed freedom.

Additional Reading

Aristotle, *The Rhetoric*, in *Basic Works of Aristotle*, ed. Richard McKeon (New York: Random House, 1941).

Ben Bagdikian, *The Media Monopoly*, 5th ed. (Boston: Beacon, 1997).

W. C. K. Guthrie, *The Sophists* (Cambridge, England: Cambridge, 1971).

Ralph Holsinger and Jon Paul Dilts, *Media Law*, 4th ed. (New York: McGraw Hill, 1997).

Robert W. McChesney, *Rich Media, Poor Democracy* (New York: The New Press, 1999).

Robert M. Pirsig, *Zen and the Art of Motorcycle Maintenance* (New York: Morrow, 1974).

Plato, "The Republic, Book VIII," trans. W. H. D. Rouse in *Great Dialogues of Plato*, eds. Eric Warmington and Philip Rouse (New York: Mentor, 1956).

Karl R. Popper, *The Open Society and its Enemies*, Vol. 1, 5th ed. (Princeton: Princeton University Press, 1966).

Notes

[1] John Stuart Mill, *On Liberty*, ed. Currin V. Shields (New York: Bobbs-Merrill, 1956), p. 21.

[2] Nina Hachigian, "China's Cyber-Strategy," *Foreign Affairs*, March/April 2001 (Online).

[3] Ibid.

[4] http://ap.tbo.com/ap/breaking/MGA3RLU8MHD.html; accessed 7-17-03; http://asia.news.yahoo.com/030714/afp/030714070210int.html; accessed 7-17-03.

[5] Ian Buruma, "What Beijing Can Learn from Moscow," *New York Times Magazine*, September 2, 2001, pp. 34–35.

[6] U.S. Department of State, "Country Reports on Human Rights Practices—2000." February 2001. (Online) http://www.state.gov/g/drl/rls/hrrpt/2000/eap/684pf.htm

[7] Geraldine Fabrikant with Graig S. Smith, "Western TV May be Nearer for Chinese," *New York Times*, September 5, 2001, pp. C1 and C4.

[8] Elisabeth Rosenthal, "China Officially Lifts Filter on Staggering Pollution Data," *New York Times*, June 14, 1998, p. A18.

[9] Ibid.

[10] http://news.bbc.co.uk/1/hi/world/asia-pacific/2913655.stm; accessed 7-17-03.

[11] U.S. Department of State.

[12] Hachigian.

[13] Salman Rushdie, "In Good Faith: The Pen Against the Sword," *Newsweek*, February 12, 1990, p. 53.

[14] Karl R. Popper, *The Open Society and Its Enemies*, Vol. 1, 5th ed. (Princeton: Princeton University Press, 1966), p. 42.

[15] The dialogue is called *The Gorgias*. For an interesting analysis of Plato's attacks on Gorgias and the teaching of persuasion, see Robert M. Pirsig's best selling biographical novel, *Zen and the Art of Motorcycle Maintenance* (New York: Morrow, 1974), especially Part IV.

[16] W. C. K. Guthrie, *The Sophists* (Cambridge, England: Cambridge, 1971), p. 270.

[17] Ibid., p. 272.

[18] Ibid., p. 183.

[19] Aristotle, *The Rhetoric*, Book I, Chapter 1.

[20] David McCullough, *John Adams* (New York: Simon and Schuster, 2001), pp. 447–48.

[21] Alexander Hamilton, James Madison, and John Jay, *The Federalist Papers*, ed. by Clinton Rossiter (New York: Mentor, 1961), p. 79.

[22] Ibid., p. 81.

[23] Jefferson quoted in Page Smith, *Jefferson: A Revealing Biography* (New York: American Heritage, 1976), p. 157.

[24] McCullough, pp. 504–05.

[25] Popper, p. 202.

[26] Frank J. Prial, "Big Growth Disclosed in List of Barred Aliens," *New York Times*, June 23, 1990, p. 24.

[27] Philip Taubman, "The Kremlin Worries That Too Many Know Too Much," *New York Times*, January 26, 1986, p. 22E.

[28] George Orwell, *1984* (New York: New American Library, 1961), pp. 5–7.

[29] Chris Hedges, "Serbs Answer To Tyranny? Get on the Web," *New York Times*, December 8, 1996, p. 1, 20.

[30] Mark Hopkins, "Watching China Change," *Columbia Journalism Review*, September/October 1989, pp. 35–40.

[31] It is against the law for a Chinese citizen to own a satellite receiver. Western program sources are carefully monitored before they are delivered via cable. See Craig S. Smith and Geraldine Fabrikant, "TV Giants Court China for a Sliver of 1.2 Billion," *New York Times*, September 10, 2001, pp. C1, C7.

[32] See, for example, Jackson Diehl, "East Europe on Cultural Fast Forward," in *Media Reader*, ed. by Shirley Biagi (Belmont, CA: Wadsworth, 1989), pp. 340–42.

[33] Robert McChesney, *Rich Media, Poor Democracy: Communication Politics in Dubious Times* (New York: The New Press, 1999), p. 185.

[34] The appreciation of the give and take of public debate is not universal. For a dissenting view see Deborah Tannen, *The Argument Culture* (New York: Random House, 1998), chapter 1.

[35] Holmes quoted in Jerome A. Barron, *Freedom of the Press for Whom?* (Bloomington: Indiana University Press, 1973), p. 320.

[36] Howard Zinn, *Disobedience and Democracy: Nine Fallacies on Law and Order* (New York: Vintage, 1968), pp. 67–87.

[37] Meg Greenfield, *Washington* (New York: Public Affairs Press, 2001), p. 93.

[38] For a review of this right see Ralph Holsinger and Jon Paul Dilts, *Media Law,* 4th ed. (New York: McGraw-Hill, 1997), pp. 214–65.

[39] Felicity Barringer, "State Dept. Protests Move by U.S. Radio," *New York Times,* September 26, 2001, p. B3.

[40] Ibid.

[41] Stephen Labaton, "Lewinsky's Lawyers to Turn Over Records of Book Purchases," *New York Times,* June 23, 1998, p. A13.

[42] J. Michael Kennedy, "Reading? Somebody May be Watching," *Los Angeles Times,* July 29, 2002 (LEXIS/NEXIS).

[43] Martin Luther King, Jr., "Letter from Birmingham Jail," in *The Rhetoric of No,* 2nd ed., eds. Ray Fabrizio, Edith Karas, and Ruth Menmuir (New York: Holt, Rinehart and Winston, 1974), pp. 301–02.

[44] Amy Harmon, "Library Suit Becomes Key Test of Freedom to Use the Internet," *New York Times,* March 2, 1998, pp. D1, D11.

[45] "The Latest Chapter: Book-Banning Attempts in Public Schools Decline Slightly," *Pittsburgh Post-Gazette,* September 5, 1996, p. A16.

[46] "Blacklisted in Oklahoma," Editorial, *The Boston Globe,* August 20, 2001, p. A10.

[47] Malcome W. Browne, "The Military vs. The Press," *New York Times Magazine,* March 3, 1991, pp. 27–30, 44–45.

[48] Stuart Elliot, "The Media Business: Advertising," *New York Times,* September 25, 2001, p. C16.

[49] Bill Carter, "CBS Pulls Show Over Concern From P & G," *New York Times,* August 17, 2001, p. C1.

[50] Russ Baker, "The Squeeze," *Columbia Journalism Review,* September/October 1997. (Online) June 23, 1998.

[51] Ibid.

[52] Ibid.

[53] Bill Carter, "60 Minutes Ordered to Pull Interview in Tobacco Report," *New York Times,* November 9, 1995, pp. A1, B15.

[54] Michael Mann's 1999 film *The Insider* effectively dramatizes this struggle.

[55] Alessandra Stanley, "Opponents of War are Scarce on Television," *New York Times,* November 9, 2001, p. B4.

[56] Ibid.

[57] Gloria Steinem, "Sex Lies and Advertising," in *Mass Media 99/00,* ed. by Joan Gorham (Guilford, CT: Duskin, 1999), pp. 173–81.

[58] Trudy Lieberman, "You Can't Report What You Don't Pursue," *Columbia Journalism Review,* May/June 2000 (Online).

[59] Ibid.

[60] Aristotle, p. 1284.

[61] Barron, p. 4.

[62] George Gerbner, "Minister of Culture, the USA, and the 'Free Market of Ideas'" in Biagi, pp. 335–39.

The Advocate and the Management of Symbols

Overview

▲ The Nature of Language
    Signs
    Symbol
    Meaning
    Functions of Language

▲ Language, Interaction, and Reality
    The Creation of Reality through Interaction
    Self as a Product of Interaction with Others
    Society as a Product of Interaction with Others

▲ Political Uses of Language
    Functions of Political Language
    Strategic Uses of Political Language
    Common Political Language Devices
        Labeling
        Doublespeak
        Hate Speech

▲ The Changing Nature of Public and Political Discourse

> *When we claim to have been injured by language, what kind of claim do we make? We ascribe an agency to language, a power to injure, and position ourselves as the objects of its injurious trajectory. We claim that language acts, and acts against us, and the claim we make is a further instance of language, one which seeks to arrest the force of the prior instance. Thus, we exercise the force of language even as we seek to counter its force, caught up in a bind that no act of censorship can undo.*[1]
>
> —JUDITH BUTLER

The attack on the United States on September 11, 2001, has been characterized as this generation's Pearl Harbor. The comparison is powerful. The surprise attack on U.S. forces on the morning of December 7, 1941—characterized by President Roosevelt as "a day that will live in infamy"—changed the course of history and the lives of a generation of Americans. In the words of Tom Brokaw, those who fought with courage, commitment, and sacrifice during World War II stayed true to the values "of personal responsibility, duty, honor, and faith."[2] As he proclaims, they are the "greatest generation any society has produced."[3] The surprise, horror, and magnitude of the attack on Pearl Harbor forced the United States into a four-year war far from its own shores.

On the evening of September 11, 2001, President George W. Bush acknowledged that "Today, our nation saw evil, the very worst of human nature."[4] Nine days later before a joint session of Congress, President Bush proclaimed, "on September the eleventh, enemies of freedom committed an act of war against our country. Americans have known wars—but for the past 136 years, they have been wars on foreign soil, except for one Sunday in 1941. Americans have known the casualties of war—but not at the center of a great city on a peaceful morning. Americans have known surprise attacks—but never before on thousands of civilians. All of this was brought upon us in a single day—and night fell on a different world, a world where freedom itself is under attack."[5] We were "at War." President Bush announced that "our war on terror begins with al-Qaida, but it does not end there. It will not end until every terrorist group of global reach has been found, stopped, and defeated."[6]

Not since the assassination of President John Kennedy did so many people stayed glued to their television sets, watching in horror as the World Trade Center buildings collapsed, the Pentagon burned, and United Flight 93 crashed. The wall-to-wall coverage of events by the networks closely adopted President Bush's war rhetoric. Within hours the attack was designated "America's New War," "War on Terror," and "War Against Terror," to name just a few.

The word "war"—taken either literally or metaphorically—set the tone for actions taken and responses to the attack. In times of war, the public places more trust in elected officials. The idea of a nation under attack buys a level of goodwill for presidents that they otherwise would not enjoy. Presidents also become more protected from political infighting and personal attacks. Criticism by members of the opposing political party is usually silenced; we easily and mistakenly jump to the conclusion that it is unpatriotic to challenge the wisdom of political or military operations against a foreign foe. Citizens are asked to make personal sacrifices, which, after September 11, meant the inconvenience of tighter security and new restrictions on some civil liberties. To be "at war" demands some form of action. At home, President Bush's early pronouncements acknowledged our shock, anger, and promise of justice. Abroad, his war rhetoric generated cause for concern. French President Jacques Chirac, while visiting the White House just a week after the attacks to show solidarity with America, stated, "I don't know whether we should use the word 'war,' but I would say that now we are faced with a conflict of completely new nature."[7]

The use of another word—"crusade"—to describe the fight against terrorism caused alarm among those in the Islamic world. For them, the term evoked images of Christian soldiers battling against Islam during medieval times. The White House apologized for the word, insisting that President Bush intended the word to mean only "a broad cause." The name the military chose for its anti-terrorism campaign was changed from "Infinite Justice" to "Enduring Freedom" because the former offended Muslim allies. To Muslims, only God can provide infinite justice.[8]

The news media were also dealing with language issues. Should the attackers be described as "terrorists" or "freedom fighters?" There was even a debate within newsrooms across the nation whether or not anchors and reporters should wear flag pins or ribbons. Reuters news service instructed reporters to preface any descriptions of attackers with "so-called."[9] The major networks, except Fox News, decided that anchors should not wear flags or ribbons. The dilemma was great for the press. Did their patriotic duties override their professional duties?

Symbols and language direct attention. Shakespeare pointed to the arbitrary nature of language symbols in *Romeo and Juliet:* What's in a name? That which we call a rose, by any other name would smell as sweet. While accurate, it is also true that words and their connotations can set a course of action from which it is sometimes impossible to recover. The childhood adage that "words can never hurt me" is often devastatingly inaccurate. In this chapter, we are going to investigate the nature of language, to identify the elements of language and meaning, to consider how language allows us to create the realities upon which we act, and to consider political uses of language.

THE NATURE OF LANGUAGE

▲

Human language is a marvelous and powerful tool. Most of our early education in language emphasizes the meaning of words, their placement in sentences, and how sentences form paragraphs. Language, however, is far more than a collection of words and rules for proper usage. Language is the instrument and vehicle for human action and expression. Contrasting the "extentional world" with the "intentional world" illustrates the importance of language. The extentional world is the world of our senses. We are aware of the room we are sitting in—the color of the walls, the texture of the carpet, the comfort of the chair—because we experience it firsthand. The intentional world is the world of language, words, and symbols. We know this world by what we read or what we are told. Even if we have never been to Europe, we can describe many European things, people, and places. We know a great deal about the Civil War (the culture, the issues, the battles) not because of firsthand experience but because of what we have read or heard. Our firsthand experiences are very limited. For most of us, the world we know and understand is based on the symbols of language.

Language can describe direct experience as well as past and future events; it can detail the reality confronting us or possibilities that do not yet exist; it is capable of transmitting both true and false messages with equal skill. Theorists often use the terms *signs, symbols,* and *meaning* to explain the capacity of language to accomplish all this. While there is debate over the terminology,[10] it is useful to explore some of the definitions because they provide insights that are helpful both for choosing language to convey a persuasive message and for dissecting messages received.

Signs

Susanne Langer describes a sign as a natural indication of the existence of a condition. Lightning is a sign that a thunderclap will be heard; fever is a sign of an illness; the tapping of a beaver's tail is a sign of danger. A sign is a symptom of a particular happening; the two are linked by a direct relationship. Another useful distinction about signs is their one-to-one relationship with what they signify. While stop signs are not a natural occurrence, they do have a simple meaning once learned. They do not invite interpretation; they signal a required behavior. Symbols do not have any such natural association with what they signify. For Langer, signs announce objects, whereas symbols induce conceptions of objects.[11]

C. S. Pierce divides signs (a category he uses to name all human signifying activity) into icons, indices, and symbols.[12] Icons are replicas of what they represent; they resemble, in some way, the objects they stand for—the universal symbols for male and female restrooms, crosses displayed in churches, or maps of territories. An index signifies an object by having been affected by it; there is a cause-and-effect relationship—dark clouds and high winds are an index of thunderstorms. Icons and indices have some connection with the objects they represent. In contrast, arbitrary signs—symbols—have no connection with what they represent and depend on the thought (the *interpretant*) that links them for meaning.

Symbols

Ernst Cassirer described three aspects of a symbol: it stimulates sensation; it stands for something other than itself; and the relationship between the symbol and what it stands for is conventional, not natural.[13] Ferdinand de Saussure divided linguistic signs (which Cassirer and Langer would have labeled symbols) into two parts. He referred to the initial sensation—the psychological imprint—as the signifier. The mental concept triggered by the signifier is the signified.[14]

Symbols, in contrast to signs, may have many relationships to the thing signified. Your name is a symbol that stands for or represents you. A minister is a symbol and stands for or represents a specific set of beliefs, values, and modes of conduct. Words are symbols that are conventionally agreed upon to represent certain things. Words are convenient symbols. They simplify the amount of information needed to communicate about something. We need only say "chair," and we know that it is an item upon which we sit. We do not need to describe and explain that a chair is an item with a seat, back, and legs that support one's weight. Symbols are flexible, arbitrary, and culturally learned.

NON SEQUITUR

Meaning

The relationship between a symbol and the thing it represents is what we call meaning. There is not a one-to-one relationship between symbols and meanings. C. K. Ogden and I. A. Richards devised the semantic triangle to articulate the relationship of the symbol, object, and meaning.[15] Their relational diagram (figure 3.1) distinguishes among the elements of thought, symbol, and referent.

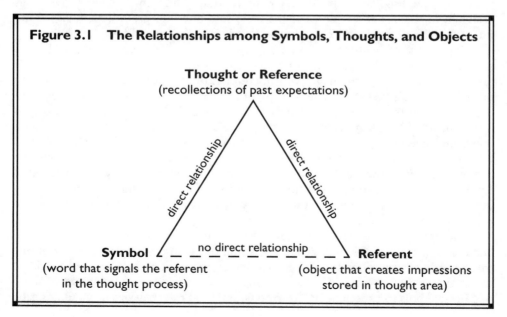

Figure 3.1   The Relationships among Symbols, Thoughts, and Objects

Thought or Reference
(recollections of past expectations)

direct relationship   *direct relationship*

Symbol   no direct relationship   **Referent**
(word that signals the referent   (object that creates impressions
in the thought process)   stored in thought area)

The simple diagram represents a very complex and varied process. At the apex of the triangle is the reference or thought the speaker has of an object or event. At the bottom right of the triangle is the referent or actual object. The symbol, at the bottom left of the triangle, abstractly stands for the object. It is important to note that there is no direct connection (thus, the dashes) between the symbol used and the referent. The only connection is through the thought. In other words, thought, symbol, and referent do not represent an equation. Meanings exist in people, not in the symbols themselves. Two individuals could see the same referent—a sleek convertible parked at the curb—use the same symbol ("Corvette") and have two radically different thoughts: "dream car" versus "overpriced, uncomfortable piece of fiberglass."

The process of using signs and symbols to represent things is called signification. Umberto Eco divides this process into four interrelated steps:

1. objects in the world

2. signs (meaning anything that designates something other than itself)

3. a repertoire of responses

4. a set of corresponding rules

Symbols are created as we develop an ever-expanding set of responses to stimuli. For there to be commonality and understanding, rules evolve to govern the structure of human communication. Words, as symbols, are arbitrary; they are created by humans and have significance only when two or more people agree to some general interpretation of the symbol. Everyone assumes the meaning of "chair" is clear, yet your mother may visualize a Queen Anne chair, while your father thinks of a big, comfortable recliner. Thus, words and symbols, even ordinary ones, have multiple meanings. In fact, the five hundred most frequently used words in the English language have more than fourteen thousand meanings assigned to them.[16] If simple concepts have so many interpretations, imagine the difficulty with abstract concepts such as freedom, equality, or liberty.

Human use of symbols allows us the capacity to see *what might be* as well as to see *what is not*. Burke referred to humans as "inventors of the negative." There is no negative in nature; the negative is a creation of language—it is a concept with no referent in the physical universe.[17] Arthur Asa Berger asks, "Have you ever wondered why it is that often when you think of a word, the opposite of the word pops into your head? . . . It is because meaning is relational. Nothing means anything in itself, and everything means something because of some kind of relationship in which it is embedded."[18] Berger continues his explanation by pointing out that rich has meaning only if we know what poor means; large is useful only as compared to small. He cites Saussure's belief that "concepts are purely differential and defined not by their positive content but negatively by their relations with the other terms of the system."[19]

The ability to see negative relationships has a companion image. We make choices about categories to which a new stimulus belongs—we decide it is not one thing but has similarities to another. We make connections between the world of the senses and the world of symbols. This is the basic process of language—connecting symbols to experience.[20] Ernesto Grassi used the term *ingenium* to describe

the human ability to see relationships.[21] The metaphor is an example of how ingenium operates in language. Aristotle long ago analyzed the usefulness of metaphor.
He described it as uncovering relationships not previously seen. Cicero used a metaphor to "illuminate" how metaphors operate. He said metaphors act as lights in
providing insight into relationships.[22] In seeking meaning, we need to be aware of
both positive and negative relationships.

Context plays an important role in establishing the meaning of symbols. I. A.
Richards believed symbols have meaning because they have previously been members of a context that made an impression on us. Words later serve as substitutes
for the part of the context missing from subsequent similar experiences. He used
the term "comparison fields" to refer to the contexts of previous experiences that
color the meaning of the present experience. Effective communication requires
common experiences—an abundance of shared comparison fields so that the experience in the hearer's mind matches the experience in the speaker's mind. Human
communication is really a stirring-up process rather than a transmitting process.
Contextual factors that influence meaning include: the social status of speakers,
the social conventions governing the speech act, the physical and social-cultural
environments, and previous discourse between the parties.

We can subdivide meaning into two categories. *Denotative* meanings refer to
formal, dictionary, agreed-upon meanings for words. The relationship between the
word and its meaning is generally universal, informative, and describes essential
properties of the referent. In this context, the word "chair" denotes an object upon
which one sits. The denotative sense of most profanity, if analyzed literally, would
have little application to the situations in which it is used. It is the *connotative*
meanings of words that provide positive or negative overtones. In this sense, the
relationship between the word and the object are individual, personal, and subject
to interpretation. If we say that an individual "sits in the chair of power," we mean
more than the object upon which the person sits. For some people, the eagle means
more than a bird, the flag more than a piece of cloth, and a cross more than a piece
of wood. As a result, words can have positive and negative meanings simultaneously. For some, abortion is murder. For others, it is a constitutional right.

The meanings of words change over time. To your parents, a "bad" suit may
imply an ugly, ill-fitting suit. To your peers, however, it may mean a sharp, good-
looking suit. Today, if something is "phat," it means it is awesome or cool; depending on your age it sounds more like a very large item. The greeting, "Hey, dude,"
popularized by Bart Simpson, may be interpreted as cool or sarcastic depending
upon the age of the speaker, the reference group, or the tone of delivery.

There are several conclusions we can generate about the relationship between
symbols and the things symbolized:

- Meanings are in people, not in words. Words evoke different meanings in
  different people. They are relative and are based on shared experiences and
  common culture. As Dan Rothwell asserts, "When we treat words as things,
  it is tantamount to eating the menu rather than the food."[23]
- As society and culture change, so do common meanings of words and their
  acceptable usages. The words "colored," "Negro," "Black," "Afro American,"

CALVIN AND HOBBES

and "persons of color" have referred to the same ethnic group during the past half-century, and each word has varied in degree of acceptability.

- No word is inherently good or bad. Society defines morality, and language is used to justify it. The acceptability of words is culturally determined.

We will explore each of these implications further as we continue our discussion of language.

Functions of Language

Language is an organized, agreed-upon, yet arbitrary system of symbols for communication. According to Ann Gill, there are several criteria for a language.[24] First, any language involves the production of physical stimuli in some channel of communication. Humans create sounds or "marks" receivable by auditory, tactical, or visual channels. Second, the stimuli created must be reproducible and receivable by a distinct group of people. In other words, a language system requires more than one person. Interaction, and hence communication, involves an exchange of symbols. Third, the stimuli exchanged must impact or affect the listener, resulting in some reaction or response. Finally, all language systems have some nonrandom rules governing the language system. Rules include syntax, punctuation, and grammar.

Language serves four broad, basic functions. First, language is a practical tool for getting things done. Each language system allows us to share information and to express desires. It allows us to function as a unit—to build, to create, and to destroy. Language is our primary means of relating to the environment and to others; language habits reflect our personality and emotional states. Through language, then, we organize reality and seek security and information. Language is the infrastructure of human culture.

Second, language facilitates thought and creativity. Edward Sapir and Benjamin Lee Whorf argued that language is the basic port of entry for nearly all forms of higher experience.[25] In any society, the linguistic system shapes ideas and guides mental activity; "the structure of a culture's language determines the behavior and habits of thinking in that culture."[26] To be sure, we don't need the word "hot" to understand that we burn a finger that is too close to a fire. Our sensory organs enable us to directly experience the heat. But most of modern life involves *characterizations* of other's actions and motives—ways of looking at the outside world that are guided by acquired vocabularies. Perception guided by language creates worlds from which it is difficult to escape. Racism in children, for example, is verbally created. If children live in a family environment that defines difference as less desirable, they are guided to see ethnic differences. It is interesting to note how our evolving vocabulary creates new sensitivities and sometimes lets old ones die. Fifty years ago Americans did not talk about attention deficit disorder, sexual harassment, post-traumatic stress syndrome, or perimenopause. The terms are new but not the states of mind or physical condition that they describe. The power to name enhances our ability to see. Vocabularies function as environments. Like all environments, they determine the limits and boundaries of our world.

Language is based on human experience. It is a way to name happenings and to establish categories that differentiate particular stimuli. At one extreme, we may argue that each word is simply a name of a category of experience, because most languages do share thousands of common categories. For example, the English word "horse" is the French word "cheval" and the German word "pferd." Some categories of language, however, are untranslatable. The reasons may be grammatical, semantical, or experiential. Each language system provides special ways of communicating about experiences; those specific ways of communicating create unique needs, responses, ways of thinking, and behavior.

Language is not just a collection of names for objects and ideas; it colors and shapes the reality perceived. As Ann Gill points out, some concepts are beyond our grasp because we have no signifier for them.[27] Without the signifier there is no signified. She creates the word "dewonks" to symbolize humans in their teens missing teeth. If dewonks became commonly accepted usage tomorrow, we would see dewonks frequently, even though yesterday we were not aware of them.

Third, language is a key element in shaping society. Most social scientists today argue that people's understandings of the world are shaped by the language available to them. If we are, as Aristotle proclaimed, social animals, then language allows us to be so. Through language we define social roles and rules of behavior; our behavior is often regulated more by words than by physical force. S. I. Hayakawa has noted that language has the same relationship to experience as a map does to an area of land.[28] A map is a pictorial representation of the territory. To be useful, it must be accurate and current. If not, we might get confused, lost, or even injured. Thus, it is important that a map reflect precisely the physical territory it represents. This is also true for language. Our language system must reflect accurately the extentional, empirical world. The symbols of "liberty," "equality," and "equal opportunity" do not reflect the real-world experience of some citizens. Frederick Douglass, an ex-slave, was invited to speak at a meeting sponsored by the Rochester Ladies' Anti-Slavery Society in July 1852 in Rochester, New York.

> Fellow citizens, pardon me, allow me to ask, why am I called upon to speak here today? . . . Are the great principles of political freedom and of natural justice, embodied in that Declaration of Independence, extended to us? . . . The blessings in which you, this day, rejoice are not enjoyed in common.[29]

Disagreements over the meanings embraced by some can escalate to violence. Hitler described a world unacceptable to other nations, and war followed. Patrick Henry articulated the importance of liberty for people that resulted in a commitment to arms. In each case, language was the vehicle for social, collective action.

Finally, language links the past with the present and makes civilization possible. We can record our ideas, thoughts, plans, and discoveries for future generations. We can then build upon our knowledge and experiences. Isolated, alone, and unable to communicate through words, we would have to rediscover again and again the making of fire, the use of tools, the treatment of disease, and so on. We are, therefore, a product of all who have preceded us. Human knowledge grows because we can record and transmit past knowledge. We do not need to start our education again each day; instead, we benefit from centuries of recorded knowledge and experience.

From a psychological perspective, Frank Dance identifies three functions of speech communication: to link an individual with the environment, to develop the higher mental processes, and to regulate both the internal and external behaviors of people.[30] From a linguistic perspective, Joshua Whatmough developed a four-fold classification system of the functions of language. There is an informative function of language that conveys information, a dynamic function of altering attitudes and opinions, an emotive function influencing the behaviors of others, and an aesthetic function of language.[31] Both these scholars recognize the persuasive function of language usage.

Although related to the ones presented thus far, Roman Jakobson provides the most comprehensive classification of the functions of language.[32] In his system, each function is associated with one of the six essential elements of human communication: source, channel, message, receiver, language, and thought (or referent). Emotive speech is associated with the speaker (source) and expresses the beliefs, attitudes, and values of the source. Phatic speech keeps channels of communication open and provides social cues for interaction; it creates social relationships. Simple greetings are examples of this speech function. Cognitive speech is associated with the message—it deals with the world of information, description, and ideas. Rhetorical speech, according to Jakobson, is the most complex of all functions of language. It seeks to influence the beliefs, attitudes, and behaviors of others. It is the language of politicians, salespeople, and the clergy. It is the ultimate speech of persuasion and influence, most associated with the receiver. Metalingual speech is talk about speech itself. It is of a higher order, is more abstract, and is associated with language, the code of communication. Finally, poetic speech structures the message in an aesthetic, distinctive, and pleasing way; it is associated with thought.

It is important to remember that any utterance may serve any number of functions. Although any speech act can have multiple functions, one function may be more dominant than others. Recognizing the many functions of language keeps us mindful of the various ways language helps us perform the tasks of daily life.

Speech and language vary in style as well as in function. Style is the way in which a communicator delivers a message—the pattern or arrangement of symbols. The difference in greetings between "Good morning, sir, how are you?" and

When your children ask where you got married,
will you have to say,
"Over there, by the unleaded?"

When we lose a historic place, we lose a part of who we are. To learn how you can help protect places in your community, visit NationalTrust.org or call 1-800-315-NTHP. History is in our hands.

NATIONAL TRUST
HISTORIC PRESERVATION

Living in a symbolic universe, humans deal with their perceptions of an object. Preservation committees work to preserve structures with historical significance and to prevent the emotional loss when such structures disappear.

"Hey, dude, what's shaking?" are differences in style, word choices, and symbol arrangement. More than two thousand years ago, Cicero identified three styles: a plain style that was direct, simple, and clearly arranged; a moderate style that was more forceful in tone; and the grand style characterized as ornate, copious, and dignified. Throughout the years there have been numerous linguistic classifications of rhetorical style. They all tend to contrast formal and informal styles, casual and intimate styles, and to identify an informative or consultative style. Factors of style will be discussed in greater detail in chapters 7 and 13.

LANGUAGE, INTERACTION, AND REALITY

▲

The Creation of Reality through Interaction

Why are so many different classes offered on the college curriculum? Most academic endeavors are attempts to understand the nature and social behavior of human beings. Formal education is a process of presenting a variety of perspectives from which to study or view reality. Sociology, psychology, communication, history, science, politics, and the humanities, to name only a few, present perspectives that individuals may use to interpret their worlds. We live in both a symbolic and physical environment. Symbolic reality is an interpretation of physical reality. A tree exists in nature. When we paint a picture of it or attempt to describe it, our interpretation is a reflection of that reality.

Language is the vehicle for sharing meanings and interpretations. Before a response to a situation can be formulated, the situation must first be defined and interpreted. We construct meanings, define situations, and provide justifications for behavior. Hence, communication and interaction with others give meaning to the world and create the reality toward which we respond and act. Humans create, manipulate, and use symbols to control their own behavior and the behavior of others.

Cassirer explained that humans live in a different reality than the physical world of sensation.[33] Humans live in a symbolic universe. Language, myth, rituals, art, music, and religion are some of the threads that weave the tapestry of our

CALVIN AND HOBBES

experience. We often see only symbolic reality; physical reality can be overwritten by symbolic experiences. We don't deal with an actual object—we deal with our perception of it, which has been influenced by a myriad of previous symbolic experiences. In Kenneth Burke's words, humans are separated from the "natural condition by instruments of their own making."[34]

Our view of the world may change as our symbol system is modified through interaction. Meanings of symbols are derived from interaction in rather specific social contexts. New interaction experiences may result in new symbols or new meanings for previous symbols. Consequently, one's understanding of the world may change. In the 1960s language played an important role in transforming perceptions of society. Black citizens challenged years of white domination and discrimination in the United States. A "brother" was a fellow black person, and "black power" represented group identity, pride, and self-awareness. The movement redefined the heritage of "Negro" into "African American," reinforced a positive self-concept of "Black is Beautiful," and declared a new political activism.

Self as a Product of Interaction with Others

Who are you? Why do you like and dislike certain things? Why do you believe the things you believe and take the positions on issues you take? The answer lies in your perception of yourself that changes through communicating with others. From birth, we send out signals for others to confirm, deny, or modify. We interpret the feedback and use it to determine who we are and where we fit. We gradually discern our status, our strengths, and our weaknesses. Through communicating with others, we become "somebody" and have opportunities to change ourselves.

The self becomes a social object that we share with others in communication. We learn who we are through our interactions with others. Throughout our lives we continue to interpret and define ourselves. Our perception of the world, how the world perceives us, and how we perceive ourselves depends on our contacts with other people.

Society as a Product of Interaction with Others

Our interactions with others also teach us what is good or bad, right or wrong. In discovering self, we identify and assume socially defined roles. We form attitudes—likes and dislikes of people, places, or things—through contact with others. As we form various attitudes, we also develop beliefs—what we know to be true about our world of people and objects. As we organize and test our attitudes through interaction, we establish values that provide general guidelines for behavior. Values are the core elements that help us interpret reality; they form the basis of how we judge or evaluate issues and concepts. For example, is loyalty more important than personal gain; is war always wrong; is honesty always good? Social control is not solely a matter of formal governmental agencies, laws, rules, and regulations. It is a direct result of identifying and internalizing the values of a group. Values become essential to our self-esteem and act to support the social order.

In addition to creating expectations of behavior, symbols create social sanctions (for example, war as God's will) or function as master symbols or "god terms" (i.e., to die for freedom). The United States sent troops to Afghanistan to "bring the terrorists to justice" and to ensure the "safety" and "security" of our citizens. MX missiles were labeled "peacekeepers" to match the rationale for the war. When followers, through socialization, have been taught significant symbols that uphold social order, they require leaders to play defined roles. Leaders must create and use symbols that unite and transcend individual and collective differences. Leaders articulate positions of superiority, inferiority, and equality; they persuade us through symbols of power, majesty, and authority.

We have certainly drawn a rather large circle in our discussion. We started with the role of language in defining and discovering ourselves and concluded with demonstrating how language maintains social order. It is useful to examine further the role of social interaction and language as a function of governing. While our focus in chapter 11 is on the forms of political persuasion, our concern here is how language structures our social relationships within a democracy and how leaders of society use language to define and interpret reality to provide a rationale for future collective action.

POLITICAL USES OF LANGUAGE
▲

Language is not just reserved for the honorable and skilled. This human tool is available to all—the good and bad, the kind and cruel, the generous and selfish. It is, therefore, open to abuse as freely as it is to proper usage.

The substance of the information the language conveys, the setting in which the interaction occurs, and the explicit or implicit functions the language performs determine whether or not language is political. According to Paul Corcoran, the very essence of language is political and, thus, persuasive. "Language in the broadest sense—ordinary conversation, symbolic expression, the grammar of social and sexual roles, the maintenance of customs and institutions, the transmission of cultural norms from generation to generation—is inevitably political because it prescribes, constrains, socializes, reinforces, and conserves the status quo."[35]

Political language is often designed to evoke reaction, not thoughtful response. Political language can be a creative instrument to stimulate passion and commitment. To control, manipulate, or structure the audience's interpretation is the primary goal of politics in general. Political discourse involves a struggle over meaning, status, power, and resources.[36] A successful politician, then, will use specific linguistic devices to reinforce popular beliefs, attitudes, and values.

It is important to understand that politics as talk does not imply politics is all talk and no action. Politics as talk *is* action in very important, although sometimes very subtle, ways. To win the public debate in defining abortion as murder is the first step toward legislative action. Compare the policy implications of whether abortion is a medical procedure or murder; whether affirmative action is a program insuring equal opportunity or governmental discrimination. As Murray Edelman reminds us, "the potency of political language does not stem from its descriptions of a 'real' world but rather from its reconstructions of the past and its evocation of unobservables in the present and of potentialities in the future, language usage is strategic."[37]

There are those within the academy who argue that facts should dominate political discussions and subsequent actions. But think of a container that by universal agreement holds six ounces of some liquid. Suppose we pour three ounces of a liquid into the container. The facts are indisputable: three ounces of liquid in a six ounce container. But from a political perspective, the issue is whether the container is *half empty or half full*. If the "reality" is that the container is half empty, then we need to allocate more time and resources to find additional liquid. If the container is half full, then there is a sense of optimism and hope. Although the facts are the same, one's view or interpretation of the facts influences one's attitudes and behavior.

Although this example is extremely simplistic, many contemporary political campaigns and legislative issues are based on similar analysis. Are we too dependent upon foreign oil? Should we drill in the Arctic reserves for additional oil? Is the risk to the environment too great? Which view of reality will prevail?

Functions of Political Language

Political symbols are the direct link between individuals and the social order. As elements of a political culture, they function as a stimulus for behavior. Using appropriate symbols can result in getting people to accept certain policies, arousing support for various causes, and obeying governmental authority. Political symbols are the means to social ends and not ends in themselves. Political symbols are also perpetuated in order to preserve the prevailing culture, political beliefs, and values. Political language creates, alters, and maintains the social state.

Political language is about power, social relationships, morals, ethics, and identity, to name only a few items. But, as Paul Corcoran warns, "while language shapes and empowers its users, the unhappy consequence is that language reproduces and reinforces exploitation, inequality, and other traditions of power."[38] Leaders win and lose; the public is empowered or enslaved; citizens are informed or misled by the strategic use of language.

Doris Graber identifies five major functions of political language: information dissemination, agenda setting, interpretation and linkage, projection for the future and the past, and action stimulation.[39] *Information dissemination* is the sharing of explicit information about the state of the nation. Government agencies are always disseminating health and safety information from new medication approvals to a new "buckle up" seat belt campaign. Such dissemination is vital to the public's understanding and support of the political system. This is especially true in democratic nations where the public expects open access to legislative debates and the decision making of government officials. However, the most important information is sometimes what is not stated, how something is stated, or when it is stated. Often, especially in messages between nations, the public must make inferences about the actual meaning and significance of official statements. Are our relations with China "open," "guarded," or "friendly"? Sometimes the very act of speaking communicates support, sympathy, or strength. Thus, the decision to speak rather than the actual words spoken conveys the meaning of the rhetorical event.

The topics politicians choose to discuss channel the public's attention. The *agenda-setting function* of political language works as follows. Before something can become an issue, a prominent politician must first articulate a problem to bring the issue to public attention. The issue can be a long-standing concern (poverty), one that needs highlighting (status of U.S. education), or created (health-care "crisis"). Political language establishes a national agenda by controlling the information disseminated to the public. Within this realm, there is always a great deal of competition because only a limited number of issues can hold public interest. While certain topics may be critically important to a person, party, faction, or group, the same topics may be perceived as meaningless or even harmful to other factions, persons, or groups.

Presidential State of the Union addresses are direct attempts by the president to set legislative goals and agendas for the pending congressional session. Four months after the attacks on the United States, President Bush outlined three goals in his State of the Union Address on January 29, 2002: "We will win this war; we'll protect our homeland; and we will revive our economy."[40] He proceeded to provide details of his budget in support of each goal. In order to win the war against terrorism, he included "the largest increase in defense spending in two decades." To protect the homeland, he proposed doubling funding in four key areas: bioterrorism, emergency response, airport and border security, and improved intelligence.

> We will develop vaccines to fight anthrax and other deadly diseases. We'll increase funding to help states and communities train and equip our heroic police and firefighters. We will improve intelligence collection and sharing, expand patrols at our borders, strengthen the security of air travel, and use technology to track the arrivals and departures of visitors to the United States.[41]

To help the economy, President Bush proposed extending unemployment benefits, providing direct assistance for health-care coverage, encouraging energy production at home, passing trade promotion authority legislation, and speeding up tax relief legislation.

Control over the definition of a situation is essential in political campaigns. Graber refers to this third function of political language as *interpretation and linkage*. Participants in election primaries, for example, all proclaim victory regardless of the number of votes received. The top vote-getter becomes the "front runner." The second-place winner becomes "the underdog" candidate in an "uphill battle." The third-place candidate becomes a "credible" candidate and alternative for those "frustrated" or "dissatisfied" with the "same old party favorites."

Again, President Bush's 2002 State of the Union Address provides an excellent example of how political language interprets current events and links the present to the past. In this case, President Bush expressed how the September 11 attacks renewed our values of citizenship.

> After America was attacked, it was as if our entire country looked into a mirror and saw our better selves. We were reminded that we are citizens, with obligations to each other, to our country, and to history. We began to think less of the goods we can accumulate, and more about the good we can do. For too long our culture has said, "If it feels good, do it." Now America is embracing a new ethic

and a new creed: "Let's roll." In the sacrifice of soldiers, the fierce brotherhood of fire fighters, and the bravery and generosity of ordinary citizens, we have glimpsed what a new culture of responsibility could look like. We want to be a nation that serves goals larger than self. We've been offered a unique opportunity, and we must not let this moment pass.[42]

A great deal of political language deals with **projection**: predicting the future and reflecting upon the past. Candidates forecast idealized futures under their leadership and predict success if their policies are followed. Some projections are formalized in party platforms or in major addresses such as inaugurals or state of the union speeches. Nearly all such statements involve promises—promises of a brighter future if followed or Armageddon if rejected. Past memories and associations are evoked to stimulate a sense of security, better times, and romantic longings. An important function of political language, therefore, is to link us to past glories and to predict a successful future in order to reduce uncertainty in an increasingly complex world.

Returning to President Bush's 2002 State of the Union Address, he used projection to articulate duty and to predict victory in the war against terrorism.

In a single instant, we realized that this will be a decisive decade in the history of liberty, that we've been called to a unique role in human events. Rarely has the world faced a choice more clear or consequential. Our enemies send other people's children on missions of suicide and murder. They embrace tyranny and death as a cause and a creed. We stand for a different choice, made long ago, on the day of our founding. We affirm it again today. We choose freedom and the dignity of every life. Steadfast in our purpose, we now press on. We have known freedom's price. We have shown freedom's power. And in this great conflict, my fellow Americans, we will see freedom's victory.[43]

Finally, and perhaps most importantly, political language mobilizes society and **stimulates action**. Language serves as the rationale for social action. Words can evoke, persuade, implore, command, label, praise, and condemn. Although political language is similar to other uses of language, it also stimulates behavior and shapes public discussion about the allocation of public resources, authority, and sanctions. In addition to calling upon Congress to take action on several legislative initiatives, President Bush in his 2002 State of the Union Address asked all Americans to commit 4,000 hours to the service of neighbors and the nation.

Craig Smith identifies five functions of *governmental* language: to unify, to legitimize, to orient, to resolve conflicts, and to implement policies.[44] These are very pragmatic and programmatic uses of political language. From a governmental perspective, language is a tool to generate a sense of inclusion and participation among citizens. Language also legitimizes and confirms the authority of governmental actions. Related to the agenda-setting function, governmental language frames our national goals, policies, hopes, and desires as well as articulates our needs, problems, and shortcomings. Social conflicts are resolved by issue discussion, explanation, debate, and negotiation. Finally, government implements policy through the creation of legislation and regulatory interpretation. From this perspective, the language of government encompasses elected officials, government agencies, and government employees.

Strategic Uses of Political Language

It is important to remember that the context and content of an interaction is what makes the use of language political. Contexts can range from a local candidate talking at a reception, to speeches in the halls of Congress, to the rally of citizens outside a courthouse, to name just a few. Below are some strategies commonly used for political purposes.

Argumentation and persuasion. Political language is used to discuss, debate, and negotiate issues and legislation. As already mentioned, political rhetoric is not neutral; it advocates a particular set of attitudes, beliefs, and values. Political language is about advocacy—creating a symbolic reality from a particular perspective for a specific purpose.

Identification. Political language creates commonality, understanding, and unity. Language is a way to relate to others, to build bridges to understanding. Politicians, both verbally and nonverbally, attempt to demonstrate they understand their constituents and are similar in beliefs, attitudes, and values. According to Kenneth Burke, "you persuade a person only insofar as you can talk the person's language by speech, gesture, tonality, order, image, attitude, identifying your ways with this person's."[45] The importance of language as it relates to nationalism can be viewed in light of the debate over English as our standard language. A "homogeneous linguistic community" is argued in terms of shared values. Social identity is another important use of political language. Language links us as a social class or ethnicity or cultural heritage. The appeal of common experiences is very strong. Language provides a rallying point for issues and a commonality of efforts.

Reinforcement. The process of persuasion is a difficult process. Most political communication is not about altering attitudes but reinforcing existing beliefs and attitudes. Most political discourse and even advertising tries to reinforce the public preferences most favorable to the source's position. Much presidential discourse is about reinforcing our national goals and values.

Inoculation. This is another message strategy designed to reinforce existing attitudes by promoting resistance to attitude change. By strengthening existing attitudes, individuals become less susceptible to subsequent persuasive attempts. What is intriguing about this strategy is that when a persuader acknowledges counterarguments or introduces negative information related to his or her own position, audiences are not only more likely to believe the speaker's rhetoric but will be less likely to entertain counterarguments or information in the future. They have been inoculated against future attempts to change their attitudes. This is most useful in political campaigns, especially in generating resistance to the influence of political attacks by opponents.

Polarization. Political language can create likenesses and commonalities; it can also distinguish or separate people, issues, and ideas. Interestingly, sometimes the best way to define an issue or position is by detailing what it is not—contrasting the concept with its opposite. Former President Ronald Reagan, for example, was good at articulating U.S. values of freedom and free enterprise by comparing us with Russia. Of course, a more direct mode of polarization is simply labeling the opposition, issue, ideology, etc. as "bad." While polarizing may divide, it does unite in the sense that it helps clarify positions, actions, and even aspects of ideology.

Defining. As mentioned earlier, in many ways campaigns are really contests to determine the winning definitions of social reality. Is the economy strong or weak? Is the crime rate high or low? Are our values strong or slipping? Is the opponent liberal or conservative? In essence, whose view of reality are voters going to believe? Once again, political language is less about changing opinions than about reinforcing prevailing views or providing the dominant view of social reality. Successfully defining issues or policies so that they resonate with the voting public is the goal of this strategy.

Expression. Many political symbols and rituals are expressive rather than instrumental. Political language allows for the expression of frustration as well as the promotion of specific policy ideas. It deals with hopes as well as fears, successes as well as failures. As the functions of political language identified above illustrate, much of political language fills this function. It is also important to recognize the contribution of political language to entertainment in U.S. popular culture. Novels, films, television, and popular journalism often explore political themes.

Power. Much of political communication is about power, domination, or control. Kenneth Hacker identifies three dimensions of power.[46] The first dimension is control over concrete political interests, revealed in policy preferences. In this case, language is objective, descriptive, and disseminates information. The second dimension of power is control over how issues are defined, debated, and acted upon. Interpretive language is critical in framing issues and defining concepts. The final dimension of power is control over agendas and decision making. Language here is once again utilitarian and concerned with getting things done and shaping society. Power in language is exhibited in many ways: arguments grounded in language that legitimizes the rule of those who govern, appeals to moral authority, or narratives of preferred behavior, to name a few. It is also important to recognize that *how* something is said adds to the power of language as much as *what* is said.

Drama. Most political events are dramatic. For some scholars, politics is living drama and worthy of study. For Hugh Duncan, "failure to understand the power of dramatic form in communication means failure in seizing and controlling power" over others.[47] It is important to remember that social dramas are not just symbolic screens or metaphors; they are forms of social interaction and integration. For example, to focus on dramas of authority one should ask: Under what conditions is the act being presented? What kind of act is it? What roles are the actors assuming? What forms of authority are being communicated? What means of communication are used? What symbols of authority are evoked? How are social functions staged? How are social functions communicated? How are the messages received? What are the responses to authority messages? The drama can involve one person or many, a symbolic (rhetorical) event or physical act, one moment or a specific period of time.

Politics, in Burkean terms, is a study of drama composed of many acts. They are acts of hierarchy, transformation, transcendence, guilt, victimage, redemption, and salvation. With an act as the pivotal concept, Kenneth Burke suggests that we investigate scenes that encompass and surround the act, for the scene provides the context for an act. Next, he suggests that we consider the agents involved in an act; the actors who mold, shape, create, and sustain movements. Likewise, consideration of the agency or the channels of communication in an act help reveal the impact of rhetorical activities. Consideration of the purpose of an act aids in discovering the ultimate motives or meaning of the act.

Drama is part of the communication process by which public issues and views are created, shared, and given life. Ernest and Nancy Bormann call this process "group fantasy." A relatively small number of people may attach significance to some term or concept such as the notions of justice, freedom, or the American dream. These fantasies are shared and passed on to others. Fantasies are contained in messages that channel through the mass media to the general public. When a fantasy theme has "chained through the general public," there emerges a rhetorical vision. "A rhetorical vision is a symbolic reality created by a number of fantasy types and it provides a coherent view of some public problem or issue."[48] Slogans or labels that address a cluster of meanings, motives, or emotional responses usually indicate the emergence of a rhetorical vision. There are several useful implications to the notion of fantasy themes. As a result of creating and sharing fantasies, there is a greater sense of community, cohesiveness, and shared culture. There are, then, common beliefs, attitudes, and values upon which to live and act. And communication is the foundation of it all.

Today, many scholars note that political campaigns are presented as dramas complete with winners, losers, good guys, and villains. Television, in particular, reduces abstract principles to human, personal components. Political issues and actions are linked to individuals. The presenter dominates in television; it is a medium for actors and animate objects rather than complex treatises. We choose among actors rather than ideologies or policies. Victims, villains, and heroes are easier to identify and address than complex issues, causes, or ideas.

Entertainment values encourage tabloid journalism, which has become the mainstay of news today.

> The tabloid reporting style is designed to heighten readers and viewers' sensory experience with the news. The details of stories are presented in graphic form. Tabloid news is written in dramatic, engaging, and readable prose presented in short paragraphs and set off with attention-grabbling headlines and visual accompaniments. TV tabloids feature quick cuts between plots and subplots, highlighting conflict and crisis.[49]

As former anchor and journalist for ABC News, David Brinkley acknowledged, "the one function that TV news performs very well is that when there is no news we give it to you with the same emphasis as if there were news."[50]

Our position is that public views on issues must be mobilized and all these strategies are key elements for that mobilization. Issues are identified and then presented to the public in symbols that appeal to past allegiances or future goals. Neither issues nor specific positions on issues exist in a vacuum. Connecting policies to the attitudes and values of the public insures that they will receive full consideration. Political office and legislation are the result of using appropriate symbols to create political followings and mass support.

Common Political Language Devices

Words can be both descriptive and evaluative. They create a specific reality toward which we act and react. The connotative, interpretive meanings of words are potentially the most dangerous and easily abused. We'll review some of the more common ways language is used to evoke specific responses in people before concluding the chapter with an analysis of the changing nature of public discourse.

Labeling.   Similar to the strategic use of defining, labeling is effective because it renders judgment by making positive or negative associations. For example, how we act toward and perceive an individual differs greatly if we are told the person is inquisitive or nosey, cool or frigid, reflective or moody, thorough or picky, forgetful or senile. Labels tell us what is important about an object and what to expect; socialization prescribes how we should act or interact with the object defined.

Labeling also forces us to make judgments and evaluations, which causes the potential for abuse. It is easier to kill a "gook" or a "Jap" than a human being. Labeling an action as communistic or socialistic produces negative connotations in the United States. How should we characterize the government's bailout of the Chrysler Corporation or the numerous savings and loan associations? What is government's role in terms of subsidies to the poor or social security? Are these examples of socialism? Perhaps. Although we value the concepts of capitalism, free enterprise, and democracy, none of these concepts exist in a pure form. If government officials had described the saving of Chrysler as a socialistic solution, the legislation probably would have failed.

The 1994 congressional elections resulted in a Republican Party majority in the House of Representatives for the first time in forty years. Newt Gingrich, a former history professor from Georgia, became the Speaker of the House. He is credited with reinvigorating the Republican Party. Throughout the 1980s, Congressman Gingrich had served as the nation's leading conservative lightning rod and had gained a reputation as a razor-tongued, oratorical street fighter. In 1990 as president of a Republican group known as GOPAC, Gingrich prepared a list of "positive governing words" and their opposites for distribution to supporters.[51] A large list of colorful adjectives, nouns, and adverbs were supposedly screened by market researchers to locate those that would have special potency with voters. The result: lists of terms of praise and condemnation that potential candidates and campaign workers could use in their local campaigns. A letter mailed to party workers entitled "Language: A Key Mechanism of Control" noted that many politicians had expressed the wish that they "could speak like Newt." The recommendations of GOPAC included the following: characterize yourself and your own record with terms like moral, proud, and hard work. Words GOPAC recommended as useful to "define our opponents" included liberal, shallow, and self-serving. Once labels of individuals or groups are publicly established, they are difficult to change. Which political party favors the rich? The poor? The educated? Big business? If you have somewhat automatic responses to these questions, you are demonstrating the power of social labels.

Doublespeak.   Members of the National Council of Teachers of English (NCTE) passed two resolutions aimed at studying and publicizing the "dishonest and inhumane use of language."[52] The resolutions were the result of growing concern about the manipulation of language by government and military officials in characterizing and reporting the Vietnam War. The NCTE later created the Committee on Public Doublespeak to monitor and combat the misuse of public language by government, public, and corporate officials. The committee began publishing a newsletter (that later evolved into the *Quarterly Review of Doublespeak*) and presenting a doublespeak award for "language that is grossly deceptive, evasive, euphemistic, confusing, or self-contradictory and which has pernicious social or political consequences."[53]

Doublespeak, according to William Lutz, is language that "pretends to communicate but really does not."[54] It says one thing but means something else. It confuses or hides the true meaning or intent of the communicator. It conceals or prevents thought. Such usage of language is certainly not helpful or informative; it is destructive. In short, doublespeak destroys relationships by corrupting thought, destroying communication, and eroding trust. As we have already suggested, language forms the basis of all human actions. We use language to think, to make decisions, and to express our thoughts and feelings on issues. Then we act as a result of processing information, which we can only do by using language. The language we hear and use in our everyday lives influences us and helps shape our opinions to a greater degree than we probably realize. If the language we hear and read is corrupt and misleading, it will corrupt and mislead our thought processes.

Not only does language affect how we think and act, but it also affects our ability to communicate with other people. To discuss issues intelligently, we must use the language that we all agree on. If some people or groups use doublespeak that hides the truth and misleads the receivers of the message, then open, honest discussion cannot take place. We cannot truly relate with people who attempt to mislead. Only through clear language do we have any hope of defining, debating, and deciding the issues of public policy that confront us.

Perhaps the most devastating effect of doublespeak is the erosion of trust. Our nation is founded on the idea of free speech—of open, honest discussion of ideas and issues. When we hear doublespeak from all sides—government, education, the advertising industry, the media—we begin to be cynical and distrustful toward these institutions. Distrust creates another barrier to true, open communication. Doublespeak is not the result of careless grammar or sloppy thinking; rather, it is the intentional use of language to mislead, to distort, and to corrupt.

Lutz identifies four kinds of doublespeak: euphemisms, jargon, bureaucratese, and inflated language. It is useful to discuss each of these in relation to public policy, as well as the related strategy of slanting.

Euphemisms are words or phrases designed to avoid negative or unpleasant reality. We use euphemisms to be courteous and sensitive to the feelings of others. For example, instead of referring to someone as "fat," we use the terms full-figured, husky, portly, or healthy, to name only a few. Firing workers has become big business in these days of re-engineering, restructuring, and downsizing. There are companies that provide termination and outplacement consulting for corporations involved in reduction activities. Just how do companies fire people? They make workforce adjustments, headcount reductions, consensus reductions, and eliminate redundan-

---

Figure 3.2   Euphemisms for Lying

white lie	terminological inexactitude	slight exaggeration
fib	dancing on the edge of the truth	misunderstanding
plausible denial	misinformation	misstatement
misrepresentation	tactical omission	stretching the truth
diversion	anomaly	inaccuracy
abnormal aberration		

---

cies in the human resources area, or initiate a program of negative employee reten-tion. Workers are dehired, deselected, repositioned, rightsized, or surplussed.

Within the realm of politics, however, euphemisms are used to mislead, cover up, or avoid sensitive issues, problems, or positions. During the bombings in Afghanistan in 2001 missiles that struck civilian areas rather than military targets did "collateral damage." Military personnel who were mistakenly and tragically killed by allied forces were casualties of "friendly fire." Such terminology is less unpleasant than the reality of our bombs killing innocent women and children or our soldiers being killed by fellow troop members.

Jargon is the specialized language created for specific functions by people in a trade or profession. The use of jargon is an efficient way to communicate with group members. However, the situation changes decisively when in-group mem-bers use jargon with individuals outside the group. At best, jargon discourages interaction, and it may also confuse or hide the truth. A "needs assessment" (a sur-vey) in order to develop an adequate "evaluation tool" (a test) for those who will manage a "transportation component" (a bus) certainly sounds like a complex and expensive project. Legal documents are full of jargon. They require special inter-pretations that make us dependent on attorneys for help, advice, and action. The medical profession also relies heavily on specialized jargon to communicate. Jar-gon reduces interference from those outside the inner circle and acts as an inhibi-tor to full, open discussion.

Bureaucratese is the piling on of compound words and complex sentences that actually communicate very little. It is often a combination of specialized jargon within rambling sentence structures. In the following example, the U.S. Tariff Commission refuses to complete a questionnaire. (Note the irony of the conclud-ing statement.)

> The problems and considerations together with ancillary ramifications, have been carefully analyzed in conjunction with manipulative and nonmanipulative factors relative to administrative equilibrium. Our conclusions, while tentative and perhaps unsuited to peripheral institutionalization, suggest in marked degree, a sub-marginal coefficient of applicability vis-à-vis the activities of the Commission, and have thus been deemed an appropriate basis for nonactional orientation toward the questionnaire accompanying your letter.
> Please advise us if further information is needed.

Inflated language—marked by euphemisms, jargon, and bureaucratese—is designed to make the common appear uncommon, the ordinary seem extraordinary. Renaming is the most common way to make everyday things more important or impressive: environmental engineers instead of garbage collectors, maintenance engineers instead of custodians, vacation specialist instead of travel agent, or relationship manager instead of salesperson, to name only a few. While the above examples at least serve the function of enhancing worker esteem, others are tragically distorted: pacification center for a concentration camp, tactical withdrawal for a military retreat, or selective deniability for lies by government officials.

Slanting is a form of outright misrepresentation where a particular implication is suggested by omitting certain crucial information. For example, a politician may proclaim that more people are employed today than ever before in our nation's history—while the percentage of people employed might well be lower than ever before. During the bombing of the Balkans in 1999, NATO held daily press briefings showing videos of the pinpoint accuracy of "smart bombs." Omitted from the briefings was any mention of the percentage of the "ordinance" that missed their targets. Without outright lying, the information presented created a different impression than all the facts warranted.

Hate Speech.   In the mid-1980s verbal abuse and violence directed at people of color and other minority groups increased. Many colleges and universities responded by developing policies and codes addressing the usage and nature of public speech acts. State and federal hate crime legislation proliferated.

Rita Whillock and David Slayden recognize hate speech as an operational tactic and rhetorical tool of persuaders. The use of hate by rhetors "is an attempt to win, to dominate the opposition by rhetorical—if not physical—force."[55] They argue that hate speech is used to "polarize particular groups in order to organize opposition, solidify support, and marshal resources toward forcing a 'final solution' to a thorny problem."[56] In effect, polarization "predisposes audiences to negate likely opposing claims, typically utilizing a literal and often highly symbolic object of hatred at which anger is focused."[57]

According to Whillock, "rather than seeking to win adherence through superior reasoning, hate speech seeks to move an audience by creating a symbolic code for violence."[58] More specifically, the goals of hate speech are to inflame the emotions of followers, denigrate the designated out-class, inflict permanent and irreparable harm to the opposition, and ultimately conquer. Hate appeals are insidious because they attract immediate attention and play upon buried cultural beliefs and stereotypes.[59]

Hate speech divides and segregates; it does not invite rational consideration of issues. Compromise is unlikely. Janette Muir suggests that opportunities for traditional persuasive attempts are limited when issues of absolute values conflict with political positions. In such situations, she argues that hate speech is used to sustain a movement "by rallying members around core doctrines and focusing their efforts against a common enemy."[60]

Hate speech is a troubling matter for people who believe in free speech. The First Amendment to the United States Constitution protects speech no matter how offensive its content. Free speech is integral to a democratic society; the freedom of all depends on each individual's right to express his or her views. Free speech advocates claim that hate speech laws cannot legislate an end to ethnic and racial violence. In fact, they argue that what is needed is more speech, not less. The goal should be to facilitate learning and understanding through open debate and discussion of all viewpoints. Dialogue and democracy are more effective tools in understanding the anatomy of hate than silence; for that reason, freedom of expression is necessary.

THE CHANGING NATURE OF PUBLIC AND POLITICAL DISCOURSE
▲

As society and technology change, so do the ways politicians campaign and govern. As a result, political rhetoric has undergone a fundamental change in both form and content. Barnet Baskerville argues in *The People's Voice* that

> societal values and attitudes are reflected not only in what the speaker says but also in how he says it—not only in the ideas and arguments to be found in speeches of the past but in the methods and practices of representative speakers and in the role and status accorded speakers by the listening public. As public tastes and public needs change, so do speaking practices—types of appeal, verbal style, modes of delivery.[61]

The United States has a rich history of political oratory. For much of our history, public speaking provided the main avenue to success and popularity. Politicians were expected to make frequent, lengthy, public orations. Political speeches were public spectacles with banners, bands, slogans, and fireworks. Beginning with Lincoln's Gettysburg Address, political oratory began to change. He established a trend toward brevity and simplicity. There was also a shift of public attention from politics to business. Business people espoused virtues of directness, conciseness, and pragmatism. In the media, the number of magazine articles and newspaper stories increased while their length decreased. Political speeches followed those trends and became shorter, more colloquial, and less airy. In fact, political oratory became public speaking with an emphasis on utility of message and the sharing of information.

The introduction of radio signaled another shift in political oratory. It introduced lively discussion shows, news reports (unlike news stories), and time constraints on both the speaker and audience. Radio crossed ethnic and regional boundaries. Public officials had to speak "at" audiences, not "with" audiences. The press became filters rather than vehicles of political communication.

The third major change in political campaign rhetoric was caused by television. By 1974, Kevin Phillips proclaimed that "in the age of the mass media, the old Republican and Democratic parties have lost their logic. Effective communications are replacing party organizations as the key to political success. . . . As the first communications society, the United States is on its way to becoming the first 'mediacracy.'"[62] We are witnessing the evolution of the new presidential rhetoric that differs in both form and content from that of only 20 years ago.

Today, we know our leaders only through the media. Television, as a medium, has changed the form and content of politics. As noted, the days of impassioned, fiery oratory presented to packed auditoriums are over. Today, presidents invite us, through the medium of television, into the privacy of their living rooms, offices, or studios for informal "presidential conversations." Kathleen Jamieson argues that the illusion of interpersonal, intimate context created through television requires a new eloquence, one in which candidates and presidents adopt a personal and revealing style that engages the audience in conversation.[63]

This means shorter speeches crafted specifically for television. Presidential speech is increasingly familiar, personalized, and self-revealing. Ronald Reagan was the first to excel at this style, which stands in marked contrast to the conversational style of Franklin D. Roosevelt, for example. The strength of Reagan's rhetoric was that we felt we knew and understood him, while the strength of FDR's was that he knew and understood us. Reagan's use of contractions—simple and often incomplete sentences, informal transitions, colloquial language, and frequent stories—transformed his formal Oval Office addresses into conversations with the people.[64] His skillful adaptation to the camera simulated direct eye contact with individuals in his audience. It had all the appearance of conversation, inviting the audience to conclude that it knows and likes presidents who use it.

Public officials adapt to the medium of television through higher levels of intimacy and expressiveness. The presumption of intimacy attempts to make the audience feel as if they know the official as a dear friend and to force the audience to render positive, personal judgments. Frequent conversations lead to friendship, trust, and intimacy with the nation. Issue disagreements are less important and are tolerated because of the appearance of friendship.[65]

While Reagan proved that television's intimacy could heighten audience identification, the 1992 presidential campaign introduced another context—Clinton's mastery of the town-hall meeting format epitomizes "presidential mediated interpersonal conversation."[66] With Clinton, presidential conversation became the primary means of conveying policy orientations and image projection. These one-on-one sessions, sometimes with viewer call-in or a live audience, seemingly moved the president one step closer to the public. Participation and interaction were encouraged. Settings gave the appearance of a casual interaction where the audience simply eavesdrops on the conversation.

Both the structure and the content of mediated presidential conversation differs from nonmediated conversation. Interviews on television differ greatly from those in print. The secret is a controlled response best suited for the medium of television. On television, how one responds is as important as the content of the response. Perceptions of personal characteristics conveyed primarily in nonverbal communication influence viewer perception of specific presidential performances. Was there a hesitation, a shift of the brow, an expression of emotion? In the infamous 1992 Richmond presidential candidate debate with Clinton and Perot, George H. Bush took a quick glance at his watch. This simple action communicated a rather callous, cavalier attitude toward the audience and the event. His glance dominated the headlines the day after the debate.

We are currently riding the crest of a new wave of technologies. The Internet, computers, fiber optics, and satellites have introduced an era of high-speed communication that greatly impacts the creation, collection, and dissemination of information and promises to enhance the public's understanding of political issues and to motivate citizen participation. The new media transcend the time and space constraints of traditional media. In addition, the new media bypass national and international boundaries.

Davis and Owen identify several major differences in the potential and actual influence between the new media and traditional media.[67] First, the new media have an anti-institutional bias. Historically, the mainstream media had, as part of their mission, public service and an obligation to cover governmental affairs. The new media have profit and entertainment as their primary concern. Thus, because the new media cover politics as entertainment, their focus is more on personalities and human-interest stories than issue education. The coverage is more personal, colorful, and conflict oriented. Second, the new media are populists in content and coverage. The focus is on conflict with an anti-establishment, anti-incumbent slant. Finally, the new media are less concerned with more traditional standards of ethics than the traditional media. There is less objectivity or even fairness in presentation. Members of the new media are more ideological and willing to use their positions to advance specific people or causes.[68]

The Internet is becoming one of the defining scientific and social innovations of this century. The information superhighway, as labeled by politicians and the media, has the ability to link people and resources in a way that was never previously possible. Users can share data, communicate messages, transfer programs, discuss topics, and connect to computer systems all over the world. The potential of the Internet as a tool for retrieving information is almost limitless. As a result of the freedom of expression allowed on this unique network, the possibilities for learning and enrichment are endless. But with a network so large (and a territory so uncharted), there is great concern about the material readily available to anyone accessing the Internet.

The role of the Internet in politics is still evolving and uncertain. It is a medium, however, that no politician can ignore. Indeed, well over 100 million American adults accessed the Internet specifically for election information during the 2000 electoral season.[69] It ranked behind television but just ahead of newspapers as the primary source of obtaining political news.[70] With each campaign cycle, we learn more about the uses of the Internet and those who use it for political purposes. Currently, most candidate sites have video, press releases, issue statements, merchandise for purchase, contribution opportunities, and opportunities to receive weekly e-mail bulletins.

In 2003 Democratic presidential candidate Howard Dean revolutionized political fund-raising with his "cyberstumping," building a solid grassroots organization.[71] In reaction to the news that the vice president was attending a $2,000 a plate fund-raising luncheon, Dean's campaign posted a picture on its Web site of the candidate eating a turkey sandwich while sitting at the computer. His appeal raised more than $500,000 in three days. Indeed, during the early months of his campaign, he received contributions totaling $7.5 million in three months from supporters reached through the Internet. The average contribution was slightly more than $100.[72] The Dean campaign reported 130,000 registered activists online, and 30,000 of them wrote handwritten notes to 60,000 undecided voters in Iowa and New Hampshire.[73]

Kevin Hill and John Hughes argue the Internet has the potential to change the flow of political information and thus revolutionize the process of political communication.[74] Prior to the Internet, the flow of political information was primarily one-way from the media to the public. The Internet now allows individuals to become, in effect, broadcasters, providing unfiltered information not shared by more mainstream media channels. They found that Internet activists tend to identify themselves as Democrats (although they vote for both parties in about equal numbers), oppose government regulations of personal activities, and are more politically active and knowledgeable than the general population. However, Internet activists are also more anti-government than the rest of society.[75]

SUMMARY

▲

We began this chapter by considering the impact and importance of presidential discourse. For some, certain words cause feelings of comfort, for others feelings of concern, and for others feelings of anger. The various reactions to President Bush's words about the September 11 attack remind us that perceptions of the same event vary dramatically. Language reveals a great deal about the speaker and the listener—and the society in which they live.

Symbols are human inventions. They have meaning or significance only when, through experience or agreement, we interpret them. Through language we construct the reality that influences our behavior. Through interaction with others, we come to know who we are, how we fit in, and what we are supposed to do.

Finally, we investigated the nature of political language, several common political uses of language, and the changing nature of political discourse. We saw how language can be used to control us, to confuse us, and to hide information from us. To communicate effectively and to understand the communication of others we must analyze the process of selection, interpretation, and symbolism used in constructing all messages.

Questions and Projects for Further Study

1. Why does it matter if we say a glass is half full or half empty?
2. Think of words or expressions that have clear meanings for you but may not be clear to your parents. Why?
3. What is your greatest strength? How do you know?
4. What is your greatest weakness? How do you know?
5. Give an example of how you define "self" through an interaction you've had with another or others.
6. Do you stop at a stop sign even if no one is around? Why?

7. What does the term "freedom" mean to you? What does the term "equality" mean to you?

8. Prepare a list of five words to describe the United States, China, and Yugoslavia. How do the lists differ? Why?

9. Find the stockholders' report for a large company on the Internet. Identify examples of doublespeak: euphemisms, jargon, bureaucratese, inflated language, and slanting.

10. Select several magazine print ads and analyze the language of the ads. What promises are implied? What does the ad not tell you?

11. Can you think of an example of hate speech? Should there be some restrictions on the use of hate speech?

12. Go to the library and select the most recent presidential State of the Union address in *Vital Speeches*. How many functions of political language were used in the address?

Additional Reading

Herbert Blumer, *Symbolic Interactionism: Perspective and Method* (Englewood Cliffs, NJ: Prentice Hall, 1969).

Robert E. Denton, Jr. and Gary Woodward, *Political Communication in America*, 3rd ed. (New York: Praeger, 1998).

Hugh Duncan, *Symbols in Society* (New York: Oxford University Press, 1968).

Murray Edelman, *Constructing the Political Spectacle* (Chicago: University of Chicago Press, 1988).

Sonja Foss, Karen Foss, and Robert Trapp, *Contemporary Perspectives on Rhetoric*, 3rd ed. (Prospect Heights, IL: Waveland Press, 2002).

Ann Gill, *Rhetoric and Human Understanding* (Prospect Heights, IL: Waveland Press, 1994).

Roderick Hart, *Campaign Talk: Why Elections are Good for Us* (New Jersey: Princeton University Press, 2000).

Kathleen Hall Jamieson, *Eloquence in an Electronic Age* (New York: Oxford University Press, 1988).

Paschal Preston, *Reshaping Communication* (Thousand Oaks, CA: Sage, 2001).

Rita Whillock and David Slayden, eds., *Hate Speech* (Thousand Oaks, CA: Sage, 1995).

Notes

[1] Judith Butler, *Excitable Speech: A Politics of the Performance* (New York: Routledge, 1997), p. 1.

[2] Tom Brokaw, *The Greatest Generation* (New York: Random House, 1998), p. xx.

[3] Ibid., p. xxx.

[4] George Bush, "Address by George W. Bush, President of the United States, Delivered to the Nation, Washington, D.C., September 11, 2001," *Vital Speeches of the Day*, Vol. LXVII, No. 24, October 1, 2001, p. x.

[5] George Bush, "Address by George W. Bush, President of the United States, Delivered to a Joint Session of Congress and the American People, Washington, D.C., September 20, 2001," *Vital Speeches of the Day*, Vol. LXVII, No. 24, p. 760.

[6] Ibid., p. 761.

[7] James Hebert, "Reigning Words: Leaders, Media Can Cause a Storm of Debate in the Labels They Use," *The San Diego Union-Tribune*, October 4, 2001, E-1.

[8] Ibid.

[9] Reed Irvine and Cliff Kincaid, "Is Reuters Kowtowing to Terrorists?" *Accuracy in Media*, November 22, 2001 (http://www.aim.org).

[10] For a succinct summary of signs, symbols, and signification, see *Rhetoric and Human Understanding* by Ann Gill (Prospect Heights, IL: Waveland Press, 1994), pp. 6–17.

[11] Ibid., p. 9.

[12] Ibid., p. 15.

[13] Ibid., p. 7.

[14] Ibid., p. 16.

[15] C. Ogden and I. A. Richards, *The Meaning of Meaning* (New York: Harcourt Brace Jovanovich, 1923).

[16] Dan Rothwell, *Telling It Like It Isn't* (Englewood Cliffs, NJ: A Spectrum Book, 1982), p. 13.

[17] Sonja K. Foss, Karen A. Foss, and Robert Trapp, *Contemporary Perspectives on Rhetoric*, 3rd ed. (Prospect Heights, IL: Waveland Press, 2002), p. 212.

[18] Arthur Asa Berger, *Signs in Contemporary Culture: An Introduction to Semiotics* (Salem, WI: Sheffield, 1989), p. 173.

[19] Ibid.

[20] Foss, Foss, and Trapp, p. 64.

[21] Ibid., p. 62.

[22] Ernesto Grassi, *Rhetoric as Philosophy: The Humanist Tradition* (University Park: University of Pennsylvania Press, 1980), p. 96.

[23] Rothwell, p. 48.

[24] Gill, p. 28.

[25] See John Carroll and Joseph Casagrande, "The Function of Language Classifications in Behavior," *Communication and Culture*, ed. Alfred Smith (New York: Holt, Rinehart & Winston, 1966), p. 491.

[26] Stephen Littlejohn, *Theories of Human Communication*, 7th ed. (Belmont, CA: Wadsworth, 2002), p. 177.

[27] Gill, p. 21.

[28] S. I. Hayakawa, *Language in Thought and Action*, 3rd ed. (New York: Harcourt Brace Jovanovich, 1972), pp. 27–30.

[29] Ronald Reid, *American Rhetorical Discourse*, 2nd ed. (Prospect Heights, IL: Waveland Press, 1995), pp. 387–92.

[30] Frank Dance, "The Functions of Speech Communication as an Integrative Concept in the Field of Communication," *XV Convegno Internazionale delle Comunicazioni* (Genoa, Italy: Instituto Internazionale delle Comunicazioni, 1967), p. 14.

[31] Joshua Whatmough, *Language: A Modern Synthesis* (New York: New American Library, 1956).

[32] Roman Jakobson, "Closing Statement: Linguistics and Poetics," *Style in Language,* ed. Thomas Sebeok (Cambridge, MA: MIT Press, 1960), pp. 350–77.

[33] Gill, pp. 9–10.

[34] Foss, Foss, and Trapp, p. 198.

[35] Paul E. Corcoran, "Language and Politics," *New Directions in Political Communication,* eds. David Swanson and Dan Nimmo (Newbury Park, CA: Sage, 1990), p. 70.

[36] Ibid.

[37] Murray Edelman, *Constructing the Political Spectacle* (Chicago: University of Chicago Press, 1988), p. 108.

[38] Corcoran, p. 53.

[39] Doris Graber, "Political Languages," *Handbook of Political Communication*, eds. Dan Nimmo and Keith Sanders (Beverly Hills: Sage, 1981), pp. 195–224.

[40] Gorge W. Bush, "The 2002 State of the Union," *Vital Speeches of the Day*, Vol. LXVIII, pp. 258–62. Quotations in this paragraph are from p. 262.

[41] Ibid., p. 260.

[42] Ibid., p. 261.

[43] Ibid.

[44] Craig Allen Smith, *Political Communication* (San Diego, CA: Harcourt Brace Jovanovich, 1990), pp. 61–62.

[45] Kenneth Burke, *A Rhetoric of Motives* (Berkeley: University of California Press, 1969), p. 55.

[46] Kenneth Hacker, "Political Linguistic Discourse Analysis," *The Theory and Practice of Political Communication Research*, ed. Mary Stuckey (Albany: University of New York Press, 1996), p. 29.

[47] Hugh Duncan, *Symbols in Society* (New York: Oxford University Press, 1968), p. 25.

[48] Ernst and Nancy Bormann, *Speech Communication: A Comprehensive Approach* (New York: Harper & Row, 1977), pp. 306–17.

[49] Richard Davis and Diana Owen. *New Media and American Politics* (New York: Oxford University Press, 1998), p. 96.

[50] Ibid., p. 260.

[51] See Michael Oreskes, "For GOP Arsenal, 133 Words to Fire," *New York Times,* September 9, 1990, Section One, p. 30.

[52] William Lutz, "Resolutions," *Beyond Nineteen Eighty-Four,* ed. William Lutz (Urbana, IL: National Council of Teachers of English, 1989), p. ix.

[53] Ibid., p. xii.

[54] William Lutz, "Notes Toward a Definition of Doublespeak" in Lutz, p. 4.

[55] Rita Whillock and David Slayden, eds. *Hate Speech* (Thousand Oaks, CA: Sage, 1995), p. xiii.

[56] Ibid., p. xiii.

[57] Ibid., p. xiii.

[58] Rita Whillock, "The Use of Hate as a Stratagem for Achieving Political and Social Goals," in Whillock and Slayden, p. 32.

[59] Ibid., pp. 32–33.

[60] Janette K. Muir, "Hating for Life: Rhetorical Extremism and Abortion Clinic Violence," in Whillock and Slayden, p. 164.

[61] Barnet Baskerville, *The People's Voice* (Lexington: University of Kentucky Press, 1979), p. 4.

[62] Kevin Phillips, *Mediacracy* (New York: Doubleday, 1974), p. v.

[63] Kathleen H. Jamieson, *Eloquence in an Electronic Age* (New York: Oxford University Press, 1988), p. 166.

[64] Ibid.

[65] Robert Cathcart and Gary Gumpert, "Mediated Interpersonal Communication: Toward a New Typology," *Quarterly Journal of Speech,* 1986, 69:267–77.

[66] Robert E. Denton, Jr. and Rachel Holloway, "Clinton and the Town Hall Meetings: Mediated Conversation and the Risk of Being 'In Touch,'" in *The Clinton Presidency: Images, Issues, and Communication Strategies,* eds. Robert E. Denton and Rachel Holloway (Westport, CT: Praeger, 1996) pp. 17–41.

[67] Davis and Owen.

[68] Ibid., p. 17–20.

[69] Lee Rainie and Dan Packel. 18 February 2001. "More Online, Doing More." The Pew Internet & American Life Project. (Online) http://www.pewinternet.org

[70] BIGResearch. February 2001. "Public Policy & Media Influence Study." Available online: http://www.bigresearch.com

[71] Jonathan Alter, "The Left's Mr. Right," *Newsweek,* August 11, 2003, p. 24.

[72] Editorial, "Dean Shakes Up the Democrats," *Chicago Tribune,* July 8, 2003, p. 20.

[73] Alter, p. 24.

[74] Kevin Hill and John Hughes, *Cyberpolitics* (Lanham, MD: Rowman & Littlefield, 1998), p. 21–22.

[75] Ibid., p. 243.

PART II

FOUR PERSPECTIVES ON THE NATURE OF PERSUASION

Persuasion and Reasoning

Overview

▲ Understanding Practical Arguments
    Analytic Arguments and Practical Enthymemes
    Demonstration and Argumentation
    Factual and Judgmental Claims
    Implied and Stated Components of Arguments
    Reasoning to Discover and to Defend
    Finding Good Reasons for Claims
    A False Distinction: Logic or Emotion

▲ Common Forms of Defective Reasoning
    Ad Hominem
    False Cause
    Non Sequitur
    Circular Argument
    Excessive Dependence on Authority

▲ How Persuasion and Logical Argumentation Differ
    Denial Often Defeats Reasoning
    Persuasion's Self-Interest and Argumentation's Public Interest

---

> *The power of reason is simply the power of the whole mind at its fullest stretch and compass.*[1]
>
> —J. E. CREIGHTON

Reasoning is about linkages. We invent, organize, and communicate ideas with the intention of establishing connections that make sense. Over the centuries logicians and philosophers have attempted to codify this process. The results have ranged from sometimes helpful to sometimes obscure, but it is important to remember that the ideal of logical thought underpins nearly every form of communication—especially persuasion. Understanding someone else involves the subtle process of taking a measure of their credibility. In virtually all forms of communication logical connections are made or missed in the continual process of estimating the significance of ideas.

Comedy is often premised on the illogical. It is one important cultural vehicle where sense becomes nonsense. Our laughter about absurd connections acts as a sign that we hold membership in the society of the sane. In *Four Weddings and a Funeral,* actor Hugh Grant's character, Charles, struggles to start a casual conversation with an apparently confused old man at a reception. As the film reminds us, miscommunication is essentially illogical communication.

Charles: How do you do, my name is Charles.

Old Man: Don't be ridiculous, Charles died 20 years ago!

Charles: Must be a different Charles, I think.

Old Man: Are you telling me I don't know my own brother![2]

The Coen brothers display their gleefully contorted logic in the film *O Brother, Where Art Thou?*. Three escaped convicts start out on a quest for freedom. But only Ulysses (George Clooney) has even a partial grasp of the English language:

Pete: Wait a minute. Who elected you leader of this outfit?

Ulysses: Well, Pete, I figured it should be the one with the capacity for abstract thought. But if that ain't the consensus view, then hell, let's put it to a vote.

Pete: Suits me. I'm voting for yours truly.

Ulysses: Well I'm voting for yours truly too.

(Both look to Delmar for the deciding vote.)

Delmar: Okay . . . I'm with you fellas.[3]

The illogical structure of these dialogues makes the statements funny to audiences precisely because we expect conversations to follow certain patterns and to be clearly reasoned. In this chapter, we define reasoning, examine some of its basic patterns, and suggest ways to estimate how patterns of reasoning vary in their power to gain compliance or command agreement. In addition, we will identify common logical mistakes that persuaders often make and some important distinctions between logical reasoning and persuasion.

Individuals are not always willing to commit the necessary mental energy to the task of determining whether conclusions have significant rational justifications.[4] Our reasons for accepting persuasive messages are sometimes more personal and eclectic than strictly logical. However, persuaders will usually fail if they do not recognize the important role of rationality in persuasion.

UNDERSTANDING PRACTICAL ARGUMENTS
▲

Stephen Toulmin, Richard Rieke, and Allan Janik note that reasoning "is a collective and continuing human transaction, in which we present ideas or claims to particular sets of people within particular situations or contexts and offer the appropriate kinds of 'reasons' in their support."[5] *Claims* linked to *evidence* or *good reasons* are what we mean when we use the term *argument*. Claims are assertions that we hope we can convince others to accept. Some claims are never stated in public because we feel we do not have the rational means to defend them. We may privately believe prejudices such as "the French are lazy," or "the Swedish drink too much." But when we *publicly* express our conclusions, we enter the realm of reasoning, because we assume that our assertions will be able to withstand the critical scrutiny of others. Phrases such as "I know . . . ," "It's true that . . . ," and "It would be difficult to doubt . . ." imply that we can provide evidence or good reasons to back up our views.

Aristotle was among the first to put practical reasoning at the center of persuasion theory. He criticized other teachers of persuasion in ancient Greece for presenting "but a small portion of the art," neglecting the important role that practical reasoning plays in winning converts. "Persuasion," he noted, "is clearly a sort of demonstration" that depends on a sequence of logically related statements or arguments. A statement is persuasive and credible either because it is directly self-evident or because it appears to be proved by other believable statements. Aristotle called these arguments containing facts or judgments acceptable to an audience "enthymemes" and noted that they "are the most effective of the modes of persuasion."[6] We will have more to say about the special nature of enthymemes shortly. But first, it is important to point out several key differences between formal arguments used by logicians and the everyday practical arguments used in persuasion.

Analytic Arguments and Practical Enthymemes

The reasoning of formal logic is very different from the enthymemes of ordinary life. Formal logic starts with the ideal of the analytic argument where claims necessarily follow from a series of premises. An argument is analytic when its conclusion is contained in (or absolutely follows from) its premises.[7] In this kind of ironclad reasoning sequence, the claim is necessary rather than probable because acceptance of the premises dictates acceptance of the conclusion.

Although the circumstances of real life rarely allow us to construct valid and true analytic arguments, this ideal provides a tantalizing model for persuaders. If we could construct arguments with the certainty of a mathematical sum, we would be very confident about the eventual outcome. We don't usually argue about mathematical outcomes, we accept them without debate if they conform to certain universal rules.

Mathematics provides the easiest language for the writing of analytic arguments because—unlike ordinary language—mathematical symbols are completely unambiguous and value free. For example, the expression

$$2 + 5 = 7$$

is analytic because its conclusion (the sum of 7) necessarily follows from its premises (universally accepted definitions of what "2," "5," and "+" mean). Similarly, the equation

$$(3 \times 6^2 \div 4) - 25 + 8 = 10$$

uses a rigid logic that leads to an unchallengeable result. Anywhere in the world, a mathematically competent person (whether a socialist, capitalist, Muslim, or Christian) could be expected to reach the same conclusion by correctly applying universally accepted rules and premises.

We can also use letters rather than numbers to represent analytic arguments. For example:

1. If A then B.

2. A.
    Therefore,
    B.

In this argument—sometimes also called deductive or syllogistic—the relationship defined in the first premise ("If A is present then B is also present") sets up a reasoning sequence that leads irreversibly to the claim. We can substitute ordinary language in place of letters or numbers to give the same argumentative form a concrete setting.

Premise: If Harry decides to go to Europe this summer, Jan will travel with him.

Premise: Harry has decided to go.

(Therefore)

Claim: Jan will also be in Europe this summer.

The most interesting characteristic of valid analytic arguments is that there is no way to deny the claim if you accept the premises. Indeed, the conclusion is contained in the premises. The prospect of developing a series of statements that implies a built-in certainty has attracted scholars and scientists for hundreds of years. The idea of asserting a series of statements of fact or judgment that cannot be refuted is extremely alluring. Philosophers from Descartes to Bentham hoped that humankind would benefit from a logic that used known premises to reach unchallengeable conclusions. They were intrigued by the possibility that people could move beyond the fictions, falsehoods, and exceptions common to ordinary discussion. As "a system of necessary propositions which will impose itself on every rational being," the idea of the valid analytic argument promises timelessness and absolute truth.[8] To them this was more than an idle pipe dream; a logic as universal as the logic of mathematics—if it could be found or invented—would be a valuable pathway that could save the human race from wars and other destructive forms of conflict.

The *force* of analytic arguments has intrigued persuaders. Just as we do not argue about the answers to basic math problems (an answer is either right or wrong), analytic arguments used in actual persuasive situations would make the conversion of listeners or readers a simple matter of explaining ironclad relationships. As a result, many persuasive statements use the general form of analytic arguments, even if their actual force is less than their form implies. Consider the controversial ruling of the Southern Baptist Convention—the country's largest Protestant denomination—on the role of women in the family. In their 1998 declaration on family life, the claim was made that a woman should "submit herself graciously" to her husband's leadership. Wives "were created to be 'helpers' to their husbands. A wife's submission to her husband does not decrease her worth but rather enhances her value to her husband."[9] Many reasons were given, but the arguments generally offered the following premises and conclusion:

Premise: Ephesians 5:22–23 notes that a husband's relationship with his wife should be like Christ's "rule" over the church.

Premise: The Bible is the word of God.

(Therefore)

Claim: Wives should submit to the leadership of their husbands.

If the Bible is the word of God and that word must be followed, then claims derived from the testimony of the Bible seem to be binding. Those who accept both premises would find it hard to reject the conclusion. Of course, the variability of biblical scholarship and alternate interpretations of scripture are additional factors that make it possible for others to reach different conclusions about the premises. Even with its strong internal structure, one still depends upon the externalities of one's own faith: for example, how we read biblical and doctrinal claims, and how we interpret them in light of changing social conventions.

There are two difficulties common to many analytic arguments on persuasive topics. The first problem results from the fact that ordinary language is affected by personal and cultural values; unanimous agreement is difficult, if not impossible, to achieve. The farther we move away from purely *denotative* languages such as mathematics, the less likely we are to locate valid analytic arguments that deal with the complexities of the real world. Language is less precise than numbers. The symbols "2" or "%," for example, have single stipulated meanings. Even relatively denotative words like "is," "allows," or "cannot" seem to define precise relationships, but they are subject to interpretation. Language carries our values and evokes personal feelings. As we move toward more *connotative* words—like "sovereignty," "democracy," "clever," or "lustful"—the possibilities for different interpretations multiply. It would be extremely odd to hear that a friend liked the number "7" better than the number "2," or grew angry at the sight of a percent sign. But it does not surprise us that thousands of years of human history have failed to produce agreement about what constitutes a democracy or even truth itself.[10] A second reason for the difficulty in making airtight analytic arguments is that most persuasive statements do not apply to all cases, categories, or people. The claim "all As are Bs" is easy to state and manipulate as an abstract expression, but it is much more difficult to make comparable categorical assertions that would help settle real human differences. People, groups, and cultures are rarely "all" of anything. In the realm of human affairs, the only statements that can be made without citing important exceptions are either obvious (water is necessary to sustain life) or trivial (all children have parents).

This is where the concept of the enthymeme is useful. Aristotle shrewdly noted that the enthymeme was "sort of" analytic, because ordinary persuasion finds its premises in the probable existing opinions of audiences rather than the categorical truths (the "alls" and "if-thens") of formal logic.[11] The conclusions of enthymemes are contingent on audience acceptance; they are not certain. Because enthymemes spell out logical relationships based on generally accepted opinions,[12] they must be at least partially judged by how well the persuader has used audience beliefs as premises for persuasion. Here, for example, is an enthymeme that Aristotle cites to show how to argue from generally accepted beliefs to persuasive claims:

> Thus it may be argued that if even the gods are not omniscient, certainly human beings are not. The principle here is that, if a quality does not in fact exist where it is more likely to exist, it clearly does not exist where it is less likely.[13]

Or, in a simpler diagrammatic form:

Premise: Even gods are not omniscient.

Premise: (Since the gods are better than people.)

Claim: Certainly human beings are not omniscient.

Note that the premise "the gods are not omniscient" is a statement of social belief. Like the declaration from the Southern Baptists, the reasoning sequence makes sense only if the premises are accepted.

NON SEQUITUR

Demonstration and Argumentation

We can approach the distinction between formal arguments and practical enthymemes from another useful perspective. Aristotle noted what many analysts of reasoning continually rediscover: the reasoning of analytic arguments is a form of demonstration; everyday persuasion requires argumentation. The differences between the two are enormous. A mathematics problem is a demonstration because its final sum is self-evidently true. The transformation of the various operations into a conclusion does not depend on discussion. No one deliberates over claims that are self-evident by definition or direct observation. In contrast, everyday argumentation is not so much concerned with truth as with the possible agreement of readers or listeners. We may argue a point to a hostile audience using a wide variety of reasoning skills, but we know that we cannot sweep away all of their doubts in the same way that we can correct an incorrect math problem.

As Aristotle noted, practical reasoning works from opinions that are generally accepted. Demonstrations work from basic premises where it would be "improper to ask any further for the why and wherefore of them."[14] There probably are no universal procedures for demonstrating conclusions such as "the United States is the most democratic society on earth." We may *argue* this point successfully before many audiences, but there is no way to *demonstrate* the point—to make claims that are immune from potential disagreement. Practical persuasion is thus always subject to the acceptance of a particular audience. In locating persuasive ideas to build arguments, we meet our audiences "on the ground . . . of their own convictions."[15]

Factual and Judgmental Claims

Another basic distinction about arguments is deciding whether they contain claims of fact or claims of judgment. Generally speaking, the force of an argument focused on a claim of judgment will not be as highly regarded as a well constructed reasoning sequence in support of a claim of fact. Facts hold out the possibility of being proven true or false. Judgments, in contrast, express priorities, preferences, or values that may justifiably differ from individual to individual.

We frequently misidentify a judgmental claim as a factual claim, thereby underestimating how much disagreement can be expected. The word "is" in a claim often creates the confusion. "Is" and other indicative verb forms (i.e., "was" and "were") have an aura of finality that makes judgmental claims sometimes seem as provable and timeless as known facts. For instance, the statement "Bill Clinton was a better president than George W. Bush" is not a statement of fact. As applied to the presidency, "better" can be legitimately defined in different ways. One person may rank a president's foreign policy decisions higher than his domestic policies; someone else may reverse these priorities. By contrast, factual claims are statements that hold the promise of being demonstrated as true or false, regardless of your own beliefs.[16] Here are some examples:

- Water at sea level boils at 210° F.
- Sirhan Sirhan killed Senator Robert Kennedy in 1968.
- The *Los Angeles Times* has the nation's largest circulation.
- There were no passenger deaths on any U.S. based airlines in 2003.
- Deaths from automobile crashes have decreased in the last ten years.

All of these statements share the possibility of being shown conclusively right or wrong. We say "possibility" because the available evidence is sometimes insufficient to discover the truth about actual events. For example, we know (it is an unchallenged fact) that the baby of aviation hero Charles Lindbergh mysteriously disappeared from his family's Hopewell, New Jersey, home. We also know that a carpenter, Bruno Richard Hauptmann, was convicted of kidnapping the baby in 1935 and was later electrocuted. But there are still doubts that Hauptmann committed the crime.[17] Persuasion frequently involves factual claims in widely varying situations: the courtroom (Hauptmann was probably innocent), the physical sciences (some deep sea plants do not need sunlight to flourish), and on social issues that attribute specific effects to specific causes (children watching violent television programs sometimes imitate the violence they see).

The most common claims in the realm of persuasion are judgmental. These cannot be proved or settled by citing supporting facts, nor can they be known in the same way that we know the truth of a statement such as "Texas was once a part of Mexico." A judgmental claim involves the assignment of personal preferences to persons, objects, or laws. The words we use in these claims indicate how we feel about what we are describing. The object of our attention is good, bad, worthwhile, dangerous, or desirable, reflecting our (and often our culture's) preferences about what is right or wrong, decent or indecent, moral or immoral, important or insignificant. Consider these samples:

- The vast U.S. system of higher education is the best in the world.
- Professional athletes are grossly overpaid.
- Door County in Wisconsin is a better vacation value than Cape Cod.
- Catholicism is superior to other forms of Christianity.
- Our criminal justice system is a national disgrace.
- Insurance companies unfairly discriminate against young drivers.
- Legalized gambling is a legitimate way for governments to raise revenue.

Note that in every statement, either an adjective or a noun gives a judgmental spin to the claim. Words like "best," "superior," "disgrace," "legitimate," and "unfairly" express feelings about the qualities of ideas or objects. We can prove to the satisfaction of most reasoning people that "smoking increases a person's chances of contracting lung cancer"—a valid cause and effect factual claim with ample proof to support it. We cannot with the same certainty prove that "Catholicism is a superior form of Christianity."

This is not to say that the old axiom warning us not to argue about religion or politics is correct. We do debate our preferences with others—and we should. Preferences and values are the basis of most of the laws and codes we live by. The only caution is that it is unreasonable to expect that argumentation will put all contrary positions to rest in the same way that a piece of evidence may prove that a defendant in a trial is guilty beyond any reasonable doubt.

Implied and Stated Components of Arguments

When we make passing comments about noncontroversial subjects, the logical relationships that contributed to the assertions rarely need to be explored. The claim that "it is too hot today" is usually accompanied by obvious evidence (high temperature and humidity, bright sun, etc.) that makes it unnecessary to provide supporting reasons. If pressed, however, we *could* make the reasoning behind almost any assertion explicit by writing down all relevant claims and premises. Our complete argument about the weather might include a factual premise ("the thermometer reads ninety-two degrees") and a judgmental premise that interprets the significance of the facts (in my opinion, ninety-two degrees is too hot). Here is the argument diagrammed as an enthymeme:

Factual Premise: "The thermometer reads ninety-two degrees."

Judgmental Premise: (implied but not stated) A temperature of over ninety-two is too hot.

(Therefore)

Claim: "It is too hot today."

As in our simple example, it is often unnecessary to make all of the premises (and sometimes even the claims) of our arguments explicit. Aristotle reminds us that we can count on our listeners to supply parts of the reasoning sequence because speakers and listeners frequently share similar assumptions about what evidence implies.

There are other times when we need to locate hidden premises in order to discover the unstated relationships on which assertions are based. We need to analyze the fragmented patterns of everyday speech and thought to detect the claims that lie beneath the surface. During the 2000 elections people who quoted "Bushisms," for example, often made an argument by offering evidence and implying the claim. Although Bush readily admitted that he could get tangled up in his own words, a BBC correspondent essentially asked readers to contemplate the language of a candidate who called people from Greece "Grecians" and referred to "tariffs and barriers" as "terriers and barriffs."[18] An unstated, but clearly implied, conclusion was his rhetoric was a sign that he was not up to the job of the presidency.

Frequently we are trying to discover the warrants for arguments. The claim is the conclusion of an argument—the destination the persuader wants us to reach. The grounds are the facts or information on which the claim is based.[19] The warrant is the portion of the argument that connects movement from the grounds to the claim. Warrants allow us to make inferences from the evidence to the claim,[20] and they often remain unstated. Suppose someone claims that "Islam promotes violence and religious intolerance." (Claims like this have been common since the attacks on the World Trade Center and the Pentagon.) The evidence cited is often the sometime murderous rhetoric and actions of Afghanistan's former Taliban regime, who helped wage a holy war against Western "infidels" such as the United States. The argument varied from source to source,[21] but it could be diagrammed as follows.

Claim: Islam is a violent religion.

Premise: Look at what the Taliban taught and advocated.

Premise: The Taliban harbored Islamic fundamentalists who unequivocally expressed their hatred for the United States.

Warrant: (Unstated but necessary: The Taliban are a representative and significant segment of Islamic thought.)

The interesting aspect of this type of construction is that the warrant is the most questionable assertion. Many thoughtful analysts have argued that the Taliban were no more representative of Islamic thought than other extremists such as the Reverend Jim Jones or David Koresh were representative of Western religious thought. The important thing to remember is that often the claims and premises most in need of a closer look are left unstated. They are, in a sense, sometimes smuggled into an argument without the benefits of full disclosure.

Reasoning to Discover and to Defend

It follows from what we have said that reasoning is used to rationalize ideas as well as to discover them. To take the second case first: we can employ the processes of logical demonstration to discover what we do not know. For example, if we subtract the entries in our checkbook from our balance, we may discover that we are overdrawn at the bank. Computers can calculate everything from shifts in the earth's crust to the movements of hurricanes. When we learn how to use existing software, we have harnessed elaborate reasoning rules that will extend our knowledge beyond its present limits.

The reasoning of persuasion, however, more commonly defends what is already known or believed. As a persuader on a given topic, your view is more or less fixed; what you hope to alter is the attitude of your listeners. Toulmin and his colleagues note that practical reasoning is better described as a way of testing ideas critically rather than discovering new ideas. Argumentative reasoning

> is concerned less with how people think than with how they share their ideas and thoughts in situations that raise the question of whether those ideas are worth sharing. It is a collective and continuing human transaction, in which we present ideas or claims to particular sets of people with particular situations or contexts and offer the appropriate kinds of "reasons" in their support.[22]

Logic in persuasion is thus often a kind of rationalization: a process of finding defensible reasons in support of cherished positions. Because of this, persuasion is open to suspicion. We are often wary of persuaders such as trial attorneys and advertisers who have adopted arguments because they are convenient rather than good.

Ideally, the best persuasion flows from arguments that were formed in the process of discovery. As discussed in chapter 2, Plato believed that elaborate efforts at persuasion without equally intense efforts to discover the best or true would result in the exploitation rather than enlightenment of an audience.[23] We are using Plato's principle when we question whether the products endorsed by celebrities have qualities that merit our attention and whether the celebrities actually use the services they endorse.

Finding Good Reasons for Claims

Having considered some of the primary components of logical persuasion, we are now in a better position to offer some practical guidelines. Karl Wallace provides an excellent foundation; he assessed practical messages in terms of a theory of good reasons. We have described the process of reasoned persuasion as the search for agreement with a claim based on relevant grounds or premises, stated or implied. The various principles, pieces of evidence, and warrants combine to create compelling arguments, the force of which will convince us to accept the claim. We can recast most of this process of finding relevant premises in the context of Wallace's theory of good reasons.

According to Wallace, "Good reasons are a number of statements, consistent with each other, in support of an ought proposition or a value-judgment."[24] They provide explanations for the judgment that the persuader hopes will be supported enthusiastically by the audience. The anticipated agreement is based on the fact that good reasons frequently summarize what members of a society already accept as right or good. As Wallace notes, "One can scarcely declare that something is desirable without showing its relevance to values." We can characterize rhetoric or persuasion "as the art of finding and effectively presenting good reasons."[25] Here is an example of a judgmental claim and its good reason premises.

> Claim: Companies that direct advertising to very young children are engaged in unethical conduct.
>
> Reason: Young children lack sufficient sophistication to discount for the "puffery" in advertising.
>
> Reason: Ethical persuaders—by definition—will not exploit gullible audiences who lack the ability to weigh the motives of communicators.

You may agree, disagree, or find fault with one or both of the reasons. Many times one person's common sense is another's irrationality, particularly if cultural traditions and differences come into play. But within the same culture you can usually sense when you have located reasons that will hold up under public scrutiny. Note that Wallace's point is especially affirmed in the second reason; it communicates a widely endorsed value that condemns exploitation. As with the first premise above, some reasons function as factual evidence; they can be tested scientifically. But practical reasoning frequently boils down to what might be called the ethical pivots of common sense. When we isolate the premises that we intend to use in support of a claim, our sense of what works is often based on judgments about conduct that we hold in common with others in the culture. Learning and rationality is the lifelong process of acquiring norms about "what goes with what," what fits, and what contexts are friendly or hostile to certain ideas. In chapter 13, we review the search for good reasons as a basis for the construction of persuasive speeches and messages.

A False Distinction: Logic or Emotion

In *The Rhetoric*, Aristotle identified three forms of proof available to the persuader: logical, emotional, and ethical (see chapter 5).[26] Although he did not mean to imply that the presence of one meant the absence of another, popular usage frequently treats these categories as distinct. Ask the average person to analyze an advertising pitch or a pamphlet from a group seeking social change. Predictably, he or she will come up with a variation of Aristotle's distinction. Some parts of the message will be identified as containing logical reasons and other parts as containing emotional appeals. Among experts who study messages closely, the wording may be fancier, but the implication that logic and emotion are opposites is still present. A law school professor regrets that "emotion can activate any behavior which has not been inhibited by reason."[27] An expert on political communication similarly notes that the statements of most politicians are "nothing more than emotional appeals."[28]

We think, however, it is a serious error to assume that the presence of emotion indicates the absence of logic. The problem with this common distinction is that reason and emotion are *complementary processes,* not opposites. In actual practice, a sense of reasoned justification usually increases our emotional attachment to ideas. When we feel that we have a strong case for a point of view, our sense of urgency in communicating that commitment is usually enhanced.[29]

Think about your experiences with the emotion of anger. Your anger probably develops in proportion to the good reasons you have for it. Reasoning motivates our emotions and serves as a register of our convictions. What we commonly call "emotion" is an outward measure of the certainty of our logic. Hence, anger, anxiety, fear, and joy have their rational origins, and we can often describe them to another person. Just because their logic may not be clear to others is not a basis for assuming that none exists.

The misplaced distinction between reason and emotion inevitably leads observers to view emotion as a kind of back door to persuasion: an illegitimate ploy that should be peripheral to the whole process. It is easy to dismiss an opponent's claims as merely appeals to emotions. But that is often an intellectually dishonest shortcut that tries to preclude thoughtful analysis of reasoning that doesn't fit our usual patterns.

In his groundbreaking analysis of Adolf Hitler's rhetoric (first published during World War II), Kenneth Burke noted that it was not enough to simply dismiss Hitler's words as the ravings of a fool. To do so, he noted, "contributed more to our gratification than our enlightenment."[30] Instead, Burke's analysis assumed that Hitler had a logic for his actions and that he had found a receptive audience. The logic was based on the treatment of Germany after World War I and the norm of widespread anti-Semitism woven into the culture. What it lacked, of course, were good reasons rooted in civil values, such as respect for religious and ethnic diversity and a healthy skepticism of governmental power.

COMMON FORMS OF DEFECTIVE REASONING
▲

Textbooks that address reasoning almost uniformly attempt to provide readers with the logician's equivalent of the Rock of Gibraltar—some sturdy reference point that will simplify the problem of navigating between good and bad reasoning. If we know what good reasoning is, then it follows that there must be systematic ways to classify forms of bad reasoning. "A *fallacy,*" notes philosopher Max Black, "is an argument which seems to be sound without being so. . . ."[31] Fallacious arguments frequently suggest more than they deliver, using the grammar and verbal patterns associated with argumentation but without the genuine links that should exist between claims and supporting statements.

Ad Hominem

This commonly cited fallacy is argument directed against persons rather than against their ideas. In ad hominem arguments a judgment is often personal and negative, deflecting attention away from the merits of an argument to alleged and largely irrelevant defects of an individual or a group. In private, former President Richard Nixon uttered what a former aide called an "undeniably ugly" range of attacks on his opponents. He was, notes Leonard Garment, "a champion hater,"[32] a fact that has been revealed in releases of White House conversations Nixon taped in the White House. A writer at the *New York Times* was "that damned Jew." Crude epithets were uttered about Supreme Court members, publishers, and his famous lists of White House enemies.[33]

The issue is less clear when we need to make decisions about an individual's capacity to perform under various circumstances. For example, where is the ethical line that separates the press's right to comment on the actions of a public official, versus simply ridiculing that person? Since governmental officials are elected to make many decisions beyond those that can be presented in a campaign, you may feel that a candidate's character—with all that implies—is relevant in determining his or her fitness for office. The trend in political commentary, however, seems toward the mean-spirited rather than toward thoughtful analysis. We have grown accustomed to empty invectives focused less on what politicians say or do and more on tangential features of their personalities. Bill and Hillary Clinton provoked levels of hate and vituperation reminiscent of southern newspaper descriptions of Abe Lincoln during the Civil War.[34] Columnists, talk radio hosts, and satirists routinely employ ad hominem attacks. Columnists and pundits regularly reflect what could be called the "politics of attitude." Consider Maureen Dowd's characterizations of a range of political leaders in just two of her columns in the *New York Times*:

> Vice Presidential nominee Dick Cheney: a "well fed, balding, bland male Republican."
>
> President Bill Clinton: a "dissolute commoner," "President Smarmy."
>
> Presidential candidate George W. Bush: "Junior" to the elder "Poppy."
>
> Al Gore: A man who fears looking like the mostly bald Senator Joe Biden.[35]

THE BOONDOCKS

© 2003 Aaron McGruder. Dist. by UNIVERSAL PRESS SYNDICATE

Dowd can be a perceptive political analyst, and in the context of modern discourse, these put-downs seem relatively mild. But like many writers seeking attention in a glutted media marketplace, she seems to find it difficult to resist the rhetoric of ridicule.

False Cause

Are tornados attracted to mobile home parks? Do the world's roosters keep the sun on schedule? A persuader who has fallen victim to the fallacy of false cause mistakenly assumes that because two events have occurred together, one has caused the other. Arguments from false cause proliferate because it is easy to mistake *correlation* for *causation*. The paragon of perfect reasoning for millions of readers and filmgoers worldwide is Arthur Conan Doyle's famous detective, Sherlock Holmes. When the available evidence of a murder seems to indicate to readers that the butler did it, the more thoughtful Holmes rejects the seeming correlation and seeks the true cause. He discovers that blows could not have been made by a right-handed person or that bodies have been dead too long.

Everyday discourse, however, is full of false cause reasoning. Individuals frustrated with social or economic problems often resort to simplistic cause-and-effect arguments that wither under close examination. In 1998 a Texas minister—frustrated by the appointment of a woman to lead a large church in Waco—unintentionally offered a classic example. Along with the Baptist church that appointed her, he blamed feminists for

> child abuse, abortion, domestic violence, divorce, teen pregnancies, drug and alcohol abuse, pornography, teen crime, gang violence, racial tensions and the ever-increasing coming out of the closet of the sodomites and lesbians.[36]

In the aftermath of the terrorist attacks on the Pentagon and World Trade Center, the conservative minister Jerry Falwell made a similar ill-fated leap from cause to effect. According to Falwell, the attacks happened because the United States had been made vulnerable by secular forces such as abortion providers, gay rights advocates, the American Civil Liberties Union, and the federal court system. All of these groups "helped this happen," he asserted,[37] only later issuing an apology after rebukes from the president and others.

Non Sequitur

A *non sequitur* occurs when a conclusion does not follow from the reasons that have been cited. One of the authors recently noticed a car with a "Conquer Cancer" slogan on its license plate, but he also noted that the driver was smoking—a non sequitur. Consider this page one newspaper headline: "BUSH APPROVES COVERT AID FOR TALIBAN FOES."[38] Can a newspaper announce *covert* plans? Viewers of the popular show *Friends* could call non sequiturs the Phoebe effect—only she seems capable of understanding the logic that ties her thoughts together.

Most non sequiturs have at least superficial connections that link claims to supporting reasons. Under closer examination, the connection is insufficient or downright inconsistent. Consider the wording of an advertisement for Alka-Seltzer Plus

Cold Medicine, as reported by *Consumer Reports*.[39] In fine print, the ad notes that the "product may cause drowsiness; use caution if operating heavy machinery or driving a vehicle." But the same message also contains testimony from Harold "Butch" Brooks, a truck driver who notes, "When I'm out on the road, bad weather, bad cold, my load's still gotta go, so I rely on Alka-Seltzer Plus." The whole ad is a non sequitur; the sum total of its claims do not fit together. Its basic inconsistency is similar to the strange reasoning used on a package of D-Con, which proudly announces that the poison is made from a "scientifically balanced blend of natural ingredients."

Non sequiturs are prevalent in advertisements. Beer ads that portray beer drinking as the key to sociability or automobile ads that imply a new car will create respect and envy make claims that don't stand up to close scrutiny. The more dangerous non sequiturs are those that arise in debates on important social issues and in the rhetoric that is offered in defense of an official action. One of the most valuable services political reporters and analysts perform is to expose the convoluted reasoning of advocates of a particular policy. Life is full of non sequiturs: the environmental stickers on the back of a gas guzzling SUV, a deadly missile called "The Peacekeeper," a president who supports public education but sends his daughter to private schools, anti-abortion politicians who cut social service programs for poor children, and so on.

Circular Argument

Sometimes the reasons given for a claim are little more than a rewording of the claim itself. Restatements appear to provide support but offer no evidence. Ad slogans such as "When you say Budweiser, you've said it all" have the structure of claims that imply good reasons, but they actually start and end with the same idea. Parents regularly use this form of argument with their children: "Do it because I said so." What follows after "because" is essentially a duplicate of what preceded. Circular arguments limit public debate on important issues by focusing on only unchallengeable claims. By August of 1968, for example, the United States had committed 541,000 troops to the Vietnam War. Many leaders in Congress and in the Johnson and Nixon administrations argued that because we were so deeply committed to the defense of South Vietnam, we should stay to see the war through to a successful conclusion. Even those who regretted having become involved in an Asian land war felt that the enormous human and economic costs already expended prohibited a withdrawal of forces. Because the deaths and misery had to serve some higher need, a quagmire of circular reasoning developed. The fact of being at war became its own justification for delaying our departure from Vietnam until the fall of South Vietnam in 1975. By that time, over fifty-eight thousand American lives had been lost.[40]

Rumors feed on circular logic. If one news outlet makes an unsubstantiated assertion about a particular event, that assertion is then covered as news by another outlet, who uses the first story as its source. This type of pattern surfaced when some media outlets reported the unsubstantiated claim that a White House aide who had committed suicide in 1993 had actually been murdered by Clinton insiders.[41] False rumors allow news operations to feed endlessly on each other's speculations.[42]

Excessive Dependence on Authority

One legitimate pattern of reasoning is to support a persuasive claim by citing the opinion of experts. Excessive dependence on authority, however, sometimes results in the premature conclusion of discussion. As Toulmin, Rieke, and Janik have noted, "Appeals to authority become fallacious at the point where authority is taken as closing off discussion of the matter in question. No further evidence is considered; the authority's opinion has settled the matter once and for all."[43]

Evaluators of effective persuasion should ask: Have I heard enough to be persuaded? If an individual has heard from only one source, the answer should probably be, not yet. Sometimes, however, a single source may have the power to change someone's mind or to motivate him or her to act. There is no shortage of experts—real or self-styled—who are prepared to argue that they should have the last (and sometimes only) word. Sometimes history has demonstrated that they could not have been more wrong. Radio pioneer David Sarnoff at one time thought it unlikely that Americans would accept advertising as a basis for the new and emerging broadcast industry. Some aviation engineers once believed that no plane or pilot could survive a flight beyond the speed of sound. More than a few Hollywood studio executives of the early 1920s doubted that film audiences would really want to hear their favorite actors talk.

Presidents, ministers, influential teachers, and therapists represent a few of the authorities who are sometimes consulted for what amounts to total documentation of a claim or a decision. Phrases like "He said so, and that's enough for me," "The only person I trust said . . .", or "She has the advanced degree, so she must know what she is saying" are clues to attitudes that have been accepted on the slender thread of a single expressed opinion. In chapter 5 we will examine in more detail persuasion based on appeals to authority.

HOW PERSUASION AND
LOGICAL ARGUMENTATION DIFFER

▲

Thus far, we have shown how a claim supported by reasonable premises can lead to persuasion. We labeled this single logical unit an argument and noted that Aristotle discovered forms of argumentation (enthymemes) that routinely appear in most types of persuasion. Does it follow that we can use the words persuasion and argumentation interchangeably? Is persuasion always subject to the rules of practical reasoning? The answer to both questions is no, because factors other than reasoning influence what people believe. We close this chapter with an explanation of why we think persuasion is more than the construction of reasoned arguments, vital though they are.

Denial Often Defeats Reasoning

Under repeated and hostile questioning from members of the opposition party, former British Prime Minister James Callahan used to respond in frustration by observing that "I can *tell* you the truth, but I *can't make you see it.*" How right he was. In the game of influence, self-interest often trumps what looks like a winning hand. As we have noted often in this book, persuasion is not easy. When we are asked to give up cherished beliefs, familiar ways of acting, and views of the world that have become part of the comfortable furniture of our lives, we frequently resist. Our worldviews immunize us against the infection of others' ideas, rejecting unwanted or unacceptable conclusions. To be sure, the line that separates universally supported conclusions from those about which reasonable people might differ is not always clear. But it would be a mistake to underestimate the human capacity for denial.

Smoking is a classic and interesting case for study. All of us have habits that could be categorized as unhealthy, but tobacco use is a special case. The health risks of smoking are printed prominently on every package of cigarettes sold and on every advertisement for the product. Appeals to quit smoking are pervasive and constructed in arguments that have a lot of force. Since the tobacco settlement agreement in 1998, major tobacco manufacturers themselves have funded campaigns to encourage children not to smoke. For example, on its Web site, Philip Morris states: "As the manufacturer of a product intended for adults who smoke, that has serious health effects and is addictive, we have a responsibility to help prevent kids from smoking."[44] The public has every reason to be acutely aware that cessation of smoking will increase the chances of a longer life and will lower the risk of debilitating illnesses. But it is easy to find smokers who will explain that (1) they understand it is a behavior that carries some risks, and (2) they still do not intend to quit. A common end-run around the evidence about the harm of smoking is to challenge some of its credibility, or ignore it.

The tendency to overrule logical conclusions about tobacco extends to some who grow it as well. As a reporter noted after an interview with a North Carolina farmer:

> When I bring up the more than 400,000 smoking-related deaths that occur in this nation every year, he tilts back in his chair, clasps his hands behind his neck and replies calmly, having expected the question. "We feel that in moderation—a pack a day—tobacco would not hurt you. . . . I do not feel, as a tobacco farmer—and I think I speak for most of them—that we are responsible for any disease. We really don't see ourselves as growing a product that's harmful to anyone. I don't think you'll find a farmer that'll feel guilty about growing tobacco."[45]

Denial routinely functions as an effective shield that can be used to ignore reasoning that takes one to an unpleasant conclusion.

Persuasion's Self-Interest and Argumentation's Public Interest

Our point about the mistake of assuming that logical and emotional appeals are discrete is relevant to a related distinction. As we have noted, someone else's logic may not be your logic. Hence, we may sometimes miss or ignore another person or group's good reasons. To put it another way, reasoning may be *personal*, appealing to an individual's needs rather than to a collective sense of reasonableness. Logic that can withstand scrutiny by many different people at the same time is the realm of argumentation. Appeals to self-interest are a central paradigm of *persuasion*. Typ-

CALVIN AND HOBBES

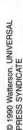

ically, trial lawyers, position papers, and debaters argue, but television commercials, family members, and sales persons are more likely to persuade. In actual practice, the route for changing minds and behaviors will often pass through both.

The difference between the two lies in the *kinds of reasons* that are offered in support of claims. All persuasion must provide a series of incentives or reasons for winning the approval of audiences, but not all legitimate persuasion involves good reasons. As we have noted, the good reasons of arguments are made with the hope that a wide diversity of people might also sense their reasonableness. By contrast, while persuaders frequently employ rational argumentation, they also rely on their abilities to use appeals to satisfy what are more clearly *personal* needs.

The distinction between persuasive *appeals* and argumentative *good reasons* is revealing. As we will discuss more fully in chapters 6 and 7, all of us have personal needs for affection, for approval from others, for high self-esteem, and so on. We can be motivated by appeals that promise to satisfy these needs. However, when we present arguments for the approval of audiences, we know that our reasoning must often move both the individual and gain acceptance from the public as a whole. For example, in a courtroom jurors are sometimes cautioned by a judge to ignore attempts at flattery directed to them by lawyers eager to win their cases. Appeals to the private need of approval, for example, are out of place in the legal system's attempt to reconstruct the historical record of what the defendant did or did not do.[46] Yet, persuasion frequently depends on just such identification—on efforts to recognize and appeal to individual needs and motivations.

One reason advertising is so effective on television is that it reaches the viewer as a private rather than a public person. We accept advertising appeals made to us in our homes that we might reject as a member of a live audience. It is revealing that a commercial viewed passively at home is sometimes greeted by groans of disbelief when shown to an audience gathered in a theater. To put our point another way, while persuasion can employ reasoning from facts and general opinions, it also reaches individuals by appeals to subjective and personal needs that have no firm basis in public opinion.

Consider the example of a skin cream ad on network television that promised to remove "ugly age spots." The commercial for Porcelana Cream opened with a picture of four middle-aged women playing a card game. One of the women is obviously ill at ease as she looks down at her hands holding the cards. We hear her say to herself, "These ugly age spots; what's a woman to do!" Porcelana promised to come to her rescue and to help her look better in the eyes of her friends.

From an argumentative point of view, the commercial is hopelessly flawed. Would friendships be at stake merely because a person had a few spots on her hands? Of course not. But the woman's anxiety and embarrassment have a certain dramatic plausibility. Based on just a few seconds of the commercial, we can believe that there are people who are anxious to be accepted by their friends; they may believe that even minor blemishes could put them at risk. The commercial appeals to the very private fear of rejection that most of us experience from time to time. To dismiss it as irrational is to miss the point. The appeal to a fear of rejection is not intended to stand up under the close scrutiny that we give arguments. But that does not deny the strong possibility that some users of the product may feel better in the knowledge that they have taken a step to improve their personal appearance. We have missed something important if we fail to recognize that there is a strong need-based logic behind most persuasion.

SUMMARY
▲

In this chapter we have looked at the role that reasoning plays in persuasion. Philosophers view logical reasoning as a source of new knowledge; persuasive arguments usually employ statements linked together to defend existing attitudes. For our purposes, we defined reasoning as the process of supporting controversial claims with premises and evidence that function as good reasons. Reasons are good when they build on value-based premises that are as sensible for others as they are for ourselves. They are said to have force when their linkages are so strong that they seem to demand our acceptance. Some of the claims and premises of arguments may involve judgments that can never fully be argued away; others may be factual and produce nearly universal acceptance.

We also noted that there is a great deal of misunderstanding about reasoning and about what it can and cannot do. For example, the most direct route to attitude change is sometimes by appealing to private but powerful motivations, such as a person's need to feel wanted by others. These individualized appeals are not necessarily irrational emotions nor unreasonable grounds for forming attitudes, but neither are they the kinds of statements that can stand up as reasons that would help shape a consensus of support in a public gathering. Advertising is full of motivating appeals, which frequently have the effect of allowing people to reward themselves or sanctioning a certain feeling. Topics of greater consequence, such as efforts to reconstruct the guilt or innocence of a defendant in a trial, demand more rigorous defenses.

Using Aristotle's writings as a guide, we looked at the unique features of practical arguments called enthymemes. Enthymemes have two special features that make them different from the formal arguments used by scientists, mathematicians, and logicians. First, the claims in enthymemes are probable or preferable, since they deal with practical subjects for which demonstrations of fact are usually impossible. Second, usually one or more of their parts (claims or premises) may be implied rather than stated; enthymemes typically build from what an audience already believes or accepts.

Like all forms of reasoning, enthymemes and other forms of argument can be made from premises of dubious quality. In fallacies like ad hominem, false cause, non sequitur, and circular argument, the premises of some arguments may present only the illusion rather than the reality of logical support. The task of the effective persuader is to avoid these superficial linkages in favor of arguments with legitimate good reasons.

Questions and Projects for Further Study

1. Locate an argumentative essay written by a newspaper columnist. After studying the column, summarize the claims and premises the author has used. Be careful to look for implied as well as stated premises. Make a judgment about the quality and adequacy of the author's arguments.

2. Observe a debate on a television talk show (CNN's *Crossfire*, PBS's *Newshour*, ABC's *Nightline*, etc.). Identify the extent to which each advocate in a program is able to communicate good reasons in defense of his or her position.

3. Using examples from magazine advertisements, locate and explain messages that contain fallacies mentioned in this chapter: ad hominem, false cause, non sequitur, circular argument, and excessive dependence on authority.

4. This chapter describes practical reasoning by comparing several categories of opposites. Briefly explain the differences between each of the following contrasting terms, indicating which term identifies a characteristic of practical reasoning:
   a. demonstration vs. argumentation
   b. reasoning to discover vs. reasoning to defend
   c. analytic arguments vs. enthymemes

5. Explain the statement in this chapter that analytic arguments offer "a tantalizing model for persuaders." Construct a simple argument with two premises and a conclusion that illustrates an analytic argument.

6. In this chapter we note that one of the most common mistakes people make with regard to reasoning is the assumption that they can prove a claim of judgment. Cite your own examples of claims of preference and claims of fact. Why is the claim of judgment not provable with the same certainty as a claim of fact?

Additional Reading

Aristotle, *The Rhetoric, The Basic Works of Aristotle,* ed. Richard McKeon (New York: Random House, 1941).

Wayne C. Booth, *Now Don't Try to Reason with Me* (Chicago: University of Chicago, 1970).

Gary Lynn Cronkhite, "Logic, Emotion, and the Paradigm of Persuasion," *Quarterly Journal of Speech,* February 1964, 13–18.

Chaim Perelman and L. Olbrechts-Tyteca, *The New Rhetoric: A Treatise in Argumentation*, trans. John Wilkinson and Purcell Weaver (Notre Dame, IN: University of Notre Dame, 1969).

Stephen Toulmin, *The Uses of Argument* (Cambridge: Cambridge University Press, 1958).

Stephen Toulmin, Richard Rieke, and Allan Janik, *An Introduction to Reasoning* (New York: Macmillan, 1979).

Karl R. Wallace, "The Substance of Rhetoric: Good Reasons," *Quarterly Journal of Speech*, October 1963, 139–249.

Notes

[1] J. E. Creighton quoted by Susanne Langer, *Philosophy in a New Key* (New York: New American Library, 1951), p. 91.

[2] All film quotes from "Memorable Quotes," Internet Movie Database (Online) http://us.imdb.com/ Quotes?0109831; accessed 8-4-03.

[3] http://us.imdb.com/Quotes?0190590; accessed 8-4-03.

[4] For a discussion on audience motivations to seek out logical relationships in persuasion, see Daniel J. O'Keefe, *Persuasion: Theory and Research,* 2nd ed. (Thousand Oaks, CA: Sage, 2002), pp. 97–99.

[5] Stephen Toulmin, Richard Rieke, and Allan Janik, *An Introduction to Reasoning* (New York: Macmillan, 1979), p. 9.

[6] Aristotle, *The Rhetoric*, Book I, Chapter 1.

[7] See Stephen Toulmin, *The Uses of Argument* (London: Cambridge University, 1964), pp. 125–35.

[8] Chaim Perelman and L. Olbrechts-Tyteca, *The New Rhetoric: A Treatise on Argumentation*, trans. John Wilkinson and Purcell Weaver (Notre Dame, IN: University of Notre Dame, 1969), p. 2.

[9] Gustav Niebuhr, "Southern Baptists Declare Wife Should Submit to Her Husband," *New York Times*, June 10, 1998, p. A1; Don Lattin, "Baptists Say Wives Must Submit," *San Francisco Chronicle*, June 10, 1998, p. A1.

[10] For further discussion of this point see Richard Weaver, *The Ethics of Rhetoric* (Chicago: Henry Regnery, 1953), pp. 7–9.

[11] Lloyd Bitzer, "Aristotle's Enthymeme Revisited," *Quarterly Journal of Speech*, December 1959, pp. 399–408.

[12] Aristotle, *Topics*, Book I, Chapter. 1.

[13] Aristotle, *The Rhetoric*, Book II, Chapter 23.

[14] Aristotle, *Topics*, Book I, Chapter 1.

[15] Ibid. For further discussion of the differences between demonstrations and arguments, see also Perelman and L. Olbrechts-Tyteca, pp. 13–14.

[16] A good case has been made by sociologists of knowledge and others that very little knowledge about human affairs is completely free of values. A good source for exploring how social values can shape what we claim to "know" is Peter L. Berger and Thomas Luckmann, *The Social Construction of Reality* (New York: Doubleday, 1967).

[17] For a convincing case arguing Hauptmann's innocence, see Ludovic Kennedy, *The Airman and the Carpenter* (New York: Viking, 1985).

[18] Gordon Corera, "Why Bushisms Matter," BBC News Online, September 5, 2000.

[19] Sonja Foss, Karen Foss, and Robert Trapp, *Contemporary Perspectives in Rhetoric*, 3rd ed. (Prospect Heights, IL: Waveland Press, 2002).

[20] Thomas Hollihan and Kevin Baaske, *Arguments and Arguing* (Prospect Heights, IL: Waveland Press, 1994), p. 89. See also Toulmin, pp. 98–99.

[21] See, for example, Andrew Sullivan, "This Is a Religious War," *New York Times Magazine*, October 7, 2001, p. 44; and Salman Rushdie, "Yes, This Is about Islam," *New York Times*, November 2, 2001, p. A25.

[22] Toulmin, Rieke, and Janik, p. 9.

[23] See Weaver, pp. 11–12, and Plato's *Phaedrus*, trans. R. Hackforth (Indianapolis, IN: Bobbs-Merrill, Library of the Liberal Arts, 1952), pp. 119–22.

[24] Karl Wallace, "The Substance of Rhetoric: Good Reasons," *Quarterly Journal of Speech*, October 1963, p. 247.

[25] Ibid., p. 248.

[26] Aristotle, *The Rhetoric*, Book I, Chapter 2.

[27] Gray L. Dorsey, "Symbols: Vehicles of Reason or of Emotion?" in *Symbols and Values: An Initial Study*, ed. Lyman Bryson, Louis Finkelstein, R. M. McIver, and Richard McKeon (New York: Cooper Square, 1964), p. 445.

[28] Murray Edelman, *The Symbolic Uses of Politics* (Chicago: University of Illinois Press, 1967), p. 137.

[29] For classic statements of this view, see Gary Cronkhite, "Logic, Emotion, and the Paradigm of Persuasion," *Quarterly Journal of Speech*, February 1964, pp. 13–18; and Samuel Becker, "Research on Emotional and Logical Proofs," *Southern Speech Journal*, Spring 1963, pp. 198–207.

[30] Kenneth Burke, *The Philosophy of Literary Form*, 3rd ed. (Berkeley: University of California Press, 1973), p. 191–92.

[31] Max Black, "Fallacies," in *Readings in Argumentation*, eds. Jerry M. Anderson and Paul J. Dovre (Boston: Allyn and Bacon, 1968), p. 301.

[32] Leonard Garment, *Crazy Rhythm* (New York: Random House, 1997), p. 199.

[33] Leonard Garment, "Richard Nixon, Unedited," *New York Times*, October 19, 2001, p. A23.

[34] See, for example, Carl Sandburg, *Abraham Lincoln: The War Years, 1864–1865* (New York: Dell/Laural Editions), pp. 661.

[35] Maureen Dowd, "A Baby Sitter for Junior," *New York Times*, July 26, 2000, p. A23; and Dowd, "Al Agonistes," *New York Times*, January 30, 1997, p. A21.

[36] Lattin, p. A11.

[37] Gustav Niebuhr, "After the Attacks: Finding Fault," *New York Times*, September 14, 2001, p. A18.

[38] Michael Gordon and David Sanger, "Bush Approves Covert Aid for Taliban Foes," *New York Times*, October 1, 2001, p. A1.

[39] "Selling It," *Consumer Reports*, April 1986, p. 279.

[40] This is admittedly a simplification of a very complex issue. There were obviously many reasons for the U.S. commitment to support the South Vietnamese. One reporter who has written extensively on both the early and later phases of our involvement is David Halberstam whose first book, *The Making of a Quagmire* (New York: Random House, 1965), points to the dilemmas brought on by heavy military involvement in a land war. His second book, *The Best and Brightest* (New York: Random House, 1972), partially reconstructs the circular reasoning behind what became the United States' "no win" situation.

[41] Jeffrey Toobin, *A Vast Conspiracy* (New York: Touchstone, 1999), p. 192.

[42] For a general discussion of this problem see Bill Kovach and Tom Rosenstiel, *Warp Speed: America in the Age of Mixed Media* (New York: Century Foundation, 1999), pp. 1–9.

[43] Toulmin, Rieke, and Janik, p. 17.

[44] http://www.philipmorrisusa.com/policies_practices/ysp.asp; accessed 8-13-03.

[45] Luisita Torregrosa, "Up in Smoke," *New York Times Magazine*, August 26, 1996, p.42.

[46] A similar distinction is sometimes made between persuasion that moves us intellectually and conviction that moves us personally. See Perelman and Olbrechts-Tyteca, pp. 26–31.

Credibility and Authority

Overview

▲ The Multidimensional Aspects of Authority

▲ The Three Meanings of Credibility
   Ethos and the Idea of Good Character
   The Rational/Legal Ideal of Credibility
   Source Credibility as Believability
   Credibility Reconsidered

▲ Strategic Dimensions of Credibility
   Legitimation
   Mystification
   Source/Placebo Suggestion
   Authoritarianism and Acquiescence

> *If he and I were crossing the Brooklyn Bridge, and he ordered me to jump over, I'd do it without asking why.*[1]
> —A FRIEND OF THEODORE ROOSEVELT

Actor Ben Affleck had been picked by the management of the Boston Beer Company as the ideal spokesperson for one of their brands. The popular actor was the perfect image of the target audience they wanted to influence: young, professional, and successful. However, when stories began to circulate that the star of *Pearl Harbor* and *The Sum of All Fears* had entered an alcohol abuse treatment center, the company had little choice but to remove Affleck's "Samuel Adams" commercials from the air.[2]

Another kind of credibility issue surfaced in 1990. California officials noted a sharp increase in consumer complaints about repairs done by Sears' Auto Service. The complaints resulted in a much publicized investigation by the Department of Consumer Affairs; agents posing as customers were overcharged almost 90% of the time. Headlines in newspapers around the state trumpeted the unnecessary repairs. As William Benoit points out, the problem was not just the initial revelations; the response to the charges was equally damaging. Sears first issued a variety of statements minimizing the complaints. It made a second mistake by having their attorneys issue defensive denials.[3] Sears eventually moved beyond self-serving defenses and demonstrated that it would take action to correct the abuses. Only then did the company begin the long task of rebuilding customer faith in its repair services.

On a more tragic scale, the loss of the Russian submarine *Kursk* left an indelible impression about the credibility of Russian officials in August of 2000. After an explosion from one of its own torpedoes damaged the *Kursk* so badly that it was unable to surface, 118 sailors died. First reports from the Russian Navy incorrectly placed the blame on a collision with another submarine. The Navy was slow to put together a rescue plan, and President Putin continued a week-long vacation as the crisis festered.

Ordinary citizens and reform-minded journalists in Russia roundly criticized the government for being slow to act and for perpetuating a cover-up. "They withheld information, stretched the truth, defined the obvious and presented xenophobic fantasies as solid facts," noted the *Moscow Times*.[4] It was all "very Soviet in nature," forcing citizens to be skeptical about government accounts of the accident in the hours and days that followed. In the end, the *Kursk* episode was a reminder to the new leader that the dynamics of Russian politics had changed since the collapse of the one-party state. In the more open and democratic Russian Republic, governmental credibility was a necessity of leadership.

The power to persuade often involves convincing others that the source is reliable and trustworthy. In these examples the effectiveness of organizations was impaired by the actions of individuals speaking on their behalf. This chapter considers how sources use their reputations to increase the prospects for successful persuasion. After a brief reminder about the difficulties in assessing credibility, the first half of the chapter explores three very different perspectives that account for how persuasive authority is established and communicated to audiences. The second half concludes with an extended examination of four related settings that are useful in understanding why certain advocates can dramatically affect audiences.

THE MULTIDIMENSIONAL ASPECTS OF AUTHORITY

Andrew King notes that the ability to control another person may include physical or psychological threats, the assignment of official authority to one person or group, or the initiation of control through personal or secret action.[5] Our attention in this chapter is primarily on the power that flows from a persuadee's conviction that *someone else* has a legitimate claim to special knowledge or expertise.

As we shall see, the processes that accompany granting authority to a more knowledgeable source are anything but simple. The complexities involved in defining and assessing credible sources force us to consider several significant limits and qualifiers about the state of our knowledge. First, as with many variables in persuasion, there is an enormous gap between the questions that we raise and the relatively incomplete answers current research is able to provide. Power relationships between people are fascinating, but they are rarely reducible to simple formulas. The reaction of audiences to high or low credibility sources are sometimes unpredictable.

Second, as our opening examples illustrate, it is important to remember that assessments of the quality of a source applies to organizations as well as to individuals. All persuasion messages have stated or implied sources. Sometimes it makes more sense to talk about the specific credibility of one individual, such as a president of the United States or a celebrity endorsing a brand of beer. At other times, it is more relevant to consider the credibility of an institution or organization, ranging from major corporations to branches of government.

Third, our emphasis on persuasive messages and sources should not obscure the fact that many of our interpersonal and professional relationships come with the prior requirement for one side to yield to another. Sometimes what looks like

NON SEQUITUR

persuasion is simply a veil that covers the necessity for people to perform their existing roles. We like to think of ourselves as free agents able to exercise choice in a wide range of situations. However, established relationships with parents, employers, mentors, and others may mean that the power structure in a given setting is more potent in defining who will yield than factors such as the credibility of a source or the quality of a message. In simple terms, the order of a superior can trump other possible persuasion effects.

And finally, it is worth remembering that advocates are their own audiences. We are deeply affected by our sense of self, which is another type of credibility. For example, the sheer act of advocacy—of attempting to persuade others—usually has the effect of deepening a persuader's conviction in his or her own message. This process of *self-persuasion* is bound up in the need to believe in our actions— and in the high credibility we normally give to ourselves. About the Mormon practice of having young men spend two years in missionary work, an older member of the church shrewdly observed: "The kids go out and may convert a few here and there, but more important, they convert themselves."[6] It is not unusual to discover that the person who has been the most effected by a persuasive message is the advocate who delivered it.

THE THREE MEANINGS OF CREDIBILITY
▲

Credibility is a pivotal term in the study of persuasion,but those who use it frequently have different—if equally valid—meanings in mind. In a general sense, estimates of credibility involve assessing how the reputation of a persuader will affect the way a given audience will respond. For some, credibility means good character, sincerity, or integrity. For others, it is a synonym for truthfulness or expertise. Social scientists often apply a third audience-centered meaning to the term: it is a trait identified with a source who is *believable* to others, even when their qualifications could be called into question. As we shall see, these three perspectives can blend together. At other times, each one presents an opportunity to explore the different ways in which sources achieve persuasive goals.

Ethos and the Idea of Good Character

One of the oldest terms associated with the qualities of an advocate is the Greek word *ethos*. For Aristotle, ethos was one of the three major forms of influence. He wrote in *The Rhetoric* that the ideal persuader should put the audience in the right emotional frame of mind *(pathos)*, state the best arguments *(logos)*, and have the right kind of character *(ethos)*. The persuader "must not only try to make the argument of his speech demonstrative and worthy of belief; he must also make his own character look right."[7]

Aristotle labeled the components of good character as good sense, good moral character, and goodwill. "It follows," he noted, "that any one who is thought to have all three of these good qualities will inspire trust in his audience."[8] Good sense and good moral character center on an audience's perception that a persuader's judgments and values are reasonable and justified. It is obvious that if the persuader seems to see the world in the same terms as the audience—a world in which good people are easily separated from less trustworthy people—they will be inclined to accept the speaker's evidence and conclusions. Add in the element of goodwill—the important idea that the persuader seems to have honorable intentions toward the audience—and we have a sense of what kinds of advocates are likely to be successful.

Ethos is the personal or professional reputation the persuader brings to the persuasive setting or constructs in the process of communicating. We usually have little difficulty recognizing the general traits of credibility. We identify high *ethos* sources as fair, trustworthy, sincere, reliable, and honest. Their knowledge about a subject may be seen as professional, experienced, and authoritative, and their manner of presentation may be perceived as energetic, active, open minded, objective, bold, or decisive.[9]

In *Zen and the Art of Motorcycle Maintenance*, Robert Pirsig talks about how character is revealed in both the large and small moments of human interaction. At one level the book is a critique of the battle between the Platonists and Sophists over the value of teaching rhetoric and citizenship: a feud we briefly examined in chapter 2. But in more prosaic ways Pirsig sees character revealed in the ways ordinary people approach their work. Consider his description of two uninvolved and distracted mechanics who had been asked to diagnose a strange noise coming from the engine of his motorcycle.

> The shop was a different scene from the ones I remembered. The mechanics, who had once all seemed like ancient veterans, now looked like children. A radio was going full blast and they were clowning around and talking and seemed not to notice me. When one of them finally came over he barely listened to the piston slap before saying, "Oh yeah. Tappets."[10]

Pirsig eventually paid a $140 repair bill for services that failed to remedy the engine problem. He later discovered that the noisy piston was caused by a damaged twenty-five cent pin accidentally sheared off by an equally careless mechanic. "Why," he wondered, "did they butcher it so?" What evidence did they provide that indicated they were less than fully competent mechanics?

> The radio was the clue. You can't really think hard about what you're doing and listen to the radio at the same time. Maybe they didn't see their job as having anything to do with hard thought, just wrench twiddling. If you can twiddle wrenches while listening to the radio that's more enjoyable.
>
> Their speed was another clue. They were really slopping things around in a hurry and not looking where they slopped them. More money that way. . . .
>
> But the biggest clue seemed to be their expressions. They were hard to explain. Good-natured, friendly, easygoing—and uninvolved. They were like spectators. You had the feeling they had just wandered in there themselves and somebody had handed them a wrench. There is no identification with the job. No saying, "I am a mechanic." At 5 PM or whenever their eight hours were in, you knew they would cut it off and not have another thought about their work. They were already trying not to have any thoughts about their work on the job.[11]

Pirsig argues that a credible mechanic is a person who can match the precise tolerances of machinery with the precise and analytic mind admired by Aristotle. The skill of an expert mechanic has little to do with "wrench twiddling," but a great deal to do with cultivating a skill for problem solving.

The Rational/Legal Ideal of Credibility

The second means of determining credibility is through formal guidelines for judging expertise and reliability. From the rational/legal perspective, statements or views deserve to be believed if their sources meet certain general standards for accuracy and objectivity. Robert and Dale Newman describe a source as believable if it tells the truth "with no concern as to whether any specific audience or reader will in fact believe it."[12]

The difference between a persuader's *ethos* and his rational credibility rests on objective criteria that exist apart from the beliefs of people in specific settings. Only an audience can decide if they believe a persuader has good character, but the legal rules for judging sources are constructed to apply to all audiences. Members of a jury, for example, may have strong suspicions that a defendant of a different social background is guilty of the charges brought against him or her. Under courtroom guidelines for assessing sources, they must disregard their personal preconceptions and decide based on the rules of evidence. Witnesses who are instantly likable because they are outwardly most like the jury members (in dress and education level, for example) may only be capable of giving hearsay (overheard or second-hand) evidence. Under the legal rules governing sources, hearsay testimony will be discounted by a judge in favor of statements from an eyewitness, even if the appearance of the eyewitness is alien to most of the members of the jury.

The abstract ideal of judging only by objective standards does not always translate into practice. Harper Lee's novel, *To Kill a Mockingbird*, explores just such a dilemma. The story is set in a small Alabama town in the 1930s. Tom Robinson, a black man, is on trial for the alleged rape of a white woman. As the narrative unfolds, it becomes clear that he is innocent. The young and disturbed woman who coaxed him into her house, kissed him, and then tried to erase her guilt by claiming that she had been assaulted illustrates the elusive nature of real-world justice. Defense attorney Atticus Finch (played in the 1963 film by Gregory Peck) tries valiantly to point out to the all-white jury that no objective review of the evidence can lead a thinking person to a verdict of guilty. Mayella Ewell has clearly fabricated the charges, knowing that an unspeakable breach of a racial code would deflect attention from the abuse of her own father. In his stirring summation to the jury Atticus concludes, "I am confident that you gentlemen will review without passion the evidence you have heard, come to a decision, and restore this defendant to his family."[13] But the twelve men succumb to their prejudices. "Atticus had used every tool available to free men to save Tom Robinson," notes Lee, "but in the secret courts of men's hearts Atticus had no case. Tom was a dead man the minute Mayella Ewell opened her mouth and screamed."[14]

What standards should have guided the jury? In the practice of law, guidelines for determining the quality of a source are relatively straightforward, although they are always harder to apply to specific cases than to summarize in the abstract. They involve two fundamental questions—one concerning a source's ability and one pertaining to probable objectivity.

Ability.   How do we determine if someone has the ability to tell the truth or to make intelligent observations about a specific subject? The first test is measuring the extent to which an authority has been in a position to observe. Were they eyewitnesses to events or did they get information secondhand from another source? Do they have the training, experience, access to information, and knowledge to know what to look for? Can testimony of one source be supported by others with knowledge in a similar area?

In 1990 Iben Browning, an expert on the earth's *climate*, predicted a massive earthquake along the New Madrid fault in southern Missouri. He based his prediction on the questionable assumption that the moon's relatively close proximity to the earth would trigger shifts in the earth's crust. Very few seismologists had faith in Browning's conclusions, pointing out that a background in climatology does not qualify someone to determine how earthquake faults will behave on specific days.[15] Those who evacuated schools and homes in response to Dr. Browning's predictions should have applied the guidelines above to evaluate Browning's credibility.

Objectivity.   After the 2001 attacks on the World Trade Center and the Pentagon, NBC News anchor Tom Brokaw was approached after a speech at Northwestern University and asked why he wasn't wearing a flag pin in his lapel. The pins had suddenly sprouted on the clothing of many news anchors after the terrorist episodes. Brokaw told the person, "I don't think it's appropriate for a journalist to wear a flag. It suggests that you approve of whatever the government is doing at that time."[16] The anchor made the assumption that even small elements of his appearance on camera should project objectivity.

Objectivity is the ability to set aside personal values or prejudices as reference points for understanding an event. Complete objectivity is impossible, but interpretations of reality can be rendered with high degrees of accuracy and fairness. Determining that a certain source lacks objectivity is not the equivalent of labeling a person deceptive or fraudulent. It is natural to see the world from a self-interested viewpoint. We expect personal investments to shape the comments and responses of groups and individuals. When they do, their credibility is said to be *willing*, and hence, somewhat suspect. *Willing* sources make claims that tend to confirm judgments or facts that are flattering or self-serving.

Suppose you heard a celebrity like CNN's Larry King talk about the positive effects of a medical treatment or medicine in the course of a news interview. You would probably assume that he was speaking from experience. If you were to discover that he had been *paid* to speak for a drug company, you might reach a very different conclusion.[17] Sources who receive compensation for messages are *willing* sources. Similarly, press releases from university press offices can be counted on to report institutional successes rather than failures. Networks like NBC tend to find important news in the Olympics only in the years when they have the rights to televise them. ABC finds similar news value in motion pictures released by their owner, the Disney company.[18]

In contrast, sources are said to be *reluctant* when they take positions that *go against* their own interests. The Newmans note that the idea of reluctant testimony is based on a sturdy principle: "It is assumed that sane individuals will not say things against their own interests unless such testimony is true beyond doubt." If a witness gains little from their own testimony, it is probably very credible.[19]

In reality, the gap between the willing and the reluctant source is an unbroken continuum that is heavily weighted at the willing end of the scale. Reluctant testimony is understandably rare. The task left to audiences searching for credible advocates is to find high-ability sources who are not so deeply tied to one point of view that they are incapable of seeing merit and truth in opposing viewpoints.

Source Credibility as Believability

A third perspective on credibility comes from comparatively recent experimental studies on the formation of attitudes. The work of psychologist Carl Hovland in the early 1950s[20] spawned hundreds of studies examining source-related traits that can affect audience acceptance of a message. A 1951 study of audience responses to high- and low-credibility sources by Hovland and Weiss is considered a classic.[21] The researchers asked students at Yale to complete opinion questionnaires that measured the students' attitudes on four different topics. After completing the questionnaires, students read pamphlets arguing pro and con positions on the same four areas. All the students read identical opinions on the four issues. The students were then randomly subdivided into different groups. Hovland and Weiss chose sources with various degrees of credibility and then told the students that a particular point of view had been authored by one of those sources. For the question "Can an atomic-powered submarine be built at the present time?" the opinion was attributed to different sources for different groups of students. One group was told that the opinion they were reading was from the Russian daily, *Pravda*. A second, demographically similar group was told that the source was the widely respected physicist, J. Robert Oppenheimer. Another topic was whether the popularity of television would decrease the number of movie theaters in operation. Again, the opinion on this subject was attributed to a high-credibility source for some readers *(Fortune Magazine)* and a low-credibility source for others (a movie gossip columnist). The study was designed to hold every variable constant except for the sources to whom the comments were attributed.

Would the attributions make a difference? Would there be greater attitude change from the groups who believed in the integrity of their sources? Not surprisingly, many of the respondents agreed with opinions when they were attributed to high-credibility sources. Oppenheimer and *Fortune*, for example, were ranked as more believable than *Pravda* and the columnist. Did high credibility translate into greater agreement with the source? The answer was a qualified yes. The experimenters measured shifts in attitudes by comparing the results of the initial questionnaires with the results of attitude surveys conducted after the experiment. The net change in attitudes was not enormous, but it was always greater for readers of trustworthy sources.[22]

Other analysts who have studied and replicated this research have noted that in order to demonstrate a measurable effect upon attitudes, the researchers had to create extreme differences in communicator credibility that,

> nevertheless, gave only a slight edge to the credible source in producing attitude change. In real-life situations, where the naturally existing differences between communicators would be much less extreme, would there still be the same enhancement of the communication by virtue of its attribution to a slightly more credible source? Some of the data suggest there would not.[23]

The problems involved in designing precise experimental studies are too complex to be outlined here.[24] The important point is that source credibility has many relevant dimensions, even when it is defined broadly from a social influence perspective. It is difficult to reduce a concept to just one measurable dimension. "One persistent theoretical problem," notes Arthur Cohen, "is that of disentangling the main components of credibility. Is it expertness or trustworthiness, perception of fairness or bias, disinterest or propagandistic intent, or any combination of factors which is responsible for the effects of credibility on attitude change?"[25] Sources can be studied by focusing on one special dimension (dress, gender, age, perceived intelligence, the decision to include both sides of an argument) or on a broader identity (a writer for the *New York Times*, a representative of the United States government, a member of the Chamber of Congress, or a felon). It may also be useful to link communicator traits to the content of a message, as has been done in studies of how the race of a speaker affects attitudes on the subject of racism.[26]

There is also evidence to suggest that the *medium* through which a message is sent affects the credibility of the source. Because they provide more personal data about a source's appearance or demeanor, for example, radio and television naturally focus more attention on demographic traits.[27] In contrast, print media give no clues about these details. Hence, many of us feel we know something about the character and personality of Dan Rather. His on-screen presence offers a specific persona. However, few Americans know anything about the executive editor of the *Washington Post*, even though that position has a significant effect on the nation's daily news agenda.

As we have noted, even the simplest communication setting contains a multitude of source variables that are difficult to isolate and study. It is hardly surprising that efforts to control for all of these factors have raised as many questions as answers. In spite of these limitations, some useful observations have come from research into the believability of sources.

1. *For many people high credibility means trustworthiness.* The concept of trust lies on or near the surface of most individual assessments of sources. What is interesting about trust is that it is implicitly an assessment of motive. Motives are read or judged in virtually every communication transaction. Assessments of motive amount to a "side calculation" that we make as we weigh another's requests on our time, attitudes, or money. Receivers are more willing to accept what a persuader says if they believe that his or her intentions are honorable. Trustworthy sources are seen as people who will not abuse their access to an audience. Audiences who believe that they are being used, deceived, or carelessly misled will pay little attention to an advocate's ideas.[28]

2. *Similarities between communicators and audiences do not necessarily pave the way for influence.* Researchers have sometimes found that listeners judge similar sources "as more attractive than dissimilar sources."[29] Most of us would expect as much. But some recent research has cast doubt on the view that attitude similarity translates into positive attraction toward a persuader.[30] The fact that there is prior agreement between people on a range of topics does not guarantee that they will more easily influence each other.

Monica Seles, Chris Evert & Mary Jo Fernandez © 2003 America's Dairy Farmers and Milk Processors

3. *Physical attractiveness increases a persuader's chances with audiences.* While intense audience involvement with a subject is usually more important, a number of researchers who have studied audience reactions to persuaders have concluded that attractive, well-dressed, and well-groomed advocates are likely to be more successful than "unattractive persuaders."[31]

4. *Prescriptive standards for judging sources (as noted in our previous discussion of rational/legal standards) often have little effect on overall persuasibility.* Similarity may be more important than expertise.[32] The sense that the expert is very different from the audience can nullify the advantages of excellent credentials. Even persuaders who carefully document the origins of their information sometimes do not fare any better than less candid advocates.[33]

5. *Audiences learn information regardless of a source's reliability.* A political campaign commercial on television may teach the viewer more about the political views of a candidate than an objective news report with ostensibly higher credibility.[34] There is a good deal of anecdotal evidence to suggest that the Internet has found audiences that are receptive to conspiracy theories, bogus medical remedies, and dubious historical facts. Some research suggests that users are not very curious about the credibility of Internet sources, assuming that there is little difference between the Web materials and more professionally edited media such as television or magazines.[35] We sometimes absorb—if not fully accept—views regardless of our assessments of the quality of the source.

6. *Audiences tend to have a shorter memory for the qualities associated with a source than for the ideas expressed.* Demonstrating what is sometimes called the sleeper effect, some studies have shown that people forget initial impressions of an advocate while retaining at least a general sense of the point of view expressed. The work of a number of researchers indicates that "the increased persuasion produced by a high-credibility source disappears. Similarly, the decreased persuasion produced by a low-credibility source vanishes."[36]

7. *The needs of receivers often override extensive consideration of a persuader's credibility.* The acceptability of a source is sometimes based on factors far removed from rational source credibility criteria. Gary Cronkhite and Jo Liska ask, "Do listeners always attend to public and television speakers because they consider the sources to be believable? Sometimes that is the reason, of course, but persuasion in such formats also proceeds as a matter of mutual need satisfaction." At times, "likability, novelty, and entertainment are valued more highly" than traditional standards of competence and trustworthiness.[37]

Credibility Reconsidered

As we have seen, the qualities that make a given source attractive to a particular audience have been the subject of much speculation. We have outlined three perspectives. For the early Greeks, who first systematically thought about the role of the advocate in persuasion, credibility was inherent in the quality of a person's character. A good persuader had to be a good and virtuous person. For logicians and historians, credibility resides in sources that have high expertise and reasonable objectivity. To social scientists who are concerned with how attitudes are formed, source credibility means believability, and it is determined by the standards of an audience.[38] Figure 5.1 presents a brief summary of these perspectives.

Figure 5.1 Three Perspectives on Credibility		
Prescriptive		**Descriptive**
1. Ethos as Good Character	2. Legal Standards for Judging Sources	3. Behavioral Studies of Believability
Good sense Good moral character Goodwill, etc.	Ability to make accurate observations Objectivity (more reluctant than willing)	Trustworthiness Honesty Expertise Similarity to receivers

STRATEGIC DIMENSIONS OF CREDIBILITY

▲

Although a message often stands or falls on the weight of its ideas and arguments, this is not the case with the four strategies discussed below. Each represents a dimension of persuasion that depends as much on an advocate's attributes as on the ideas presented. The use of a source's prestige to confer *legitimacy* on ideas or groups, the use of *mystifications* to telegraph a source's expertise or power, the potency of *source/placebo suggestion*, and the sometimes dangerous reliance on *appeals to authority* all play special roles in persuasion settings.

Legitimation

A few leaders have the power to add legitimacy to almost any idea or cause they endorse. Their presence insures the success or importance of a gathering, such as when a president chooses a local forum for an appearance. Or their endorsement can lend an aura of prestige to an object or cause. These high-ethos figures may be politicians, business leaders, entertainers, artists, clergy, or local civic leaders. Their names may be as recent and familiar as Tiger Woods, Russell Crowe, or Bill Gates, or as distant as the folk heroes Charles Lindbergh and broadcaster Edward R. Morrow. What all of these figures have exhibited is the power to gain acceptance for a point of view because of who they are.

Sources that have the power of legitimation are usually either celebrities or charismatic leaders. Richard Sennett argues that the trivia that flows from the

HE'S ONE IN A MILLION.
WE ARE HAPPY TO ANNOUNCE,
SO IS SHE. Meet Janette Saldana, the one-millionth kid to take the first step in turning her dreams into reality, thanks to StartSomething.[SM] With support from Target, this nationwide youth program from the Tiger Woods Foundation has reached a major milestone that we're very proud to celebrate. If you're ready to begin making your own mark, go to target.com and scroll down to the TigerWoodsStartSomething logo for more information or to sign up.

TARGET

Target Corporation

celebrity-making machinery of the mass media increasingly eclipse a person's genuine accomplishments. It may now be easier to be a celebrity—to be well known—than to sustain public attention on an agenda for social action.[39] Being an interesting personality may now be more important than having something to say. One reason actors get involved in political campaigns, Robert Redford has noted, is sheer guilt. A lot of actors feel they are in a shallow profession. "Other people are out there digging trenches and working in dangerous jobs. . . . That guilt produces some desire for credibility, so they go into campaigns."[40] In this case legitimacy is reciprocal. Actors gain from their association with serious causes, and the causes gain from the celebrity status of the actors. Celebrities have influence because of name recognition. Advertising has relied on celebrities for years. As early as the 1880s, tobacco companies linked their products with athletes and actors.[41] Endorsements by celebrities reached their peak on network television in the late 1950s when many stars, program hosts, and even some news reporters were expected to sell their sponsor's products.

Throughout the California gubernatorial recall election in October 2003, Arnold Schwarzenegger quickly emerged as a front-runner. His celebrity status allowed him to attract instant support before he had defined a single position on social issues or a plan to repair the state's broken economy.[42] Fellow actor Rob Lowe coordinated a group called Celebrities for Arnold. The surge of interest in his candidacy was remarkable in an era where candidates usually must seek support of special-interest groups, which would normally mean expressing views those groups want to hear. As one reporter stated, the sheer power of celebrity allowed Schwarzenegger to move "onto political center stage with a force resembling his entrances in the *Terminator* movies."[43] Schwarzenegger won with 48.6 percent of the vote in a crowded field.

Legitimacy through charismatic leaders has traditionally been associated with gifted moral and political figures who have gained prominence through challenges to formal channels of authority. Sociologist Edward Shils describes charismatic leaders as "persistent, effectively expressive personalities who impose themselves on their environment by their exceptional courage . . . self-confidence, fluency, [and] insight. . . ."[44] They seem to be a force of history, a presence who demands respect and attention from others. Figures as diverse as Mohandas Gandhi in India, Nelson Mandela in South Africa, and Martin Luther King, Jr. in the United States were sometimes as powerful as the official authorities they confronted in their quests for independence and civil liberties. But, as Shils notes, "it is also possible to apply the general characteristic of charisma to all individuals who can establish ascendancy over human beings by their commanding forcefulness or by an exemplary inner state which is expressed in a being of serenity."[45] A number of leaders from recent world history owed part of their effectiveness to the force of their public images and personalities—among them, Theodore Roosevelt, Franklin Roosevelt, Louisiana's Huey Long, France's Charles de Gaulle, and Cuba's Fidel Castro. To be sure, charisma does not buy instant success with an audience. But the presence of this elusive quality primes most audiences to levels of receptivity that ordinary sources usually cannot match.

Mystification

Mystification is the use of special symbols and technical jargon to communicate special authority and expertise to which others should defer. The use of specialized language or an office environment that announces particular skills can discourage opinions that differ from those of the persuader. For example, a physician in her office can use both language and the clinical environment to persuade clients—who understand few of the Latin-based terms of the health sciences, to accept a diagnosis. Mystifications are perhaps the only forms of communication that succeed by offering impressive but not fully understood vocabularies and symbols.

Persuaders may not employ mystifications in a calculated attempt to suppress opposition, but the result may be the same. If we interpret the jargon of a profession as an indication of authority, we may willingly decide that the language we cannot decode is itself a reason to yield.

Mystifications are also a way of "pulling rank." Anything but obedience somehow seems wrong or risky. Appeals for compliance are sometimes worded in vague but evocative symbols. An advocate is unlikely to impress us by simply stating, "Too many cooks spoil the broth." But this cliché can be whipped into something that implies the necessity to yield to a superior level of knowledge.

> Undue multiplicity of personnel assigned either concurrently or consecutively to a single function involves deterioration of quality in the resultant product as compared with the product of the labor of an exact sufficiency of personnel.[46]

Consider Thurman Arnold's classic analysis of the confusing mysteries of jurisprudence, the impressive term used to designate the study of legal philosophy. "Here is a subject," he notes, "which not even lawyers read. Its content is vague; its literature is abstruse and difficult. Nevertheless there is a general feeling that under this title are hidden the most sacred mysteries of the law."[47] He notes that the confusing jargon of the legal profession "performs its social task most effectively for those who encourage it, praise it, but do not read it."[48] For most of us, legal language remains a mysterious but impressive set of codes that provide a reason for placing our faith in its highly trained specialists.

Source/Placebo Suggestion

One of the most fascinating forms of source-induced influence is the placebo effect. A placebo is a harmless and chemically neutral agent presented as treatment for an illness. Its most familiar form is a sugar pill, but it may also include impressive machines, bundles of herbs, or virtually any object or symbol system invested with special powers. Part of the potency of placebos lies in their powers of mystification. The inability to understand the medical terminology, complicated apparatus, medicines, and equipment may actually enhance the possibilities for a cure. Ironically, a more thorough understanding of the limitations of treatments might remove the mystery, which is the basis of the cure. The remarkable fact about placebos is that they sometimes work. When administered by medical authorities, placebos can have very real therapeutic benefits that defy biological explanations. Often, the mere *suggestion* that a person is receiving a therapeutic treatment is sufficient for actual healing to begin.

The power of suggestion triggers expectations, which can create significant physical and mental effects. As Jerome Frank notes, "a patient's expectations have been shown to affect physiological responses so powerfully that they can reverse the pharmacological action of a drug."[49] Some studies indicate that success in treatment with placebos ranges from 30 to 60 percent. For the treatment of conditions with a subjective dimension—such as pain and allergies—effectiveness may even be higher.[50] The most common explanation for this link between mind and body is that placebos trigger the release of endorphins that can block symptoms and create an enhanced sense of well-being. Recent studies have challenged some of the claims made for placebos in clinical trials of specific drugs and treatments.[51] But there is little doubt that treatments involving subjective outcomes (i.e., pain or a sense of well-being) are greatly affected by medical symbols and the high expectations associated with them.[52]

The primary lesson of the placebo effect is an important one for persuaders. Sources can create the *expectation* of physical or mental transformation. Whether we take a placebo in a medical study or decide that a doctor's language qualifies him or her as an expert, our expectations may lead to compliance and (in certain kinds of treatment) substantive improvement. Any agent or object that enjoys the unqualified faith of a persuadee—shaman, faith healer, acupuncturist, psychotherapist, or motivational speaker—can activate expectations that lead to improvement. Results from placebo studies often demonstrate that we cannot afford to be too eager to dismiss faith-based or alternative treatments. In this realm of our psychology, the science of healing must sometimes be subordinated to the potency of expectant attitudes.

Authoritarianism and Acquiescence

History is filled with examples of strong leaders who have used threats and persuasion to reshape the attitudes and actions of compliant people. Hitler, Mussolini, and Japan's Tojo were widely portrayed in the United States as having hypnotic control over their followers during World War II. Many believed these leaders could persuade their supporters to do almost anything. Like Jim Jones or David Koresh, their powers seemed strong enough at times to justify mass suicide. The popular press often portrays such persuasion in overly simple terms. A group of "gullible" people are taken in by a "cult" and "brainwashed" by a clever and demonic figure. These terms place all the responsibility on an evil, strong leader. But they miss what appears to be a natural tendency among many to defer to unambiguous authority. In his classic study of the true believer, Eric Hoffer noted that especially for people who see themselves as society's victims rather than beneficiaries, strong insurgent leaders can be especially seductive. In Hoffer's words:

> People whose lives are barren and insecure seem to show a greater willingness to obey than people who are self-sufficient and self-confident. To the frustrated, freedom from responsibility is more attractive than freedom from restraint. . . . They willingly abdicate the directing of their lives to those who want to plan, command and shoulder all responsibility.[53]

The first major English language analysis of social conditions and personality traits that give rise to obedience to authority was *The Authoritarian Personality* by

T. W. Adorno, Else Frankel-Brunswik, and their associates in 1950.[54] The authors, some of whom had escaped from Austria before the Nazi attacks on Jews, traced the origins of a multitude of personality traits, including anti-Semitism, "susceptibility to antidemocratic propaganda," ethnocentrism (judging others by one's own cultural values), and predispositions toward fascism. Their efforts to determine how patterns of upbringing instilled such traits is less important here than the fascinating questions their study brought into focus. Are certain kinds of listeners overly susceptible to appeals based on authority, especially official sources? Are some types of audiences too willing to look past the natural ambiguities of everyday life for the rigid ideological certainties of a demagogue (i.e., Hitler's stereotypes of Jewish "failings")? What psychological needs are satisfied when total allegiance is promised to a leader?

The F (Anti-Democratic) Scale questionnaire was developed to locate the authoritarian type, to discover the signs of authoritarian submission, and to find evidence of an uncritical attitude toward idealized moral authorities. It consisted of several agree-disagree claims. Listed below are some of the typical statements in the questionnaire. A respondent was asked to agree or disagree with each.

- Obedience and respect for authority are the most important virtues children should learn.

- Every person should have complete faith in some supernatural power whose decisions will be obeyed without question.

- What this country needs most, more than laws and political programs, are a few courageous, tireless, devoted leaders in whom the people can put their faith.[55]

In analyzing scores of responses to questions like these, the authors discovered that anti-Semitism, rigidity, ethnocentrism, undue respect for power, and many other traits tend to cluster within many of the same people and are probably tied to certain styles of family life. They learned that authoritarianism can be identified and recognized in segments of almost any population. What remains unanswered, however, is whether such people represent a unique persuadable type.

The dilemma raised by obedience to authority is that, while every society has an important stake in the rule of law, the failure of ordinary people to challenge leaders who support unjust or inhumane acts can coarsen or even destroy a society. There have been times (in colonial America, for example, or in the decisions of all the Soviet republics to declare autonomy) when disorder arguably brought about a better order. The advantage of hindsight helps gauge when the price of obedience has been too costly. For instance, it is now easy to criticize the average German soldier's obedience to Hitler and his lieutenants during World War II. Nearly every discussion of that conflict questions how so many people in Germany could have accepted the blatant xenophobia and racism of the Third Reich.[56] But others have also questioned why many Americans accepted the decision to jail thousands of Japanese Americans in the same period. Why was the nation silent when it became federal policy to detain 117,000 *American citizens* of Japanese ancestry in prison camps on the West Coast?[57] What made the official propaganda line that a San Francisco "Jap" could be as dangerous as a Tokyo "Jap" acceptable? The rhetoric of our leaders and slick Hollywood war films played their parts.[58] Governments, businesses, and institutions have enormous interests in protecting their own authority.

Psychologist Stanley Milgram strikingly illustrated how people accept oppressive authority. His well-known and controversial work in the 1960s measured the degree to which ordinary people would follow problematic orders from a responsible official. Although his research design would be rejected by most university research boards today, it clearly demonstrated the dangers of obedience to authority. Milgram advertised for volunteers to help conduct a learning experiment. Those whom he selected were asked to assist him in teaching a learner who was, in reality, a Milgram confederate. Every time the learner incorrectly answered a question, the volunteer would be instructed to act as the teacher and to administer an electrical shock. This scheme of reward and punishment was ostensibly designed to help improve the skills of the learner.

In *Obedience to Authority*, Milgram explained how the volunteers were introduced to the setting.

> After watching the learner being strapped into place, he is taken into the main experimental room and seated before an impressive shock generator. Its main feature is a horizontal line of thirty switches, ranging from 15 volts to 450 volts, in 15 volt increments. There are also verbal designations which range from slight shock to danger-severe shock. The teacher is told that he is to administer the learning test to the man in the other room.

> The learner, or victim, is an actor who actually receives no shock at all. The point of the experiment is to see how far a person will proceed in a concrete and measurable situation in which he is ordered to inflict increasing pain on a protesting victim.[59]

The dilemma the teacher faced was one of obedience. At what point should he reject the commands of the experimenter to keep going?

> For the subject, the situation is not a game; conflict is intense and obvious. On one hand, the manifest suffering of the learner presses him to quit. On the other hand, the experimenter, a legitimate authority to whom the subject feels some commitment, enjoins him to continue.[60]

Many did continue, even when the learner cried out in agonizing pain. Had the learners actually been wired to the shock box, many would have died a slow and painful death.

To witnesses of this research, the volunteers who obeyed Milgram appeared sadistic. Milgram concluded otherwise, citing the very human tendency to shift responsibility to a higher and seemingly legitimate authority. He noted that "relatively few people have the resources needed to resist authority. A variety of inhibitions against disobeying authority come into play and successfully keep the person in his place."[61]

Admittedly, there are differences between a setting in which a volunteer agrees to carry out the orders of a researcher and a persuasive situation in which a popular advocate elicits support from an autonomous collection of individuals.[62] The volunteer's desire to be helpful is probably greater than the average listener's motivations to accept the views of many persuaders. We doubt that most people in open societies are the "servile flock . . . incapable of ever doing without a master" that Gustave LeBon described in his famous study of social movements.[63] Even so, any casual observer of the workplace, the classroom, and scores of other hierarchical settings will readily see how references to authority function as effective appeals.

SUMMARY
▲
_____

In human communication, the content of a message is almost always understood in terms of the quality and acceptability of a source. As we noted at the beginning of this chapter, there are many questions about the nature of authority that still need answers, and there are many ways to describe how credibility enables persuaders to succeed. Three forms of credibility were outlined. Audiences expect that those seeking their support will demonstrate positive traits of character, common sense, and goodwill. Persuasion theorists from Aristotle onward have described such traits of good character as essential to all individuals who would call themselves worthy advocates. In settings such as the courtroom and the laboratory where audiences are prepared to weigh evidence to determine truth, sources are best measured by reference to their abilities to observe events accurately and objectively. We called this second form of credibility the rational/legal model of credibility. A third type involves the idea that specific personal attributes of persuaders are likely to be attractive or unattractive to particular types of people. This believability standard has less to do with the search for truth or good character than with audience attitudes.

Credibility is central to the study of persuasion. An audience's awareness of the personal biography of an advocate is often the first important moment in the communication process. In addition, for public figures and persuaders reaching large audiences, the presence of charisma or a mystifying expertise may double or redouble the impact of a message. The sheer force of a dominating public character can generate an intensely loyal following—sometimes because of the extraordinary nature of an advocate's leadership, at other times because individuals may have a strong and sometimes dangerous desire to relinquish responsibility to others.

Questions and Projects for Further Study

1. Recall the arrangement and layout of a doctor's office that you have visited recently. Analyze that space in terms of the subtle technical symbols and mystifying messages it communicates. Be sure to consider specific categories such as dress, use of technical jargon, and the presence of scientific equipment. What are some of the common effects these elements have on patients? How would demystifying some of these elements change some of the effects you have cited?

2. Observe some of the experts and spokespersons who appear in a network news program (i.e., CNN's _Larry King Live_, PBS's _Newshour_, ABC's _Nightline_, etc.). They may be seen making observations about the day's events from

their vantage points in government, business, the arts, and so on. Note if the introduction of the guests lays out their *ethos* for the audience. Assess the credibility of one or two experts using both the rational/legal model and the experts' own claims.

3. Locate several magazine ads that use prestige and legitimation as a persuasive strategy. Describe the verbal and visual symbols that help sell the product.

4. Attend a portion of a criminal trial in your area. Study the way the prosecution and defense attorneys attempt to establish or discredit the credibility of specific witnesses. (A film that provides the same kind of experience is Francis Ford Coppola's *The Rainmaker*.)

5. Identify and describe a character from films or television who seems to exhibit some of the characteristics of the authoritarian personality.

6. Using a standard search engine such as Yahoo or Google, pick a controversial topic and generate a random list of Web sites relating to the topic. Answer some of the following questions: Do any of the Web sites make statements about their own credibility? What cues or signals are included to suggest high credibility? How do you think individuals would respond to the absence or presence of credibility claims?

7. You may have noticed that this chapter poses a dilemma that could also be a contradiction. Persuasion admittedly requires deference to many types of experts and authorities. But we concluded with a caution about the dangers of persuasion that exploit the symbols of expertise and authority (as illustrated by Milgram). Attempt to explain the differences between persuasion based on genuine credibility and persuasion that abuses an audience's faith in authority. Cite a real or hypothetical example.

8. In "Factors of Source Credibility" by Jack Whitehead (*Quarterly Journal of Speech*, February 1968, pp. 69–63), a number of traits identified with high-credibility sources are listed. Choosing from his list below, identify and defend eight credibility traits that would most help (1) a male member of a persuasion course advocating a compulsory year of government service for all eighteen-year-olds or (2) a senator from your state urging a cross-section of citizens to support a 15 percent pay increase for all members of Congress. The traits include the following:

fair	good speaker	respectful
good	right	honest
trustworthy	loyal to listeners	admirable
just	patient	correct
sincere	straightforward	reliable
valuable	unselfish	nice
virtuous	has goodwill	calm
moral	frank	friendly
professional manner	experienced	energetic

authoritative	has foresight	bold
aggressive	active	open-minded
decisive	proud	
objective	impartial	

Additional Reading

T. W. Adorno, Else Frankel-Brunswik, Daniel J. Levinson, and R. Nevitt Sanford, *The Authoritarian Personality* (New York: Harper and Brothers, 1950).

Gary Cronkhite and Jo R. Liska, "The Judgment of Communicant Acceptability," *Persuasion: New Directions in Theory and Research*, eds. Michael Roloff and Gerald Miller (Beverly Hills: Sage, 1980), pp. 101–39.

Andrew Flanagin and Miriam Metzger, "Perceptions of Internet Information Credibility," *Journalism and Mass Communication Quarterly*, Autumn 2000, pp. 515–40.

Carl Hovland, Irving L. Janis, and Harold Kelley, *Communication and Persuasion* (New Haven, CT: Yale, 1953).

Charles A. Kiesler, Barry E. Collins, Norman Miller, *Attitude Change: A Critical Analysis of Theoretical Approaches* (New York: John Wiley and Sons, 1969).

William J. McGuire, "Attitudes and Attitude Change," *Handbook of Social Psychology*, Vol. II, 3rd ed., eds. Gardner Lindzey and Elliot Aronson (Mahwah, NJ: Lawrence Earlbaum, 1985), pp. 262–69.

Stanley Milgram, *Obedience to Authority: An Experimental View* (New York: Harper & Row, 1974).

Robert P. Newman and Dale R. Newman, *Evidence* (Boston, MA: Houghton Mifflin, 1969).

Daniel J. O'Keefe, *Persuasion: Theory and Research*, 2nd ed. (Newbury Park, CA: Sage, 2002).

Carolyn W. Sherif, Muzafer Sherif, and Roger E. Nebergall, *Attitudes and Attitude Change* (Philadelphia: W. B. Saunders, 1965).

Notes

[1] Woodbury Kane quoted in Edmund Morris, *Theodore Rex* (New York: Random House, 2001), p. 117.

[2] Laura Holson, "The Show Must Go On," *New York Times*, August 12, 2001, sec. 3, p. 2.

[3] William Benoit, "Sears' Repair of its Auto Service Image: Image Restoration Discourse in the Corporate Sector," *Communication Studies*, Spring 1995, pp. 94–95.

[4] Pavel Felgenhauer, "Drowning Reality of *Kursk*," *The Moscow Times* (Online), August 31, 2000.

[5] Andrew King, *Power and Communication* (Prospect Heights, IL: Waveland Press, 1987), p. 138.

[6] Lawrence Wright, "Lives of the Saints," *The New Yorker*, January 21, 2002, p. 50.

[7] Aristotle, *The Rhetoric*, Book II, Chapter 1.

[8] Ibid.

[9] These are high credibility indicators cited by Jack L. Whitehead, Jr. in "Factors of Source Credibility," *Quarterly Journal of Speech*, February 1968, p. 61.

[10] Robert M. Pirsig, *Zen and the Art of Motorcycle Maintenance: An Inquiry Into Values* (New York: William Morrow, 1974), p. 32.

[11] Ibid., pp. 33–34.

[12] Robert P. Newman and Dale R. Newman, *Evidence* (Boston: Houghton Mifflin, 1969), p. viii. We are indebted to the authors of this book for the general scheme developed in this section.

[13] Harper Lee, *To Kill A Mockingbird* (New York: Popular Library, 1962), p. 208.

[14] Ibid., p. 244.

[15] William Robbins, "Watching and Waiting for a Quake to Happen," *New York Times*, December 4, 1990, p. A22.

[16] Bill Carter, "An Energized Brokaw Is in the Middle of the Story," *New York Times*, November 5, 2001, p. C1.

[17] Melody Petersen, "Heartfelt Advice, Hefty Fees," *New York Times*, August 11, 2002, sec. 3, pp. 1, 14.

[18] Robert McChesney, *Rich Media, Poor Democracy* (New York: The New Press, 2000), p. 54.

[19] Newman and Newman, p. 79.

[20] Carl Hovland, Irving L. Janis, and Harold Kelley, *Communication and Persuasion* (New Haven, CT: Yale, 1953).

[21] Carl Hovland and Walter Weiss, "The Influence of Source Credibility on Communication Effectiveness," *Public Opinion Quarterly*, 1951, 15:535–60.

[22] For a critique and review of this study see Philip G. Zimbardo, Ebbe B. Ebbesen, and Christina Maslach, *Influencing Attitudes and Changing Behavior*, 2nd ed. (Reading, MA: Addison-Wesley, 1977), pp. 94–98, 125–27.

[23] Ibid., p. 126.

[24] For more detailed analyses of experimental research on source credibility see: Kenneth Andersen and Theodore Clevenger, Jr., "A Summary of Experimental Research in Ethos," in *The Rhetoric of Our Times*, ed. J. Jeffrey Auer (New York: Appleton-Century-Crofts, 1969), pp. 127–51; Jesse G. Delia, "A Constructivist Analysis of the Concept of Credibility," *Quarterly Journal of Speech*, December 1976, pp. 361–75; Icek Ajzen and Martin Fishbein, *Understanding Attitudes and Predicting Social Behavior* (Englewood Cliffs, NJ: Prentice Hall, 1980), pp. 13–27, 218–28; and Dominick A. Infante, Kenneth R. Parker, Christopher H. Clarke, Laverne Wilson, and Indrani A. Nathu, "A Comparison of Factor and Functional Approaches to Source Credibility," *Communication Quarterly*, Winter 1983, pp. 43–48.

[25] Arthur R. Cohen, *Attitude Change and Social Influence* (New York: Basic Books, 1964), p. 26.

[26] Andersen and Clevenger, p. 132.

[27] See, for example, Steve Booth-Butterfield and Christine Gutowski, "Message Modality and Source Credibility Can Interact to Affect Argument Processing," *Communication Quarterly*, Winter 1993, pp. 77–89.

[28] For more on assessments of motives, see our discussion of attribution theory in chapter 6.

[29] Herbert W. Simons, Nancy N. Berkowitz, and John Moyer, "Similarity, Credibility, and Attitude Change: A Review and Theory," *Psychological Bulletin*, January 1970, pp. 2–4.

[30] Michael Sunnafrank, "Attitude Similarity and Interpersonal Attraction in Communication Processes: In Pursuit of an Ephemeral Influence," *Communication Monographs*, December 1983, pp. 273–84.

[31] For general discussions of these findings see: Mark L. Knapp, *Nonverbal Communication and Human Behavior* (New York: Holt, Rinehart, and Winston, 1972), pp. 63–90; and Raymond S. Ross, *Understanding Persuasion*, 4th ed. (Englewood Cliffs, NJ: Prentice Hall, 1994), pp. 99–100.

[32] William J. McGuire, "Attitudes and Attitude Change," *Handbook of Social Psychology*, Vol. II, 3rd ed., eds. Gardner Lindzey and Elliot Aronson (Mahwah, NJ: Lawrence Earlbaum, 1985), p. 263.

[33] Wayne N. Thompson, *Quantitative Research in Public Address and Communication* (New York: Random House, 1967), pp. 54–55.

[34] Thomas E. Patterson and Robert D. McClure, *The Unseeing Eye: The Myth of Television Power in Politics* (New York: G.P. Putnams, 1976), pp. 22–23.

[35] Andrew Flanagin and Miriam Metzger, "Perceptions of Internet Information Credibility," *Journalism and Mass Communication Quarterly*, Autumn 2000, pp. 515–40.

[36] Charles Kiesler, Barry E. Collins, and Norman Miller, *Attitude Change: A Critical Analysis of Theoretical Approaches* (New York: John Wiley and Sons, 1969), p. 108.

[37] Gary Cronkhite and Jo Liska, "The Judgment of Communicant Acceptability," in *Persuasion: New Directions in Theory and Research*, ed. Michael Roloff and Gerald Miller (Beverly Hills: Sage, 1980), p. 104. See also Daniel J. O'Keefe, *Persuasion: Theory and Research* (Newbury Park, CA: Sage, 1990), pp. 130–57.

[38] For a more detailed discussion of different assumptions for assessing credibility, see Cal Logue and Eugene Miller, "Rhetorical Status: A Study of its Origins, Functions, and Consequences," *Quarterly Journal of Speech*, February 1995, pp. 20–28.

[39] Richard Sennett, *The Fall of Public Man* (New York: Vintage, 1978), pp. 282–87.

[40] Ronald Brownstein, "Hollywood's Hot Love: Politics," *New York Times*, January 6, 1991, pp. 13, 16, 17.

[41] Daniel Pope, *The Making of Modern Advertising* (New York: Basic Books, 1983), p. 228.

[42] Vincent Schodolski, "Is Arnold a Democrat in GOP Clothing?" *Chicago Tribune*, August 18, 2003, pp. 1, 14.

[43] Schodolski, p. 1.

[44] Edward Shils, "Charisma," in *The Encyclopedia of the Social Sciences,* Vol. 2, ed. David Sills (New York: Macmillan, 1968), p. 387.

[45] Ibid.

[46] Quoted in Richard Weaver, *The Ethics of Rhetoric* (Chicago: Henry Regnery, 1953), p. 200.

[47] Thurman Arnold, *The Symbols of Government* (New York: Harcourt, Brace and World, 1962), p. 46.

[48] Ibid., p. 70.

[49] Jerome D. Frank, *Persuasion and Healing* (New York: Schocken, 1974), p. 137.

[50] Margaret Talbot, "The Placebo Prescription," *New York Times Magazine,* January 9, 2000, pp. 34–39, 44, 58–59; F. J. Evans, "Placebo," in *The Encyclopedia of Psychology,* Vol. 3, 2nd ed., ed. by Raymond Corsini (New York: John Wiley and Sons, 1994), pp. 91–92.

[51] Gina Kolata, "Placebo Effect is More Myth Than Science, Study Says," *New York Times,* May 24, 2001, p. A20.

[52] Fred Guterl, "How Real is the Placebo Effect?" *Newsweek,* June 18, 2001, p. 49.

[53] Eric Hoffer, *The True Believer: Thoughts on the Nature of Mass Movements* (New York: Harper and Row, 1966), p. 109.

[54] T. W. Adorno, Else Frankel-Brunswik, Daniel J. Levinson, and R. Nevitt Sanford, *The Authoritarian Personality* (New York: Harper and Brothers, 1950). The study is considered a classic, although serious questions have been raised about its complex attitude-research methodology in 1950. See for example, Roger Brown, *Social Psychology* (New York: Free Press, 1965), pp. 509–26.

[55] Adorno, et al., p. 248.

[56] See, for example, Daniel Goldhagen, *Hitler's Willing Executioners: Ordinary Germans and the Holocaust* (New York: Knopf, 1996).

[57] Charles Goodell, *Political Prisoners in America* (New York: Random House, 1973), p. 87.

[58] David Hwang, "Are Movies Ready for Real Orientals?" *New York Times,* August 11, 1985, sec. 2, pp. 1, 21.

[59] Stanley Milgram, *Obedience to Authority: An Experimental View* (New York: Harper and Row, 1974), pp. 3–4.

[60] Ibid., p. 4.

[61] Ibid., p. 6.

[62] For a useful discussion of Milgram's study and the problem of obedience, see Roger Brown, *Social Psychology,* 2nd ed. (New York: Free Press, 1986), pp. 1–41.

[63] Gustave LeBon, *The Crowd* (New York: Viking, 1960), p. 118.

The Psychology of Persuasion

Overview

▲ Logic and Rationality
▲ Components in Attitude Change
   Beliefs
   Attitudes
   Values
▲ Behavioral Theories of Persuasion
   Stimulus-Response Theory
   Reinforcement Theory
   Attribution Theory
   Consistency Theories
   Social Judgment Theory
   Long-Term Attitude Change
   Elaboration Likelihood Theory
   Theory of Reasoned Action

> *By becoming aware of our ways of talking and how effective they are,*
> *we can override our automatic impulses and adapt our habitual*
> *styles when they are not serving us well.*[1]
>
> —DEBORAH TANNEN

Much of the research on persuasion has tried to pinpoint the processes individuals go through in deciding whether to accept or to reject a particular message. Think about the decisions you make daily. How many people try to convince you to behave one way or another? From your parents to your friends to your teachers to your boss to the advertisers in countless media, the attempts to influence are pervasive. If someone were to discover a fail-safe method to dissect the private deliberations of individuals, that ability would give them awesome power to influence others. Fortunately, fears about a Svengali mastermind can be put to rest, since most theories of persuasion address *tendencies* of certain people in certain contexts. While these theories provide useful information about numerous processes, no single theory can predict with absolute certainty how one person will behave at all times.

In this chapter we will investigate various behavioral theories of persuasion. The persuader who is thinking like a psychologist attempts to determine what happens "inside" individuals when they are confronted with appeals urging change. Specifically, we will consider various theories that attempt to account for internal changes that occur when we feel compelled to alter our beliefs and attitudes. We will also discuss several persuasive strategies correlated with behavioral theories.

LOGIC AND RATIONALITY
▲

If you were to ask people how they make decisions, most would reply that they think about possible alternatives and choose the one that makes the most sense. While they might not use the terms rational and logical, they would be describing the exercise of reason—the ability to think, infer, and comprehend in an orderly, intelligent fashion. Yet, if most of us believe we are rational beings, how do we explain seemingly irrational behavior? Why do people continue to smoke when the evidence clearly indicates that smoking is a health risk? Why do people with children keep loaded guns in their homes when evidence about firearm accidents is plentiful? Why do people consume illegal drugs when such usage is personally harmful? Logic would dictate that we should avoid smoking, storing loaded firearms in our homes, and consuming illicit drugs. How can large numbers of people ignore the seemingly obvious?

Human logic is a complex and sometimes subjective notion comprised of more than just facts. How we interpret pieces of information and assign meaning and significance to them depends on which process we decide to use in categorizing inputs received. Interaction between speaker and listener affects both the information retained and the assessment process. A teenager with a sense of immortality and a strong desire to belong can easily find enough evidence to categorize cigarettes as emblems of adulthood. Persuasion is more than an exercise in formal logic, because humans are more than machines.

Context, knowledge, experiences, and socioeconomic variables affect how we interpret persuasive attempts. In most communicative and thus persuasive contexts, there are content and relational levels of communication. How well we know or feel about a person impacts reception of a message—often more than the content of the message.[2] There can never be absolute predictable behavior as long as there are choices and human motives. There are too many situations, emotions, and differences among people for there to be singular solutions or arguments. Persuasion is a bridge across these differences. Persuasion is not something one does to someone; rather, it is a cooperative venture with another person.

COMPONENTS IN ATTITUDE CHANGE
▲

In chapter 1, we defined persuasion as the process of preparing messages to alter or strengthen the beliefs, attitudes, or behaviors of the intended autonomous audience. The clearest evidence of successful persuasion is some form of overt behavior. The ultimate goal of most persuasive endeavors is to get someone to do something. That action usually only follows after important internal changes. Traditional persuasion theory argues that behavior change or modification is predicated on attitude change. Consequently, attitude change is the core concept in nearly all theories of persuasion.

Beliefs, attitudes, and values are theoretical or hypothetical constructs. You cannot point to them as you can to a tree, a car, or a house. As a result, they are difficult to define, difficult to measure, and difficult to manage. Yet, the concepts provide the basis for all social scientific investigations of human persuasion. Before we can discuss behavioral theories of persuasion, we need to explore the concepts of beliefs, attitudes, and values. We separate the three terms and note some distinguishing features, but it is important to remember that the three work together. Not everyone agrees on how to define these elements or even whether we can distinguish one from the other. Attempting to delineate differences does, however, help us sort out human tendencies and focuses our attention on the myriad influences on our behavior.

Beliefs

A belief is what we personally "know" to be true or false—our convictions— even if others disagree. There are many types of beliefs. Deeply held beliefs become core values; we also hold beliefs about matters that are more incidental to our lives. For example, we might believe that honesty is a requirement for good character; we can also believe that *Friends* is more entertaining than *Frasier*. There are beliefs in a thing—the high probability that something exists. There are also beliefs in a particular relationship between an object and something else. We can believe that Mount Everest is the highest mountain in the world, and we can believe that climbing it is dangerous. Beliefs are informational statements that link specific attributes to an object.[3] Our perceptions of how two or more things are related determine the categories to which we assign information. One's attitude toward an object is a function of one's *salient* beliefs—those that are stronger and more important than incidental beliefs. Salient beliefs provide the basis for our attitudes toward the object.[4]

Valence is a term used to describe the direction of classification of information—whether it is added as supporting evidence for other beliefs or rejected as not fitting our belief system. Valence looks at *how* information influences our beliefs. Weight is another important element in classifying inputs; it is a function of credibility. If we believe the statement is true, it has a heavier weight in our system. Weight measures *how much* we accept the relationship between an object and an attribute. We reason about a statement and then decide whether it makes sense. How we interpret information and assign meaning to it depends on both weight and valence.

Beliefs are components in our cognitive system. Cognition is the term that refers to the process of knowing—how we learn. Learning theories focus on the relationships between stimuli and responses. Martin Fishbein has developed a number of theories about how people assimilate and integrate information.[5] Later in the chapter, we'll look at his theory of reasoned action. In the next section, we'll discuss his expectancy-value theory, which relates an attitude toward an object to beliefs about the object. Included here are two of his findings about how an attitude is formed.

1. Attitude toward an object depends on the number of beliefs about the object, the strength of those beliefs, and the evaluation of the connection between the object and beliefs about it.

2. Information often changes the weight of a belief or adds new information.

Earlier in the text we discussed how persuasion is often directed to reinforcing opinions. One of the reasons for this is that most new information reinforces strongly held opinions. However, if an opinion is based on little information, new information can change a belief. How we integrate new information with our existing beliefs and attitudes determines whether we reinforce or change our thinking about a particular topic.

Consider, for example, some potential beliefs that may contribute to one's attitude about abortion:

1. The purpose of sexual intercourse is procreation.

2. Children should be raised in a family environment, not in a single-parent environment.

3. Life begins at conception.

4. Having a child outside of marriage would greatly embarrass my family.

5. A woman should decide what happens to her body.

6. Human life does not begin until the fetus can survive outside the womb.

7. Our regard for the human fetus is a test of our own compassion for all humans.

8. People who care so much for unborn fetuses should show at least as much compassion for children who are now on this earth.

9. Some religious beliefs view abortion as the murder of innocent life.

10. Government has no role in private decision making.

There are many other potential beliefs on the issue of abortion. The important point is that one individual would rank some of these beliefs as more important than others. Another person might rank them in exactly the opposite order. The ranking would be based on each individual's particular experience and knowledge, which would affect the depth of feeling and the confidence to evaluate the issues. Our ranking of beliefs changes over time. Life events may greatly influence the ordering or reordering of beliefs relevant to an issue. For example, it is reasonable to expect the life event of becoming a parent to influence one's view of abortion. One of the co-authors of this book has changed his views on the issue of capital punishment three times—sometimes religious considerations prevailed in forming his attitude; at other times, more legalistic arguments dominated his thinking; more recently, scientific advances in DNA technologies influence his opinion because wrongful conviction is less likely given the reliability of DNA testing.

It follows that the more information we have or know about an issue or topic, the more certain our beliefs will be. While one new bit of information may not have much effect, multiple inputs may cause us to question some of the beliefs that contributed to an attitude. With the issue of abortion, one strategy to alter attitudes would be to present information that addresses the issue of when life begins. To confirm or challenge an individual's belief about the beginning of life will strengthen or weaken an individual's attitude on the issue. For some, however, the issue of freedom of choice may be more salient than the conception of life. Because audience members differ in terms of which beliefs are more salient, multiple persuasive messages are essential for effective persuasion.

Attitudes

Beliefs provide the foundation for attitudes, which become knowledge structures or *schemas* informing everyday living. For example, stereotypes are forms of schemas that serve as shortcuts for interaction and behavior.[6] Every opinion is based on one or more beliefs about a topic; attitudes are a combination of beliefs and the weight we assign to them. Attitudes evaluate;[7] they express opinions about an issue. In other words, attitudes involve our awareness about something (belief) and our judgment about it. There are attitudes toward an object and attitudes toward the consequences of acting on that predisposition. For example, a person can have a positive attitude about chocolate cake but a negative attitude about consuming too many empty calories. Because they are an expression of how one feels, attitudes are predispositions to behave a certain way.

Attitudes comprise our likes and dislikes of people, places, or things; they influence our responses to stimuli and ultimately our behavior. Thus, when we evaluate some symbol in the world as desirable or undesirable, we are forming an attitude. If we say "abortion is bad," we are expressing an attitude. Attitudes are learned predispositions—tendencies to react favorably or unfavorably. They are learned patterns of response based on past personal experiences or the experiences of trusted others.

Gass and Seiter identify several definitional characteristics of attitudes. First, as already mentioned, attitudes are learned; they are not innate. Second, attitudes precede and therefore influence individual behavior. They provide mental short-cuts to guide behavior. Third, attitudes have an evaluative dimension signaling direction of response and intensity of feeling. Finally, attitudes are directed toward some specific object. The object could be a person, group, idea, policy, event, etc.[8]

Figure 6.1   Belief Structure of an Attitude

Attitude: I don't like "rap" music.

Beliefs:

rap music is atonal	rap lyrics are often violent and profane	rap glorifies gang lifestyle	rap degrades; it does not inspire

Values: conservative, respect

We develop our attitudes through social interaction with others, gathering information from a variety of sources that influence our attitudes on a wide range of topics. In addition to face-to-face interactions, we obtain a great deal of infor-mation from the mass media. Many of our attitudes are influenced by what we see in the media, such as attitudes toward sex, violence, or fashion—to name only a few. Indeed, scholars fear the long-term influence of the media on society's beliefs, attitudes, and values.

We also form attitudes based on direct experience. The loss of a loved one or friend in an accident caused by a drunk driver significantly impacts our attitudes toward drinking and driving. Likewise, exposure to ultrasound images of fetuses may well influence one's views toward abortion. Related to direct experience is observational learning, sometimes called modeling or vicarious modeling. By watch-ing others, we form attitudes about what is right and wrong, good and bad. When we emulate those we admire, our attitudes are influenced in any number of ways.

We also formulate attitudes through the process of social comparison. We are in a constant state of comparing our attitudes with others. As social animals, we seek social acceptance and validation. If we "hang out" with a group whose values differ from our own, there will most likely be some adjustment. Parents often fear that the college experience will endanger the values of their children. In truth, a university environment provides a diversity of attitudes and opinions. A good edu-cation will force each of us to question our fundamental beliefs and values. In gen-eral, we usually retain the attitudes formed throughout the years. We tend to socialize with those who are similar to us—in background, socioeconomic status, and, yes, attitudes. It is not surprising that we are most comfortable with those who are similar to us.

Finally, there are a few studies that suggest a genetic basis for the development of at least some attitudes. Some scholars suggest that some phobias or personality traits may be inherited; thus, some individuals are more predisposed toward certain

Vanessa Short Bull, Oglala Lakota.

Political Science major, dancer,

Miss South Dakota USA 2000,

spokesperson for Native American

cancer awareness, stand-up

comic. Nearly 60% of our graduates

go on to a non-Indian college

or university. This exceeds the

transfer rate of community

college students nationwide.

AMERICAN INDIAN COLLEGE FUND◊
EDUCATION IS STRENGTH

For more on tribal colleges, call

800.776.3863 or go to collegefund.org.

Courtesy of the American Indian College Fund, Denver, CO

attitudes than others. For example, identical twins are more likely to have similar attitudes than non-identical twins. While still somewhat controversial, investigating the genetic connection with attitude formation is a growing area of study.[9]

How do we discover the attitudes of others? There are numerous techniques to measure attitudes. First, we can simply ask people; self-reports are one method of measuring attitudes. Second, we can observe people's behavior—what they say in daily conversation or by their actions. This method usually involves some attempt to correlate attitudes to behavior. For example, it is reasonable to assume that if someone wears a jacket with a Yankees logo every day, the person probably likes and favors the team. Third, people tend to associate with others who hold similar beliefs, attitudes, and values. By identifying a person's business and social associations, one might ascertain an attitude profile of an individual. For example, if someone belongs to the National Rifle Association, there is a reasonable probability that his or her attitudes about a range of social and political issues will match those of other NRA members. This tendency becomes more pronounced as people age. Finally, there are a number of physiological devices and methods to measure attitudes. Galvanic skin responses measure the electronic conductivity of the skin. Drastic changes of responses reflect intensity of feelings about a subject or topic. Measuring pupil dilation is another example of a physiological technique of measuring attitudes.[10]

Mary John Smith identifies four factors that determine the strength of any specific attitude: the number of beliefs an individual has regarding some area of experience; the extent to which one's beliefs are hierarchically arranged in an interrelated, supportive structure; the degree to which individuals judge their beliefs to be "true"; and the intensity of one's affective evaluation of each belief.[11]

The formation, maintenance, and evolution of attitudes are ongoing and lifelong processes. Crime, for example, may not be viewed as a major problem until one becomes a victim. Direct experience, as mentioned earlier, is one component in attitude formation. Attitudes on the emotional issue of abortion often result from our interactions at home and among friends. We form many attitudes based on vicarious or symbolic experience. Much of what we know is based on what we read, are told, or see on television. We also form many of our attitudes based on stereo-

NON SEQUITUR

WILEY

8-25

© 1997 Wiley Miller, Dist. by UNIVERSAL PRESS SYNDICATE

types—assumptions resulting from limited and largely inaccurate information. Attitudes of this nature abound. Statements of sexism and racism reflect attitudes based on stereotypes. This is why it is important that the sources of our information be accurate and fair. Otherwise, the very basis for our attitudes may be questionable.

Decades of research demonstrate that sometimes people act in accordance with their attitudes—and sometimes they do not. Attitudes provide insights into human behavior. First, understanding attitudes helps explain behavior. In the vernacular, when we know "where someone is coming from" (i.e., understand their attitudes), we can infer the reason for a certain behavior or reaction. Second, understanding how attitudes impact behavior informs us about how to modify the behavior of others.[12] Third, attitudes help predict behavior. If we understand how attitudes are formed and shaped, we can design specific strategies for target audiences to improve the chances that they will respond the way we wish.

The value we expect to receive from something determines our attitude. To persuade, we need to examine what consequences are associated with an issue. The goal is to change or to reinforce (depending on the outcome we hope will happen) the receiver's perceptions about what will result from the action we're advocating. Fishbein's expectancy-value theory addresses this effect. Attitudes and beliefs are usually based on the consequences expected from a particular course of action.[13] As mentioned earlier, attitudes toward an object depend on the number of beliefs held about it, the strength of those beliefs (salience), and the evaluation of the connection between the object and related beliefs. For every attitude about a person, place, or object, we recognize the attributes, limits, and consequences of holding a specific view.

There are three factors that influence the link between attitudes and subsequent behavior. *Situational factors* are perhaps the strongest influence. Social roles and norms guide what we say and how we say it. There are pressures for public consistency between attitudes and our behavior. *Individual differences* are the second factor. In general, the stronger the attitude held on an issue, the more consistency between attitude and behavior. High self-monitoring individuals display more consistencies. Direct experience has a significant impact leading to more consistency. Finally, *specificity of linkage* influences the strength of attitude-behavior consistencies.

Generally, people who are inner-directed and in touch with their feelings display greater attitude-behavior consistency than do people who rely on cues from others or from the situation to determine behavior.[14] Studies indicate that the degree of vested interest in an issue also affects attitude-behavior consistency; the greater the potential impact on the individual, the greater the consistency.[15] Some research demonstrates that under strict time constraints, individuals will rely on attitudes to direct behavior. Attitudes based on direct experience have more impact on behavior than do general arguments. Finally, it appears that the more information people have about a particular issue, the greater the attitude-behavior consistency.[16]

Daniel O'Keefe identifies three strategies to encourage attitude-consistent behavior. The first is to demonstrate a link between a specific attitude and subsequent behavior. For example, the act of going to church could be linked to the attitudes of being a "good" person. Some medication commercials for prescription drugs link taking care of oneself with the necessity to be there when needed by family members in the future. Enhancing the perceived relevance of attitudes to a specific behavior helps ensure consistency. A second strategy is to induce feelings of hypocrisy. As will be mentioned in our discussion about cognitive dissonance, highlighting a disconnect between someone's attitude and behavior is a good way to get an individual to adjust their behavior more in line with the attitude. The third strategy is to encourage anticipation of feelings. Basically, one invites the target to think about how they will feel if they behave in a certain way. The latter two strategies involve feelings of guilt, regret, maybe even embarrassment.[17]

There is no fail-safe correlation between attitudes and subsequent behavior. However, studies do indicate that attitudes can predict broad classes of behavior.[18] It is important to remember that most attempts at persuasion are not about changing attitudes, much less beliefs and values. Rather, most attempts seek to maintain or reinforce particular beliefs, attitudes, and values. Certainly, one-shot attempts are less effective than multiple attempts. In terms of progression, attitudes are easier to influence than beliefs or values.

Persuasion occurs by a matter of degrees. Herbert Simons identifies several ways attempts at persuasion influence our beliefs, attitudes, and values. *Response shaping* occurs when people acquire new beliefs or are socialized to learn new attitudes that may impact values. *Response reinforcement* attempts to strengthen currently held attitudes, beliefs, and values, thus making us more resistant to change. *Response changing* is the conversion of others' beliefs, attitudes, or values. The latter, of course, is the most difficult to achieve.[19]

Values

Values are our central, core ideals about how to conduct our lives. They represent what we consider intrinsically right or wrong. As a result, values are far more stable than attitudes and beliefs. In general, we learn our value system in childhood, and it remains essentially unchanged throughout our lives. As we will see in chapter 7, many values are a product of our culture. In the United States values of democracy, liberty, freedom, and equality are culturally based. Another source of values is intense lifetime experiences. Strong religious values, for example, may result from early training and church attendance, or perhaps from a conversion experience. A strong work ethic may be a product of early poverty. Although our values rarely change, they may assume more or less importance at different stages in our lives. At one point, social awareness of others may be the predominant focus; at other times we might value solitude. One may become more conservative as one grows older because of work and social experiences and an increased desire to protect what one has accumulated.

Thus, values are ideals, overarching goals that people wish to obtain. Values are more global and general than attitudes. We may have many attitudes that comprise a single value. If we value freedom, we may have specific attitudes on gun control laws, mandated taxes, or uniform school curricula that may appear to limit individual freedoms.

Now that we have sketched some distinctive features of beliefs, attitudes, and values, let's return to the concept that the three interact. As mentioned at the beginning of this section, the goal of persuasion is to stimulate a preferred action.

The likelihood that we will accept or reject a message and act accordingly depends on three dimensions. The *cognitive* dimension focuses on our beliefs—what we know about the object. The *affective* dimension focuses on our attitude—how we feel about the object. The *behavioral* dimension reveals the probability of our acting in accordance with our attitudes and beliefs. For example, supporters of more stringent gun laws attempt to tap into strong feelings and memories of tragedies resulting from handgun violence. Handgun Control Inc. sponsors campaigns that link handguns with deaths. Their ultimate goal, of course, is to combine negative feelings about guns with specific information that will encourage individuals to act on their attitudes and beliefs. The behavioral outcome of this goal is to solicit contributions to counteract the legislative clout of the powerful National Rifle Association. The NRA uses much of the same attitude-belief-behavior linkage. Editorials in *The American Rifleman* tap into existing views that gun control threatens basic freedoms. Members are encouraged to vote for political candidates who support the NRA. The motivating language is both graphic and masculine: "It means a total commitment to safeguarding your firearm freedoms on every front with a square jaw and an iron fist."

Many of our beliefs and values are the result of *unexamined inheritances*. As rational beings, it is likely that we can be persuaded to take a look at the underpinnings of certain beliefs and to reassess our opinions. We have a number of attitudes that have been formed without a sufficient amount of information. These are subject to change. Both attitudes and beliefs are relatively easy to ascertain. We express them daily in conversations. Values are much more elusive. We don't as frequently discuss them—perhaps we could not even name some of the principles guiding our actions. Thus, values are the least likely candidates for change through persuasion.

Let's review the functions our belief-attitude-value systems play in our daily decision making. The first is a utilitarian function—influencing our behavior. As we attempt to cope with people, ideas, and situations, our attitudes incline us toward or against certain actions and responses to daily social life.[20] The crush of information, requests, and solicitations we receive daily would overwhelm and paralyze us if we had to assess the consequences of each proposal without any shortcuts. Attitudes provide familiar scripts—a pattern of response which has been effective in the past. Scripts provide a shorthand method of response that allows us to follow a "cognitive course of least resistance."[21] We simply don't have the time, energy, or capacity to analyze everything exhaustively.

Attitudes also serve an ego-defense function by helping us know who we are and what we stand for; thus, they reduce internal, mental conflict.[22] They help mask truths known to us that we prefer others not see, and they protect us from unpleasant realities. We can infer now, for example, that the class bullies of our youth lacked self-confidence and self-esteem. The tough attitudes displayed masked the true feelings of low self-worth and abilities.

Third, there is a knowledge function. Our value system gives meaning to the world around us by providing frames of reference and cues for accepted behavior.[23]

Attitudes help us form the "dos" and "don'ts" of daily life. The danger is, of course, that some attitudes and beliefs are comprised of stereotypes or misinformation. In times of war, sentiments about protecting one's country and dislike of those threatening the security of a nation may be helpful in uniting people against a common enemy. Such beliefs can be dangerously unfair, as was the incarceration of United States citizens of Japanese descent during World War II. In times of peace, such attitudes and beliefs are harmful since they reflect only negative feelings—fear, dislike, hatred—that do nothing to address or correct the underlying causes of resentment. Today, Japanese purchases of U.S. companies and properties have recreated some anti-Japanese attitudes in the United States.

Finally, there is a value-expressive function[24]—a vehicle for expressing our core feelings, beliefs, and values about self, society, and others. We display our attitudes and beliefs proudly. Patriotism was manifested in the proliferation of flags after September 11, 2001, and the invasion of Iraq in 2003. Such displays reinforced our feelings about the United States, our support for freedom, support for the troops, and our heroic conflicts of the past. By understanding the functions of beliefs, attitudes, and values, a persuader may formulate more appropriate strategies for attitude change.

BEHAVIORAL THEORIES OF PERSUASION
▲

The study of persuasion from a behavioral perspective began as early as World War I. The focus of much of this research was on propaganda. The researchers investigated patterns of response based on elements of information and misinformation. This very early research laid the structural foundation for studies to follow. World War II stimulated additional studies in the area. This time, however, the research was more exploratory and experimental and focused on the relatively new concept of attitudes. The Yale studies directed by Carl Hovland had a profound impact on persuasion theory. Hovland and his colleagues perceived persuasion "as a process of teaching persuadees to learn new attitudes or modify old ones, in much the same way that animals in a learning laboratory are trained to traverse a maze or to modify past maze-crossing habits."[25] Behavioral theories of persuasion are grounded in social psychology and are characterized by experimental laboratory research concerned with how beliefs, attitudes, and values impact human behavior. While we cannot be exhaustive, we will review some of the more important behavioral theories of persuasion.

Stimulus-Response Theory

Robert Cialdini argues that we have preprogrammed scripts of behavior. They serve as mental shortcuts that we use in making everyday judgments. For example, we are conditioned to equate expensive items with quality or social status. Named brands become emblems of taste, elevating them over generic brands of equal quality. As mentioned previously, the advantages of preprogrammed shortcuts is conservation of time, energy, and mental capacity. Disadvantages include being

CATHY

vulnerable to costly mistakes, placing too much credence on just one decision factor, and an increase in errors of judgment. Indeed, much of the process of getting people to comply with requests and suggestions is based on the tendency for automatic, shortcut responses to external stimuli.[26]

A simplistic behavioral model for persuasion is the stimulus-response model of learning theory. The most famous example of this theory is Pavlov's dog. Each time the dog was fed, a bell was rung. Soon, upon only hearing the bell, the animal began to salivate. Learning theories center on the relationship between stimuli and responses. Infants enter the world with a "clean slate." They *learn* what behavior is acceptable, what is right, and what not to do. Most learning theories assume reinforcement is necessary to induce learning.[27] Positive rewards reinforce certain attitudes and behavior. If we are told enough that we are good, beautiful, or smart, we begin to believe it and act accordingly. The stimulus of a teacher's praise for a student is obviously designed to reinforce the motivation of doing good work. To the extent this linkage works, a *conditioned response* is a predictable outcome. Throughout life we learn to seek favorable rewards and to avoid unfavorable ones. We tend to give more credence to attitudes and behaviors that occur in the presence of positive reinforcements. We will have more to say about the reinforcement role of attitudes in the next section.

Conditioned response has another effect on social interactions. Research demonstrates that we are more likely to be attracted to those who hold similar attitudes. The social stimulus in this example is the discovery of shared attitudes. Subsequent behavior is attraction. Attitudes that are rewarded grow stronger. Similar attitudes have a reward value for us because the interaction confirms our view of the world and related issues.

Learning theory is important in persuasion. As discussed earlier, people make decisions by learning to associate consequences with proposals. The persuader wants the audience to associate particular feelings with a proposal. Persuasion involves introducing new feelings about the proposal to weaken previous associations that would be less favorable. The goal is to extinguish the relationship between the proposal and unfavorable associations. Feelings about good consequences become connected with the object. In the language of learning theory, we are conditioned to expect a particular result. Thereafter, we identify the proposal itself with our feelings about the consequences. Conditioning works by arousing a dislike or like without the necessity of repeating the consequences—just the mention of the object is sufficient.

Advertising uses this concept daily. What do we think of when we think of Michelob—friends, good times, women, or men? Why does that trademark create these associations? Because the ads keep giving us messages that cause us to identify certain things with Michelob. This is a form of stimulus-response. If you were to exchange an expensive wine and a cheap wine in the bottles, which do you think would win a taste contest among your friends? Would the stimulus of an expensive label predispose them to favor that bottle? If you were to purchase two paintings from a local artist and sign one Smith and the other Picasso, which do you think would receive more money at an auction? The same process is used when advertisers use a famous spokesperson for ads. They hope we will suspend judgment and attach our good feelings about the celebrity (the stimulus) to their product. As a result, we respond to the person and not to the attributes of the product. The key is the power of association between objects and images.

Although the structure of the stimulus-response model is rather simple, its variables can become complex. Focusing on the nature of the stimulus highlights factors of human motivation and conditioning. For example, what makes us recognize and value a Picasso painting more than one by Smith? Focusing on the nature of the response evaluates factors of choice and reasonableness. What rationale would we provide for a preference for the Picasso painting? And finally, focusing on response emphasizes factors of background, beliefs, and values. What motivates an interest in paintings or in cubism in general? In many ways, the stimulus-response model provides the basic premises for all the other behavioral theories of persuasion.

Reinforcement Theory

In the late 1940s and early 1950s, scholars were interested in understanding how people change attitudes. A body of research known as reinforcement theory draws primarily from the principles of human learning behavior. The theory essentially argues that attitude changes result from learning generated through reinforcement. As already noted, attitudes are rather stable unless an individual undergoes a new learning experience. Persuasive communication encounters provide incentives for changing an attitude. The incentives could be some form of evidence, new information, reason, or argument.

The process of acquiring new attitudes moves from attention to comprehension to acceptance. Attending to a message depends on familiarity with the issue and its importance to the audience. The incentives to give our attention to a topic need to be reasonable, clearly understood, and relevant. The operation of the variables of attention and comprehension are the same for the process of persuasion as for ordinary learning. According to theorists, incentives offered for an attitude change create expectations that reinforce acceptance. Expectations often involve social approval or acceptance. Reinforcement of attitudes occurs in many ways. Our attitudes are reinforced each time we hear others whom we admire express similar beliefs. Some argue that Rush Limbaugh not only provided a forum for conservative views but empowered many conservatives to become more vocal. The process of classical conditioning is a blatant form of attitude reinforcement.

Attribution Theory

Attribution theory attempts to explain how people account for the actions of others. A strong component of human nature is to try to make sense of the world and the behavior of others. We receive messages, decode them, and interpret them. By analyzing the broad situation or context of an action, we attribute a motive, cause, or reason for a behavior. Attributions of motives are a part of the subtext of all communication. For example, suppose you are a car salesperson and you begin a conversation with a potential customer by complimenting his or her clothing. How will the customer interpret the compliment? It could be read as a sincere gesture, as a ploy to gain rapport, or as an invitation to start a social relationship. The entire communication that follows is understood in terms of the customer's perception of the persuader's intent. Similarly, a fascinating feature of most films, plays, and novels is the way authors weave cues about the intentions of particular characters into the script. Part of the pleasure we derive from fiction is in learning whether we were right in judging that a character had evil or honorable intentions. Every James Bond story, for example, features at least one or two women whose loyalty to Bond is in doubt.

The task for the persuader is to figure out how certain messages or behaviors will be interpreted. What makes the process complex is that human perception plays a major role in interpreting the messages of others. Perception is comprised of a multitude of variables that function differently in each individual. Because no two people process information the same way, attributions of intent can vary within an audience exposed to the same persuasion. One person may praise a president for making a courageous defense of policy; another may condemn the very same effort as a collection of cleverly worded half-truths.

There are two classifications of attributions: situational and dispositional.[28] *Situational* identifies factors in the environment that are believed to cause people to act in certain ways. A classic example is attributing criminal behavior to environmental factors such as poverty, broken homes, or ineffective schools. In chapter 7, we will see that an important source of attitudes is the peer group and the varied audiences they represent. For example, one of the authors of this text comes from the Appalachian region of North Carolina. In that region, there is a great deal of sensitivity toward issues of poverty, hunger, education, and the role of government in addressing those issues. Thus, the coauthor tends to favor governmental involvement in financing educational programs and scholarships as well as social welfare programs.

Dispositional attributions identify internal, personal factors that are believed to cause people to behave in certain ways. Such reasons for behavior lie at the core of individual beliefs or values. For example, elements of religion or philosophy may influence behavior. A privileged individual with inherited wealth may favor a social role of government in addressing poverty because of a strong belief in a high

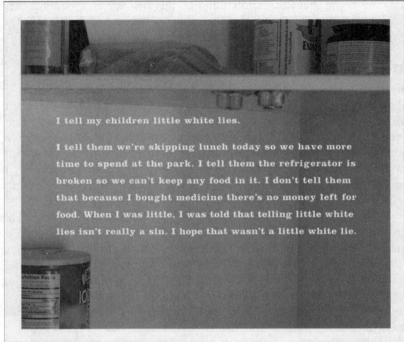

I tell my children little white lies.

I tell them we're skipping lunch today so we have more time to spend at the park. I tell them the refrigerator is broken so we can't keep any food in it. I don't tell them that because I bought medicine there's no money left for food. When I was little, I was told that telling little white lies isn't really a sin. I hope that wasn't a little white lie.

Food or medicine? **1 in 5** kids in America faces hunger because of decisions like this. To help in your community, call 800-FEED-KIDS or visit feedingchildrenbetter.org. Hunger. A choice no one should have to make.

Insert Your Local Food Bank or Food Rescue Program Here

standard of life for all Americans. In chapter 5 we noted that certain personality traits (authoritarianism, for example) may correlate with predictable attitudes, such as excessive faith in the judgments of authority figures. To relate to the previous example, the coauthor from the mountains of North Carolina tends to be rather "conservative" on social issues such as abortion because of the social values and Baptist upbringing of his youth.

There are problems with this approach. There is no certainty of correct or precise interpretation of individual motives, and such an approach encourages oversimplification of human behavior. Each day our actions are influenced by the roles we play. The authors at various times assume the roles of teacher, parent, husband, and citizen—all of which impact behavior. We may show compassion as a parent and husband but show little sympathy for poor performance as a teacher or citizen. In the example above, it would be just as easy for a privileged person not to favor a social role of government because of the belief that poor people are lazy and undeserving of governmental financial help.

It is important to remember that although attribution theory does not have universal application, the process of analyzing possible motives provides useful information about how persuasion works. An essential first step is to analyze our own behavior. Determining the factors that contribute to our beliefs and attitudes helps us understand the behavior of others. We can then provide more informed reasons to justify the behavior we would like our persuasion to encourage.

Consistency Theories

Some persuasion theorists focus on the mind as the intermediary between stimulus-response.[29] The mind organizes incoming, often unrelated, stimuli into useful patterns. *Balance theories* assume individuals are uncomfortable with inconsistency and will work to reduce any discrepancies between new information and their attitudes and beliefs. For example, if you overheard a friend whose honesty you never questioned telling a lie, how would you feel? If you felt uneasy, would you change your beliefs about honesty? Would you change your attitude about your friend? Would you rationalize about the situation in which the lie was told? Persuasive strategies, according to balance theory, should highlight inconsistencies while providing more acceptable (consistent) alternatives for behavior.

To imagine how imbalance produces change, consider that—for any attitude—there is at least one related attitude that should be consistent. If the related attitude is inconsistent, calling attention to that inconsistency may produce change. For example, if you have a high regard for the president but a low regard for the military service, your attitude toward the president's decision to support a policy reinstituting the military draft will be in a state of imbalance.

Psychological consistency is both internally and externally motivated. Internal influences are guided by attitudes based on our beliefs and values. External influences for consistency are motivated by desires to be accepted, to project a prescribed image, or to save face.[30]

How does a person resolve the discrepancy created when a respected person takes on a disliked idea? Balance theory predicts that the disparity will be resolved

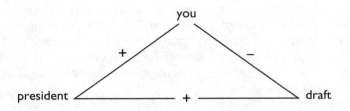

by altering one or both of the two original attitudes. If respect for the president is roughly equal to dislike for the draft, we would expect a process of change that would bring the two elements in consonance. That is, the person's enthusiasm for the president will moderate, and/or his dislike of the draft will be less intense. In short, the balance is restored by changing attitudes to create consistency, as revealed in comments like, "I still think he's a pretty good president" or "I don't like the idea of the draft, but there may be times when it is necessary." Such comments reveal that there has been a change that reduces the inconsistency between the two elements.

The concept of cognitive dissonance was introduced by Leon Festinger in 1957.[31] The theory has been refined and modified by many since it was first proposed; here we outline only its basic assertions. Revealed inconsistency produces dissonance or mental stress. The intensity of discomfort of inconsistency varies. If an issue is rather minor and not central to one's belief system, then the discomfort is small. For example, one may support preserving the environment but still accept plastic bags at the grocery store. If, however, the issue is central to one's beliefs, then the discomfort is great.[32] The removal of the stress may take the form of changing an attitude or behavior to reduce the inconsistency. Roger Brown has offered a concise summary of dissonance theory.

> A state of cognitive dissonance is said to be a state of psychological discomfort or tension which motivates efforts to achieve consonance. Dissonance is the name for a disequilibrium and consonance the name for an equilibrium. Two cognitive elements, A and B, are dissonant if one implies the negation of the other: i.e., if A implies not-B. Two cognitive elements are consonant when one implies not the negation of the other element but the other element itself: i.e., A implies B. Finally, two elements, A and B, are irrelevant when neither implies anything about the other. Dissonance is comparable to imbalance: consonance to balance. . . .[33]

The basic assumptions of Festinger's theory—that dissonance causes tension and that inconsistency will motivate people to do something to reduce the uncomfortable imbalance—are similar to other consistency theories. The difference is that the theory of cognitive dissonance emphasizes the activities people employ to justify changes in attitudes and/or behaviors after they have been convinced to do something.[34] Stephen Littlejohn lists the situations where dissonance is likely: decision making, forced compliance, initiation, effort, and social support.[35] The more important or critical the decision, the more dissonance one experiences.

The magnitude of difference between elements of the decision increases the potential of experiencing dissonance. The choice between purchasing toothpaste versus purchasing a car has a very large magnitude of difference. In contrast, the more similar the choices, the less potential for dissonance. For example, deciding between two televisions will create less dissonance than choosing between purchasing a television or a new video camera. In addition to the importance of the decision and the similarity between two alternatives, Littlejohn states that two other variables affect the amount of dissonance experienced. The attractiveness of the choice we made will either alleviate or increase the dissonance, and the perceived attractiveness of the alternative not chosen will similarly affect how we feel about a decision.[36] For example, if your parents decided to replace the wiring in their house instead of taking a trip to Hawaii, the level of dissonance would depend on which option had more attraction for them.

When a person is forced to do something contrary to his or her beliefs, the resulting dissonance may lead to attitude change. Being forced to do something we do not want to do (for example, in the military, in school, by parents, or by employers) is sometimes called *enforced discrepant behavior* by psychologists. We naturally want to lessen the discrepancy between the enforced behavior and the inconsistent attitude. The outcome may be that we may like a person more if we are forced to say nice things to them in public, or we may come to share the belief that military discipline is good training for later life. These changes in attitude give meaning and consistency to positions we have expressed publicly.

Interestingly, the stronger the threat of punishment or the higher the reward, the less dissonance an individual may experience. As Littlejohn states, the less external justification (such as reward or punishment), the more prominence internal inconsistency assumes.[37] Initiation ceremonies can be linked both to strong rewards/threats and to effort. Robert Cialdini relates a number of incidents—from tribal coming-of-age ordeals to hell week campus activities to military boot camps to freshman hazing at West Point—to illustrate the concept that the severity of an initiation ceremony heightens commitment to the group.[38] Despite experiencing pain, exposure to the elements, hunger, thirst, and embarrassment, there is less dissonance about the group that inflicted the torment than milder initiation activities would cause. Cialdini quotes William Styron on his Marine boot camp experience: ". . . who does not view the training as a crucible out of which he emerged in some way more resilient, simply braver and better for the wear."[39]

Researchers have tested the theory that people who exert great effort or go through pain and hardship to gain something will value the results more highly than those who achieve the same thing with minimal effort.[40] Personal effort or investment plays a role in the amount of dissonance one may experience. The greater the personal effort, the more likely we will rationalize our behavior or attitude as correct. Finally, social acceptance of behavior drastically lessens dissonance. As the parents of older children frequently lament, strong peer pressure can virtually eliminate a lifetime of value training.

Two important qualifications are important to remember when applying consistency theories to the study of particular messages. First, there is no internal inconsistency if two concepts are not related or if a person's attitudes toward two concepts are similar. For example, if a president we did not like proposed a policy we feared, there would be no psychological need for change. As the model suggests, both attitudes are already aligned. The model provides a simple guide to whether a communication situation is balanced. An odd number of negative signs indicates imbalance; a positive number of negative signs (or zero) indicates balance.[41]

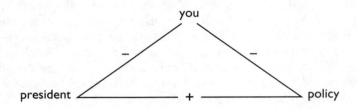

The second caution is that the human mind, when confronted with an inconsistency, provides many different options, not all of which call for adjusted attitudes. First, you can simply dismiss the source or validity of the conflicting information. For example, one may not accept data about teen smoking from the Tobacco Institute or gun safety from the American Rifle Association. Second, one may reduce dissonance by finding new supportive or consonant information or sources. For example, one may reason that it is far better to be a little overweight than to keep smoking. Or one may disregard messages that drinking wine or any alcohol has risks in favor of studies that suggest that drinking wine reduces the likelihood of heart attacks. One simply gives more weight to particular information, thus reducing the overall dissonance.

Gass and Seiter identify several additional strategies for resolving inconsistency. Suppose someone has recently committed to not eating meat, but thinks eating seafood is fine. *Overt denial* is ignoring any inconsistency. The individual simply does not view seafood as meat. *Bolstering* is rationalizing or making excuses. The harvesting of seafood is not as cruel as slaughtering cattle or fowl. *Differentiation* is separating the attitudes in conflict. Fish are less physiologically complex than cows or other livestock. *Transcendence* is focusing on a higher level issue. We all need protein and some seafood helps lower cholesterol. Finally, one may simply attempt to *convert* others to their position.[42]

The various cognitive elements (bits of information) that comprise the attitude become critical. For example, Philip Zimbardo and his colleagues analyzed the issue of smoking.[43] There is now undeniable evidence that smoking causes cancer. Other elements can, however, mitigate the threat of cancer. A smoker may only consume low tar cigarettes or may believe that smoking is good for relaxation or weight control. The smoker may also espouse the old adage that you've got to die of something; the relationship between smoking and cancer thus becomes less important.

Factors such as self-concept and the potential for rewards and punishments are among the most important reasons for people maintaining consistency among their beliefs, attitudes, and values. However, it is important to remember that there is no direct relationship between attitudes and behavior. Seldom is there one attitude that dictates behavior. There are many attitudes that influence us. For this reason, it is difficult for anyone to achieve consistency at all times for all beliefs, attitudes, and values.

Social Judgment Theory

When we say it is cold outside, just how cold is it? It depends on how warm it was in the very recent past. On the first 60 degree day following winter, the temperature seems balmy. However, the first 60 degree day following summer seems very cool. Social judgment theory grew out of the work of psychologist Muzafer Sherif.[44] The theory suggests that any attempt at persuasion must focus on the receiver of the message. The beliefs and biases of the target audience are key elements in deciding what type of message will be most effective. Sherif argues that people do not evaluate messages based on merit alone. People compare arguments with their current attitudes and then decide if they should accept the advocated position. Their current attitudes serve as reference points or anchors for their evaluations.[45] For example, if an experimenter turned on a light in a darkened room and said the wattage was 100, that brightness would become the anchor, the reference point. If you were asked to judge the brightness of four other lights, you would probably see the ones closest in intensity to the anchor as even more similar than they really are; this is the assimilation effect. Thus, you might judge a 75 watt light as the same as the 100. You would probably judge dimmer lights as even less similar than they actually are; this is the contrast effect. When we perceive a contrast among attitudes, we detect a shift away from our anchor points. When we find attitudes in line with our own, we see them clustering around our anchor points.

Sherif applied these principles to how we judge messages, with current beliefs serving as the anchor point. He added one more critical ingredient—ego involvement. This theory treats attitudes and beliefs as a continuum in which there is a range of acceptable positions, a range of neutral feelings, and a range of unacceptable positions. Individuals judge messages based on both internal anchors and ego involvement. The more relevant an issue is to one's self-image, the stronger the anchoring opinion.

In understanding how our internal anchors or reference points function in terms of attitude change, there are three important concepts to consider: latitudes of acceptance, rejection, and noncommitment. The *latitude of acceptance* is the range of attitudinal positions clustering around the anchor. On most issues, there is a range of positions or statements that people could accept. Even those who are generally against abortion may favor exceptions in cases of rape or incest. Persuasive messages that fall within the audience's latitude of acceptance are more likely to be successful.

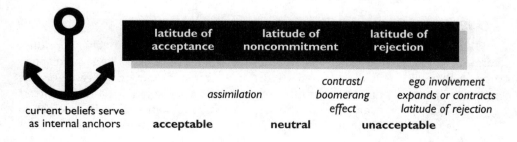

Messages that fall into the *latitude of noncommitment* are interesting. Because of the assimilation effect, certain messages in this range may be perceived as similar to the anchor point, while those farther along the continuum may be pushed into the unacceptable range by the contrast effect. Again, ego involvement will determine the width of each band. Low ego involvement with a message results in a wide attitude of noncommitment and the possibility of persuasion.

In contrast, the *latitude of rejection* is the cluster of positions that are absolutely unacceptable. Obviously, messages that fall within this category will not encourage attitude change. In fact, just the opposite often occurs. Messages that fall within this region tend to reinforce existing attitudes or positions—the boomerang effect. Therefore, it is important to know where the latitude of acceptance ends and the latitude of rejection begins. For example, when does one person's free speech become another person's obscene language? When does one advocate's plea for equal opportunity become the receiver's perception of discriminatory preferences? When one is highly ego-involved, the latitude of rejection is quite large and the latitude of noncommitment is small. Highly ego-involved people are difficult to persuade.[46]

The theory's implications for persuasion are many. Assimilation constitutes persuasion; contrast effect represents failure to persuade.[47] Individuals with wide latitudes of acceptance are open to greater changes in attitudes than those with narrow latitudes of acceptance. Individuals who are more ego-involved on certain topics or issues tend to have larger latitudes of rejection and are thus more resistant to persuasive attempts to change attitudes. If our audience is known to favor an idea similar to ours or is at least noncommittal, it may take only one or two attempts to have our messages assimilated into the latitude of acceptance. If the audience is highly ego-involved and opposed to our position, a single message will probably be contrasted and rejected. "Persuasion would require many messages over a long period of time, each gradually expanding the latitude of acceptance and slowly moving the favorite position (anchor belief)."[48]

According to Richard Perloff, this theory has special implications for politicians and political actors. Political communicators must always moderate their messages for very diverse audiences. During most campaigns, candidates are not really interested, nor do they have the time or money to change attitudes or opinions. They are trying to gain support by sharing their views with the largest number of voters. In social judgment theory terms, candidates want "to encourage voters to assimilate the candidate's position."[49] It is not surprising, therefore, that politicians often straddle the fence on issues. From the perspective of social judgment theory, it is an effective strategy of persuasion.

Long-Term Attitude Change

Kathleen Reardon argues that there are three main steps in achieving long-term change.[50] First is receiver motivation. A listener must have some predisposition to change. If not, the persuader must create an environment for change. This may require efforts on a number of fronts to create a sense of trust and support. It is not enough, for example, to explain the medical benefits of losing weight to overweight people. Supportive family and friends are essential to successful weight loss. Influencing motivation "involves finding out what matters to the persuadee and shaping one's initial message(s) to address those concerns and needs."[51] Simply saying that smoking is unhealthy does not address concerns such as weight gain, nicotine addiction, or psychological dependency.

The second step is participation. The receiver must be able to participate in the elements of change. We know that people are more accepting of a decision if they participate in the decision-making process. Sometimes, calling for small changes first may lead to larger, long-term changes in attitudes and behavior. A call for action is an important part of the attitude change process.

The final step is reward. There must be some positive reward for a changed behavior, belief, or attitude. Since most of us do not feel comfortable with uncertainty, we usually do not seek change and prefer the status-quo—a known quantity. If there is to be long-term change, there must be some visible or noticeable reward for the changed attitude or behavior. The greater the reward, the greater the potential magnitude of change.

Elaboration Likelihood Theory

After decades of studies, it is still difficult to explain how to change attitudes. Most studies show that nearly every "independent variable" under investigation would indeed influence persuasion in some situations, have no effect in others, and decrease persuasion in still others. How can this be? Earlier in the chapter, we discussed the tendency to rely on shortcuts or "scripts"—patterns of response that have been successful in previous experiences. As Robert Cialdini states,

> You and I exist in an extraordinarily complicated environment, easily the most rapidly moving and complex that has ever existed on this planet. To deal with it, we *need* shortcuts. We can't be expected to recognize and analyze all the aspects in each person, event, and situation we encounter in even one day. We haven't the time, energy, or capacity for it. Instead, we must very often use our stereotypes, our rules of thumb, to classify things according to a few key features and then to respond without thinking when one or another of these trigger features is present.[52]

Richard Petty and John Cacioppo developed elaboration likelihood theory to explain the different methods individuals use to process persuasive messages. The shortcut method described above fits the *peripheral processing route*. The receiver employs some simple decision rule to evaluate the advocated position. The decision mechanism could be communicator credibility or expertise. The *central processing route* involves thoughtful analysis using critical thinking to assess the arguments presented in the message. Central processing involves extensive issue-relevant thinking; careful examination of the information contained in the message, close scrutiny of the message's arguments, consideration of other issue-related material, etc. The focus of the central route is the message. In the peripheral route, characteristics of the speaker or the context are more influential. Rather than testing whether the ideas presented in the argument make sense (central route), we are influenced by affective factors such as whether the source is likeable or attractive.

In a persuasive context, elaboration refers "to the extent to which a person scrutinizes the issue-relevant arguments contained in the persuasive communication."[53] Sometimes receivers will engage in extensive issue-relevant thinking while at other times very little effort is extended. Research demonstrates that persuasion occurs at each interval along the continuum of high incidences of issue elaboration to virtually no issue elaboration. When conditions encourage people to engage in issue-relevant thinking, elaboration likelihood is high. To be salient in this context, appeals must contain well-constructed arguments supported by strong evidence. Studies have revealed numerous factors that may influence the degree of elaboration. Some of the factors include: receiver's mood, the degree to which the attitude is based on a mixture of positive and negative elements, the presence of multiple sources with multiple arguments, the personal relevance of the topic to the receiver, and the receiver's degree of need for cognition or to engage in thinking.[54]

Petty and Cacioppo argue that people want their attitudes to be consistent with behavior, but they also want to be correct. We learn from our environment if our attitudes are right, wrong, acceptable, etc.; we must identify some standard for judgment. For some, it may be religious doctrine, political philosophy, or written documents. For many, it results from merely comparing one's attitudes to those of others. We know, for example, that holding similar opinions to those of others increases our confidence in the validity of our opinions.

Two key elements affect the probability of choosing one route over the other: ability and motivation. The ability to elaborate is affected by our knowledge about the subject matter presented in the persuasive message, the ease of understanding the message as presented, message repetition, and the number of distractions at the time the message is received.[55] Motivation is affected by our involvement with the issues presented—how important we believe the consequences of accepting the message will be to us. The number and variety of arguments presented also affect motivation. If we hear a number of competing views, the central route may be the only means available to process and organize the information. One other factor influencing motivation is personality. Some people thrive on analyzing issues and weighing possibilities; others find the process stressful. The higher one's ability and motivation, the more likely the central route will be employed. If an issue is important enough to us to activate our powers of reasoning to understand it, we use the central route. If the issue is important but we don't feel qualified to assess the argument, our emotions will seek cues from the situation.

According to the model, the central route of elaboration requires both ability and motivation. If ability is high and motivation is low at the time of message exposure, little argument processing will occur. Any influence will be the result of some contextual cue associated with message. For example, the highly credible or well-liked source of the message may be the most influential component. In contrast, if motivation is high and ability low, the desire to process the message will not be matched by the capacity to do so. Again, situational cues may play a major role of influence.

Since the probability of elaboration depends on a number of factors, individuals will differ in how they react to messages. As was true with social judgment theory, there is a likelihood continuum for individuals. Some issues will fall squarely

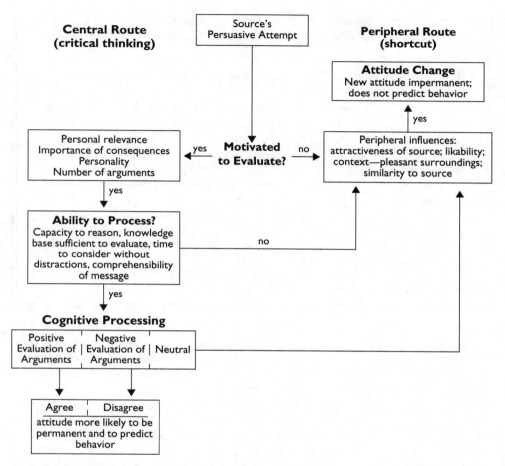

Adapted from Richard E. Petty and John T. Cacioppo, *Communication and Persuasion: Central and Peripheral Routes to Attitude Change.*

in the central route while others will almost certainly be peripheral. For issues between those two extremes, persuasion may involve cues associated with both the central and peripheral routes.[56] For example, a doctor who has seen that marijuana is an effective pain reliever for glaucoma patients would have both the ability and the motivation to process messages relating to the legalization of marijuana via the central route. A parent who believes any drug use will lead to addiction will reject such a proposition without listening to the arguments, possibly by labeling the source irresponsible. A college student without strong feelings about the subject could be persuaded by either argument and by feelings about the source.

As stated in postulate 5, the most consistent, powerful, long-term, and influential attitude change results from the central route of elaboration. It is important to understand that the peripheral route of persuasion, although short-term, is still very effective. This is why the use of emotional appeals in advertising is very suc-

---

Postulates of Elaboration Likelihood Theory of Persuasion

1. People are motivated to hold correct attitudes.

2. People vary in the amount and nature of issue-relevant elaboration in which they are willing or able to engage to evaluate a message.

3. Variables can affect the amount and direction of attitude change by (a) serving as persuasive arguments, (b) serving as peripheral cues, and/or (c) affecting the extent or direction of issue and argument elaboration.

4. As motivation and/or ability to process argument is decreased, peripheral cues become relatively more important determinants of persuasion. Conversely, as argument scrutiny is increased, peripheral cues become relatively less important determinants of persuasion.

5. Attitude changes that result mostly from processing issue-relevant arguments (central route) will show greater temporal persistence, greater prediction of behavior, and greater resistance to counterpersuasion than attitude changes that result mostly from peripheral cues.

Source: Richard Petty and John Cacioppo, *Communication and Persuasion: Central and Peripheral Routes to Attitude Change* (New York: Springer-Verlag, 1986), pp. 5–24.

---

cessful. Attitude change generated through the central route of elaboration is relatively permanent, resistant to counterpersuasion, and predictive of behavior. Under the peripheral route, attitude changes are more temporary, susceptible to counterpersuasion, and less predictive of behavior.

The theory raises interesting issues for persuaders. Is their message more likely to be processed centrally or peripherally? What constitutes an understandable message for what audience? Messages processed through the central route seem to result in longer lasting attitude change. If a persuader judges that the peripheral route is more likely for a particular message, what is the best strategy to enhance the chances for central processing? While the peripheral route may not lead to long-term attitude change, is it easier to trigger acceptance through this route, even if short-term? For some messages, that strategy could be useful.

Theory of Reasoned Action

Icek Ajzen and Martin Fishbein have developed a theory of reasoned action that helps explain how attitudes guide behavior. The theory has generated a great deal of empirical research in recent years. Studies validating the theory have investigated such topics as: voting, consumer purchases, family planning, seat belt use, recycling, and exercise, to name just a few.[57] Ajzen and Fishbein argue:

> People consider the implications of their actions before they decide to engage or not engage in a given behavior. For this reason we refer to our approach as a "theory of reasoned action." . . . We make the assumption that most actions of social relevance are under volitional control and, consistent with this assumption, our theory views a person's intention to perform (or to not perform) a behavior as the immediate determinant of action.[58]

Intentions are the key element in this theory. People's intentions are affected by both their attitude toward a possible behavior and the subjective norms regarding that behavior. The attitude component refers to the specific action under consideration (e.g., to buy the car or not). The norm component considers the expectations of other people or perceptions of the social pressures to perform or not to perform the behavior in question. According to the theory, "the individual constructs this attitude toward the behavior by a careful analysis of available information. This attitude is a function of the person's beliefs concerning the likely outcomes to result from performing the behavior and the person's positive or negative feelings about those outcomes."[59]

CALVIN AND HOBBES

In essence, individuals calculate the costs and benefits associated with social behavior. There is, as Ajzen and Fishbein call it, a "conscious deliberation" of factors. There are four components to the theory: attitude toward the behavior, subjective norm, behavioral intention, and actual behavior. Our attitudes toward a behavior result from our general beliefs about the potential consequences of the behavior and our evaluation of the likelihood of such consequences or outcomes of the behavior. The second component of the model, subjective norm, considers whether or not individuals or groups would approve of the behavior and our degree of motivation to comply with the views of others. These considerations influence our intention or commitment to perform the behavior.

While this model is somewhat commonsensical, it does identify factors of influencing a behavior or decision. The model acknowledges that attitude change may be achieved in a variety of ways, influenced by a number of factors. It also provides insight into why attitudes may not predict behavior. For example, we may well think there is great health risk in smoking, but peer pressure and the act of smoking by well-liked "heroes and celebrities" may influence the decision to smoke.

A Schematic Diagram of Ajzen and Fishbein's Theory of Reasoned Action

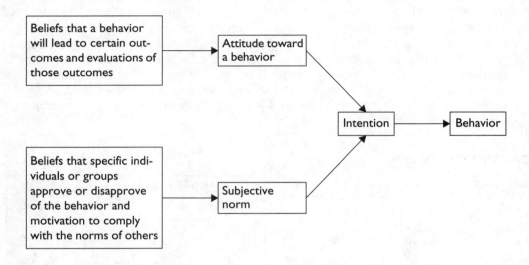

Adapted from Icek Ajzen and Martin Fishbein, *Understanding Attitudes and Predicting Social Behavior.*

SUMMARY

▲

In this chapter, we discussed how the concepts of beliefs, attitudes, and values provide the basis for our behavior. In addition, we highlighted the importance of perception and social situations in influencing our actions. Human nature basically seeks rewards and attempts to avoid punishment. Stimulus-response theory explores this tendency. A number of other theories build from this one. Attribution theory explains the desire to make sense of the behavior of others and ourselves. We attribute motives for actions taken. Our belief that attitudes and behavior should be consistent is explored in consistency theories. What happens when we confront an inconsistency? How do we learn what behaviors are acceptable, and how do we decide how to judge the behavior of others? Social judgment theory alerts us to the anchors and reference points we use for analyzing messages. Elaboration likelihood theory recognizes that we sometimes apply full reasoning powers to messages and sometimes we rely on automatic responses that have worked in the past. The theory of reasoned response suggests behavior results from the conscious consideration of and deliberation about one's attitude and its implications for a given course of action. All of these theories help us make sense of the world and the behavior of ourselves and others. If we take the time to reflect on the processes revealed by the theories, we will be much more likely to recognize—and to construct—effective persuasive encounters.

Questions and Projects for Further Study

1. Select a television advertisement and see how many specific techniques and behavioral theories of persuasion you can find.

2. Select a magazine advertisement and see how many specific techniques and behavioral theories of persuasion you can find.

3. Select a contemporary controversial political issue and identify the underlying beliefs, attitudes, and values on each side of the issue. Attempt to construct a belief structure of the attitudes identified as illustrated in figure 1 of the chapter.

4. Select a contemporary controversial political issue and identify the positive or negative attitudes about the various factors of the issue. Attempt to isolate the source of each attitude, i.e., direct experience, symbolic experience, and/or stereotypes. How do these attitudes compare with those of a friend?

5. How would your persuasive strategies differ if you were to advocate mandatory military service when speaking before an audience comprised of veterans, women, or college students? Would socioeconomic status make a difference? Why?

Additional Reading

Robert B. Cialdini, *Influence: Science and Practice*, 4th ed. (Boston: Allyn and Bacon, 2001).

Phil Erwin, *Attitudes and Persuasion* (Sussex, England: Psychology Press, Ltd., 2000).

Leon Festinger, *A Theory of Cognitive Dissonance* (Evanston, IL: Row, Peterson, 1957).

Martin Fishbein and Icek Ajzen, *Belief, Attitude, Intention, and Behavior* (Reading, MA: Addison-Wesley, 1975).

Robert Gass and John Seiter, *Persuasion, Social Influence, and Compliance Gaining*, 2nd ed. (Boston: Allyn and Bacon, 2003).

Harry Mills, *Artful Persuasion* (New York: AMACOM, 2000).

Richard Perloff, *The Dynamics of Persuasion* (Hillside, NJ: Lawrence Erlbaum, 1993).

Richard Petty and John Cacioppo, *Communication and Persuasion: Central and Peripheral Routes to Attitude Change* (New York: Springer-Verlag, 1986).

Milton Rokeach, *Beliefs, Attitudes, and Values* (San Francisco: Jossey-Bass, 1968).

Notes

[1] Deborah Tannen, *You Just Don't Understand: Women and Men in Conversation,* (1990) New York: Ballantine Books, p. 295

[2] Herbert Simons, *Persuasion in Society* (Thousand Oaks, CA: Sage, 2001), p. 49.

[3] Martin Fishbein and Icek Ajzen, *Belief, Attitude, Intention, and Behavior* (Reading, MA: Addison-Wesley, 1975), pp. 222–28.

[4] Daniel J. O'Keefe, *Persuasion: Theory & Research*, 2nd ed. (Thousand Oaks, CA: Sage, 2002), pp. 53–54.

[5] Stephen W. Littlejohn, *Theories of Human Communication*, 7th ed. (Belmont, CA: Wadsworth, 2002), pp. 124–26.

[6] Simons, p. 32.

[7] Martin Fishbein and B. Raven, "The AB Scale: An Operational Definition of Belief and Attitude," *Human Relations*, February 1962, 15:42.

[8] Robert Gass and John Seiter, *Persuasion, Social Influence, and Compliance Gaining*, 2nd ed. (Boston: Allyn and Bacon, 2003), pp. 43–44.

[9] Phil Erwin, *Attitudes and Persuasion* (Sussex, England: Psychology Press, Ltd., 2001), pp. 21–41.

[10] Gass and Seiter, p. 51.

[11] Mary John Smith, *Persuasion and Human Action* (Belmont, CA: Wadsworth, 1982), p. 39.

[12] Gass and Seiter, p. 43.

[13] Richard Perloff, *The Dynamics of Persuasion* (Hillsdale, NJ: Lawrence Erlbaum Associates, 1993), pp. 81–95.

[14] Dominic Infante, Andrew Rancer, and Deanna Womack, *Building Communication Theory*, 4th ed. (Prospect Heights, IL: Waveland Press, 2003), p. 107.

[15] Perloff, p. 85.

[16] Russell Fazio and David Roskos-Ewoldsen, "Acting as We Feel," in *Communication and Persuasion*, eds. Richard Petty and John Cacioppo (New York: Springer-Verlag, 1986), pp. 74–82.

[17] O'Keefe, pp. 21–23.

[18] Perloff, pp. 81–95.

[19] Simons, pp. 30–31.

[20] Gerald Miller, Michael Burgoon, and Judee Burgoon, "The Functions of Human Communication in Changing Attitudes and Gaining Compliance," in *Handbook of Rhetorical and Communication Theory*, eds. Carroll Arnold and John W. Bowers (Boston: Allyn and Bacon, 1984), pp. 442–44.

[21] Infante, et al., p. 104.

[22] Miller, et al., pp. 442–44.

[23] Ibid.

[24] Ibid.

[25] Herbert W. Simons, *Persuasion: Understanding, Practice and Analysis*, 2nd ed. (New York: Random House, 1986), p. 29.

[26] Robert B. Cialdini, *Influence: Science and Practice,* 4th ed. (Boston: Allyn and Bacon, 2001), pp. 2–17.

[27] Burgoon, Hunsaker, and Dawson, *Human Communication*, 3rd ed. (Thousand Oaks, CA: Sage, 1994), p. 188.

[28] Philip Zimbardo, Ebbe Ebbesen, and Christina Maslach, *Influencing Attitudes and Changing Behavior* (Reading, MA: Addison-Wesley Publishing, 1977).

[29] Burgoon, et al., p. 192.

[30] Gass and Seiter, p. 58.

[31] L. Festinger, *A Theory of Cognitive Dissonance* (Evanston, IL: Row, Peterson, 1957).

[32] Gass and Seiter, p. 59.

[33] Roger Brown, *Social Psychology* (New York: Free Press, 1965), p. 584.

[34] Burgoon, et al., p. 200.

[35] Littlejohn, p. 127.

[36] Ibid., pp. 127–28.

[37] Ibid., p. 128.

[38] Cialdini, pp. 76–80.

[39] Ibid., p. 80.

[40] Ibid., p. 79.

[41] Burgoon, et al., p. 196.

[42] Gass and Seiter, p. 60.

[43] Zimbardo, et al., pp. 66–67.

[44] See Muzafer Sherif and Carl Hovland, *Social Judgment: Assimilation and Contrast Effects in Communication and Attitude Change* (New Haven: Yale University Press, 1961); Carolyn Sherif, Muzafer Sherif, and Roger Nebergall, *Attitude and Attitude Change: The Social Judgment-Involvement Approach* (Philadelphia: W. B. Saunders Company, 1963); Smith, pp. 264–74; Littlejohn, pp. 130–32.

[45] Infante, et al., p. 124.

[46] Littlejohn, p. 131.

[47] Infante, et al., p. 125.

[48] Ibid., p. 126.

[49] Perloff, p. 206.

[50] Kathleen Reardon, *Persuasion in Practice* (Newbury Park, CA: Sage, 1991), pp. 10–11.

[51] Ibid.

[52] Cialdini, p. 7.

[53] Richard Petty and John Cacioppo, "The Elaboration Likelihood Model of Persuasion," in *Communication and Persuasion* (New York: Springer-Verlag, 1986), p. 7.

[54] O'Keefe, p. 141.
[55] Infante, et al., p. 135.
[56] Ibid., p. 136.
[57] O'Keefe, p. 105.
[58] Icek Ajzen and Martin Fishbein, *Understanding Attitudes and Predicting Social Behavior* (Englewood Cliffs, NJ: Prentice-Hall, 1980), p. 8.
[59] Fazio and Roskos-Ewoldsen, p. 83.

Persuasion, Audiences, and Social Learning

Overview

▲ The Idea of an Audience

▲ A Conceptual Baseline: Social Learning

▲ The Audience Analysis Process
   Wiring the Audience: Dial Group Testing
   The Principle of Identification
   Universal Commonplaces
   Audience-Specific Norms

▲ Advocates, Messages, and Audiences
   Believing in Our Words
   High Credibility/High Agreement Persuasion
   High Credibility/Low Agreement Persuasion
   Low Credibility/High Agreement Persuasion
   Low Credibility/Low Agreement Persuasion

▲ Unintended Audiences

163

> *The other, not the self, should be the center of whatever "communi-cation" might mean.*[1]
>
> —JOHN DURHAM PETERS

The psychological explanations of persuasion discussed in the preceding chapter generally account for the internal processes that occur when individuals are confronted with messages that reinforce or challenge existing attitudes. For the psychologist, the ultimate subject is the individual, and the primary outcomes for study include an individual's attitudes and behaviors. By contrast, theories of persuasion rooted in *social* explanations assume that the personalities of specific individuals are reflections of the society in which they live. Social theorists look at the power of culture to shape values and beliefs. They start with the premise that we are largely what our contact with others has made us. As soon as we enter the world, we begin to acquire attitudes from a maze of contacts that give our lives meaning and purpose.

This socialization process begins with the family, but it is soon shaped by a variety of forces: school, work, church, and the casual associations of daily life. Émile Durkheim was one of the founders of modern sociology. He noted that our world is governed by networks of obligations and memberships through which we acquire and share common attitudes:

> Sentiments born and developed in the group have a greater energy than purely individual sentiments. A man who experiences such sentiments feels himself dominated by outside forces that lead him and pervade his milieu. He feels himself in a world quite distinct from his own private existence. . . . Following the collectivity, the individual forgets himself for the common end and his conduct is oriented in terms of a standard outside himself.[2]

The familiar claim that we are social animals is basic to the study of persuasion. By nature we are learners and imitators. Successful communication happens when messages produce a "direct sharing of consciousness."[3] This chapter explores the complex processes of identifying and appealing to audiences. We begin with a caution about the problematic labeling of audiences as targets of appeals. The remainder of the chapter presents several models that help characterize the varied relationships that can exist between persuaders and their audiences.

THE IDEA OF AN AUDIENCE

The study of public persuasion would be unmanageable without the convenient idea of the audience—the process of aggregating individuals into a larger and cohesive unit. Key assumptions in this process include an expectation that members assigned to the audience have some similar beliefs and demographic and lifestyle characteristics (age, sex, income, region of residence, gay versus straight, and so on). Media outlets often sell their audiences to advertisers based on some of these features. Virtually every record, film, and television producer targets a particular niche or market. Even so, the concept of the audience rarely works as well in fact as it does in theory.

Although we are sometimes slow to acknowledge it, audiences brought together by the mass media rarely turn out to be as uniform or homogeneous as we assume. As James Webster and Patricia Phalen note, "audiences are not naturally occurring 'facts,' but social creations. In that sense, they are what we make them."[4] Even the basic grouping of people by the fact that they have voluntarily come together in the same space at the same time has some complications. The motives of those who self-select themselves into the same group can be surprisingly diverse, as is usually the case when audience members gather to listen to a political campaigner who makes a campus stop. Many come to support the speaker; some come as skeptics. Others may have been urged to attend by a friend or are there to complete a class project. It would be a mistake to assume the audience shared the same ideological or personal reasons for attending.

There are other problems associated with the concept of audience. The idea of the audience was born in a simpler period. The audience when Aristotle wrote his text, *The Rhetoric*, consisted of a few hundred citizens of a small city, meeting in the same place at the same time. American participatory democracy in the late 1700s similarly consisted of a very restricted citizenry of white male landowners. Today, by contrast, audiences are sometimes defined in the millions, with the wide demographic variations common to such large numbers.

In contrast to the rhetorical tradition that embraced the idea of inclusion (e.g., "All men are created equal"), modern life has fostered a greater consciousness of racial, gender, lifestyle, and class distinctions. While these sensitivities have helped secure the civil rights objectives of many communities, one of the prices we have paid for these advances is a fraying of our faith in the idea of a true national community. Beyond our love of shopping malls and mass-market films and television, do we share something deeper, something approaching a common civic culture?[5] Are there universal national values and ideals that define our national life? Some social theorists have noted that we are less a melting pot that blends away our differences than a culture that more or less accommodates them.[6] If that is the case, the idea of an audience of members more or less sharing the same values and priorities may be an illusion.

The largest of our mass media—especially the commercial television networks—have made diverse audiences a given. The permeability of media intended for specific groups means that many forms of persuasion have secondary or unintended audiences. *Lifetime* television and *Cosmopolitan* magazine are billed as media for women, but men consume them as well. As Joshua Meyrowitz has pointed out, the electronic media now make it easy for individuals to eavesdrop on messages intended for others.[7] Difficulties arise when a message intended for one group is reported via the mass media to a second group who may not have the same expectations as the primary group. Sociologist Orrin Klapp has noted that this is one of the challenges for leaders and celebrities who must conduct much of their work in public.[8] It can be extremely difficult for persuaders to construct and maintain a consistent public image as they move through various settings with

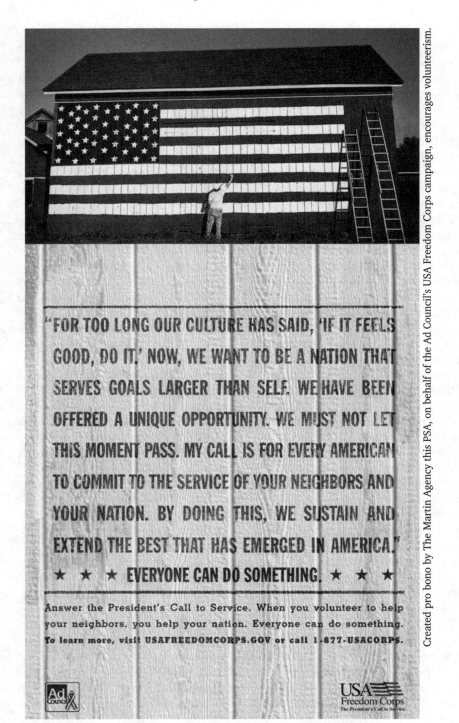

Created pro bono by The Martin Agency this PSA, on behalf of the Ad Council's USA Freedom Corps campaign, encourages volunteerism.

The Freedom Corps encourages service for the good of the community.

notably different communication requirements. During the 2000 presidential campaign George Bush whispered to Dick Cheney that a certain *New York Times* reporter was "a major-league a------,"[9] unaware of the microphone that broadcast his comment. Ronald Reagan similarly prepared for a radio "fireside chat" in 1984 by warming up with the jocular observation that he would begin bombing the Soviet Union "in five minutes." He did not know that journalists were already listening and gleefully jotting down his comments.[10] Such is the nature of our times that persuasion messages—even ones intended to remain private—often are carried far beyond their intended audiences.

Even with all of these reservations, it is hard to think about persuasion very long without making estimates about how a given group exposed to the same message will respond. The idea of audiences with shared attitudes is a necessary tool in the process of designing and measuring the effectiveness of appeals. But persuaders must avoid simple or glib judgments about the potential shared features of audiences.

A CONCEPTUAL BASELINE: SOCIAL LEARNING

▲

Among the few principles common to almost all forms of persuasion is the idea of social learning, which is sometimes also called *social proof*. The principle states that what we believe or do is often dominated by our interest in conforming to others. Robert Cialdini notes that "we view a behavior as correct in a given situation to the degree that we see others performing it."[11] Whether we are deciding the appropriate topics of conversation in a restaurant, if we should laugh out loud in a movie theater, or if we should voice our opinion about a politician, we often look for cues from other people.

> The tendency to see an action as appropriate when others are doing it works quite well normally. As a rule, we will make fewer mistakes by acting in accord with social evidence than by acting contrary to it. Usually, when a lot of people are doing something, it is the right thing to do.[12]

However, this shortcut to determining how we should act has its dangerous side.

Cialdini's assessment of the tragedy of Guyana (see chapter 1) provides an illustration of the dangers of relying on the principle of social proof. Those who followed Jim Jones found themselves totally isolated in an environment completely alien to anything in their previous experience. In such a state of uncertainty, they were particularly susceptible to following the example of others—not just the charismatic Jones, but all the similar others who were in Jonestown. Cialdini notes that Jones's real genius as a leader was to recognize the power of social influence.[13] No leader can be totally persuasive for all members of a group all the time—but he or she can rely on social tendencies that operate when similar others are present. To defend ourselves from social influence, we must learn to recognize when we are most vulnerable to it.[14]

Social learning is one of the few iron laws of human interaction. We often overlook the fact that everyone looks for social evidence; that is, while we are observing the reactions of others to determine the best course of action, they are also watching and learning.[15] We use attitudes as markers in our interactions— basic indicators of our place in the environment.[16] The principle of social proof works best when we observe the behavior of people similar to ourselves.[17]

In most Western cultures the socialization process is complex and sometimes contradictory. Consider the problematic dimensions of alcohol use in society. Our society spends millions of dollars constructing messages warning about the costly effects of alcohol use. Drug and alcohol programs exist in virtually every corner of organizational life. Universities, for example, have hired more and more people in an attempt to curb campus drinking, a major cause of deaths, injuries, and sexual assaults on the nation's campuses. Numerous solutions have attempted to deal with the culture of drinking. One interesting approach is called *social norms marketing*. Ads and posters in the campaign indicate that most students are only moderate drinkers.[18] The idea is to resocialize students by giving them statistical information on the actual attitudes and behaviors of their peers, presenting the view that they have overestimated the extent to which other students consume alcohol. The campaign encourages students to use the behavior of others as a benchmark.

THE AUDIENCE ANALYSIS PROCESS
▲

Experienced persuaders usually give their messages a trial run prior to the actual presentation. This auditioning may be informal, such as when we attempt to gauge the probable reaction of a friend before expressing an opinion. Or it may be formal, as in the elaborate and expensive survey research and audience analysis studies used by broadcasters and advertisers. The goal is the same: to locate points of identification that will bridge whatever gulf exists between persuaders and those they want to influence.

Wiring the Audience: Dial Group Testing

Various marketing, media, and testing organizations turned the auditioning process into something approaching a science. ASI Entertainment, for example, conducts market research to test audience responses to everything from television shows to game show hosts. At Preview House on Sunset Boulevard, participants (who received free tickets to screenings) begin their roles as audience members by completing questionnaires about their television-viewing and product-purchasing habits. They are then seated in the comfortable theater. Each chair has a five-position (very good, good, fair, dull, and very dull) dial that the participant turns to relay their opinions about the action unfolding on the screen.[19] These dials are connected to a computer that provides a real-time graph of the audience's collective reaction to whatever is on the screen. A pilot for a new television series tests well if the collective response of the group registers higher than fair. Producers of the show may learn that one character does not work for most members in the audience, and that character (and the actor or actress playing the role) may be written out of the script.

Presidential candidates may suffer a similar fate, as Bob Dole discovered in the 1996 campaign against Bill Clinton. In both private and media studies, the acerbic Dole did not do well. His attacks on Bill Clinton in the New Hampshire primary debate sent a CNN audience's dials plunging, as did his mere presence on the television screen.[20] Even references to his impressive war record failed to make the

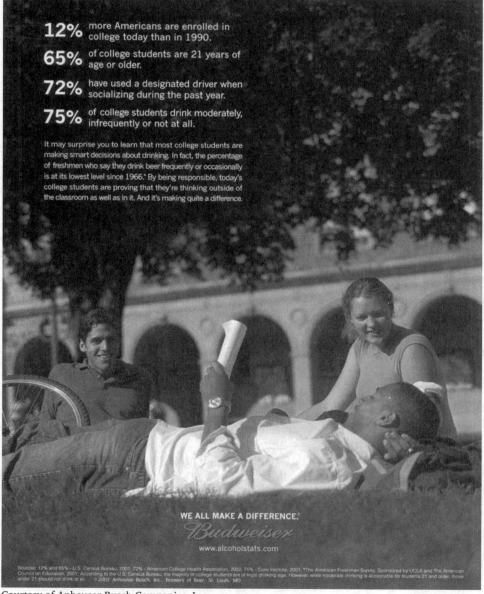

12% more Americans are enrolled in college today than in 1990.

65% of college students are 21 years of age or older.

72% have used a designated driver when socializing during the past year.

75% of college students drink moderately, infrequently or not at all.

It may surprise you to learn that most college students are making smart decisions about drinking. In fact, the percentage of freshmen who say they drink beer frequently or occasionally is at its lowest level since 1966.* By being responsible, today's college students are proving that they're thinking outside of the classroom as well as in it. And it's making quite a difference.

WE ALL MAKE A DIFFERENCE.

Budweiser

www.alcoholstats.com

Sources: 12% and 65% - U.S. Census Bureau, 2001. 72% - American College Health Association, 2002. 75% - Core Institute, 2001. *The American Freshman Survey, Sponsored by UCLA and The American Council on Education, 2001. According to the U.S. Census Bureau, the majority of college students are of legal drinking age. However, while moderate drinking is acceptable for students 21 and older, those under 21 should not drink at all. © 2002 Anheuser-Busch, Inc., Brewers of Beer, St. Louis, MO

Courtesy of Anheuser-Busch Companies, Inc.

dials move into more positive territory. Dole was wounded in World War II, but test audiences thought commercials pointing out his heroic military service were part of a "pity quest."[21] Although the press generally gave Dole high marks as a political debater, television audiences did not find his personality appealing.

The Principle of Identification

Since some communication is not intended to win over audiences, not all communicators are persuaders. For example, some writers and musicians may work to please only themselves or to achieve a private aesthetic goal. For them the act of self-expression may be its own reward. Even though most art is rhetorical (that is, artists usually seek receptive audiences), it is plausible that a creator of some form of art might say "I like it, and that is all that's important." Persuaders, however, *must* always go further; they must construct messages that narrow the gap between their attitudes and those of their audiences. In ways not demanded of other manipulators of words and images, they must reconcile their differences with those they seek to influence. Identification is the primary tool for achieving this goal.

The principle of identification may be the most universal of all the elements of communication. Think of a film, television drama, or novel with a character with whom you have no psychological alignment. What are your feelings about that character? We seek connections with others and resonance with the ideas and experiences of others. For example, music would lose much of its appeal if we could not identify with the lyrics or if hearing the melody did not transport us to a familiar experience.

Critical to reaching an audience is an advocate's ability to understand the collective beliefs of the members of the audience: what they like and dislike, what they take for granted, and what they are likely to challenge. St. Augustine noted that a person is persuaded if she or he "embraces what you commend, regrets whatever you build up as regrettable, rejoices at what you say is cause for rejoicing"—in short, when the person thinks as you do.[22] Persuasion may be described as a process that uses the familiar to gain acceptance for the unfamiliar.

Opportunities for identification are more varied than one might first suppose.[23] In our casual usage of the term, we often observe that identification is the product of various forms of similarity, for instance: ideological ("I agree"), demographic ("We are both men"), or shared circumstances ("Both of us grew up in Colorado"). What more intensive study reveals, however, is our remarkable capacity to extend our empathy to people and situations even when there seems to be no obvious analogues in our own experience. Given the inclination to do so, we are surprisingly adept at "standing in another person's shoes."

We can establish identification on many different levels. Our manner of dress and style of delivery can communicate physical similarity, while the expressions and examples we use can reassure an audience that we share similar experiences. This method can be seen in the seminal work of Tony Schwartz, who has become something of a legend in the history of radio and television commercials. Schwartz believes that the most effective persuasion acts to trigger beliefs and feelings that

NON SEQUITUR

© 1996 Wiley Miller. Dist. by UNIVERSAL PRESS SYNDICATE

already exist within a person. Effective advocacy depends as much on calling forth what individuals already believe as it does on advancing new ideas. Schwartz notes that an audience is the persuader's "workforce." A persuader "must deeply understand the kinds of information and experiences stored in his audience, the patterning of this information, and the interactive . . . process whereby stimuli evoke this stored information."[24] Identification is the sharing of experiences and values; it is achieved when listeners and readers sense that what is being said expresses their own attitudes.

Universal Commonplaces

Identification flows from a sense that advocate and audience share the same cultural beliefs. Known as commonplaces, these beliefs represent the core thoughts and ways of thinking that characterize a particular society. According to the French social theorist Jacques Ellul, a commonplace "serves everyone as a touchstone, an instrument of recognition. It is rarely quoted, but it is constantly present; it is behind thought and speech; it is behind conversation. It is the common standard that enables people to understand one another. . . ."[25]

The earliest compilers of commonplaces were Greek and Roman rhetoricians, notably Aristotle and Cicero.[26] Both identified habitual patterns of thought common to particular segments of their societies. More recently, anthropologists and sociologists have used commonplaces to map the ideological landscape of a tribe, nation, or culture. In 1935 researchers Robert and Helen Lynd studied a city dubbed "Middletown" to discover the attitudes held in common by large sections of the community. They catalogued the essential commonplaces of the city: "the things that one does and feels and says so naturally that mentioning them in Middletown implies an 'of course.'"[27] A sampling from their list of attitudes on the general subject of "the proper roles for government" points out the durability of many commonplaces:

- The government should leave things to private initiative.
- The American democratic form of government is the ideal form of government.
- The Constitution should not be fundamentally changed.

- Americans are the freest people in the world.
- The United States will always be the land of opportunity and the greatest and richest country in the world.[28]

Alan Wolfe's similar study in 1998 entitled *One Nation, After All* identified a number of areas of general agreement. He surveyed eight middle-class suburbs around the nation, but the statements for which he found substantial agreement are probably universal to the culture as a whole. Among them:

- The problems of inner cities are largely due to people's lack of personal responsibility for their own problems.
- Even though it has its problems, the United States is still the best place in the world to live.
- It has become much harder to raise children in our society.
- There are many different religious truths, and we ought to be tolerant of all of them.[29]

Not every individual would accept all of these fundamental starting points, nor do they always remain unchanged from generation to generation.[30] They are universal in the sense that they reflect mainstream public opinion at a specific time. We can isolate them as the building blocks of persuasion of a particular time because they are readily accepted by so many within a culture.

Awareness of key commonplaces makes it easier to initiate a sequence of persuasive appeals. Almost any persuasive message can be shown to have broad-based commonplaces as key starting points. Presidents, for example, frequently employ many of the items from the above lists. In his 1992 inaugural address, Bill Clinton emphasized the limits of government and the virtues of helping for the good of the community. "We must do what America does best," he noted, "offer more opportunity to all and demand more responsibility from all."

> It is time to break the bad habit of expecting something for nothing from our government or from each other. Let us all take more responsibility, not only for ourselves and our families, but for our communities and our country.[31]

These statements reflected the general view of the Clinton administration toward welfare reform, but they also built on long-standing American suspicions about the ability of governments to perform efficiently. George W. Bush's 2001 Inaugural Address offered the same commonplaces. "America, at its best," he noted, "is a place where personal responsibility is valued and expected." Government must do some things, "yet compassion is the work of a nation, not just a government."[32]

Audience-Specific Norms

Some topics require persuasion that uses more specific and sometimes more controversial starting points. Audience-specific norms differ from universal commonplaces by appealing to a limited number of groups within a society. Divisive subjects such as abortion rights, controls on the sale of firearms, the death penalty, and farm subsidies for tobacco growers evoke passionate responses from both sides. As issues become more specific, individuals become more selective in the values and attitudes they accept. American society consists of thousands of organizations and coalitions, some formal and some informal. All of us are in the mainstream of opinion on some topics and in the minority on others. Our membership in a complex society inevitably means that we will be moving with the tide of public opinion sometimes and swimming against it at other times.

With some accuracy we could predict the audience-specific norms for Handgun Control Incorporated (handguns are too abundant in the United States), the National Rifle Association (the Second Amendment protects the private ownership of firearms), or the People for the Ethical Treatment of Animals (animals have rights). To persuade groups who embrace specific ideologies, we must find norms they will find acceptable. The search for audience-specific norms is a reminder that groups differ in their definitions of what is "good," "just," "fair," and "important."

It is interesting to note how audience-specific norms are frequently at the root of discussions about the political correctness of certain expressions or attitudes. When members of one group are faulted for misnaming the members or actions of another, it is usually specific terms that either offend or affirm certain in-group sensibilities. Phrases such as "women's issues" or "gay rights" confer legitimacy on clusters of politically correct norms important to women and homosexuals. References to "broads" or "sexual deviants," for example, both deny the norms these groups embrace and reveal the ideologies of the user.

The question of what constitutes modern feminism is an interesting case of competing ideas. Political adviser Mary Matalin, for example, offered her view of why "the feminist movement has a problem." Matalin stated that women who are asked why they are not feminists are likely to respond, "I don't want to emulate men to succeed—I like being a woman; I respect the right of women to stay home; I don't hate men."[33] Matalin uses these short responses to counter what she sees as the norms of the movement. Other writers such as Susan Faludi and Gail Dines identify very different feminist norms: for example, oppression and women as victims of sexual violence[34] or "the white-male patriarchy."[35]

This battle of norms illustrates what writer Naomi Wolf has described as the very different traditions that modern feminists must deal with. The older tradition of "victim feminism," she argues, is giving way to a newer "power feminism" that defines women as free agents capable of setting their own agendas. Unlike an older feminism that was sometimes "antisexual," and preached a doctrine that asked women to "identify with powerlessness," new and different norms define a "power feminism" that:

> Is unapologetically sexual . . .
> Hates sexism without hating men . . .
> Seeks power and uses it responsibly, both for women as individuals and to make the world more fair to others . . . [and]
> Encourages a woman to claim her individual voice . . .[36]

The long-term debate over the goals of this movement is far more complex than these few examples indicate, but they do illuminate how norms compete for political legitimacy.

There are two ways to learn about audience norms. One is to arrive at estimations about what the audience thinks based on *demographics*. Certain attributes such as age, occupation, and religious affiliation can predict attitudes. The second method is to test for attitudes by doing *systematic polling* of samples of an audience. The dial groups in the discussion of Preview House are one example of polling. Most persuaders do not have the time or money to conduct survey research, so demographic assessment is the most common means of predicting audience attitudes and norms.

Demographics literally means "measurement of the people." Every audience can be profiled by standard demographic categories: age, sex, income level, education, geographical location, and membership in formal associations. Since most groups show greater similarities than differences in at least some traits, it is possible to make cautious generalizations about group attitudes. Radio stations and their advertisers, for example, generally find that preferences for musical formats correlate with particular kinds of listeners (teens, older adults, suburban adults, men, and so on). Similarly, television networks attempt to show prospective advertisers that their programs reach commercially lucrative segments of the population, such as adult women who make a high percentage of all household purchases. Consumer magazines such as *Money* attract potential advertisers by demonstrating that their audiences have high-income levels.

Inference making is partly a matter of guesswork. It involves using known facts to arrive at conclusions about unknown facts. Although such inferences are inexact, it is advantageous to make estimations about the attitudes of people based on what is known about their personal and social situations. Audiences with heavy concentrations of farmers will respond differently than audiences of bankers, retirees, union members, or college seniors. Persuaders addressing these groups should work backwards from general traits to an estimate of probable attitudes and values each group could be expected to endorse or condemn.

Jury selection in trials remains one of the most interesting forms of inference making about audiences. In criminal trials lawyers and judges have the right to reject prospective jurors. In the age of the televised "mega-trial," the attempts by defense attorneys to seat twelve sympathetic individuals on the jury are highly visible. A number of consultants were paid for their expertise in selecting jurors in O. J. Simpson's prolonged 1994 trial. According to several prominent defense attorneys and jury consultants the ideal panel to return a "not guilty" verdict for Simpson should have included men rather than women, older rather than younger members, African Americans, and "football buffs rather than football widows."[37] The common thread is a clear—if simplistic—notion of identification. The ideal jury was thought to be a group with as many similarities as possible to the defendant.

ADVOCATES, MESSAGES, AND AUDIENCES

▲

The forces that work for or against an advocate can be reduced to three simple but important variables. For persuasion to occur, there must be an advocate (someone or some group with a viewpoint to express), a message (the point of view the advocate wants listeners to accept), and an audience (listeners, viewers, or readers). Removal of any variable makes communication impossible. Figure 7.1 is a model of this process based on the work of researchers who looked at how people maintain and change their attitudes.[38]

For any persuasive setting it is reasonable to estimate relationships between the three variables as positive (+) or negative (–). A positive sign indicates approval, a negative sign indicates disapproval. The model illustrates the ways advocates, audiences, and messages directly interact with each other. Its six different configurations show the possibilities that flow from two key questions that should be asked about any persuasive encounter: Does the audience like the advocate? Does the audience share the advocate's point of view? Depending on the negative or positive relationships between the variables, the model predicts audience acceptance or rejection of the advocate and the message. For example, the most difficult form of persuasion is diagrammed in figure 7.1-f. In this case the audience has negative feelings toward both the persuader and the ideas. In the remainder of this chapter, we will discuss what the model reveals about six possible types of persuasive encounters.

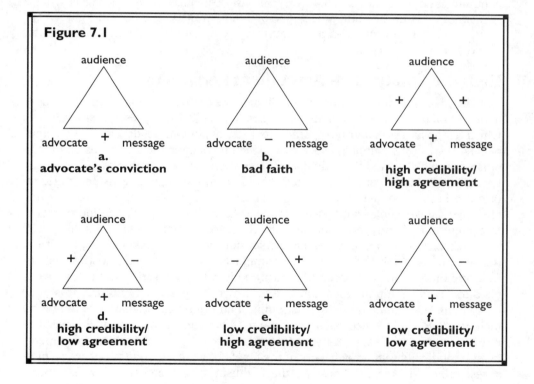

Figure 7.1

a.
advocate's conviction

b.
bad faith

c.
**high credibility/
high agreement**

d.
**high credibility/
low agreement**

e.
**low credibility/
high agreement**

f.
**low credibility/
low agreement**

Believing in Our Words

Figure 7.1-a diagrams the only relationship that should be (but is not always) constant: the advocate's positive faith in the rightness of the ideas presented. Although what an audience thinks about a topic may range from approval to disapproval, the audience rightly assumes that the persuader's expressions of support for his or her idea are sincere. Assuming no coercion, people are unlikely to argue for what they do not believe. An ethical presumption underlying all forms of persuasion is that advocates truly believe in what they want others to accept.

If we learn that a persuader deceptively supported a position, we may feel used. Bad-faith communication is diagrammed in figure 7.1-b; the minus sign indicates that a speaker is saying one thing but believing another. To be sure, there are times when people are required to *front* for someone else's viewpoints. Fronting may be required when individuals must represent the views of organizations or individuals to which they are attached, as when a governmental press aide defends an official policy with which she or he privately disagrees. We all face the challenge between loyalty and honesty in our lives, either as retail or service workers, or in the defenses we feel obligated to make on behalf of coworkers, family members, or friends. But beyond a limited range of professional and personal loyalties, we will assume that individuals are authentic in their expressed support for an idea: what a person professes is what he or she actually believes. To assume otherwise makes communication an endless chain of funhouse mirrors, where nothing is what it seems. The default presumption of personal authenticity is shown in figure 7.1-a. The interests of honesty and personal integrity dictate that the plus sign on this side of the triangle is constant.

High Credibility/High Agreement Persuasion

The ideal communication environment is one in which the audience is positive about both the message and its presenter. Figure 7.1-c represents situations in which enthusiastic supporters gather to hear a popular leader recite esteemed beliefs. Democratic campaign speeches spoken to Democratic audiences and Methodist sermons delivered to Methodist congregations are two examples of "preaching to the choir." Audiences attentive to a candidate appearing on television or face-to-face are heavily populated by people who already appreciate the source and the message.[39] Basic persuasion research suggests that "people pay attention primarily to content that already interests them and that is congenial to their point of view."[40]

High credibility/high agreement persuasion may seem unnecessary, but it is a mistake to overlook the need for communication to reinforce existing beliefs. Rhetoric that fits in with an existing attitude is extremely satisfying; it fulfills our need for membership in associations, and it involves practically no risk. It is obviously more rewarding and less threatening than the reverse, which would involve facing an audience whose members have doubts about us and our message. Such reinforcement may seem empty and ritualistic, but organizations and movements must periodically remind believers of the tenets basic to their faith. Speeches, messages, rallies, and leaflets prolong the enthusiasm of members who need occasional renewal.[41]

Persuasion for reinforcement sometimes also benefits from mass media exposure, which allows it to reach secondary audiences who are not so unified. In some instances, a message that seems to be intended for people who are already true believers may actually be designed to use the enthusiasm of those believers to infect a larger and previously indifferent mass media audience. The primary audience's support becomes part of the persuasive message, generating enthusiasm that may impress others who see the event secondhand. Laugh tracks on television comedies serve a similar purpose. The laughter reminds us that we should be having a good time—others are laughing at the dialogue or the antics. Political conventions similarly exploit this dual audience arrangement. They know that potential voters watching on television may be influenced by the zeal on the convention floor. The excitement of the supporters is a perfect backdrop to attract the attention of the undecided 5 or 6 percent, who could make the difference between electoral success and failure.

High Credibility/Low Agreement Persuasion

One of the most fascinating political events at the close of the 1980s was the rise of Vaclav Havel from obscure playwright to president of the Czech Republic. The remarkable transformation of one of the most repressive Communist regimes to an innovative democracy captured the attention of the world. Havel was at the center of this Cinderella story. He had been jailed by the old government for criticizing its actions in his plays and essays; by 1989 he reluctantly agreed to serve as the head of state. A hero's welcome in Washington and an invitation to address Congress made him the symbol of the tide of democracy sweeping through the old Eastern bloc. He was a symbol that ideas matter and that sometimes the pen can be mightier than the sword, and he was represented as a Czech version of Thomas Jefferson.

Not everything Havel said, however, added to the gloss of his new image. In July 1990 he told an international gathering of journalists who were meeting in Prague that journalism must honor the right of governments to keep their secrets and that press freedoms were not necessarily absolute.[42] He expressed concern about the social unrest that a truly free press can create, leading some writers at the meeting to wonder if Havel had conveniently set aside the memory of his own repression.

His new message of caution was at odds with his image as an uncompromising foe of repressive governments. This high credibility/low agreement setting diagramed in figure 7.1-d. is a classic case of persuasion. Typically, an advocate has earned the goodwill of the audience but tests that goodwill by arguing the merits of an unpopular idea. Political leaders often test the patience of their most ardent supporters by advocating ideas that do not conform to the norms of the supporters. In 1964 Lyndon Johnson assured voters that he would avoid the military solutions attributed to his opponent, but he committed thousands of troops to the war in Vietnam. President Clinton bitterly disappointed many political liberals by supporting more restrictive welfare benefits for children as well as adults. Many of George W. Bush's supporters expressed disappointment that he did not act more decisively after a series of accounting scandals in the summer of 2002.[43]

Two very different strategies fit the high credibility/low agreement setting. One is to intensify audience identification with the favorable public image of the advocate ("if such a terrific person believes this, maybe my own view is wrong"). With this approach, the advocate's association with the proposal is emphasized but the ideas associated with it are downplayed. Most celebrity endorsements of products function this way. In advertisements very little is said on behalf of the product other than the fact that it is associated with a person we admire. A second strategy—and one which has far greater merit—is to make the best case possible in defense of the idea to which the audience is indifferent or hostile. The advocate's reputation is sufficient to guarantee that an audience will listen to a reasoned presentation. Havel and his supporters had no choice but to explore the second high credibility/low agreement strategy, pointing out that it takes time to establish an open society where citizens must assume more independence and personal responsibility. It is not unreasonable to expect that former totalitarian states will need more than a few years to evolve into liberal democracies with similar guarantees; the United States has had over two hundred years to refine its freedoms.

A high credibility/low agreement setting is not without risks. Since a well-liked person is affirming a position that many do not accept, it is possible that the personal prestige of the advocate will suffer. The bright star of Minnesota Governor Jesse Ventura seemed to fade quickly after a series of statements and acts pushed the populist to the margins of mainstream life. Ventura's fiscal conservatism and "live-and-let-live" social agenda arguably matched the views of many in his state, but his criticism of religion and moonlighting as a sports announcer overshadowed the antigovernment populism that was the original source of his power.[44]

Low Credibility/High Agreement Persuasion

The situation represented in figure 7.1-e represents an arrangement that is the exact reverse of what we just discussed. Unlike the well-liked persuader outlining what an audience does not want to hear, the audience in this situation fundamentally agrees with the ideas being expressed but has low regard for the advocate.

A persuader might analyze this situation and conclude, "Why bother? I'm content if the audience agrees with me. There's no need to attempt to persuade if my presence may be counterproductive, risking a loss of support for the very attitude that I want them to hold." As a member of a township planning board, one of the authors witnessed a boomerang effect—receivers of a message responding in ways that are the reverse of the desired action. Members of the community spoke for or against land-use proposals. Some of the persuasion was so inept or hostile that virtually every word had the effect of *increasing* the distance between the advocate and the board. Their goals would have been better served by remaining silent.

An advocate with more effective skills can find at least one major reason for using low credibility/high agreement persuasion: the opportunity to increase personal credibility. By exploiting the audience's agreement on an issue, he or she may be able to reverse any negative personal feelings. Like the chameleon that blends in with the colors of a landscape, the advocate may gain protection against an audience's hostility by carefully cultivating shared ideas as an enhancement of his or her character. Ideas serve as membership cards to groups that would otherwise reject the low credibility speaker.

One of the most difficult audiences for Bill Clinton to address was the one present for a 1993 Memorial Day address at Washington's Vietnam Veterans Memorial. To many of the veterans and military leaders who had gathered, Clinton did not have the required credentials to be a Veterans Day speaker. His reputation as a draft dodger had endured beyond the bitter 1992 campaign. Like many other college students of his day, he avoided service in Vietnam and protested against the continuance of the war. When he spoke he was greeted with both applause and boos, but he persisted with ideas that resonated with his audience. He was eloquent in identifying common ground and in making a plea to put the negative feelings generated by Vietnam in the past.

> Let us continue to disagree, if we must, about the war, but let us not let it divide us as a people any longer. No one has come here today to disagree about the heroism of those whom we honor, but the only way we can really honor their memory is to resolve to live and serve today and tomorrow as best we can. . . . Surely that is what we owe to all those whose names are etched in this beautiful memorial.[45]

The primary strategy of a persuader confronting audience perceptions of low credibility is to identify shared values, experiences, and ideas—commonplaces that can function as bridges between a suspicious audience and the persuader. Garrison Keillor's parody of the etiquette for meeting famous people reminds us of the importance of the ways we act as evidence of who we really are.

1. Never grab or paw the famous. They will instantly recoil and you will never win their respect. Stand at least thirty-two inches away. If your words of admiration move him or her to pat your shoulder, then of course you can pat back, but don't initiate contact and don't hang on. Be cool.

2. Don't gush, don't babble, don't grovel or fawn. Never snivel. Be tall. Bootlicking builds a wall you'll never break through. A simple pleasantry is enough—e.g., "Like your work!" If you need to say more than that (I think you're the most wonderful lyric poet in America today), try to modify your praise slightly (but your critical essays really suck). Or cough hard, about five times. That relieves the famous person of having to fawn back. . . . Famous people much prefer a chummy insult to lavish nonsense: a little dig about the exorbitant price of tickets to the star's show, perhaps, or the cheesiness of the posters.[46]

We are always advocates attempting to cultivate our personal credibility in addition to promoting our positions on issues. As we noted in more detail in chapter 5, the question of what makes a source credible has produced many different and sometimes conflicting answers. It is evident here that credibility can be sought by taking public positions that will be embraced by an approving audience.

Low Credibility/Low Agreement Persuasion

As mentioned earlier, figure 7.1-f represents the persuasive situation that carries the heaviest burdens. It indicates a lack of audience support for *both* the persuader and his or her ideas. Not unexpectedly, most people do not joyfully tackle such an arrangement. Indeed, more than a few students have suggested that a persuader should come to this setting only with bodyguards and a familiarity with possible escape routes! Reality is usually less ominous.

Films and novels occasionally portray a single-minded persuader who faces the low credibility/low agreement double dilemma. David Mamet has made a career writing fascinating screenplays populated by men and women in such conflict (*The

Spanish Prisoner, Hoffa, Glengarry Glen Ross, The Verdict, Heist, and others). Actual results are less dramatic than either our imaginations or Hollywood suggest. Real audiences are rarely won over by such attempts, but they are also usually less hostile than the model implies.

Senator Ted Kennedy has made it a career-long policy to address audiences sharply at odds with his generally liberal political views and somewhat flamboyant public persona. In one of his most famous appearances, he accepted an invitation from Jerry Falwell to visit Liberty Baptist College, which was then the center of the religious right's crusade against the politics represented by Kennedy and others. He emerged successfully from that encounter, even if his audience's attitudes on abortion, school prayer, and the Equal Rights Amendment were probably unchanged.[47] While many observers might view such efforts as exercises in complete futility, there is often considerable value in making listeners a little less comfortable with their own beliefs.

Former First Lady Barbara Bush also faced an audience with some of the features of the low credibility-low agreement model. She had been invited to give the commencement address at Wellesley College in 1990. As news of the invitation spread, so did objections that she was not an appropriate role model for the women students. Their reasoning was that her identity was created largely by her husband's position. Some students made it known that Bush was the school's second choice, after author Alice Walker declined. A full quarter of the senior class signed a petition asking for another choice. Other speakers might have declined to attend in the face of such animosity, but Bush persisted and offered a heartfelt speech celebrating the freer choices available to women today, but also embracing the connections to family that men and women need to make.

> For several years you've had impressed upon you the importance to your career of dedication and hard work, and of course that's true. But as important as your obligations as a doctor, a lawyer, a business leader will be, you are a human being first and those human connections with spouses, with children, with friends are the most important investment you will ever make.[48]

The combination of low agreement and low credibility means that it will be difficult to leverage a position: for example, using high agreement to gain credibility or using high credibility to gain agreement. The task for the persuader starting with both low credibility and low agreement is to find commonplaces or norms that can be initial stepping stones to increasing both variables. Used as sources of identification, those initial steps can narrow the gaps that divide advocate and audience.

UNINTENDED AUDIENCES
▲

As we noted at the outset, persuasion theory usually presupposes that messages will be targeted to specific audiences. Implied in this observation is the unstated but often important corollary that these messages will be ignored by nearly all others. Often this is precisely what happens, especially when communication takes place in relatively private settings. Even so, actual events and the realities of the communication age have a way of working against perfect isolation of messages.

Many forms of communication are now easily carried to others beyond primary audiences, often to unintended audiences leading to unintended effects. The results may be humorous, as in the 1988 farce *The Naked Gun*, where the forgetful Inspector Frank Drebin concludes a speech to a large gathering and forgets to remove his cordless public address microphone before visiting the rest room. This silly sequence makes an important rhetorical point: in many different ways the electronic media make it less possible to isolate audiences from each other.

Consider George W. Bush's decision to address an audience at Bob Jones University in the midst of the 2000 presidential campaign. After losing the New Hampshire primary, Bush needed a win in South Carolina, where the university is located. He also needed to outflank his rival, John McCain, by appealing to conservative activists in the state. That strategy made the choice of Bob Jones tactically useful. However, the university has a reputation as an institution that is hostile to African Americans, Catholics, gays, and others. Some newspapers reported Bush's brother Jeb would not have been able to date his wife at the school because of its policies against interracial dating.[49] In the end, Bush gave a noncontroversial speech at the university. But many in the rest of the nation that made up his unintended audience interpreted the appearance as an endorsement of the school's alleged intolerance.

SUMMARY: THE ETHICS OF ADAPTATION

▲

The central theme of this chapter has been that successful persuasion must be measured against the necessity to adapt to specific audiences. We need to assess our strengths and weaknesses in relation to those we want to influence. Sometimes our strengths lie in who we are; in many instances they reside in the specific ideas we intend to communicate. Commonplaces and group-specific norms establish important points of identification between persuaders and receivers. In its most elemental form, persuasion is the strategy of building acceptance by communicating in the common currency of shared experience and attitude. The use of these materials to establish identification with a reluctant audience is an essential communication process. *There are simply few other persuasion skills that matter as much as the ability to link one's own persuasive message to relevant audience values.*

Built into this theme is what many consider the troubling question of when adaptation goes too far. Plato called excessive adaptation to audience beliefs pandering and claimed that it was a common feature of persuasion. "Isn't it highly likely," modern counterparts to Plato might argue, "that audience-based persuasion encourages a persuader to sacrifice personal beliefs as the price for winning audience approval? Doesn't the presence of the audience and its norms put enormous burdens on a persuader, even though his or her personal vision may be superior to that of the group whose support is sought?"

These are evocative questions, but they pose several false dilemmas. They presuppose that many forms of communication are not audience based—that somehow in other settings we are truer to our authentic selves. In truth, the reactions of others are factors in almost every communication context. The admonishments to "be ourselves" and "not to worry about what others think" sound good but are almost impossible to obey. Unless we are entirely self-sufficient economically and socially, we confront and accommodate both audience demands and private convictions every day.

Moreover, the process of considering how our words affect others does not preclude asserting ourselves. There is ample room for us to learn how to be rhetorically accommodating without "selling out." Much of the activity of daily life is a constant process of mediation between our own and other people's beliefs. We are fit company for others largely because of our willingness to engage in this accommodation. We heap a great deal of praise on personalities who show the courage to "do and say what they think without regard for what others may say." Film stars like Harrison Ford, Tom Hanks, and Julia Roberts have played their share of independent-thinking heroes, perhaps serving as surrogates for the rest of us who like the fantasy of the defiant outsider. But successful accommodation to audiences is not by itself an intellectual crime.

The ethical line is crossed when adaptation extends beyond the natural process of mediation and reaches into the denial of authentic convictions. The persuader who deliberately ignores beliefs for the sake of performance has violated the acceptable threshold of accommodation. It is reasonable and shrewd to determine and to coordinate with audience values that also support a deeply held personal belief, but it is unethical to sacrifice personal feelings simply for the sake of winning over others.

Finally, it is important to remember that the audience is often asked to do most of the giving in many persuasive situations. The persuader's intention to transform the attitudes or actions of a group of people implicitly says, "Give me both your attention and the benefit of your agreement." It seems more reasonable to expect that audience adaptation should be a dialogue between the advocate and audience. The persuader who seeks change from a group of people but is at the same time unwilling to give their ideas serious consideration is perhaps more unreasonable than the person accused of pandering too much.

Questions and Projects for Further Study

1. Look for commonplaces in an article in a mass-market magazine such as *Reader's Digest*. Locate more specialized group norms in a magazine with a narrower audience such as *Maxim* or *Ms*. Describe how some of these elements function as appeals to the audience.

2. *Broadcasting & Cable* and *Advertising Age* are two trade magazines that are filled with discussions of audiences and their characteristics. *Broadcasting & Cable*, for example, contains numerous ads for syndicated programs that stations may rent, programs that already attract certain kinds of audiences. *Advertising Age* contains articles describing the plans of companies for reaching certain audiences. Prepare a written or oral summary of the audience that one advertiser or program producer wants to reach. Which programs defy the idea that there is a single audience type that would be receptive to it?

3. In spite of the fact that we believe that we are responsible for our own commitments, a theme in this chapter is that we acquire most of our attitudes through our associations with others. What authorities or associations can you identify that have influenced your beliefs and attitudes?

4. At one point in the chapter, the authors note that an ethical presumption that goes with all forms of persuasion is that persuaders should believe in what they want others to accept. Publicly arguing for a position in which one does not personally believe is sometimes called fronting. Cite an instance of fronting that involved you, or cite some situations where fronting is common and perhaps necessary. Do any of these situations suggest that fronting may be ethical?

5. Using examples from television, films, or recent news events, illustrate what is meant by the following terms:

Boomerang Effect

Low Credibility/Low Agreement Persuasion

Norms

Pandering

6. Most libraries have copies of *Vital Speeches of the Day*, which reprints speeches given in a wide variety of fields and indicates the nature of the audiences. Using the scheme presented in figure 7.1, look through several recent issues and diagram three different kinds of communication settings (such as 7.1-c, -d, and -e).

7. Pick an issue or position on which you hold strong views. Given your position on the particular question chosen (i.e., defending a politician, a controversial policy, or group), identify an organization that would hold contrary or different attitudes. Imagine that you were invited by this organization to explain your convictions. After giving your invitation some thought, describe the norms and commonplaces you think the hypothetical audience holds and how you would bridge your differences to increase their support or understanding of your point of view.

Additional Reading

Robert Cialdini, *Influence: Science and Practice*, 4th ed. (Boston: Allyn & Bacon, 2001).

James Hay, Lawrence Grossberg, and Ellen Wartella, eds., *The Audience and its Landscape* (Boulder, CO: Westview Press, 1996).

Charles Kiesler, Barry E. Collins, and Norman Miller, *Attitude Change: A Critical Analysis of Theoretical Approaches* (New York: John Wiley, 1968).

Robert S. Lynd and Helen Merrell Lynd, *Middletown in Transition: A Study in Cultural Conflicts* (New York: Harvest, 1937).

William McGuire, "Attitudes and Attitude Change," *Handbook of Social Psychology*, Vol. II, 3rd ed., eds. Gardner Lindzey and Elliot Aronson (Mahwah, NJ: Lawrence Earlbaum, 1985), pp. 233–46.

Tony Schwartz, *The Responsive Chord* (New York: Anchor, 1974).

James Webster and Patricia Phalen, *The Mass Audience: Rediscovering the Dominant Model* (Mahwah, NJ: Lawrence Erlbaum Associates, 1997).

Alan Wolfe, *One Nation After All* (New York: Viking, 1998).

Notes

[1] John Durham Peters, *Speaking into the Air* (Chicago: University of Chicago Press, 1999), p. 265.

[2] Émile Durkheim quoted in Hugh Dalziel Duncan, *Symbols and Social Theory* (New York: Oxford, 1969), pp. 152–53.

[3] Peters, p. 4.

[4] James Webster and Patricia Phalen, *The Mass Audience: Rediscovering the Dominant Model* (Mahwah, NJ: Lawrence Erlbaum Associates, 1997), p. xiii.

[5] For a discussion of this question see Robert N. Bellah, et al., *Habits of the Heart*, Updated Edition (Berkeley: University of California Press, 1996), pp. 275–307.

[6] Todd Gitlin, *The Twilight of Common Dreams: Why America is Wracked by Culture Wars* (New York: Henry Holt, 1995), p. 203.

[7] Joshua Meyrowitz, *No Sense of Place* (New York: Oxford University Press, 1985), p. 73–92.

[8] Orrin E. Klapp, *Symbolic Leaders* (Chicago: Aldine, 1964), pp. 101–75.

[9] Marjorie Hershey, "The Campaign and The Media," in *The Election of 2000*, ed. by Gerald Pomper (New York: Chatham House, 2001), p. 58.

[10] Larry Speakes, *Speaking Out* (New York: Avon, 1988), p. 312.

[11] Robert Cialdini, *Influence: Science and Practice*, 4th ed. (Boston: Allyn & Bacon, 2001), p. 100.

[12] Ibid., p. 100.

[13] Ibid., pp. 132–33.

[14] Ibid., p. 111.

[15] Ibid.

[16] William McGuire, "Attitudes and Attitude Change," *Handbook of Social Psychology*, Vol. II, 3rd ed., eds. Gardner Lindzey and Elliot Aronson (Mahwah, NJ: Lawrence Earlbaum, 1985), pp. 233–346.

[17] Cialdini, p. 119.

[18] Susan Okie, "Drinking Lessons: As Alcohol Problems Grow, Colleges Seek New Remedies," *The Washington Post*, April 16, 2002, p F1.

[19] Todd Gitlin, *Inside Prime Time* (New York: Pantheon, 1983), pp. 36–40; Ron Miller, "At Preview House, Viewers are the Guinea Pigs," *Philadelphia Inquirer*, August 16, 1983, p. 6E.

[20] CNN, New Hampshire Primary Debate, February 15, 1996.

[21] Pamela Hunter, "Using Focus Groups in Campaigns: A Caution," *Campaigns and Elections*, August 2000 (LEXIS/NEXIS).

[22] Augustine quoted in Kenneth Burke, *A Rhetoric of Motives* (Berkeley: University of California, 1969), p. 50.

[23] For a more detailed discussion see Gary C. Woodward, *The Idea of Identification* (Albany: State University of New York Press, 2003).

[24] Tony Schwartz, *The Responsive Chord* (New York: Anchor, 1974), p. 25.

[25] Jacques Ellul, *A Critique of the New Commonplaces*, trans. Helen Weaver (New York: Knopf, 1968), p. 13.

[26] See, for example, Aristotle, *The Rhetoric*, Book I, Chapters 5–7, trans. W. Rhys Roberts (New York: Modern Library, 1954); Cicero, *Topics*, trans. H. M. Hubbell (Cambridge: Harvard University Press, 1960), pp. 383–459.

[27] Robert S. Lynd and Helen Merrell Lynd, *Middletown in Transition: A Study in Cultural Conflicts* (New York: Harvest, 1937), p. 402.

[28] Ibid., pp. 413–15, 418.

[29] Alan Wolfe, *One Nation After All* (New York: Viking, 1998), pp. 62, 177, 205, 155.

[30] Some commonplaces in the Lynds' study have become antiques, for example, "a married woman's place is first of all in the home and any other activities should be secondary to 'making a good home for her husband and children'" and "married people owe it to society to have children." Lynd and Lynd, p. 410.

[31] Bill Clinton, Inaugural Address, in Michael Osborn and Suzanne Osborn, *Public Speaking*, 3rd ed. (Boston: Houghton Mifflin, 1994), p. B24.

[32] "President George W. Bush, Inaugural Address," *The San Diego Union-Tribune*, January 21, 2001, p. A8.

[33] Mary Matalin, "Stop Whining!" *Newsweek*, October 25, 1993, p. 62.

[34] Susan Faludi, "Who's Hype?" in Ibid., p. 61.

[35] Gail Dines, quoted in Sarah Crichton, "Sexual Correctness: Has It Gone Too Far?" in Ibid., p. 55.

[36] Naomi Wolf, *Fire with Fire* (New York: Random House, 1993), pp. 135–37.

[37] David Margolick, "Ideal Juror for O. J. Simpson: Football Fan Who Can Listen," *New York Times*, September 23, 1994, p. A1.

[38] This model is adapted from one originally proposed by psychologist Fritz Heider. For a review of his model and other variations on it see Charles A. Kiesler, Barry E. Collins, and Norman Miller, *Attitude Change: A Critical Analysis of Theoretical Approaches* (New York: John Wiley, 1968), pp. 155–78.

[39] Thomas Patterson and Robert D. McClure, *The Unseeing Eye: The Myth of Television Power in National Politics* (New York: G. P. Putnams, 1976), p. 121.

[40] Kurt Lang and Gladys Engle Lang, *Politics and Television* (New York: Quadrangle, 1968), p. 16.

[41] To cite studies of just two types of messages, see Arthur M. Schlesinger, Jr., "Annual Messages of the Presidents: Major Themes of American History" in *The State of the Union Messages*, Vol. 1, 1790–1860, ed. by Fred L. Israel (New York: Chelsea House/Robert Hector, 1966), pp. xiii–xvi; Donald Wolfarth, "John F. Kennedy in the Tradition of Inaugural Speeches," *Quarterly Journal of Speech*, April 1961, pp. 124–32.

[42] Bill Kovach and Tom Winship, "Havel: Prison for Journalists?" *New York Times*, July 15, 1990, p. E19.

[43] David Gergen, "Time To Step Up to the Plate," *U.S. News and World Report*. (Online) July 29, 2002.

[44] James Pinkerton, "Ventura Byway: A Sad End to Wrestler's Excursion into Politics," *Pittsburgh Post-Gazette*, July 27, 2002 (LEXIS-NEXIS).

[45] Bill Clinton, Memorial Day Address, 1993, C-SPAN. Purdue University Video Archives.

[46] Garrison Keillor, *We Are Still Married* (New York: Viking/Penguin, 1989), p. 297.

[47] See Gary Woodward, *Persuasive Encounters: Case Studies in Constructive Confrontation* (New York: Praeger, 1990), pp. 53–75.

[48] Barbara Bush, "Commencement Address at Wellesley College," June 1, 1990, C-SPAN. Purdue University Video Archives.

[49] John Leo, "The Company He Keeps," *U.S. News and World Report*, March 6, 2000, p. 15.

PART III

THE CONTEXTS OF PERSUASION

8

Interpersonal Persuasion

Overview

▲ Dimensions of Interpersonal Communication

▲ Variables of Interpersonal Persuasion
    Verbal Characteristics
    Nonverbal Characteristics
    Power and Control
    Compliance-Seeking Messages
    Conflict
    Gender Differences
    Culture and Diversity
    Leadership

▲ Contexts of Interpersonal Persuasion
    Organizations
    Sales
    Interviews

> *Effective participation in contemporary life demands that we understand varied individuals with whom we interact and that we cultivate a range of communication skills in ourselves.*[1]
>
> —JULIA T. WOOD

We experience the process of persuasion in a wide variety of contexts ranging from sitting alone thinking to participating in a mass demonstration. The three basic levels of persuasion are: intrapersonal, interpersonal, and public. Although the essential processes of persuasion are alike for each level, there are noticeable differences in appeals, strategies, and tactics. Intrapersonal persuasion is communication with oneself; it provides cues for interpreting sensations, images of who we are, and motives for our behavior. Interpersonal persuasion, the topic of this chapter, focuses on face-to-face interaction with others. We address public persuasion in the next chapter.

Much of our face-to-face interaction—whether among family, friends, or strangers—is purposeful and persuasive. It may be as simple as requesting someone to bring you a book, as important as asking someone to hire you, or as emotional as asking someone to marry you. Within the interpersonal context, persuasive efforts may be characterized as:

1. Dynamic—participants send and receive signals continually and simultaneously; the situation is not static.
2. Interactive—participants influence each other; they are interdependent. Each person is constantly aware of the other and assumes the roles of both sender and receiver, which involves constant adaptation and adjustment.
3. Proactive—involves the total person. Beliefs, attitudes, values, social background, and previous transactions all influence the nature of the interaction.
4. Contextual—environmental and situational factors influence the interaction.
5. Intense—content of the interactions are most often personal, intimate, and revealing, thus producing the risks of rejection, withdrawal, exposure, and even weakness.

After reviewing in greater detail those elements of persuasion most related to interpersonal interaction, we will focus on the specialized contexts of organizations, interviews, and sales. The persuasive potential of interpersonal persuasion is particularly apparent in these three areas.

The various theories, strategies, and tactics of persuasion are applicable to any level or context of human communication. They may differ, however, in terms of degree and effectiveness. The forms of dyadic (two-person) communication range from the most social (intimate), to the most formal (interview), to the most stressful (interrogation). Within these areas, persuasive strategies and tactics may range from the subtle to the overt, the rational to the psychological, and the verbal to the nonverbal.

Interpersonal persuasion is challenging, difficult, and complex. Kathleen Reardon defines it as the behavior that takes place "when two or a few people interact in a way that involves verbal and nonverbal behaviors, personal feedback, coherence of behaviors (relevance or fit of remarks and actions), and the purpose (on the part of at least one interactant) of changing the attitudes and/or behaviors of the others."[2]

DIMENSIONS OF INTERPERSONAL COMMUNICATION

▲

To illustrate the cognitive or rational dimension of the persuasive interpersonal communication process, suppose you wanted to sell your old car. How much information should you share in the sales pitch—mileage, motor size, oil usage, miles per gallon, prior accidents, etc.? What type of opinions will you offer about the car's condition, treatment, value, etc.? Planned persuasive strategies include language choice, attitudes, logic, and credibility. Most interactions are purposeful; the parties have a goal to accomplish. During the encounter, information, opinion, and action will be exchanged. Information shared may be incomplete, inaccurate, or biased. Opinions expressed may be unwarranted based on the information presented. The actions or behavior desired may reveal the persuader's motives.

The second dimension of persuasive interpersonal communication is relationships. William Schultz argues there are three primary human needs that interpersonal communication can help fulfill.[3] The first is the need for inclusion. As social animals, we need to belong, to be accepted, and to be recognized. Through interaction we establish friends and relationships, prestige and status, commitment and group participation. A well-adjusted person is usually characterized as one who has self-confidence, is well liked by others, and is comfortable in a wide variety of social settings. Social inclusion is important for acceptance, compliance, and task performance.

Control is the second basic human need; it implies more than just power over others. It includes knowing when to defer to others as well as when and how to assert one's self-interests. The military is primarily organized by control. Roles are very clearly defined. In most other organizations, control is a process of give and take, negotiating different opinions, experiences, skills, and knowledge. We will have more to say about the role of control in interpersonal persuasion later in the chapter.

The third need is for affection. This need progresses beyond the emotional support and relationships associated with the notion of inclusion. All humans need affection—to love and to be loved. Through interpersonal communication, we grow in relationships from first introductions or greetings to personal intimacy. We know, for example, that it is easier to persuade someone if they know us, trust us, and like us.

Our car example might not seem the best illustration of relational processes. However, even if you sell the car to a stranger, the first part of the interaction would be to establish trust and to build linkages of identification. You must persuade the person that you are honest and have nothing to hide; the potential buyer must convince you that he or she intends to buy the car and has the funds to pay for it. You might emphasize similarities and commonalities between you and the potential buyer such as mutual friends, places, or experiences to establish a mini-relationship during the transaction.

VARIABLES OF INTERPERSONAL PERSUASION
▲

As we have already noted, some would argue that all persuasion is interpersonal in the sense that some source creates and sends a message received by another person who renders judgment and responds to the message. We will revisit elements introduced in previous chapters in the context of face-to-face interactions.

Verbal Characteristics

In chapter 3, we discussed the nature of symbols and language in creating the reality within which we act. Human communication is a purposeful process of selection, interpretation, and symbolism. We select our verbal behaviors largely based on interactions that were successful in the past. We repeat verbal behaviors that created satisfying exchanges; those that led to ineffective exchanges are eliminated from our repertoire of possible behaviors.

Interpersonal communication is a very complex process. Joe DeVito has identified several characteristics of effective interpersonal communication that have strategic implications for persuasive interpersonal interactions.[4] Interpersonal communication in honest and satisfying relationships involves openness, empathy, supportiveness, positiveness, and equality. These qualities stimulate the perceptions of honesty, trust, and accessibility. How do you enhance humanistic qualities in interpersonal conversation? Be willing to reveal information not commonly known about yourself. Respond spontaneously to the communication and feedback of others. Be sensitive to the desires and feelings of others. Be less judgmental and evaluative of others. Be pleasant and engage in behavior that acknowledges the presence and importance of others.

A *pragmatic* approach to interpersonal effectiveness focuses on communicative behaviors that help the speaker or listener accomplish desired goals or outcomes. Such communication is other-oriented and characterized by confidence, expressiveness, immediacy, and interaction management. Other-oriented communication and immediacy generate attentiveness and interest; it also demonstrates consideration and respect for the interaction participant. Confidence and expressiveness generate trust and involvement. Interaction management techniques maintain the proper pacing of an interaction toward a decision or issue resolution. Enhance pragmatic qualities by linking yourself to others in the conversation by using terms such as "we," "our," or "us." Echo the feelings expressed by others by relating similar stories or experiences. Reinforce the comments of others with head nods, smiles, and physical touches of friendship (nonverbal behaviors, which are discussed below).

We tend to develop and maintain relationships that provide more rewards than costs. Obviously, the most satisfying relationships are those where the rewards and costs are equal to those of our partner. At the heart of this approach to interpersonal communication is the conscious effort to provide positive rewards in our daily interactions. Some examples are simple behaviors such as saying "thank you," inquiring how people are feeling, or acknowledging their efforts. Both the structure and content of an interpersonal interaction help establish a relationship that will provide a context for future compliance and receiver behavior. Today's conversation will impact future conversations. For example, in a job where you depend on others for task completion, the quality of your interpersonal interactions will affect your job performance and evaluations.

Nonverbal Characteristics

Nonverbal codes and symbols have many of the same characteristics as verbal codes and symbols. They convey distinct meanings within a culture or society. Both nonverbal and verbal meanings are arbitrary; they are formed as a result of social interactions. Nonverbal communication is an essential part of all human communication. Some scholars argue that the meaning we get from interactions comes primarily from the nonverbal dimensions of message exchange.[5] Nonverbal messages may emphasize or accent a particular part of a verbal message. A certain look, gesture, or increase in volume may provide clues to the attitude or emotion of the communicator. Nonverbal messages may complement or contradict what is stated verbally. In addition, they regulate the flow of interactions. From certain nonverbal cues, we learn when it is our turn to speak or when someone wishes to interrupt. Nonverbal messages also substitute for verbal messages. A simple nod of the head or shaking of a finger is all the reply one may need to a question.

CALVIN AND HOBBES

There are numerous nonverbal codes or systems in our culture.[6] Body communication refers to the various messages sent by our physical presence, such as gestures, posture, movements, and appearance. Facial and eye communication include smiles, frowns, raised eyebrows, scowls, winks, and eye movements such as eye contact and pupil dilation. Artifactual communication includes all the material objects accumulated by people such as clothing, cars, and pens. Artifacts communicate social class, status, or success. There are often expectations of style and dress, for example, associated with many professions. Most research indicates that certain artifacts, especially clothing, can indeed influence compliance and persuasiveness. Spatial communication deals with human use of personal space and territory. Tactile communication focuses on touch and physical contact. Paralanguage refers to the sounds and the meanings associated with *how* words are spoken. Vocal rate, pitch, volume, and pauses all affect the meaning communicated in our verbal messages. Smell, as a code system, deals with how odor communicates. Besides natural scents and perfumes, there are cultural differences in reactions to smell. Finally, temporal communication focuses on human uses of time. This brief explanation of the many types of nonverbal codes emphasizes how pervasive and important the role of nonverbal communication is in everyday conversation.

There are three aspects of nonverbal behaviors that affect persuasion. First, the level of animation, expression, or enthusiasm shown during an interaction enhances persuasion and the effectiveness of the message. Vocal variety, affirming nods and gestures, and maintaining eye contact are a few behaviors that enliven contact with others. Second, nonverbal behaviors that express liking and attraction also enhance message reception. Increased proximity, smiling, and touching are obvious ways to show attraction. Finally, the level of relaxation displayed during an interaction is important in gaining trust and the appearance of truthfulness. A relaxed posture and the absence of vocal anxiety are important elements in establishing credibility. General persuasiveness increases when nonverbal behaviors communicate enthusiasm, attraction, and relaxation.

Scholars have reported other findings about eye contact, body movements, distance, touching, and vocal delivery that link persuasiveness and nonverbal behaviors. Those who engage in more direct eye contact are more persuasive and are perceived as more trustworthy.[7] Studies have shown that direct eye contact during 60 to 90 percent of the interaction is most effective. Several studies also demonstrate the impact of facial expressions. By smiling and/or nodding, waitresses earn more tips, therapists are judged to be warmer and more competent, job interviewees create positive impressions of themselves and are more likely to get jobs, and students pay more attention to teachers.[8] In general, more dynamic speakers are more persuasive. Specific examples of dynamic behavior include frequent gesturing, hand movements, head nodding, smiling, and high levels of energy. Of course, these activities must appear natural, genuine, and sincere or the issue of credibility will outweigh any persuasive gains from dynamic presentation.

Touching can be a powerful tool of reinforcement for compliance. For example, studies revealed that bookstore customers who were touched on the arm shopped longer and bought more; supermarket customers who had been touched were more likely to taste and purchase food samples; restaurant customers provided a 20–30 percent increase in tips if they had been touched during ordering and service.[9] While touching tends to stimulate feelings of liking, trust and interpersonal involvement, there are cultural norms and limitations to such behavior. In making a request, a slight touch on the arm may increase compliance. However, a sustained touch may increase anxiety and stress. How well you know the participant in the interaction is crucial in deciding how and when to touch someone.

The same is true when considering the distance of interaction. Standing close to the persuadee is more likely to gain compliance. Part of the reason is that we tend to stand closer to people we like. In contrast, when personal space is invaded, there is an intimidation factor at play. The persuader may be perceived as demanding, desperate, or needful.[10]

Speech fluency is another important factor to consider. Speech pauses, hesitations, and vocal repetitions decrease speaker credibility and perceived competence, thus reducing the persuasiveness of a message. Communication scholars have identified language characteristics that result in powerless types of speech. Forms of powerless speech include: hesitations ("uh," "ah," "well," "um," or "you know"), hedges ("kinda," "I think," or "I guess"), tag questions ("isn't it?", "wouldn't it?", or "right?"), disclaimers ("Don't get me wrong, but," "I'm not sure, but"), accounts (excuses or justifications), and side particles ("like," "simply," "you know," or "that is"), to name a few. The use of these speech forms in conversation and even more so in formal presentations lowers credibility, perceptions of competence, and trustworthiness.[11] A conversational style of delivery is perceived as more competent, knowledgeable, sincere, and trustworthy. A more passionate presentation tends to be perceived as emotional. Of course, the purpose and context of the event would dictate the style of presentation. At the very least, a confident speaker will be more successful than a tentative, hesitant one.

Power and Control

In the process of negotiating meaning through verbal and nonverbal codes, the need for control is often the agenda hidden in our interactions with others. We tend to react negatively to overt displays of power and control. Yet, we generally admire those whom we perceive as having influence. Space does not permit a detailed discussion of the concepts of interpersonal power and control, but we will highlight a few of the elements important to influence and persuasion.

Power should not be confused with authority. Authority is a legal or managerial right to make decisions, assign tasks, and ensure satisfactory performance; it is delegated. Properly used power is a force that enhances authority. Therefore, authority is the *right* to do something; power is the *ability* to do something. Michael Hackman and Craig Johnson define power as "the ability to influence others."[12] At the base of power is a relationship structure. While one may exert more influence than others in a group, there is still some form of relationship and mutual influence and interdependence.

In their classic study, John French and Bertram Raven identify five sources of power.[13] Coercive power is based primarily on the use of punishments or threats to induce desired behavior. Coercive power is not an enduring form of influence, and it may cause resentment and a lack of trust among acquaintances. Reward power is the ability to give something of value to others in exchange for desired behavior. Rewards can range from a simple "thank you" to more tangible items such as money or a larger office. The use of rewards to stimulate compliance can enhance cooperation and motivation. Legitimate power is based on the authority of a position. The manager can expect compliance based on her position, although the employee may find that type of power less satisfying and effective than other forms of power. Expert power is based on the skills and general competence of a person. Compliance results from mutual trust and respect. In effect, one earns power as a result of expertise. This form of power is positive and long lasting. Finally, French and Raven identify referent power that results from feelings of admiration, affection, and loyalty. People comply with requests out of respect and a willingness to return favors for past actions. This form of power takes a long time to develop.

Generally, the most useful forms of power for persuasive purposes are those based on personal qualities of individuals rather than those based on the authority of position or coercion. DeVito observes that in any interpersonal relationship, the person who holds the power is the one less interested in and less dependent on the rewards and punishments controlled by the other person. In short, the more you depend on a relationship, the less power you have in it.[14]

Power plays are patterns of communication that take unfair advantage of another person. They rob people of opportunities to make their own choices, free of harassment or intimidation. One such power play is "nobody upstairs," where receipt of requests are simply not acknowledged. The "you owe me" power play results when others do something for you and then demand something in return. The "you've-got-to-be-kidding" play is an emotional attack on another by expressing such disbelief in a statement that it appears silly or stupid. There are many attempts at power plays. The important thing to remember is that they are verbal strategies that enhance compliance through fear, intimidation, humiliation, or social pressure. In such situations, one may ignore the power play without altering behavior, or one could treat the episode as an isolated instance by objecting to it. If you choose the latter alternative, you should express your feelings, describe the behavior to which you object, and offer to discuss salient issues of contention openly.[15]

Julia Wood argues that all relationships are organized in terms of power and the degree of interdependence.[16] She identifies three types of organizing structures for interpersonal relationships; many relationships are a blend of the three structures. Relationships are not static, they evolve over time and structures may change.

Figure 8.1   Forms of Relationships

Relationship Type	Power	Dependence
Complimentary	Unequal	Highly Interdependent
Parallel	Distributed	Moderately Interdependent
Symmetrical	Equal	Highly Independent

Complementary relationships involve unequal power and high interdependence. In the past, when husbands worked and wives stayed at home, men had greater power in terms of social positions and jobs. Women needed economic security and shelter; men needed comfort, support, and someone to nurture the family. Within such relationships, roles were clearly defined, as were rules of interaction and behavior expectations. Despite the mutual interdependence, men enjoyed more social power and status, and the problems due to such discrepancies are obvious. Ironically, fully complementary relationships may be very stable, and studies show that they may be quite satisfying for those who desire distinct role definitions within relationships. Many relationships are predicated on complementary structures: teacher-student; parent-child; supervisor-employee. These relationships emphasize differences. If based on expert, legitimate, or reward power, they can be efficient and harmonious. In other instances, these relationships stagnate and prohibit personal growth.

In symmetrical relationship structures, each person strives for the same amount of power and status and has an equal share of responsibilities. Individuals in these relationships are very independent. Emotional and social links are shared values, life philosophies, and common experiences. Studies show that satisfaction tends to be lower for couples in such relationships, and the couples tend to have fewer children. Symmetrical relationships, however, are the structure of most friendships. Differences are minimized in symmetrical relationships, but the parties can become very competitive when equality is constantly negotiated. As a result, the relationships are often less stable and are prone to hostility and stress.

Parallel structures provide moderate interdependence and distributed power in relationships. Partners define themselves as equal, but each has differing amounts of power and authority in certain realms based on each party's area of competence. Parallel relationships are actually a blend of the complementary and the symmetrical. In certain areas, one partner will assume the role of expert while the other willingly takes the role of subordinate. On a different issue, the roles may be reversed. Alternatively, some issues will be resolved by each person taking symmetrical roles. Parallel relationships are thus marked by flexibility and a focus on understanding what each person's expectations are in particular situations. Blending expert and referent power usually characterizes parallel relationships.

Compliance-Seeking Messages

Compliance-gaining research focuses on influence in interpersonal, face-to-face contexts—attempting to find what strategies are most effective in getting people to comply with requests. Robert Gass and John Seiter argue that this is one of the top areas of research in communication.[17] Some compliance-gaining techniques are very obvious, such as offering rewards or threatening punishment, while others are more subtle, such as persuading another to comply by establishing one's expertise or credibility. Not all strategies are appropriate in all situations. Power imbalance, intimacy, relational consequences, degree of resistance, and perception of benefits are several situational factors that affect which strategies are appropriate.[18] Some scholars would argue that all compliance-gaining strategies are persuasive—that is, intentional verbal and nonverbal attempts to influence the beliefs, attitudes, values, or behaviors of others. All the strategies are grounded in some form of interpersonal power.

Erwin Bettinghaus and Michael Cody have developed a useful typology of strategies for persuading people to comply with one's wishes.[19] There are seven general categories in their typology. *Direct requests* are the most common strategy of getting others to do what we want them to do. The context and social dynamics of the situation affect compliance with direct requests. Responding to a friend or boss is different than responding to a total stranger. In addition, the size or magnitude of the request impacts compliance.

Rationality strategies involve providing reasons and evidence to support one's request. The supporting data legitimize the request as well as provide motivation for compliance. This general strategy works well when making requests of strangers or of fellow workers. Providing details develops trust and rapport and does not obligate the requester beyond the necessity to provide good reasons.

Exchange strategies seek some mutual benefit for complying with a request. These strategies may be as simple as trading favors ("I'll drive today if you drive tomorrow") or as elaborate as negotiating the exchange of money or more tangible items.

Manipulation strategies are more varied and complex. They seek compliance through emotional appeals. The most common is to "butter up" an individual prior to making a request. The use of high praise and flattery may enhance compliance. This strategy can fail, however, if the praise and flattery are viewed as shallow or insincere. Inspirational appeals are attempts to arouse enthusiasm by appealing to an individual's values, ideals, aspirations, hopes, and dreams. Another tactic, especially in the workplace, is to demonstrate sufficient competence, worth, and likability to produce trust and confidence in one's judgment. A strong and favorable image provides motivation and justification for others to comply with various requests. However, this strategy can evolve into an expertise strategy, which is somewhat coercive. The full and only justification for the request for compliance is based on one's knowledge and expertise. Rewards are another form of manipulation strategies; for example, a car dealer can offer a bag of popcorn and a beverage. The most common form of manipulation is to make a promise for future favors if compliance occurs. Negative emotional appeals can also gain compliance. Displays of anger, disappointment, and hurt often force compliance through guilt. Negative appeals are very effective in the short term but may hinder future compliance.

Coercive strategies employ the use of negative sanctions and threats for non-compliance. These are the most extreme and harsh tactics. While certainly effective, they do not enhance future compliance and may decrease motivation for cooperation even with simple requests.

Indirect strategies involve dropping hints about a desired behavior without actually making a direct request. Coalition tactics involve using the support of others or specific groups to convince the target to agree. For example, stating that it is important to have the phones answered immediately when the store opens or mentioning that the phones start ringing even before the store opens may motivate employees to arrive to work and be at their desks a few minutes early every day. The key is to provide enough information, needs, or desires so that the target will recognize the desired behavior.

The final category of compliance strategies identified by Bettinghaus and Cody is *emotional appeals,* involving love and affection. These appeals are more intimate and are based on personal commitments. An example would be appealing to your parents to take better care of themselves or to get regular physical examinations because of your love for them or personal desire for their well-being.

Situational factors influence compliance.[20] The degree of intimacy is a powerful factor affecting our willingness to comply with requests. The more intimate the relationship, the more we tend to rely on emotional appeals. Compliance-gaining strategies also vary with the degree of dominance in the relationship. A subordinate tends to use nonconfrontational strategies and rational or indirect appeals with a superior. Superiors use more direct tactics, since they have more power in the relationship. Similarly, the response to resistance also depends on the nature of the relationship. Threats are most likely when there is a power differential and when one is not afraid of putting an interpersonal relationship at risk.

The context of a request is an important consideration, as are prior interactions with the individual and our own personal motives. We comply with requests for a multitude of reasons. We may respond to a superior's request not out of fear of sanctions but out of respect. We may respond to a friend's request out of a sense of loyalty and value rather than out of an anticipated exchange of future favors. The strategic dimensions of a request or compliance may not be apparent from the verbal statement.

It is important to remember that one-shot persuasive attempts are not very successful. It generally takes several attempts. Studies show that a succession of influence tactics are best.[21] These tactics are called *sequential influence techniques*. One such technique is the *foot-in-the-door* tactic. This tactic assumes that people will comply with a second, larger request if they first agree to a smaller initial request. Scholars find that this technique is more successful if the request is prosocial, that is, it benefits someone other than the requestor. The effectiveness of the size of the request is less certain. It appears that both too small and too large initial requests may inhibit acceptance of the second request.[22] Another technique is the *door-in-the-face* tactic. Here, the first request is so large that it is certain to be declined. The second, smaller request is granted, which is what the person wanted in the first place. The basis of this tactic is to start high and scale down. Another example of multiple attempts at compliance is called *low balling*. With this tactic, compliance is obtained by starting low and then scaling up or adding to the original requests. The difference among all of these examples is the magnitude of the initial request.

How does one resist persuasion? There are several strategies that might be successful. Nonnegotiation is the overt refusal to comply. Identity management is the strategy of manipulating images of the other person—for example, responding to a request with "I would never ask you to do such a thing." Justifying is the process of pointing out the potential negative outcomes of compliance. Finally, negotiation is the process of proposing alternatives to the request. For example, you could agree to cook dinner tonight if you did not have to do so tomorrow night.[23] Interpersonal persuasion is challenging, difficult, and complex. It is also a daily occurrence. The nature of the relationship is the key to strategy selection.

Conflict

Peter Kellett and Diana Dalton define interpersonal conflict as "interaction between people expressing opposing interests, views, or opinions."[24] Resistance to persuasion can lead to open conflict just as open conflict can lead to attempts at persuasion. The process of persuasion assumes differences of attitudes, beliefs, values, and behavior among people. Therein lie the seeds of conflict. The fact of the matter is that conflict is not an external reality but an increased perception of incompatible differences, the loss of perceptions of credibility, and the dissolution of perceived similarity.[25] Communication plays a dual role in conflict and conflict management. Communication—the particular verbal and nonverbal symbols chosen—probably created the original conflict. Improperly managed, more communication may worsen the conflict. On the other hand, skillful communication may also be the only path to ending or lessening the problem.

Today it is increasingly difficult to have disagreements without anger or hostility. Talk shows and the evening news broadcast images of international conflict, hate, and anger. Since most of us feel uncomfortable in conflict situations, we often blindly follow the models of behavior seen at home, with friends, or displayed by the media. In an increasingly strident society, the differences between disagreement and conflict are often forgotten, which can be disastrous for relationships. Disagreements are rather common, but they do not need to escalate into conflict. The communication strategies one chooses often determine whether disagreements are resolved or conflicts erupt. As William Cupach and Daniel Canary advise, "Communication provides the means by which we recognize and express conflict. In addition, communication most often distinguishes productive conflict from destructive conflict."[26] The more competent we are as communicators, the more likely we can manage conflict so that it does not harm our interpersonal relationships. Indeed, "conflict necessarily involves interpersonal influence and the use of strategies to establish, reinforce, or alter others' thoughts, emotions, and behaviors."[27]

Tolerance for disagreement differs among people. In addition, the degree of friendship and likability between individuals affects the likelihood of disagreement growing into conflict. Conflict, of course, can lead to relationship deterioration and even dissolution. However, interpersonal conflict can also force people to examine a problem and to work toward a solution that would not be reached if the conflict did not surface. If productive conflict management strategies are utilized, the relationship may well emerge from the encounter stronger and more satisfying.[28]

There are several different levels and different types of conflict. There can be interpersonal conflicts over *specific behaviors*, such as what movie to see on Friday night or whether to serve pork or beef. Another level of conflict is *relational roles*, such as who is willing to commit to taking the relationship to the next level or whether a partner should accept a job in another city. The third level is conflict about *personal characteristics and attitudes*, such as political preferences or jealous behavior.[29] *Content* conflicts are the most common type of conflict involving disagreement over facts, definitions, goals, or interpretation of information. More interaction between the parties is critical in solving content conflicts. More interaction often results in more mutual understanding. Sometimes the interaction reveals that the differences are not so great as originally believed. Such cases could be labeled pseudoconflicts because perceived differences are greater than the actual incompatibility.

Ego conflicts are potentially the most harmful. If proving that one has superior power, knowledge, and expertise is linked to the outcome of the conflict, the possibilities for a mutually satisfying resolution are slim. More interaction alone will have little impact on resolving ego conflicts. *Value* conflicts are the most difficult to solve. Recall from chapter 6 that values rest at the core of our being and are stable ideals that most of us will not readily change. Finding strategies to convince others to adopt our values can be difficult, if not impossible. Indeed, depending on the values in conflict, these types of conflicts can also be the most intense or violent.

There are many different ways people cope with adversity and conflict. Some people are very passive. In situations of conflict they are reluctant to state their opinions or feelings. More specifically, some individuals withdraw physically or psychologically, thus removing themselves from the situation. This strategy, of course, does not address or solve the conflict. Others surrender or give in to the opposition in order to avoid further conflict or to spare themselves emotional turmoil. They may even submit to demands regardless of the consequences. While this may seem sensitive to the feelings of others, it is really being dishonest and often causes resentment and anger to build up internally. It is better to deal with conflict than to hold feelings of hurt and anger inside.

Other people become more aggressive in confrontational situations. They lash out with highly charged, emotional responses. Aggressive behavior tends to be judgmental, dogmatic, and coercive. Outright displays of aggression are likely to result in lose-lose situations. Such behaviors are not in the best interest of a relationship and may escalate the degree of hostility. Finally, some people adopt assertive behavior. Here the person stands up for him- or herself by expressing opinions and feelings— while keeping the potential response of the receiver in mind. In short, assertive people employ persuasive techniques, including discussion and negotiation.

The essence of interpersonal persuasion involves strategies of bargaining and negotiation. Craig Johnson and Michael Hackman distinguish between the two concepts.[30] For them, bargaining is a "win-lose" situation. Bargaining often involves an adversarial relationship—one or more parties taking rather extreme positions. The bargaining process also involves clashes of wills, demands for concessions, the use of threats, and sometimes even deception. Negotiation, according to Johnson and Hackman, is a process of problem solving often resulting in a "win-win" situation. The focus is on a common goal, not emotional clashes or a test of wills. Objectivity and fairness are important characteristics of the negotiation process.

They describe four basic steps in the negotiation process. First, separate the people from the problem so that the focus is on the issue at question, not the egos or personalities of the individuals involved. If the problem becomes personal, then solving the conflict will be most difficult. Second, focus on the interests of those involved, not their positions. Another way to view this step is to focus on the end result—the mutual goal of the individuals—and to work from there. Third, invent options for mutual gain. Time spent brainstorming possible solutions or resolutions to problems or conflict is a good tactic that reveals alternatives. Finally, use mutually agreed-upon objective criteria to determine the terms of resolution.[31] Ultimately, successful negotiation results from fostering a climate of cooperation while reducing one of competition. Characteristics of a cooperative climate include open and honest communication, an emphasis on similarities or items of commonality, portrayals of trust, mutual problem solving, and a reduction of conflicting interests.[32]

Some people are naturally resistant to any persuasive effort. Those who are highly ego-involved in an issue or those who possess an extreme conviction or position on an issue will not be open to opposing views. In addition, those who are rigid, authoritarian, and older tend to be less open to persuasive attempts. Persuasion is also difficult when listeners have been rewarded for their positions in the past and are unfamiliar with the speaker's background and opinions.

In terms of your own persuasive efforts, there are specific communication styles or behaviors that encourage conflict and thus should be avoided. First, avoid negative, derogatory labels for the actions of others (such as bad, silly, crazy, etc.). Second, avoid personal attacks. Third, avoid presenting "all or none" distinctions or alternatives; they polarize the disagreement, reducing the likelihood of a cooperating solution. The essential ingredient in persuasion is to keep the lines of communication open. People who have not firmly committed to one action or position are more receptive to calmly reasoned presentations. Fourth, avoid speaking in broad generalities. Always provide specific facts and examples to support arguments. Fifth, avoid speaking from an authoritarian perspective. Remember, the best solution is created jointly, in collaboration with the other person. Position the discussion as an exploration of alternative perspectives, not a debate on values. Finally, avoid emotional verbal and nonverbal communications. Emotional outbursts dilute arguments by redirecting attention to the outbursts rather than to the arguments. Aggression, hostility, tension, or rivalry seldom help in accomplishing long-term goals and objectives.

There are numerous suggestions for managing conflict. They generally revolve around good practices of persuasion and human communication. For example, Kellett and Dalton suggest four interaction skills that can help you to negotiate and manage interpersonal conflict. *Responsive listening* requires a conscious, genuine effort to hear and process what the other individual is saying without interruption.

CALVIN AND HOBBES

Perception checking involves using paraphrases to gauge whether you are correctly interpreting the thoughts and feelings of the other person. *Value clarification* is an attempt to understand the assumptions and objectives of the other person. Sometimes our preconceptions or assumptions are incorrect. These skills help determine the content goals (what each party wants) and the relational goals (how interdependent the parties are) in the conflict. The fourth interaction skill involves the need to be included and respected. If one or both parties feel that their identities are threatened (a loss of face), the conflict can escalate beyond the original disagreement. *Face management skills* (such as helping others increase their self-esteem, displaying goodwill, avoiding criticism) are ways to deal with conflict while showing respect for the other individual.[33]

William Wilmot and Joyce Hocker suggest that the dialogue process is an act of commitment to both the relationship and to one's own principles. Dialogue involves actively listening to understand the other viewpoint and having a deep respect for the other person.[34] The following communication strategies contribute to effective dialogue and help create an atmosphere of trust.

- Speak your mind and your heart
- Listen well
- Summarize and ask questions
- Express strong feelings appropriately
- Avoid harmful statements
- Give and take

Timothy Borchers identifies four variables in interpersonal conflicts: The *attributes* (personalities, needs, attitudes, etc.) of the parties in conflict; the *conflict issues* (causes of the dispute and the positions involved); *relationship variables* (degree of trust, power, interdependency); and *contextual factors* (the environment in which the conflict occurs). Avoiding a defensive climate is one step toward creating a positive atmosphere for conflict resolution. Critical evaluations, attempts to control the other party, hidden agendas, and rigid adherence to one's own position are all examples of behaviors that create a negative climate.[35] In contrast, the following help create a supportive climate.

Description: Use evidence to describe the issues or positions; do not use emotional terms or appeals. Be as specific as possible in defining the problem.

Problem orientation: Focus on the task at hand without attacking the other person. Deal with one aspect, issue, or factor at a time.

Empathy: Make an effort to understand the feelings of the other person.

DeVito describes a five-step model of conflict management.[36] The first is to define the problem in very specific terms. It is important for both parties to agree as to the nature, scope, or form of conflict. The next step is to examine possible solutions. There is usually more than one way to solve a conflict. Some solutions are more desirable than others; participants weigh the costs and benefits that each solution will entail for both parties. Participants are looking for "win-win" solutions where both parties feel good about the proposed resolution. While there is no such thing as a perfect solution, interaction contributes to consensus. The next step is to test the solution mentally. We reflect on how we feel about the solution and its implications. Next we evaluate the solution. Is this the best alternative? Will it really solve the problem? This step focuses more on operational considerations while the others focus on personal, emotional responses. Finally, one must either accept or reject the solution.

It would be a mistake to view all conflict as bad. Conflict can be productive, especially if each party gains something. The difference between helpful and non-helpful conflict is "the extent to which it dominates interaction and the degree to which it is or is not balanced by more positive communication."[37] Conflict can establish social interactional boundaries; reduce tensions; clarify roles, objectives, or differences; and provide the basis for negotiation and continued interaction.

Several strategies help make conflict productive rather than nonproductive. First, learn to ask good questions in order to explore all aspects of the conflict. Second, make understanding conflicts a priority. Third, attempt to learn from your previous conflicts or other people's conflicts. And finally, learn to manage conflicts more effectively through strategies of negotiation.[38]

Kellett and Dalton identify several myths about conflict. The first is that "more communication always creates more clarity." The quality of the communication is much more important than the quantity. Focus on defining the problem and contributing to mutual understanding. The second myth is that "there is always an answer or solution to a conflict." Some conflicts cannot be resolved; others are difficult and require persistence. The third myth is that "managing conflict is primarily about doing things differently." The basis for many conflicts is not the specific behavior but the attitudes and feelings surrounding the issue. Unless the emotional and relationship dimensions are addressed, a change in behavior about the content issue will not resolve the conflict. The final myth is that "peace is the absence of conflict." If conflict is submerged, the relationship may appear to be peaceful, but the areas of disagreement continue unabated. Unless the conflict surfaces and is addressed with quality thinking and understanding, the parties cannot move forward."[39]

Gerald Miller finds conflict desirable because humans are creative through conflict; it is also a form of human relationship or contact.[40] Conflict, according to Saul Alinski, is an essential element of life. He asserts, "Life is conflict and in conflict you're alive."[41] From this brief overview, we can characterize conflict as: inevitable, based on communication, both harmful and beneficial, varying in degree based on communication style, and sometimes incapable of resolution.

Gender Differences

Differences in communication behavior develop because of cultural and societal influences plus individual backgrounds and experiences. Generally, there are several areas of gender differences in conversation and discourse, including voice, pronunciation, intonation, choice of words, argumentation styles, lexicon, syntax, interactional and conversational behavior, as well as visual features and nonverbal communication.[42] For more than a decade, scholars have debated about the degree of genuine gender differences. Most scholars recognize that differences between men and women are both biologically and culturally based. However, the causes, implications, and magnitude of differences are in dispute.[43] Furthermore, other identity factors (such as ethnicity, geographical location, and economic status) may account for some of the differences. For example, scholars are discovering that differences in ethnic and cultural backgrounds contribute more to overall differences than does gender. Our purpose here is to look at the role of communication.

The research literature describes masculine and feminine styles of communication. One style is not superior to another, nor do they necessarily correlate with specific sexes. Some women may be socialized in the masculine style while some

men may show more characteristics of a feminine style of communication. Deborah Tannen urges that recognizing the differences between men and women means seeking understanding—not placing blame or rendering judgment. As Tannen observes, "recognizing gender differences frees individuals from the burden of individual pathology. . . . If we can sort out differences based on conversational style, we will be in a better position to confront real conflicts of interest—and to find a shared language in which to negotiate them."[44]

Masculine and feminine styles identify specific communication behaviors, goals, and rules. Essentially, men and women differ in frequency of talk; with whom they talk; amount of disclosure; and use, purpose, and content of talk. From a social perspective, women speak and hear a language of connection and intimacy. Men speak and hear a language of status and independence. For women, the language of conversation is one of rapport, a way to develop and maintain relationships. For men, talk is more "report talk," a means to preserve independence and to maintain status in the social hierarchy.[45] The masculine style is characterized as competitive, assertive, and task oriented. Communication tends to be more individualistic, instrumental, and reserved. In contrast, the feminine style is characterized as cooperative, supportive, and relational. Communication tends to be more expressive and focused on interpersonal relationships.[46]

There are several specific behaviors associated with the different styles of communication. Men tend to interrupt others more frequently, to talk for longer periods of time, to be less self-disclosing, and to control the situation by offering opinions, suggestions, and information. Women tend to disclose more information about themselves, use more euphemisms and emotional terms, provide greater frequency and longer duration of eye contact, and are more likely to respond, offering agreement or disagreement.[47]

Men and women also tend to differ in the amount of listening or turn taking in conversations. From a role perspective, men lecture and women listen. Through listening, women seek to build rapport and establish a closer relationship with others. Women use listening cues as signs of paying attention and interest. Men use fewer listening cues, are more likely to change topics, and use less relational elements in general conversation. Men are not showing disrespect but are reflecting a more pragmatic style of communication.[48]

According to Shari Kendall and Deborah Tannen, the workplace provides several unique constraints that impact gender communication: a hierarchical ranking system, a history of greater male participation, requirements for evaluation of performance, and the requirement to interact regularly with others.[49] Within the workplace, men are more likely to speak in ways that call attention to themselves and to receive credit for contributions. Women, in contrast, are more likely to preface statements with a disclaimer, speak at a louder volume, and be more succinct in speaking. Women also tend to minimize status differences between themselves, while men tend to use rhetorical strategies that reinforce status differences.

Conversational conventions are particularly noticeable in the workplace environment. For example, men often use opposition rituals such as banter, joking, teasing, and playful put-downs. In contrast, women's rituals tend to focus on the nature of the relationships by maintaining an appearance of equality, taking into account the effect of the exchange, and attempting to downplay displays of authority.[50] In communication styles, men tend to be more direct, sometimes to the point of rudeness. Women, on the other hand, are more indirect in making requests of others. The degree of conversational directness communicates power and comfort with one's authority. Men are more likely to be indirect when expressing a weakness or an error, or when sharing a problem.[51] Of course, difficulties arise when various rituals and strategies are misunderstood. Male oppositional strategies may appear hostile and arrogant to some. Women using conversational strategies to demonstrate empathy and to avoid appearing boastful may be interpreted as displaying a lack of confidence and questionable competence.[52]

Women and men also differ in nonverbal messages. Women smile more, stand closer, and touch more often than men. Men extend their bodies, literally taking up greater areas of space than women. When speaking, both men and women look at men more than at women.[53]

Finally, men and women differ in how they engage in and resolve conflict. Men tend to withdraw from conflict situations. In contrast, women want to confront conflict directly, talk about it, resolve it, deal with it in an immediate fashion. In arguments, women tend to display more emotion and men more logic. In the literature, this is referred to as "conflict feelers" and "conflict thinkers."[54]

John Gray (who gained national attention with his book *Men Are from Mars, Women Are from Venus*) advises:

> Without a positive understanding of our differences, many possibilities for cooperation and mutual trust and respect are overlooked and go untapped. Too often men do not recognize the value that women bring to the workplace, while women mistrust the support that is possible to receive from men. Through understanding our differences in a more positive light, both men and women at all levels of the workplace can begin to appreciate each other more."[55] To improve the interpersonal communication between the sexes, Tannen recommends taking "each other on their own terms rather than applying the standards of one group to the behavior of the other.[56]

Perhaps "women could learn from men to accept some conflict and difference without seeing it as a threat to intimacy, and many men could learn from women to accept interdependence without seeing it as a threat to their freedom."[57] Tannen concludes her best-selling book with the notion that "understanding the other's ways of talking is a giant leap across the communication gap between women and men, and a giant step toward opening lines of communication."[58]

Culture and Diversity

Culture encompasses all the integral components of an individual's life: language and gestures; personal appearance and social relationships; religion; philosophy; values; courtship, marriage, and family customs; food and recreation; economic systems; and government, to name just a few.[59] Intercultural communication is the study of face-to-face interactions among people of diverse cultures,[60] and it is increasingly important as technology makes it easy to communicate with others anywhere in the world. Examples abound where businesses have generated communication problems across cultures:

- Chevrolet failed to successfully market its Nova automobile in Latin American countries. "No va" in Spanish means "does not go" or "it doesn't run."

- In Brazil, Braniff Airlines promoted "rendezvous lounges" on its flights. In Portuguese, rendezvous is "a place to have sex."

- Kentucky Fried Chicken's slogan "finger-licking good" in China was translated as "eat your fingers off."[61]

Fred Jandt argues that communication and culture are inseparable.[62] For him, successful intercultural communication requires message skills, behavioral flexibility, interaction management, and social skills.

> Message skills refers to the ability to understand and use the language and feedback. Behavioral flexibility is the ability to select an appropriate behavior in diverse contexts. Interaction management means handling the procedural aspects of conversation, such as the ability to initiate a conversation. Interaction

management emphasizes a person's other-oriented ability to interaction, such as attentiveness and responsiveness. Social skills are empathy and identity maintenance. Empathy is the ability to think the same thoughts and feel the same emotions as the other person. Identity maintenance is the ability to maintain a counterpart's identity by communicating back an accurate understanding of that person's identity.[63]

While we do not have the space to discuss cultural sensitivity in depth, some general principles are outlined below.

- Address people of other cultures with the same respect you would like to receive.
- Describe your perceptions of the world as accurately as possible; expect to discover that perceptions vary from culture to culture.
- Encourage people of other cultures to express their uniqueness.
- Attempt to emphasize commonalities of cultural beliefs and values rather than focusing on differences.
- Practice self-monitoring behaviors; be aware of proper and appropriate verbal and nonverbal messages, since verbal and nonverbal communication patterns vary from culture to culture.
- Avoid stereotypical and prejudicial associations, descriptions, or assumptions.

Leadership

The study of leadership continues to grow; universities are adding academic majors and minors in leadership studies. Few hold to the belief that "leaders are born." Instead, most believe that leadership is a set of skills and values that can be taught and that becoming an effective leader is a lifelong process. Successful leaders are willing to interact with others and have developed effective communication skills.[64]

Although the concept of leadership is difficult to define, we agree with Michael Hackman and Craig Johnson that "leadership shares all of the features of human communication."[65] Leaders use symbols to create reality, communicate about the past/present/future, and often use persuasion to accomplish goals. Leadership may be viewed as a special form of human communication. At the core of nearly all definitions of the term is influence. Hackman and Johnson define leadership as "human (symbolic) communication, which modifies the attitudes and behaviors of others in order to meet shared group goals and needs."[66]

Legal authority or a designated title does not guarantee leadership status. Ultimately, the role of leader is granted by the follower; as a result, leadership is a special circumstance of interpersonal communication. Although certain aspects of leadership are more suited to group, organizational, or mass contexts, the foundation is the relationship between each leader and follower. Research identifies traits of leaders that relate to ability, sociability, motivation, and communication skills. In terms of ability, leaders exceed other group members in the areas of intelligence, scholarship, insight, and verbal facility. In terms of sociability, leaders are more dependable, active, cooperative, and popular. In areas of motivation, leaders exceed others in terms of initiative, persistence, and enthusiasm.[67]

According to Hackman and Johnson, the following communication strategies enhance leadership effectiveness: develop perceptions of credibility, build and use power bases effectively, empower followers, make effective use of verbal and non-verbal influence cues, develop positive expectations for others, foster creativity, manage change, gain compliance, negotiate productive solutions, develop argumentative competence, and adapt to cultural differences.[68] We discuss many of these activities in describing the leaders of social movements in chapter 9.

Styles of leadership impact both the effectiveness and the popularity of the leader.[69] An authoritarian style exhibits group control, direction, and conflict. Although this style may result in increased productivity and task performance, it may also result in less satisfaction and more aggression among followers. A more democratic style of leadership attempts to involve followers in setting goals and encourages group interaction and teamwork. This leadership style tends to foster better follower morale, participation, innovation, and commitment. Communication skills and abilities are essential in developing and maintaining a democratic leadership style. The laissez-faire style of communication characterizes a leader who is easygoing and offers little guidance or support. As a result, productivity, cohesiveness, and satisfaction suffer. Some would argue that this style appeals to individuals who value autonomy and self-rule. If working with peers similar in rank, age, or experience, the laissez-faire style would be effective. The various styles are summarized in figure 8.2.[70]

Figure 8.2   The Effects of Authoritarian, Democratic, and Laissez-Faire Leadership Communication Styles

Authoritarian Leadership	Democratic Leadership	Laissez-Faire Leadership
Increases productivity when the leader is present.	Lowers turnover and absenteeism rates.	Decreases innovation when leaders abdicate, but increases innovation when leaders provide guidance as requested.
Produces more accurate solutions when leader is knowledgeable.	Increases follower satisfaction.	
Is more positively accepted in larger groups.	Increases follower participation.	Decreases follower motivation and satisfaction when leaders abdicate.
	Increases follower commitment to decisions.	
Enhances performance on simple tasks and decreases performance on complex tasks.	Increases innovation.	Results in feelings of isolation and a decrease in participation when leaders abdicate.
Increases aggression levels among followers.	Increases a follower's perceived responsibility to a group or organization.	Decreases quality and quantity of output when leaders abdicate.
Increases turnover rates.		Increases productivity and satisfaction for highly motivated experts.

Some leaders have a task communication orientation; others focus on an interpersonal communication orientation. Task-oriented communication stresses the successful completion of task assignments. The concern for getting the work done is greater than the concern for individuals. In contrast, the interpersonal orientation emphasizes relationships and follower feelings and general welfare. The interpersonal orientation incorporates many of the characteristics of the democratic style: teamwork, cooperation, and supportive communication.[71]

Followers also play an important role in the leadership process and need to develop their communication skills as well. Robert Kelley identifies three sets of skills that characterize exemplary followership. First, followers add value to the organization and to meeting its objectives. They are committed and share in the organization's values; they actively seek the skills necessary to ensure the success of the organization. Second, good followers fully integrate themselves within the organizational social structure by joining teams and building relational bridges to others throughout the organization. Finally, exemplary followers are guided by courteous and ethical behavior at all times. Such behavior reduces internal conflict and increases morale.[72]

Do you want to be a leader? If you do, Rudolph and Kathleen Verderber suggest that you be knowledgeable about particular tasks, work harder than anyone else, be personally committed to group goals and needs, be willing to be decisive at key moments in the discussion, interact freely with others, and develop skill in maintenance functions as well as in task functions.[73]

CONTEXTS OF INTERPERSONAL PERSUASION
▲

Every interaction takes place within a specific situation or environment. We conclude the chapter with three specialized situations of interpersonal persuasion: organizations, interviews, and sales.

Organizations

In the twenty-first century, changes occur rapidly in the workplace. Markets are global and the workforce is diverse. Technology impacts every facet of an organization, from product development and manufacturing to mass marketing and product delivery. Likewise, the workforce is very different than it was just two decades ago. Employees are more mobile, less loyal to corporate America, and desire more balance among career, family, and community. Job satisfaction often outweighs the size of the paycheck. Communication has never been more important or critical to the very survival of organizations.

Organizations are usually defined as collectivities of individuals organized to achieve some purpose or goal. In some cases, the purpose may be economic—to produce some product or to provide a particular service that can be sold in the marketplace. In other cases, the purpose of the group may be more social—people brought together because of common beliefs, ideology, or community function. Hackman and Johnson argue that "organizations are formed through the process of communication . . . communication is not contained within the organization. Instead, communication *is* the organization."[74]

Because all organizations are purposeful and structured, they impact the nature of human communication in very specific ways. The notion of organization involves concepts such as rules, roles, power, specialization, leadership, hierarchy, and control, to name only a few. The structure of organizations often masks the fact that a majority of the communication interactions that take place are interpersonal. The nature of the relationships is often affected by the hierarchical nature of superior/subordinate roles and by the culture of the organizational environment, but the theories and approaches to interpersonal persuasion still apply.

Today, corporate communication includes a number of internal and external communication activities, such as public relations, investor relations, employee relations, community relations, advertising, media relations, labor relations, government relations, technical communications, training and employee development, marketing communications, and management communications. According to Michael Goodman, executives use corporate communication to lead, motivate, persuade, and inform both employees and the public.[75]

Communication activities within organizations can be formal or informal. Formal communication activities are those officially sanctioned by the organization and are usually task oriented. These include items like memos, policy statements, and newsletters. Informal communication activities are those that occur among the individuals of an organization. Some would argue that informal communication activities are sometimes more important than formal organizational communication activities.

The flow of communication is usually characterized by the direction from which it originates. Upward communication consists of messages sent from lower levels of the organization to upper levels of the hierarchy. For managers, upward communication is the primary source of information about worker problems and issues. As a process, upward communication encourages employee participation and provides an outlet for conflict and tension. Upward communication, however, is difficult. Workers are usually reluctant to share negative messages with superiors. Mid-level supervisors may actively discourage upward messages because they feel threatened. They may feel that upward communication intrudes on their power and jeopardizes their job security. Thus, how one communicates dissatisfaction or general problems becomes a serious dilemma for employees at all levels of an organization.

Downward communication—messages from higher to lower levels—is the most obvious and prevalent within organizations. It ranges from direct verbal orders to more formal activities such as employee performance evaluations. Downward communication provides the primary means for sharing job-related information and organizational goals and philosophies. The challenge, of course, is for downward communication to be respectful of employees and to enhance their job performance.

Lateral communication describes messages shared between equals (those at the same level in the hierarchy) within an organization. This form of communication is also very important. In addition to improving teamwork and worker morale, it facilitates task coordination and completion. It provides an informal network of employee support and information. Nevertheless, even lateral communication endeavors can be problematic. A lack of cooperation and trust among colleagues, as well as power-hungry peers, may sour the work environment.

Phillip Tompkins summarizes some of the research findings related to the flow of communication:[76]

1. Those higher in an organization communicate more while performing their jobs than do those lower in the organization.

2. Job responsibilities significantly impact the quantity and direction of communication activities.

3. Communication within organizations is usually initiated by the person of higher status.

4. Those of the same level or status within an organization are more likely than those of differing status to discuss problems and solutions.

5. Message content influences who will transmit it, who receives it, and message accuracy.

6. Job satisfaction, trust in superiors, and mobility aspirations influence willingness to engage in upward communication.

7. Physical proximity results in more interaction.

8. The number of interactions a person initiates within an organization is related to the number the person receives.

9. Most employees do not have the opportunity to send a great amount of information upward in their organizations.

10. Most employees receive their information through interpersonal, informal channels of communication.

Kathleen Reardon talks about three models of organization-employee interaction.[77] The first is called the *exchange model*. Organizational incentives and rewards provide employee motivation for productivity. In essence, the organization exchanges money, benefits, and social outlets in return for work performed. Employee participation is limited, and rules are seldom challenged. The second model is the *socialization model*. The organization actively persuades employees about the value of organizational goals and objectives. Corporate culture, peer pressure, and leadership by example are key factors in securing employee cooperation. While there is more individual autonomy, there is still little direct employee participation in the life of the organization. The final approach to organization-employee interaction is the *accommodation model*. Employees actively participate in shaping organizational rules as well as production goals. The structure of the organization attempts to maximize the skills, abilities, and unique characteristics of each employee. They become partners in the problem-solving and decision-making activities of the organization.

Eric Eisenberg and Harold Goodall argue that positive interpersonal relationships are crucial to the very survival of individuals, teams, and organizations. In fact, for them, positive interpersonal relationships at work are a necessity, not a luxury.[78] One of the important interpersonal interactions is with customers (specific strategies and techniques are discussed in the sales section of this chapter). Responsiveness, courtesy, and good listening skills are vital to positive customer service. Communicating with supervisors is another important interpersonal interaction on the job. Employees tend to choose one of four approaches when dealing with superiors: *ingratiating*—the employee is overly friendly and warm; *tactician*—the employee uses reason and evidence in support of statements and requests; *bystander*—the employee generally avoids contact with the supervisor; and *shotgun*—where the employee relies on a variety of approaches. Some scholars suggest that discussing nonwork issues with superiors adds stability, trust, and predictability to the relationship.[79]

From a strategic perspective, Eisenberg and Goodall suggest the tactic of *managing up*—a performance that makes the boss look good. The best way to do this is through advocacy, "learning how to read a superior's needs and preferences and designing arguments to accomplish goals."[80] They suggest several guiding principles: plan a strategy; determine why the supervisor should listen, or connect your argument to something important to the boss; tailor the arguments to the supervisor's style and characteristics; assess the supervisor's technical knowledge of the issue; build coalitions within the organization; and develop your own presentation skills.[81]

Today most employees in the United States work in some type of team-based unit. There are numerous classifications of teams. Usually they fall within three general categories: project teams, work teams, and quality-improvement teams. Project teams are organized around the design and development of new products or services. Work teams are most often responsible for the entire task process that delivers a product or service to a client. Quality-improvement teams focus on customer satisfaction and team performance evaluation leading to reduce costs.[82]

Through interaction with others, we begin to develop various organizational roles. Within teams, individuals usually assume one of three different roles. In the *task role*, members summarize and evaluate ideas, playing a major part in idea generation and performance progression. The *maintenance role* is when members are active in reducing tension or conflict to maintain team harmony and morale. The *self-centered role* is harmful to teams. The individual dominates all aspects of the project and communication exchanges.[83] As is the case in small groups, members will play a variety of roles during task performance and completion. Successful teams are characterized by exhibiting mutual respect among members, a high degree of cooperation, and self-monitoring behaviors that focus on others rather than self.

Today, scholars are approaching organizational communication from a cultural perspective, emphasizing the importance of establishing the corporate climate, socializing employees, and establishing expectations of behavior. For example, how does the corporate culture of McDonald's differ from that of Burger King? IBM from Hewlett-Packard? One author learned very quickly how corporate culture can differ while working in advertising. Some advertising agencies emphasize creativity while others focus on account management. Some agencies are more traditional in terms of offices and division of labor while others have no walls or assigned accounts. In the latter case, individuals work on numerous accounts, based on their area of expertise.

We can look at corporate culture along three dimensions.[84] The first is artifacts and patterns of behavior. This includes such elements as the corporate logo, the company's headquarters, annual reports, even the general business attire of the office staff, all of which provide the outward, observable manifestations of corporate beliefs and values. Artifacts revealing culture include architecture, furniture, technology, dress, written documents and art, to name just a few. How people address each other, for example, reveals aspects of formality, power relationships, and status.

The second dimension—corporate values and beliefs—reflect how things ought to be done in an organization. Slogans or ad campaigns, such as Ford Motor Company's "Quality is Job 1" or General Electric's "We bring good things to life," communicate corporate values. Of course, organizations don't actually have values, individuals do. The people who formed or who currently lead the company have a consensus about how things should be done or what the goals, priorities, and objectives should be. The corporate leader may exert a strong influence on values and hence on the organization's culture. Employees who share these values are recruited and hired, strengthening the values that pervade the corporate culture.

The third level of consideration, basic assumptions of the organization, is more abstract and difficult to assess. It requires analysis of the differences between what a company says and what it does. For example, poor treatment at a bank that advertises itself as warm and customer friendly may result in a loss of confidence and trust, two very important elements in the financial community.[85]

In a positive corporate culture, employees will understand the organization's vision, values, process of communication, nature of compensation, quality of work environment, and personnel decisions. Figure 8.3 provides statements for each category to ensure a healthy corporate culture.

To understand how some of the communication variables of content, direction, channel, and style relate to behavior and its impact on an organization's culture, consider the various possibilities in figure 8.4.

Change is an inevitable part of life; in addition, communication and change are intricately connected. As George Cheney, Lars Christensen, Ted Zorn, and Shiv Ganesh state, "Communication is more than a tool for change; *communication constitutes change.*"[86] Many organizations emphasize change in their mission statements. In addition, organizations face constant decisions about how to change to meet global demands or how to incorporate new technologies. For employees, change is a personal issue, not just one of policy or business. Thus, how change is communicated and implemented are important elements of corporate culture. In order to cope with change effectively, Michael Goodman suggests managers should share information honestly; involve employees in decisions; communicate about change initially in face-to-face interactions; allow for autonomy and flexibility; show appreciation for people's efforts; and consider the meaning and purpose of work for subordinates.[87] As Goodman observes, executives cannot "make plans without considering the strategic value of communication in day-to-day activity and in the long-term vision of the corporation."[88]

Figure 8.3   Positive Corporate Culture[89]

Vision
Management has a clear vision about the future direction of the organization.
The organizational vision is one all employees can support.

Values
Management models organizational values through their behavior.
Employees can clearly identify the organizational values.

Communication
At work, people freely pass on information that might be helpful to others.
Management listens attentively to the needs of employees.

Compensation
All employees share in the financial success of the organization.
Merit pay is based on clearly defined, objective data.

Work Environment
Management creates an environment free of harassment.
Personal information is kept confidential.

Personnel Decisions
Employees are aware of the career paths available to them.
Hiring, firing, promotions, and transfers are clearly linked to the objectives of the organization.

Figure 8.4   Communication Variables and Orientations

Variable	Orientations	Effect on Culture
Communication content	Task	Productivity important
	Social	Human relationships important
	Maintenance	Human relationships important
Communication direction	Downward	Authoritative; one-way communication
	Upward	Less authoritative; interactive
	Horizontal	Team oriented; interactive
Communication channel	Written	Productivity important; formal
	Electronic (phone, fax, e-mail)	Productivity important; less formal
	Face-to-face	Human relationships important
Communication style	Formal	Authoritative; task oriented
	Informal	Human relationships important

Sales

Selling can be viewed as a special form of interpersonal communication. In a sense, we are all salespeople whether advocating a specific position, idea, service, or product. Regardless of occupation, anyone who is successful is an effective salesperson. The basic appeals, strategies, and tactics of persuasion are essential to successful sales.

There are multiple approaches to sales. The *selling formula approach* treats all customers alike. Sales result from taking the customer through a series of mental states: attention, interest, desire, and action. The salesperson has a developed script or canned presentation. The idea is that there are certain product appeals or attributes that will be attractive to all individuals regardless of situation or context.

A more recent approach to sales assumes that purchases are made to satisfy needs. In order to make a sale, one must discover the customer's needs and demonstrate how the products or services will meet those needs. This *need-satisfaction approach* requires greater skills of conversation and persuasion. Because each customer is unique, the salesperson discovers through conversation which appeals to voice and which ones to avoid. There are three distinct phases to this process. In the need development phase of the conversation, the salesperson encourages the prospect to talk about his or her needs or requirements while actively listening to the information shared. As the salesperson gains insight into the customer's needs and desires relevant to the product or service, the conversation shifts to the need awareness phase of the conversation. The salesperson talks more, repeating the salient needs and observing whether the customer confirms the desires. In the final phase, need fulfillment, the salesperson demonstrates how the product or service will fully meet the needs discussed. In this phase, the seller is doing all the talking. Notice that in this approach, the sales pitch is tailored to the specific needs or requirements of the customer. It is critical for the salesperson to know the features of the product or service as well as how to phrase questions for the need-development phase. The goal is to control the interview without seeming to do so. The best way to obtain both customer participation and information is to ask questions.

Every sales transaction is based on some form of interpersonal relationship between customer and salesperson. The higher the risk or costs to both parties, the more involved the relationship. Dan O'Hair and Gustav Friedrich offer five basic rules of conduct that salespeople can employ to have successful customer relationships:[90]

1. Know the customer.
2. Take responsibility for customer satisfaction.
3. Avoid unresponsive behavior.
4. Employ effective communication skills.
5. Treat customers with respect.

Rolph Anderson offers a seven-stage model of personal selling.[91] The first stage is prospecting and qualifying—identifying potential customers based upon a set of criteria, such as financial capability, social rank, organizational authority, or general favorableness toward the product or service. Planning the sales call is the second stage. Five specific activities should be considered. (1) Establish the objective of the call: the motivation to generate sales, to develop a contact list, to maintain current customers, etc. (2) Choose a persuasive strategy: foot-in-the-door, door-in-the-face, need satisfaction, etc. (3) Plan for an effective and efficient meeting: do not waste the customer's time. (4) Prepare for the customer's reactions: give thought to how to handle objections likely to be raised. (5) Display confidence and professionalism: set a tone that will enhance the sales attempt.

The third stage is approaching the prospect, and the initial impression is critical. Verbal and nonverbal behaviors—from the firmness of the handshake, to how one is dressed, to the level of comfort with the interaction, to knowledge about the product or service—will determine how receptive the customer will be to the next stage. The fourth stage is making the sales presentation. After articulating the features and benefits of the product or service, the next stage is negotiating resistance or objections. To overcome objections, differentiate between valid objections about the product or service from excuses for avoiding a decision. Try to turn objections—which are an indication that the customer is seriously thinking about how the product or service might be used—into a positive: link price objectives with quality or proven customer service, for example. The sixth stage is closing the sale. The seventh and final stage is servicing the account. The old saying, "it is easier and less expensive to keep customers than to win new customers," highlights the importance of this stage.

The Million Dollar Round Table (MDRT) argues that the building of mutual trust is one of the most effective sales strategies. How do you build trust? The same way you do in any interpersonal relationship: by being yourself, being genuine, engaging in appropriate self-disclosure, and displaying empathy. The MDRT provides seven basic rules for closing a sale:[92]

- Establish your credibility.
- Know your product.
- Know your client.
- Keep it simple.
- Sell concepts and benefits.
- Communicate your enthusiasm, your certainty and your commitment.
- Take a chance, ask for the close.

There are several techniques used most often to close a sale. The *presumption technique* involves acting as if the deal is done, such as writing up an invoice or going to the cash register. The *choice technique* is based on closing the sale on a minor aspect of the product or service. In essence your presentation is offering choices among features and benefits of the product, rather than asking whether the customer intends to make a purchase. For example, the question asked may be, "Do you prefer an IBM compatible or a Macintosh?" The *inciter technique* is a last resort effort to close. The technique involves incentives such as free delivery, no interest, free gift, or some special discount. The rationale is to prevent the prospect from waiting until tomorrow to consider the purchase. The *report technique* is rather inventive. The salesperson shares a story that parallels the prospect's situation. The anecdote demonstrates how the purchase solved an identical problem.

Obviously, in order to maintain trust, the story or anecdote must be true, using real names, etc. Finally, one of the most common closing techniques is *comparison and contrast*. A precise and honest comparison of the features and benefits of one's product or service with a competing brand can result in a sale.[93]

While we mentioned how to handle objections briefly, this can be the most critical part of any sales presentation. There are several techniques salespeople use to handle objections. First, anticipate possible objections. The better you know the prospect and motivations, the better you can anticipate possible objections. This being the case, you can preempt specific questions or objections by addressing them within the body of the presentation. Another general rule is to answer objections immediately. If you hesitate or delay responding, the prospect will focus even more on the objection. However, there are two situations when delaying a response may be advantageous: when the objection is not related to the point under consideration and when questions about price are raised before you have completed your presentation.[94]

There are other successful techniques as well. One is called the *boomerang*, turning an objection into a reason for buying the product. Another is *I'm coming to that*, a tactic used when the salesperson wants to convey critical information before jumping to the point of objection. If they must concede the objection, they often will use a *yes, but* technique of quickly following the objection with an advantage or positive product attribute. The *offset* technique admits the validity of the objection but then follows with a superior point that more than compensates for the original objection. Sometimes by asking questions relevant to the objection, the salesperson forces the prospect to provide support or evidence for the objection. Finally, a simple *direct denial* can be effective by attributing the objection to a misunderstanding or wrong interpretation of information.[95]

In sales situations, you may encounter a difficult customer—one who is unsatisfied with a product or service or who may even be hostile. You have a responsibility not only to address the issue at hand but also to properly represent your organization. There are several things you can do in such difficult situations: let customers talk, reassure them that their concerns will be heard, do not personalize the issue (the anger is not aimed at you), acknowledge instances where the customer is correct, apologize and provide immediate corrective action when the company or yourself is at fault, and be sure to ask the customer to suggest how the problem or issue could be avoided in the future.[96]

We would be remiss if we did not highlight some of the problematic areas of sales in relationship to traditional persuasive theory. Especially in a democratic society, persuasion is based on the concept of informed choice. Despite the phrase *caveat emptor* (let the buyer beware), the ethical burden is on the persuader to ensure that products are fairly presented. There are also other issues to consider. Does the seller really believe in the product? Does the buyer really need the product or service? In terms of persuasion there is little difference between the selling of ideas and the selling of products. Both are important to our society and utilize the same tools of persuasion.

Interviews

In many ways the interviewing process is also a type of sale. When you interview for a job you are both the product and the salesperson. You need to be prepared to talk about your unique features and product benefits. Your resume and cover letter are just the first steps toward employment.

It is possible to argue that nearly all dyadic communication is a form of interviewing. Even in social conversation with another person there is the rotation of roles and the exchange of information that provides the basis for future transactions and behavior. However, here we are referring to a more formal, prescribed form of dyadic communication. Charles Stewart and William Cash define interviewing as "an interactional communication process between two parties, at least one of whom has a predetermined and serious purpose, that involves the asking and answering of questions."[97] The concepts key to this definition lie in the words "predetermined and serious purpose." Thus, according to Stewart and Cash, an interview is a formal communication transaction where one or both of the parties have specific behavioral objectives in mind (i.e., altering a belief, attitude, or action). Even mini-interviews—those that seek to elicit the opinions of colleagues, etc.—may mask a persuasive intent. The questioner may appear to have an open mind but may, in reality, have no intention of accepting the interviewee's position.

Today with almost instantaneous communication (such as e-mail, cell phones, and PDAs) are face-to-face interviews necessary? Stewart and Cash think they are essential and offer several examples of when face-to-face interviews are most beneficial.[98] If it is necessary to verify that the interviewee is who he or she claims to be or if it is necessary to challenge or to ask for clarification about information on an application, face-to-face interactions are an excellent discovery tool. In addition, much valuable information is revealed through the nonverbal dimensions of a face-to-face conversation. Answers to questions in face-to-face interviews are often longer and more detailed than in written questionnaires. Interviewees are more willing to share personal information in face-to-face conversations, thereby increasing the likelihood of revealing their attitudes, beliefs, and values.

In an interview situation, the interviewer and interviewee share dual roles. In the best interviews, participants freely rotate between the roles. Without such an exchange, participants sacrifice power, control, and personal motives. This perspective recognizes that each participant in an interview has a purpose and thus needs to prepare for the encounter.

There are many types of interviews: informational, employment, appraisal, or counseling, to name only a few. The differences distinguishing each type are the general purposes and contexts of the interviews. In most interviews, the same strategies and tactics are found as in other persuasive contexts, such as public speaking and advertising. Before entering an interview, you should analyze all of the elements thoroughly. What should be accomplished? What can be expected? How can you best present yourself? Many of the suggestions provided in this book relating to other persuasive topics can be used in your analysis (see especially chapter 13).

Minimally, you should consider the persuasive situation and topic and then carefully develop appropriate strategies and tactics. In terms of the person you want to persuade, you should analyze the person's values and background in order to gain insight into what motivates that individual. The goal is to understand better how the receiver will perceive the situation. You will then be able to develop strong arguments and appeals for your points and objectives. When and where the interview takes place will impact such persuasive elements as attention, control, and length of the interview. Finally, you should spend as much time preparing the content of the interview as you would a public presentation. You should structure your argument carefully by identifying key appeals and supporting your ideas with examples and evidence.

Stewart and Cash suggest a basic structure to follow for a persuasive interview.[99] In the opening, it is important to establish rapport with the other party. This may be accomplished with an exchange of greetings and small talk about weather, sports, or the headlines. The goal is to establish an open climate where there can be a free exchange of ideas and information. A feeling of trust and mutual goodwill between the participants is important. Once a good communication climate has been established, a brief orientation is needed to explain the purpose and nature of the interview.

Stewart and Cash recommend preparing an interview guide that provides a structured outline of topics and subtopics to be addressed. Of course, the degree of structure may vary depending on the degree of formality of the interview. At one author's university, the list of specific questions asked during employment interviews for staff members must be provided to the personnel office and the questions must be asked of each referred applicant. Formal interviews require very specific topic and subtopic planning.

There are several patterns one could follow in developing questions.[100] A topical pattern is the most common. Questions flow from the particular subject being discussed. A time sequence pattern develops questions in some chronological order. This could be in terms of stages or the order in which events happen. A cause-to-effect sequence is an option in which possible causes of the issue are explored, followed by a discussion of effects. Related to this pattern is the problem-solution sequence where first there is an attempt to understand the perceived problem and then an exploration of possible solutions. The purpose of any of the patterns is to develop mutual understanding and, depending upon the purpose of the interview, agreement.

In the closing portion of the interview, it is important to summarize what has been discussed and to review agreements reached. The closing usually occurs in three stages. When appropriate, you begin to focus on the solution and ask "yes-response" questions to verify positions. The agreement stage of the closing is the most dangerous period. At this point, you should obtain a final agreement and commitment from the interviewee. While being pleasant and reassuring, you want to eliminate any doubt about the action to follow. Finally, it is a good idea to arrange for a follow-up interview. This is useful to establish rapport once again and to check the status of commitment expressed throughout the interview. Your leave-taking should be relaxed and positive. Do not bring up any new issues or items to discuss; take some time for small talk, if possible. Be sincere and honest. Don't make promises you cannot keep. Also, don't rush the closing. This is an opportunity to strengthen rapport.

Interviewing is a good example of how persuasion is an integral part of most communication. The key ingredients for all forms of communication are planning and preparation.

Figure 8.5   Tips for Successful Employment Interviewing

- Keep smiling.
- Be enthusiastic.
- Be honest.
- Make frequent eye contact.
- Remain positive.
- Less can be more.
- Keep things conversational.
- Be prepared to ask questions.
- Take time to think before you respond.
- Don't ask about time off, salary, or benefits until the interviewer asks.
- Avoid negative comments about former employers and colleagues.
- Prepare a closing statement/argument.

SUMMARY

▲

The foundation for all persuasion is a thorough understanding of the audience—whether an audience of one or millions. We engage in interpersonal persuasion much more frequently than we recognize. The amount and type of persuasion we use (or are exposed to) depends on the nature of particular interpersonal encounters. We may seek the approval of others to satisfy the relational needs of acceptance, affection, and respect. We frequently seek compliance to accomplish specific tasks: to finish a project, to sell a product, or to be hired. Many interpersonal encounters involve both cognitive and relational processes. The verbal and nonverbal symbols we choose to communicate our intentions affect the outcome. Compliance depends on the strategies we select, the situation or context, and the nature of the relationship.

Conflict often results from prolonged, intense efforts of interpersonal persuasion. Frequently, a negative reaction results not from the actual facts of the disagreement but from the quality of the communication exchanged. The most important aspect to remember about conflict is that it must be managed. If we apply the knowledge we have gained about how to communicate effectively, we should be able to conduct our participation in interpersonal exchanges—including conflict—successfully.

In the twenty-first century, our society and workplace are more diverse than ever before. Therefore, sensitivity to issues of cultural and gender communication are vitally important. While interpersonal communication within the organizational context ranges on a continuum from formal to informal, much of the work accomplished depends on effective interpersonal communication. While interviews and sales are formal forms of interpersonal persuasion, they rely on the same principles of communication we have identified and discussed throughout this book.

Questions and Projects for Further Study

1. In terms of the three types of relationship structures, how would you categorize your relationship with your father? mother? teacher? employer? girlfriend? boyfriend? classmates?

2. Can you think of a time when you and an intimate friend had an argument? What happened? Analyze the conversation and argument in terms of gender differences discussed in this chapter.

3. You have a 2002 Honda Accord automobile you wish to sell. Develop the sales appeals and arguments for persuading a friend, a stranger, or a middle-aged man or woman to purchase the car. How do the appeals differ and why?

4. For the above automobile, prepare a specific appeal that would address buyer motivations of profit and thrift, safety and protection, ease and convenience, pride and prestige, sex and romance, love and affection, adventure and excitement, performance and durability.

5. Describe the leadership qualities you like best and explain why. Describe the leadership qualities you do not like and explain why.

6. You are the manager of a department at a large clothing store. Prepare questions for a job interview, a work appraisal interview for a problem employee, and an employee termination interview. How do these interviews differ in strategies and appeals?

7. From your own experience, provide an example of a pseudoconflict, a content conflict, and an ego conflict.

8. You have been working in a furniture store for one year. Prepare arguments you would use in asking for a raise.

9. Discuss the ethical issues, dimensions, and implications of:

    a. attempts to sell a $50 Bible to a family of six with an income of $20,000 a year.

    b. attempts to sell a used car that had been in a major accident and recently repaired.

10. Describe the nonverbal behaviors associated with interactions with friends, acquaintances, and employers.

11. If you work for an organization or company, how would you describe its values and climate? With whom do you interact the most on the job? Do you feel free to make suggestions for job improvement to superiors?

Additional Reading

Daniel Canary and Kathryn Dindia, eds., *Sex Differences and Similarities in Communication* (Mahwah, NJ: Lawrence Erlbaum, 1998).

Joseph A. DeVito, *Messages: Building Interpersonal Communication*, 5th ed. (Boston: Allyn & Bacon, 2002).

Eric Eisenberg and Harold Goodall, *Organizational Communication*, 3rd ed. (Boston: Bedford/St. Martin's, 2001).

Robert Gass and John Seiter, *Persuasion, Social Influence, and Compliance Gaining*, 2nd ed. (Boston: Allyn and Bacon, 2003).

John Gray, *Mars and Venus in the Workplace* (New York: Harper Collins, 2002).

Laura K. Guerrero, Joseph A. DeVito, and Michael L. Hecht, *The Nonverbal Communication Reader: Classic and Contemporary Readings*, 2nd ed. (Prospect Heights, IL: Waveland Press, 1999).

Michael Hackman and Craig Johnson, *Leadership: A Communication Perspective*, 4th ed. (Prospect Heights, IL: Waveland Press, 2004).

Frederic Jablin and Linda Putnam, eds., *The New Handbook of Organizational Communication* (Thousand Oaks, CA: Sage, 2001).

Fred E. Jandt, *Intercultural Communication*, 3rd ed. (Thousand Oaks, CA: Sage, 2001).

Peter Kellett and Diana Dalton, *Managing Conflict in a Negotiated World* (Thousand Oaks, CA: Sage, 2001).

Charles Stewart and William Cash, *Interviewing: Principles and Practices*, 10th ed. (New York: McGraw-Hill, 2003).

Deborah Tannen, *Talking from 9 to 5* (New York: William Morrow and Company, 1994).

Notes

[1] Julia T. Wood, *Gendered Lives,* 3rd ed. (Belmont, CA: Wadsworth, 1999), p. 16.

[2] Kathleen Reardon, *Persuasion in Practice* (Newbury Park, CA: Sage, 1991), p. 112.

[3] See William Schultz, *Firo: A Three-Dimensional Theory of Interpersonal Behavior* (New York: Holt, Rinehart and Winston, 1958); and "The Postulate of Interpersonal Needs," in *Messages,* ed. by Jean Civikly (New York: Random House, 1977), pp. 174–84.

[4] Joseph A. DeVito, *The Interpersonal Communication Book,* 10th ed. (New York: Allyn & Bacon, 2004).

[5] Laura K. Guerrero, Joseph A. DeVito, and Michael L. Hecht, *The Nonverbal Communication Reader* (Prospect Heights, IL: Waveland Press, 1999), p. 4.

[6] Ibid., p. 7.

[7] Robert Gass and John Seiter, *Persuasion, Social Influence, and Compliance Gaining,* 2nd ed. (Boston: Allyn & Bacon, 2003), pp. 175–76.

[8] Ibid., p. 177.

[9] Herbert W. Simons, *Persuasion in Society* (Thousand Oaks, CA: Sage, 2001), p. 107.

[10] Gass and Seiter, p. 183.

[11] Michael Hackman and Craig Johnson, *Leadership: A Communication Perspective,* 4th ed. (Prospect Heights, IL: Waveland Press, 2004), pp. 135–36.

[12] Ibid., p. 126.

[13] John French and Bertram Raven, "The Bases of Social Power," in *Studies in Social Power,* ed. by D. Cartwright (Ann Arbor, MI: Institute for Social Research, 1959), pp. 150–67.

[14] Joseph DeVito, *Messages: Building Interpersonal Communication Skills,* 5th ed. (Boston: Allyn & Bacon, 2002), p. 350.

[15] Ibid., pp. 333–34.

[16] Julia T. Wood, *Relational Communication* (Belmont, CA: Wadsworth, 1995), pp. 160–63.

[17] Gass and Seiter, p. 235.

[18] Ibid., p. 240.

[19] Erwin Bettinghaus and Michael Cody, *Persuasive Communication,* 5th ed. (New York: Harcourt Brace, 1994), pp. 185–88.

[20] Richard Perloff, *The Dynamics of Persuasion* (Hillsdale, NJ: Lawrence Erlbaum Associates, 1993), p. 267–68.

[21] Ibid., pp. 283–90.

[22] Timothy Borchers, *Persuasion in the Media Age* (Boston: McGraw-Hill, 2002), p. 339.

[23] Gass and Seiter, p. 241.

[24] Peter Kellett and Diana Dalton, *Managing Conflict in a Negotiated World* (Thousand Oaks, CA: Sage, 2001), p. 166.

[25] James McCroskey and Virginia Richmond, *Fundamentals of Human Communication: An Interpersonal Perspective* (Prospect Heights, IL: Waveland Press, 1996), p. 61.

[26] William R. Cupach and Daniel J. Canary, *Competence in Interpersonal Conflict* (Prospect Heights, IL: Waveland Press, 1997), p. xiii.

[27] Kellett and Dalton, p. 166.

[28] DeVito, *Messages*, p. 311.

[29] Cupach and Canary, p. 13.

[30] Hackman and Johnson, pp. 173–75.

[31] Ibid., pp. 183–86.

[32] Ibid., p. 181.

[33] Kellett and Dalton, p. 166.

[34] J. Hocker and William Wilmot, *Interpersonal Conflict*, 6th ed. (New York: McGraw-Hill, 2001), pp. 256–57.

[35] Borchers, pp. 407–08.

[36] DeVito, *Messages*, pp. 319–22.

[37] Wood, *Relational*, p. 263.

[38] Kellett and Dalton, pp. 10–11.

[39] Ibid., pp. 13–15.

[40] Gerald Miller, "Introduction: Conflict Resolution through Communication," in *Conflict Resolution through Communication*, ed. by Fred Jandt (New York: Harper & Row, 1973), p. 3.

[41] Saul Alinski, *Rules for Radicals* (New York: Vintage Books, 1969), p. vii.

[42] Ruth Wodak, *Gender and Discourse* (Thousand Oaks, CA: Sage, 1997), p. 11.

[43] See one of the essays in Daniel Canary and Kathryn Dindia, eds., *Sex Differences and Similarities in Communication* (Mahwah, NJ: Lawrence Erlbaum, 1998).

[44] Deborah Tannen, *You Just Don't Understand* (New York: Ballantine Books, 1990), pp. 17, 18.

[45] Ibid., p. 77.

[46] Wood, *Relational*, p. 134.

[47] McCroskey and Richmond, pp. 301–06; and Tannen, p. 129.

[48] DeVito, *Messages*, p. 105.

[49] Shari Kendall and Deborah Tannen, "Gender and Language in the Workplace," in *Gender and Discourse*, ed. by Ruth Wodak (Thousand Oaks, CA: Sage, 1997), pp. 81–91.

[50] Deborah Tannen, *Talking from 9 to 5* (New York: William Morrow and Company, 1994), p. 23.

[51] Ibid., pp. 114–15.

[52] Ibid., p. 23.

[53] DeVito, *Messages,* p. 160.

[54] Ibid., p. 293.

[55] John Gray, *Mars and Venus in the Workplace* (New York: Harper Collins, 2002), p. 4.

[56] Tannen, *You Just Don't Understand*, p. 121.

[57] Ibid., p. 294.

[58] Ibid., p. 298.

[59] Fred E. Jandt, *Intercultural Communication*, 3rd ed. (Thousand Oaks, CA: Sage, 2001), p. 8.

[60] Ibid., p. 38.

[61] Ibid., pp. 3–4.

[62] Ibid., p. 28.

[63] Ibid., p.63.

[64] Hackman and Johnson, p. 20.

[65] Ibid., p. 6.

[66] Ibid., p. 12.

[67] Verderber and Verderber, p. 378.

[68] Hackman and Johnson, pp. 23, 25.

[69] For a very good discussion and summary of research, see Hackman and Johnson, chapter 2.

[70] Ibid., p. 43.

[71] Ibid., pp. 46–47.

[72] Robert Kelley, *The Power of Followership* (New York: Doubleday, 1992), pp. 142–48.

[73] Verderber and Verderber, p. 382.

[74] Hackman and Johnson, p. 222.

[75] Michael Goodman, *Corporate Communications for Executives* (Albany: State University of New York, 1998), p. 2.

[76] See Phillip K. Tompkins, "The Functions of Human Communication in Organization," in *Handbook of Rhetorical and Communication Theory,* eds. Carroll Arnold and John Bowers (Boston: Allyn & Bacon, 1984), pp 683–98; and DeVito, *Human Communication,* 9th ed. (Boston: Allyn & Bacon, 2002), pp. 697–98.

[77] Reardon, pp. 143–46.

[78] Eric Eisenberg and Harold Goodall, *Organizational Communication,* 3rd ed. (Boston: Bedford/St. Martin's, 2001).

[79] Ibid., p. 234.

[80] Ibid., p. 235.

[81] Ibid., p. 235.

[82] Ibid., pp. 265–70.

[83] Ibid., p. 271.

[84] Edgar H. Schein, *Organizational Culture and Leadership* (San Francisco: Jossey-Bass, 1985),

[85] Goodman, p. 30.

[86] George Cheney, Lars Thøger Christensen, Theodore E. Zorn, Jr., and Shiv Ganesh, *Organizational Communication in an Age of Globalization: Issues, Reflections, Practices* (Long Grove, IL: Waveland Press, 2004), p. 320.

[87] Goodman, p. 44.

[88] Ibid., p. 1.

[89] Ibid., p. 4.

[90] Dan O'Hair and Gustav Friedrich, *Strategic Communication in Business and the Professions,* 3rd ed. (Boston: Houghton Mifflin, 1998), p. 186.

[91] Borchers, pp. 398–400.

[92] The Million Dollar Round Table Center for Productivity, *Million Dollar Closing Techniques* (New York: John Wiley & Sons, 1999).

[93] Ibid., pp. 25–35.

[94] Ibid., pp. 118–21.

[95] Ibid., pp. 121–27.

[96] O'Hair and Friedrich, p. 190–92.

[97] Charles Stewart and William Cash, *Interviewing: Principles and Practices,* 10th ed. (New York: McGraw-Hill, 2003), p. 1.

[98] Ibid., pp. 9–11.

[99] Ibid., pp. 316–23.

[100] Ibid., pp. 86–87.

9

Public and Mass Persuasion

Overview

▲ Public Communication and Persuasion
    Characteristics of Public Communication
    Public Opinion and Persuasion

▲ Persuasive Campaigns
    Product or Commercial Campaigns
    Public Relations Campaigns
    Political Campaigns
    Issue Campaigns
      Grassroots Lobbying
      Corporate Advocacy/Issue Management
    Social Movements
      Characteristics
      Persuasive Functions
      Life Cycle
      Leadership
      Resistance to Social Movements

▲ Campaign Implementation

> *Democracies depend on citizens to have the necessary competencies for participation in the ongoing deliberations that identify and resolve public concerns.*[1]
>
> —GERARD A. HAUSER

Public persuasion involves interactions on a societal scale. Through public communication, we discuss issues, formulate and debate policy, campaign for public office, and implement societal reform and changes. As our society becomes more complex, individual and independent actions are no longer sufficient to guarantee success or survival. Group efforts impact us daily, and we join forces with others to ensure that our views are heard and our needs are met.

Shearon Lowery and Melvin DeFleur argue that the United States has become a "mass society." For them, a mass society means more than a large number of citizens. It refers to "a distinctive pattern of social organization . . . a process of changing social organization that occurs when industrialization, urbanization, and modernization increasingly modify the social order."[2] Since World War II, people have expanded their identification with the goals of formal organizations such as unions, interest groups, professional associations, and political alliances. Contacts with formal organizations help establish social power and provide an outlet for exercising and developing skills.

At the very heart of democracy is public communication. The quality of that public communication directly impacts the quality of our democracy and society at large. In this chapter, we investigate the nature of public communication and persuasion. Our focus is on the multiple strategies of various public persuasive campaigns.

PUBLIC COMMUNICATION AND PERSUASION
▲

As we noted in chapter 2, public persuasion has been a sophisticated art for centuries. Over 2,000 years ago, Aristotle's *Rhetoric* detailed the strategies for convincing others. Verbal skills were highly valued and a necessity for public life. The master of public discourse was eloquent, ethical, and civic minded. The Greeks trusted and preferred oral, face-to-face interaction to the written word. With the advent of the printing press, literacy was no longer a privilege of the aristocracy. With the printed word, public communication and persuasion extended beyond immediate audiences. Electronic communication further extended the power and impact of human communication and persuasion. In our modern world, oral, written, and electronic communication is an essential and pervasive part of our lives. However, the growth in frequency and availability of public communication has not necessarily improved the human condition. Some argue that increased public communication has amplified public deception, confusion, interpersonal isolation, and the complexity of modern life.

Characteristics of Public Communication

We define public communication as intentional efforts to change or modify the beliefs, attitudes, values, and behaviors of an audience through the use of symbols in a public forum. Our broad definition of public communication identifies persuasion as its goal, the use of symbols as its means of meeting its objective, and the public arena as its context of interaction.

Public communication is marked by several characteristics that distinguish it from other forms of communication. These distinctions have been mentioned in other chapters, but it is useful to review them briefly.

- Public communication is simply more *public*. The interactions are not private, and intimacy is sacrificed. Consider, for example, that although ABC's Barbara Walters frequently interviews celebrities within the seemingly comfortable security of their homes, their responses will be heard by millions of people.

- Communication *settings* are less relevant. For example, a politician's comments before an Iowa caucus are not limited to the immediate audience; they are broadcast throughout the nation.

- *Audiences* are larger, more diverse, and anonymous. Because a message will be heard by people with varying backgrounds, beliefs, and values, appeals are general and few specifics are detailed. The politicians campaigning in Iowa cannot make promises to farmers that could upset urban voters in another region.

- Public communication is *mediated*. The form and content of messages depends on the medium selected. Television is naturally better suited for movement, action, and drama than is radio. Newspapers and magazines offer expanded space for written messages allowing for more examples, details, and argumentation. The use of mass media restricts audience feedback, and the interpretation of the message is thus vulnerable to misunderstanding.

- Public communication provides an *opportunity for change*. People, groups, and opinions can be mobilized quickly. Mass persuasion is best at linking ideas and potential audiences for some common action.

Public communication provides several social functions, including information, persuasion, entertainment, and culture dissemination. Public communication shares information needed to conduct business and to regulate social life. It has a persuasive function that provides opportunities for various viewpoints or ideas to be presented, discussed, and debated. The entertainment function often blends several purposes. For example, *Saving Private Ryan* won several academy awards in 1999 for its portrayal of the personal struggles and challenges facing soldiers during the Normandy invasion of World War II. Although entertaining, the film was also informative in its depiction of the horrors of battle and the personal issues of life, death, and humanity in times of war. The movie also portrays the heroic efforts of what Tom Brokaw calls "the greatest generation."

Public communication preserves and disseminates all the rituals and ceremonies of our culture. Films, speeches, lectures, television programs, and other events weave a cultural fabric that unites people, groups, and ideas. Through public communication, humans give cultural meaning to a bewildering variety of daily events.

Public Opinion and Persuasion

Over the last decade, public opinion polls have proliferated exponentially. Phrases such as "margin of error," "sample size," and "favorable approval ratings" have become part of our national political vocabulary. Polls are used not only to inform us about our collective beliefs, attitudes, and values, but also to persuade and even manipulate our attitudes and behavior. Polls have become an integral part of print and broadcast news coverage on virtually all social issues, as well as public and political campaigns.

There are many types of polls beyond those conducted by the media. Commissioned polls are those conducted on behalf of an organization. They are not necessarily designed for public consumption but are useful in guiding the decision making of the organization. Commercial firms as well as special-interest organizations may commission polls to gauge public trust and confidence in a product or a position on an issue. If the results are favorable, especially to a special-interest group, the results may be released for pubic awareness and support. For example, the Sierra Club releases polls demonstrating that the majority of Americans support keeping public lands free from development, mining, or logging activities.

Pseudo-polls are those where print and electronic media organizations encourage audiences to register their opinions on a topic or subject matter. These are not valid polls because the sample of respondents is self-selected, not random, and response rates are very low. Even the questionnaires that members of Congress distribute to constituents are unreliable. These types of polls are more of a public relations gimmick than a valid attempt to gather information on public attitudes.

In general, the public is becoming more skeptical of polls—especially those used during elections. Exit polling at voting locations has received special scrutiny. Indeed, the lack of precision by the networks attempting to identify the winner during the 2000 presidential elections was embarrassing. In fact, after much effort and expense to improve the technology and method of analyses for exit polling, errors were so great that networks declined to report the data during the mid-term elections of 2002. Although accuracy is not always assured, public opinion, revealed through countless polls, has emerged as a critical factor in public persuasion today.

We tend to think of public opinion as a monolithic entity. Leaders espouse views and positions based on the "public's opinion" with great certainty. However, the truth is that public opinion is not static, and polls are just another tool of persuasion. In order to understand the persuasive potential and impact of polls and public opinion, we need to look briefly at the nature of public opinion.

The more abstract the goal or objective, the greater the consensus of opinion. For example, nearly everyone wants to curb the increase in crime. There is much less agreement about *how* to lower crime. The more specific a claim, the less consensus one will find among the public. Thus, many politicians are very general in their pronouncements and calls to action. There is more risk in being specific.

Carroll Glynn and his colleagues provide four reasons why public opinion is an important consideration for public persuasion.[3] First, a democratic government should reflect the will of those governed; policy should be based on public opinion.

Second, respect for public opinion is a safeguard against demagoguery. Third, public opinion provides clues about culture. Public sentiment toward specific issues provides insight into contemporary norms and values. Fourth, sometimes public opinion must be mobilized. During times of national crisis, elected officials strive to mobilize public sentiment and support. As will be discussed later in the chapter, a major task of all social movements is to mobilize public support for an issue, event, or prescribed action.

Public opinion may be thought of as "the collective expression of opinion of many individuals bound into a group by common aims, aspirations, needs, and ideals."[4] Few issues inspire opinions or feelings from the entire citizenry. At the heart of any opinion is the issue of salience or self-interest. We may offer opinions on many issues, but there are few that motivate us to take action, whether writing a letter, going to a public rally, or sending money to an organization. To motivate people to take action, persuasive appeals and messages often focus on the commonality of the group.

Public opinion does not anticipate events; it only reacts to them. Events become crucibles for public opinion. For example, the Exxon oil spill in Alaska generated a great deal of public attention and support for environmental actions. Memberships in environmental groups increased, and regulatory legislation was drafted at state and federal levels. The tragic bombing of the federal building in Oklahoma City in 1995 focused a great deal of attention on civilian paramilitary groups. United States involvement in Kosovo as part of a NATO action in 1999 sparked debate about the role of our military in the post-Cold War world. The tragic attack on the United States on September 11, 2001, raised questions about immigration, the extent of government surveillance on its citizens, and our role in fighting international terrorism. A social issue may languish for lack of attention until dramatized by an event. Awareness and discussion may lead to crystallizing opinions and attitudes. However, even dramatic events rarely sway public opinion for an extended length of time.

Public opinion is intertwined with a variety of cultural forces and institutions; it evolves as standards change. For example, twenty-five years earlier, former president Bill Clinton probably would have resigned before the impeachment hearings began. However, in 1998, many Americans distinguished between the private actions of a president and the pubic management function of government.

William Paisley argues that there are three social forces influencing public communication campaigns: public distrust, episodic issues, and the rise of issue literacies.[5] Americans have become increasingly critical of government since Watergate and the presidency of Richard Nixon; the growing number of political, social, and corporate scandals and crises have amplified public cynicism and distrust. In addition, issues continually rise and fall on the national agenda; there are more and more special-interest groups competing for national attention. Nearly every issue is portrayed as a "crisis." Citizens feel less confident about finding solutions and distrust those who portray themselves as specialists or experts on the issues.

PERSUASIVE CAMPAIGNS

▲

The term *campaign* comes from military vocabulary. In a general context, a campaign is a connected series of operations designed to bring about a particular result. It involves planning, strategy, competition, winners, and losers.

Herbert Simons defines persuasive campaigns as "organized, sustained attempts at influencing groups or masses of people through a series of messages."[6] This definition of persuasive campaigns emphasizes three key characteristics. First, campaigns are generally well-organized events; they are not spontaneous public events. There is an identifiable organizational structure with leaders, goals, and established routines. Campaigns most often have beginning and ending dates. The second major characteristic of a campaign is a large audience size. As already discussed, this factor greatly influences the form and content of messages. The third characteristic of persuasive campaigns is the use of multiple messages to alter the beliefs, attitudes, values, or behaviors of a segment of the general public.

Public persuasion campaigns are fundamentally communication exercises about politics (broadly defined to include elections or mass social movements), issues, products, and services. A communication approach to campaign analysis challenges the basic assumption of behaviorists that public campaigns play a minor role or have little influence in citizen decision making. Communication scholars argue that campaign research has focused too much attention on individual attitude change or voter conversion. Such research ignores the long-term, cumulative effects of public persuasive campaigns.

As argued in chapter 3, we create and manipulate reality through symbols. Campaigns are exercises in the creation, recreation, and transmission of significant symbols. Communication activities are the vehicles for action—both real and perceived. Samuel Becker advises that "any single communication encounter accounts for only a small portion of the variance in human behavior."[7] He characterizes our communication environment as a *mosaic*.[8] The mosaic consists of an infinite number of information bits on an infinite number of topics scattered over time and space; exposure is varied and repetitive; and the bits are disorganized. As these bits become relevant or address a need, they are attended. We must arrange these bits into a meaningful cognitive pattern. Public campaigns are great sources of potential information and contain, however difficult to identify or measure, elements that impact decision making. New information bits can replace other bits to change or modify our worldview, attitudes, or opinions. Broadly speaking, there are five types of campaigns. While specific strategies and tactics of persuasion may overlap, these types of campaigns contain unique elements and specific processes of persuasion.

Product or Commercial Campaigns

Product or commercial advertising campaigns are the focus of chapter 10. The purpose of such campaigns is to sell specific ideas, products, or services. Advertising is the most pervasive form of persuasion in the United States. It is both a creative and a scientific process. Advertising campaigns are intricate and complex, utilizing psychological strategies and tactics to move consumers along a continuum from awareness to knowledge, to liking, to preference, to conviction, and to purchase. Because of their scope and impact, advertising campaigns are significant elements of public communication, fulfilling both social and economic functions.

Public Relations Campaigns

Richard Campbell argues that the difference between advertising and public relations is that "advertising is controlled publicity that a company or an individual buys; public relations attempts to secure favorable media publicity (which is more difficult to control) to promote a company or client."[9] Don Schultz and Beth Barnes claim public relations is one of the most diverse areas in marketing communications: "Public relations, broadly defined, concerns an organization's communications with its various publics. Those publics can include the company's suppliers, its employees, its stockholders, its products' consumers, and the community at large."[10] Emma Daugherty characterizes public relations messages as persuasive rhetorical messages that go beyond mere presentations of data.[11] Because public relations involves so many communication strategies, and a wide array of activities, the term is difficult to define. From a broad perspective, public relations refers to "the entire range of efforts by an individual, an agency, or any organization attempting to reach or persuade audiences."[12]

The practice of public relations generally include the activities of advertising, promotion, publicity, propaganda, special events, internal communication, public affairs, issues management, press agentry, media relations, government relations/lobbying, community relations, industry relations, and minority relations.[13] Each activity requires the construction of carefully crafted messages designed for specific targets or audiences. In short, each activity is about purposeful, persuasive communication. Some PR activities are done by agencies and some are done by "in-house" corporate professionals.

By 2002, there were well over 2,000 PR firms in America and over 3,000 worldwide. Most companies and corporations have dedicated departments devoted to public relations activities.[14] Among the audiences public relations activities target are consumers, the general public, company employees, shareholders, media organizations, government agencies, and community and industry leaders.[15]

Most corporate communication professionals argue that public relations is a social science utilizing the latest communication skills, theories, and technologies. From a corporate perspective, the practice of public relations is the way institutions explain, justify, and package their interests in terms of the common good.[16] From an industry perspective, public relations serves three primary functions in business and society: to control publics by directing what people think or do in order to satisfy the needs or desires of an institution; to respond to publics by developing specific reactions to problems, situations, or initiatives of others; and to achieve mutually beneficial relationships among all the publics of interest to an organization by fostering positive interactions among its constituencies.[17]

In short, public relations campaigns are designed to address an issue, to solve a problem, or to improve a situation. Doug Newsom, Judy Turk, and Dean Kruckeberg identify four types of public relations campaigns.[18] A *public awareness* campaign is designed simply to make people aware of something. This type of campaign ranges from something as simple as the date of a school opening to a local civic event. A *public information* campaign goes beyond citizen awareness of an event and also shares some vital information. A *public education* campaign goes an additional step beyond awareness and information to explanation of the material to the extent that the public can apply the information to daily behavior. Some of the contemporary campaigns on drugs, smoking, and drunk driving, for example, either reinforce existing attitudes or attempt to modify existing behavior. Finally, *behavior modification* campaigns are the most difficult and complex. The defining focus of the various types of public relations campaigns is the behavior desired from the targeted audience.

Crisis communication has become a specialty function of public relations. A crisis is "a major occurrence with a potentially negative outcome affecting an organization as well as its publics, services, products, and/or good name."[19] A crisis may not necessarily mean the end of a company or even a product. Recall the tainted Tylenol scare that led to more secure packaging of products; the pain reliever enjoyed a full market recovery. Remember also the Exxon *Valdez* oil spill. The corporation spent millions to handle the crisis. Crisis communication involves "the verbal, visual, and/or written interaction between the organization and its publics (often through the news media) prior to, during, and after the negative occurrence."[20]

Forward-thinking companies prepare contingency plans in case they confront a crisis. They develop strategic communication considerations for each of the five stages. *Detection* is the first stage, during which the organization watches for warning signs. The second stage is *preparation/prevention*. In this stage, the organization prepares a proactive campaign to address a potential crisis or, if possible, to avoid one. In stage three, *containment*, the communication is designed to limit the duration of the crisis or to keep it from becoming more serious. The fourth stage is *recovery*, where the organization attempts to get out of the news and back to business as usual. Finally, the learning stage consists of careful evaluation of the crisis and a review of actions taken.[21]

Political Campaigns

For communication scholars, the essence of politics is human interaction. The interaction may be formal or informal, verbal or nonverbal, public or private—but always persuasive, forcing individuals to interpret, to evaluate, and to act.

Political campaigns are our national, state, and local conversations. They are highly complex and sophisticated communication events: communication of issues, images, social reality, and personas. They are essentially exercises in the creation, recreation, and transmission of significant symbols through human communication. As we attempt to make sense of our environment, political bits of communication contribute to our voting choices, worldviews, and policy preferences.

Michael Pfau and Roxanne Parrott identify three unique features of political campaigns.[22] First, political campaigns are more person oriented than product or service oriented. Thus, the message will focus on a person running for office or appeals to voters. Second, political campaigns are more restricted to a specific time frame. The beginning and ending points are more pronounced than with other types of campaigns. The time frame impacts strategies and the choice of media outlets, as well as the types of appeals presented. Third, political campaigns incorporate multiple media—speeches, debates, news media, paid advertising, brochures, posters, and bumper stickers, to name a few.

Modern political campaigns follow three or four relatively distinct phases: preprimary, primary, nomination conventions for presidential campaigns, and general election. Communication functions differ in each phase of a campaign. During the preprimary phase, communication activities define the candidate's image, inform the public about positions on issues, and create a sense of viability and legitimacy for the candidate's campaign. During the primary phase, the candidate engages opponents, responds to attacks, and attempts to generate support and motivate supporters. At conventions, especially during presidential campaigns, candidates participate in rituals providing a sense of legitimation, reaffirmation of candidacy, and demonstration of party unity. Many of the communication functions for the general election phase revisit strategies from the previous phases: reinforce image, compare and contrast issue positions, respond to attacks, and motivate support.

The various forms of political communication surface and resurface throughout the campaign: announcement speeches, the basic campaign speeches, news conferences, debates, political advertising, and acceptance speeches. Political campaign communication is heavily mediated. In order to reach the greatest number of voters, candidates rely on television, radio, newspapers, direct mail, and now the Internet.

The *limited effects model* of campaign communication research dominated scholars' views for nearly 40 years. The model was based on data from the 1940 elections presented by Lazarsfeld, Berelson, and Gaudet in *The People's Choice*.[23] At that time, most voter decisions were based on attitude predispositions, group identification, and interpersonal communication; mediated messages contributed little to converting voters from one candidate to another. Thirty years ago, campaigns were conducted by volunteers and party activists. Face-to-face canvassing was essential to winning. Beginning in the 1960s, new communication technology changed campaigns. With the decline of political parties, the increase of single-issue politics, the prominence of mass media, and the sophistication of social science research, the terrain today differs significantly from that of the 1940s and 1950s.

Daniel Shea and Michael Burton distinguish new style campaigns from old style in four ways: new players, new incentives, new tactics, and new resources.[24] In the old style, parties ran candidates for office. Today, individuals run for office. The party has less control over who runs, especially in primaries. Individuals with money (like Steve Forbes in 1996 or Ross Perot in 1992) or people with name recognition but little political experience no longer need to rely on party affiliation. Access to television is more important than party support. The decline of parties and the increasing importance of political action committees have encouraged "lone-ranger" campaigns.

Campaign professionals have replaced volunteers. Previously, volunteers and activists played an essential role in generating grassroots support and getting out the vote. Today, campaign people and money come from outside the geographic area of the election race. Money rules the day in terms of staff, advertising, and the use of campaign technology. Campaign management and services have become an industry. For consultants, political ideology or public policy are less important than the number of clients. The ideal of the citizen legislator has been replaced by the professional, career politician. Government service provides a path to corporate jobs and big money. Many of these changes are at the higher levels of electoral politics. There still are citizen legislators at the state and local level, although there is an increasing professionalization of political campaigns even at those levels.

Old-style politics involved traditional strategies of group-based appeals with traditional party messages. The goal was voter education and broad mass appeal. Today, the strategies and tactics are more narrowly defined and targeted. Voter preferences are revealed through scientific research, and candidates target their messages to voter segments. The Internet allows candidates to attract supporters and donations. It also provides instant, inexpensive feedback through e-mail.

Campaigns perform both instrumental (task goal) and consummatory (meta associations) functions.[25] Three instrumental functions are: behavioral activation, cognitive adjustment, and legitimation. Campaigns motivate behavior (whether helping with a campaign or voting on election day), reinforcing voter attitudes. By discussing issues, campaigns stimulate awareness; reflecting on a candidate's views can result in the voter modifying his or her policy preferences. Campaigns legitimize both the newly elected and the rules, laws, and regulations they pass.

Consummatory functions go beyond tasks such as the selection of candidates or enactments of legislation. They help create the metapolitical images and social-psychological associations that provide the glue that holds our political system together. Campaigns provide personal involvement in many forms: direct participation, self-reflection and definition, social interaction and discussion, and aesthetic experiences of public drama and group life. Campaigns also provide the legitimization of the electoral process, reaffirming commitment to our brand of democracy, debate, and political campaigning.

Political campaigns, then, communicate and influence, reinforce and convert, increase enthusiasm and inform, and motivate as well as educate. As Bruce Gronbeck argues, campaigns "get leaders elected, yes, but ultimately, they also tell us who we as a people are, where we have been and where we are going; in their size and duration they separate our culture from all others, teach us about political life, set our individual and collective priorities, entertain us, and provide bases for social interaction."[26]

The *uses and gratifications model* of campaign effects is increasing in popularity. This model basically argues that campaign effects on voters depend on the needs and motivations of the individual voter. Voters may turn to campaign messages for information, issue discussion, or pure entertainment. Currently, the most popular approach to the study of campaign communication is *agenda-setting theory*. Basically, the theory states that the media do not tell the public what to think but do decide what information to present and therefore do tell the public *what to think about*. By highlighting some items and not others, the media influence our topics of discussion, reflection, and opinion formation. The powerful media effects of *priming* and *framing* will be discussed in chapter 11.

NON SEQUITUR

Ultimately, it is important to remember that political campaigns do more than elect public officials. They reinforce voter attitudes and help change voter preferences. They also motivate specific action, such as volunteering to help with campaigns or casting ballots on election day. By discussing issues, campaigns stimulate awareness about vital national concerns. Political campaigns help to legitimize our brand of democracy by facilitating new leadership. Political campaigns offer personal involvement in many forms, including direct participation, self-reflection and definition, social interaction and discussion, and aesthetic experiences of public drama and group life. Political campaigns, then, communicate and influence, motivate and inform, reinforce and convert. We will discuss political campaigns in greater detail in chapter 11.

Issue Campaigns

Although related to political campaigns, issue campaigns attempt to get audiences to support a certain course of action or belief independent of official political structures, systems, or procedures. Organizations generating such campaigns include political action committees, religious organizations, schools, and hospitals, to name only a few. Campaigns range from specific lobbying efforts to general public awareness campaigns.

The federal government and most state agencies refer to their public campaigns as *public affairs* or *public information* activities. Despite the language, these are persuasive campaigns. Consider the 60-year-old Smokey Bear fire prevention campaign. In surveys, 98 percent of the people know who Smokey Bear is and his purpose. In addition, most people are familiar with his adage, "Only you can prevent wildfires." (Prior to 2000, the wording was "forest fires.") The Smokey Bear campaign is credited with reducing forest fires by 50 percent since 1944. It was designed to reduce the staggering costs of severe wildland fires and to instill a personal responsibility for the prevention of such fires (http://www.smokeybear.com). Smokey is so popular and receives so much mail, he even has his own zip code (20252).[27] Smokey now has help in reaching his goal. The Firewise Campaign (http://www.firewise.org) advises homeowners about measures they can take to protect their property.

Water-retaining succulents and foliage. Planting them around your home is a simple way you can make it more defensible against wildfires. Discover other ways you can protect your home and your loved ones. Visit Firewise.org.

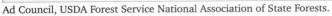

Ad Council, USDA Forest Service National Association of State Forests.

There is an increasing trend toward the "organized dissemination of government information." According to Dennis Wilcox and his colleagues, the factors of increasing urban population, social mobility, societal complexity, citizen demands, and public scrutiny have all contributed to increasing volume, variety, and frequency of informative communication endeavors. News releases, press conferences, posters, reports, bulletins, special events, exhibits, broadcast public service announcements, brochures, and paid advertising are rather routine governmental communication endeavors. In fact, the federal government spends nearly $3 billion a year on activities related to public affairs and employs an estimated 12,000 communication specialists.[28]

Because the government does not publish its own newspaper or operate radio or television stations, it must rely on communication professionals to transmit vital information to the general public. Today, it is not unusual to see local, state, or federal governments launch campaigns using press releases, press conferences, media events, and advertising. In the mid-1980s, for example, the U.S. Army was spending nearly $70 million a year for recruitment advertising. Recent campaigns include such diverse topics as antismoking, AIDS awareness, prevention of drunk driving, and seat belt safety, to name a few.

According to Ron Faucheux, "in the modern world, few major issues are merely lobbied anymore. Most of them are now managed, using a triad of public relations, grassroots mobilization, and lobbyists."[29] Many large public affairs firms are now organized by the divisions servicing governmental relations, public relations, and grassroots lobbying.

Grassroots Lobbying. Grassroots lobbying is the "process by which an interest group identifies, recruits, and activates citizens to contact public officials, usually legislators, on behalf of their shared public policy views."[30] Citizens targeted for mobilization usually have some affiliation with the organization and are predisposed to support the cause advocated.

The goal of grassroots lobbying is to create massive pressure to move a legislator toward the desired position of an organization and to convince him or her to cast a key vote. The more individualized or personalized the appeal, the better. The most effective grassroots programs are those that allow constituents to communicate in their own words to legislators. To supplement the various contacts of voters, organizations sometimes use television commercials to educate the public on specific legislation or to describe an issue. Often they urge you to call your congressman or senator and provide you with the phone number and specific legislative bill number for you to encourage or to discourage passage.

Like most campaigns, grassroots lobbying efforts follow distinct phases (see figure 9.1). The first phase is research, when public attitudes as well as legislative voting records are reviewed. During this phase, the basic strategy is devised and the campaign plan is prepared. In the targeting phase the organization determines which public officials need to hear from constituents and which constituents should be mobilized. Sensitizing is a phase unique to grassroots campaigns. The goal of this phase is to create the right political climate for the message by using public relations events, press conferences, ad campaigns, editorial board meetings, and

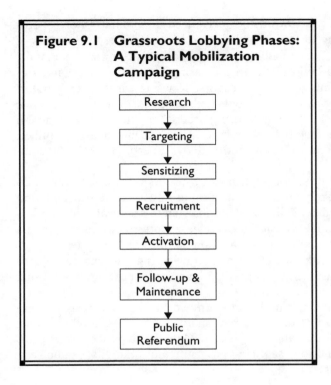

Figure 9.1   Grassroots Lobbying Phases: A Typical Mobilization Campaign

Research

↓

Targeting

↓

Sensitizing

↓

Recruitment

↓

Activation

↓

Follow-up & Maintenance

↓

Public Referendum

other similar strategies. Recruitment is another unique and important phase to grassroots lobbying campaigns. During this phase, direct mail, phone banks, and other methods are used to recruit volunteer activists. Activation is the phase of getting volunteers to write, fax, call, or visit elected officials. This phase usually occurs while legislatures are in session and focuses on key votes or issue debates.

Because the ultimate success of grassroots campaigns depends on volunteers, the follow-up/maintenance phase is important for successive mobilization attempts. Organizations express appreciation to volunteers and regularly communicate with them. While listed as a discrete phase in our diagram, communication with activists is really an ongoing and fundamental task of any interest group. Finally, if an issue goes to ballot or a public referendum, a political campaign must be organized and orchestrated. This often requires a new and distinct campaign initiative.[31]

Citizen action groups must make four strategic decisions concerning issues and tactics: (1) whether to encourage input from members—in many large citizen action groups, participation is usually limited to those who have made financial contributions to the organization; (2) whether to reject compromises and lobby publicly on highly visible issues that receive extensive media attention or to work behind the scenes and to bargain with opposition groups; (3) whether to use direct lobbying by the organization's staff or to rely on grassroots efforts; and (4) whether to join coalitions with other groups or to lobby alone.[32]

Just how do grassroots campaigns work? Let's examine a few examples of this type of advocacy. The National Federation of Independent Business (NFIB) is one of the largest and most sophisticated associations in the United States. It has over 600,000 members. The association built a state-of-the-art membership database that includes names, addresses, phone and fax numbers, geographic region, legislative districts, number of employees, type of business, issue positions, and political backgrounds. The computer network is connected to fax machines that make instant communication possible. The association has 50 state directors and employs 600 field representatives, whose jobs include membership growth and some lobbying activities. NFIB divides the membership list into several categories.

The AIDS Memorial Quilt is an excellent example of a highly successful grassroots program.

There are 400,000 members who responded to at least one direct mail solicitation; this is the *A-list*. Refining that list to members who responded to more than one direct mail solicitation yields the *AA-list*, with 200,000 members. The *guardian list* consists of the 40,000 most active members. Finally, the most valued list is the 3,000 *key contact* members, who have close relationships with public officials and decision makers. While direct mail is the mainstay of their communication efforts, NFIB uses extensive "telelobbying" efforts to connect members to elected officials. They report a response rate among members of 66 percent. Another technique is *rolling mail*. This involves timing mailings among congressional districts in order to maximize the flow of member response to legislative officials.

The American Association of Retired Persons (AARP) also uses a variety of methods to mobilize their more than 35 million members. Founded in 1958, AARP exerts a great deal of influence, especially on issues related to health care and social security. The association relies on their Web site, a monthly magazine, a monthly newspaper, a quarterly Spanish newspaper, a national radio network series *(Prime Time)*, direct mail, and telephone trees to mobilize their most active members. In addition, they use paid ads, video teleconferencing, and community meetings to reach members. AARP has staffed offices in every state. Volunteers are the heart of the organization. All members of the Board of Directors, all national officers, state presidents, and thousands of legislative and program leaders are unpaid volunteers. They are involved in advocacy at the national and state levels plus innovative community service and education programs such as tax preparation assistance (Tax-Aide), a driver safety program, grief and loss counseling, independent living programs, and a senior community service employment program (SCSEP). AARP's revenue in 2002 was $636 million, and their expenditures on legislative advocacy and research totaled $57 million.[33]

The National Rifle Association is a very high profile and extremely active grassroots lobbying organization. Members are primarily sporting-gun enthusiasts and people interested in protecting Second Amendment rights. The organization has been around since the Civil War; it was started by Union officers to promote the improvement of marksmanship among members. However, the assassination of President Kennedy and the passage of the Gun Control Act of 1968 fundamentally changed the purpose and scope of the organization. The act prohibits "unlicensed persons from buying, selling, or otherwise transferring rifles, shotguns, handguns, or ammunition outside of their home state or in any form of interstate commerce."[34] The NRA opposed the act on the basis of serious infringements on Second Amendment rights. The NRA has a full-time staff of more than 300 individuals. Membership benefits include various types of insurance, training, and discounts on everything from hotels to airline tickets. The organization is comprised of more than 10,000 state associations or local clubs and publishes several different magazines. Nearly 50,000 attended its annual convention in 2001.[35]

The NRA becomes very vocal in defending its positions, particularly when national events could threaten a loss of membership. The 1995 bombing of the Murrah Federal Building in Oklahoma City, the 1999 Columbine High School shooting in Colorado, and the sniper attacks around the Metro Washington, D.C., area in 2002 all caused the NRA to initiate aggressive public relations activities. From a political perspective, the NRA has five levels of involvement.[36] (1) It grades candidates on their positions about firearms and publishes those ratings in *American Rifleman*. (2) The organization endorses candidates. (3) The NRA contributes funds to political candidates. (4) It also makes "in-kind" contributions, such as fund-raising activities on behalf of candidates. (5) The organization may use its own funds to produce radio, television, or direct mail advertising on behalf of candidates. For example, in the 2000 Senatorial race in Virginia, the NRA sent out mailings, ran 378 television ads and 155 radio ads, and set up a network of members to help "get-out-the-vote" on behalf of Republican George Allen. In total, they contributed over $500,000 to his candidacy. Between 1978 and 2000, the NRA has contributed over $26 million to candidates running for election; $22.5 million for Republicans and $4.3 million for Democrats.[37]

There are numerous strategies and tactics in grassroots lobbying. Member mobilization involves organizing supporters to demonstrate a show of strength to a public official on a certain issue. Mass or volume grassroots programs involve getting sympathizers to sign petitions, to mail preprinted postcards or form letters, or to send Mailgrams to public officials. *Astroturf* refers to manufacturing instant public support for a point of view; this mass grassroots program plays on the emotional reactions of the public to a specific event or news story. An *action alert* is a letter, newsletter, Mailgram, phone call, fax, e-mail, or other communication from an interest group to supporters, designed to activate a response. In order to generate a response, most direct mail solicitation stresses conflict and extremism rather than compromise or moderation. Negativism and emotional appeals characterize the vast majority of messages.[38] A *grasstops* action by an interest group involves the identification, recruitment, and activation of a small number of opinion leaders and influential citizens to contact public officials through personalized letters, phone calls, or visits.

More specific tactics include telephone patch-throughs, bounce-backs, satellite conferencing, and interactive kiosks. A telephone *patch-through* is when an organization calls members and, if the reaction is suitable, immediately forwards the calls to an elected official so the members can deliver a personal message or view. *Bounce-backs* are direct mail response vehicles signed by members and forwarded to officials to register a specific message or opinion. *Satellite conferencing* is an electronic meeting in which group constituents in a targeted legislator's district can discuss a specific issue or pending legislation. *Interactive kiosks* are exhibit booths at conventions or related conferences where interested citizens or group members may forward phone calls, faxes, or messages to elected officials.[39]

Information technology has transformed U.S. culture and politics. One result is that corporations and trade associations are building public constituencies for their issues. The number of national citizen action groups increases each year. All such groups have a particular issue to protect, define, and/or promote. Although citizen action groups have existed since the beginning of our nation's history, political action committees (PACs) are a more recent phenomenon. In 1974 there were 608 registered PACs; by 2000, the number had grown to 3,900.[40] Beyond serving as an essential source of political campaign funding, organizational PACs often run their own issue campaigns. There are two major types of political action committees: affiliated and independent. Affiliated PACs include labor unions, corporations, cooperatives, and professional organizations (trade and health). Each group is separate and collects funds from individuals associated with the sponsoring organization. Independent PACs include those organized to support a particular politician or issue.[41]

In the beginning, PACs were oriented to business or labor concerns and were created to give money to political candidates. Over the years, political action committees have changed from representing large industry groups to working on behalf of smaller subsets focusing on just a few issues. PACs are now more specialized and ideological, more likely to represent a narrow wing of a national party or special interests on a specific issue. Unlike the traditional business PAC, the new *leadership* PACs want to inject their issues into the national political debate. As Peter Dickinson, co-executive director of Campaign for Working Families, a conservative PAC headed by Gary Bauer (a 2000 Republican presidential contender and advisor to the Reagan administration) says, "We're not an organization interested in gaining access to members. We want to impact elections and help to drive issues, perhaps on a national level."[42] For example, The People for the American Way, a liberal organization, formed its own PAC and placed ads criticizing the impeachment process of President Bill Clinton.

Interest groups, labor unions, corporations, political parties, and even private individuals often engage in issue advocacy activities. Although contributions to individuals are restricted, donated funds can pay for commercials that do not *explicitly* call for the *election* or *defeat* of an individual without limitation. Of course, it is rather easy to structure an advertisement that clearly expresses preference without naming individuals. For example, an ad that ran in the fall of 2000 by the American Conservative Union contained shots of babies with the voice-over stating, "In New York, all babies like these have something in common." Following the shot of a baby wearing a New York Yankee baseball cap, the announcer stated, "They've lived here longer than Hillary Rodham Clinton." On the screen appeared: "Learn more at http://www.conservative.org. Paid for by the one million members and supporters of the American Conservative Union." Issue advocacy communication is often much more attack oriented than advertisements for candidates. During the 2000 campaign, seventy-four groups spent well over $90 million on television issue advocacy commercials.[43]

Modern grassroots lobbying is one of the hottest trends in politics today. Interest groups expand and quickly become professional organizations; the news media can spotlight group activities, and technology makes building volunteer organizations as simple as soliciting financial support and creating/maintaining a computer database. Corporations such as Philip Morris, R. J. Reynolds, and WBX Technologies use proactive, grassroots mobilization for controversial issues such as the sale of cigarettes or waste removal. Organizations such as the National Rifle Association and the American Association of Retired Persons are extremely accomplished at mobilizing grassroots support. Orchestrated grassroots activities alarm many political observers. Some view grassroots lobbying as a weapon of powerful and rich corporations and special-interest groups. Others, however, view such efforts as ways to reinvigorate and educate the public on issues of great importance to our nation. The orchestration of public opinion to promote a particular view is nothing new; it falls squarely within our democratic tradition. Grassroots lobbying will undoubtedly increase in both level of activity and intensity in the future.

Corporate Advocacy/Issue Management.   Corporate advocacy and issue campaigns have increased in prominence and thus merit special consideration. In the early 1970s, corporations were suffering from a variety of social and economic problems: recession, inflation, oil crises, decline of public trust, increase of public hostility toward large companies, and increased legislative restrictions and controls. In this social and political environment, corporations developed extensive public relations staffs whose jobs were to present the companies' policies to the public through the distribution of information. Today, many corporate communication endeavors advocate specific viewpoints on issues. Although corporations recognize the value of maintaining public goodwill, they are also willing to engage in open debate about a variety of social issues. They compete to influence public attitudes and/or behavior. In exercising their First Amendment right of freedom of speech, companies aggressively assert their social, political, and economic agendas. The participation in the formation of public opinion is now an essential element of corporate public relations. Such activities are part of a genre of advertising known as corporate advocacy and issue management. Practitioners must possess the skills necessary for developing and executing strategic communication campaigns and activities. They require the skills of anticipation, interpretation of public opinion, research, campaign implementation, and evaluation.

Prakash Sethi defines advocacy advertising as "the propagation of ideas and elucidation of controversial social issues of public importance in a manner that supports the position and interests of the sponsor while expressly denying the accuracy of facts and downgrading the sponsor's opponents."[44] The goals of advocacy advertising are to counteract public hostility to corporate activities, to counter the spread of misleading information by critics of the organization, to educate the public on complex issues of importance to an organization, to counteract inadequate access to and bias in the news media, and to promote the values of free enterprise.

Issue management encompasses more strategic activities than does advocacy advertising. Issue management includes proactive public relations activities designed to head off problems between corporations and their publics. According to Robert Heath and Kenneth Cousino, this means the involvement of public policy experts in strategic business planning and management, issue monitoring and analysis, communicating about issues and efforts to meet changing standards of corporate social responsibility.[45]

One of the earliest, now classic, advocacy campaigns was the ExxonMobil op-ed advertising program. For over 30 years ExxonMobil has placed full-page editorials in newspapers, news magazines, and service-club magazines like *Rotarian, Kiwanian,* and *Elks.* Their goal is "to encourage thought and dialogue by informing the public about our industry, explaining our views on key issues of the day and presenting responsible policy proposals. We welcome comments and reactions to the opinions expressed."[46] The approach was to "take the offensive without being offensive."[47] "In political terms," according to Herb Schmertz, former public affairs director, "the ads constitute the platform on which we run. Each week, in effect, we add another plank or reinforce a previous one. To continue the analogy, we are continually seeking new supporters among the undecided, and one way we do this is by a continuing series of position papers on the important issues of the day."[48]

When ExxonMobil began the campaign in 1970, three major issues faced the oil industry: oil cutoffs from foreign nations, environmental concerns from the public over oil drilling and excavation, and low public confidence in the credibility of corporations. The first op-ed piece appeared on October 19, 1970, with the headline: "America has the world's best highways and the world's worst mass transit. We hope this ad moves people." The ad was not self-serving but actually addressed the need for more and better mass transit systems to reduce oil consumption. Ultimately, ExxonMobil wants to portray itself as a credible champion of the public interest. Based on content analyses of ExxonMobil's op-ed ads from 1982–86, Gerri Smith and Robert Heath found both moral and expertise appeals.[49] The moral appeals involved traditional values and sought to convince the audience that it was morally wrong not to agree or comply with the message. The use of expertise appeals attempted to enhance the company's image and credibility. From the beginning, ExxonMobil accepted the long-term perspective, realizing that it would take years for the campaign to yield results.

Corporations are primarily concerned with how issues and legislation about the environment, public health and safety, and governmental regulations affect their business. For example, oil and chemical companies usually address environmental issues of conservation and pollution. Tobacco companies address freedom

Africa's health crisis

There is an unprecedented health crisis in sub-Saharan Africa.

Malaria has rebounded steadily since the 1970s, largely due to the end of antimalarial spraying. Of the one million people who die of malaria every year worldwide, at least 70% are African children.

Nearly 30 million people there are living with HIV/AIDS, including 10 million between the ages of 15 and 24 and three million children under 15. Last year 2.4 million Africans died of AIDS, and 3.5 million were newly infected.

HIV also brings tuberculosis (TB) in its wake. Together, HIV and TB are a lethal combination, each speeding the other's progress.

The economic impact of the three scourges of malaria, AIDS and TB has been enormous. For example, HIV/AIDS strikes hardest at people in the prime of their lives and leaves behind orphans and destitute elderly dependents. Because it can ravage the adult population of rural areas, it contributes to agricultural decline and malnutrition, even starvation.

Just as there is a gathering crisis, there is a gathering response. Global institutions and governments are joining the fight. One example is the Global Fund to Fight AIDS, Tuberculosis and Malaria. This is a newly formed intergovernmental organization funded largely by the major industrialized countries. It recently distributed its first round of grants. And President Bush has

asked Congress for substantial additional funds to fight AIDS in Africa.

Several other organizations deserve special mention: the Global Business Coalition on HIV/AIDS, the Global Health Initiative Task Force of the World Economic Forum, the World Health Organization's Roll Back Malaria initiative and the Corporate Council on Africa. These organizations and others like them are dedicated to mobilizing the resources and skills of private companies in improving public health. ExxonMobil is actively involved in their work.

Private companies benefit from healthy communities and a healthy workforce. That is why we help provide clean water and vaccination programs, and why we support the initiatives just mentioned. We are also well acquainted with the local communities where we operate. In addition to financial aid the private sector can, because of this familiarity, provide employee involvement, logistical support, training, local health infrastructure and, most important of all, a path to better living conditions in the form of employment and economic development.

The health crisis in Africa is too big for the governments there to handle by themselves. They need help — from other countries, from responsible NGOs and from the private sector. All can join together to help offer an effective response to deadly disease — and hope to millions.

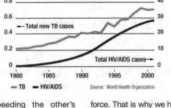

Africa Disease Trends
1980—2001 (Millions of cases)

— Total new TB cases

Total HIV/AIDS cases

— TB   — HIV/AIDS   Source: World Health Organization

ExxonMobil

Exxon Mobil Corporation

of choice and smokers' rights. Insurance companies actively support seat belts and airbags for automobiles.

Brad Hainsworth argues that corporate issues evolve in a rather predictable manner.[50] The process is composed of four stages: origin, mediation and amplification, organization, and resolution. In the origin stage, "an issue arises when an organization or public attaches significance to a perceived problem that is a consequence of a developing political, economic, or social trend."[51] Awareness and concern are expressed by identifiable publics or social groups. Conflict begins to emerge over the perceived problem, and there are calls to do something about the issue. Corporations must constantly survey the social and political environment for such issues.

Figure 9.2   Planning an Event for News Coverage

An important part of the process of designing persuasive campaigns involves planning public events that may be covered as part of the day's news. Press conferences, open meetings, rallies, and protests can become powerful forums for the communication of a group's social or political agenda. Many now routinely employ guidelines developed by political campaigners, who have always needed to reach potential supporters via the free news media. Here is a list of common rules for promoting the coverage of an event by the broadcast and print media:[52]

- Schedule events early in the day, at times convenient for the media from whom you want coverage. If you want to make a noon newscast, plan a 9:30 to 10:00 a.m. starting time.

- Organize the event around one basic theme. Determine the lead you want the press to write, then organize the event to achieve it.

- Make sure your primary spokesperson is well briefed with accurate information and knowledge of the questions he or she may be asked.

- Call assignment editors and ask for coverage. In the unsubtle publicity arts, shyness is not a virtue.

- Make your event as visual as possible. The announcement of a lawsuit against a local polluter will be more interesting to television if it is made at the site of the pollution rather than in an organization's office.

- Prepare packets of information to back up your basic message. Make it as easy as possible for reporters to get the necessary facts.

- Consider the convenience of the reporters from whom you want coverage. Will they need telephones, suitable background and lighting for video, a common audio feed for the public address system, a place to sit, etc.?

- If the goal is television and radio coverage, break up your statement into short, quotable segments. In a perfect world the average television news story would run longer than 40 seconds. Because short stories are the rule, your advocate will probably receive a 15-second sound bite. Make it count.

- If members of the press fail to attend, send them coverage of the event anyway: press releases with relevant quotes to the print media or your own videotape to the television media.

The process of mediation and amplification occurs when multiple publics (i.e., interest groups, professions, and industries) expand the discussion of the issue through specialized media and begin to address policy implications. Regulations may be drafted or legislation proposed. Theorists argue that it is at this stage of issue development that an organization may have the greatest influence on further development and resolution of the issue.

The organizational stage emerges when publics unite around the issue and support specific actions of resolution. Public visibility is heightened, and the issue is propelled into public debate and policy process. Opinion leaders and public officials rally around the issue and seek a resolution to the conflict. The resolution stage is when the issue or conflict is addressed through legislation or regulatory policies.

An aggressive corporate advocacy and issue management perspective allows large companies to become active players in the political process, which is a legitimate cause for concern. Large corporations have access to media and multimillion-dollar budgets, unlike most citizens and civic groups. How will opposing viewpoints or legitimate challenges to corporate claims and information be disseminated? Should corporations pay for such ads from after-tax profits, or are these campaigns general business expenses and thus tax deductible?

Social Movements

There have been times in our nation's history when large groups of citizens mobilized to express anger, support, or ideas about a wide variety of issues and topics. Groups were organized by race, sex, age, and social or political beliefs. Actions ranged from advocacy to violent demonstrations. In the eighteenth century, a social movement led to the Revolutionary War and our independence. In the nineteenth century, social movements fought to free the slaves, end child labor, improve the working conditions of factory workers, gain voting rights for women, and abolish the legalization of alcohol. In the twentieth century, many of the earlier movements continued to engage supporters while new causes such as advocating world peace, abortion rights, protection for the environment, and protection of the rights of the elderly, gays, African Americans, Latinos/as, and Native Americans gained traction. As we enter the twenty-first century, many of the same movements seek political, social, and religious justice.[53] Americans have always joined together to exercise, and sometimes even stretch, the principles of democracy. Such social collective actions are called social movements and are a special form or type of persuasive campaign. Their primary purpose is to bring about or to resist change. Charles Stewart, Craig Smith, and Robert Denton argue that social movements are unique, with special characteristics that distinguish them from other forms and functions of mass persuasion, such as political parties, advertising campaigns, lobbying or other special-interest group campaigns.[54]

Characteristics.   Social movements are an *organized collectivity with minimal organization*. Some movements are more organized than others. During the 1960s, the civil rights movement was well organized, with Martin Luther King recognized as the major leader; the American Indian movement was less visible and much smaller in scope. It should be noted that there may be many organizations within

How can you help protect
the prairie and the penguin?

Simple. Visit www.earthshare.org and learn how the world's
leading environmental groups are working together under one
name. And how easy it is for you to help protect the prairies and
the penguins and the planet.

www.earthshare.org

One environment. One simple way to care for it.   **Earth Share**

Earth Share Campaign created by Foote, Cone & Belding, Chicago.

the same basic movement. For example, within the pro-life movement there are various religious and secular organizations that seek legislation limiting abortions. Social movements may encompass numerous campaigns by different organizations to achieve specific goals.

Social movements are *uninstitutionalized collectivities* because they operate outside the established social order. This means that access to institutional channels of power, communication, and funding are not available. The activities of most labor unions, PACs, and legislative committees are not social movements. Such groups, however, may have been part of an earlier movement. For example, the United Auto Workers was at one time a movement organization; today it is part of the established order. Thus, social movements are always an "out-group."

Movements must be *significantly large in scope*. Movements must be large enough in terms of geographic area, time, and participants to accomplish specified programs and tasks. The larger the movement, the greater the visibility and funding possibilities. Movements grow from the ground up rather than from the top down.

Movements *propose or oppose programs for change in societal norms, values,* or *both*. The rhetoric of movements prescribes what must be done, who must do it, and how it must be done. Innovative social movements, for example, hope to replace existing norms or values with new ones. Examples of innovative movements include women's rights, civil rights, or gay liberation movements. Revivalistic movements work to return to the norms or values of an idealized past; the Native American, pro-life, and environmental movements are revivalistic. Finally, resistance movements work to prevent changes in existing norms or values. Often, such movements favor the status quo and arise in opposition to newly formed movements. Examples of resistance movements include anti-civil rights, Aryan superiority, and pro-choice movements.

Movements *encounter opposition in a moral struggle*. Movement members believe they possess moral authority and legitimacy of purpose. They view their actions as a moral imperative—a mission to correct social injustice or evil. Challenges to social norms and the status quo generate opposition from various organizations or established institutions such as universities, churches, businesses, regulatory bodies, and so on. The opposition believes equally fervently that their goals to preserve the status quo are principled and righteous.

Finally, *persuasion is pervasive* in social movements. Through verbal and nonverbal symbols social movements work to change audience perceptions and behavior. Although violence is sometimes associated with social movements, it is incidental and used primarily for symbolic purposes. Persuasion is the primary means for satisfying the major functions and requirements of social movements.

Persuasive Functions. Social movements must fulfill a number of roles if they hope to contribute significantly to change. Stewart, Smith, and Denton identify six basic persuasive functions: transform perceptions of reality, alter self-perceptions of protestors, legitimize the social movement, prescribe and sell courses of action, mobilize for action, and sustain the social movement.[55] Transforming perceptions of reality include altering perceptions of the past, present, and future. Movements must challenge accepted ways of viewing historical events and people in order to emphasize the severity of a problem and the need for drastic action. For example, the women's movement had to confront and to change the established view that a woman's place was in the home caring for children while a husband established a career and provided for the family.

There are several ways movements alter perceptions of the present. For example, renaming or redefining an event or object provides an opportunity for people to view the circumstance differently. Within the pro-life movement, language referring to the fetus as a baby and abortion as murder has a strong impact on listeners. Movements use *god terms* and *devil terms* to create clear images of good and bad behavior or thought. For most Americans god terms include democracy, freedom, liberty, equality, and justice, to name only a few. Devil terms would be opposite notions such as communism, slavery, or prejudice. Another common way to alter perceptions of the present is to provide information that counters or demonstrates inconsistencies with the information provided by the established order. Like political candidates, social movement leaders must provide a utopian vision of a future full of hope and optimism. To accomplish this, the rhetoric includes bleak images of what the future will be if the goals of the movement are not met.

An ongoing task is to enhance perceptions of the movement and its members. This is often accomplished by contrasting selfless movement members altruistically working for the common good with opponents who have selfish motives with no redeeming value. Opponents are grand conspirators who have secretly committed a crime against the people. The movement is at war with the opposition.

Social movements must transform self-perceptions of members to believe in the righteousness of their cause and in their power to accomplish the goals of the movement. For example, the women's liberation movement conducted consciousness-raising groups to enhance self-concept, dignity, and worth. Through this transformation, women could recognize their potential and gain strength to compete in a "man's world." In the 1960s, blacks chose the word *black* to replace the word *Negro*, which had been selected by whites. Black power became the symbol for independence, power, and dignity.

One of the most difficult tasks for a movement leader is to maintain the legitimacy of the movement and to confer that legitimacy on movement members. Strategies include both finding common ground and defining dissimilarities. *Common ground* strategies involve creating a sense of identification by emphasizing similarities, shared experiences, and a common cause with targeted audiences. *Conflict strategies* emphasize dissimilarities and conflict with those who oppose the movement's goals.

In prescribing courses of action, social movements must first explain what should be done. Movements must not only develop a program of change with specific demands, actions, and solutions to problems; they must also sell, defend, and justify the program. Movements also specify who is most qualified to do the job. They provide rationales for why their organization, leaders, and members provide the best means of creating the desired change. Finally, movements must articulate how the changes should be instituted. This may be one of the more critical persuasive tasks. Movement members differ in terms of intensity of feeling, identification with the cause, and patience. The more radical factions may prefer ultimatums, confrontation, or terrorism to bring about the desired change. Others may prefer nonviolent resistance tactics such as sit-ins, boycotts, or strikes. Others may simply wish to petition the establishment for a fair hearing, preferring to work within the legislative structure to bring about the desired change.

Leaders must be sufficiently persuasive to inspire people to join and participate in the movement. They must continually disseminate the movement's message in order to attract new members and to maintain old ones and to mobilize members to work for the movement's goals. Leaders must unify, organize, and energize a diverse membership.

Sustaining a movement is a major persuasive task. It is easier to start a movement than to sustain one. Leaders must justify setbacks and remain optimistic about accomplishing movement goals. For the movement to be successful, it must remain visible and viable. As a movement becomes older, these tasks become more difficult. Movements use special ceremonies, annual conventions, and anniversary celebrations to keep the movement visible.

Life Cycle.   Although it is nearly impossible to divide movements into separate phases, there are recognizable patterns of development. Stewart, Smith, and Denton identify five stages of social movements: genesis, social unrest, enthusiastic mobilization, maintenance, and termination.[56] As a movement matures, the persuasive requirements evolve and change among the various stages.

The genesis stage consists primarily of intellectuals or prophets articulating some imperfection in society through essays, editorials, songs, poems, pamphlets, lectures, or books. They identify a problem and visualize a bleak future if the problem is not solved. Bob Dylan and others addressed the dangers inherent in the Vietnam War in folk songs nearly a year before the Gulf of Tonkin incident that escalated U.S. involvement. Betty Friedan's book entitled *The Feminine Mystique* initiated the women's movement by describing the status quo and the need for change. Such works provide a source for public discussion about key issues. Sometimes a special event will trigger attention to an issue or cause. The *Roe v. Wade* decision in 1973 by the Supreme Court allowed abortion in all fifty states and provided the impetus for the pro-life movement.

In the social unrest stage, prophets and intellectuals become agitators, and the goals of the movement began to coalesce. Concerned citizens alerted to the problems become active members. The movement produces its own literature, often including a manifesto or declaration presented at a convention or conference. The ideology clearly identifies the "devils" responsible for the problem and the "gods" who will forge solutions. In attempting to transform perceptions of society, such we-they distinctions are extremely important. Most rhetorical energies during this stage involve petitioning the groups perceived to be responsible for the status quo.

The enthusiastic mobilization stage of a social movement is exciting. The charismatic leader emerges and captures a great deal of attention for the movement and its issues. Membership expands to include sympathizers from both the general public and the establishment. All available channels and means of communication are utilized to advance the cause. The movement now confronts serious opposition, and the strategies must extend beyond legislative petition and discursive measures. Mass rallies and demonstrations are used to disseminate the movement's message, to draw attention to itself, and to pressure the opposition. The persuasive goal of the movement during this phase is to raise the consciousness level of the public and to force the establishment to comply with movement demands.

It is difficult to maintain the energy and enthusiasm of the earlier stages. As defeats mount and goals are not immediately realized, the members become impatient, and the public becomes bored. In the maintenance stage, persuasive tactics focus on legislative measures, membership retention, and fund raising. The leadership changes from agitators to statesmen. The primary channels of communication are newsletters, journals, and the occasional television talk show. Sweeping demands are compromised, and the rhetoric is moderated.

In the termination stage, the social movement ceases to exist. The movement may have accomplished its goal (as did the antislavery movement of 1865 with the passage of the Thirteenth Amendment to the Constitution) or it may be transformed into part of the establishment (as was the Nazi movement in Germany). Some movements die while others become pressure groups, such as the American Indian Movement or the consumer rights movement. Few social movements are totally successful in their efforts. Some members become disaffected and drop out or join a splinter group, while others simply become part of "the system."

Each stage requires specific persuasive skills, personalities, and tactics. In open societies, social movements are often the primary initiators of social change. Thus, although all social movements end, they do impact society in a variety of ways, such as new laws, social awareness, or new social groups, to name only a few.

Leadership. Social movement leaders are frequently from higher strata groups—teachers, students, professionals, clergy, and so on.[57] Perhaps the most important function of social movement leaders is as the symbol of their movement. They are identified with its mission and cause and are responsible for the members' actions. While they are decision makers, they lack the powers of reward and punishment usually associated with more traditional views of leadership. Movement leaders are confronted with a variety of tasks, pressures, and audiences. Most leaders must be capable of handling diverse and often conflicting roles on a daily basis. They must be able to communicate with the media and establishment members, while maintaining the trust of the "true believers" of the movement.

Movement leaders obtain their positions by being perceived as charismatic, prophetic, or pragmatic. Charisma refers to a public presence that inspires confidence and attracts followers. Prophecy relates to the leader's ability to articulate movement principles, values, and beliefs. Of course, a leader must ultimately get something done. A mere ideologue will not be sufficiently pragmatic to be able to sustain a leadership role. Movement leadership is a difficult and challenging task. Without question, most movement leaders are admired by some and hated by others. They must be able to handle diverse and conflicting roles, change as the movement changes, adapt to events, and lead without getting too far ahead or too far behind their movements.

Resistance to Social Movements.   Because establishments have a strong commitment to the status quo, it is not surprising—in fact, it should be expected—that they will respond to disruptions and challenges.[58] In a democratic society, just how strong should the response be? While the First Amendment protects freedom of speech, there are certainly limits of expression. When does a shout become disruptive? When does a gesture become obscene? In essence, how does the establishment balance its legal obligations and the rights of society against the rights of individuals, minorities, and/or unpopular ideas or opinions?

There are five general strategies employed by the established order to confront and resist social movements.[59] The strategy of evasion is usually the first strategy employed. The movement is largely ignored. Establishment figures refuse to acknowledge or meet with movement leaders.

The strategy of counterpersuasion occurs when the establishment can no longer ignore the movement. In this case, institutions actively challenge the goals, assumptions, and leaders of the movement. Leaders are discredited. Goals of the movement are characterized as dangerous. Opponents may claim that the movement threatens democracy and promotes anarchy. Movement leaders are characterized as extremists or fanatics. Such rhetoric will often generate fear among the "silent majority." From a bureaucratic perspective, government agencies can postpone action on movement requests or deny permits for meetings or parades.

A more aggressive approach is the strategy of coercive persuasion that involves tactics ranging from general harassment to labeling movement leaders as criminal to prosecution of movement leaders and members. Coercion attempts can include police arrests, creation of secret files, tax audits, military reclassifications, or challenges to government funding or loans—to name only a few. Such tactics send a powerful message to movement leaders and followers, creating fear and hesitation among movement members.

The strategy of adjustment gives the appearance of working with the movement, providing some concessions without accepting movement demands or goals. Symbolic gestures may include appointing special committees or commissions to study proposals, firing or replacing midlevel personnel who were targets of attacks, or incorporating movement leaders and sympathizers within the institutional structure.

The strategy of capitulation is the total acceptance of a movement's goals, beliefs, and ideology. This rarely occurs. The established order controls communication channels and has too many resources at its disposal. However, over a period of time, many movement goals and objectives find their way into mainstream American life.

CAMPAIGN IMPLEMENTATION
▲

Allan Cigler and Burdett Loomis observe four trends in contemporary public persuasion. First, the number of special-interest groups that attempt to influence policy outcomes has increased. Second, lobbying efforts extend beyond the halls of Congress to media blitzes and grassroots efforts aimed at key constituencies. Third, the government itself engages in public campaigns. Finally, there is a declining distinction between the politics of elections and the politics of policy making. Public persuasion contributes to an activated social culture.[60]

The key to the execution of any successful campaign is systematic planning. The basic steps in developing a campaign are the same regardless of its size, scope, or focus. Figure 9.3 identifies six basic considerations that would be appropriate for nearly all types of campaigns.[61]

Figure 9.3   Campaign Implementation Overview

Stage	*Components*
1. Situation analysis	target audience; product/issue/idea; competition or opponent
2. Objectives	missions; goals; outcomes
3. Strategies	messages; media; presentation activities
4. Budget	labor; material; media; talent; production
5. Implementation	timing; follow-up
6. Evaluation	what people say; what people think; what people do

---

The primary purpose of the *situation analysis* step of campaign planning is to gather needed information that will become the basis for designing the persuasive message, strategies, and execution. A careful situation analysis provides an assessment of the potential audiences or market and the social environment in which they are located plus the strengths and weaknesses of the product or idea. From an advertising perspective, the situation analysis includes investigations of the consumer, the product, and the competition. An issue campaign perspective focuses on the elements of the problem and the targeted audiences. Research is vital for this phase of campaign planning. *Secondary research* involves finding relevant information that has already been collected by others; it provides a general orientation. The major source of secondary research is the local library. *Primary research* is original research conducted to gather specific information. For example, although secondary research could reveal a national trend toward more healthy food and drink, a specific survey may be needed to isolate probable successful appeals and which categories of food items to target. Three descriptive variables of the audience are investigated. Demographic characteristics are derived from statistical studies of the population. Such characteristics include age, sex, income, education, family size, and occupation. Geographic characteristics focus on differences among urban, suburban, and rural areas of the country as well as regional differences. Finally, psychographic analysis attempts to describe markets based on lifestyle issues, activities, interests, and opinions.

After research has been conducted and analyzed, the next step is to determine *objectives*—what the campaign seeks to accomplish. Different objectives will influence how the campaign is developed. Objectives are clear, specific, and measurable statements of desired outcomes of the campaign. Clear objectives help reduce uncertainty, aid in direct message formation, and provide standards for evaluation. Some objectives may be stated in terms of unit or dollar sales. Others may be set in terms of some type of behavioral activity by the audience. For example, the targeted audience of the campaign may be asked to purchase a product, call a number, return a reply card, seek more information, contribute to a cause, vote for a specific candidate, or attend an event. Sometimes the objectives focus on communication effects such as general awareness, message recall, product knowledge and preference, or issue-position conviction. Objectives may range from: general outcomes desired by a campaign; more specific task outcomes or end points of activities to be completed by workers in order to execute a campaign; very specific, measurable or observable end results that a campaign must attain.

Objectives target *what* needs to be done; *strategies* explain *how* to do it. Strategic areas of concern include message construction, media selection, tactics, publicity, and promotions. The goal of the message strategy is to construct a message or series of messages that will influence a target audience to think, act, or behave in the desired way. The key to most successful strategies is to isolate the appeals, promises, solutions, or benefits that will have the greatest impact on the target audience. One of the best known techniques for structuring effective, persuasive communications is the *AIDA formula*: an acronym for attention, interest, desire, and action. Good research provides the clues to message creation and tactic selection. (Message construction strategies are discussed in detail in chapters 4, 6, and 13.)

Whether conducting a commercial advertising campaign or a political campaign, *budget* impacts all other elements of campaign design and development. For some campaigns, budgets are of little concern; for others, funds may be limited. Today, with the cost of media, labor, and material, the campaign budget becomes a vital consideration in the formation of a campaign. It is often useful to generate several possible budgets for a campaign—from an optimal budget that satisfies every possible need to a more modest budget that will accomplish fewer, but still important, objectives. The creation of multiple budget scenarios increases flexibility in campaign execution.

Timing is critical for the next step: *implementation* of the plan of action. Follow-up activities reinforce initial impressions and provide the foundation for the final step.

Finally, a systematic *evaluation* of the campaign reveals what worked and what did not work; it also allows for the fine-tuning of various campaign elements in order to maximize effectiveness. Measures and criteria of evaluation are planned ahead of time; they should be used from the start of the campaign all the way through to the conclusion. Commercial advertising campaign evaluation is a form of research that attempts to determine what actually happened in the marketplace and why. There are many things to measure other than a win-lose situation. Elements of awareness (knowledge, recall, or recognition), attitude (perceptions, feelings, or preferences), and behavior (purchase, vote, or support) are examples of areas to assess and evaluate. Thus, the evaluation of a campaign involves more than just the visible outcomes, especially if one wishes to learn for future efforts. Many of the same research techniques used in analyzing the situation can be used in evaluating the persuasive campaign.

SUMMARY

▲

Public persuasion differs from interpersonal persuasion in size and scope. The larger the audience, the more elements of persuasion that are needed to alter beliefs, attitudes, and values. Mass persuasion requires numerous messages, numerous appeals, and numerous communication channels. Persuasive campaigns, therefore, are a highly organized series of messages designed to meet all of these criteria. The messages must appeal to large numbers of people.

The systematic execution of a campaign includes analyzing the situation, developing objectives, planning strategies, preparing budgets, implementing the campaign, and evaluating its success. These processes are true for all types of campaigns: product advertising, political, and issue, which includes grassroots and corporate advocacy/issue management.

Although a form of public persuasion, social movements are unique collective phenomena that are more complex than the other types of campaigns. Persuasion is the essence of social movements. It is the key ingredient needed to transform conceptions of history, alter current perceptions, prescribe courses of action, mobilize for action, and sustain the movement. Across the various stages of a movement—genesis, social unrest, enthusiastic mobilization, maintenance, and termination—persuasion requirements evolve and change.

Social movements have played an important role in our society. They have stimulated argument and debate about human rights, war, and peace. They have provided the catalyst for social change and legislative action. Public persuasion is a vital part of a democratic society. It influences what we want, what we buy, what we think, and how we interact with others.

Questions and Projects for Further Study

1. Select a product and find ads for it in 8 to 10 different magazines. How are the ads similar? How do they differ?

2. Select an example of the following types of campaigns: commercial advertising, political, governmental, corporate advocacy and issue management. How are they similar? How do they differ?

3. Formulate a hypothetical product and develop a campaign according to the steps presented in the chapter.

4. Construct a national public relations campaign on the issue of alcohol abuse using awareness, information, education, reinforcement, and behavior modification approaches. How are they similar? How do they differ?

5. According to the criteria presented in the chapter, which of the following is a social movement? Why?

survivalists	Nazi
consumer rights	Gray Panthers
ecology	tax reform
American Indian	Greenpeace

6. Select a social movement and demonstrate how the movement fulfills the persuasive functions identified in the chapter.

Additional Reading

Allan Cigler and Burdett Loomis, eds., *Interest Group Politics*, 6th ed.(Washington, DC: Congressional Quarterly Press, 2002).

Robert E. Denton, Jr. and Gary Woodward, *Political Communication in America*, 3rd ed. (Westport, CT: Praeger, 1998).

Stewart Ewen, *PR! A Social History of Spin* (New York: Basic Books, 1996).

Robert L. Heath, ed., *Handbook of Public Relations* (Thousand Oaks, CA: Sage, 2001).

Ronald Rice and Charles Atkin, eds., *Public Communication Campaigns,* 3rd ed. (Thousand Oaks, CA: Sage, 2001).

Fraser P. Seitel, *The Practice of Public Relations,* 8th ed. (Englewood Cliffs, NJ: Prentice-Hall, 2001).

Daniel Shea and Michael Burton, *Campaign Craft: The Strategies, Tactics, and Art of Political Campaign Management* (Westport, CT: Praeger, 2001).

Charles Stewart, Craig Smith, and Robert E. Denton, Jr., *Persuasion and Social Movements*, 4th ed. (Prospect Heights, IL: Waveland Press, 2001).

Judith Trent and Robert Friedenberg, *Political Campaign Communication*, 5th ed. (Lanham, MD: Rowman & Littlefield, 2004).

Notes

[1] Gerard A. Hauser, *Introduction to Rhetorical Theory* (Long Grove, IL: Waveland Press, 2002) p. 96.

[2] Shearon Lowery and Melvin DeFleur, *Milestones in Mass Communication Research*, 3rd ed. (New York: Longman, 1995), p. 11.

[3] Carroll J. Glynn, Susan Herbst, Garrett O'Keefe, and Robert Shapiro, *Public Opinion* (Boulder, CO: Westview Press, 1999), pp. 4–11.

[4] Dennis Wilcox, Phillip Ault, Warren Agee, and Glen Cameron, *Public Relations: Strategies and Tactics*, 6th ed. (New York: Longman, 2000), p. 210.

[5] William Paisley, "Public Communication Campaigns: The American Experience," in *Public Communication Campaigns*, 3rd ed., eds. Ronald Rice and Charles Atkin (Thousand Oaks, CA: Sage, 2001), pp. 16–20.

[6] Herbert Simons, *Persuasion*, 2nd ed. (New York: Random House, 1986), p. 227.

[7] Samuel Becker, "Rhetorical Studies for the Contemporary World," in *The Prospect of Rhetoric,* eds. Lloyd Bitzer and Edwin Black (Englewood Cliffs, NJ: Prentice-Hall, 1971), p. 21.

[8] Ibid., pp. 21–43.

[9] Richard Campbell, *Media and Culture* (Boston: Bedford/St. Martin's Press, 2003), p. 425.

[10] Don Schultz and Beth Barnes, *Strategic Advertising Campaigns* (Lincolnwood, IL: NTC Publishing, 1995), p. 241.

[11] Emma Daugherty, "Public Relations and Social Responsibility," in *Handbook of Public Relations*, ed. by Robert Heath (Thousand Oaks, CA: Sage, 2001), p. 406.

[12] Campbell, p. 425.

[13] Campbell, p. 433.

[14] Ibid., p. 431.

[15] Ibid., p. 433.

[16] Stewart Ewen, *PR! A Social History of Spin* (New York: Basic Books, 1996), p. 34.

[17] Doug Newsom, Judy Turk, and Dean Kruckeberg, *This is PR: The Realities of Public Relations*, 6th ed. (Belmont, CA: Wadsworth, 1996), p. 190.

[18] Ibid., pp. 453–56.

[19] Kathleen Fearn-Banks, "Crisis Communication," in *Handbook of Public Relations*, ed. by Robert Heath (Thousand Oaks, CA: Sage, 2001), p. 480.

[20] Ibid., p. 480.

[21] Ibid., p. 480.

[22] Michael Pfau and Roxanne Parrott, *Persuasive Communication Campaigns* (Boston: Allyn & Bacon, 1993), pp. 332–33.

[23] Paul Lazarsfeld, et al., *The People's Choice* (New York: Columbia University Press, 1948).

[24] Daniel Shea and Michael Burton, *Campaign Craft: The Strategies, Tactics, and Art of Campaign Management*, Revised Edition (Westport, CT: Praeger, 2001), pp. 7–10.

[25] Bruce Gronbeck, "Functional and Dramaturgical Theories of Presidential Campaigning," *Presidential Studies Quarterly*, Fall 1984, 14:490.

[26] Ibid, p. 496.

[27] Newsom, et al., p. 457.

[28] Wilcox, et al., p. 332.

[29] Ron Faucheux, "The Grassroots Explosion," *Campaigns & Elections*, December/January 1995, p. 20.

[30] Faucheux, p. 22.

[31] Ibid., p. 23.

[32] Kenneth Godwin, *One Billion Dollars of Influence* (Chatham, NJ: Chatham House, 1988), p. 74.

[33] AARP Fact Sheet; AARP Annual Report 2002, p. 10. Both available at http://www.aarp.org/aboutaarp; accessed10-14-03.

[34] Kelly Patterson and Matthew Singer, "The National Rifle Association in the Face of the Clinton Challenge," in *Interest Group Politics*, 6th ed., eds. Allan Cigler and Burdett Loomis (Washington, DC: CQ Press, 2002), p. 57.

[35] Ibid., pp. 58–59.

[36] Ibid., pp. 67–72.

[37] Ibid., p. 71.

[38] Godwin, p. 94.

[39] Faucheux, p. 22.

[40] http://www.cfinst.org/studies/vital/tables/3-9.htm; accessed 10-14-03.

[41] Margaret Conway, et al., "Interest Group Money in Elections," in *Interest Group Politics*, 6th ed., eds. Allan Cigler and Burdett Loomis (Washington, DC: CQ Press, 2002), pp. 121–25.

[42] Derek Willis, "PAC Plays," *Campaigns & Elections*, April 1999, pp. 241–46.

[43] Conway, et al., p. 149.

[44] S. Prakash Sethi, *Advocacy Advertising and Large Corporations* (Lexington, MA: Lexington Books, 1977), p. 57.

[45] Robert Heath and Kenneth Cousino, "Issues Management: End of First Decade Progress Report," *Public Relations Review*, Spring 1990, 16(1):10.

[46] http://www2.exxonmobil.com/Corporate/Newsroom/OpEds/Corp_NR_OpEds_Overview.asp; accessed 10-14-03.

[47] Herb Schmertz, *Good-Bye to the Low Profile: The Art of Creative Confrontation* (Boston: Little, Brown & Co., 1986), p. 138.

[48] Ibid., p. 134.

[49] Gerri Smith and Robert Heath, "Moral Appeals in Mobil Oil's Op-Ed Campaign," *Public Relations Review*, Winter 1990, 16(4):48–54.

[50] Brad E. Hainsworth, "The Distribution of Advantages and Disadvantages," *Public Relations Review*, Spring 1990, 16(1):34–36.

[51] Ibid., p. 34.

[52] For additional information on planning news events and developing media relations strategies, see Carole E. Howard and Wilma K. Mathews, *On Deadline: Managing Media Relations* (Prospect Heights, IL: Waveland Press, 2000).

[53] See Charles Stewart, Craig Smith, and Robert E. Denton, Jr., *Persuasion and Social Movements*, 4th ed. (Prospect Heights, IL: Waveland Press, 2001), p 53.

[54] Ibid., pp. 1–25.

[55] Ibid., see chapter 3, pp. 51–82.

[56] Ibid., see chapter 6, pp. 129–50.

[57] Ibid., see chapter 5, pp. 103–28.

[58] Ibid., see chapter 14, pp. 319–40.

[59] John Bowers, Donovan Ochs, and Richard Jensen, *The Rhetoric of Agitation and Control*, 2nd ed. (Prospect Heights, IL: Waveland Press, 1993), pp. 9–64.

[60] Allan Cigler and Burdett Loomis, eds., "Introduction," in *Interest Group Politics*, 6th ed. (Washington, DC: CQ Press, 2002), pp. 10–12.

[61] There are numerous classifications of campaign planning and execution. The one presented here is one of the most basic in structure. However, all of the important variables are identified.

Advertising as Persuasion

Overview

- ▲ What Is Advertising?
- ▲ The Evolution of Advertising from a Communication Perspective
- ▲ The Role of Psychology in Advertising
- ▲ How Advertising Works
- ▲ Advertising as Myth
- ▲ Common Advertising Appeals
     - Power
     - Meaning
     - Norms
     - Isolation
     - Self-Esteem
     - Guilt
     - Fear
     - Sex
- ▲ How to Critique Ads
- ▲ Criticisms of Advertising
     - Deception
     - Language
     - Children
     - Consumerism
     - Social Effects
     - Freedom of Speech
     - Private versus Public Interests
- ▲ What Can I Do?

> *The historians and archeologists will one day discover that the ads of our times are the richest and most faithful daily reflection that any society ever made of its entire range of activities.*[1]
> —MARSHALL MCLUHAN

Advertising is undoubtedly the most pervasive form of persuasion in our society. Just a decade ago, we were exposed to approximately 1,600 ads a day. Today, that number has risen to over 3,000 per day.[2] In 2001, an hour of network prime-time programming contained an average of 16 minutes, 8 seconds of advertising, an all-time high.[3] If the average family views 47 hours of television per week, it sees 12 hours of advertising. One-third of daytime television is taken up by commercials. Many people will spend at least three years of their lives watching television commercials.[4] Most radio stations present 40 minutes of advertising per hour of programming. Sixty percent of newspaper space is devoted to advertising. The Sunday edition of the *New York Times* contains on average 350 pages of ads.[5]

Advertising continues to expand and invade our daily lives. Monthly bills are full of ads; clothing items have become billboards for products like Coca-Cola; professional golfers wear hats and shirts paid for by sponsors; video and DVD rentals have commercials before the feature; ads pop up on log-ons to the Internet. Ads are now shown at theaters before the movie begins, and products are strategically featured in many films. Ads are on the sides of buildings, on taxis, and in the restrooms of restaurants. Ads are even in the schools. Channel One provides free equipment to schools for educational satellite programming. Imbedded within a 12-minute newscast are 2 minutes worth of advertising.[6]

Companies spend well over $200 billion a year in advertising.[7] That amount exceeds what the entire nation spends on higher education. Although we represent about 6 percent of the world's population, the United States absorbs nearly half of the world's advertising expenditures.[8]

Many commercials, produced and directed by the most talented people in the entertainment industry, rival the network shows. As consumers, we pay dearly for those commercials. According to Donna Cross, 20–40 percent of a product's price represents the production costs of commercials.[9] In fact, ads cost more on a per minute basis than most major Hollywood feature films. The average cost to produce a 30-second television commercial in 2001 was $358,000.[10] In Cross's opinion, this amounts to "double shafting." Manufacturers use advertising to persuade us to purchase their products and then charge us for the advertising expenses.

The new star in celebrity endorsements is golf professional Tiger Woods. In 2001, he received over $54 million in endorsements, compared to *just* $45 million for Michael Jordan in his best year. Tiger Woods's endorsements include Nike, American Express, Electronic Arts video games, *Golf Digest*, All Star Café, Rolex, Titleist golf equipment, Wheaties, CBS Sportsline, ABC, ESPN, Warner Books, TLC Laser Eye Centers, General Motors, and Asahi Beverages of Japan, to name just a few.[11]

Commercials are such a feature of daily life that many advertising symbols and slogans become part of our culture. Advertisers focus attention on certain aspects of culture and ignore others. Advertising creates role models, heroes and heroines. We can easily identify our favorite commercial characters, slogans, and songs. In some way, we are all experts on advertising. We know what we like, what is in good taste, what is clearly right or wrong. Ironically, according to Stewart Alter, we do not believe advertising influences our buying decisions.[12] In a telephone survey, only 14 percent of the respondents said they were influenced by advertising. Interestingly, however, respondents believed that women, young people, and people in low-income groups are more affected by advertising than other groups. Individuals from those groups disagreed. As a society we tolerate, remember, and enjoy advertising messages but are quick to dismiss their value or impact.

Today, we witness the full circle of promotion: license merchandizing, product placement within films, and cross-promotion with fast food restaurants. In 1937, Disney was the first studio to link films with merchandise, when they marketed toys and other items based on *Snow White and the Seven Dwarfs*. The proliferation of cross-selling has grown exponentially since then. Consider the placement of products in movies. In 1982, sales of Reese's Pieces increased 300 percent when E.T. ate the candy. When Tom Cruise wore Ray-Ban aviator sunglasses in *Top Gun*, sales increased by 40 percent. Over 50 firms specialize in product placement in movies and television programs. Firms review scripts scene-by-scene looking for opportunities to display products. For example, in the summer of 2000, Universal Pictures was planning the sequel to *The Mummy*. The chairperson, Stacey Snider, admits that *The Scorpion King* "is one of the only movies I can think of that was completely engineered to extend the franchise." In previous eras, films began with a screenplay, director, and cast. Today, a franchise film works backward from "the Happy Meal to the plot." The movie *Scooby-Doo* brought in an additional $30 million in profits from coloring books and stuffed animals.[13]

Having started the trend, Disney continues to create tie-ins to existing properties. They have produced a series of movies based on their long-standing theme park rides: *The Country Bears*, *Pirates of the Caribbean*, and *The Haunted Mansion*. As Disney studios chairman Dick Cook explains: "You are talking about Disney icons that thousands of millions of people have experienced at our parks. . . . You are capitalizing on what is part of pop culture right now."[14]

There is even product placement in video games today. For example, the game *Madden NFL* features the Fox Sports logo on end-zone billboards. Likewise, *Andre Agassi Tennis* features logos of Nike and Canon on the walls of the tennis court.[15]

The final frontier for advertisers may well be cyberspace. The Internet is just 30 years old. In its first 15 years, it was populated by about 1,000 hosts. In its second 15 years, the number grew to 45 million. The average annual growth rate continues to increase exponentially. Over 60,000 new domain names are registered each week.[16] By March of 1999, the Internet reached over 240 countries and nearly 200 million people. Commercial companies operate over 85 percent of all Web sites. Web sales topped $300 billion in 1998 and continue to account for a significant and increasing percent of the global economy.[17] In 2002, advertisers spent nearly $8 billion on the Internet.[18]

James Twitchers characterizes advertising as ubiquitous, symbiotic, profane, and magical. Advertising surrounds us; it is also symbiotic and invokes heroes and cultural icons, playing on what is perceived as good and bad. Michael Jordan and AirJordan shoes, Tiger Woods and Nike, or Britney Spears and Pepsi are examples of strong associations. Advertising is profane. Today the limits of taste are stretched; often the goal of advertising is to shock, leading to the characterization of advertising as profane. Finally, contemporary advertising is magical. Ads promise that products will accomplish amazing things, from promises of love and success to looking younger.[19]

Jean Kilbourne argues that media are simply devices to deliver audiences with specific criteria to companies. "Magazines, newspapers, and radio and television programs round us up, rather like cattle, and producers and publishers then sell us to advertisers. . . ."[20] An ABC executive is quoted as saying, "What we are is a distribution system for Procter & Gamble."[21] Juliann Sivulka observes, "No single institution has played a greater role in both reflecting and shaping American life. . . . Advertising both mirrors a society and creates a society."[22]

In this chapter, we investigate the persuasive dimensions of advertising. First we will present an overview of advertising. Then, after identifying the tactics and techniques of persuasion used in advertising, we will examine how we can become better critics of advertising and more knowledgeable consumers. Finally, we will look at some of the negative aspects of this form of communication.

WHAT IS ADVERTISING?
▲

In the traditional sense, advertising is a function or tool of marketing. Most definitions from this perspective emphasize four major characteristics.

1. Advertising is a *paid* form of communication.

2. Advertising is a *nonpersonal, presentational* form of communication distinct from face-to-face sales presentations.

3. Advertising messages present *ideas, products,* and *services.* Although we often associate advertising only with products, increasingly it addresses ideas and services.

4. Sponsors of advertising messages are *identified.*

We can also look at advertising in terms of what it *does.* In the early 1900s, N. W. Ayer (who later founded the first advertising agency in the United States) defined advertising as "keeping your name before the public."[23] This awareness function eventually was combined with information. Most commercial messages contain a great deal of information about product purpose, usage, price, or availability. Although the messages inform, they are also highly controlled. Great care is given to message content, direction, and length. Persuasion is now an essential element of advertising. Advertising does not pretend to present both sides of a purchasing decision—nor is it required to do so. Advertising is perhaps the strongest form of advocacy. Advertising does many things other than just sell products. It can build market penetration by attracting new users, defend a brand's market share by reinforcing brand loyalty, slow down market share losses, increase frequency of product purchase, stimulate trial usage, and emphasize brand values.

A communication definition of advertising recognizes the importance of the mass media in carrying the messages. The various media impact the style, content, and presentation of any message. Advertising uses strong narratives, influential language, nonverbal expressions, sophisticated lighting, sound effects, and editing to project its messages.

Still another way to gain insight into the nature of advertising is to review the methods of classifying advertising. One classification scheme is by audience. Some ads are aimed at large, general audiences while others are aimed at small, perhaps regional audiences. Some are designed for audiences with specific demographic characteristics (age, sex, income, or occupational status), while other ads appeal to specific lifestyles or psychographic variables based on audience beliefs, attitudes, or values. Advertising is also classified according to the types of advertisers: national (general) or local (retail), business (industrial, trade, professional) or noncommercial (government, civic groups, religious groups), product (service, goods) or corporate (image, ideas), primary (create a demand for generic product for entire industry) or selective (create a demand for a specific brand of product).

Finally, social scientists investigate advertising from a theoretical perspective. They view advertising as the most influential institution of socialization in modern society. Sut Jhally, for example, argues that advertising plays an important role in the mediation of the relationship between people and objects. Jhally defines advertising as a "discourse through and about objects."[24] Most of this chapter will discuss the social implications of advertising.

Defining advertising is not a simple task. It is a vital force in our economy and a powerful means of communication. It influences who we are, how we live, and how we judge others. For our purposes, advertising is defined as *communication by a specific group or industry utilizing mass media for the purposes of selling a product, service, candidate, or idea to a target audience.* This definition recognizes that the most effective form of persuasion is created with a specific audience in mind. An effective commercial speaks to the wants, desires, and problems of a specific group.[25] It gains attention, addresses needs, and solves problems. The definition also recognizes the importance of media adaptation. Today's technology is more than just a conduit for the transmission of symbols. Its role is as important to the reception and understanding of the message as is the package in enticing us to select a product.

Although advertising is mediated, a well-crafted message functions much like interpersonal communication. Advertising is targeted communication; successful appeals are tailored to the receiver demographically and psychographically. On a power/impact dimension, cognitive response resembles interpersonal exchange. Attention, retention, and response compare favorably with those elements in interpersonal communication. Indeed, the audience sometimes responds to advertising characters as real people.

Advertising, as with most persuasion, is both a science and an art. As a science, advertising must observe, measure, and analyze individuals, groups, and institutional behavior. It must establish cause-and-effect relationships and provide a rationale and evidence for the conclusions reached. Advertising is also an art; it embraces intuitive judgment, encourages creative application of symbols (both verbal and nonverbal), and harnesses subjectivity to connect with the audience it wants to persuade.

While informing us about products, advertising also informs us about ourselves, society, social values, and behavior. We learn from the roles and models presented in ads. The more pervasive and persuasive, the more invisible advertising becomes in terms of influence and impact. Its presence and images become natural, expected, and even desired. The irony is that the less we notice, the more open we are to the persuasive message. We must pay attention to the world presented and to the tactics and techniques of presentation. Decades ago, Vance Packard recognized the potential impact of advertising and warned, "the result is that many of us are being influenced and manipulated far more than we realize, in the patterns of our everyday lives."[26]

THE EVOLUTION OF ADVERTISING FROM A COMMUNICATION PERSPECTIVE

▲

William Leiss, Stephen Kline, and Sut Jhally analyzed the evolution of what they term the *cultural frames* for goods (see figure 10.1).[27] They argue that individuals become acquainted with the meanings of objects through society's culture and customs. As mentioned earlier, advertising is the primary means for imparting the meaning of objects to people.

The *idolatry frame* took place from 1890 to 1920. The focus was on the product; the approach was rational, descriptive, and informative. Products were devices to meet the utilitarian needs of consumers. *Iconology* lasted from 1920 to 1950. It shifted attention away from the attributes of products to what the product represents. A brand of soap did more than get you clean; it also demonstrated caring. Products developed social meaning through symbolic attributes. *Narcissism* extended from 1950 to 1970, and the advertising during this period explained how products would meet individual needs. Products were less symbolic and more transformative—vehicles for personal change and satisfaction. The insight of psychology provided the emotional strategies for ad development and execution. *Totemism* reflects a synthesis of the other three frames and covers the period from 1970 to 1980. Products became emblems of group membership. Product usage defines self within a larger context or social group. Thus, the advertising is more specific and targeted to lifestyle variables.

These brief historical synopses highlight the evolution of advertising messages from what a product *does* to what a product *says*. Clothes are worn for fashion rather than warmth, for social status rather than durability, for personal style rather than utility. Products are portrayed as having unique personalities, emotions, and significance beyond their chemical and physical characteristics.

Since 1886, Coca-Cola has employed nearly 200 slogans praising its product. In the early years, the medicinal properties of the beverage were highlighted: "For headache and exhaustion, drink Coca-Cola" or "The favorite drink for ladies when

Figure 10.1 Cultural Frames for Goods

Cultural Frames	Idolatry products meet utilitarian needs	Iconology products embody attributes approved by society	Narcissism products transform self and satisfy personal needs	Totemism products signal group membership
Period	1890 1900 1910	1920 1930 1940	1950 1960	1970 1980
Media for Advertising	Newspapers/ Magazines	Radio	Television	
Marketing Strategy	Rational	Non-Rational	Behaviorist	Segmentation
Advertising Strategy	Utility	Symbols	Personalization	Lifestyle
Elements in Ads	product qualities price use	symbolic attributes of products	products as vehicles for personal change	people in specific activities, settings
Themes in Ads	quality useful descriptive	status family health social authority	glamour romance sensuality self- transformation	leisure health groups friendship

thirsty, weary, and despondent." Later, the focus was on the taste and thirst quenching attributes of the drink. More recently, the focus is on the social uses of the product. We were told that "Things go better with Coke," "It's the real thing," "Coke adds life," "Have a Coke and a smile," "Coke is it," "Can't beat the feeling," "Always Coca-Cola," and "Coca-Cola . . . Real."

Coca-Cola had been the most successful product in history and dominated the soft-drink industry. When it began losing market share to Pepsi, management decided to investigate changing its formula. As Roy Stout, head of market research for Coca-Cola USA, said, "If we have twice as many vending machines, dominate fountain, have more shelf space, spend more on advertising, and are competitively priced, why are we losing share? You look at the Pepsi Challenge, and you have to begin asking about taste."[28] After spending $4 million on research, the company introduced the new Coke on April 23, 1985 with great fanfare. By June, it became clear that the public would not acquiesce to the "new and improved" strategy for a beverage it had enjoyed for almost a century. On July 10, the company brought back the original formula. Contrary to the predictions of taste tests and market research, the public was unwilling to accept change to an emblem that had become ingrained in U.S. culture.[29]

Figure 10.2   Coca-Cola Slogans

1886 Drink Coca-Cola.

1900 Deliciously refreshing. For headache and exhaustion, drink Coca-Cola.

1904 Coca-Cola is a delightful, palatable, healthful beverage. Coca-Cola satisfies. Delicious and Refreshing. Drink Coca-Cola in bottles—5¢.

1905 Drink a bottle of carbonated Coca-Cola. Coca-Cola revives and sustains. Drink Coca-Cola at soda fountains. The favorite drink for ladies when thirsty, weary, and despondent. Good all the way down. Flows from every fountain. Sold in bottles.

1906 The drink of quality. The Great National Temperance. Thirst quenching—delicious and refreshing.

1907 Delicious Coca-Cola, sustains, refreshes, invigorates. Cooling . . . refreshing . . . delicious. Coca-Cola is full of vim, vigor and go—is a snappy drink.

1908 Sparkling—harmless as water, and crisp as frost. The satisfactory beverage.

1909 Delicious, wholesome, refreshing. Delicious, wholesome, thirst quenching. Drink delicious Coca-Cola. Whenever you see an arrow think of Coca-Cola.

1910 Drink bottled Coca-Cola—so easily served. It satisfies. Quenches the thirst as nothing else can.

1911 It's time to drink Coca-Cola. Real satisfaction in every glass.

1912 Demand the genuine—refuse substitutes.

1913 Ask for it by its full name—then you will get the genuine. The best beverage under the sun. It will satisfy you. A welcome addition to any party—anytime—anywhere.

1914 Demand the genuine by full name. Exhilarating, refreshing. Nicknames encourage substitutions. Pure and wholesome.

1915 The standard beverage.

1916 It's fun to be thirsty when you can get a Coca-Cola. Just one glass will tell you.

1917 Three million a day. The taste is the test of the Coca-Cola quality. There's a delicious freshness to the flavor of Coca-Cola.

1919 Coca-Cola is a perfect answer to thirst that no imitation can satisfy. It satisfies thirst. Quality tells the difference.

1920 Drink Coca-Cola with soda. Delicious and refreshing. The hit that saves the day.

1922 Quenching thirst everywhere. Thirst knows no season. Thirst can't be denied. Thirst reminds you—drink Coca-Cola.

1923 Refresh yourself. A perfect blend of pure products from nature. There's nothing like it when you're thirsty.

1924 Pause and refresh yourself.

1925 Six million a day. The sociable drink. Stop at the red sign and refresh yourself.

1926 Thirst and taste for Coca-Cola are the same thing. Stop at the red sign.

1927 Around the corner from anywhere. At the little red sign.

1928 A pure drink of natural flavors.

1929 The pause that refreshes.

1930 Meet me at the soda fountain.

1932 Ice-cold sunshine. The drink that makes the pause refreshing.

1933 Don't wear a tired, thirsty face.

1934 Carry a smile back to work. Ice-cold Coca-Cola is everywhere else—it ought to be in your family refrigerator. When it's hard to get started, Start with a Coca-Cola.

1935 The drink that keeps you feeling right. All trails lead to ice-cold Coca-Cola. The pause that brings friends together.

1936 What refreshment ought to be. Get the feel of wholesome refreshment.

1937 America's favorite moment. Cold refreshment. So easy to serve and so inexpensive. Stop for a pause . . . go refreshed.

1938 Anytime is the right time to pause and refresh. At the red cooler. The best friend thirst ever had. Pure sunlight.

1939 Coca-Cola goes along. Make lunch time refreshment time. Makes travel more pleasant. The drink everybody knows. Thirst stops here.

1940 Bring in your thirst and go away without it. The package that gets a welcome at home. Try it just once and you will know why.

1941 A stop that belongs on your timetable. Completely refreshing.

1942 The only thing like Coca-Cola is Coca-Cola itself. Refreshment that can't be duplicated. Wherever you are, whatever you do, wherever you may be, when you think refreshment, think ice-cold Coca-Cola.

1943 That extra something. A taste all its own. The only thing like Coca-Cola is Coca-Cola itself. It's the real thing.

1944 How about a Coke. High sign of friendship. A moment on the sunnyside.

1945 Whenever you hear "Have a Coke," you hear the voice of America. Passport to refreshment. Happy moment of hospitality. Coke means Coca-Cola.

1947 Coke knows no season. Serving Coca-Cola serves hospitality. Relax with the pause that refreshes.

1948 Delicious and refreshing. Where there's Coca-Cola there's hospitality. Think of lunchtime as refreshment time.

1949 Coca-Cola . . . Along the highway to anywhere.

1950 Help yourself to refreshment.

1951 Good food and Coca-Cola just naturally go together.

1952 Coke follows thirst everywhere. What you want is Coke. The gift of thirst.

1953 Dependable as sunrise.

1954 For people on the go. Matchless flavor.

1955 Almost everyone appreciates the best. America's preferred taste.

1956 Feel the difference. Friendliest drink on earth. Makes good things taste better.

1957 Sign of good taste.

1958 Refreshment the whole world prefers. The cold, crisp taste of Coke.

1959 Cold, crisp taste that deeply satisfies. Make it a real meal.

1960 Relax with Coke. Revive with Coke.

1961 Coke and food—refreshing new feeling.

1962 Enjoy that refreshing new feeling. Coca-Cola refreshes you best.

1963 A chore's best friend. Things go better with Coke.

1964 You'll go better refreshed.

1965 Something more than a soft drink.

1966 Coke . . . after Coke . . . after Coke.

1970 It's the real thing.

1971 I'd like to buy the world a Coke.

1975 Look up America.

1976 Coke adds life.

1979 Have a Coke and a Smile.

1982 Coke is it!

1985 We've got a Taste for You (Coca-Cola and Coca-Cola Classic). America's Real Choice.

1986 Catch the wave (Coca-Cola). Red White & You (Coca-Cola Classic).

1989 Can't Beat the Feeling.

1990 Can't Beat the Real Thing.

1993 Always Coca-Cola.

2001 Life tastes good.

2003 Coca-Cola . . . Real.

Music is an influential persuader. Fans mimic how musicians dress and talk; people in other professions who receive acclaim are approvingly called "rock stars" as evidence of their impact on their audiences. When music videos became popular in the 1980s, the possibilities for influence increased. The artists could incorporate mini-dramas with their music to raise social consciousness or to express political views or social critiques. Advertising quickly capitalized on this popular form of entertainment.

Hit songs of musical artists provided the background music for diverse products. For example, the music of Sting was used by Jaguar automobiles, Fatboy Slim for Mercedes-Benz, *NSYNC for McDonald's, Backstreet Boys for Burger King, and Britney Spears for Pepsi, to name a few. The artists were featured prominently in some of the ads so that association of the product with the artist would create new markets or increase sales.

The structure and nature of advertising is directly related to the political and social structure of society. In countries where tradition and the status quo are valued and there is little technological innovation, advertising is not needed and thus has little social impact. In authoritarian countries, advertising is tightly controlled and is used to promote national goals and specific consumption patterns. In the United States, where self-interest, individualism, rationality, competition, and the freedom of choice are highly valued, advertising plays to those tendencies. Capitalistic society encourages consumerism. For many immigrants, North America was presented as a "land of milk and honey" where they might find an abundance of goods. The wage system of labor encouraged consumption. Advertising is vital to advanced capitalistic societies, where it is necessary to motivate people to work hard so they can accumulate money, which can then be used to buy products.[30]

From this brief overview of the evolution of advertising, we can make several assumptions about its practice in the United States. Advertising must be considered within the cultural context of a nation. Advertising messages are extremely complex—utilizing rational, emotional, and social elements. Thus, the messages are open to various interpretations, and the actual effects cannot be predicted with certainty.

THE ROLE OF PSYCHOLOGY IN ADVERTISING

▲
_____

As early as 1954, several professional publications began devoting more and more attention to what they called "motivation research."[31] By the 1980s, many large ad agencies hired psychologists and anthropologists to provide information on human nature and behavior in order to learn about human needs and purchasing behaviors.[32] Advertisers began looking for ways to link *extra-psychological values* to products in order to increase their appeal. A general orientation to product definition that plays on individual strengths, weaknesses, hopes, and fears is known in the advertising industry as product positioning.[33] From this perspective, the advertiser does not begin with the product but with the mind of the consumer. That is, advertising does not try to change minds; instead it ties product attributes to the existing beliefs, ideas, goals, and desires of the consumer.

We react favorably to attitudes or behaviors that match prior knowledge and experience. To say that a cookie tastes "homemade" or "like Mother used to make" does not tell whether the cookie is good or bad, hard or soft, sweet or bland. Rather, the statement invokes memories of the aroma of fresh-baked cookies and nostalgia for Mother's baking. Advertisers are more successful if they position a product to capitalize on established beliefs or expectations of the consumer.

Product brand selection or loyalty says more about who we wish to be than who we are. John Jones, who spent over 25 years in the advertising business, argues that "in product design, in packaging, in promotion, in direct-response materials—in short, in every piece of communication directed to consumers—there is a speaker, someone who is making assumptions about the reader. And there is a mock reader, the person you and I are supposed to become."[34]

A positioning approach to advertising is a response to an overcommunicated society. Each year there are thousands of new books published, numerous new cable channels, a proliferation of specialty magazines, and more and more Web sites crowding the Internet—all vehicles for introducing thousands of new products. During a year, the average American will view nearly two thousand hours of television, listen to over one thousand hours of radio, spend over three hundred hours reading newspapers and magazines, and additional hours searching for products and services on the Internet. There is a great deal of competition for our attention. Product positioning provides a way to cut through the clutter and to take a shortcut to the brain.

Simplified messages tied to consumer experience and knowledge do not require logic, debate, or lengthy explanations. The most effective ads are those that work on a stimulus-response motivation. How can Bill Cosby be so effective pitching Jell-o® products? Is it because he is an expert on children and nutrition? Probably not. Since he is funny and likeable, people are attuned to his message because of his public persona. Cosby's credibility profits from his celebrity status and the characters he has portrayed on television shows. Michael Jordan is the most celebrated athlete in the United States and probably in the world. His six world championships and instant recognition have helped sell everything from Nike shoes to Chevy Blazers to Ball Park Franks to long distance telephone service. Numerous viewers want to "Be like Mike," and sales of the products he promotes reflect that desire.

There is another important reason why psychology invaded the advertising community. In the early 1970s, the purchasing power of the dollar decreased by 60 percent, and many households required two paychecks to survive.[35] As inflation grew, the "Woodstock generation" became cynical. Bigger was not better. Change for the sake of "progress" was suspect, and the advertising industry needed to find another means to stimulate the public to buy. The solution to the problem was image transformation. Advertisers attempted to increase the perceived value of mass-produced products. The primary strategy was to offer an emotional reward for using a product. In short, *brand personality* became more important than *brand performance*. Sexy jeans have a stronger appeal than long-lasting jeans. A stylish watch is favored over an accurate one.

Behavioral psychologists can find parallels between Ivan Pavlov's conditioning experiments and advertising. In his famous experiment, Pavlov rang a bell whenever he presented food to a dog; the food stimulated salivation. After a number of repetitions, the dog would salivate at the sound of the bell—even when no food was presented. A communications research manager at Coca-Cola remarked: "Pavlov took a neutral object and, by associating it with a meaningful object, made it a symbol of something else; he imbued it with imagery, he gave it added value. That is what we try to do with modern advertising."[36] While the power of a single advertisement to shape any one individual's behavior may be minimal, repeated advertising images and slogans can have an impact. The use of humor in advertising is another means of conditioning. If listeners find the message funny, they may associate those good feelings with the product. Purchase of that product is then linked to good times and pleasure.

The term *psychographics* was coined in 1968 to describe market research that classifies population groups according to psychological variables such as attitudes, interests, and opinions. Arnold Mitchell incorporated psychographics in a model he created to explain changing values and lifestyles in the 1970s; its acronym was VALS. After its inauguration as an SRI International product in 1978, VALS was recognized by *Advertising Age* as "one of the ten top market research breakthroughs."[37] In 1989, the typology was reworked to maximize its ability to predict consumer behavior. Personality traits replaced social values as the mechanism for segmenting the marketplace because individual differences affect purchase behavior more directly than social trends and are more stable over time. The foundation of the VALS™ approach is that independent psychological traits control behavior. Demographics such as gender, age, and education are not sufficient to predict how people consume goods and services. Personality traits such as leadership, innovativeness, and vanity affect decisions in combination with the material resources available.[38]

The first dimension along which VALS™ classifies consumers is motivation; the three primary motivations are ideals, achievement, and self-expression. The primary motivation influences what products, services, and activities individuals will view as characteristic of themselves and will, therefore, choose. Consumers motivated by ideals are guided in their choices by principles—abstract and idealized criteria to determine what is best. Consumers with an achievement orientation make choices in relation to the reactions, concerns, and desires of others in the groups to which they belong or aspire to belong; they are motivated by symbols of success. Finally, consumers motivated by self-expression are guided by the desire for social or physical activity, variety, and excitement; they are action oriented and make choices that emphasize individuality.

The second dimension is resources, which refers to both material and psychological resources (such as income, health, energy level, and self-confidence). From these two dimensions, VALS™ identifies eight groups of consumers that exhibit distinct behavioral and decision-making patterns. The groups are labeled as innovators, thinkers, believers, achievers, strivers, experiencers, makers, and survivors. See figure 10.3 for a summary of the eight market segments.

Groups can have similar characteristics to those that border them on both dimensions (horizontal = motivation; vertical = resources). Thus, thinkers and achievers both have substantial resources, and their primary motivations may blend at the edges. While experiencers also are high on resources, they do not overlap in motivation with thinkers, but could have some similarities to achievers. Similarly, believers, strivers, and makers all have low resources, but strivers could exhibit similarity in motivation to both while makers would not overlap with believers. The segment at the top of the figure, innovators, exhibits all three primary motivations and has abundant resources. This group has a significant impact on the marketplace. Survivors, in contrast, have few resources and often feel powerless; they do not exhibit a primary motivation.[39]

Firms use the VALS™ system to design new products and services, target products and markets, position products in the marketplace, extend product lines, and develop ad campaigns. For example, a telecommunications campaign used VALS™ to identify early-adopter consumers for a new product. The research helped the campaign develop the prototype and to prioritize the features and benefits that would appeal to early adopters. The research also helped select the best name,

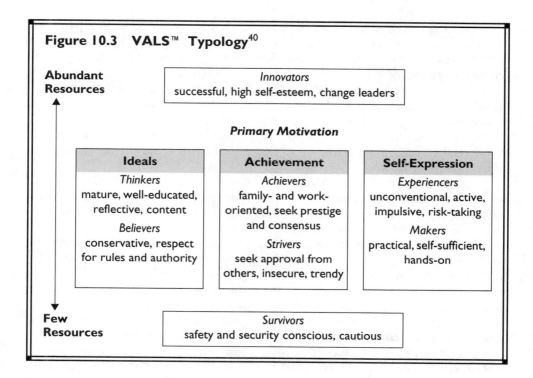

Figure 10.3   VALS™ Typology[40]

Abundant Resources ↑

Innovators
successful, high self-esteem, change leaders

Primary Motivation

Ideals	**Achievement**	**Self-Expression**
Thinkers mature, well-educated, reflective, content	*Achievers* family- and work-oriented, seek prestige and consensus	*Experiencers* unconventional, active, impulsive, risk-taking
Believers conservative, respect for rules and authority	*Strivers* seek approval from others, insecure, trendy	*Makers* practical, self-sufficient, hands-on

Few Resources ↓

Survivors
safety and security conscious, cautious

logo, positioning strategy, and the price. A Japanese automobile manufacturer repositioned its product base in the United States after using VALS™ to target consumer perceptions. The advertising based on that research resulted in a 60% increase in sales in six months. Prior to selecting a spokesperson for a television campaign to increase the customer base for long-distance service, a company used VALS™ to insure that they selected a spokesperson to whom the targeted audience would relate.[41]

HOW ADVERTISING WORKS

▲

There are four basic models of buyer behavior.[42] *Psychological models* are based on the idea of stimulus-response. The models predict how humans will respond to external stimuli in the environment and focus on the possible forms of stimuli that will create mass response. *Economic models* assume that people are rational and make reasoned purchasing decisions based on price, quality, pleasure, or esteem. The difference between psychological and economic models is the underlying assumption concerning human behavior. The psychological model views humans as robots: buying decisions are automatic as long as the right stimulus is used. In contrast, the economic model assumes that people will acquire the necessary information to make a decision. The model does not judge the quality of the reasons; it simply states that people calculate their decisions.

Sociological models of buying behavior argue that specific social groups directly influence consumer desires, preferences, and purchases. Thus, such variables as status, lifestyle, and reference groups dictate buying habits. Finally, *statistical models* of buying behavior focus on the purchasing patterns of groups or types of consumers. For example, a statistical model could predict that higher-income, well-educated, professional individuals often buy items from direct mail catalogs. In addition, the frequency of catalog purchase is related to the timing of the purchase. The more recent the last purchase, the greater the likelihood of another purchase. For a retailer, this model would mean that sending two or three catalogs a month should increase sales.

Each of these models provides insight into why people buy when they do. Basically, all advertising attempts to move a consumer along a continuum from awareness, to knowledge, to liking, to preference, to conviction, and finally to purchase—in short, to persuade (see figure 10.4).

At each stage of the continuum, ads address various behavioral dimensions and use different types of appeals and techniques. From awareness to knowledge, ads use slogans or jingles to capture attention and attempt to provide the consumer with product information and facts. To move the consumer from liking to preference, the ads use image, status, and glamour appeals to play upon emotions and feelings. To reinforce conviction and repeat purchases, ads attempt to stimulate and to direct consumer desires through price appeals and testimonials.

From this rather simple continuum of consumer reaction, we can see four distinct levels of persuasion.[43] The most simple and basic level is what Kim Rotzoll and James Haefner call *precipitation*. At this level, the advertising messages must

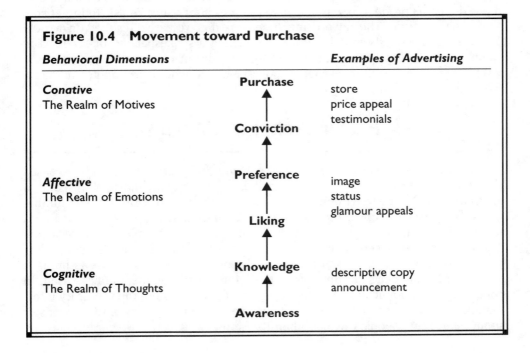

Figure 10.4   Movement toward Purchase

Behavioral Dimensions		*Examples of Advertising*
Conative The Realm of Motives	**Purchase** ↑ **Conviction**	store price appeal testimonials
Affective The Realm of Emotions	**Preference** ↑ **Liking**	image status glamour appeals
Cognitive The Realm of Thoughts	**Knowledge** ↑ **Awareness**	descriptive copy announcement

fight clutter and penetrate the mind of the consumer; the persuasive goals are brand awareness and knowledge. The second level is *persuasion*. At this level, the messages appeal to human feelings and emotions and attempt to induce purchase. This level is the most powerful and perhaps the most subtle. The third level is *reinforcement*. Here the goal is to legitimize and validate a purchase. *Reminder* is the final level of persuasion, which reinforces brand loyalty. For example, most McDonald's ads are designed to remind the public to revisit—to maintain "top-of-mind" awareness.

Critics of advertising allege that it creates demand, which wouldn't exist without the promotion and that it often influences consumers, who are unaware that they have been persuaded. William Leiss, Stephen Kline, and Sut Jhally summarize the three ways advertising creates this demand.[44] First, *technological manipulation* creates demand by utilizing the latest in psychographic and demographic research—resulting in better knowledge about consumers than they have of themselves. In addition development of media technology allows advertisers to reach mass audiences, with no requirement for literacy skills. Some critics allege television, in particular, is persuasive and manipulative—discouraging any critical thought process. Advertising also creates demand through *false symbolism*. Products become symbols for desired attributes. Articles of clothing are presented as emblems of status or group identification; perfumes are portrayed as promising sex. Products are acquired because of what they symbolize instead of what they do. Finally, advertising creates demand through *magic in the marketplace*. Advertisers imply that their products will transform consumers' lives. They offer simple answers to complex problems—easing the pains of loneliness or failure, for example. Through the magic of purchase, the consumer changes his or her life.

Another interesting explanation of how advertising works is provided by the advertising agency of Foote, Cone & Belding (FCB).[45] Their model suggests that purchasing decisions are based on the degree of involvement in the decision and the degree to which thinking or feeling provides the basis for making a decision. These elements can be visualized as two continuums that cross to form a matrix. One has high and low involvement as its endpoints; the other has thinking and feeling (see figure 10.5).

Each quadrant of the matrix has a different ordering of three key elements in making a purchasing decision. We buy something *(do)* based on the product information provided *(learn)* or based on some feeling or emotion about use of the product *(feel)*. In order to illustrate these orientations, let's consider each quadrant separately.

High Involvement–Thinking

According to the FCB model, purchasing major, expensive items such as houses, cars, or household furnishings requires high consumer involvement and careful thinking. Consumers seek product information to ensure product value and quality. The consumer is reflective, seeks the best deal, and bases the decision on product information and demonstration. From this perspective, consumers follow a *learn-feel-do* sequence in making a purchasing decision. Note too that this sequence provides insight into how to create the advertising. Advertising for products in this

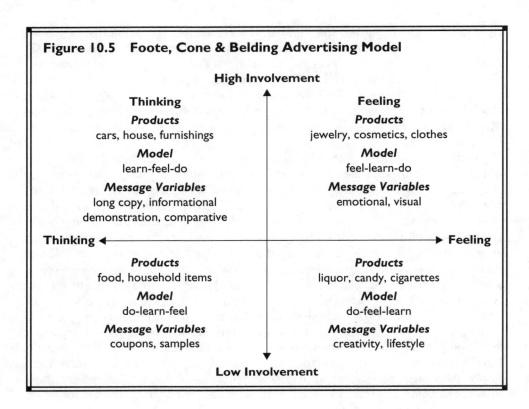

Figure 10.5   Foote, Cone & Belding Advertising Model

High Involvement

Thinking

Products
cars, house, furnishings

Model
learn-feel-do

Message Variables
long copy, informational
demonstration, comparative

Feeling

Products
jewelry, cosmetics, clothes

Model
feel-learn-do

Message Variables
emotional, visual

Thinking ◄————————————————————► **Feeling**

Products
food, household items

Model
do-learn-feel

Message Variables
coupons, samples

Products
liquor, candy, cigarettes

Model
do-feel-learn

Message Variables
creativity, lifestyle

Low Involvement

category requires a substantial amount, including detailed descriptions, comparative product analyses, and visual demonstrations.

High Involvement–Feeling

Some products (such as jewelry, cosmetics, clothing, or other fashion products) are based primarily on subjective, emotional reactions while also demanding a great deal of consumer time and involvement. The products often have more expressive, symbolic meaning than functional usage; thus, purchase decisions are rather personal. Because product information is less important than consumer attitudes, the purchasing sequence is *feel-learn-do*. For products in this category, advertising must rely on emotional and visual elements as well as on the psychological needs of the consumer. We purchase these products to signal to others how we want to be perceived and understood.

Low Involvement–Thinking

Food and small household items comprise this category of products. How much emotion can we generate in deciding what toothpaste or detergent to purchase? Brand loyalty is strong for these products, and purchasing is based on habit rather than major product differentiation. Developing brand loyalty does involve some rational thinking. We ultimately decide to use a product because it is cheaper or better. The buying sequence here is *do-learn-feel*. Most of the advertising for this category is to provide top-of-mind awareness and to counter any "invasion" from advertisements for other products. Free sample offers facilitate both doing and learning in an effort to create a positive feeling for the product. Coupons provide a reason for subsequent purchase and encourage loyalty to the brand.

Low Involvement—Feeling

In many ways, this category is a catch-all for a variety of products ranging from candy, cigarettes, or liquor to movies. The key is that these products are highly subjective and depend on personal taste. They are low involvement primarily because they are relatively inexpensive and consumed quickly. They involve feelings because preferences are personal and many of the items are promoted using imagery. The sequence for this category is *do-feel-learn*. Instant gratification and self-satisfaction are the primary goals of much of the advertising. The messages stress creativity and self-indulgence. Some products in this category (alcoholic and nonalcoholic beverages, for example) also stress lifestyles.

The FCB model is challenging but useful. It recognizes that there are many reasons and variables in making a decision to purchase an item. It suggests approaches for creating effective advertising messages based on the sequence of buying decisions. Perhaps most importantly, it addresses the variety of consumer buying decisions, ranging from what type of gum to buy to what type of house to purchase. Advertising is persuasive because it adapts its messages to the complexity of the situation.

It is important to recognize that advertising, in many ways, counters traditional ideas about how we learn and how we acquire attitudes. Many scholars argue that the learning process is linear and consistent. Information is transmitted; once the information is understood, attitudes may change or some reorganization of belief structure will occur. Once an attitude alters, then a corresponding behavior follows. The FCB model counters this notion. Emotion can be a primary motivating factor. Linear models don't account for affective elements and nonrational preferences.

We purchase some products simply because we remember advertisements for them that pique our interest and we want to try them. We may then like the product and form a favorable attitude. In other cases, the advertising causes an attitude to form without ever experiencing the product, as in the belief that Mercedes are superior automobiles. We attach emotional significance to the products (status or prestige, for example) before any purchase takes place. In this sequence, we start with an attitude change, develop emotional ties, and then, if circumstances allow, purchase the car.

Two important concepts in advertising are reach and frequency. *Reach* is how many people in the target audience will actually see or hear an ad. *Frequency* is how many times the target audience will see or hear the ad within a specified timeframe. A certain frequency of seeing an ad is required in order to evoke product awareness and eventually a purchase. The ideal is to maximize both reach and frequency, but it may be too expensive to reach a total target market with the required frequency.

Psychologist Herbert Krugman believes that before advertising can induce behavior, three steps must be taken: (1) stimulate interest; (2) prompt product evaluation and recognition; and (3) reinforce message variables. The three steps are accomplished through multiple repetitions of messages.[46] Research has shown that a relatively small volume of advertising, usually two or three exposures, can influence short-term sales. Greater frequency may influence long-term sales. Price reductions have a similar effect. They can increase sales in the short term, and repeated price reductions can extend this effect.[47]

John Jones found that advertising had a positive but short-term effect in 70 percent of the cases he reviewed. Both long-term and short-term effects were noted in 46 percent of the cases. Short-term refers to an immediate sales boost when a specific brand is advertised. Long-term impact means a continuation of short-term effects, a result strong enough to be detected over a year and measured by an improvement in the brand's market share.[48] In comparing advertised and unadvertised brands, Jones found that the average market share of advertised brands is between five and seven percent higher than unadvertised brands. In addition, there is greater *brand penetration* of advertised brands. Over the course of the study, the average proportion of households buying one of the advertised products was 17 percent compared to just 10 percent for unadvertised brands. This study also found that advertised brands command higher prices (14 percent higher than unadvertised brands) and thus greater profits.[49]

One of the more interesting findings of advertising research in the last decade is that well-liked advertising sells very well. One school of thought is that likability enhances persuasion. Liking a message predisposes the individual to believe its message content. Another hypothesis is that liking an ad generates a positive affect that is transferred from the commercial to the product. Others claim that commercials that are liked get better exposure. The basis of this hypothesis is that well-liked ads will be watched more than disliked ads. When we see well-liked ads we are less likely to leave the room or change channels. Still others think that liking is a surrogate for cognitive processing. The basis of this hypothesis is that when consumers actively process messages, they are more likely to act on those messages. Finally, it is thought that liking evokes a gratitude response. While perhaps a stretch, it is thought that part of subsequent consumer behavior is based on having enjoyed the advertising itself and wanting to reward that pleasurable experience.[50]

John Jones argues that successful advertising campaigns have three characteristics. The intrinsic properties of the advertisement itself reward viewers for watching the ad by making the commercial entertaining and amusing. Second, these campaigns communicate visually rather than verbally. Finally, the advertisement becomes an "emotional envelop."[51] In short, successful advertising campaigns are intrinsically likable, highly visual, and encourage viewer engagement by communicating their promises in terms relevant to the consumer.[52]

Jan Zimmerman identifies four steps to Internet marketing: (1) Gain attention; video, sound, graphics, or animation draw people to the Web page and keep them there. (2) Create interest; relevant or desired information must be provided quickly to keep people interested. This involves constant updating of Web pages to keep them exciting and current. The goal is to keep people on the site to motivate them to return often. (3) Build desire through interactivity as viewers move through the site. (4) Induce action. This final step is the same for all marketing and sales campaigns. In many ways, having an individual take action on the Internet is easier than with other media. With a click on an icon, an item can be ordered, a thought shared, or service requested.[53]

Some people believe advertising uses subliminal messages—messages that allegedly target the consumer's subconscious—to sell products and services. The idea of subliminal advertising originated in a famous study that projected messages of "eat popcorn" and "drink Coca-Cola" on movie screens for 1/3,000 of a second. The messages increased sales of popcorn by 57 percent and sales of Coke by 10 percent.[54] Whether advertisers hide symbols or phrases in their messages is widely disputed. Wilson Bryan Key, in his controversial books *Subliminal Seduction* and *Media Sexploitation*, provided numerous examples of sexual symbols, words, and pictures he believed were embedded in ads.[55] According to Key, such messages succeed on two levels: people remember the ads and the targeted behavior is stimulated.

> The basis of modern media effectiveness is a language within a language—one that communicates to each of us at a level beneath our conscious awareness, one that reaches into the uncharted mechanism of the human unconscious. This is a language based upon the human ability to *subliminally* or *subconsciously* or *unconsciously* perceive information. . . . It is virtually impossible to pick up a newspaper or magazine, turn on a radio or television set, read a promotional pamphlet or the telephone book, or shop through a supermarket without having your subconscious purposely massaged by some monstrously clever artist, photographer, writer, or technician. As a culture, North America might well be described as one enormous, magnificent, self-service, subliminal massage parlor.[56]

There are several problems with the notion of subliminal advertising. First, the original study was conducted during the movie *Picnic* that contained several scenes of people eating and drinking during hot summer weather. Was the audience responding to the subliminal advertisement or simply mimicking the behavior in the movie? In addition, the study has never been replicated with the same dramatic results. In fact, scholars Anthony Pratkanis and Elliot Aronson reviewed over 150 academic articles and more than 200 professional papers on subliminal advertising. They concluded that "in none of the papers is there clear evidence that supports the proposition that subliminal messages influence behavior."[57] Also, industry professionals continue to deny the widespread use of subliminal techniques—for the very practical reason that they simply do not work. John O'Toole, former chairman of the advertising agency of Foote, Cone & Belding, emphatically states, "I don't like to destroy cherished illusions, but I must state unequivocally that there is no such thing as subliminal advertising. I have never seen an example of it, nor have I ever heard it seriously discussed as a technique by advertising people."[58]

Of course, as we have already argued, the appeals are very subtle. Subliminal advertising may be in the eyes of the beholder, because many of the appeals are a matter of perception. For example, a product that uses a movie star as a spokesperson might appeal to one consumer because the star has successfully portrayed practical, down-to-earth characters. Another consumer might focus on the celebrity's fame and wealth. Another might find the star's physical attractiveness appealing. Appeal is emotional and depends on the receiver's perception of the star.

Even the most subtle actions may generate a strong appeal. As noted at the beginning of this chapter, products that appear as props in movies have a subtle but powerful impact. Another example is the advertising for perfume or cologne that shows an attractive couple in bed. One appeal is the person, the other is sex. One approach is subtle, the other is more direct and plays on our human interest in sex. Advertising utilizes deeply ingrained desires and motives of human nature.

In September 2003 a British apparel and fragrance company, French Connection Group, began a marketing campaign for their products sold under the acronym FCUK (French Connection United Kingdom). The company strategically played on the suggestive acronym to attract the attention of teenagers who have already been exposed to countless sexually-oriented messages in advertising, music videos, and video games. "Whether it shocks or amuses you, FCUK certainly makes the consumer think," claimed Anderea Hyde, president of the holding company.[59] The advertising campaign for FCUK fragrance featured the headline "Scent to Bed" over the image of a young, attractive, half dressed couple snuggling on a bed. A purchase of $38 or more received a free T-shirt with the "Scent to Bed" slogan. Despite protests by parents who resented the marketing strategy, the company maintains its focus on the acronym. On the Web site for the company, when the viewer clicks on fcukbuymail.com, the pop-up reads: "Where the fcuk are you? Choose your country below."[60]

Timothy Joyce recognizes four major changes in contemporary advertising. First, we are continually exposed to more and more advertising. In all forms of media, the number of ads continue to increase each year. Second, advertising messages have become shorter. For television, fifteen-second ads account for 35 percent of all network spots. In terms of print, ads have become more visual and less wordy. Third, especially with television, there is more emphasis on creativity and on likability of the advertising message. Finally, there is a growth of the use of consumer and trade promotions, including price discounts, coupons, point programs for repeated purchases, etc.[61]

The advertising industry relies on the subtle and the obvious, the rational and the absurd, the everyday and the novel in order to lead us from awareness to ultimate purchase. Keeping that in mind, we will now consider some of the more common tactics and approaches to persuasion in U.S. advertising.

ADVERTISING AS MYTH
▲

From a cultural perspective, there is a growing trend toward viewing advertising as myth. Ancient Greek and Roman mythologies were stories of explanation, a way to understand the universe based on heroic stories. According to Joseph Campbell, myths help us realize the wonder of the universe and our place in it; they also validate the customs and social rules of our culture.[62] Myths are enduring stories that teach valuable lessons as well as entertain.

Nearly all advertising tells a story; they are narratives that describe situations and solve problems. Richard Campbell finds three common mythical elements in most ads: (1) they feature characters, settings, and plots; (2) they involve conflicts, usually pitting one set of characters or social values against another; and (3) the conflicts are resolved by using the product. In effect, the products become the hero. Richard Campbell argues that "ads are most effective when they create attitudes and reinforce values. Then they operate like popular fiction, encouraging us to suspend our disbelief."[63] Thus, most ads are a narrative fiction that communicate information about a product in the context of the values, lifestyles, and culture of the target audience. Advertising is the means of creatively tapping the mind's perceptual inventory—encouraging the linking of images, symbols, and feelings to the object or idea being sold. Over time, advertising creates mythical worlds and characters that become associated with specific brands.

As myth, the power of advertising is at the unconscious level. Carl Jung, the famous psychologist, argued that our unconscious contains archetypal or universal images that can be traced back to the origin of the human species. These images function somewhat like instincts to influence and control our behavior. For Jung, the power of mythology and the symbols that drive it (i.e., archetypal images) come from our collective, unconscious psyche. He cautioned against overestimating the role of rationality in decision making. He discussed the intentional and unintentional contents of the mind. The unintentional content can influence behavior without our being aware of it. This distinction helps explain why so many people believe they aren't affected by advertising. They are not conscious of any influence and believe they rationally evaluate all such messages.

Sal Randazzo explains how advertising can operate below the radar of awareness.

> Each advertisement or commercial represents an individual mythology, which also contributes to the overall brand mythology. . . . Megabrand advertising doesn't just sell product, it creates an emotional bond between the brand and the consumer. Advertising creates this bond by mythologizing the product; by humanizing it; and by giving the product a distinct identity, personality, and sensibility. Advertising mythologizes brands by wrapping them in consumers' dreams and fantasies.[64]

The advertising for McDonald's is an excellent example of this process. McDonald's is more than a restaurant. Through the years of advertising, it is seen as a mythical and magical place where kids and parents are happy, where everyone is welcomed, and where everyone can be forever young at heart.

Mythic archetypes provide many of the story lines and characters found in commercials. For example, there are two major Western archetypical female images: the mother and the maiden. The mother archetype possess the attributes of warmth, nurturance, comfort, and security. Roles include mother, teacher, homemaker, cook, and gardener, to name just a few. The maiden archetype emphasizes youth, beauty, enchantment, and seduction. It runs a continuum between virgin and harlot, with roles such as damsel or siren. There are also two major Western masculine archetypal images: father and warrior. The father image reflects the attributes of reason, order, law, protector, and provider. The roles are coach, teacher, leader, etc. The warrior reflects independence, strength, and courage, as evidenced by cowboys, sports stars, or soldiers.

There have been many archetypal roles and stories in advertising. Campbell's soup ads often use the mother archetype, showing a loving and nurturing caretaker to the rescue with a bowl of wholesome soup. Betty Crocker has been the corporate symbol of General Mills since 1921. The first Betty Crocker looked like a homemaker of the 1930s. Her image has been refined to reflect a more contemporary, universal mother.

An example of the maiden archetype is the Breck girl, who appeared in shampoo ads for more than 50 years. John Breck formulated one of the first shampoos in 1930 as a gentle alternative to bar soap, which he blamed for his hair loss. In 1936, his son, Edward Breck, hired commercial artist Charles Sheldon to draw pastel likenesses of models, with soft focus and haloes of light and color to create highly romantic images of feminine beauty and purity. The first national advertising campaign for Breck began in 1946, and the Breck girl's image (haloed blonde profile, with a defiantly uplifted chin in dynamic tension with downcast eyes) was registered as the company's trademark in 1951. Advertising executives crafted idealized images of a woman both desirable and chaste—images that resonated powerfully and resulted in one of the longest running ad campaigns in U.S. history. There were more than 200 Breck girls including Brooke Shields, Kim Basinger, Jaclyn Smith, and Cybil Shepard, to name just a few. The Breck girl was an icon as instantly recognizable as Nike's swoosh. The Smithsonian includes an exhibit of this highly successful advertising campaign, which was discontinued around 1978. There have been three attempts to revive the campaign, the last beginning in late 2002.[65]

An example of the father archetype is the Quaker Oats Man. This image was created in 1877 by the Quaker Mill company. The original image resembled the picture of William Penn in Quaker clothes. It was meant to convey confidence, trustworthiness, and value. On a more unconscious level, the Quaker Oats man represents a religious father figure. The basic image has been revised only four times in over 100 years. The Maytag repairman is another fatherly figure; he is calm, patient, and tirelessly dependable. The Mr. Goodwrench character represents the protective and caring aspects of the father archetype. The Marlboro Man is a warrior archetype—the lone cowboy as a symbol of a rugged, pioneering spirit. The Marlboro Man is one of the most successful examples of brand image and personality in the history of U.S. advertising.

The brand personality of Budweiser beer is the masculine, hard working, and self-assured male, and the brand positioning in the consumer's mind is "a premium beer for the average Joe."[66] The product is linked to specific qualities: Beechwood aging, the Budweiser heritage, and commitment to quality.

Budweiser masterfully uses its team of Clydesdales as another association with its brand. The horses are a complex symbol of strength and power, representing the heritage, dignity, and pride of the working-class male. They also represent a bygone era. The Anheuser-Busch eagle on the company logo also has positive brand associations of power and as a symbol of the United States and patriotic tradition.[67] The letter "A" on the logo represents Anheuser—but also first in alphabetical order and the best or highest grade.

Martin Green summarizes well the symbolic nature of contemporary advertising.

> In the mythic world of advertising, products displace the world of the spirit. Life becomes defined by the products accumulated or used. Community, love, fam-

ily, and religion are expressed through icons of industrial production. Pepsi is youth and youth is Pepsi, forever frolicking in an Eden of sun-filled streams and beaches, engaging in an eternal baptism of innocence. McDonald's restaurants serve as social centers and nurturing institutions, locales of conviviality, providers of food and drink in never-ending abundance.[68]

COMMON ADVERTISING APPEALS
▲

We have already noted the complex nature of advertising. Some ads attempt to motivate consumers to purchase products; others position candidates or causes in a particular light. The basis of almost all advertising today is emotion. While it is beyond the scope of this chapter to identify all the various techniques advertisers use, there are several basic emotional appeals common to most advertising messages.

Power

There are many kinds of power—economic, physical, political, and social, to name only a few. Many advertising messages offer products as a means of obtaining power. Advertisements present vignettes, images, icons, or emblems of power—all available for the price of a product or service. For example, Marlboro cigarette ads present the iconic cowboy. While few of us aspire to be a cowboy, we do aspire to be strong and independent. Many truck and car ads emphasize power elements. Chevy claims to be built "like a rock." Sport utility vehicles are wildly popular. The ads emphasize powerful engines and huge tires. They have a strong masculine appeal, emphasizing the ability to go anywhere in any weather. The names are rugged and project powerful images: Mountaineer, Blazer, Pathfinder, Navigator, Expedition, Durango, and Explorer. For years, cars have been identified with animals: cougars, mustangs, and vipers, for example. The association is with a primitive, wild form of power. Some auto appeals are more subtle. One campaign for Jaguar avoided an overt display of aggression and power. The copy proclaimed that the Jaguar possesses "confidence born of proficiency and power" providing an "authoritative response."[69]

Power appeals abound in nearly every product category. Cologne ads for both men and women promise sexual strength and power. Some ads offer economic power with such headlines as "You can lease a BMW for only $400 per month" or "You now qualify for an additional $10,000 line of credit on your Visa or Master-Card." Of course, many political ads offer us power as members of certain groups whose views and needs will be heard in Washington if we elect the right person. Sometimes the product itself is used to epitomize power. For example, we know that Dodge trucks are "ram tough," that Sears Die-Hard batteries are "heavy duty," and that Glad's Alligator garbage bags are "puncture proof." Most products, we are told, give us some kind of additional power or strength.

Meaning

We live in a complex world. Advertising offers products that will make it easier to be effective and to navigate the complexities of our environment. We can combat hunger by giving ten dollars per month to sponsor a child in a foreign country; General Electric will help us bring good things to life; we'll be in good hands with Allstate; we can have a good weekend if we drink Michelob. Ads tell us what is the best, the ultimate, the chic, and so on.

Carol Moog is concerned about the language of advertising where appeals target people's searches for identity. "The trouble with the advertising mirror is that we never see ourselves reflected; we only see reflections of what advertisers want us to think their products will do for us."[70] In effect, advertisers sell definitions of who we are. Thus, all we need to do to acquire a desired identity is to buy the product.

The United States is a society that relies on marketing. In fact, people learn to market themselves. Using brand names is a shortcut in that marketing process. It gives people a sense of security that their behavior will be approved. We use products that announce to others our socioeconomic level, our taste, and our impression of who we are. Our personalities become products, sometimes based on the material culture we embrace.

Fashion and style are shaped by advertising. In this sense, advertising is a central institution that helps shape collective consciousness and behavior. Ask yourself, what are the characteristics of style? Where did you get such criteria? Moog argues that *Glamour* is in the business of making women a bit more uncomfortable with who they are, while offering dreams, promises, or guidance that will help them become something more.[71] Several years ago, she notes, the models in the magazines were flawless in appearance and make-up. Next, they were more real and used less make-up for a more natural look. Now, sexiness and glamour are back. In short, each new image is largely initiated by advertisers. A general review of ads in fashion magazines tells us that men should be powerful, rich, confident, and athletic, while women should be beautiful and thin. As Michael Jacobson and Laurie Mazur observe, "personhood is defined by what we buy, never mind such traits as honesty, generosity, and loyalty."[72]

De Beers's "Diamonds are Forever" slogan links diamonds to love and marriage. The link is universally accepted but totally created by advertising. The slogan was first used back in 1947. Today, the slogan implies more than the strength of diamonds; it links diamonds with love, marriage, and anniversaries; diamonds have become part of our marriage ritual. Meaning and identity are packaged and sold like commodities.

Norms

Advertising tells us what is good or bad, in or out, right or wrong. Fashion advertising, as discussed above, establishes specific norms for behavior. Ads reveal how we should look, dress, and eat. It is interesting to note the transformation of blue jeans from pants indicating a lower working class to a symbol of protest to a status symbol of high fashion. During the civil rights movement and the anti-Vietnam years, jeans symbolized resentment, protest, and denial of the norms of what constituted acceptable apparel in society. Jeans were the uniform of the counterculture. In 1977, Jordache used television commercials to advertise tight jeans using sexy models. Jeans were then transformed into a fashion statement, and prices skyrocketed as fashion designers competed for the newly created market. Today, jeans are accepted as a standard of casual and comfortable dress for all ages, while certain brands still represent status symbols.

Product usage defines us socially and can even disclose what we believe. Many people find the billboards for Hooters restaurants offensive and judge people who spend their money there accordingly. It is important to remember that advertising appeal is not monolithic. Individuals will accept or reject the norms in the message based on their values and experiences.

Isolation

Many ads play on the fear of individual isolation and loneliness. From watching a sporting event to relaxing with friends, ads usually portray an intimate or a social setting. Product appeals provide a means of identifying with a particular crowd or protecting against an imagined faux pas. Many liquor ads depict a man or woman in a party setting with friends. A well-known vodka ad proclaims "Friends are worth Smirnoff." The message establishes a norm that equates caring with spending money. The visual implies that popularity will be the result of using the product. To be liked and accepted as part of a group is a powerful appeal.

Self-Esteem

A number of ads play on feelings of self-esteem. As mentioned earlier, products promise to make us better. The message of a Diet Center ad reads, "First I changed my body, then I changed my mind . . . I'm more confident, more in control." Researchers have found that women's magazines contain 10 times as many ads and articles promoting weight loss as men's magazines, the exact ratio of eating disorders between the sexes. Studies at Stanford University and the University of Massachusetts found that 70 percent of college females reported feeling worse about their own looks after reading women's magazines.[73] In a *Glamour* magazine survey with over 33,000 women participating, 75 percent of the respondents between the ages of 13 and 35 thought they were fat, while only 25 percent of them met the medical definition of overweight. Even 45 percent of the underweight women respondents thought they were fat.[74] Forty to 80 percent of fourth-grade girls are dieting. At least one-third of 12- to 13-year old girls are actively trying to lose weight. One survey found that 63 percent of high school girls were on diets compared to only 16 percent of boys.[75]

Models are becoming thinner and less representative of the general population. A generation ago, the typical model weighed 8 percent less than the average woman; today she weighs 23 percent less. Most models are thinner than 95 percent of the general female population.[76] According to Jacobson and Mazur,

> Girls and teenagers are perhaps the most vulnerable to beauty-industry propaganda. For them, advertising is a window into adult life, a lesson in what it means to be a woman. And lacking the sophistication of their older sisters and mothers, girls are less likely to distinguish between fact and advertising fiction.[77]

Jean Kilbourne is very concerned about the impact of advertising on young women. "Primarily girls are told by advertisers that what is most important about them is their perfume, their clothing, their bodies, their beauty."[78] Advertising plays on desires to improve looks and health and to be liked. Most ads present images that make us feel inadequate, not normal, or socially alienated—hoping that we accept the implication that using the product will alleviate our shortcomings. The influence goes well beyond the self-image of women. In a study on a well-known college campus, males who were shown centerfolds from *Playboy* and *Penthouse* were much more likely to find their own girlfriends less sexually attractive.[79]

Guilt

Perhaps the most prominent appeal used in advertising is guilt. We are urged to buy products to ensure the safety, health, intelligence, and social well-being of loved ones. As an appeal in advertising, guilt works in a number of ways. Diamond ads state "if you love her enough." The implication is that the only way to show your love for a partner is by giving diamonds. Some advertisements specify the amount of the expenditure: "you should spend no less than three months' wages on an engagement diamond." Guilt can motivate behavior to compensate for a wrongdoing—for example, sending flowers for missing an appointment. It can also play on a desire to repair a self-image—sending a gift to "start over." Guilt is a potent incentive to purchase what the marketer is trying to sell.

Fear

Advertising can make us fearful of many diverse situations—from burning in a fire to smelling bad at a party. There are many types of fears, including physical, social, and psychological. Consumers are more likely to remember ads that use fear appeals than those using positive, upbeat appeals.[80] Products will either prevent disaster, solve our problems, or at least reduce the risk of embarrassment. Fear appeal is so basic that it is difficult to find an ad that does not use it in some fashion. One of the most overt appeals to fear has been utilized by Volvo for several years. Their commercials focus on safety rather than styling, gas mileage, or resale value. Some critics have suggested that American Express commercials have heightened fears about foreign travel almost as much as the threat of terrorist attacks.

For products such as deodorants, mouthwash, or dandruff shampoos, hidden fear appeals are used to invoke anxiety followed by use of the product to solve the potential embarrassing problem. Since 1950, Dial soap has successfully played on the fear of body odor with the tagline, "Aren't you glad you use Dial? Don't you wish everybody did?" Fear can also be the main ingredient in political advertising. Doom is the predicted result if an opponent is elected. Consultants have discovered that it is easier to get citizens to vote against a candidate than to influence them to vote for a candidate.

When advertising increases apprehensions, it may succeed in convincing us to behave according to its plan, but it leaves a residue of unaddressed emotion. Before products can solve problems, they must first convince us that we have a problem. For more than a decade, there have been numerous ad campaigns based on fear appeals related to smoking, drinking, and AIDS. Yet, most recent studies indicate an increase in smoking, especially among young people. Too strong a fear appeal can cause a person to feel helpless and without control over the situation, thus decreasing attention and the effectiveness of the message. Fear appeals work best when they offer specific recommendations for overcoming the threat—and when the recommended action is perceived as reasonable, realistic, and effective. The antidrug campaign of "Just Say No" in the 1980s was generally thought to have failed because its solution was not realistic.

Sex

Advertisers are increasingly using sexual appeals to sell products of all sorts. We are accustomed to the use of allusions of sex in perfume, lingerie, and liquor ads, but now it can be found in ads for such products as cheese, soft drinks, junk food, and even power tools. Recall Häagen-Dazs ice cream's use of sex as a metaphor for sensual indulgence in the 1990s, not to mention several shampoo ads that invited an "organic experience."

Sexual appeals range from subtle to overt and appear in the majority of all advertising. Michael Phillips reports that since 1964, sexual illustrations have become more overt; sexual elements are more likely to be visual than verbal; and female models are more likely than male models to be suggestively clad, partially clad, or nude.[81] According to research, sexual images increase the amount of time spent looking at the ad, which can translate into higher message recall and positive associations. More subliminal uses of sexual appeals are also common. Product placement, model positions, and provocative graphics arouse interest. The intent is to increase the time spent viewing the ad and to aid recall.

The most overt and provocative use of sex in ads is to gain attention. Nudity certainly gains attention, but it is less successful in aiding the recall of the advertising message. Sexual innuendo in advertising abounds. One of the more celebrated attempts was a young Brooke Shields in a Calvin Klein ad where she proclaimed, "Nothing gets between me and my Calvin Klein jeans." Hennessy cognac has enjoyed a successful campaign since 1984 that utilizes a sexy sell. Although the tagline simply states, "Hennessy, the civilized way to keep warm," the various scenes reveal a romantic couple in various stages of coziness, seduction, and undress. In a 1994 Hyundai television commercial, two women evaluate men's physical endowments based on the car they drive. They prefer the "confident" Hyundai driver who doesn't need to rely on an expensive car to make an impression and they ask, "Wonder what he's got under the hood?"

Historically, Calvin Klein's Obsession ads are among the most controversial, using nudes of both genders in various configurations, often with no text. The sexual imagery is bold. Such scenarios gain audience attention and are used for fantasy fulfillment and stimulation. In 1995, Calvin Klein once again provoked controversy by using very young models in suggestive poses. In some of the ads, the model's underwear is clearly visible. Critics of the ads charged Klein with supporting child pornography. In fact, a government investigation confirmed that all the models were over the age of eighteen. Nevertheless, within weeks, Klein canceled the ad campaign. Some observers noted that the company benefited more from the publicity of the controversy than they would have from repeated airings of the commercial. He later came under criticism for using models who appeared to be "strung out on drugs."

It's even more brazen in England. A poster for Coca-Cola shows a naked woman with her curves replicating the contours of a glass Coke bottle. The tagline states, "Get your hands on a contour." One for women shows a man's firm "six-pack" stomach also resembling the ribbing on a Coke bottle. Again, the tagline is "Get your hands on a six-pack."

Sexual appeals in advertising help define sex roles in society. Through ads we learn our roles and behavior in courtship, fashion, and other types of social behavior. Of major concern to many social scientists is the perpetuation of sexual stereotypes of power, dominance, and success. Many of the ads using sexual appeals reinforce sexist notions about the idealized woman and man; they also exploit human sexuality. In the former case, the ads give us unrealistic notions about our bodies, feelings, and emotions. In the latter, they encourage us to think of sex as a commodity.

Pop artist Madonna turned underwear into outerwear. In the 1980s, designers began the trend toward less coverage in clothes. Ad campaigns for juniors, then teenage girls, and then younger children featured midriff tops and hip huggers. Stores such as Wet Seal, Hot Topic, and Gadzooks started carrying the Playboy line and Hotkiss. Britney Spears videos spurred the acquisition of similar clothing styles by her fans. By 2002, bikinis and bright colored bras were sold at GapKids and even in the children's department at Sears. Abercrombie, the kids' store of Abercrombie & Fitch, sells thongs for girls 7 to 14 years of age. The campaign showed images of cherries and such messages as "Wink Wink" and "Eye Candy." Public outrage caused the company to remove the thongs from their shelves and from their catalog. Some groups charged the campaign encouraged pedophilia and further erodes the self-esteem of young girls. The primary concern for many is that as we see more and more explicit and suggestive themes in TV shows, movies, and videos, products will also follow the trend in their advertising (recall the earlier discussion of the FCUK campaign).

HOW TO CRITIQUE ADS
▲

A primary goal of this book is to provide tools of analysis for the persuasion we encounter in various contexts. Because of the extensive daily exposure to advertising, we should look beneath the surface of ads to understand how images create an impression. Judith Williamson claims advertisements are one of the most important cultural factors molding and reflecting our life today.[82] Every ad creates structures of meaning. Advertisements transform statements about things into statements of significance to people. For example, if a characteristic of a car is high gas mileage, then this characteristic is translated to notions of economy and rationality. The key is to transform the language of objects to the language of people.

As a critic, one should look at the textual relationships between the parts of the message and the meaning created. Through ads, diamonds come to mean love—a transformation beyond mineral and rock to a purely human sign. In some ads, the objects communicate the human message such as "say it with flowers" or "gold says I love you." In other ads, people are identified with the objects such as "I'm a Pepper."

The visual image plays a very important role in the meaning created. In a famous television ad for Apple computers reminiscent of George Orwell's *1984*, a striking woman hurls a sledgehammer through the video screen that hundreds of people have been watching in a trance. The spot was a media sensation and won several creative awards. Words cannot, of course, adequately describe the visual power of the commercial. Some of the implications of the ad were that the new Apple Macintosh computer would allow individual creativity and freedom, releasing us from the world of domination and "big brother" control. Another highly visual campaign is for the Infiniti automobile. For the first two years of the television and print campaign, the car was never shown. The words were poetic and the visuals were of sweeping landscapes. The Infiniti is more than a car, the experience more than transportation.

Using a textual approach, we look for meanings within the ad. What are the appeals? What does the product promise in human terms? The product may promise smooth skin but imply younger looks. The product may promise a close shave but imply greater female approval. Careful analysis of advertising forces us to become more critical of the claims made.

When analyzing advertising, look for patterns of similarities and differences. For example, how are people portrayed in print ads—as housewives or executives, smart or dumb, fat or thin? How frequently are certain roles portrayed? What gender roles and/or models for expected behavior are presented? First, focus on the attributes, claims, and promises of the product. Next, analyze the images, stereotypes, and placement/positions of the visuals. Finally, consider the implied audience, claims, warrants, and the evidence—the specific wording of the message. By analyzing surface and implied meanings of advertising messages, we can better recognize the persuasive appeals and assess their validity.

Use the following questions as a general guideline when reviewing an ad.

1. What does the ad promise?
2. What does the ad *not* say?
3. What are the claims being made?
4. What reasons are given for purchasing the product?
5. What was the first thing that caught your attention?
6. What are the social relationships being portrayed? Who is in charge? Who holds the power?

While analyzing these specific elements, remember the following:

- People often buy more than products. A Mercedes is more than transportation; we buy the world that it represents.
- There is no relationship between the brand and its image.
- Read all the fine print.
- We participate in our own persuasion.

CRITICISMS OF ADVERTISING

▲

Although we accept advertising as a daily practice, there has always been some criticism of the industry. We seem to have a love-hate relationship with advertising. For most businesses, advertising is a necessary evil. For consumers, the commercial interruptions are sometimes pleasant, sometimes informative, but always intrusive. There are several issues of advertising that deserve special attention.

Deception

Most of us would agree that advertising is a business based on deception and half-truths. However, most of the factual messages presented in ads are true, and the factual statements can be verified. The problem is that there are few factual statements in most advertising messages. Consumers do not make distinctions between factual statements and value judgments. As noted in chapter 4, statements of fact are verifiable, whereas statements of value express opinions that are, to say the least, very subjective and judgmental. What does it mean when an ad claims that a restaurant has the best hamburgers? Does it mean they have the best hamburgers in terms of taste, size, toppings, or price? Certainly, several restaurant chains can claim to have the best hamburgers, but can they all claim to have the biggest? Perhaps they can. Some restaurants may have the biggest based on weight before cooking or after cooking, or based on size by using very large buns or by using thin but large-in-circumference hamburgers.

There is a difference between false advertising and misleading advertising. False advertising means claims are explicitly and literally false. Most ads make claims that are explicitly true but generate false meanings. The implied claims are the most powerful and motivate consumers to purchase the product. Thus, most advertisers settle for the subtle half-truth. For example, an ad for Klondike Lite ice-cream bars proclaimed that it was "the 93 percent fat-free dessert with chocolate-flavored coating." Can you detect anything wrong with this ad? The bars are indeed 93 percent fat-free, if you don't count the coating. If you count all the calories—including those in the coating that comes "with" the bar—the product actually contains 14 percent fat—twice as much as claimed in Klondike's advertising.[83]

Some ads are misleading because of the nature of the comparisons made in their presentations. Bayer aspirin claims that "All aspirin is not alike. In tests for quality, Bayer proved superior." The implication is that Bayer is better in relieving pain than other brands of aspirin. However, the tests referred to in the ad were tests for quality conducted by Bayer, which showed that Bayer's tablets were "superior" because they were whiter and less breakable than other brands tested.[84] Implied superiority claims abound in product ads and are becoming even more subtle. For example, if all pain capsules take about the same amount of time to work, one brand can claim that "no pain reliever works faster!" Although the literal claim is true, the consumer is led to infer that the brand is superior to all others. Other examples include "Nobody builds a more productive line of farm equipment" (International Harvester); "Nobody does it better" (Winston Light cigarettes); "No leading brand gets rid of dandruff better than Selsun Blue"; or "No other cereal has more natural food fiber than Kellogg's All-Bran."

Such claims state equality but imply superiority. Research has shown that consumers not only accept implied claims and puffery from ads but also tend to elaborate on the claims presented.[85] Studies consistently reveal that the vast majority of assertions made in advertising are subjective rather than factual claims. We must be careful in accepting the claims made in comparative advertising.

Other ads mislead by implying results that the product can't deliver. If we resist the appealing images, we can usually challenge the rationality of claims made in ads. Can the product really make us more beautiful, rich, young, successful, or sexy? Is there a logical relationship between the problem presented and the solution offered? For example, consider the Coast soap commercials. If you feel sleepy and sluggish in the mornings, will a shower with Coast make you feel instantly alert, happy, and energetic? Improving your nutrition or going to bed earlier would be logical solutions to the problem of sluggishness; showering with a particular brand of soap is not.

Visual lies and distortion also reinforce an implied claim. In a 1990 Volvo commercial, a monster truck drove across a line of cars, crushing all of them except the Volvo. Although never stated, the implied claim was that Volvo was stronger and thus safer than the other automobiles. However, the audience was not informed that the visual demonstration was false. The Volvo wagon had been reinforced with steel and wood and the other cars were weakened for the shot. Volvo paid over $600,000 in fines because of the misleading nature of the commercial.[86]

Advertising is misleading when it provides incomplete or exaggerated descriptions of products or services. An ad may state that a desk is made of "all wood" but omit that the wood is actually compressed wood parts. The more ludicrous ads will often contain small print caveats about the claims made. Ads touting high-yield investments will tell you in small print that they require a large amount of money for participation; free checking requires a large minimum monthly balance; a new car for $100 a month requires a large down payment—the examples are endless.

Most advertising focuses on trivial aspects of products—elevating the insignificant to significant status. Minor qualities are exaggerated. In fact, differences among most brands or product categories are slight. Much of the distortion in advertising is accomplished in the visual aspects of the message. Food looks better, clothes fit better, and gadgets are handier in commercials and pictures than after a purchase has been made. Ivan Preston argues that the primary cause of deceptive advertising is that "advertisers typically sell brands rather than just products. Because a brand must be presented as different from other brands although they are not, advertisers are tempted to create false differences."[87]

The consumer is deceived by exaggerated product differences and by contrived competition.[88] For example, Pert Plus, Pantene Pro-V, VS Sassoon, Physique, and Herbal Essence are all Procter & Gamble shampoo products; Tide, Gain, Era, and Ivory belong to the Procter & Gamble stable of detergents. Kool-Aid, Country Time, and Crystal Light powdered drink mixes are all Kraft Foods brands, as are Maxwell House, Maxim, and Sanka coffees. Such abundance of products gives us the illusion of choice, and each one tells us they are superior to their "competitors."

Ads can be deceptive through:

- Pseudo claims—An ad for toothpaste may claim to "fight cavities," but is it the chemical composition of the paste, the movement of the toothbrush, or regular brushing that fights cavities?
- Comparison with an unidentified other—An ad for toothpaste may claim that it "has superior cleaning action," but is it superior to another brand or to not brushing?
- Comparison of the product to its earlier form—An ad for a toothpaste may claim that the product is "new and improved." In what way is it better; what was wrong with the old version?
- Irrelevant comparisons—An ad may claim that the toothpaste is the "best selling of its kind." What does "kind" mean? Best among whiteners? Among gels? Among those that have fluoride?
- Pseudo survey—An ad for toothpaste may claim that "4 out of 5 dentists recommend the toothpaste." What was the criterion of selection? Were the dentists paid in any way?[89]

Perhaps the most difficult question involving deception concerns the motives of the advertiser. Many local retailers advertise a sale on low-end merchandise, hoping to sell more expensive models once the consumer gets in the store. Thus, while the ads are not deceptive, their purpose is not to offer the consumer a good value or necessarily a good product; the primary purpose is "bait-and-switch."

Language

Advertising has a tremendous impact, and many educators are concerned that advertising debases our language. For Carol Moog, America's "second tongue" is product language.[90] The violation of rules of grammar and punctuation is commonplace. For years there was a running debate about the grammar used in the phrase, "Winston tastes good like a cigarette should." Many people believed that the grammatically correct sentence is "Winston tastes good as a cigarette should." Advertising copy contains a multitude of dashes, hyphens, and sentence fragments. The United States Army received hundreds of letters each year from teachers and students questioning the punctuation in the slogan, "Army. Be All That You Can Be." There is also the problem with misspelling of words in titles and names of products. Some scholars argue that the constant use of superlatives in ads cheapens and lessens the power of words and language. How many times can a product be "new and improved"? Words like "quick," "easy," "amazing," or "best" lose their power when used frequently.

Children

Children are special targets for advertisers. For more than 25 years, there has been a national debate on the impact and influence of advertising on children. The concern centers on the fact that children are unable to defend against the persuasive messages. They have not yet learned the critical thinking skills encouraged in the section on how to critique ads. Advertisers in the United States direct more than $1 billion a year toward children. And their efforts are rewarded. It is estimated that children under 14 years of age spend more than $24 billion; teenagers spend about $100 billion a year.[91] In addition, research shows that children are the primary influencers of family spending on consumer goods to the tune of $200 billion a year. For example, the concept behind using Ronald McDonald is to entice young children to ask parents to take them to McDonald's. Hyatt mails promotional brochures to children who have stayed at the hotels, encouraging them to come back for another visit. Advertisers know if they can create brand loyalty when a child is young, they may well have a customer for the next 60 or 70 years.[92]

Children watch an average of 3 hours of TV a day during weekdays and 6 to 8 hours on weekends. After age two, the majority of children are exposed to over 20,000 commercials per year.[93] Children's programming has more ads per hour than adult or general audience programming. Studies reveal that of the advertising on children's programming, 3 percent is for healthy foods compared to 22 percent for cereals and breakfast food, 18 percent for snacks and drinks, 6 percent for fast foods, and 34 percent for toys.[94]

Marketing research shows that by the age of 6 months, babies are already forming images of corporate logos and mascots, and by age 3, most children are making specific brand-name requests for products. Studies show that children exhibit high recall of ads, details about the characters, story lines, brand names and products, and even packaging.[95] The detail of knowledge of commercials is alarming. Advertisers use bright colors, fast-paced editing, animation, and special sound effects. Most cartoons are nothing less than program-length commercials to sell toys and products. Because children's critical thinking skills are undeveloped, commercials can take advantage of them by distorting product attributes. Toys seem larger, more exciting, and easier to operate than is actually the case. For teenagers, products are offered to solve life's problems—from unmanageable hair to the lack of friends. Eight million children in schools receive the daily Channel One broadcasts consisting of ten minutes of news and two minutes of commercials. The sad fact is, according to Roy Fox, "More than any other experience or text, commercials are 'read' by more students, more often, than *Romeo and Juliet*, or *A Tale of Two Cities,* or *Huck Finn*, or *The Catcher in the Rye.*"[96]

Research shows that advertising influences kids in gender-role, racial, and social stereotyping, as well as in sexual and physical identity creation. Especially among young children, studies show verbal, physical, and mental "replay behaviors" resulting from exposure to advertising. Examples of verbal replays include singing popular jingles or talking to friends about favorite ads or advertising characters. Physical replays are when children act out or imitate scenes or actions from commercials. Mental replays are when children think or daydream about commercials they have seen.[97] Studies also reveal that advertising makes kids more materialistic, generates friction between parents and children, and limits the formation of moral and ethical values.[98]

In the last decade, cross-promotion and licensing have become a mainstay of advertising aimed at children. Perhaps the industry's most successful licensing effort was with the Teenage Mutant Ninja Turtles in 1990. The Turtles generated

200 licensed products and earned nearly $2 billion in revenues compared to $135 million in movie ticket sales. This amount, of course, pales in comparison to the toy merchandizing efforts supporting the latest *Star Wars* movie epic "prequel." Psychologists claim that children may actually suffer lower self-esteem if they do

not own a popular toy, such as the Cabbage Patch doll of 1985, the Teenage Mutant Ninja Turtles of 1990, or the "right" tennis shoes, to name just a few. In the last decade, there were increasing incidents of violence associated with teenagers stealing $100 gym shoes, like Nike AirJordans, and satin Starter jackets. As a result, several public school systems have proposed that students wear uniforms to school to avoid the social problems related to clothing issues.

There can be little argument that children are especially vulnerable to the persuasive impact of advertising. Many social groups are calling for more regulation and control. The nations of Belgium, Denmark, Norway, Sweden, and the Canadian province of Quebec ban all advertising aimed at children on radio and television. Roy Fox makes several recommendations relevant to children and advertising: ban electronic and print advertising in schools, establish media education curricula in schools, reduce the number of commercials in children's programming, and classify all toy-based programs as infomercials, thus allowing greater regulation by the Federal Communication Commission.[99] The American Academy of Pediatrics recommends, among other things, that children under the age of 2 not watch any television.[100]

Consumerism

The word *consumer* did not always have positive connotations. In its original French usage, consumption was viewed as an act of pillage, destruction, and waste. Americans represent about 6 percent of the world's population, but we use almost 30 percent of the planet's resources. We have more than 30,000 supermarket items with over 200 kinds of cereal alone.[101]

With industrialization, the idea of using things up became associated with prosperity. The sole purpose of advertising is to entice us to buy products; critics argue that it makes people too materialistic. Christopher Lasch, in his book *The Culture of Narcissism*, argues that "advertising manufactures a product of its own: the consumer, perpetually unsatisfied, restless, anxious, and bored. Advertising serves not so much to advertise products as to promote consumption as a way of life."[102] If happiness and success are measured by the things we possess, the race to "keep up with the Joneses" is an endless cycle. Advertising perpetuates the cycle by supplying images that fuel unhappiness with ourselves and our possessions.

John O'Toole (former chairman of Foote, Cone & Belding) acknowledges that advertising sells things people do not need. He claims that people only need air, food, and water. For him, the distinction is that advertising cannot sell things people do not want.[103] To avoid stagnation and a depressed economy in a capitalistic system, goods must be consumed. Advertising creates false needs by responding to the needs of manufacturers rather than to the needs of consumers.

Advertisers do more than encourage us to buy what we do not need; they go to great lengths to make what we already have obsolete. We then have no choice but to update equipment, cars, or appliances (particularly if the manufacturers stop making the replacement parts necessary for repairs). The Huffy Corporation came out with a new 12-speed bike despite the fact that market research revealed that most people do not even use 10 speeds when riding. Why? According to then President Harry Shaw, "People don't really need the two extra speeds. The bike may not do so much for you but it should help to obsolete the 10-speeder."[104]

Social Effects

With the erosion of the influence of traditional social institutions (the family, the church, and schools) young people learn social skills and values from television shows and commercials. Critics are concerned about the social influence of advertising in defining who we are, our values, and our self-esteem. Jean Kilbourne summarizes the social influence of advertising:

> It often sells a great deal more than products. It sells values, images, and concepts of love and sexuality, romance, success, and, perhaps most important, normalcy. To a great extent, it tells us who we are and who we should be. We are increasingly using brand names to create our identities.[105]

We briefly discussed the tendency of commercials to stereotype people. Women, old people, and minorities in particular are often stereotyped by the advertising industry in terms of looks, occupations, roles, and behavior. Kilbourne goes even further. She thinks advertising turns people into objects. "Women's bodies, and men's bodies too these days, are dismembered, packaged, and used to sell everything from chain saws to chewing gum."[106]

Also mentioned earlier was the tendency of advertising to feed our hopes and desires while profiting from our insecurities. Michael Hyman and Richard Tansey caution about the ethics of what they call "psychoactive ads," defined as those that cause viewers to feel anxious, hostile toward others, or to lose self-esteem."[107] For example, a public service ad that has appeared on television shows a raw egg and asks the viewer to pretend the egg is the viewer's brain. The announcer then breaks the egg and drops it into a hot skillet and says that this is what drugs do to brains. The goal of the ad is to discourage teenagers from using drugs. However, the scare appeal creates such anxiety in some drug users that they become suicidal. The fact is that emotion-arousing commercials may generate unintended, harmful influences and effects.

There is also concern about the impact of advertising on the cultural climate of our nation. Some ads are in poor taste, yet find public approval. Twenty years ago, advertisements for hemorrhoid treatments, contraceptives, and douche products would have shocked the public. Advertisements today are more suggestive and challenge traditional values. The pressure for AIDS education and prevention has stimulated further debate about what is acceptable for public broadcast.

Freedom of Speech

We know that the First Amendment to the U.S. Constitution guarantees and preserves our freedom of speech. Commercial speech differs in that a fee is charged to air the message. In one case, we are concerned about the expression of thoughts, beliefs, and opinions. In the other case, the concern is with speech designed to promote products, services, or issues. Not everyone has equal access to the means of expression of commercial speech.[108]

Advertising can have a large impact on freedom of speech in the United States. In terms of special issues, corporate images, or political advertising, only those organizations or individuals with money have access to the media to disseminate their messages. As mentioned in chapter 2, private interests often dictate what will be broadcast or published. Some critics suggest that influential sponsors of programs or advertisers in newspapers and magazines even direct the content of the news by threatening withdrawal of advertising support. Negative news stories jeopardize major corporate sponsorship. Perhaps even more damaging is the impact on how we address each other about the social issues confronting us. Politicians compete for exposure and must speak in "sound bites" that fit a one-minute news story. It is common to hear on the radio that "the news is brought to you by. . . ." Shouldn't we have access to news regardless of whether or not someone will pay for it?

Advertisers increasingly influence entertainment program content. Product boycotts have become a major weapon for citizen groups that desire to get a program off the air. If shows, characters, or plots are too controversial, advertisers will pull support from the program. Diane English, the creator of a long-running CBS series, was mindful of the influence when the title character, Murphy Brown, became pregnant in 1991. English knew that abortion was not an option for discussion on the show because sponsors would not approve.[109] After Ellen Degeneres revealed she was a lesbian on her television show in 1997, some advertisers withdrew support. The following season, the show was canceled.

Private versus Public Interests

Advertising is often selfish; it shows very little responsibility to society. Its goal and responsibility is to serve the marketing goals of the company paying the bills. John Kenneth Galbraith argues that ads primarily serve private rather than public interests.

> Advertising operates exclusively. . . on behalf of privately produced goods and services. . . . Every corner of the public's psyche is canvassed by some of the nation's most talented citizens to see if the desire for some merchantable product can be cultivated. No similar process operates on behalf of the nonmerchantable services of the state."[110]

Michael Hyman and Richard Tansey argue that advertisers should be more responsible to public interests; they advocate three simple practices.[111] First, advertisers should carefully assess both the medium and the market. Some images used in advertisements can have a negative impact on some groups, such as AIDS victims, Vietnam combat veterans, young men and women, and gamblers, to name only a few. Second, Hyman and Tansey suggest that advertisers should clearly label psychoactive ads with an introductory announcement. They cite as a model news programs that caution viewer discretion because of strong imagery or themes discussed. Finally, they suggest that advertisers avoid the use of shocking dramatizations, such as a young child killed in a car accident because of a drunk driver.

Michael Jacobson and Laurie Mazur summarize the problems of private versus public interests—commercialism—in a democracy:

Any culture that surrenders its vision and its self-sustaining human values to the narrow judgment of commerce will be neither free nor just. Commercialism does serious damage to the substance of democracy; if not to its forms. It leads to censorship or self-censorship of the media, to invisible chains that keep people from speaking out, to the indentured status of politicians, and to an overall coarseness that deprecates the humanitarian impulses and the creative drives of a culture in balance, a culture having commerce without commercialism.[112]

WHAT CAN I DO?
▲

There is growing concern about the negative impact of commercials on our culture. Some suggested remedies violate individual freedom of speech and decision making. Many recommendations focus on specific areas or audience groups. For example, some argue commercial messages of all types should be banned in schools. Others suggest that very early in their lives, students should be taught elements of media literacy and effects. Some advocacy groups even argue media issues should be treated and viewed as public health issues. Others suggest that we create "ad-free zones," especially on public land, parks, and scenic parkways.

If you are serious about minimizing the influence of advertising on your purchasing behavior and want to show concern for the environment, below are several things you can do:

- Don't "go shopping." Don't go to a store unless you need a specific item.
- Live within your means. Avoid using credit when making purchases. This will reduce impulse purchases.
- Take care of what you already own to extend the useful life of the item.
- Postpone buying new items.
- Do it yourself—learn to fix items.
- Research value, quality, and durability. Become a comparative shopper.
- Get it for less. Buy items only on sale and do comparative shopping for major items.
- Buy it used. Today there are many used and secondhand outlet stores selling everything from office furniture to clothes.

SUMMARY
▲

Our purpose in this chapter was to identify the functions, techniques, tactics, and appeals of contemporary advertising. Advertising is as powerful, subtle, and intensive as any face-to-face encounter. It is both a creative and a scientific process. Advertising messages are inherently persuasive; they seek to convert the individual by playing on human emotion, hopes, and fears. People's interests are targeted based on demographic characteristics such as age, sex. income, or lifestyle. Our society is characterized by material possessions that often carry symbolic significance for the owner.

The quantity of advertising is increasing, and the distinctions between advertising and other forms of communication, such as news and information, are increasingly blurred. Advertising, like all persuasive communication, is not neutral and will always involve a battle of psychological wits. To balance the pervasive presence of advertising, consumers must engage in constant, critical analysis of advertising's messages and influence.

Questions and Projects for Further Study

1. Using the Foote, Cone & Belding advertising model, provide a contemporary example of an ad for each quadrant of the model.

2. Select a print ad, a radio ad, and a television commercial and critique the ads following the questions and guidelines provided in the section on "How to Critique Ads."

3. Thumb through a monthly or weekly magazine; find examples of ads that create appeals based on:

   a. power

   b. meaning

   c. norms

   d. isolation

   e. self-esteem

   f. guilt

   g. fear

4. Select a magazine ad and perform a detailed content analysis of both the explicit and implicit meanings and promises contained in the ad.

5. Select an issue of *Gentlemen's Quarterly* and *Vogue*. How are men and women portrayed in each magazine? Do the portrayals differ? If so, how? What type of relationships, roles, and social status are the models portraying?

6. Record all the ads you see in one day from these sources: television, radio, newspapers, magazines, World Wide Web, billboards, and "point of sale" displays in stores. How does the list you compiled compare to the lists of others in your class?

7. Think about the items you have purchased in the last two weeks. How did you learn about them? Why did you buy one particular brand rather than another?

8. Select one product category and one major magazine (for example, automobiles and *Time* Magazine). Go to the library and find back issues of the publication and see how the advertising for the product has changed for each decade since 1940.

9. Take one product category and see how many different appeals are used in ads for the product appearing in magazines written for varying reader interests.

10. Watch one hour of television and write down the number of ads seen.

Additional Reading

Roy Fox, *Harvesting Minds: How TV Commercials Control Kids*, 2nd ed. (Westport, CT: Praeger, 2000).

Katherine T. Frith, ed., *Undressing the Ad: Reading Culture in Advertising* (New York: Peter Lang, 1997).

John Jones, *The Ultimate Secrets of Advertising* (Thousand Oaks, CA: Sage, 2002).

Jean Kilbourne, *Deadly Persuasion* (New York: The Free Press, 1999).

Carol Nelson and Herschell Lewis, *Handbook of Advertising* (Chicago: NTC Business Books, 1999).

Michael J. Phillips, *Ethics and Manipulation in Advertising* (Westport, CT: Quorum Books, 1997).

Juliann Sivulka, *Soap, Sex, and Cigarettes* (Belmont, CA: Wadsworth, 1998).

Jan Zimmerman, *Marketing on the Internet* (Gulf Breeze, FL: Maximum Press, 2000).

Notes

[1] Marshall McLuhan, *Understanding Media: The Extensions of Man*, (New York: McGraw-Hill, 1964), Part II, Chapter 23.

[2] W. James Potter, *Media Literacy*, 2nd ed. (Thousand Oaks, CA: Sage, 2001), p. 135.

[3] Richard Campbell, *Media & Culture*, 3rd ed. (Boston: Bedford/St. Martins, 2003), p. 385.

[4] Jean Kilbourne, *Deadly Persuasion* (New York: The Free Press, 1999), p. 58.

[5] Potter, p. 137.

[6] Ibid.

[7] Kilbourne, p. 33.

[8] Potter, p. 135.

[9] Donna Cross, *Media-Speak* (New York: Mentor Books, 1983), p. 14.

[10] http://www.icommag.com/november-2002/november-page-1b.html; accessed 10-22-03.

[11] Campbell, p. 385.

[12] Stewart Alter, "Influenced by Ads? Not Me, Most Say," *Advertising Age*, June 10, 1985, p. 15.

[13] "Franchise Fever!" *Newsweek*, April 22, 2002, p. 58.

[14] Ibid., p. 59.

[15] Kilbourne, p. 374.

[16] Jan Zimmerman, *Marketing on the Internet* (Gulf Breeze, FL: Maximum Press, 2000), p. 5.

[17] Ibid., p. xxiii.

[18] Ibid., p. 21.

[19] Cited in Timothy Borchers, *Persuasion in the Media Age* (Boston: McGraw-Hill, 2002), p. 358–59.

[20] Kilbourne, p. 34.

[21] Ibid., p. 35.

[22] Juliann Sivulka, *Soap, Sex, and Cigarettes* (Belmont, CA: Wadsworth, 1998), p. 425.

[23] John O'Toole, *The Trouble with Advertising* (Chelsea House, 1981), p. 15.

[24] Sut Jhally, *The Codes of Advertising* (New York: St. Martin's Press, 1987), p. 1.

[25] William Meyers, *The Image-Makers* (New York: Times Books, 1984), p. 43.

[26] Vance Packard, *Hidden Persuaders* (New York: Pocket Books, 1957), p. 1.

[27] William Leiss, Stephen Kline, and Sut Jhally, *Social Communication in Advertising* (New York: Routledge, 1990), pp. 327–48.

[28] Robert M. Schindler, "The Real Lesson of New Coke: The Value of Focus Groups for Predicting the Effects of Social Influence," *Market Research*, December 1992, p. 28.

[29] Thomas Oliver, *The Real Coke, The Real Story* (New York: Random House, 1985), p. 98.

[30] Arthur Gerger, *Media Analysis Techniques* (Beverly Hills: Sage, 1982), p. 57.

[31] Packard, p. 21.

[32] Campbell, p. 395.

[33] See Al Ries and Jack Trout, *Positioning: The Battle for Your Mind* (New York: McGraw-Hill, 1981).

[34] John Jones, *Does It Pay to Advertise?* (Lexington, MA: Lexington Books, 1989), p. 345.

[35] See Meyers.

[36] "Coca-Cola Turns to Pavlov," *The Wall Street Journal*, January 19, 1984.

[37] http://www.sric-bi.com/VALS/; accessed 10-28-03.

[38] VALS™ Framework and Segment Descriptions; http://www.sric-bi.com/marketing/VALS/VALSFramework2002-09.pdf.

[39] A sample questionnaire is available at http://www.sric-bi.com/VALS/surveynew.shtml.

[40] Adapted from The VALS™ Segments, http://www.sric-bi.com/VALS/types.shtml.

[41] http://www.sric-bi.com/VALS/projects.shtml.

[42] Don E. Schultz, *Essentials of Advertising Strategy* (Chicago: Crain Books, 1981), pp. 16–17.

[43] Kim Rotzoll and James Haefner with Steven Hall, *Advertising in Contemporary Society: Perspectives toward Understanding*, 3rd ed. (Urbana: University of Illinois Press, 1996), p. 114.

[44] Leiss, et al., pp. 22–26.

[45] R. Vaughn, "How Advertising Works: A Planning Model," *Journal of Advertising Research*, 1980, 20:27.

[46] John Jones, *When Ads Work* (New York: Lexington Books, 1995), p. 37.

[47] Ibid., p. 59.

[48] Ibid., p. 27.

[49] Ibid., p. 32.

[50] Alexander Biel, "Likeability: Why Advertising That is Well Liked Sells Well," in *How Advertising Works*, ed. Joe Jones (Thousand Oaks, CA: Sage, 1998), pp. 111–20.

[51] John Jones, *The Ultimate Secrets of Advertising* (Thousand Oaks, CA: Sage, 2002), p. 10.

[52] Ibid., p. 33.

[53] Zimmerman, pp. 56–57.

[54] Courtland Bovee and William Arens, *Contemporary Advertising* (Homewood, IL: Irwin, 1986), p. 152.

[55] See Wilson Bryan Key, *Subliminal Seduction* (New York: Signet Books, 1973), and *Media Sexploitation* (New York: Signet Books, 1976).

[56] Key, *Subliminal*, p. 11.

[57] Anthony Pratkanis and Elliot Aronson, *Age of Propaganda* (New York: W. H. Freeman and Company, 1992), p. 201.

[58] O'Toole, p. 21.

[59] http://www.edifyingspectacle.org/sexuality/blog/archives/amorous_capitalism/fcuk_you.php

[60] http://www.frenchconnection.com/flash/index_small.html

[61] Timothy Joyce, "The Advertising Process," in *How Advertising Works*, ed. Joe Jones (Thousand Oaks, CA: Sage, 1998), pp. 15–16.

[62] Joseph Campbell, *The Power of Myth* (New York: Doubleday, 1988), pp. 4–8; see also Joseph Campbell, *Transformation of Myth Through Time* (New York: Harper & Row, 1990).

[63] R. Campbell, p. 406.

[64] Sal Randazzo, *Mythmaking on Madison Avenue* (Chicago: Probus Publishing Company, 1993), pp. 49–50.

[65] http://www.smithsonianmag.si.edu/smithsonian/issues00/jan00/breck.html

[66] Randazzo, p. 12–14.

[67] Ibid., p. 260.

[68] Martin Green, "Some Versions of the Pastoral: Myth in Advertising; Advertising as Myth," in *Advertising and Culture*, ed. Mary Cross (Westport, CT: Praeger, 1996), p. 41.

[69] Carol Moog, *"Are They Selling Her Lips?": Advertising and Identity* (New York: William Morrow and Company, 1990), pp. 93–94.

[70] Ibid., p. 35.

[71] Ibid., p. 116.

[72] Michael Jacobson and Laurie Mazur, *Marketing Madness* (Boulder, CO: Westview Press, 1995), p. 13.

[73] Kilbourne, p. 133.

[74] Jacobson and Mazur, p. 77.

[75] Kilbourne, p. 134.

[76] Jacobson and Mazur, p. 77.

[77] Ibid., p. 79.

[78] Kilbourne, p. 132.

[79] Ibid., p. 133.

[80] Michael Hyman and Richard Tansey, "The Ethics of Psychoactive Ads," *Journal of Business Ethics*, 1990, 9(2):108.

[81] Michael J. Phillips, *Ethics and Manipulation in Advertising* (Westport, CT: Quorum Books, 1997), p. 120.

[82] Judith Williamson, *Decoding Advertisements* (New York: Marion Boyars, 1983), p. 11.

[83] Jacobson and Mazur, p. 144.

[84] Cross, p. 16.

[85] See Robert Wyckham, "Implied Superiority Claims," *Journal of Advertising Research*, February/March 1987, pp. 54–63.

[86] Ivan Preston, *The Tangled Web They Weave: Truth, Falsity, and Advertisers* (Madison: University of Wisconsin Press, 1994).

[87] Ibid., p. 53.

[88] Cross, pp. 28–29.

[89] Kathleen Jamieson and Karlyn Kohrs Campbell, *The Interplay of Influence*, 3rd ed. (Belmont, CA: Wadsworth, 1992), pp. 195–98.

[90] Moog, p. 89.

[91] Carole Macklin and Les Carlson, *Advertising to Children* (Thousand Oaks, CA: Sage, 1999), p. xi.

[92] Jacobson and Mazur, p. 21.

[93] Roy Fox, *Harvesting Minds: How TV Commercials Control Kids* (Westport, CT: Praeger, 2000), p. 31.

[94] Potter, p. 142.

[95] Ibid., p. 31.

[96] Ibid., p. 8.

[97] Ibid., pp. 91–146.

[98] Fox, p. 19.

[99] Ibid., pp. 161–65.

[100] Potter, p. 143.

[101] Ibid., p. 144–45.

[102] Christopher Lasch, *The Culture of Narcissism* (New York: Warner Books, 1979), pp. 137–38.

[103] O'Toole, p. 53.

[104] Cross, p. 21.

[105] Kilbourne, p. 74.

[106] Ibid., p. 27.

[107] See Hyman and Tansey.

[108] R. Campbell, p. 406.

[109] Hyman and Tansey.

[110] John Kenneth Galbraith, *The Affluent Society*, 3rd ed. (Boston: Houghton Mifflin, 1976), p. 198.

[111] Hyman and Tansey, pp. 111–13.

[112] Jacobson and Mazur, p. 9.

Political Persuasion

Overview

▲ Four Cases of Political Persuasion
  Winning the Vote in 1920
  The Campaign for Health Care Reform
  The Politics of Religious Doctrine
  Selling the City

▲ Forms of Political Persuasion
  Administrative Persuasion
  Legislative Persuasion
  Campaign Persuasion
  Persuasion through Symbolic and Status Issues
  Persuasion in the Context of Entertainment

▲ What We Can Learn from Political Persuasion
  Limited Effects Model
  Significant Effects Model

▲ Politics and Trust

> *Public business, my son, must always be done by somebody. It will be done by somebody or other. If wise men decline it, others will not; if honest men refuse it, others will not.*[1]
> —JOHN ADAMS, ENCOURAGING HIS SON TO ENTER PUBLIC LIFE

As members of communities, we have a significant interest in the terms of that membership. Politics is the means for negotiating these terms. We are all politicians. Our political selves endlessly negotiate a range of power relationships—from the ways we present ourselves in a job resume to the vows we write for a wedding ceremony.

We establish contacts and ties that bind us together and sometimes pull us apart, whether on a personal or a governmental level. The fraying of relations within human groups can lead to violence. An alternative is to manage them through political institutions, using persuasion, negotiation, and compromise as tools for problem solving. To be sure, we are often cynical about politics, and especially professional politicians whom we frequently judge to be the agents of special interests. But politics is an indispensable process for negotiating our differences. Public business, free choice, and persuasion are inseparable. Open societies require political activity and the bartering that comes with it. As John Bunzel has noted, the presence of a political situation implies the absence of agreement that has created patterns of influence. "Only in a closed society, where people are accustomed to accept what the rulers are convinced is 'good' for them, can the distinctive context of politics be totally removed in favor of the art of imposition."[2]

NON SEQUITUR

© 1997 Wiley Miller. Dist. by UNIVERSAL PRESS SYNDICATE

FOUR CASES OF POLITICAL PERSUASION

▲

While no single set of traits makes political persuasion completely unique, we can identify many essential forums and features. Political persuasion is usually concerned with several broad goals: the selection of individuals to serve in a public office, the adoption of legislation, the "selling" of administrative objectives by leaders, and the formulation of policy. Each of the four representative cases that follow move beyond these broad categories to illuminate the details that make politics such a rich setting for the study of persuasion.

Winning the Vote in 1920

Whether political decisions are made with great foresight and courage or made poorly, we are affected by them. How fast we can legally drive, how much tuition we pay, when we are declared legally dead, when we may marry or divorce, even how many hours we work in a day are a few examples of the local and national codes that touch our lives. Basic privileges we now take for granted, such as the right to vote, were won through diligent political action.

Women in the United States won suffrage only in 1920 when Tennessee became the 36th state to ratify the Twentieth Amendment to the Constitution. Congress had passed the legislation three years earlier proclaiming that "the right of citizens of the United States to vote shall not be denied or abridged . . . on account of sex. . . ." The first meeting to campaign for the "social, civil, and religious rights of women" had been organized seventy-two years earlier by Elizabeth Cady Stanton, Lucretia Mott, and others.[3]

Like so many other causes then and now, the women's suffrage movement depended on the mastery of the art of political persuasion. Virtually every strategy used in the years prior to ratification is still used today. The most dramatic persuasive tactics involved pickets in front of the White House ("Mr. President, how long must women wait for liberty?"), mass parades, and rallies. Arrests of women in virtually every major city of the United States made daily headlines. Some of those given jail sentences went on hunger strikes, undergoing agonizing pain when jailers resorted to the use of stomach feeding tubes.[4]

The most effective forms of persuasion undertaken by supporters of women's suffrage were less dramatic but no less important. The key activity involved lengthy and sustained efforts at lobbying individual legislators and members of Congress. The well organized National American Woman's Suffrage Association (NAWSA) was especially effective at securing the agreement of individual members of Congress and the state legislatures. One of the lobbyists, Maud Wood Park,

> was concerned with finding just the right woman to make a favorable impression on the member being interviewed. She always sent a woman from a man's own region if possible, recognizing the difficulty a New England woman might have, for example, with a congressman from Georgia. She thought on balance her most successful lobbyists were women from the middle-west, middle-aged, and "rather too dressy," but "possessed of much common sense and understanding of politics in general, as well as of the men from their districts."[5]

Like most movements, the campaign for women's rights faced internal disputes about the kinds of tactics that were appropriate to produce change. Park and others in NAWSA favored quieter persuasion and less open conflict than the more confrontational Congressional Union. In the end, years of effort from many groups finally succeeded in winning the support of the men who dominated Congress and most of the state legislatures.

The Campaign for Health Care Reform

Perhaps no recent presidential initiative has been more thoroughly studied by students of political persuasion than the 1992 attempt of the Clinton administration to introduce a federally supported program of universal health care. A promise of massive reform to control high medical costs and equalize access was a cornerstone of Bill Clinton's 1992 political campaign. The First Lady was enlisted as one of the key policy makers, only to become a lightning rod that attracted more attention than she wanted from the insurance industry and other opponents. Clinton personally committed a great deal of presidential time to the campaign, which would have restructured 15 percent of the U.S. economy. It was an enormous political risk in a society that usually favors only modest and incremental reform.

Throughout 1993 and the first half of 1994, Hillary Rodham Clinton was a formidable advocate for establishing federal mandates for employers and insurance providers. But "Hillarycare," as the administration's various plans came to be known, quickly created opposition, especially in the private health insurance industry. Lining up its own supporters to lobby Congress and to influence public opinion, the insurance companies elaborated the dangers of what one of their television commercials described as "mandatory government health alliances run by tens of thousands of new bureaucrats."[6]

By the summer of 1994 both camps had engaged in numerous attempts to persuade the public. Some of the more interesting strategies are listed below.

> In early 1993 an industry group opposed to universal health coverage began a multi-million-dollar television ad blitz to raise fears that the new legislation would take away the health benefits Americans already had. One of the most quoted spots featured a couple (Harry and Louise) sitting in their kitchen, reacting in horror to the alleged injustices of the Clinton plan. In their words, government administrators would end up dictating the doctors a patient could see and the kinds of treatment that would be covered.[7]

> Hillary Clinton scheduled weekly visits to various locations around the country to urge support for universal health care. One typical event was held on a summer afternoon in Seattle. As the First Lady took the microphone in front of thousands at an outdoor rally, she spoke of the need to make guaranteed health coverage "a human right" and a matter of "social justice." Many cheered. Others (urged to attend by a conservative radio station) waved signs of protest, among them: "Hillary, Hands Off My Health Care!" Nearly all of the visits in this campaign were designed for widespread media coverage. At many open meetings victims of illness who had been bankrupted by hospital and doctor fees told heartbreaking stories.[8]

> President Clinton's pollster, Stan Greenberg, selected the themes for presidential speeches and other appearances through polling and intensive interviews of eight or nine people at a time (focus groups). Greenberg advised Clinton on several occasions that support for the objectives

of health care reform remained high, even while doubts grew about the workability of various proposals.[9]

In the summer of 1994, several unions sponsored a bus tour across the United States. The riders included nurses, survivors of serious injuries, and family members whose finances had been destroyed by payouts for expensive medical procedures. At some stops, protesters who opposed reform met the bus with placards opposing "socialized health care."[10] When the bus reached the White House, Clinton was visibly moved by the account of a man who had lost his wife to a chronic disease because the couple could not afford treatment. Clinton had difficulty delivering his proposed comments.

By midsummer of 1994, it was clear that the Clinton administration would reject alternative Republican proposals (he had announced in the 1994 State of the Union Address that he would veto any bill that offered less than full universal coverage), and Congress would rebuff the Clinton plan. Each side had invested heavily in the public debate over the adequacy and affordability of American health care. In the political post mortems about the campaign, some observed that the Clinton administration had not invested enough energy in finding common ground.[11] Bruised by the hostility exhibited by opponents, the administration refused to compromise.

The Politics of Religious Doctrine

Formal religion cannot escape the issues and conflicts of secular life. One of the most contentious issues for many churches is what position to take on "ceremonies of union between members of the same sex." And religious denominations are not the only institutions placing barriers on such unions. Though increasingly common in Canada and Europe, Vermont is the only state that gives gay couples many of the legal protections that heterosexual couples have, such as the right to inherit the property of a deceased partner.

Many churches are grappling with the symbolic side of this issue. Do the scriptures implicitly forbid the recognition of homosexual couples? Or is "the love and compassion expressed by Christ in the Bible" an invitation to incorporate modern social conventions in older religious doctrines?[12] Agitation for acceptance of these ceremonies came primarily from urban parishes. Opposition was often expressed in terms of whether these ceremonies undermine biblical doctrines that permit the church to bless commitments only if made between a man and woman.

Though many Catholics and some priests have confronted the question, the church's more hierarchical structure gives them less room to challenge the Vatican's view that homosexuality is "an objective disorder." Southern Baptists take a similar view, while Reform Judaism and Unitarians have affirmed their interest in celebrating the union of gay couples.[13] In the middle, many centrist Protestant faiths have agonized over what their church policies should be. The issue has been heavily debated by Presbyterians, United Methodists, Episcopalians, and Evangelical Lutherans,[14] a process encouraged by the fact that their parent organizations have structured themselves after the model of open governmental assemblies. In each denomination significant numbers of local ministers have officiated at ceremonies of union.

For many of the 8.5 million United Methodists it was not possible to overlook differences on this issue. Some were disturbed by a growing number of congregations that had joined a Reconciling Congregation Program, with the goal of welcoming all persons regardless of sexual orientation.[15] After a church jury narrowly acquitted an Omaha minister for performing a ceremony of union for two women from his congregation, the judicial and legislative hierarchy of the church was forced to act. At issue was whether a rule in the church's Book of Discipline barred ministers from performing gay marriages or simply advised against it.[16] A judicial council ruled in favor of an outright ban. In the words of one journalist who covered the debate, ministers who wish to offer all the rituals of the church to gay members learned "the sometimes treacherousness, blood-letting and duplicity of ecclesiastical politics."[17] Given the visibility of the issue and the strength of feelings on both sides, the church decided it needed to take a stand. While some clergy, church leaders, and lay activists had attempted to negotiate their differences and viewed the issue as a matter of conscience and faith, the religious institution implemented the votes of its decision makers.

Selling the City

In his book *A Prayer for the City,* Pulitzer Prize winning author Buzz Bissinger illuminates the daily demands for effective advocacy that are placed on a big city mayor.[18] In many ways, cities are where political intentions are tested most severely. In municipal politics, there are few places to hide. Ideas, good intentions, and staff are never enough to protect a mayor from the effects of leadership. The nation's mayors know their victories and failures will be evident to anyone who uses a city's streets and sidewalks.

Bissinger documents the municipal career of Ed Rendell, a former district attorney who became one of the nation's most respected and innovative mayors (1992–1999). Imagine the swagger and intensity of the actor Michael Douglas, then add a few pounds and years, and you have a fairly accurate image of Rendell. He was raised in affluence on the upper West Side of Manhattan, but his beefy countenance made him more comfortable among workers at the Naval Shipyard in South Philadelphia than with the affluent constituents along the "Main line."

It is an understatement to say that Philadelphia has never been an easy metropolis to govern. Previous mayors had polarized the city along racial and ethnic lines—or had made decisions that drained away any sense of pride. Perhaps the nadir of the City of Brotherly Love came in 1985, when Mayor Wilson Goode made the horrifying decision to drop a bomb from a police helicopter on a group of squatters in a West Philadelphia row house. The resulting fire that burned over 60 homes and caused 11 deaths left deep wounds. In a city that was already strapped by a declining industrial base, crippling taxes, and an infrastructure of aging homes and utilities the catastrophic fire was an appalling new injury.

Rendell did not bring the patient back to perfect health. His moves to cut costs and privatize many city services provoked many critics. But his effective advocacy did restore a considerable degree of pride to the city, along with a remarkable legacy of civic improvements. After pulling the government back from the brink of insolvency, he suddenly seemed to be everybody's favorite mayor—in demand as a speaker and adviser to other urban leaders who hoped to reinvent municipal government.[19] He became Governor of Pennsylvania in 2003.

As mayor, one of Rendell's greatest strengths was his tireless energy in attempting to win friends and financial allies for Philadelphia. He rarely missed an opportunity to convince residents that they lived in a world-class city. He seemed to have an endless source of energy to do whatever it took to get another donation from a corporation or to use his appearance at a neighborhood function to convince residents that he cared. Here are a few efforts from midway through his term:

- In exchange for declaring one day in July as "Hot Dog Day" and for sharing the stage with a live pig, Rendell collected a gift of cash from a meat company for the city's recreation department.

- In the same week he negotiated the sale of $500 million in bonds, largely on his ability to get concessions from unions and other city contractors.[20]

- Rendell was instrumental in raising millions of dollars from donors for a new performance center for the Philadelphia Orchestra. Orchestrating a coalition of groups that would have impressed a seasoned member of Congress, he won large contributions from Pennsylvania legislators, many corporations, and a number of wealthy foundations. The complex cost a staggering $240 million. After some arm twisting, industrialist Sidney Kimmel donated $17 million and the complex was named the Kimmel Center. In 2001 the enormous glass-enclosed complex of theaters and restaurants opened, creating even a little envy from visiting Parisians.

- Working with other leaders, Rendell concluded that if Philadelphia was no longer going to be a major manufacturing city, it would have to survive partly by selling its history. Turning a former industrial metropolis into a tourist and convention destination was not easy. Most visitors were accustomed to visit Independence Hall and call it a day. But building on the work of past mayors, Rendell helped complete a new convention center, new hotels, and even won an unusual prize for a Democrat—selection of the city as the site of the national convention of the Republican Party in 2000.

Every big city mayor must plead for support from members of the legislature, reporters, business leaders, and others. But Rendell seemed born to the challenge and inexhaustible in his determination. As Bissinger notes, "He hated the tag of supersalesman, this notion of him as some amalgam of Deepak Chopra and Lou Costello, this big-city mayor who never saw a pool opening or a groundbreaking he could resist . . . but he never stopped pumping on behalf of the city."[21]

FORMS OF POLITICAL PERSUASION
▲

As all of the above cases illustrate, political persuasion is primarily about two things. It is both the *process* for negotiating differences that surface in our organizational and community life and an *outcome* that gives power to some and inevitably takes it from others. In this section we turn our attention to some of the major features of *administrative, legislative, and campaign persuasion*. Each offers its own problems and possibilities and suggests a range of strategic options that are useful in many contexts beyond politics.

Administrative Persuasion

The formal powers of most governmental leaders rarely fall in the category of unilateral orders that are swiftly carried out. Consider the opinion of one of our most powerful presidents: Franklin Roosevelt. In his lifetime he thought he had very little power, once telling an amused gathering of reporters,

> The Treasury is so large and far-flung and ingrained in its practices that I find it almost impossible to get the action and results I want. . . . But the Treasury is not to be compared with the State Department. You should go through the experience of trying to get any changes in the thinking, policy, and action of the career diplomats and then you'd know what a real problem was.

And the Navy? "To change anything in the Na-a-vy," mused Roosevelt, "is like punching a feather bed."[22]

For presidents, mayors, and officers of corporations, persuasion is the result of leadership. Leadership is persuasion. While these people are listed at the top of the organizational chart they still need leadership skills for effective persuasion. A judge in a court of law renders decisions and sentences, but most other leaders know that they cannot govern only by decree. As Bill Clinton once noted, being president is like being the captain of an unresponsive boat. "That is, I can steer it, but a storm can still come up and sink it. And the people that are supposed to be rowing can refuse to row."[23] The need to win the allegiance of their own bureaucracies—not to mention the support of members of Congress and the mass media—dictates that constant attention must be paid to techniques of persuasion.

Leaders are, by definition, individuals who are both symbols and symbol makers. We look to leaders for more than the daily management of governmental affairs. We expect their actions and words to embrace our goals and values. The success that any single leader enjoys is partly a function of skill in evoking a public sense of participation and acceptance of governmental initiatives. In the fall of 2002, for example, the Bush administration leaked plans for a U.S. invasion of Iraq, noting that the country harbored terrorists and possessed weapons of mass destruction. These plans met intense resistance in the Middle East and in Europe; even some members of the President's party did not approve. While many disliked the regime in Baghdad, they felt that a military invasion was too extreme. The administration failed to convince the rest of the world that their plans had merit. Secretary of Defense Donald Rumsfeld dismissed the need to spell out the administration's reasons, leaving commentators like Anne Applebaum to puzzle over the reluctance of the administration to "make its case."[24]

Broadly speaking, administrative persuasion sets the public agenda, builds coalitions, and channels public attitudes into a workable course of action.

Setting the Public Agenda.   One measure of any leader's success is how well he or she can focus attention on a common problem and dramatize its significance. At any given time, public attention is limited to a relatively small number of issues that dominate newspaper headlines and evening news broadcasts. A governor with an eye on shaping a state's agenda may repeatedly focus on a limited number of urgent issues in order to orchestrate news coverage that will alter public opinion. This is sometimes called "staying on message," or "managing the news agenda." For example, former Pennsylvania governor Richard Thornburgh sought to end a state monopoly on the sale of all liquor by waging a highly visible rhetorical campaign against the inefficiency and poor customer service of state liquor stores. It was Thornburgh's intention to rally public opinion by encouraging news coverage of the unpopular Pennsylvania Liquor Control Board. His goal was to use public opinion to leverage the legislature to act. In the end he succeeded in making the state agency more unpopular, but fell short of getting the legislature to end the state's domination of liquor sales.

The Reagan administration in the early 1980s was highly successful in managing the news agenda. Reagan combined his considerable personal charm with a unique ability to stay "on message." Access to the president in unguarded moments was limited, and advisers Michael Deaver and James Baker kept the press busy with at least one "message of the day" and one photo opportunity. As one unhappy journalist noted, "together they sold the official myths of Reagan's presidency to the American public by developing a sophisticated new model for manipulating the press."[25]

Building Productive Coalitions.   The essence of political leadership is coalition building. Finding ways to get groups with different goals to work together is a powerful skill. Effective leaders know when to make alliances and when to end them. Those who are brought together may be foreign states (such as those who expressed solidarity with the United States after the attacks on the Pentagon and World Trade Center in 2001), political factions (the "truth and reconciliation" process undertaken by South Africa's Nelson Mandela), or traditional foes like environmental, farming, and hunting interests (at times brought together by various Secretaries of the Interior, or organizations such as the Sierra Club).

Bill Clinton used a strategy of "triangulation" between Republicans and Democrats to put together coalitions on a range of issues including free trade, family leave, and welfare reform. As noted earlier, however, he failed to build a coalition on health care reform in his first term and also failed to build a coalition to prevent his impeachment in his second term. While George Bush built a coalition for his early efforts against the war on terrorism, he failed to win international understanding for the abandonment of the ABM missile treaty with Russia and the Kyoto accords to prevent global warming. Many Europeans came to view Bush as a unilateralist content to ignore the opinions of other nations.[26]

Portraying and Using the National Mood.   Interestingly, early presidents like Thomas Jefferson rarely addressed Congress or the public in person. But their modern counterparts are expected to express the collective grief, anger, joy, and resolve of their constituents. Theodore Roosevelt declared the White House a "bully pulpit," and each succeeding leader has understood the role of president as encompassing an important public dimension. By the end of Bill Clinton's first year in office, he had made nearly 600 public speeches in scores of formal and informal settings.[27]

We expect the president to be, in Mary Stuckey's words, our "interpreter in chief." As she notes, the holder of the highest office in the land has become "the nation's chief storyteller," offering narratives of "what sort of people we are, [and] how we are constituted as a community."[28] George Bush's first address to Congress after the terrorist attacks on New York and Washington, like Ronald Reagan's effective eulogy to the crew lost in the explosion of the space shuttle *Challenger,* voiced what most Americans already felt. These presidents found the right expressions of national resolve and grief.

At other times, a political figure will seek a way to press for his or her own agenda by making someone else's victimization or triumph a representation of what is "good" or "just" or "wrong" with ourselves or others. In many of his speeches President Reagan made a point of identifying an individual "just like the rest of us" whose experiences illustrated something important about our national character. Sometimes it was a neighbor who was frustrated with all the paperwork required before building a new house; at other times it was an ordinary person who engaged in highly visible acts of kindness, selflessness, and courage.[29] Politicians often seek examples of our national identity in the isolated moments of individual lives.

Legislative Persuasion

In the endless cycles of deliberative politics, new initiatives are proposed, the problems they are intended to remedy are discussed, and decisions are made that eventually result in the enactment or defeat of legislation. The single most important function of any legislative body—from local town councils to the United States Congress—is the consideration of laws. The policy under discussion may be as narrow as a town council's ruling on whether satellite dish antennas can be placed in front yards, or as complex as a constitutional amendment prohibiting abortions.

Since policies are specific actions taken to remedy social or economic problems, their explanation and defense usually hinges on a problem-solution sequence. Successful policy defenses are based on convincing persuadees that (1) a problem is severe and (2) a proposed course of action will alleviate either the causes of the problem or at least its worst symptoms.

In both predictable and unpredictable ways, legislatures are arenas for persuasion. The sometimes heated exchanges that occur before a key vote often present the most memorable images of legislators engaged in influencing each other, but floor debate is not where most legislative persuasion occurs. To understand how various representatives make up their minds on how they will vote on any item, we usually have to look elsewhere. Four important pressure points occur as a bill moves from introduction to final passage.

Legislative Leadership.   The most predictable source of leadership comes from chief executives and legislative leaders, who regularly engineer plans for transforming issues of public concern into legislative proposals. While management traits vary, most effective leaders know their goals and stick to them—finding the right mix of idealism and practicality. They usually lead through example, making their character an extension of the core beliefs they want others to share. Most importantly, as James McGregor Burns has noted, political leadership is *collective*. "Leaders, in responding to their own motives, appeal to the motive bases of potential followers."[30]

The presidency of Lyndon Johnson is an especially interesting example. Before becoming president he was a powerful Senate leader. Even after moving to the White House, he continued to work closely with other leaders in the Senate. Between 1963 and 1965, Johnson introduced a number of major proposals to deal with racial discrimination, hunger, and poverty. Most dramatically, he persuaded members of Congress to pass the landmark Civil Rights and Voting Rights Acts of 1964 and 1965, which guaranteed the right to vote, to work, and to use public facilities. He did it by identifying with his former colleagues in the Congress and by indicating his resolve to achieve an unassailable objective. The legislation changed the face of southern politics forever, opening local and national offices to talented African American leaders.[31] Johnson was not a natural public speaker, but as a southerner his speeches on the effects of racial segregation and the need for legislative remedies were highly effective. The public presentations of his agenda combined with his legendary ability to win converts with heavy one-on-one arm twisting[32] established an eloquent rationale for ending devices such as poll taxes and literacy tests designed to prevent black citizens from voting.

Lobbying.   As with the campaign to win the vote for women in 1920, many public laws start with the efforts of an organized group and the sympathy of a handful of legislators. Lobbyists represent businesses, unions, and organizations— and fully exploit the First Amendment right to petition the government. The term lobbying comes from the fact that before legislators had private offices, they used to meet individuals seeking to influence legislation in the foyer immediately outside a legislative chamber. The noun has become a verb; to lobby is to attempt to influence a legislative or administrative decision in government.[33]

At the federal level over 20 percent of all lobbyists are former members of Congress, working near the federal offices of the representatives they seek to influence. They collectively spend about $1.5 billion to win support in Congress. The banking and credit industry alone paid an estimated $40 million to shape legislation on personal bankruptcy and other financial issues.[34]

Some groups such as the well financed National Rifle Association, National Association of Broadcasters, and the AFL-CIO may actually draft legislation or amendments to bills that are then introduced by sympathetic legislators in Washington and the various states. The more routine work of lobbying involves supplying facts and arguments to legislators, usually prior to a key legislative vote.[35]

For many Americans, lobbying borders on bribery—using money, food, sex, or whatever represents a legislator's weakness—in order to win special favors for an interest group. While lobbyists do have power, their persuasion tactics are often far less exotic than the perceived sinister behavior. The most common lobbying strategies include telling a legislator what constituents back home think, making suggestions for how he or she can defend a vote, and supplying arguments about the positive or negative consequences of a certain legislative decision. Most lobbying is low-key and directed to sympathetic or undecided lawmakers.[36] This kind of persuasion is sometimes called "wholesale" politics because it is directed to lawmakers and not to the general public. "Retail" political persuasion involves activities intended for general public consumption such as speeches, press conferences, television, or direct-mail advertisements.

Hearings.   One of the most potent forums for the persuasion of both the U.S. public and individual legislators is the committee hearing. This venue is where much of the work of legislating and negotiating is done. In 1973, the three major commercial networks devoted over 235 hours to the presentation of Senate hearings into the Watergate affair.[37] The political history of the United States could be partly written from the minutes of the legislative hearings that have taken place in the nation's capital—ranging from Joseph McCarthy's attempts in 1954 to find Communists in the State Department to the hearings that began in 1994 surrounding the conduct of Bill Clinton in the Whitewater/Lewinsky scandals. Millions of Americans become transfixed by the theater of such high-visibility proceedings.

Hearings are conducted by the members of committees who have jurisdiction over specific types of proposed legislation. They present an ideal setting for supporters and opponents of legislation to dramatize their concerns. Victims, experts, and lobbyists regularly appear before committees that consider early drafts of proposed legislation. Committee members often count on the presence of the press—especially television cameras—to place issues of concern before the general public. Hearings have an inherent drama—whether a heated exchange between a committee member and someone called for questioning or the prepared statements of those who have suffered a loss. The testimony of victims is often graphic and dramatic; the narratives highlight innocent victims and the villains who have harmed them. For example, the Enron employees who lost their jobs and their pensions fuelled public anger against the company executives called by House and Senate committees to explain their accounting practices.[38] Committee leadership can orchestrate hearings to sway public opinion and to make a convincing case for new legislation.

Constituent and Party Pressure.   Members of legislatures are also the recipients of influence *from* constituents and colleagues. Traditionally, in representative democracy messages from constituents are given attention, if not always acted upon. Letters, faxes, phone calls, and e-mail from a legislator's district can all be factors in determining how he or she will vote on a pending question.[39] Their power is offset somewhat by the growing use of letter-writing campaigns by large lobbying groups, including corporations.[40] But a staffer usually keeps a tally of how opinion is running on an issue. The best letter writing campaigns will have several hundred individually written letters from constituents arriving in a period of about a week.[41]

Another source of influence is the party. Political parties are less dominant than they once were, but they are still important. Parties in Washington and the state capitals used to be able to "deliver" the votes of their members with great regularity. Prior to the 1950s, the act of going against one's party was a risky business. Powerful leaders like Lyndon Johnson in the Senate and Sam Rayburn in the

House of Representatives headed well-drilled teams of floor managers and whips who would regularly deliver the votes of members on questions that had been defined as party issues.

The same structure is still in place and still imposes a degree of party discipline. Consider Steven Waldman's description of the Clinton administration's efforts to assure legislative victory for the AmeriCorps program. The bill that eventually became law offers help for students who want to attend college in exchange for community service. Republicans were lukewarm to the idea, complaining that it duplicated other federal college programs such as work-study. Some tried to kill the bill outright or to attach amendments to it that would cripple its chances of passage. The presidential aide responsible for helping get the legislation through the Senate intact was Eli Segal.

> Segal and his team set up a "war room" just outside the chamber in a small office used by the vice president when he presided over the Senate. They each had assignments. Robert Gordon would work on talking points for senators. A rotating cast of young staffers and volunteers would monitor the floor debate on TV. (Shirley) Sagawa would keep track of the dozens of amendments under consideration. Jack Lew would handle negotiations over budget numbers. And Segal would work the senators.[42]

As Waldman indicates, Segal had his work cut out for him because some members of the president's own party had doubts about the program.

> His next stop was a meeting of the Sunbelt Caucus, made up of mostly moderate and conservative lawmakers. If the White House lost these Democrats, it could be defeated. . . . With this group Segal . . . tried to assure the caucus that this was not going to be a big, reckless spending program. "Young people have a right to a college education, but they have to pay for it," he said. He spoke about how national service would combat "centrifugal forces by enabling people of different backgrounds to work together."[43]

One-on-one, Segal would attempt to assure a senator that the vote was justified, at the same time attempting to head off the arguments of opponents. One phone call from the war room was typical:

> "How are you?" Segal said. "I missed you back in the state." The small talk lasted just about ten seconds. "I'm essentially calling to let you know where we are and make sure you're comfortable with where we are." This was Segal at his best. "Are you aware of any major problems we have ahead of us? Anything you want to run through?"[44]

By looking for members with doubts and trying to head them off, Segal engaged in an old and common process of tallying votes. He skillfully reassured members that their votes were essential and reminded them that the president was watching the outcome closely.

Campaign Persuasion

A third and archetypal form of political persuasion occurs in the context of campaigns. By definition, a campaign is a concerted effort to influence a targeted group over a limited time frame. Lobbying directed toward a legislature, advertising intended for the general public, and other forms of organized persuasion have many of the features of campaigns and are discussed elsewhere in this book. (See, for example, chapter 10.) Our focus here is on electoral campaigns to put a person in public office. Before discussing several characteristics shared by all campaigns, we want to mention the influence of the media.

Our perception of campaigns is governed and to some extent distorted by a modern paradox. There are thousands of officeholders in the United States who are *personally* known to many individual residents, but who are not the subject of much *media* coverage. We primarily think of the political world as the actions of the 537 elected members of Congress plus the presidency. Our windows on this world are known primarily by their initials—CNN, ABC, MSNBC, and so on. While these networks broadcast images rich in expressive content, including people reacting to events that have affected them, they naturally cast us more as observers than participants. Ironically, our relationship to political events mimics the intimacy of personal contact, but ultimately denies it. Dan Rather, Peter Jennings, George Bush, and Tom Daschle are people we "know." And yet they are part of a complex information web that has made us spectators to global events over which we have little influence. Television, rather than the party organization, now binds the nation together. No political party can match the ability of the three networks to convey attitudes and information to the nation. Perhaps because the national level of electoral politics is mediated through so many external filters, we are less accepting and more wary of its messages.

Short-Term Orientation.   A campaign is always governed by a limited time frame. Political candidates must work to have public attitudes peak at just the right moment—election day. The idea of the campaign itself owes its imagery to the battlefield. Strategies and tactics are defined, and the troops are mobilized on voting day to produce a final victory. In war, as in politics, battles may not always be decisive, but on any given day there will be a winner.

Use of Public Relations Professionals.   There was a time in the United States when candidates did much of the routine work of the campaign themselves. They often hired printers, rented halls, wrote their own speeches, and depended on a close cadre of friends and associates. Even President Woodrow Wilson was not beyond taking time out of his schedule to write (at the typewriter or in shorthand) a specific statement or campaign speech. But today, with the exception of the most local of public offices, candidates for higher-level positions employ professional public relations specialists.

Scores of full-time campaign consultants operate in virtually every state with clients that include individuals, political parties, and pressure groups organized to defeat ballot questions. Full-service consulting firms such as Washington's Matt Reese Associates or New York's Garth Associates Inc., are capable of managing virtually every aspect of a politician's campaign.[45] Like most complex businesses, the firms run by these consultants also subcontract more specialized work to professionals with highly prized talents. Over the last several decades the best known have included:

- Dick Morris—an advisor to both Republican Senator Trent Lott and President Bill Clinton. Morris is credited with developing intensive polling techniques and campaign strategies to foil Republican attempts to win back the White House in 1996. Successful strategies included *triangulation*, which Morris described as a combination of "the best theme from each side: 'opportunity' from the left and 'responsibility' from the right."[46]

- Karl Rove—started his consulting business in 1981. He worked on numerous Texas campaigns and was a pivotal adviser for both George H. Bush and the younger George Bush in 2000, and stayed on as a senior White House Adviser.

- Richard Vaguerie—direct-mail campaigns for conservative candidates and causes. Vaguerie is credited with being one of the first political operatives to refine methods for targeting voters through direct mail. Most large campaigns use techniques he developed to solicit funds and to identify supporters.

- Tony Schwartz—radio and television commercials. Schwartz produced some of the most memorable political commercials in the 1960s and 1970s, including the "Daisy spot" that implied that presidential candidate Barry Goldwater would use nuclear weapons in Vietnam. Schwartz is considered a master of the soft sell, using ads that imply more than they state.[47]

- Alex Castellanos—a skillful designer of hard-hitting advertising for the GOP. Castellanos was brought into the Dole campaign in 1996 to revive its sagging image, and worked on the 2000 campaign of George Bush. He is a specialist in attack ads,[48] and enjoyed playing the relatively simple Bush persona against the complex and contradictory images of the preceding administration.[49]

- James Carville—helped manage an upset senate victory in Pennsylvania that demonstrated the vulnerability of President Bush prior to the 1992 campaign. Carville went on to be the star political consultant to Bill Clinton[50] but proved less successful in advising an incumbent who lost a hotly contested New Jersey governor's race won by the GOP's Christine Todd Whitman.

A vast range of campaign events now unfold with a professional gloss that matches other forms of advertising and public relations—with a price tag to match. Services offered include speechwriting, scheduling events, press relations, ethnic and trade press contacts, issue research, satellite scheduling (for television interviews), radio services, on-line services, staff and volunteer recruitment, campaign finance, and polling.

Evolutionary Change.   Typically, campaigns must evolve through stages of growth that will enable them to gain new resources, such as money and workers, and to increase credibility and visibility. Some of the features of persuasive campaigns are discussed in the next chapter. Our attention here is on the four basic phases of electoral campaigns described by Judith Trent and Robert Friedenberg.[51]

The first stage is *surfacing*; individuals seeking public office attempt to establish their basic honesty and credibility with the U.S. public. They try to be as visible as possible and attempt to gain recognition as serious contenders for a particular office. Fundraising efforts are intense in this stage. Fundraising via the Internet became a viable option in 2000. Presidential challengers like Bill Bradley and John

McCain were surprisingly effective in quickly raising campaign cash via the Internet.[52] As mentioned in chapter 3, Howard Dean was phenomenally successful in using the Internet to solicit contributions in 2003.

For the relatively unknown Bill Clinton, the surfacing phase before the 1992 elections required months of grueling campaign appearances. Clinton was young, the governor of a low-profile southern state, and a novice without a national following. He used a carefully crafted series of speeches in the summer of 1991 to attract media attention as a "different kind of Democrat."[53] By contrast George W. Bush had a relatively easy time during this phase. Most early challengers to his nomination in 1998 and 1999 dropped away. And even with a late challenge by Senator John McCain, the press had long written about Bush as the presumptive nominee of his party.[54]

The *primary stage* focuses on the party elections that give individuals the right to be the official nominees of a party for an office. At the presidential level, they include the early winter contests in New Hampshire and the March "Super Tuesday" selections made by the parties in Florida, Massachusetts, and many other states. Primaries sap the energies and resources of even the most ambitious and energetic presidential candidates. Huge sums of money are spent on local television in efforts to win sizable chunks of each state's party members. Some are elected as pledged delegates to the summer political conventions. The support of others makes the candidate look strong in polls that measure comparative popularity with contenders from the same party. Throughout the primary process, consultants and media specialists are hired, organizations move into high gear, and messages are fine-tuned. In addition, elaborate networks of fundraisers are established for the costly process of activating generally uninterested voters. Buying access to the U.S. public via television is exorbitantly expensive, making the primary phase a test of the contender's ability to tap the resources of organized interest groups in order to reach the less organized masses.[55]

The third phase is dominated by the *nominating conventions*. In the past, contenders in the same party fought for the right to represent it in the fall elections, but the conventions now have a more ritualistic function. The primary season now yields the party's likely nominee; conventions confirm that choice. However, they still play an important part in defining the issues that are likely to dominate the upcoming campaign. In 2000, both of the parties' conventions attracted unusual interest because they offered two new candidates. The Democrats met in Los Angeles amidst a great deal of media discussion about the prominence given to the Clintons, resulting in somewhat damaging discussions that Gore was still in the shadow of the dynamic Clinton. The Republicans met in Philadelphia and went out of their way to avoid the decisive rhetoric that in previous conventions had made them seem a less than inclusive party. The convention also was the pivotal point where George Bush would be measured as presidential material. He used his opportunities well, emphasizing that he was a "uniter not a divider."[56]

In the fourth stage, the *general election*, strategic decisions are weighed and carried out, and scores of questions must be answered. From a persuasion perspective several of the most interesting include the following:

- Should the candidate avoid debates or welcome them? Traditionally, front-trunners and incumbents are less inclined to agree to debates than challengers and other candidates lagging in popularity.

- Should the emphasis of television advertising be on attacking your opponents—what consultants euphemistically call "raising the negatives of the opposition"—or ignoring them?[57] Strategists remind candidates that a two-way race really means that voters have four choices. They can vote for or against either candidate. Sometimes campaigns calculate that they can gain more by motivating voters to register their dislike of a candidate.

- How prominent should surrogates or other representatives of the candidate be? In 2000, the candidates for vice president played significant roles. Dick Cheney had much more experience and more "presence" than Bush. While that was a benefit, the older and more eloquent Cheney could also upstage Bush. Joe Lieberman helped Gore put some distance between himself and Bill Clinton; he was given a high profile in the campaign.

From late August to election day, presidential candidates operate extensively from an airplane—within the constant presence of members of the national press and a close cadre of advisers. In Washington and other major cities, scores of additional workers work on future appearances, coordinate with local leaders of the political parties, and continue to contract for television, radio, and print advertising.

In this final period, campaigns take on a character that is quite unlike anything else—partly a well-designed machine and partly a firestorm that can suddenly flare up beyond anyone's ability to control it. A Gore staffer experienced the control problem, noting with great frustration that no message his team devised seemed to help the candidate benefit from the generally strong economy of the Clinton years.[58] By contrast, Karl Rove has reflected on the good luck of the Bush campaign, winning states such as West Virginia and Tennessee that "we should not have won."[59] In campaign years when the American public is fortunate (and the authors are of two different minds about 2000), campaigns are much more than intellectually empty exercises in self-praise. They can be great national conversations. And they can allow us to catch some rare glimpses of the nation's collective will.

Emphasis on Character. Electoral campaigns are usually presented as a chance to debate the *issues* of the day. But more than anything else, campaigns are about character: what journalist Charles Peters has defined as "the ability to rise above all the forces that keep us from thinking clearly—not only about what will work, but about what is right."[60] We expect that election campaigns will provide evidence of the fitness of a candidate's character and will give us reason to put our faith in his or her judgment. As important as specific issues are, we realize that they will change over time, while the fundamental capacities and good sense of a leader will remain essentially unchanged.[61] When we talk about particular politicians, it is usually in terms that describe the kind of person we think they are. We see them as generous, ambitious, serious, calculating, friendly, obsessed, self-serving—or any of hundreds of other character traits. Political commercials are largely exercises in ethos building. Campaigns generally feature candidates in the same way that dramatists mold characters to be representatives of good or bad traits. We see politicians making statements and taking positions, but many of the statements are secondary to the calculated image or public persona that is projected.

Emphasis on Strategy Reporting. A wealth of research has contributed to our understanding of how the routines and formulas of newsgathering shape political attitudes. While many analyses resist global generalizations to all instances and contexts, some broad conclusions have emerged. The ambitious Campaign Mapping Project undertaken by Rod Hart and his colleagues sampled a range of media and other texts from 1948 to the present. Their content analyses revealed the surprising durability of key journalistic norms such as *pessimism* and *detachment*:[62] norms that

---

**Figure 11.1 The Logistics of a Campaign:
Developing Basic Strategies and Resources**

Although no two campaigns are exactly alike, there are certain basic requirements for planning and executing political campaigns. The list below applies to those seeking offices ranging from the presidency to a seat in the House of Representatives.

Period	Planning and Research	Campaign Activities
Pre-Primary:	Use polls to measure visibility with potential voters; engage in issues research; make profile of strengths and weaknesses; learn about campaign finance and ballot requirements; seek advice of potential supporters.	Organize staff; begin fund-raising; seek assistance and support of party activists; participate in newsworthy events; meet with local or national opinion leaders and editors; open and equip campaign office; establish campaign committees.
Primary:	Continue polling; identify contributors; research opposition; test basic campaign themes; fine tune basic speech; build grassroots organization.	Deliver basic campaign message, respond to attacks; hold fundraising events; begin direct-mail campaign to increase name recognition and to identify supporters and contributors.
Convention:	Identify supporters and potential workers; seek party help; purchase media time and space for the general election campaign.	Address delegate's concerns; identify issues for party support; seek roles for surrogates in public events and party hierarchy.
General Election:	Schedule events to target undecided voters; begin planning for get-out-the-vote activities on election day; use tracking polls to measure efficiency of various messages and media; continue to refine basic themes.	Appear in best-chance districts; seek media coverage of appearances; (if behind in polls) challenge opponent to public debates; seek newspaper endorsements; ask contributors for additional support; (if affordable) use television for late campaign blitz; increase campaign appearances to five to ten each day.

others have assumed are of more recent vintage. These conventional attitudes are continually reflected in stories that encourage the audience to be suspicious about the motives of politicians who are portrayed as constantly seeking advantage in a chess game of moves and countermoves. In practice, these norms mean that the positions taken by candidates will be reported less frequently than the motives behind their campaigns. Joseph Cappella and Kathleen Jamieson call this *strategy* reporting, noting that it feeds a climate of cynicism about politics and politicians.[63]

If campaigns are presented as a collection of strategic decisions designed only to win support on election day, who can fault the American public for tuning out? Some remedies include journalism that emphasizes substance rather than process; replacing sound bites with long-form coverage from C-SPAN and the press, extended one-on-one-debates, and greater direct access for candidates to the public without the intervening narratives of political journalists.[64]

Importance of Media Framing and Priming.   Increasingly, analysts of the electoral process and other forms of political persuasion point to the power of the press to significantly impact attitudes by *framing* their narratives and *priming* news consumers. Framing and priming are two pivotal concepts that focus on how the placement or deletion of story details can alter audience attitudes about political agents. Priming theorists Shanto Iyengar and Donald Kinder note that it is possible to dramatically alter an audience's judgment about the competence and integrity of a politician by altering the *sequence* of presentation for certain story details.[65] If a campaign story about a candidate starts with a negative fact about her, that fact will loom as a significant measure of the candidate for the rest of the story. It is notoriously difficult to induce attitude change from a television or a news story. But it is comparatively easy to use television news or ads to build a sense of importance for a topic. As Iyengar and Kinder note:

> Political persuasion is difficult to achieve, but agenda setting and priming are apparently pervasive. According to our results, television news clearly and decisively influences the priorities that people attach to various national problems, and the considerations they take into account as they evaluate political leaders or choose between candidates for public office.[66]

Framing is similar, but more general. It represents a persistent pattern for structuring stories, always reminding us that "the devil is in the details." Frame analysts do not necessarily argue that the media employ a secret tool to smuggle attitudes into ostensibly objective reporting. They instead note that all stories must start from a specific perspective—and that perspective dictates what facts and details will be relevant.[67] It is useful to think of a media frame as a window with a limited view of the terrain outside. Other windows in different locations might offer a very different perspective. The press, in essence, chooses the window from which we look at the territory. As Regina Lawrence notes, frames amount to "an exercise (intentional or, quite often, unintentional) of journalistic power."[68]

In 2000, as mentioned earlier, the activities of Al Gore were often reported through the *media frame* of the personality and activities of Bill Clinton. The activities of the president loomed as a dominant context for assessing Gore's performance.[69] But framing applies to all forms of political reporting well beyond campaigns. One recent study indicated a tendency of American and European news-papers to organize coverage of the 1991 civil war in Somalia in terms of military rather than humanitarian issues.[70] One effect of the military frame was to couch the problem more in terms of warlords and factions than peacekeeping. As we write this, reporting on the activities of Vice President Dick Cheney has often been filtered through the frame of his former leadership of an oil company that is now under fed-eral scrutiny: a pattern concurrent with a news agenda dominated by stories about poor corporate accounting practices.[71] Alternate frames, such as his considerable governmental experience in previous administrations, have been rejected.

Persuasion through Symbolic and Status Issues

Thus far, we have described political persuasion in instrumental terms. Cam-paigns and discussions of policy are about gaining or using power to achieve cer-tain specific goals. As obvious as this observation is, it should not obscure the equally compelling uses of politics as expression. Like all of the popular arts, polit-ical discussion sometimes exists more for the emotional lift it gives its participants than for the specific effects it may produce in the nation's governmental and civil life.[72] Politics has a dramatic and expressive function in any society. A Memorial Day tribute to troops killed in battle—filled with music, flags, and soldiers—hardly lends itself to a discussion of the possibly disastrous foreign policy decisions that caused the deaths of those being honored. The cross, the flag, and their verbal counterparts are not instruments of discussion as much as expressive symbols of affirmation. *Political language defines who we are or who we want to be, as often or more often than it contributes to social change.*

Sometimes a specific issue matters less for how it might evolve into legislative proposals than for what our position on it says about who we are. In his interesting discussion of what he calls *status politics*, sociologist Joseph Gusfield notes that we tend to combine our attitudes toward specific issues with stereotyped attitudes about certain kinds of people.[73] A topic becomes a status issue when a group col-lectively makes the judgment that *where* other people stand on a question demon-strates their superiority or inferiority. In short, status issues are linked to identity.

For example, how should the western expansion of the United States be por-trayed in school history books? Was government negotiation and compensation with Indians fair? Did the Army and government policy serve the nation or enforce harsh terms on indigenous people with prior land claims? Story lines for history books are hotly debated by many school boards in many states.[74] Similarly, should golfer Tiger Woods continue to play on courses that restrict membership by race or gender? The vast majority of Americans would not be affected by his decision, but his actions still matter to many as confirmations or denials of self-worth.[75]

Heated debates about gay rights, veterans' benefits, affirmative action, and women's issues all speak to the vital issue of self- and group esteem. When state-ments are made that confirm the prestige of groups with which we identify, our own sense of self-esteem is confirmed. A victory for the group is a victory for us as well. The concept of status politics is a potent reminder that political persuasion is not only about objective changes in policy, but also about our sense of solidarity or estrangement from others.

The Vietnam Memorial is a tribute to the many soldiers killed in that war.

Persuasion in the Context of Entertainment

Much of the persuasion we have discussed above comes from a fairly narrow sector of public discourse: those involved in the political institutions of government. What of the other vast riches of American discourse in novels, film, television, and popular journalism? Are they outside the realm of politics, or a further extension of it? We believe that many segments of popular culture have political dimensions. In drama, for example, political attitudes are often latent or subtextual elements of character, content choice, and content avoidance.

In writing about film actor John Wayne, Garry Wills notes that his outsized western characters created a political attitude. Wayne was an "American Adam," an evocative carrier of "mythic ideas about American exceptionalism—contact with nature, distrust of government, dignity achieved by performance, skepticism toward the claims of experts."[76] In films like *Stagecoach* and *Rio Bravo* Wayne enacted an ideology within an image that had the power to persuade.

The process of selection about what goes into these portraits inevitably forces the creators of all entertainment forms to make choices about preferred ways of viewing the elements of our culture. The narrative structure of our popular entertainment communicates praise or blame about institutions, values, and social priorities. These images of the powerful and the weak, the rich and the poor, heroes and fools, give legitimacy to some and deny it to others. As such, the judgments passed on to us by the entertainment media are at least implicitly political because they offer compelling visions of what we should fear or whom we should honor. In Todd Gitlin's apt phrase, television and its content represent our "national dream factory." Its relentless presence in our living rooms gives it the power to "reproduce larger ideologies" and "grander fantasies" than might ever be communicated by less pervasive institutions.[77] Film theorist James Monaco has similarly noted that movies communicate the details of the social contracts that govern our lives, including challenges or affirmations of the "basic ideals of community, family, and relationships."[78] Commercial films communicate what we collectively want to praise or condemn in our national life. Small towns may be sentimentalized as American Edens (*Back to the Future, My Girl, The Best Years of Our Lives*), with suburbs as their opposite (*American Beauty, Fargo*). Businesses may be populated by cunning and corrupt figures (*Wall Street, The Insider, Jerry Maguire*). Many films provide portraits of women who defy conventional boundaries of class or sexism (*Working Girl, Thelma and Louise, The Business of Strangers*).

The recurring fantasies of countless television series are usually more positive and idealistic than feature films. We are subtly attracted to the social order and bedrock stability of the generally happy and adaptable families of prime time. But sometimes even mainstream television can produce interesting social subtexts. NBC's *Frasier*, for example, offers sharp commentary.

> In many small ways the writers of the series poke fun at the pretensions of America's professional class. *Frasier* observes the world of two overeducated sons—Niles and Frasier—whose pampered lives are the subject of sharp wisecracks from their salt-of-the-earth father, a retired policeman. Both brothers are perfect images of insecure yuppiedom. Despair can set in for the slightest of reasons: a wine that is too warm, upscale restaurants that forget a reservation, and especially the decision of Martin, Frasier's father, to move in. An old easy chair held together by duct tape is a reminder of the class and generational differences that separate father and son. It sits in Frasier's glittering Seattle apartment in silent rebuke of his pretensions. Martin's sensibilities are far more working class. He often speaks for the political and social sensibilities of the audience. When Niles says the food at a favorite restaurant is "to die for," Martin typically punctures his son's class and generational pretensions. "Niles, your country and your family are to die for. Food is to eat."[79]

An additional tool that helps us discover the political overtones in content is *negative evidence*. It is an invaluable concept for the persuasion analyst, because sometimes the most interesting feature of a message is what is not present in it—the *absence* of something one might reasonably expect to find. As television's Linda Ellerbee has noted,

> When we point the camera at one thing, we are pointing it away from another. Thus, one of the first things to look at when viewing the media is what you cannot see.[80]

In assessing the content of the broadcast networks' nightly newscasts, for example, one would expect to find stories on certain topics, such as the failures of savings and loan banks in the mid-1980s. Ironically, however, little was reported at the time, leading to discussions about how such an important event was ignored.[81] Among huge stories that were seriously unanticipated and underreported in the American media—especially television news—we would include the looming collapse of the Soviet Union in the 1980s, and the failure of the business press in 2001 to see the deceptive accounting practices of companies such as Enron and Worldcom.

Advertiser-supported media generally produce some interesting patterns of negative evidence. Many studies confirm that media content—in news or entertainment—generally plays to our fantasies and beliefs rather than to our mistaken impressions.[82] Indeed, journalists who truly report the unexpected sometimes pay a high price for the business and power interests they offend.[83]

WHAT WE CAN LEARN FROM POLITICAL PERSUASION
▲

We sometimes assume that political persuasion is pervasive and relatively easy, but that is not necessarily the case. As with virtually all contexts for persuasion, shaping political attitudes is a struggle. How much of a struggle is still open to debate. We can simplify the discussion for our purposes by looking at two different camps, one that holds that political agents—especially the mass media—have a great deal of power to shape attitudes. The other camp acknowledges that persuasion occurs but that its effects are more limited.

Limited Effects Model

It can be extremely difficult to isolate the effects of messages and mediums from the other influences that ebb and flow through our lives.[84] But we do have some important conclusions that suggest the stability rather than the volatility of political attitudes. We know that core political attitudes tend to be quite stable. For example, Republicans, Democrats and Independents are likely to retain their identities for long periods of time, if not entire lifetimes. One axiom cited by campaign professionals is that "40 percent of the people will always vote for your party, and 40 percent will never vote for your party, and the remaining 20 percent are up for grabs."[85] As this assertion suggests, individual messages like political commercials are heavily discounted by consumers wary of their claims, though negative ads often do shape attitudes.[86] During campaigns, many citizens tend to tune out messages until the final phases of the campaign.[87] Even the Internet seems to have had only a moderate impact,[88] though it has been touted as the medium that will reinvigorate a sense of political participation.[89] As Melvin DeFleur and Everette Dennis note, the media "are quite limited in their influences on people who select and attend to any particular message."[90] Media content plays a significant role in helping us justify our decisions,[91] but the public is subject to less manipulation from political or media sources than most observers assume.

Significant Effects Model

The other side of this argument is represented by a number of observers who have argued that media portrayals of politics are difficult to measure, concealing significant effects. This view is put forth by John Zaller:

> [T]he true magnitude of the persuasive effects of mass communication is closer to "massive" than "small to negligible" and . . . the frequency of such effects is "often." Exactly as common intuition would suggest, mass communication is a powerful instrument for shaping the attitudes of the citizens who are exposed to it, and it exercises this power on an essentially continuous basis.[92]

Zaller's reasons are complex, but they basically involve the methodological point that traditional measures of political impact are too clumsy to detect the significance of changes. The changes are there; we just need to do a better job of measuring them. For example, part of the "large effects" hypothesis makes more sense when one distinguishes between relatively demanding changes in *attitude* and more subtle but important changes in *awareness*. As we noted with regard to framing and priming, the media seem to have more power to create awareness of a subject than to create a particular attitude toward it. This is called *agenda setting*, and it is a cornerstone of study for all kinds of mass media effects.[93]

Consider, as well, a statistic we gave in support of minimal effects. We quoted Kathleen Jamieson's observation that perhaps only 20 percent of the voters in an election can be influenced by campaign messages.[94] But who could argue that one fifth of an audience's attitudes or votes are insignificant? The presidential election of 2000 was decided by just a tiny fraction of that percentage. Many Congressional races, referenda, and local campaigns are also decided on razor thin margins. One of the important lessons *any* persuader can take from the study of politics is that even voters on the edges can spell the difference between victory and defeat.

POLITICS AND TRUST
▲

We close with a cautionary word about our national distrust of politics and political messages. The commonly accepted stereotype of the political persuader is a human weather vane whose persuasion is shaped by whatever direction the winds of public opinion are blowing. Some of the most compelling figures in dramatic literature are characters caught between a sense of personal duty and the need to maintain a public face. Shakespeare made this a central feature in many plays; strong and decisive heroes, such as Coriolanus, were forced to balance their private ideals against the need to say the politically correct things to satisfy potential allies. Of the honest Coriolanus who says what he thinks even when it is impolitic, a friend observes that "his nature is too noble for the world." Because he has little interest in winning the support of others, he stands out as the nonpolitical hero, a man who "would not flatter Neptune for his Trident."[95]

Ours is a very different time, but the dilemma of serving the needs of many while remaining true to oneself remains. The images of politicians as men and women dominated by expediency rather than principles are generally nurtured by a cynical press.[96] But like all stereotypes, they tend to fall apart when examined more closely.

From a persuasion perspective, democratic politics should be seen as a process for turning conflict into consensus. We should expect that the diversity of political opinions on any one question will reflect the diversity of opinions in society as a

NON SEQUITUR

THE REHABILITATED WHITE-COLLAR CRIMINAL

PAROLE BOARD

AND I CAN ASSURE YOU THAT I WILL NEVER PARTAKE IN SUCH FRAUDULENT ACTIVITY AGAIN, UNLESS, OF COURSE, I'M ELECTED TO CONGRESS, WHERE IT'S STANDARD PROCEDURE...

WILEY

11-5

© 1997 Wiley Miller. Dist. by UNIVERSAL PRESS SYNDICATE

whole *and that political figures will attempt to adjust to these opinions as well as attempt to change them.* The hero Coriolanus is not a politician precisely because he is *disengaged.* He stands apart from the community and makes minimal attempts to play a role in it. Ironically, we honor him and his modern counterparts who have dismissed the political world, but as John Adams suggests at the beginning of this chapter, at what price?

The process of seeking consensus requires attitudes that will flex and positions that must be compromised. Not all consensus builders are liars or weak-willed opportunists. Indeed, many of the heroes of the world's great moral and social movements—for example, Elizabeth Cady Stanton, Nelson Mandela, Martin Luther King—can be productively studied for their attempts to accommodate the views of others even while pressing their own demands.[97] Imagine the costs to their supporters and their causes had these leaders decided to disengage, to live apart from the political world. What if they had decided that an ongoing conversation with their complex and imperfect societies would be more of a bother than it was worth? We are perhaps too comfortable with the idea that those who shun the give and take of public life have somehow preserved their good character. We think one good lesson can be taken from the engagement that is the essential work of politics: we can be too quick to dismiss the honor and dedication that is bound up in the messy but essential business of serving the public interest.

SUMMARY

▲

In this chapter, we have illustrated the scope of U.S. political persuasion by surveying some of the communication patterns common to politics in a variety of contests: administrative, campaign, and policy-making activities, as well as expressive forms of persuasion tied to status issues and messages embedded in popular entertainment. No single overview is adequate to describe the wealth of thought and research that has been directed to the processes involved in shaping public opinion. However, we have offered some broad conclusions that students of persuasion should keep in mind.

- We are all political, both as agents of groups seeking influence and as the recipients of the appeals of others.
- Politics is not only about the state and its institutions but also about how *all* kinds of institutions reach decisions and accommodate differences.
- Administrative and legislative persuasion thrives on coalition-building activities. Political leadership requires listening more than demanding, accommodation as well as idealism.
- Political campaigns represent ideal case studies for the processes and difficulties of persuasion. They provide opportunities to see the effects of media agenda setting, framing, and priming. They also are a reminder of the variety of media that can be used to deliver messages, ranging from television ads to the Internet.
- At the national level, political persuasion is increasingly a professionalized process involving the technologies of news management and mass communication.
- It would be a mistake to consider political activity as separate from other forms of popular culture, especially novels, films, and prime-time television. Popular media reflect the values and attitudes of our political culture.
- Measures of persuasion effects are inexact. If the key yardstick is *attitude change*, effects seem to be minimal. If other yardsticks such as *increased awareness* are included, the effects of various efforts may be greater than we can now measure.
- Changing political attitudes is often limited by the necessity to communicate to constituents through the filters of the news media, which tend to personalize coverage in terms of a political agent's strategies rather than their ideas.

Questions and Projects for Further Study

1. Attend a city council meeting, a session of the state assembly, legislative hearings, or an address given by a prominent political leader. After observing one of these events, compare your overall impressions with the coverage provided by newspapers, radio, or television stations in your area. Did framing or priming occur? Was the coverage focused on strategy or messages? How well was the public served by the news story?

2. Plan a group viewing of the classic 1993 campaign film, *The War Room* (available on DVD and videocassette). This documentary by Chris Hegedus and D. A. Pennebaker traces the work of advisers George Stephanopoulos and James Carville in the 1992 presidential campaign of Bill Clinton. It also provides an interesting look at modern campaigns. After the film, compare your impressions. Specific questions to discuss might include:

   - Does the film explain why the Clinton campaign was successful in 1992?
   - What personal characteristics worked for or against Carville as an advocate for his candidate?

- What is the most interesting persuasive strategy you observed?
- How would you like to see political campaigns change?
- Which of the settings (political commercials, television news reports, rallies, and debates) offered the best opportunity for reaching and persuading voters?

3. The authors argue that most forms of entertainment, such as films and television programs, have at least latent political content. After reviewing their arguments in the section, "Persuasion in the Context of Entertainment," (a) argue against their position or (b) identify further examples that confirm their conclusions.

4. The speeches of all modern presidents are available in most libraries as part of a continuing series of volumes collectively titled *Public Papers of the Presidents of the United States*. The White House Web site also publishes recent speeches (www.whitehouse.gov). Using George Bush's September 20, 2001, address to Congress on terrorism, illustrate coalition building, the president as "interpreter in chief," and leadership agenda setting.

5. In this chapter we mention several social movements that have pushed for legislative action in civil rights, voter rights, abortion, and so on. What major social issues are most visible now? Do the activists in those movements share any of the tactics cited in the 1920 campaign to secure the vote for women? Are any of the current movements justifiably seen as raising status issues?

6. The authors assert that even organizations such as churches follow political processes. Beyond the examples cited in the book, illustrate this conclusion with your own recent experiences in a nongovernmental organization. What made specific advocates persuasive or ineffective?

7. View Warren Beatty's film, *Bullworth*, that satirizes national politics. What does it reveal about politics, persuasion, and political participation? Does it argue for or against the authors' assertion that politics *should* be about accommodation and can be a noble calling?

Additional Reading

Joseph Cappella and Kathleen Jamieson, *Spiral of Cynicism: The Press and the Public Good* (New York: Oxford, 1997).

Robert E. Denton, Jr. and Gary C. Woodward, *Political Communication in America*, 3rd ed. (New York: Praeger, 1998).

Murray Edelman, *The Symbolic Uses of Politics* (Urbana: University of Illinois, 1963).

Roderick Hart, *Campaign Talk: Why Elections are Good For Us* (Princeton: Princeton University Press, 2000).

Kathleen Hall Jamieson and Paul Waldman, *Electing the President 2000: An Insider's View* (Philadelphia: University of Pennsylvania, 2001).

Mary Matalin and James Carville, *All's Fair* (New York: Random House/Touchstone, 1994).

Dick Morris, *Behind the Oval Office* (New York: Random House, 1997).

Stephen Reese, Oscar Gandy, Jr., and August Grant, eds., *Framing Public Life* (Mahwah, NJ: Lawrence Erlbaum, 2001).

Judith Trent and Robert Friedenberg, *Political Campaign Communication*, 3rd ed. (Westport: Praeger, 1995).

Steven Waldman, *The Bill*, Revised and Updated (New York: Penguin, 1995).

John Zaller, "The Myth of Massive Media Impact Revived: New Support for a Discredited Idea," in *Political Persuasion and Attitude Change*, eds. Diana C. Mutz, Paul Sniderman, and Richard Brody (Ann Arbor: University of Michigan Press, 1996).

Notes

[1] Adams quoted in David McCullough, *John Adams* (New York: Simon and Schuster, 2001), p. 415.

[2] John H. Bunzel, *Anti-Politics in America* (New York: Vintage, 1967), pp. 7–8.

[3] Ann Scott and Andrew Scott, *One Half of the People* (New York: J. B. Lippincott, 1975), p. 9.

[4] Sherna Gluck, ed., *From Parlor to Prison* (New York: Vintage, 1976), p. 22.

[5] Scott and Scott, p. 39.

[6] Robin Toner, "Ads Are Potent Weapon in Health Care Struggle," *New York Times*, February 1, 1994, p. A14.

[7] Ibid.

[8] Michael Wines, "Sales Pitch for (Which?) Health Care Plan," *New York Times*, July 25, 1994, pp. A1, A13.

[9] Bob Woodward, *The Agenda: Inside the Clinton White House* (New York: Simon and Schuster, 1994), p. 315.

[10] Catherine S. Manegold, "Health Care Bus: Lots of Miles, Not So Much Talk," *New York Times*, July 25, 1994, p. A12.

[11] Joe Klein, *The Natural* (New York: Doubleday, 2002), pp. 124–26.

[12] Larry Witham, "Churches Debate Role of Homosexual Unions," *Insight*, August 7, 2000 (LEXIS/NEXIS).

[13] See, for example, Hanna Rosin, "Gay Issues Pose Pastoral—and Personal—Dilemmas," *The Washington Post*, August 18, 2001, p. B9; and Eric Goldscheider, "Going Inside the Church for Same-Sex Unions," *New York Times*, March 16, 2002, p. B6.

[14] "Homosexuality and Church Unity," *The Christian Century*, March 11, 1998, p. 253.

[15] Maureen Byrne, "Ban on Same-Sex Unions Debated," *Seminole (Fl.) Times*, August 29, 1998, p. 6.

[16] Gustav Niebuhr, "Methodists Act Against Homosexual Unions," *New York Times*, August 12, 1998, p. A10.

[17] Michael Howard, "Methodist Pastor Obeys Her Conscience, Not Church," *Rocky Mountain News*, August 20, 1998, p. 6A.

[18] Buzz Bissinger, *A Prayer for the City* (New York: Random House, 1997).

[19] Steven Meyers, "Government Reinvention: A Seminar with a Master," *New York Times*, March 6, 1994, p. A35.

[20] Bissinger, pp. 238–39.

[21] Ibid., p. 239.

[22] Roosevelt quoted in Emmet John Hughes, *The Living Presidency* (New York: Coward, McCann and Geoghegan, 1972), p. 184.

[23] Woodward, p. 330.

[24] Anne Applebaum, "Iraqniphobia," *Slate*. (Online) August 8, 2002.

[25] Mark Hertsgaard, *On Bended Knee: The Press and the Reagan Presidency* (New York: Schocken, 1988), p. 345.

[26] "Bush Unpopular in Europe, Seen as Unilateralist," *Pew Research Center for the People and the Press*. (Online) August 15, 2001.

[27] Carol Gelderman, *All the President's Words* (New York: Walker, 1997), p. 156.

[28] Mary Stuckey, *The President as Interpreter in Chief* (Chatham, NJ: Chatham House, 1991), p. 1.

[29] Paul D. Erickson, *Reagan Speaks: The Making of An American Myth* (New York: New York University, 1985), pp. 32–50.

[30] James MacGregor Burns, *Leadership* (New York: Harper and Row, 1978), p. 452.

[31] Michael Oreskes, "Civil Rights Act Leaves Deep Mark on the American Political Landscape," *New York Times*, July 2, 1989, p. 16.

[32] See, for example, Michael Beschloss, *Taking Charge: The Johnson White House Tapes* (New York: Simon and Schuster, 1997), pp. 165–238.

[33] William Safire, *Safire's Political Dictionary* (New York: Ballantine, 1978), pp. 383–84.

[34] Center for Responsive Politics, http:/www.opensecrets.org/lobbyists/index.asp; Jill Abramson, "The Business of Persuasion Thrives in Nation's Capital," *New York Times,* September 29, 1998, p. A1.

[35] For a critical assessment of the power of Washington lobbyists see Jeffrey H. Birnbaum, *The Lobbyists* (New York: Times Books, 1992).

[36] An interesting case study of legislative lobbying is T. R. Reid's *Congressional Odyssey: The Saga of a Senate Bill* (San Francisco: W. H. Freeman, 1980).

[37] Stephen Hess, *The Ultimate Insiders: U. S. Senators in the National Media* (Washington: Brookings, 1986), p. 38.

[38] Richard Oppel, Jr. and Richard Stevenson, "Enron's Many Strands: The Overview," *New York Times,* February 27, 2002, p. A1.

[39] Richard F. Fenno, Jr., *Home Style: House Members in Their Districts* (Boston: Little, Brown, 1978), pp. 217–18.

[40] Alison Mitchell, "A New Form of Lobbying Puts Public Face on Private Interest," *New York Times,* September 30, 1998, pp. A1, A14.

[41] Marlowe and Company, "People's Guide to Influencing Congress." (Online) August 19, 2002.

[42] Steven Waldman, *The Bill,* Revised and Updated (New York: Penguin, 1995), p. 198.

[43] Ibid., p. 186.

[44] Ibid.

[45] Larry J. Sabato, *The Rise of the Political Consultants* (New York: Basic, 1981), p. 351.

[46] Dick Morris, *Behind the Oval Office* (New York: Random House, 1997), p. 339.

[47] For a fascinating look at campaign tactics see Tony Schwartz, *The Responsive Chord* (New York: Doubleday, 1972).

[48] Nora Fitzgerald, "Political Punch," *Adweek,* Eastern Edition, August 10, 1998, p. 22.

[49] Kathleen Hall Jamieson and Paul Waldman, *Electing the President 2000: An Insiders' View* (Philadelphia: University of Pennsylvania, 2001), pp. 188–89.

[50] See Mary Matalin and James Carville, *All's Fair* (New York: Random House/Touchstone, 1994).

[51] This four-part list is based on a discussion of campaigns in Judith S. Trent and Robert V. Friedenberg, *Political Campaign Communication,* 4th ed. (New York: Praeger, 2000), pp. 17–53.

[52] Anthony Corrado, "Financing the 2000 Elections," in *The Election of 2000,* ed. by Gerald Pomper (New York: Chatham House, 2001), pp. 101–02.

[53] Jack Germond and Jules Witcover, *Mad as Hell: Revolt at the Ballot Box, 1992* (New York: Warner Books, 1993), pp. 99–100.

[54] William Mayer, "The Presidential Nominations," in *The Election of 2000,* ed. by Gerald Pomper (New York: Chatham House, 2001), pp. 26–29.

[55] The extent to which political campaigns depend on fat war chests has been called a national disgrace. For an overview of the problem of excessive money in American electoral politics see W. Lance Bennett, *The Governing Crisis,* 2nd ed. (New York: St. Martins, 1996), pp. 136–56.

[56] Mayer, pp. 38–40.

[57] In the last 10 years a great deal has been written about attack advertising—campaign advertising that denigrates opponents. Estimates vary on how well attack ads work. One general strategy adopted by candidates who fear the effects of attack ads involves inoculating audiences against the effects of these ads. See, for example, Michael Pfau and Henry C. Kenski, *Attack Politics: Strategy and Defense* (New York: Praeger, 1990), pp. 13–60.

[58] Jamieson and Waldman, p. 175.

[59] Ibid., p. 204.

[60] Charles Peters, *How Washington Really Works* (Reading, MA: Addison Wesley, 1980), p. 132.

[61] James David Barber, *The Presidential Character: Predicting Performance in the White House* (Englewood Cliffs, NJ: Prentice Hall, 1972), p. 446.

[62] Roderick Hart, *Campaign Talk: Why Elections are Good For Us* (Princeton: Princeton University Press, 2000), pp. 169–98.

[63] Joseph N. Cappella and Kathleen Hall Jamieson, *Spiral of Cynicism: The Press and the Public Good* (New York: Oxford University Press, 1997), pp. 3–86.

[64] See Gary C. Woodward, "Narrative Form and the Deceptions of Modern Journalism," in *Political Communication Ethics: An Oxymoron?,* ed. by Robert E. Denton, Jr. (Westport, CT: Praeger, 2000), pp. 139–42.

[65] Shanto Iyengar and Donald Kinder, *News That Matters* (Chicago: University of Chicago, 1987), pp. 63–89.

[66] Ibid., p. 117.

[67] Stephen Reese, "Prologue—Framing Public Life: A Bridging Model for Media Research," in *Framing Public Life*, eds. Stephen Resse, Oscar Gandy, Jr., and August Grant (Mahwah, NJ: Lawrence Erlbaum, 2001), pp. 10–11.

[68] Regina Lawrence, "Game-Framing the Issues: Tracking the Strategy Frame in Public Policy News," *Political Communication*, 2000, 17(2):93.

[69] E. J. Dionne, Jr., "The Clinton Enigma: Seeking Consensus, Breeding Discord," in *The Election of 2000*, ed. by Gerald Pomper (New York: Chatham House, 2001), pp. 1–11.

[70] Philemon Bantimaroudis and Hyun Ban, "Covering the Crisis in Somalia: Framing Choices by *The New York Times* and *The Manchester Guardian*," in *Framing Public Life*, eds. Stephen Resse, Oscar Gandy, Jr., and August Grant (Mahwah, NJ: Lawrence Erlbaum, 2001), pp. 175–84.

[71] See, for example, Allan Sloan and Johnnie Roberts, "Sticky Business," *Newsweek*, July 22, 2002, p. 26.

[72] For a broad discussion of this perspective see Jack M. McLeod and Lee B. Becker, "The Uses and Gratifications Approach," in *The Handbook of Political Communication*, eds. Dan D. Nimmo and Keith R. Sanders (Beverly Hills, CA: Sage, 1981), pp. 67–99. A less technical discussion of this perspective is also developed in Murray Edelman, *The Symbolic Uses of Politics* (Urbana: University of Illinois, 1967), pp. 1–43.

[73] Joseph R. Gusfield, *Symbolic Crusade: Status Politics and the American Temperance Movement* (Urbana: University of Illinois, 1963), pp. 1–22.

[74] Todd Gitlin, *Twilight of Common Dreams* (New York: Metropolitan Books, 1995), pp. 7–36.

[75] Linda Greene, "At Augusta, It's Symbols That Mean the Most," *New York Times*, August 4, 2002, section 8, p. 11.

[76] Garry Wills, *John Wayne's America* (New York: Simon and Schuster, 1997), p. 311.

[77] Todd Gitlin, ed., *Watching Television* (New York: Pantheon, 1987), pp. 4–5.

[78] Quoted in Terry Christensen, *Reel Politics* (New York: Basil Blackwell, 1987), p. 2.

[79] Anita Gates, "Yes, America Has a Class System. See 'Frasier'" *New York Times*, April 19, 1998, sec. 2, p. 35.

[80] Quoted in Naomi Wolf, *Fire with Fire* (New York: Random House, 1993), p. 78.

[81] Ellen Hume, "Why the Press Blew the S & L Scandal," *New York Times*, May 24, 1990, p. A25.

[82] See, for example, Neil Postman, *Amusing Ourselves to Death: Public Discourse in the Age of Show Business* (New York: Penguin, 1985), pp. 3–15; Jeffrey Scheuer, *The Sound Bite Society* (New York: Four Walls, Eight Windows, 1999), pp. 1–59; Bill Kovack and Tom Rosenstiel, *Warp Speed: America in the Age of Mixed Media* (New York: Century Foundation, 1999), pp. 1–32.

[83] For a collection of recent case studies see Kristina Borjesson, ed., *Into the Buzzsaw: Leading Journalists Expose the Myth of a Free Press* (New York: Prometheus Books, 2002).

[84] For an interesting discussion of the problems associated with estimating political effects through television see Ken Goldstein and Paul Freedman, "Lessons Learned: Campaign Advertising in the 2000 Elections," *Political Communication*, 2002, 19:5–6.

[85] Kathleen Hall Jamieson, *Everything You Think You Know About Politics* (New York: Basic Books, 2000), p. 5.

[86] For a clear review of the effects of television on campaigns, see Thomas Hollihan, *Uncivil Wars: Political Campaigns in a Media Age* (Boston: Bedford/St. Martins, 2001), pp. 104–14.

[87] Jamieson, *Everything You Think You Know About Politics*, p. 5.

[88] For a summary of one way the Bush campaign used the Internet in 2000, see Jamieson and Waldman, pp. 193–94.

[89] Margaret Scammell, "The Internet and Civic Engagement: The Age of the Citizen-Consumer," *Political Communication*, 2000, 17:351–55.

[90] Melvin DeFleur and Everette Dennis, *Understanding Mass Communication*, 6th ed. (Boston: Houghton Mifflin, 1998), p. 456.

[91] Doris Graber, *Mass Media and American Politics*, 5th ed. (Washington, DC: Congressional Quarterly Press, 1997), p. 262.

[92] John Zaller, "The Myth of Massive Media Impact Revived: New Support for a Discredited Idea," in *Political Persuasion and Attitude Change*, eds. Diana C. Mutz, Paul Sniderman, and Richard Brody (Ann Arbor: University of Michigan Press, 1996), p. 18.

[93] See, for example, Maxwell McCombs, "The Agenda Setting Approach," in *Handbook of Political Communication*, eds. Dan Nimmo and Keith Sanders (Beverly Hills, CA: Sage, 1981), p. 121; and Everett Rogers and James Dearing, "Agenda Setting Research: Where Has it Been and Where is it Going," in *Communication Yearbook*, Vol. 11 (Beverly Hills, CA: Sage, 1988), pp. 555–94.

[94] Jamieson, *Everything You Think You Know About Politics*, p. 5.

[95] William Shakespeare, *Coriolanus,* ed. by Reuben Brower (New York: Signet, 1966), pp. 244–55.

[96] Cappella and Jamieson, pp. 17–37. In contemporary dramas Congress is especially filled with self-important windbags, such as Richard Dreyfus' Senator Bob Rumson in *The American President* and Gene Hackman's Senator Keeley in *The Birdcage*.

[97] For example, Martin Luther King, Jr. campaigned for Lyndon Johnson in 1964 and then campaigned to keep the pressure on for civil rights legislation after Johnson was elected. See Taylor Branch, *Pillar of Fire: America in the King Years: 1963–1965* (New York: Simon and Schuster, 1998), pp. 518–23.

PART IV

ISSUES AND STRATEGIES OF MESSAGE PREPARATION

Calvin and Hobbes

TODAY AT SCHOOL, I TRIED TO DECIDE WHETHER TO CHEAT ON MY TEST OR NOT.

WATTERSON © 1993

I WONDERED, IS IT BETTER TO DO THE RIGHT THING AND FAIL ...OR IS IT BETTER TO DO THE WRONG THING AND SUCCEED?

ON THE ONE HAND, UNDESERVED SUCCESS GIVES NO SATISFACTION. ...BUT ON THE OTHER HAND, WELL-DESERVED FAILURE GIVES NO SATISFACTION EITHER.

OF COURSE, MOST EVERYBODY CHEATS SOME TIME OR OTHER. PEOPLE ALWAYS BEND THE RULES IF THEY THINK THEY CAN GET AWAY WITH IT. ...THEN AGAIN, THAT DOESN'T JUSTIFY *MY* CHEATING.

THEN I THOUGHT, LOOK, CHEATING ON ONE LITTLE TEST ISN'T SUCH A BIG DEAL. IT DOESN'T HURT ANYONE.

...BUT THEN I WONDERED IF I WAS JUST RATIONALIZING MY UNWILLINGNESS TO ACCEPT THE CONSEQUENCE OF NOT STUDYING.

STILL, IN THE REAL WORLD, PEOPLE CARE ABOUT SUCCESS, NOT PRINCIPLES.

...THEN AGAIN, MAYBE THAT'S WHY THE WORLD IS IN SUCH A MESS.

WHAT A DILEMMA!

SO WHAT DID YOU DECIDE?

NOTHING. I RAN OUT OF TIME AND I HAD TO TURN IN A BLANK PAPER.

ANYMORE, SIMPLY ACKNOWLEDGING THE ISSUE IS A MORAL VICTORY.

WELL, IT JUST SEEMED WRONG TO CHEAT ON AN ETHICS TEST.

Ethical Considerations of Persuasion

Overview

▲ Ethics, Values, and Principles

▲ Communication, Ethics, and Society
    Persuasion and Communication Ethics
    Sources of Attitudes and Values
    Categories of Communication Ethics

▲ Considerations for Ethical Communication
    Communicator Considerations
    Message Considerations
    Medium Considerations
    Receiver Considerations
    Ethical Values of Communicators

▲ Areas of Special Concern
    Media and New Technologies
    News Journalism
    Politics and Political Communication
    Public Discourse

> Transforming *leadership . . . occurs when one or more persons*
> *engage with others in such a way that leaders and followers raise*
> *one another to higher levels of motivation and morality.*[1]
> —JAMES MACGREGOR BURNS

Since the beginning of time, humans have expressed a concern for ethics. Plato's *Republic* is essentially a work of political ethics, as is Aristotle's *Nicomachean Ethics*. For both Plato and Aristotle, the good person was a conscientious citizen contributing to the city-state. The notion of civic virtue implies a citizenry that is informed, active, selfless, enlightened and, above all, just.

Life today is more individualistic. We are concerned with self-actualization, success, comfort, convenience, property, and the pursuit of happiness. For more than a decade, there have been increasing numbers of studies, polls, and news articles lamenting the decline of ethical behavior in America. As early as 1987, the cover of *U.S. News & World Report* asked "A Nation of Liars?" and *Time* magazine "Whatever Happened to Ethics?" *Atlantic Monthly* in 1992 and *Newsweek* magazine in 1995 explored the absence of a sense of shame as a norm in our culture. Lying and cheating among adults and among children has become rather commonplace. More recent surveys show that 80 percent of high school students admit to having cheated at least once—with half stating they did not believe cheating was necessarily wrong. In fact, many indicated that it is *necessary* to lie, cheat, or steal in order to succeed. Even 54 percent of middle schoolers admit they have cheated on an exam. Ninety-two percent of high-school-age children report that they regularly lie to their parents.[2]

The numbers for college students are equally disappointing. Seventy-five percent of college students admit to cheating. As of the summer of 2002, there were well over 300 Internet term paper sites offering essays on thousands of subjects, even offering to write custom papers for an exorbitant fee. During this timeframe, a poll conducted by Zogby International revealed that 73 percent of college students agreed with the statement that "what is right and wrong depends on differences in individual values and cultural diversity" versus the 25 percent who believed that "there are clear and uniform standards of right and wrong by which everyone should be judged." Two percent were not sure.[3]

Sadly, the same general disregard for ethical behavior can be found among the general public. A national poll revealed that 30 percent of individuals admit to putting extra work experience or educational experience on their resume, 40 percent telling someone that "the payment is in the mail" when actually it isn't; and 55 percent lying about their age in order to get a special discount, to name just a few examples.[4] What words do we use to describe behavior that is a little bit wrong? If you make personal phone calls at work, are you stealing? What about downloading songs from the Internet? Is it dishonest to reuse a stamp that wasn't cancelled by the post office?[5]

We ended the twentieth century with a president who was impeached, ultimately disbarred, and found in contempt of court for lying under oath, not to mention to the American public. We began the twenty-first century with the largest number and scope of corporate scandals and transgressions since the years before the Great Depression.

The fragmented nature of society today makes defining ethical behavior more difficult. We separate our world into personal, business, political, and religious realms. We approach each realm with a different set of behaviors. The segmentation can be an excuse to ignore ethical behavior appropriate in one context if we're operating in a different realm. We might find lying to our spouse completely unacceptable but could soften the stance on lying if talking to a supervisor. Deception and fraud abound in society across all occupations and socioeconomic groups. Individuals from the fields of entertainment, business, politics, and others too numerous to list are frequently in the news as a consequence of acts of deception. These examples don't remove the responsibility of conducting ourselves in an ethical manner, but they offer abundant rationales if we're looking for an excuse.

Ethical decisions are not always about scandals or personal misconduct. On a daily basis we are confronted with choices and decisions that have ethical implications: Do I repeat a rumor I heard about another person? Do I answer a question honestly, even if it may hurt a friend's feelings?

It is indeed a sign of the times that nearly all textbooks, regardless of subject matter, now include a chapter on ethics. A cynic would argue that such a treatment is rather useless. How can a few pages and perhaps a class lecture or two succeed where years of religious instruction or family life have failed? Nevertheless, it is helpful to reflect on our personal behavior and the potential consequences of our actions. According to the Hastings Center, instruction and discussion of ethics may result in stimulating the moral imagination, recognizing ethical issues, eliciting a sense of moral obligation, developing analytical skills, and tolerating disagreement.[6]

We realize that the subject of ethics is open to a wide range of definitions and interpretations. In the limited scope of this chapter, we cannot address the philosophical questions of ethics such as: Do we judge actions (behavior, consequences, results) as ethical or do we judge the actor (the individual's intentions)? Do we consult principles or rules to judge whether a specific act is ethical, or must we look only at the consequences of the act? If we strictly follow rules, is morality reducible to authority? If we look only at consequences, do we reduce morality to expediency? Is there a universal right or wrong, or is all behavior relative? Immanuel Kant believed he should never act in any way that he would not want to become universal law. He also declared that in a legal system people are guilty if they violate the rights of others, but in ethics they are guilty if they only think of doing so.[7] Can his standards apply to society today?

Stephen Toulmin argues that the social function or purpose of ethics is to reconcile conflicts of interest and to prevent avoidable suffering. A simplified version of Toulmin's approach to ethics is to test individual actions by rules and to test those rules by their consequences.[8] Our position in this chapter follows his suggestions and could be rephrased as: ethical communication should be fair, honest, and designed not to hurt other people.

ETHICS, VALUES, AND PRINCIPLES

▲

According to Conrad Fink, "ethics is a system of principles, a morality or code of conduct. It is the values and rules of life recognized by an individual, group, or culture seeking guidelines to human conduct and what is good or bad, right or wrong."[9] From this perspective, ethics refers to standards of conduct based on moral duties and virtues derived from principles of right and wrong. There are two behavioral dimensions to ethics. The first is the ability to *discern* right from wrong; the second is a commitment to do what is right, good, and appropriate. Thus, there is an action dimension to ethics. It implies more than words, it involves active compliance with rules or standards of behavior. Moral virtue refers to moral excellence, characteristics, or conduct worthy of admiration, such as generosity, kindness, or valor.

The terms *values* and *ethics* are not the same thing. Ethics are concerned with modes of conduct and behavior. Values, as discussed in chapter 6, are the composite beliefs and attitudes that determine how someone actually behaves. Ethical values directly relate to beliefs concerning what is right and wrong. Our core values define our personal character and personality. Often, our values may conflict. For example, our commitment to honesty and fairness may conflict with our desire for wealth and success in some situations. Obviously, when values conflict, choices must be made. Our choices are based on the ranking in importance of our values.

Whether we know it or not, we all have some form of personal moral value system that reflects how we rank competing values in deciding how we will behave. Our personal value system encompasses our values of right and wrong, good and evil. From individual value systems we collectively form general moral principles or expectations of behavior. Ethical principles are the rules of conduct derived from a culture's ethical values. For example, honesty is a value. From this value, we form many principles: be truthful, don't mislead, don't cheat, etc. Sometimes principles become laws to ensure social compliance. Some might argue that government has gone too far trying to legislate morals. Others see the decline of morals and advocate even more principles or laws regulating human behavior.

COMMUNICATION, ETHICS, AND SOCIETY

▲

The disciplines of rhetoric and communication studies have long been interested in the subject of ethics. There is universal agreement that human communication demands concern for ethics. Richard Johannesen argues that "potential ethical issues are inherent in any instance of communication between humans to the degree that the communication can be judged on a right-wrong dimension, involves possible significant influence on other humans, and that the communicator consciously chooses specific ends and communicative means to achieve those ends."[10]

Because communication involves the process of symbol selection, choice, and creation, some scholars argue that all intentional communication transactions inherently involve some degree of persuasion. As you may recall from chapter 3, language is the vehicle for social interaction, a practical tool for getting things done. It is also a form of social behavior. Through language, we define social roles and rules for behavior. Interaction with others creates the reality toward which we respond and act. Indeed, it makes a difference if we convince someone that a glass is either half-full or half-empty. In the former, there is a sense of hope and optimism. The latter involves caution and perhaps even despair. Ethical choices about language are mandatory in a society that negotiates boundaries of conduct through communication.

Historically, Americans place great faith in the ability of people to make rational and reasonable decisions in life. We also believe strongly in the guarantees of the First Amendment: the freedom of speech and the freedom of the press.[11] These values and practices place a special burden on those who communicate with others. With that freedom comes responsibility—responsibility for the form and content of our communication behavior. The importance of this point becomes clear when considering the essential characteristics of a democratic form of government.

The notion of *accountability* is essential to a representative democracy. Because citizens delegate authority to those who hold office, politicians must answer to the public for all actions and deeds. *Information* is critical for citizens to make informed judgments and evaluations of elected officials. Incomplete or inaccurate information can lead to bad public decisions. *A free marketplace of ideas* is vital to the concept of democracy. Diversity of thought and respect for dissent are hallmarks of the values of freedom and justice. When multiple viewpoints are heard and expressed, the common good prevails over private interests. Finally, we enjoy a process of what Dennis Thompson calls *collective deliberation* on disputes about issues and fundamental values.[12] It is national and public debate that determines the collective wisdom and will of the people.

The notion of authority is a central concept in social and political thought. There are many forms of authority: bureaucratic, technical, or professional, to name a few. The role of authority in government is to establish moral, ethical, and intellectual standards and also to guarantee social and political freedom—acting as a barrier to centralized, arbitrary, and despotic power. We use authority to protect our rights, to provide order and security, to manage conflict, and to distribute the benefits and burdens of society.

The authority of the U.S. government originates from the Constitution. The *moral* authority of government originates from the collective beliefs, attitudes, and values of the citizens. Moral authority consists of the felt obligations and duties derived from shared community values, ideas, and ideals. From a democratic perspective, the very nature of authority as the ability to evoke purely voluntary compliance must be moral in form and content. Otherwise, social violence, chaos, and coercion will be the norm. Moral authority rests on voluntary consent.

A government is only as good, decent, and moral as its citizens. Individual integrity, responsibility, and accountability are the best check on government abuse. The collective social values of the citizens become the conditions necessary for the existence of political authority. The government that encompasses and expresses our collective values ensures the respect and voluntary compliance of all citizens. Political authority rests on the assumption that it exists to promote the good of those who accept it, that the common good will prevail, not the self-interests of the those in authority or by the exercise of force.

We need to reaffirm ourselves to our national civic values—the principles embodied in the Declaration of Independence, the Constitution, and the Bill of Rights—that bring us together as a people. The ideals of freedom, equality, democracy, and justice provide the basis for building community and trust in the United States today. Civic responsibility, accountability, and initiative should once again become a keystone of social life. Moral discipline means using social norms, rules, customs, and laws to develop moral reasoning, self-control, and a generalized respect for others. Such an approach to social life will help citizens recognize the values behind the laws and why these laws are necessary. Democracy makes government accessible and accountable to ordinary citizens. Finally, of course, we desperately need moral leadership in the future, not defined by a specific set of standards or dogma, but clearly recognized by the public as possessing the moral authority of governing. In short, in order to elect better leaders we must become better citizens, friends, and neighbors.

Thus, at the very heart of democracy is public communication. The quality of that public communication directly impacts the quality of our democracy and society at large. According to philosopher Jack Odell,

> A society without ethics is a society doomed to extinction. . . . Ethical principles are necessary preconditions for the existence of a social community. Without ethical principles, it would be impossible for human beings to live in harmony and without fear, despair, hopelessness, anxiety, apprehension, and uncertainty.[13]

In the past, religions were the primary source for ethical standards. In the United States, the political separation of church and state has created separation in other arenas as well. Steven Carter decries the trend in our political culture to treat religious beliefs as arbitrary and unimportant to social life. Those who espouse religious beliefs, attitudes, and values in public are often portrayed as ignorant, extreme, and even potentially harmful. Carter believes that religious beliefs and values should inform public policy. "Democracy is best served when the religions are able to act as independent moral voices interposed between the citizen and the state."[14]

Persuasion and Communication Ethics

Persuasion is a tool of communication. It can be used by both good and bad people for equally good or bad purposes. Strategies and tactics of persuasion are not inherently good or bad. It is the motives of persuaders that determine if the use of specific strategies is good or bad. These motives provide a context for judgment. For example, most academics and politicians complain about the use of overtly emotional rather than more rational or logical appeals. However, one could argue that to use a strong emotional or fear appeal in producing a teenage anti-drunk driving ad may well be appropriate. But someone using a fear appeal as a threat or blackmail to disclose some personal information would not.

To illustrate the complexity of judging the appropriateness of various strategies and tactics of persuasion, consider the following dilemma. Suppose a terrorist group has threatened to explode a bomb in a city, potentially killing thousands of people. The police arrest a member of the group, but he or she refuses to talk. Should the police torture the terrorist to obtain the location of the bomb in order to save thousands of lives? Which outcome is worse: the torture of one individual or the failure to save thousands of innocent people? Is this a case where coercion may be warranted?

By its very nature, persuasion forces us to consider the ethical consequences of our own acts. When we communicate with a persuasive intent, we are usually seeking change in others rather than in ourselves. We expect those we address to risk changes in their attitudes or behaviors, even while we remain relatively comfortable in our own. Thus, the persuader gives up nothing while asking others to alter their lives. Under these circumstances, there is an understandable need to consider whether a communication transaction that places most of the risk on the receiver meets certain minimal standards of fairness and decency. The risks persuaders may ask others to accept may be financial ("This product is worth your hard-earned dollars."), psychological ("Your fear of large animals is irrational; you'll enjoy an afternoon of horseback riding."), social ("No one will think less of you for agreeing to serve as an unpaid volunteer."), or physical ("You haven't lived until you've tried hang gilding.").

The concern for communication ethics is about social relationships and trust. Sissela Bok argues that "there must be a minimal degree of trust in communication for language and action to be more than stabs in the dark. This is why some level of truthfulness has always been seen as essential to human society, no matter how deficient the observance of other moral principles."[15] She cautions that trust in some degree of veracity is a foundation for relationships among human beings; without it, institutions would collapse.

One could begin with the simple assumption of St. Augustine that "it is evident that speech was given to man, not that man might therewith deceive one another, but that one man might make known his thoughts to another. To use speech, then for the purposes of deception, and not for its appointed end, is a sin."[16] We have choices in what we say and how we say it. The distinction for many scholars between truth and lying is the *intent* to mislead or not disclose. As communicators, we have a responsibility for veracity beyond personal motives.

For example, consider that television programs directed to children also sell to children. Advertisers seeking exposure on children's programs target their young audiences by using appeals that will motivate them to buy (or lobby their parents to buy) products such as cereals or toys. The ethical line here is a thin one. By their nature, children are not yet savvy consumers. The match between marketing experts and vulnerable four-year-olds is grossly uneven. Because children lack an adult's ability to discount the advertising puffery that is part of most product advertising, corporations obviously have special obligations to their young audiences.

Sources of Attitudes and Values

In chapter 6, we defined the concepts of beliefs, attitudes, and values and argued that attitude change is the core concept in nearly all theories of persuasion. But where do our attitudes, beliefs, and values originate? Louis Day identifies four influential sources: our family, peer groups, role models, and societal institutions.[17]

Early in our lives, parents provide our rules for behavior. Through instruction and discipline, we gain a sense of right and wrong. As we grow older, we learn not so much from what our parents tell us as we do from observing their behavior. We learn a powerful lesson about deception when we see Dad call in sick and then go golfing. As children we learn attitudes and form values partially from what parents tell us and more specifically from what our parents do.

As we reach adolescence, peer groups gain importance in developing our attitudes and values. Our peer groups evolve and change. Initially we learn from others in our neighborhood, church, school, social clubs, and, eventually, our workplace. These groups exert pressure and challenge our core values.

Role models other than our parents are another influence on our values and attitudes throughout our lives. Role models may be people we know, historical figures, or sports and media celebrities. By becoming psychologically involved with role models, we assume their ideas, attitudes, and behavior. Some social observers worry about the lack of genuine heroes today. Many parents are concerned about the influence of rock or media stars, such as Britney Spears or Howard Stern, on the values of their children.

Even as adults, however, we are still influenced by real or fictionalized characters. A telling moment for political observers was when President Ronald Reagan repeated Clint Eastwood's line, "Go ahead, make my day," to Congress in promising to veto a tax increase. The allusion was very clear. The statement portrayed Reagan as strong, defiant, even heroic. Media celebrities and media stars routinely provide testimony before Congressional committees encouraging more spending and legislation in areas of special interest. Christopher Reeve is outspoken on issues of cloning and the use of fetal tissues for research. Mary Tyler Moore addresses issues of diabetes research and funding. Alec Baldwin has become a noted activist on environmental issues, animal rights, and gun control. For years, Richard Gere has been outspoken on issues of human rights and the movement to free Tibet from Chinese occupation. Special causes enjoy the publicity associated with celebrities. However, because of the powerful impact of celebrities, many citizens believe that media stars and athletes have a moral obligation to set higher standards of social conduct than does the public at large. Interestingly, a growing number of athletes deny any such responsibility. They are paid to play the game, that's it.

Social institutions are also important in influencing, changing, or reinforcing social values. We associate specific values and expectations of behavior with institutions such as churches, government, and various professional organizations. We are shocked and disappointed when we learn of corruption within government, the police, or the medical profession, for example. There is a growing debate about the proper role of social and governmental institutions in instilling values among the populace. Should values education be taught in schools? Have we gone too far in removing religious values and principles from government? Within the last few years, several states have passed legislation to require the recitation of the Pledge of Allegiance, required moments of silence, and character education programs.

The process of socialization begins early in life. Our beliefs, attitudes, and values are a product of all that we experience throughout our lives. They form the basis of our character as individuals and as a society. Our daily interactions, whether formal or informal, verbal or nonverbal, test our current beliefs and attitudes and shape our future values.

Categories of Communication Ethics

Ronald Arnett reviewed studies related to communication ethics published from 1915 to 1985 in journals of the field. His review revealed five categories of or approaches to communication ethics that have become a starting place for most scholars: democratic ethics, universal-humanitarian ethics, procedural or code ethics, contextual ethics, and narrative ethics.[18]

Democratic ethical concerns, as already mentioned, focus on how to improve the functioning of democracy in the United States. Guidelines address the needs for openness, accuracy, mutual respect, and justice.

The *universal-humanitarian approach* to communication ethics goes beyond concerns for democracy. This approach attempts to identify universal, concrete guidelines for social interaction. Concepts important to this approach are: wisdom, morality, social and human values, rationality, character, commitment, and responsibility, to name only a few.[19] This approach often resembles Platonic idealism but also recognizes the importance of individual honesty, truth, and dignity.

Almost every organization and profession has developed standards of conduct—a *procedural code* approach to ethics. They range from the very narrow and specific to the most broad and idealistic. Even a casual reading finds many of the guidelines rather optimistic, especially in light of contemporary practices. For example, members of the American Association of Political Consultants sign a code pledging to "use no appeal to voters which is based on racism or discrimination," to "refrain from false and misleading attacks on an opponent," and to "be honest in my relationship with the press." In light of such guidelines, few political ads would qualify. As discussed in chapter 11, political ads routinely violate one or more of the above guidelines. Of course, the value of professional codes for an organization or profession is a public acknowledgement of acceptable standards of behavior. The codes offer ideal standards for decision making about ethical practices.

If you search the Internet, you will find a number of organizational and professional codes. A quick reading reveals great similarity in the values and goals espoused in the various statements. Many of the statements could work for nearly any profession or social endeavor.

Contextual ethics in some ways counter the universal orientation. Proponents of this perspective argue that one must consider the dynamics and elements of the situation when rendering ethical judgments. Audience adaptation, symbolic choice, and flexibility become key issues. Lying may even be acceptable if the contextual requirements dictate such a strategy. For example, the Defense Department during a war might deny that an air crew had been shot down in a hostile country; security concerns would override the necessity to tell the truth. While there may be problems identifying and articulating absolute ethical standards, few scholars would advocate complete reliance on a situational approach to communication ethics.

Of the various approaches, *narrative ethics* is the newest and most theoretical. In many ways, it is a combination of all the others. At the heart of this approach is the belief that social drama, vision, and storytelling interact to construct community values. A code emerges from public discussion and interaction. Public narratives provide the rationale for action and social definitions. In essence, this

Figure 12.1   Code of Professional Ethics[20]

As a member of the American Association of Political Consultants, I believe there are certain standards of practice which I must maintain. I, therefore, pledge to adhere to the following Code of Professional Ethics:

• I will not indulge in any activity which would corrupt or degrade the practice of political consulting.

• I will treat my colleagues and clients with respect and never intentionally injure their professional or personal reputations.

• I will respect the confidence of my clients and not reveal confidential or privileged information obtained during our professional relationship.

• I will use no appeal to voters which is based on racism, sexism, religious intolerance or any form of unlawful discrimination and will condemn those who use such practices. In turn, I will work for equal voting rights and privileges for all citizens.

• I will refrain from false and misleading attacks on an opponent or member of his or her family and will do everything in my power to prevent others from using such tactics.

• I will document accurately and fully any criticism of an opponent or his or her record.

• I will be honest in my relationship with the news media and candidly answer questions when I have the authority to do so.

• I will use any funds I receive from my clients, or on behalf of my clients, only for those purposes invoiced in writing.

• I will not support any individual or organization which resorts to practices forbidden by this code.

approach recognizes the dynamic nature of ethical considerations, a process produced through a constant public/private dialectic."[21]

These five approaches to ethics represent attempts to understand a complex topic from varying perspectives. While the categories may seem artificially segmented, they need not be viewed as mutually exclusive. Descriptive labels should not be confused with prescriptive rules. If we are attuned to our communication behaviors and attempts at persuasion, we will recognize the frequency with which we confront ethical dilemmas. Attempting to classify the dilemma will probably not be our first concern, but the background knowledge of how others have analyzed and approached similar dilemmas will help us determine the ethical considerations in a given situation.

CONSIDERATIONS FOR ETHICAL COMMUNICATION
▲

There are several basic procedures to guide our decision making about ethical persuasive appeals. First, search your conscience. Reflect on the lessons and values of your upbringing. Would you ask your parents to follow the prescribed action? Would your grandparents approve? How would your favorite teacher react? A second test is peer consultation. We can discuss our ideas, appeals, or approaches with friends, mentors, or other people we respect and trust. Interpersonal discussion may help us sort out our motives, suggest our biases, and help focus on the primary issues of conflict. The third test is publicity. Here you test ideas or arguments with representatives of the people most likely to be affected by your opinions. For example, suggest a smoking ban to a smoker or gun restrictions to an avid hunter. Finally, look for personal, religious, or professional guidelines. Many samples are provided throughout this chapter. Some ethicists argue that the only guideline necessary is the golden rule, "Do unto others as you would have them do unto you."

Sissela Bok has several recommendations to avoid deceiving others. She suggests that people can

> decide to rule out deception wherever honest alternatives exist, and become much more adept at thinking up honest ways to deal with problems. They can learn to look with much greater care at the remaining choices where deception seems the only way out. They can make use of the test of publicity to help them set standards to govern their participation in deceptive practices. Finally, they can learn to beware of efforts to dupe them, and make clear their preference for honesty even in small things.[22]

A casual survey of communication textbooks and codes provides a wide range of "do's" and "don'ts" to ensure ethical persuasive communication. Below we identify and summarize some of the most common standards in relation to the communicator, the message, the medium, and the receiver. We conclude by providing a list of desired ethical values of communicators.

Communicator Considerations

1. Do not misrepresent personal knowledge, experience, or skills.
2. Do not conceal personal motives or purposes for persuasive appeals.
3. Do not misrepresent, distort, or ignore consequences of actions advocated.
4. Do not advocate ideas, positions, or actions in which you do not believe.
5. Do not advocate actions or behaviors of others that are dangerous, illegal, or unethical.
6. Do not use coercion or manipulation to achieve ends.
7. Respect the diversity of opinions.
8. Encourage full discussion and debate of issues.
9. Provide the very best thinking and reasoning based on the most current evidence in developing an argument.
10. Respect individuals' right to privacy.
11. Recognize that during moments of utterance, you are the sole source of argument and information.
12. Select and present facts and opinions fairly.
13. Reveal sources of information and opinions.

Message Considerations

1. Do not use false, fictitious, distorted, or irrelevant information or evidence to support arguments or claims.

2. Do not intentionally use misleading or illogical reasoning.

3. Do not oversimplify complex issues, positions, or situations into polar views or choices.

4. Do not artificially link ideas or arguments to emotional appeals or claims.

5. Do not use language that is confusing or misleading to an audience.

6. Do not attack the personal character of opponents.

7. Do not use sexist or racist language or appeals.

8. Do not make false or misleading comparisons.

9. Do not offer quotations from testimonies of others out of context or in such a way as to distort original intent.

10. Avoid offensive appeals or materials.

11. Utilize the most timely and accurate information available in presentations.

12. Clearly distinguish among assumptions, opinions, and facts.

Medium Considerations

1. Do not use "subliminal perception" or other techniques that convey information or views without the full awareness of the audience.

2. Do not use visual devices, effects, or techniques that distort information or deceive the audience (for example, exaggerated camera angles, lighting, etc.).

3. Do not use sound effects or devices that distort or deceive the audience (for example, the use of compressed speech, background music, etc.).

4. Do not use visual, symbolic artifacts such as flags, children, or animals that generate emotional support or divert attention away from the issue or evidence presented.

5. The technology of or the access to the medium should not be the determining factor of influence, information, or message understanding.

Receiver Considerations

1. Be open to dissent and the opinions of others.

2. Listen critically in order to analyze, synthesize, and properly interpret and evaluate ideas or arguments presented.

3. Be prepared to provide a response or feedback to the ideas or arguments presented.

4. Do not be defensive or ego-involved in responses.

5. Do not judge an argument or position based on the speaker's race, religion, sex, or cultural heritage.

6. Be honest in responses.

Ethical Values of Communicators

Ethical persuasive discourse is essentially identical to all other ethical communication. The following values are characteristics of an ethical communicator.

1. Honesty—individuals are truthful, open, sincere, and objective
2. Integrity—individuals are principled with a sense of values and willing to take a stand
3. Caring—individuals are empathetic and concerned about the feelings and circumstances of others
4. Respect—individuals believe in the dignity and value of all humans
5. Fairness—individuals are committed to the expression of diversity of opinion and equal justice for everyone—even if expressed opinions are radically different
6. Democracy—individuals advocate the values of liberty, equality, and the process of open debate and discussion of ideas and issues
7. Responsibility or accountability—Individuals are willing to be responsible for actions and ideas advocated
8. Civic virtue—individuals are committed to public service and the exercise of responsible citizenship
9. Competence—individuals are knowledgeable, intelligent, and capable of performing or completing tasks as claimed
10. Reliability—individuals are dependable, consistent, and loyal

Much of the information in this textbook is directed to an audience with fairly similar worldviews. Today, the idea of community has expanded on some levels to global proportions. This means the Western worldview encounters Eastern beliefs or third-world philosophies. The anger and frustration of Middle Eastern Islamic nations against the United States, as reflected in the extreme attack on the World Trade Center in New York on September 11, 2001, is a case in point. Is there a generic ethical code that allows people of diverse backgrounds to communicate ethically?

Joseph Juhasz and Lester Shepard call for "people of goodwill everywhere to agree on a universal basis for moral conduct."[23] Developments in information technology, communication, and travel have reduced distances. To preserve world peace and continued prosperity, there is a need for globally accepted ethical norms. Seven key values are summarized below.

1. Benevolence—goodwill or good intention, cooperation, peace, loyalty, solidarity, compassion, caring, and humility; readiness to help instead of harm, to sympathize rather than being judgmental, and to respect others
2. Equality—avoidance of domination and oppression. Exercising the least possible force, constraint, violence, threat, or power over the other. Refraining from the exploitation of perceived weakness, such as infirmity, old age, vulnerability, ignorance, gullibility, or any handicap. Absence of racial, ethnic, religious, sexual, class, and cultural prejudice as well as of social exclusion

3. Truthfulness—lies, pretense, and fraud work against the creation of a better world; honesty and truth are the building blocks for a better future

4. Equity—implying social justice; people must be provided with the basic necessities of life; abject poverty makes moral conduct almost impossible; information should be free; everyone with a desire to learn must be guaranteed the opportunity for an education to her/his fullest potential

5. Environmental protection—protect the environment to the extent possible given a society's needs for the basic necessities of life

6. Freedom—everyone should enjoy freedom of action as long as it doesn't interfere with the freedom of others

7. Treat others as you wish that others treat you—the golden rule is unequaled in succinctly summing up the right moral conduct; although one can cite exceptions to its validity on technical grounds, the point is that any person of adequate intelligence can grasp its intent and understand its applicability in concrete cases

AREAS OF SPECIAL CONCERN
▲

As we have seen, ethical communication behaviors are critical for interpersonal relationships and individuals. They are also essential elements of any professional endeavor. In addition, some professions or communication industries tend to generate special ethical concerns. These include media and new technologies, news journalism, and politics. While the "sins" are easy to describe and illustrate, our purpose here is to illustrate general concerns and to suggest some actions.

Media and New Technologies

Computers, fiber optics, and satellites have introduced an era of high-speed communication that greatly impacts the creation, collection, and dissemination of information. Our laws and social expectations have not kept up with the rapid changes in communication technologies. The Internet is becoming one of the defining scientific and social innovations of the twenty first-century. The "information superhighway," as labeled by politicians and the media, has the ability to link people and resources in a way that was never previously possible. Users can share data of all types, communicate messages, discuss topics, and connect to computer systems all over the world. By 2002, in the United States alone, well over 200 million people had Web access either from work or home.[24] The potential of the Internet as a tool for retrieving information is almost limitless. As a result of the freedom of expression allowed on this unique network, the possibilities for learning and enrichment are endless. But with a network so large (and a territory so uncharted), there is great concern about the quality of material readily available to anyone accessing the Web.

The Internet is unique; every individual connected to it defines his or her corner of cyberspace. There is no Internet, Inc., no board of directors, no president, and very few rules, if any. Each person logging on to the system is generally given access through a service provider—a large company or organization that has paid to install and maintain a high-speed Internet connection and either give or sell that access to users. Whether the service provider is a commercial on-line service such as CompuServe or Prodigy, or an organization such as General Electric, or a university, the service provider's obligation usually ends when its customer opens a connection. From that point, it is up to each user to seek out information, assess its accuracy, and decide whether to transfer it to the user's own computer.

Misrepresentation and outright lying are rather commonplace on the Web. Individuals in discussion groups who seek on-line conversations and computer friendships may encounter others who lie about their age, sex, looks, income, or occupation. There is special concern for child and teenage safety on the Internet. Some of the risks include exposure to inappropriate material, emotional vulnerability from sharing personal information with strangers, or harassment from demeaning or belligerent e-mail or bulletin board messages. With the increased placement of Internet connections in public schools, educators are faced with numerous issues and concerns. Imagine, for example, a middle-school student researching a paper on the history and construction of the White House. A simple query to "Whitehouse.com" leads to a pornographic site whose page contains full nudity and proclaims, "We are the Worldwide Leader in Adult and Political Entertainment."

Jan Alexander and Marsha Tate, research librarians, suggest a five-point checklist for Web site credibility:

1. Authority—who is responsible for creating the information?
2. Accuracy—are sources of information identified; can they be checked easily?
3. Objectivity—is information, news, advertising, or opinion clearly identified and separated?
4. Currency—is it clear how often the files are updated?
5. Coverage—does it seem as if the subject is adequately discussed?[25]

Kevin Hill and John Hughes argue that the Internet has the potential to change the flow of political information and thus revolutionize the process of political communication.[26] Pre-Internet, the flow of political information was primarily one way from the media to the public. The Internet now allows individuals to become their own broadcasters, providing unfiltered information not shared by the more mainstream media channels. They found that Internet activists tend to identify themselves as Democrats, oppose government regulations of personal activities, and are more politically active and knowledgeable than the general population. However, Internet activists tend to vote between the political parties in equal numbers but are more anti-government than the rest of society.[27]

Most service providers and user organizations have created guidelines for acceptable Internet usage. Likewise, many public schools have found it necessary to develop both student and parental agreements outlining the rules and risks of Internet usage.

In the workplace, questions of privacy and ownership of communication are becoming the subject of policy formation. Defining what is private in the workplace is becoming more difficult and complex. Is computer e-mail private and confidential? Does your host system or organization keep records of your destinations on the Internet? Do computer files on office machines belong to you or to your organization? Employers are monitoring phone calls, reading e-mail, installing hidden video cameras, conducting routine background checks, and obtaining a wide range of personal and medical information that may influence performance or promotion evaluations. Issues of privacy have become especially acute as technological advances change the nature of work, communication, and supervisory functions in the workplace.

Of course, there are other general privacy issue concerns related to the Web. Computers record every message and purchase made through a network. Buying products online provides a customer profile of purchasing behavior. Organizations and firms imbed *cookies* on computers. A cookie is information that a Web server puts on your hard drive that remembers specific details of how you use the Web, such as site visits, frequency of visits, banner ads displayed, etc. Over time, the provider can customize the site in terms of your likes and preferences, largely without your knowledge or awareness.

Another example of technology's impact on communication is the increasing use of photo manipulation, which is now virtually impossible to detect. Some manipulations may seem harmless and even humorous. *Spy* magazine superimposed First Lady Hillary Clinton's face on a model dressed in leather, holding a whip. *TV Guide*, in doing a cover story on Oprah Winfrey, superimposed Oprah's face on the body of Ann-Margaret. These examples may be in bad taste or disrespectful, but are they dishonest? Consider *National Geographic* publishing a picture of the pyramids of Giza with one moved closer to another for a "tighter shot composition," or the removal of a soft-drink can from the photo of a Pulitzer prize-winning photographer. A quick search by Google reveals some 198,000 companies offering services for photo manipulation or photo illustration. Some editors and publishers argue that manipulated photos or videos are a disservice to history. People do not have the right to alter what is true and actual. Others argue that manipulated photos do not convey accurate information and thus, by definition, distort reality. Such photos are simply false and misleading. At the very least, scholars and observers contend that all manipulated photographs should carry proper disclosure and explanation.[28]

Some examples of outright distortion are obvious. Others are more subtle. The arrest of O. J. Simpson for the murder of his wife and an acquaintance became a fast-breaking news story in 1994. The mug shot of Simpson became the cover photo for both *Time* and *Newsweek* magazines. However, the photo used by *Time* was a darkened image of Simpson that led to a storm of controversy. The differences between the two magazine covers was vivid. Many African American journalists described *Time* magazine's image as racist, making Simpson look more sinister, and thus guilty. *Time* magazine denied any racial implication or imputation of guilt associated with the cover photo. While they used the technique of "photo-illustration" in creating the cover, the managing editor argued that

> photojournalism has never been able to claim the transparent neutrality attributed to it. Photographers choose angles and editors choose pictures to make points. . . . And every major news outlet routinely crops and retouches photos

to eliminate minor, extraneous elements, so long as the essential meaning of the picture is left intact. Our critics felt that Matt Mahurin's work changed the picture fundamentally; I felt it lifted a common police mug shot to the level of art, with no sacrifice to truth.[29]

There is an international movement by photojournalists to develop a code of conduct relevant to manipulated or enhanced photos used in news stories. Many think that no journalist should knowingly cause or allow the publication or broadcast of a photograph that has been manipulated unless that photograph is clearly labeled as such. Manipulation does not include normal dodging, burning, color balancing, spotting, contrast adjustment, cropping and obvious masking for legal or safety reasons. Unacceptable photographic or video imagery manipulation techniques would include repositioning an element in an image; changing the size, shape or physical appearance of an element; merging two or more visual elements into one; adding an element to an image; changing spatial relationships or colors in an image; or removing a visual element from the image.

Some of the problems associated with technology may be regulated. However, as is the case with most questions of ethics, they become issues of human judgment. As we enter the twenty-first century, ethical implications of the use of technology will fuel public debate.

News Journalism

There is a growing concern about the practice of broadcast journalism in the United States. Criticisms of the press range from allegations of distortion to outright lying. Generally, the public thinks that the press has become too powerful, too negative, and too biased in its news coverage. In fact, 52 percent of Americans "don't trust" journalists. In addition, just 22 percent think journalists have "high ethical standards."[30]

Davis and Owen contend that "the news media's populist bent and democratizing influence are more accidental than deliberate, more elusive than real. While there is a potential for news media to facilitate democratic discourse and to foster participant norms, there is no guiding principle that is leading toward these goals."[31]

Much of the criticism of contemporary journalism focuses on the coverage of politics and political campaigns. According to Larry Sabato, "It has become a spectacle without equal in modern American politics: the news media, print and broadcast, go after a wounded politician like sharks in a feeding frenzy. The wounds may have been self-inflicted, and the politician may richly deserve his or her fate, but the journalists now take center stage in the process, creating the news as much as reporting it, changing both the shape of election-year politics and the contours of government."[32]

A review of the plethora of books about television news reveals four major areas of concern. First, there is concern about how the media cover people, places, and events. Some argue that the coverage is largely irrelevant to the average citizen. Journalists tend to ask questions for themselves rather than questions that reflect the interests of citizens. For example, during the 2000 presidential primary, Democratic Senator Bill Bradley focused on his initiatives in health care and education. The media, however, focused on his personality and personal health issues.[33]

Figure 12.2 National Press Photographers Association, Inc. Code of Ethics[34]

The National Press Photographers Association, a professional society dedicated to the advancement of photojournalism, acknowledges concern and respect for the public's natural-law right to freedom in searching for the truth and the right to be informed truthfully and completely about public events and the world in which we live.

We believe that no report can be complete if it is not possible to enhance and clarify the meaning of words. We believe that pictures, whether used to depict news events as they actually happen, illustrate news that has happened or to help explain anything of public interest, are an indispensable means of keeping people accurately informed; that they help all people, young and old, to better understand any subject in the public domain.

Believing the foregoing we recognize and acknowledge that photojournalists should at all times maintain the highest standards of ethical conduct in serving the public interest. To that end the National Press Photographers Association sets forth the following Code of Ethics which is subscribed to by all of its members:

1. The practice of photojournalism, both as a science and art, is worthy of the very best thought and effort of those who enter into it as a profession.

2. Photojournalism affords an opportunity to serve the public that is equaled by few other vocations and all members of the profession should strive by example and influence to maintain high standards of ethical conduct free of mercenary considerations of any kind.

3. It is the individual responsibility of every photojournalist at all times to strive for pictures that report truthfully, honestly, and objectively.

4. As journalists, we believe that credibility is our greatest asset. In documentary photojournalism, it is wrong to alter the content of a photograph in any way (electronically or in the darkroom) that deceives the public. We believe the guidelines for fair and accurate reporting should be the criteria for judging what may be done electronically to a photograph.

5. Business promotion in its many forms is essential, but untrue statements of any nature are not worthy of a professional photojournalist and we condemn any such practice.

6. It is our duty to encourage and assist all members of our profession, individually and collectively, so that the quality of photojournalism may constantly be raised to higher standards.

7. It is the duty of every photojournalist to work to preserve all freedom-of-the-press rights recognized by law and to work to protect and expand freedom-of-access to all sources of news and visual information.

8. Our standards of business dealings, ambitions, and relations shall have in them a note of sympathy for our common humanity and shall always require us to take into consideration our highest duties as members of society. In every situation in our business life, in every responsibility that comes before us, our chief thought shall be to fulfill that responsibility and discharge that duty so that when each of us is finished we shall have endeavored to lift the level of human ideals and achievement higher than we found it.

9. No Code of Ethics can prejudge every situation, thus common sense and good judgment are required in applying ethical principles.

James Fallows believes that these problems are the result of journalists moving away from their central values. In essence, "mainstream journalism has fallen into the habit of portraying public life in America as a race to the bottom, in which one group of conniving, insincere politicians ceaselessly tries to outmaneuver another."[35]

Tabloid journalism has become the mainstay of news today because of its ability to entertain the audience. "The tabloid reporting style is designed to heighten readers and viewers' sensory experience with the news. The details of stories are presented in graphic form. Tabloid news is written in dramatic, engaging, and readable prose presented in short paragraphs and set off with attention-grabbling headlines and visual accompaniments. TV tabloids feature quick cuts between plots and subplots, highlighting conflict and crisis."[36] As former anchor and journalist for ABC News David Brinkley acknowledged, "the one function that TV news performs very well is that when there is no news we give it to you with the same emphasis as if there were news."[37] In the last five days of the 2000 presidential campaign, news about Bush's drunk-driving conviction generated twice the number of stories on his background and character than during the week of the Republican convention.[38]

The growing trend of checkbook journalism (paying sources for exclusive interviews) has become so widespread that even more traditional news outlets are forced to make indirect payments to sources in the form of consultant fees, travel and entertainment expenses, etc. Such practices are the result of efforts to increase the entertainment and dramatic value of a story, but they raise questions of conflicts of interests, source integrity, and motivation.[39]

The second major area of concern by media critics is the negativity of the press, which has contributed to the public becoming alienated from the political process. Increasingly since the 1970s, journalists have added their own more negative spin and interpretation of events and issues. In 1996, for example, journalists got six times more airtime than the candidates they were covering. The dominant news value in campaign stories is conflict, with less focus on issues.

This negative, anti-political bias of the press is an alarming historical trend. A historical analysis of media coverage by Rod Hart reveals that "the media are considerably more negative than politicians and those differences have not abated during the last fifty years."[40] A study by Thomas Patterson shows that "candidates of the 1960s got more favorable coverage than those of the 1970s, who in turn received more positive coverage than those of the 1980s."[41] The overall change is dramatic. Of all the evaluative references to Kennedy and Nixon in 1960, 75 percent were positive. Network news portrayal of recent presidential campaigns reveal an alarming trend toward negative coverage. During the 1992 presidential campaign, more than 80 percent of the network news stories on the Democratic Party were negative as well as 87 percent of all references to the Republican Party.[42] During the 1996 campaign, 53 percent of television news stories about Bill Clinton and 59 percent of stories about Bob Dole were negative.[43] This trend of negative coverage has occurred in news magazines as well. Thus, for Patterson, "there can be no doubt that the change in the tone of election coverage has contributed to the decline in the public's confidence in those who seek the presidency."[44]

Third, much of the criticism of contemporary journalism focuses on the coverage of politics and political campaigns. Joseph Cappella and Kathleen Jamieson argue that the contemporary journalistic culture and its focus on strategy, conflict, and motives encourage public cynicism.[45] Specifically, they claim that voters exposed to news framed in terms of campaign strategy report higher levels of cynicism than those who saw it framed in the more traditional problem-solution story formats.[46] Campaign strategy coverage is comprised of several characteristics: winning and losing are the central concerns; the language of war, games, and competition dominates; stories with performers, critics, and audience hold attention; performance, style, and perception of the candidate are central features; and there is heavy reliance on polls.[47] During the 2000 primary season, only 13 percent of news stories focused on issues while 80 percent focused on campaign strategies, tactics, and projected winners or losers.[48]

For Cappella and Jamieson, strategic coverage of campaigns and government is problematic, inviting "the attribution of cynical motives to political actors in campaigns and public policy debates, not because voters are distanced from the process but precisely because they are drawn into it and, through a rational analysis of the politicians whose motives they have come to know, reject the actors and ultimately the process."[49] The result is a "spiral of cynicism" in which "reporters and politicians justify their own cynical discourse by saying that it is required by the other. By producing the predicted discourse, each reinforces the assumption the other brought to the exchange."[50]

Richard Davis and Diana Owen express the fourth concern about the media: the rise of an elite corps of "celebrity journalists" that increasingly become integral parts of news stories and events.[51] They enjoy celebrity status in terms of pay, perks, fan clubs, and huge speaker fees; they have their own "star system" and compete for airtime. With this trend is also the rise of interpretive content of news. Each story has a slant and has become shorter in order to accommodate more segments for viewer interest. In addition, there are a growing number of individuals who move from political jobs into the newsroom. These partisan pundits "masquerade as reporters on newscasts and talk shows."[52] There is no expectation or pretense of objectivity or independence. Some "celebrity" journalists appear in movies as well as in product commercials. How are we expected to know what is real and who to believe?

Thomas Patterson advises that journalistic values and political values are at odds with one another, which results in a news agenda that misrepresents what is at stake when voters choose among candidates. Journalistic values introduce an element of random partisanship into campaigns, which works to the advantage of one side or the other. Election news, rather than serving to bring candidates and voters together, drives a wedge between them.[53]

> The problem is that the press is not a political institution. Its business is news and the values of news are not those of politics. Election news carries scenes of action, not commentary on the values reflected in those scenes. Election news emphasizes what is controversial about events of the previous twenty-four hours rather than what is stable and enduring. The coverage is framed within the context of a competitive game rather than being concerned with basic issues of policy and leadership. It projects images that fit story lines rather than political lines. Election news highlights what is unappetizing about politics rather than providing a well-rounded picture of the political scene."[54]

Much has been written about the media and media ethics. We want to emphasize that broadcast news is a human communication endeavor. "News" is selected, created, and communicated by people. News is much more than just facts. It is a story, an argument, a process of the "symbolic creation of reality," as explained in chapter 2. News stories influence how readers and viewers perceive reality. As observed by Kathleen Jamieson and Karlyn Campbell, "news is gathered, written, edited, produced, and disseminated by human beings who are part of organizations and who have beliefs and values. . . . These beliefs, values, functions, and interests are bound to influence the messages these networks publish and broadcast."[55]

As television viewers, we need to recognize that news broadcasts contain very persuasive messages. News and the truth are not the same thing. News reporting is just one version of the facts—a created sequence. Some aspects are magnified; others are downplayed. Likewise, the notion of objectivity does not address the issue of truth. Rather, it simply acknowledges the attempt to present both sides or perspectives of an issue. Objectivity is a worthwhile, but impossible, goal to imple-

---

Figure 12.3

What kind of news drives prime-time newsmagazines? The Project for Excellence in Journalism studied five shows on the three major networks during six weeks in 1998 and analyzed them by subject. Four traditional hard news topics are listed first, then three softer feature areas, and then 11 other general news subjects.

	20/20 (ABC)	48 Hours (CBS)	60 Minutes (CBS)	PrimeTIME Live (ABC)	Dateline (NBC)
Government	0%	0%	0%	0%	1.4%
Military/Nat'l Sec.	0	0	5.6	0	0
Foreign Affairs	3.3	0	0	13.3	0
Law/Justice	6.7	10.0	16.7	0	12.3
Entertainment/Celeb.	3.3	5.0	5.6	13.3	5.5
Human Interest	10.0	45.0	0	26.7	4.1
Personality/Profile	3.3	5.0	22.2	0	19.2
Consumer Business	16.7	0	5.6	13.3	15.1
Health/Medicine	26.7	0	5.6	0	12.3
Crime	10.0	5.0	11.1	26.7	13.7
Education	0	0	5.6	0	0
Social Welfare	10.0	0	5.6	0	4.1
Economy	0	0	0	0	0
Science/Technology	0	25.0	5.6	6.7	1.4
Religion	6.7	5.0	5.6	0	1.4
Arts	0	0	5.6	0	0
Weather/Disaster	0	0	0	0	9.6
Sports	3.3	0	0	0	0
TOTAL	**100**	**100**	**100**	**100**	**100**

Source: Project for Excellence in Journalism and the Medill News Service Washington Bureau

ment. We are all shaped by our own beliefs, attitudes, and values. There are some reasonable factors to consider. First is story selection—selecting stories that consciously or subconsciously fit your own way of thinking. Second is source selection—selecting those who will mirror opinions that agree with you or your preferred position. Third is fact selection and arrangement—reporting both sides in a balanced manner. Fourth is language selection—selecting language devoid of bias or emotion. Finally, the factors of timing and context are important—providing the proper context for story, facts, and opinions.

Terrorism presents some very special challenges in terms of media coverage, sources, and balance. Media can be used by terrorists, but just how patriotic should broadcasters be? Should media outlets avoid participating in negotiations with terrorist groups? Should they reveal secret military information?

Some of the persuasive dimensions of the news include technology (camera angles, editing, special effects), the newsgathering process (deadlines, reliability and truthfulness of sources), story structure (drama, conflict, action, novel), interpretation (personal bias, ideological orientations), and social action (agenda setting, initiating public debate).

Neil Postman offers several recommendations when viewing news programming:[56]

1. In encountering a news show, you must come up with a firm idea of what is important—one needs some basis, knowledge, or criteria for evaluating the significance of "news." In order not to be manipulated by news, viewers need to have some concrete idea of what is significant and of value in their lives.

2. In preparing to watch a TV news show, keep in mind that it is called a "show"—the priority of local stations and networks is not citizen education. News is a business endeavor to garner viewers for commercial purposes. This consideration helps us to remember that news is portrayed in dramatic and stylistic ways.

3. Never underestimate the power of commercials—as presented in chapter 10, commercials are planned, purposeful attempts of persuasion.

4. Learn something about the economic and political interests of those who run TV stations.

5. Pay special attention to the language of newscasts—language frames the pictures, creates the reality toward which we act. Language reflects our view of issues, places, events, and the world.

6. Reduce by at least one-third the amount of TV news you watch—there is a tremendous amount of redundancy in news, and less than half of the stories are really "news" rather than stories chosen for their entertainment value.

7. Reduce by one-third the number of opinions you feel obligated to have—not all views are equally correct or deserve your attention. One needs to be reflective and base attitudes and beliefs on experience and reasonable factors.

8. Do whatever you can to get schools interested in teaching children how to watch a TV news show.

Without question, there are special and unique ethical considerations for the press: good news versus bad news, issues of privacy and objectivity, degree of explicitness of video footage, use of hidden cameras and recorders, use of unnamed sources, and "off-the-record" versus "on-the-record," to name only a few. While our intent is not to provide a laundry list of ethical journalistic rules and practices, we do suggest that the practice of journalism should reflect the social values of our nation. Such values include honesty, justice, humaneness, social responsibility, stewardship, and freedom.

Politics and Political Communication

Historically, there has always been great skepticism about the practice of politics and, above all, about politicians. In many public opinion polls, people find that politicians are more dishonest than car salespeople and attorneys. Part of the problem is the continual string of shocking behavior by many politicians: the Watergate scandal during the Nixon administration and the allegations of sexual misconduct in office by former Senator Gary Hart and Bill Clinton are a few of the events that generated concern among voters. Some ethical dilemmas arise because of the difference between campaigning and governing. George H. Bush's reversal of his pledge not to raise taxes in 1992 was portrayed as an act of willful deception and outright lying, not as an act of leadership and conscience. Some scholars attribute his reversal as a major reason for his defeat in 1996. Other concerns are raised about the actual process of getting elected. Many citizens assume that politicians will say or do almost anything to get elected. For many, the critical question becomes whether ethical politics is possible or whether the phrase is an oxymoron.

NON SEQUITUR

To address campaign ethics is a daunting task for several reasons. First, political campaigns are mediated events. Few Americans experience campaigns firsthand. We experience campaigns, the candidates, and the issues through media portrayals. In the United States, television has become the primary medium for political campaigning. To complicate matters more, how we form political attitudes and candidate images of competence, leadership, and character depends largely upon the mediums viewed and messages attended. Seldom does one message determine preference. In some cases, years of media exposure condition specific responses during campaigns. Given the complexity of the media's role in electoral politics, it is difficult to trace all the strands of campaign ethics.

Second, there are many players involved in campaigns: candidates, consultants, reporters, editors, etc. There are certainly no uniform considerations of ethics among all the players. However, each has some role in determining how the candidate is portrayed or presents him- or herself and in the strategy of a campaign.

Third, there are multiple media and candidate activities involved in campaigns, from bumper stickers to political advertising, to two-minute news packages, to the talking-head political shows, to the constantly increasing number of candidate debates. The ethical concerns or decisions lie not in the "machinery" of campaigns but in the people who use the media, strategies, and tactics. While true, this rationale is too simplistic and only part of the story. Of course, intentionality is a variable of ethics, but so is capability or access. For example, television is usually targeted as the source of numerous social and political ills: reduced voter turnout, decline of political parties, decline of political participation, reduction of issue discussion to sound bites, automatic reelection of incumbents, increased use of symbolic rather than problem-solving strategies of leadership, and increase of general public distrust and cynicism, to name only a few. Are these concerns the results of the medium itself, the content, access, control, or socialization (i.e., how we *use* a medium)?

Fourth, there really is no single set of standards, criteria, or behavior that defines political campaign ethics, despite the proliferation of individual codes of ethics for professional groups. Everyone would pay lip service to the necessity to tell the truth in political ads. But do we need to tell the "whole truth and nothing but the truth?" While what is said may be true, what is *not* said could be more useful in voter decision making. To claim an opponent voted a certain way, it might be more informative to know whether the vote was in committee, on the floor, for a specific bill or for an amendment. Or consider the attack ad that claims an opponent cast the "deciding vote" on an issue that passed by one vote. Who is to say it was the deciding vote? Consider too journalism's distinction between "objectivity" and "fairness." In order to meet the standard, one simply needs to present both sides of an argument or issue, whether the dissenting voice is legitimate, logical, reasonable, representative or in any way valid. Does such reporting inform the citizenry?

In essence, the ethical concerns or issues associated with politics and political campaigns are no different than those of other areas of life. They revolve around a speaker, a message, and an advocated behavior (i.e., "vote for me"). Because campaigns result in granting an individual public trust and social power if elected, they lend themselves to special concerns and judgments.

Royce Hanson draws on the moral principles and metaphors of war to describe campaigning and democratic governance.[57] He views campaigns as surrogates for civil war where ballots are substituted for bullets. The vocabulary of a campaign is rich in the language of warfare (i.e., victory and defeat, attack and counterattack, strategy and tactics, rallying the troops, etc.). However, there are interesting differences of ethical considerations between war and democracy. For example, during war, ethical constraints are relaxed. It is not unethical to mislead the enemy, spy on them, withhold information from your own citizens and soldiers to protect strategic advantages. However, democracy demands ethical principles. Voters must have access to the information necessary to make informed decisions. Democracy condemns lying and secrecy as political and governing strategies. Misinformation is dangerous to informed choice.

In campaigns, "truth" is assumed to emerge from the competition between candidates. Hanson notes that unlike trials by jury, campaigns follow no rules of evidence. No one is under oath, everything is admissible and deniable. Under the rules of political engagement, we expect each candidate to present views and positions most favorable to his or her campaign and most damning to the opponent. Truth and collective wisdom emerge from the campaign process. From this perspective, a campaign is the means to governing, the implementation of the candidate's promises and fulfillment of constitutional duties. The duties include obligations to address issues of public concern truthfully.

Bruce Gronbeck developed a model to assess ethical issues of presidential campaigns.[58] He views campaigns as corporate rhetorical ventures in which it is becoming increasingly difficult to place blame on individuals. Gronbeck argues that in order to make ethical assessments, citizens reduce campaigns to comprehensible dramas where they examine the action (motives), people (character), and thought (competence as politicians) of the candidates. These dramas can be assessed from four moral vantage points: message makers, message consumers, the messages themselves, and situation expectations. In constructing a 3 × 4 matrix (see figure 12.4), Gronbeck generates 12 questions voters should ask in assessing the ethical dimensions of presidential candidates.

Figure 12.4   Questions to Guide Voters' Ethical Judgments in Presidential Campaigns

	Ethical Pivots		
Moral Vantages	Motives	Character	Competence
Message Makers	Are candidates' motives acceptable?	Are candidates' characterological styles acceptable?	Have candidates demonstrated political competence?
Message Consumers	What political motives do sets of voters find acceptable?	What characterological styles do sets of voters find acceptable?	What measures of political competence are used by particular sets of voters?
Messages	Are candidates' motives expressed in acceptable ways?	Are candidates' characterological styles depicted in acceptable ways?	Are candidates illustrating their political competence in messages and in responses to opponents' messages?
Situations	What motives are acceptable in various situations?	What characterological styles are expected in various situations?	Are candidates handling various political situations competently?

Of course, all of our knowledge about campaigns is not firsthand. We form judgments based on the bits and pieces of information we glean from friends and from the media. For Gronbeck,

> ethical assessment is a complex negotiatory process, whereby the causes and effects, rights and wrongs that politicians, the press, and other public commentators isolate and assess are framed in sociodramas that each of us views and judges in terms of our individual experiences.[59]

Political ads are the primary source of campaign information for the vast majority of voters. Research indicates that political ads educate viewers about issues, influence voter perceptions about candidates, and especially influence late-deciding or undecided voters.[60] In addition, scholars have found that attack or negative political ads influence voters because they are more compelling, more memorable, and more believable than more neutral ads.[61]

Lynda Kaid provides one of the most comprehensive analyses of some of the ethical concerns related to political advertising.[62] She expresses concern about the use of ads as a means of "buying access to voters." This becomes an increasing concern with corporate or organizational issue and advocacy advertising. Without question, the greatest expense of most campaigns is advertising. It is a simple fact that those with abundant resources are most able to get their message out to the general public. If, as some argue, that money equates with free speech, then some politicians and organizations have more "free" speech than others.

Another enduring criticism of political advertising is the dependence upon emotion and strong visuals to convey meaning rather than a more rational, logical discussion of issues. In essence, political spots tend to detract from rational decision making by concentrating on images instead of issues, resulting in emotional, not logical, vote choices.

Another criticism is that political spots tend to oversimplify issues, thus debasing and even trivializing the electoral process. It is nearly impossible to fully explain the complexity of most issues in 30 or 60 seconds. As a result, most ads are superficial, containing half-truths and some distortion of information.

A growing concern among scholars is the use of media manipulation to enhance or even alter reality. The most common uses of television technology include editing techniques, special effects, visual imagery or dramatizations, and computerized alteration techniques. Examples of each have become commonplace. In some cases, the "morphing" technique transforms objects or candidates (such as the Pinocchio effect—elongating an opponent's nose to imply lack of truthfulness). In other cases, photo manipulation is used. In the 1996 U.S. Senatorial Campaign in Virginia, incumbent John Warner aired an ad that placed the face of his opponent in a group shot of "liberals" including Edward Kennedy.

Scholars have recently investigated the role and impact of attack or negative ads. As already mentioned, they have found that attack or negative political ads influence voters because they are more compelling, more memorable, and more believable than positive ads.[63] However, Stephen Ansolabehere and Shanto Iyengar (1995) find that the heavy reliance upon negative political ads result in lower voter turnout and general public cynicism. "Attack advertisements resonate with the popular beliefs that government fails, that elected officials are out of touch and quite corrupt, and that voting is a hollow act. The end result: lower turnout and lower trust in government, regardless of which party rules."[64]

A final concern is the failure to disclose information. Even when the sources of allegations are disclosed, the references are on the screen for just a matter of seconds and often out of context. In addition to the failure to disclose the source of communication, other common concerns include the lack of providing adequate or complete information and the ambiguity and/or inconsistency of messages. Visual impressions may lead viewers to "see what they want to see."

While there may be many ethical issues and concerns about political campaigns and communication, we believe strongly that democratic life carries responsibilities for audiences and citizens as well as for politicians. The polity must share the praise or blame that it heaps on its leaders. Their failures are, in many ways, our failures. Becoming an informed, educated, and critical voter is your best safeguard against unethical political advertising.

Public Discourse

Finally, it is important for us to give some consideration to the essential role of ethical public discourse. According to Celeste Condit, public morality is "constructed by collectivities through their public discourse in a process of reflexive reproduction that utilizes the capacity of discourse simultaneously to create, extend, and apply moral concepts."[65] The public and the individual interact to produce morality. More specifically, "it is through the arguments of individuals about enactment of particular moral rulings that the collective moral code is built."[66] The process of constructing public morality "fulfills the human urge for goodness, creativity, and perfection."[67]

Ronald Collins and David Skover fear the "death of discourse" in America. They point to the irony of "discourse dying in America, yet everywhere free speech thrives."[68] For them, discourse is interaction characterized by reason, by method, and with purpose. It is not trivial talk. Discourse is not mere expression for expression's sake; rather, as in the Aristotelian sense, it is in the service of the public good. It is about values, policies, and national character.

We need to ask ourselves if we engage in healthy political discourse—and if we do, to what degree? Collins and Skover distinguish the principles of political discourse characterized by rational decision making, civic participation, meaningful dissent, and self-realization from contemporary political speech characterized by entertainment, passivity, pleasure, and self-gratification. For them, we are on the border of equating "amusement with enlightenment, fantasy with fact, and the base with the elevated."[69] A candy bar is food, but is it nutritional? How much junk food do we consume? How much junk food can we ingest before the body becomes sick? We have plenty of food, but we are starving. Similarly, how much of our so-called political discussion is actually trivial talk? In how much trivial discourse can we participate before we as a nation become critically naive and uninformed?

One should note that the concern is not about *persuasive* oratory, the genuine engagement of ideas. As Keith Felton argues, there is power in purposive oratory. When poetic in its reach, when deservedly acclaimed, oratory outlives the moment of utterance, and enters a universal lexicon of expression to become a permanently recorded part of the march of ideas. The influence of language upon history is ineluctable . . . (it) buoys civilization over its perennial perils.[70]

We agree with Kathleen Jamieson when she posits that good political persuasion is a

discourse that argues rather than asserts, seeks the common rather than private good, relates a candidate's past to his or her promises and those to governance, grants the goodwill of all parties to the dialogue, and engages the issues raised by others while being engaged by them as well. It is a discourse that restores the genres of speeches, debates, press conferences, interviews, and ads to their distinct and distinctly useful roles in the campaign menu.[71]

SUMMARY
▲

Louis Day makes the case that all societies need a system of ethics for social stability. According to him, "ethics is the foundation of our advanced civilization, a cornerstone that provides some stability to society's moral expectations."[72] A system of ethics serves as a moral gatekeeper by identifying and ranking the norms and morals of a society. A system of ethics also helps societies resolve conflicts and establishes rules and laws for behavior. Finally, a system of ethics helps clarify competing values and new social dilemmas. The current debate over such issues as genetic engineering and assisted suicide are examples of new ethical and moral dilemmas confronting America.

Throughout this book, we have identified and explained various tools of persuasion. We have also attempted to note problems and abuses of the practice of persuasion. Like any instrument, the tools of persuasion can be used for good or bad purposes. In this chapter we explored ethical considerations of persuasion and summarized some of the specific rules of application. However, we believe that if there is a problem with ethics in the United States, it begins with each individual interaction. We cannot depend on teachers, politicians, the media, or religious leaders to correct the real or perceived problems of American ethics. The task is ours. Only as citizens can we alter or affect the quality of our society. As Ronald Arnett observes,

If we are to be concerned about ethical issues in communication and do not wish to place ourselves at the mercy of expert opinion, then argument, debate, and public discourse over what is and is not ethical must continue. If we are to be good choice makers, we must actively pursue opportunities to ask ethical questions about the process and the content of communication.[73]

Your study of persuasion may well be a significant factor in your ethical growth. Learning how to find good reasons to support your ideas, learning how to present your opinions so that an audience will listen, and learning to express yourself clearly and intelligently will help you become an active, contributing member of society. Ethics is not a separate subject for study; it is an integral part of each individual and every action. Likewise, persuasion is not an isolated topic; it occurs constantly. We are both receivers and creators of persuasion—just as we both experience and create ethical behavior.

Questions and Projects for Further Study

1. What values do you think your parents taught you? Friends? Teachers? Role models? How do they compare and contrast?

2. Select five magazine ads and analyze them according to the Advertising Code of American Business (http://www.theaapc.org/content/aboutus/codeofethics.asp). How do they conform to the specified standards?

3. Reflect upon the list of ethical values of communicators provided in the chapter. Do you think it is possible for someone always to reflect these values? Why or why not?

4. Share with the class your current or childhood heroes. What makes them special? What do you emulate in them?

5. Describe the main values of democracy. Give a concrete example of each and explain how ethical communication contributes to each value.

6. Videotape two evening news broadcasts for the same day. Compare the broadcasts: order of story topics, length of time of stories, visuals used, etc. Compare and contrast reports on the same topic or story. How are they similar? How are they different?

7. Should the media treat rape as any other crime, i.e., give names of victims and names of alleged rapists? Should newspapers report the cause of death in the obituaries if the cause is AIDS or suicide?

8. You interviewed three people for a position in your company. How much detail do you provide to those not selected for the position? What influenced your decision?

9. From your perspective, is it ever "ok" to lie? If so, under what circumstances? Is there a difference between lying about public and private matters? Personal or business matters?

10. If available through your instructor, view several political ads. Do they increase voter knowledge? Do they tell the "whole" truth? How would you go about verifying the facts and claims presented in the ads?

Additional Reading

Sissela Bok, *Lying: Moral Choice in Public and Private Life* (New York: Vintage Books, 1989).

Joseph Cappella and Kathleen Hall Jamieson, *Spiral of Cynicism: The Press and the Public Good* (New York: Oxford University Press, 1997).

Stephen Carter, *The Culture of Disbelief* (New York: Basic Books, 1993).

Robert E. Denton, Jr., ed., *Political Communication Ethics: An Oxymoron?* (Westport, CT: Praeger, 2000).

James Fallows, *Breaking the News: How the Media Undermine American Democracy* (New York: Vintage Books, 1997).

Roderick Hart, *Campaign Talk* (Princeton, NJ: University of Princeton Press, 2000).

Richard Johannesen, *Ethics in Human Communication,* 5th ed. (Prospect Heights, IL: Waveland Press, 2002).

George Lakoff, *Moral Politics* (Chicago: University of Chicago Press, 1996).

Len Marrella, *In Search of Ethics* (Sanford, FL: DC Press, 2001).

Thomas Patterson, *Out of Order* (New York: Vintage, 1993).

Philip Seib, *Campaigns and Conscience: The Ethics of Political Journalism* (Westport, CT: Praeger, 1994).

Notes

[1] James MacGregor Burns, "Transactional and Transforming Leadership," in *Leader's Companion: Insights in Leadership through the Ages,* ed. by J. Thomas Wren (New York: The Free Press, 1995), p. 101.

[2] Glenn C. Altschuler, "Battling the Cheats," *Education Life,* January 7, 2001.

[3] http://www.zogby.com

[4] Carolyn Kleiner and Mary Lord, "The Cheating Game," *U.S. News & World Report,* November 12, 1999.

[5] Eric Zorn, "Line on Sharing Music Is Drawn in Shades of Gray," *Chicago Tribune,* September 11, 2003, sec. 2, p. 1.

[6] James Jaksa and Michael Pritchard, *Communication Ethics: Methods of Analysis* (Belmont, CA: Wadsworth, 1994), p. 12.

[7] Immanuel Kant, *Fundamental Principles of the Metaphysics of Ethics* (1785), trans. T. K. Abbott.

[8] As quoted in Andrew G. Oldenquist, *Moral Philosophy* (Prospect Heights, IL: Waveland Press, 1978), pp. 16–17.

[9] Conrad Fink, *Media Ethics* (New York: McGraw-Hill, 1988), p. 8.

[10] Richard Johannesen, *Ethics in Human Communication,* 5th ed. (Prospect Heights, IL: Waveland Press, 2002), p. 2.

[11] For a detailed discussion of democratic values and communication, see Robert E. Denton, Jr., "The Primetime Presidency: The Ethics of Teledemocracy," in *Ethical Dimensions of Political Communication,* ed. by Robert E. Denton, Jr. (New York: Praeger, 1991), pp. 91–114.

[12] Dennis Thompson, *Political Ethics and Public Office* (Cambridge: Harvard University Press, 1987), p. 3.

[13] As quoted in John Merrill and Jack Odell, *Philosophy and Journalism* (New York: Longman Press, 1983), pp. 2, 95.

[14] Steven Carter, *The Culture of Disbelief* (New York: Anchor Books, 1993), p. 16.

[15] Sissela Bok, *Lying: Moral Choice in Public and Private Life* (New York: Vintage Books, 1989), p. 18.

[16] In Bok, p. 18.

[17] Louis Day, *Ethics in Media Communications: Cases and Controversies* (Belmont, CA: Wadsworth, 1991), pp. 11–13.

[18] Ronald Arnett, "The Status of Communication Ethics Scholarship in Speech Communication Journals from 1915 to 1985," in *Conversations on Communication Ethics,* ed. by Karen Joy Greenberg (Norwood, NJ: Ablex, 1991), pp. 55–72.

[19] Ibid., p. 60.

[20] http://www.theaapc.org/content/aboutus/codeofethics.asp. Numerous codes of ethics are available online. One source listing a number of codes is: http://www.iit.edu/departments/csep/PublicWWW/codes/codes.html. In addition, the Ethics Resource Center (http://www.ethics.org/) has a number of interesting articles and guidelines for developing codes.

[21] Bok, p. 68.

[22] Bok, p. 243.

[23] http://www.ethics1.org/united.html

[24] Paul Lester, *Visual Communication: Images with Messages,* 3rd ed. (Belmont, CA: Wadsworth/Thompson, 2003), p. 375.

[25] Ibid., p. 376.

[26] Kevin Hill and John Hughes, *Cyberpolitics* (Lanham, MD: Rowman & Littlefield, 1998).

[27] Ibid., p. 243.

[28] Visit http://graphicssoft.about.com/cs/digitalphotoethics/ for a number of articles on the ethics of photo manipulation.

[29] "To Our Readers," *Time*, July 4, 1994, p. 4.

[30] Provided by *The Polling Report, Inc.*, January 9, 1999.

[31] Richard Davis and Diana Owen, *New Media and American Politics* (New York: Oxford University Press, 1998), p. 243.

[32] Larry Sabato, *Feeding Frenzy* (New York: The Free Press, 1991), p. 1.

[33] Thomas Hollihan, *Uncivil Wars* (Boston: Bedford/St. Martin's Press, 2001), p. 77.

[34] http://www.nppa.org/ethics/default.htm. See also, APME Code of Ethics http://www.apme.com/about/code_ethics.shtml.

[35] James Fallows, *Breaking the News* (New York: Random House, Vintage edition, 1997), p. 7.

[36] Davis and Owen, p. 96.

[37] Ibid., p. 260.

[38] Marjorie Hershey, "The Campaign and the Media," in *The Election of 2000*, ed. by Gerald Pomper (New York: Chatham House Publishers, 2001), pp. 46–72.

[39] Davis and Owen, p. 253.

[40] Roderick Hart, *Campaign Talk* (Princeton, NJ: University of Princeton Press, 2000), p. 172.

[41] Thomas Patterson, *Out of Order* (New York: Vintage Books, 1993), p. 20.

[42] Ibid., p. 18.

[43] Diana Owen, "The Press Performance," in *Millennium: The Election of 1996*, ed. by Larry J. Sabato (Boston: Allyn and Bacon, 1997), p. 207.

[44] Patterson, p. 43.

[45] Joseph Cappella and Kathleen H. Jamieson, *The Spiral of Cynicism* (New York: Oxford University Press, 1997), p. 31.

[46] Ibid., p. 96.

[47] Ibid., p. 33.

[48] Hollihan, p. 89.

[49] Cappella and Jamieson, p. 37.

[50] Ibid., p. 237.

[51] Davis and Owen, pp. 189–209.

[52] Jim Squires, "The Impossibility of Fairness," *Media Studies Journal*, 1998, 12(2):66–71.

[53] Patterson, p. 52.

[54] Ibid., p. 208.

[55] Kathleen Jamieson and Karlyn K. Campbell, *The Interplay of Influence* (Belmont, CA: Wadsworth, 1992), p. 30.

[56] Neil Postman, *How to Watch TV News* (New York: Penguin Books, 1992), pp. 159–68.

[57] Royce Hanson, "Reading Lips and Biting Sound: The Ethics of Campaign Communications," in *Morality of the Mass Media*, ed. by Lawson Taitte (Dallas: University of Texas, 1993), pp. 157–206.

[58] Bruce E. Gronbeck, "Ethical Pivots and Moral Vantages in American Presidential Campaign Dramas," in *Ethical Dimension of Political Communication*, ed. by Robert E. Denton, Jr. (New York: 1991), pp. 49–68.

[59] Ibid., p. 66.

[60] Montague Kern, *30-Second Politics* (New York: Praeger, 1989), p. 5.

[61] Michael Pfau and Henry Kenski, *Attack Politics* (New York: Praeger,1990), p. xiii.

[62] Lynda Kaid, "Ethics and Political Advertising," in *Political Communication Ethics: An Oxymoron?*, ed. by Robert E. Denton, Jr. (Westport, CT: Praeger, 2000), pp. 146–77.

[63] Pfau and Kenski, p. xiii.

[64] Stephen Ansolabehere and Shanto Iyengar, *Going Negative* (New York: The Free Press, 1995), p. 148.

[65] Celeste Michelle Condit, "Crafting Virtue: The Rhetorical Construction of Public Morality," in *Contemporary Rhetorical Theory*, eds. John Lucaites, Celeste Condit, and Sally Caudill (New York: Guilford Press, 1999), p. 320.

[66] Ibid., p. 321.

[67] Ibid., p. 321.

[68] Ronald Collins and David Skover, *The Death of Discourse* (Boulder, CO: Westview), p. xix.

[69] Ibid., p. 203.

[70] Keith Felton, *Warriors' Words* (Westport, CT: Praeger, 1995), p. xv.

[71] Kathleen Hall Jamieson, *Dirty Politics* (New York: Oxford University Press, 1992), p. 11.

[72] Day, p. 19.

[73] Arnett, p. 69.

Constructing and Presenting Persuasive Messages

Overview

▲ Strategic Considerations of a Set Presentation
Know the Audience
Determine Your Objectives
Determine Your Thesis
Develop Main Points
Amplify and Support the Main Points
Write the Introduction
Prepare the Outline
Presenting the Message

▲ Strategic Considerations of Discursive Messages
When to Reveal the Thesis
Whether to Recognize Opposing Views
How to Use Persuasive Language

▲ Strategic Considerations for Nondiscursive Persuasion
The Visual Image
Honoring Gestalt Values
Set Modest Goals
Keep the Message Simple and Thematically Consistent
Use Effective Aural and Visual Analogues
Position Your Message as Entertainment or Information
Use a Sympathetic Figure or Key Icons
Frame the Discussion in the Imagery of Heroes, Villains, and Victims

---

> *From eloquence comes the surest and safest protection for one's friends.*[1]
> —CICERO

In this chapter we will explore the composition of persuasive messages. Even if you do not anticipate a career as a professional advocate, a look at how persuasive messages are put together provides an opportunity to see how specific strategies of persuasion produce concrete results. The process of constructing and designing arguments and appeals reveals a range of possible strategies. The first part of the chapter offers practical guidelines for preparing *discursive* messages: longer statements such as face-to-face presentations that depend primarily on verbal arguments rather than on visual images or symbols. The final section explores selected strategic considerations for organizing and presenting *nondiscursive* messages. These shorter forms of communication usually depend on symbols—pictures, icons, slogans, headlines—for much of their meaning. Typical nondiscursive messages include billboards, Web sites, and advertising. They are especially enticing because they invite a whole world of possibilities for visually enhanced persuasion.

STRATEGIC CONSIDERATIONS OF A SET PRESENTATION
▲

People often say that they are "writing a speech," but a speech on paper is only a guide for what really matters: the actual presentation to an audience. Just as the building produced by an architect is more than the blueprints, a speech is more than words on paper. A speech is a type of communication that takes place between listeners and speakers at a particular point in time. What we actually write is a *plan for that moment*.

In the sequence described below, there is more thinking than writing. The suggested steps produce a sentence outline that serves as a flexible guide to every key idea, appeal, and phrase you want to use. This process avoids the tedious task of writing down every word to be spoken but provides a sequence for locating the essential points of the message. The sentence outline allows enough freedom to adapt to unexpected situations and opportunities. As you read through these steps, it will also be apparent that this plan is a practical application of the logic of the good reasons approach discussed in chapter 4. Though our model here is a speech, abstracting *any* form of persuasive message in outline form is a useful way to see and to critically examine its structure and arguments.

Know the Audience

Persuading an audience is similar to a journey over unfamiliar terrain. Your route has to be adjusted to fit the landscape of existing attitudes. As we indicated in chapter 7, a fundamental requirement of communication is an understanding of the person or persons you wish to influence. It is admittedly difficult to be precise about the attitudes, values, and interests of groups. People are too complex to be reduced to simple stereotypes. But because persuasion involves "adjusting ideas to people and people to ideas,"[2] thorough preparation starts with questions about the audience.

- How will they respond to your point of view?
- Will they consider you a qualified advocate?
- What is the extent of their prior knowledge?
- Has anything happened recently that would affect the audience's interest and attitudes?
- What position have opinion leaders in the audience taken on the topic?
- What core values or attitudes will your own message challenge?
- Which existing audience values can be used as good reasons?

Questions like these will help you assess the audience to decide what you can hope to accomplish in the message.

Determine Your Objectives

After determining the makeup of your audience and their attitudes toward your message, you are in a position to set realistic goals about what you can achieve. In some cases you may want an audience to agree to cooperate: to give money, volunteer time, pass on a message to others, or buy a product. In other cases the goal may be more closely linked to a person's sense of self, as when a listener is urged to think or act differently about an entrenched or addictive behavior (i.e., drinking, gambling, aggressive driving). Don't settle for vague objectives such as "informing," or "increasing awareness." You have successfully found the objective for a message when you know *exactly* what you want from your contact with the audience. Here are some examples.

- To encourage a jury member to vote "not guilty"
- To sign up volunteers or pledges for a campus organization
- To have listeners vote for a straight ticket on election day
- To make a sale
- To discourage the purchase of products that your group is boycotting
- To flood legislators with letters in support of legislation
- To encourage changes in the eating, drinking, or smoking habits of friends
- To encourage an audience to respect the work of a controversial author, artist, or musician
- To win supporters for a different philosophy
- To encourage people to accept the merits of an unpopular position
- To remind people that the beliefs they already hold are worth keeping
- To move listeners incrementally closer to accepting an attitude they still reject

Some desired purposes are impossible to achieve in one attempt, such as a complete reversal of a group's opposition to a proposed law. Base your expectations on the fact that a single persuasive event will have limited impact. It is unlikely, for example, that a current member of the United States Senate could successfully convince most of her colleagues that they should press for an end to the long-standing economic boycott of Cuba. Even so, the hope that she might weaken support for the boycott in the Senate may not be out of the question. Good objectives consider what is realistically possible given the specific circumstances you are likely to encounter. Even though you probably will not state them to your audience, write down your objectives and keep them in mind.

Determine Your Thesis

To this point, your preparation has been largely concerned with defining the unique persuasive situation governed by your message, your audience, and what the audience knows about you. The next task is to draft the most important sentence of the whole message. Write the *thesis* that you want to communicate. Think of the thesis statement as the *primary conclusion of the message*, the statement to which everything else that is said is subordinate. It should be the one idea listeners recall weeks later.

Inexperienced communicators are tempted to skip the thesis-writing stage and begin preparing the rest of the message, or they may substitute a one- or two-word topic for a genuine thesis statement. Failure to establish one central idea in your planning can result in much wasted time and disorganization. Likewise, stating a general topic rather than a specific thesis falls short of providing the guidance necessary to prepare the rest of the message. For example, it is not enough to prepare a persuasive case centered on phrases such as "federal standards for truck emissions" or "gun control." Both topics are ripe for advocacy, but persuasive attempts on these issues should be constructed from more sharply defined declarative sentences. Consider the following thesis statements.

- The federal government should dramatically raise its minimum standards for light truck emissions.
- Federal law should require gun manufacturers to equip handguns with safety locks.
- Our state should close failing schools and provide full tuition vouchers to their students.
- Television networks neglect the needs and interests of older Americans.
- Credit card vendors should be banned from university retail areas.
- The NCAA does not adequately protect student athletes from exploitative athletic programs.

Although no two people will develop identical messages from the same thesis statement, the construction of a clear thesis is essential to trigger the mental processes necessary for the next stage—constructing the main points that are the framework for the body of the message.

Develop Main Points

After determining your thesis, the next step is to locate the good reasons that justify the thesis. As we noted in chapter 4, reasons are good when they make sense to you and are likely to make sense to your audience as a defense for the thesis. Not all good reasons will be universally accepted. However, you should work to establish reasons that are consistent with what you believe and what you think an audience will accept. For example:

Thesis: Light trucks for personal use should have to conform to the same auto fuel efficiency standards as automobiles
(because . . .)
I. Standards that exempt trucks are meaningless since they represent well over half of all vehicles sold in many parts of the country.
II. These trucks are not used primarily to haul heavy goods, but to provide the same functions—such as commuting to work—as passenger cars.
III. Owners of trucks should share equally in the minimal costs needed to improve the air we all breathe.[3]

In this preliminary outline, the main points are worded as declarative sentences, making their relationship to the thesis clear and apparent. The insertion of "because" between the thesis and each of the main points is a useful test of this relationship, since main points should "make sense" when bridged by this word. If a main point does not seem to follow, it may not be a good reason. Imagine, for instance, an added fourth point for the above example:

IV. Trucks are manufactured by most of the big auto-makers.

If you read the thesis statement followed by the conjunction "because," the statement above doesn't make sense. Unlike the other points that invite agreement and move a listener closer to the thesis, agreement with statement IV is largely irrelevant. In terms of practical logic, it has no force. One could agree and still oppose the thesis.

Amplify and Support the Main Points

The few sentences developed so far are essential to the successful preparation of the message, but general assertions by themselves lack the impact of specific evidence and examples. Many listeners will remember only two things: your general point of view and your most interesting example or illustration.

There are two basic ways to make ideas vivid and memorable: amplification and proof. These forms of support fill out the body of the message, appearing as indented subpoints (A, B, C, and so on) under the main points designated with Roman numerals. For example:

Thesis
   I. Main point
     A. Amplification or evidence
      1. Further explanation

Amplification dramatizes the familiar or ordinary; *evidence* seeks to prove what may be doubted. Amplification is important but often neglected because we sometimes confuse merely stating a point with making it clear. Simply saying what you think does not guarantee that interest or understanding will follow. Ideas must be sufficiently explained so their relevance and implications are instantly apparent.

Few statements are so novel or fresh that merely stating them will command our attention. Listeners discover the significance of ideas through application to specific situations. Examples, extended illustrations, comparisons, and analogies are the basic explanatory tools. Inexperienced communicators frequently overestimate the ability of a few sentences to create interest or clear away confusion; they forget that their own familiarity or interest in a topic may not be shared by the audience. A good teacher, for example, does not simply talk about a subject; she or he *teaches* it—making the vague much clearer.

Consider the subject of "writing." For most of us any talk about putting words on paper is something that is—on the surface—pretty self-evident and maybe not very interesting. But in compilations about how authors work, such as Brian Lamb's *Booknotes*, there are hundreds of small but interesting facts that revive the idea of writing in all of its creative and sometimes peculiar details. A few examples:

Shelby Foote, historian: I write with a "dip pen," which causes all kinds of problems—everything from finding blotters to pen points—but it makes me take my time, and it gives me a feeling of satisfaction . . . you have to dip it in the ink and write three or four words and dip it again. It has a real influence on the way I write.[4]

Christopher Hitchens, an editor of Vanity Fair: I sometimes write in bars in the afternoons. I go out and find a corner of a bar. If the noise isn't directed at me—in other words, there's not a phone ringing or a baby crying or something—I quite like it if the jukebox is on and people are shouting the odds about a sports game. I just hunch over a bottle in the corner. . . . Then when I've got enough (written) down, I start to type it out, editing it as I go. I don't use any of the new technology stuff.[5]

bell hooks, poet, feminist, and professor: I like to write in really tiny, enclosed spaces, and I don't know why this is. I like them to have a window, but I like them to be very small. . . . I handwrite everything, and then I put it on computer. I think, for me, there's something about handwriting still that slows down the idea process. When you're working on the computer, I find you can just zoom ahead, and you don't have those moments of pause that you need. . . . I primarily write in the morning. I'm a meditator, so I get up to meditate . . . and then I like to write with fierce intensity for a few hours, and then I like to play for the rest of the day.[6]

Reading how authors work adds detail to a vague process. In samples like these a simple process that we think we all know is given new life through the rituals and routines of well-known authors.

The second key form of message development is evidence, which aspires to providing proof—sometimes factual, sometimes informed opinion—for a controversial claim. Evidence is used to reduce doubts and reservations in a skeptical audience.[7] Since the qualities of credible sources of evidence were thoroughly discussed in chapter 5, our focus here is on what evidence can and cannot do in overcoming audience resistance.

While it is rare to find evidence that makes claims absolutely certain or true, persuaders usually attempt to cite evidence that may be hard for opponents to dismiss. A speech by the former president of the American Medical Association on the rising costs of coverage uses examples and statistics to urge change.

Let me tell you what I've seen in the last few weeks. I met a family at a pediatric hospital in Des Moines, Iowa. One of the parents told me that their daughter needs medications that cost $5,000 a month. And their insurance requires a co-payment of 20%. Now I don't have to do the math for you to have your figure out that's $12,000 that family has to pay every year. Just for medications alone. . . . And then, there was the story that still makes my blood run cold. A story I will never forget. Because I met another man that day (who) had just turned 62. And he said to me, "Doctor, I lost my job to a young man when I was 59. And I lost my health coverage. Now, I have a lung tumor. And I have to decide whether to spend my resources on radiation and chemotherapy to buy an extra year of life or to forego treatment now and leave something for my wife." No one in the United States of America should ever have to make a decision like that.[8]

Similarly, in remarks at the University of Texas President Bill Clinton rolled out a variety of evidence forms as proof that the ideal of racial justice was still unfulfilled. He delivered his address, "Tearing at the Heart of America," on the same day as the 1995 Million Man March calling for pride and responsibility in black men.

[Statistics]
And blacks are right to think something is terribly wrong when African American men are many times more likely to be victims of homicide than any other group in this country; when there are more African American men in our corrections system than in our colleges; when almost one in three African American men in their 20s are either in jail, on parole or otherwise under the supervision of the criminal justice system—nearly one in three.

[Testimony]
Abraham Lincoln reminded us that a house divided against itself cannot stand. When divisions have threatened to bring our house down, somehow we have always moved together to shore it up.

[Hypothetical Example]
Imagine how you would feel if you were a young parent in your 20s with a young child living in a housing project, working somewhere for $5 an hour with no health insurance, passing every day people on the street selling drugs, making 100 times what you make. Those people are the real heroes of America today, and we should recognize that.

[Statistical Comparison]
And there is still unacceptable economic disparity between blacks and whites. . . . The truth is that African Americans still make on average about 60 percent of what white people do; that more than half of African American children live in poverty. And at the very time our young Americans need access to college more than ever before, black college enrollment is dropping in America.

[Personal example]
The single biggest social problem in our society may be the growing absence of fathers from their children's homes, because it contributes to so many other social problems. . . . This, of course, is not a black problem or a Latino problem or a white problem; it is an American problem. . . . I know from my own life it is harder because my own father died before I was born, and my stepfather's battle with alcohol kept him from being the father he might have been.[9]

Although these evidence forms vary in what they might convince a listener to accept, all provide compelling forms of support for major contentions.

Write the Introduction

After the main and supporting points of the speech have been outlined, the remaining task is the completion of the introduction. While the introduction is the first part of a speech, it is the last to be written. Just as it would be difficult to introduce a person you did not know, so it is awkward to write an introduction before the body of a message has been completed. At this stage, you know what attitudes or behaviors you want the intended audience to accept. Now you are in a position to build a bridge between the audience's existing attitudes and those you want them to hold at the end of the message.

A good introduction prepares an audience to accept the main points that you will present, reducing resistance to your ideas and arguments. Each of the following is worth considering, although it is unlikely every introduction will need to achieve all of these objectives.

Gain Interest and Attention.   An audience cannot be motivated to accept an idea until it has been motivated to listen. Stories, relevant personal experiences, or vivid statistics are good ways to begin speeches. Abstract ideas are more accessible when explained through the actions of particular people. Note how former Attorney General Janet Reno began a speech to law school graduates about the importance of life's smaller lessons. The subject was the small Florida house that her mother built when she was still a child:

> My father didn't have enough money to hire a contractor to build the house and my mother announced that she was going to build the house. And we said, "What do you know about building a house?" She said, "I'm going to learn."
>
> And she went to the brick mason, to the electrician, to the plumber, and she talked to them about how to build a house; and she built the house. She dug the foundation with a pick and shovel, she laid the block, she put in the wiring and the plumbing; and my father would help her with the heavy beams when he came home from work at night.
>
> She and I lived in that house till just before she died, before I came to Washington when she died. And every time I came down the driveway and saw that house standing there, as a prosecutor, as a lawyer having a difficult problem to solve, that house was a symbol to me that you can do anything you really want to if it's the right thing to do and you put your mind to it.[10]

The image of this tenacious woman building her own home provided an interesting story and an appropriate symbol for Reno's commencement speech.

Establish Goodwill.   The greater the gulf that separates speaker and audience, the greater the need to say something that will establish a sense of goodwill between the two. A speaker may start by noting that differences should not overshadow common values and goals. One of the strengths of an open society is the belief that differences of opinion can be productive and can flourish without producing walls of hostility. For example, members of the United States Senate may oppose each other in speeches given from the floor, but many continue to be friends in less partisan settings. The custom of addressing even vehement opponents as "the distinguished member from Virginia" or "my colleague from New Jersey" is not merely good politics, it also part of a healthy framework for persuasion.

One common device for gaining goodwill is to refer to values the audience and speaker hold in common. This was the strategy of an editor at *Playboy* at the beginning of a speech to Southern Baptists, few of whom could be counted on to share the *Playboy* philosophy. He tactfully combined references to shared concerns with comments on the spirit of openness within the audience:

> I am sure we are all aware of the seeming incongruity of a representative of *Playboy* magazine speaking to an assemblage of representatives of the Southern Baptist Convention. I was intrigued by the invitation when it came last fall, though I was not surprised. I am grateful for your genuine and warm hospitality, and I am flattered (though again not surprised) by the implication that I would have something to say that could have meaning to you people. Both *Playboy* and the Baptists have indeed been considering many of the same issues and ethical problems; and even if we have not arrived at the same conclusions, I am impressed and gratified by your openness and willingness to listen to our views.[11]

Use Humor (Carefully) to Soften Opposition. Humor can take away the "edge" sometimes associated with advocacy, at the same time softening an impression an audience may hold that the speaker knows all the answers. When he was president of AT&T, Robert Allen started a speech to an audience at Pennsylvania State University by kidding himself and his audience about some of the low points of the previous year. "So here's my deal," he noted. "I won't mention the Nittany Lions football season—if you won't mention that *Fortune* magazine recently described me as 'dull as flannel.'"[12] Similarly, George W. Bush humorously acknowledged his occasional grammatical and pronunciation difficulties, showing journalists a photo of the First Lady with her hand over his mouth. He explained in a mock serious tone, "she is helping me pronounce Azerbaijanis."[13]

Preview the Scope of the Message. Comprehending a message takes significant effort, especially if the message is delivered orally and challenges some of our views. It therefore must be introduced with some care. A crucial part of the opening is a clear statement of what you will cover. This is sometimes called a "roadsign" or "overview" statement. Just as runners pace themselves according to the distances that are set in advance, listeners should be given advance notice of the length and scope of the topic in which they are investing their attention. Lack of information about the length of the speech and the range of topics to be considered is as frustrating as not knowing the distance of a foot race until the finish line.

Your introduction should tell the audience what topics you will discuss, what topics will be excluded, and how long the presentation will take. By mentioning what will be excluded, for example, you can lay to rest misunderstandings about the scope of your speech and provide a better match between what an audience expects and what they will hear. In a speech attacking the National Rifle Association's persuasion tactics, for example, Raymond Rodgers provided an initial indication of the framework of his remarks. He stated his thesis, referred to what he did not have time to talk about, and concluded with a summary of his main points.

> In the brief time available today, I would like to discuss several standard argu-
> ments of the NRA against handgun control by measuring them against some
> standard logical and rhetorical fallacies. Those fallacies are: (1) failure to define
> terms; (2) use of the "big lie"; (3) the fallacy of the "slippery slope"; (4) bully
> tactics; and (5) the fallacy of improper appeals to authority.[14]

This overview not only communicated the thesis and main points, but also signaled the scope of ideas to be addressed.

Define Key Terms.   Successful communication sometimes depends on the
way words or phrases are used. Some terms are misunderstood because they are
technical, others because ordinary usage may not coincide with the meanings you
have in mind. In either case, definitions are useful.

DILBERT

In the following example, a historian begins an address on the relationship
between sports and television with a redefinition of two familiar words that imply
two different worlds.

> Sport, I am convinced, is the best known yet least understood phenomenon in
> American society. Much of our misunderstanding and misconceptions about
> sports stems from our failure to make meaningful distinctions among the vari-
> ous components of the sports world. . . . One is sport. Sport is an extension of
> play involving two or more persons. Sport turns on games and contests which
> are highly organized, competitive, characterized by the established rules; but
> like play, sport has as its primary purpose fun for the participant.
>   Athletics, on the other hand, derives not from play at all, but from work. Ath-
> letics, as they have been referred to from the ancient Greeks on, refers to
> intensely competitive confrontation between specially trained performers
> whose primary objectives are (a) spectator entertainment and (b) victory.
> Although the game involved in sport and athletics may be the same, as, for
> example, basketball, the two activities are worlds apart in terms of purpose and
> attitude. . . . I would simply call your attention to the obvious difference that
> we understand between intramural sport and intercollegiate athletics.

The speaker then uses the distinctive meanings of the two terms to state his
thesis: "The telecommunications industry is interested in athletic contests, not
sporting events."[15]

It may appear that an introduction containing all five elements discussed above would consume half the allotted time for a speech. Even if this assessment were accurate, the minutes would be well spent if the receptivity of the audience was increased. The more unfamiliar an audience is with a topic or the more hostile they are toward your thesis, the greater the need to take the time to establish an appropriate foundation for the persuasive appeals.

Prepare the Outline

As mentioned earlier, going through the strategic processes discussed in this section generates an outline for your planned presentation. After completing all the stages, finalize your working outline; it will contain key ideas and concepts you want to cover. Organize it clearly, type it using a large point size, and make the major ideas and divisions of the speech easy to locate at a glance. Every outline is different. Some speakers use full sentences throughout while others may work out a system of key words or topics below the main point (I, II, etc.) level. The following model is a general guide. This style of indention allows the speaker to see at a glance major ideas and their support.

INTRODUCTION
  A.
  B.
  C.
Thesis:
BODY
I.
  A.
  B.
    1.
    2.
II.
  A.
  B.
III.
  A.
  B.
SUMMARY
Restate main points and close with a final capstone example, illustration, or quote.

The sample outline on the following pages represents the kind of organizational style extemporaneous speakers should develop. In order to make it possible for a reader to understand the speaker's points, we have made the outline slightly more wordy than would be desirable for a working outline. Some speakers may even reduce their notes to an outline of key words and phrases. The outline illustrates a basic organizational style that works well in speech preparation: a limited number of points and the expectation that the specific language, transitions, and some detail will be added during delivery.

The Advantages of Being a "Near Vegetarian"

Introduction

    A. A friend of mine says she won't eat anything that has eyes . . . unless it's pota-toes. Actually, she eats some fish, but she is in good company, sharing a diet with millions around the world, from Paul Newman to Paul McCartney, from Pythagoras to Plato.

    B. We can no longer dismiss vegetarians as skinny people who live on twigs and berries.

        1. A diet based on little or no meat is no longer a fad.

        2. You don't need to be a customer of juice bars or health food stores to take advantage of what we now know about how to eat well without loading your body and your veins with the residues caused by high-fat diets centered on meat.

    C. We are what we eat: some medical specialists estimate that half of the people occupying hospital beds are in them because of problems brought on by their diets. Among the most common: colon cancer, heart disease, obesity, and perhaps the sharp rise in the number of instances of breast cancer in the United States.

        1. My point is not to convince you to become a particular kind of vegetarian, or even a total vegetarian.

(But the evidence continues to build demonstrating that . . .)

***Thesis*: You can live a healthier life—and one that makes less demands on the resources of the planet—by eating a largely vegetarian diet.**

    I. We pay a heavy personal and global price for meat consumption.

        A. The personal cost of eating meat is a diet rich in fat.

            1. Dr. Bonnie Liebman writes in *Nutrition Action*, "The meat industry may insist on denying the health benefits of vegetarian diets, but research on heart dis-ease, cancer, high blood pressure, diabetes, and obesity argues otherwise."[1]

            2. The *New York Times'* Jane Brody, a widely respected science writer, has come to the same conclusion. She recently wrote, "The central question about vegetarian diets" is no longer whether it is "healthy to eliminate meat. . . ." "The answer," she notes, "seems to be yes."[2]

            3. Pathogens in ground beef are especially dangerous, and a major cause of the 200,000 food poisoning cases every day in the United States.[3]

        B. The global price of meat consumption is the depletion of range and forest land, and the inefficient use of our grain harvests.

            1. You need 16 pounds of grain to produce one pound of beef. But you need just one pound of grain to produce a large loaf of bread.[4]

            2. Food advocate John Robbins estimates that it takes nearly four acres to feed a meat eater for a year, but only one acre to feed a vegetarian.[5]

    II. Vegetarians eat well.

        A. A vegetarian diet offers most of the variety and taste available to non-vegetarians.

            1. Most of our current cravings can be met without meat.

                a. Green Giant and other leading companies have developed good vegetable imitations of meat items.

                b. Some "veggie-burgers" and "chicken" patties made by these companies are nearly indistinguishable from meat, but contain less saturated fat and calories.

2. Most of the world's great cuisines are built on flavors and textures that occur in vegetable form: pasta sauces; the wonderful tastes and textures of grains used in Chinese, Middle Eastern and American southwestern cooking, especially rice and wheat; and grains used in great French and English breads and beers.

3. The sweetest and most intense flavors we know are herbal and vegetable.

   a. When you use mustard, salsa, or ketchup, you are using vegetable and herbal flavoring frequently to cover the "off taste" of animal flesh.

B. Vegetarians and near vegetarians consume food with a better nutritional balance.

   1. The enemy is saturated fat, so common in most kinds of meat.

      a. There is no doubt that cholesterol contributes dramatically to deaths from heart disease.

      b. Animal fats are major contributors of cholesterol; they also tend to retain pesticide residues with their own side effects.[6]

      c. Vegetables, including grains, have virtually no cholesterol.

   2. Vegetarians generally have cholesterol levels that make heart attacks less likely, according to researchers in the well-known Framingham, Massachusetts heart study.[7]

III. Life is sacred: We don't have to sacrifice other mammals to feed ourselves.

A. All of us would be horrified to see the conditions we create for the 9 million animals we slaughter every day.

   1. A person doesn't have to be a die-hard animal lover to recognize how inhumane it is to subject animals to factory farming methods.

      a. A short life in a cage in a darkened building is all that most chickens, pigs, and calves raised for their meat have.

      b. Cattle are forced to eat grains they can barely digest in order to stimulate meat production, only to be shipped often wounded or crippled to feedlots, and then to their deaths.[8]

B. It seems reasonable to extend our basic wish for quality of life to other living creatures, especially the mammals we now consume.

Summary (Restate main points and add closing)

I was at a restaurant in Florida with a friend. . . . She saw "dolphin" on the menu and was horrified. . . . The waiter assured us that we "weren't eating 'Flipper.'" "Dolphin" can also mean a kind of scale fish. But the moment struck me as odd. Many of the animals we raise for food don't have cute names, but they are intelligent creatures living lives that—I believe—should only come to natural rather than violent ends.

Sources

[1] B. Liebman, "Are Vegetarians Healthier than the Rest of Us?" *The Nutrition Debate: Sorting Out Some Answers*, eds. John Dye Gussow and Paul Thomas (Palo Alto, CA: Bull Publishing, 1986), p. 192.

[2] Brody quoted in A. C. Prabhupada, *A Guide to Gourmet Vegetarian Cooking* (Los Angeles: Bhaktivedanta, 1983), p. 1.

[3] E. Schlosser, *Fast Food Nation* (Boston: Houghton Mifflin, 2001), pp 193–195.

[4] F. Lappe, *Diet for a Small Planet* (New York: Ballintine, 1982), p. 9.

[5] J. Robbins, *May All Be Fed* (New York: William Morrow, 1992), p. 33.

[6] O. Schell, "Modern Meat," in *The Nutrition Debate*, pp. 181–184.

[7] Liebman, p. 193.

[8] M. Pollan, "Power Steer," *New York Times Magazine*, March 31, 2002 (LEXIS/NEXIS).

Presenting the Message

While there is no single formula for translating ideas from the page into an effective face-to-face presentation, there are a number of solid guidelines to consider.

- Practice delivering your message several times, but do not memorize it or read it. Because an outline can be understood at a glance, the actual explanation of points can be made in the conversational language you choose at the moment. The outline provides all of the landmarks that are necessary to talk your way through the message, but in a style that is closer to everyday conversation than to oral reading. As Otis Walter and Robert Scott have noted, we tend to be more expressive in voice and gesture if we *think about our ideas as we say them.* An outline encourages thinking; reading does not.[16]

- For your outline, use double-spaced large type (16 point or larger) on full sheets of paper. Small note cards are too hard to read while trying to maintain audience eye contact.

- Be flexible about cutting or adding items to the outline. The actual circumstances of delivery (running out of time, unanticipated comments made by a previous speaker) may force you to vary your speech from its original form. The outline can easily accommodate change.

- Use a systematic pattern of indenting so that key points can be easily located along the left-hand margin. If you lose your place, for example, you can always relocate the main points of the speech by searching them out on the left margin. Reserve Roman numerals for major contentions in the body of the speech that will be repeated several times.

- Avoid writing a conclusion that introduces new ideas that have not been developed in the body. The real conclusion of the speech is the thesis. An extended conclusion may involve a review of all main points and perhaps a closing story or illustration.

- A major goal should be to *communicate your conviction.* Don't be overly concerned about pauses, the urge to rephrase an idea, or the desire to make another attempt to clarify a point. These are natural features of all oral communication. It is more unnatural to read to someone in a way that makes their presence seem marginal rather than central to your reason for speaking.

- Use media support sparingly. PowerPoint, video, and computer illustrations can help amplify main points, but they can also create their own distractions and disrupt the flow of ideas. Use display and visual media *only if they actually add to your persuasiveness.* And since equipment can malfunction, prepare a message that will work even without media support.

DILBERT

STRATEGIC CONSIDERATIONS FOR DISCURSIVE MESSAGES

▲

To this point, we have described a general method for translating a persuasive intent into an actual message. We turn now to several additional concerns about persuasion strategies in longer, discursive forms of communication.

When to Reveal the Thesis

Ideally, you should state the thesis in the introduction to give direction to the remarks that follow. In some instances, however, this strategy might alienate the audience. If their hostility to the thesis is known to be very strong, you might withhold it until you have established common ground and evidence for the conclusions you want them to reach.[17]

In his famous "Funeral Oration," for example, Marc Antony begins by praising Brutus, one of the assassins of Caesar, as an honorable man. He does so because Brutus has just given his speech in which he has convinced the crowd that Caesar deserved to die. The lines Shakespeare writes for Antony initially give no hint as to the eventual conclusion he wants his audience to reach:

> Friends, Romans, countrymen, lend me your ears;
> I come to bury Caesar, not to praise him.

Only later in the speech is it evident that he has actually come to do the reverse: to bury Brutus and to praise Caesar. Antony concludes that Brutus is the true villain only when he thinks the audience is ready to hear it. This attitude gradually emerges from the signs of Caesar's goodness that Antony weaves into his observations, seemingly as afterthoughts. Finally, the repeated phrase that Brutus was an honorable man achieves its intended irony.

> When that the poor have cried, Caesar hath wept:
> Ambition should be made of sterner stuff;
> Yet Brutus says he was ambitious;
> and Brutus is an honorable man.[18]

Whether to Recognize Opposing Views

When we think of a persuader or a passionate advocate, we usually assume that the ideas to be presented will be one-sided. Few persuaders, whether they are consumer advocates testifying in a congressional hearing or people selling cars, will give equal time to ideas or attitudes they oppose. Successful persuasion frequently requires a commitment to one side of a case because the communicator's conviction must be apparent. Part of what makes a persuader credible is the evident passion he or she has for a cause.

Yet audiences do not live only in the persuader's world. In many cases, their awareness about a topic includes significant information about the other side of a controversial question. They have been subject to counterpersuasion—persuasion intended to weaken the impact of opposing advocates—and will be subject to it again. In the case of heavily advertised products such as beer and automobiles, for example, counterpersuasion frequently occurs within a matter of hours or even minutes.

There have been many experimental studies conducted to measure how attitudes are affected by single and two-sided persuasion.[19] One conducted by Carl Hovland and his associates found that a two-sided presentation may not be as effective for an audience that already agrees with your point of view.[20] However, individuals hostile to a speaker's thesis responded positively to the recognition given the other side of a question. This was especially evident in "better educated" listeners.[21]

As a general rule, the greater the audience's "working knowledge" of a topic the more a persuader will need to state and deal with counterarguments.[22]

Even if members of an audience lack knowledge of counterarguments, it may be beneficial to present some of what the other side thinks before opposing ideas are raised. This interesting strategy is called inoculation.[23]

> The situation is similar to that in the medical field when a person is brought in a germ-free environment and is suddenly exposed to germs. That person's body is vulnerable to infection because it has not developed any resistance. Such a person can be given resistance either by supportive treatment—good diet, exercise, rest, and so forth—or by inoculation, a deliberate exposure to a weakened form of the germ that stimulates the development of defenses.[24]

How to Use Persuasive Language

We offer one final observation about discursive message design. Sometimes we may get so involved in the structure of the outlined speech that we overlook the importance of key terms. A finished speech outline is like a completed but unpainted car. The basics are in place, but how we react to it depends to a great extent on the exterior color that is applied. Just as paint color can make a car acceptable or unacceptable in our eyes, so can the semantics of the speech make a difference in our attitudes toward an idea. Look especially at adjectives, nouns, and verbs that make up the major headings. Phrase them in ways that contribute forcefully to your appeals and arguments.

Roosevelt University

Here are two main points of a rough-draft outline for a speech arguing that employers should not use lie detectors to assess the honesty and performance of employees:

I. *Lie detectors are unreliable, and*

II. *Lie detectors violate our personal liberties.*

While these ideas may be well chosen, their wording could be greatly improved. First, a speech that is arguing against these devices should not use the inexact and misleading phrase "lie detector." Although the term is a common one, its use works against a main point of the speech (that these machines do not detect lies). A less loaded term is polygraph. Second, you could intensify the impact of the main points with more vivid and specific language. Consider, for example, the nouns, adjectives, and verbs added to these points to increase their impact:

I. *Polygraphs are supposed to detect "lies," but the outdated machine is itself a notorious liar.*

II. *The forced use of the polygraph destroys our rights to privacy, freedom, and honor.*

Although the ideas in the original and revised drafts are essentially the same, the wording of the second attempt is worded more persuasively. A machine that "lies" is a more obvious threat to our liberties.

STRATEGIC CONSIDERATIONS FOR NONDISCURSIVE PERSUASION
▲

Persuasion can be visual as well as verbal. Any survey of design strategies would be incomplete without consideration of messages that rely as much or more on images and other visual and aural elements to convey meaning. Any consumer of Web sites, direct-mail flyers and advertising sees how graphics, photo art, and audio can have an impact on message comprehension and acceptance. There may be some truth to the notion that we have never been more *ocularcentric*—defining what we know by what we can see.[25] But it has always been the case that the representational world offers immediate and universal signs and symbols: images and sounds that cross beyond the borders of language to communicate in universal terms.

Nondiscursive media depend on the instant connections made by visual information because they usually have less time to make their point. They frequently exist in a media environment that is cluttered with many other competing messages. In the language of the elaboration likelihood model discussed in chapter 6, they are likely to be processed using the "peripheral" route. Attention to them is brief and depends on the initial impact of key words and images. Complex relationships and statistical data are usually given graphic representations or visual reference points that are easy to follow.[26] Text headlines must communicate an attitude clearly and directly. Implications of danger or safety, threat or reassurance, approval or rejection often must be communicated in the familiar iconography of the culture.

Turkish Culture and Tourism Office

The Visual Image

Carefully selected visual imagery is usually a key element in the compression of a message into the limited time and space of a nondiscursive message. Images provide effective analogues to complex ideas; they can easily represent the essence of a message. Thus, a campaign that urges parents to take greater responsibility for some aspect of their children's health might include an ad of a child's small fingers holding an adult's hand. The dependency on adults is easily reflected in such an image. Pictures also function as commentary. They may be visual puns that play on familiar shapes and objects (Absolut vodka ads), representations of values more easily shown then discussed (the use of multi-ethnic actors in Coke ads), or invitations to share the same evocative fantasy (television car ads shot in Utah's stunning Monument Valley). They have branded their products with images that can stand-in for verbal messages. With sufficient repetition—and without scandals such as Enron's, which destroy carefully constructed associations—images trigger more or less reliable attitudes. Add in representations of human faces, human forms, and a flood of feelings and sensitivities can be evoked.

Images can also function as icons. Icons are graphic or pictorial representations that are instantly recognizable to members of a culture, or a sub-group within it. In some ways they function as the visual counterparts to commonplaces and norms. They instantly communicate a recognized feature of the culture. Logos such as McDonald's arches, Coca-Cola's white on red cursive script, and Microsoft's primary colored butterflies are instantly recognizable; they are burned into our consciousness. Commercial art relies on the iconic image to enhance recall and favorable recognition for a product or service.

NON SEQUITUR

Some icons also trigger strong feelings. Before September 11, 2001, directors of films like *Working Girl* and *Town and Country* often used the Manhattan skyline as a backdrop in helicopter shots casually sweeping from the dense skyscrapers of Midtown southward to the slender towers of the financial district. Among the images captured in these tableaus meant to convey the city's energy and vitality are shots of the World Trade Center. But no more. The twin towers are now iconic.

Pictures of them cannot be casually used as a background. Their familiar shapes carry too much meaning to be used for anything less than a statement about loss and an unexpectedly hostile world.

Honoring Gestalt Values

The design and layout of messages using text, graphics, and images are governed by many more strategies and aesthetic considerations than can be fully represented here. But there are at least some core variables to keep in mind.

Gestalt theory was a complete psychological system that arose at the end of the 1800s. Its theorists believed that individuals had to be understood in the specific context of their lives, not simply as physical agents. "To the Gestaltists," notes Roy Behrens, "things are affected by where they are and by what surrounds them . . . so that things are better described as 'more than the sum of their parts.'"[27] Much of the Gestaltists' psychological work has been discredited, but their core guidelines for how we perceive relationships between elements of an image have provided a useful terminology for design. A Gestalt approach to the layout of images and text assumes that certain choices create messages that are unified and perceptually satisfying. Although the Gestalt concepts are not strictly models for persuasion, they help explain how we perceive images, and indicate what seem to be certain hard-wired human predispositions for processing visual information. They include:

- *Figure and ground. We perceive objects against the context of their surroundings*. We expect that a background is a fitting and appropriate setting for foreground action. In the simplest form of this law, ground should not dominate a figure (text or images). Ground dominates only when the message intends to suggest the vulnerability of a figure, as when a surfer is photographed against an enormous wave.

- *Similarity. We group similar things in the same frame together.* Images should have obvious contextual connections to each other. Text (headlines as well as amplification) should use consistent fonts, rhetoric, and syntax within the same message or frame.

- *Proximity. We assume connections and relationship between the same things or people if they are in the same location.* For example, the closer individuals are to each other, the more we will seek to interpret the basis of their relationship. Their status as coworkers, friends, relatives, or intimate partners becomes a significant part of the message.

- *Continuation. The layout of a message visually creates a line or natural curve.* The delicate business of framing representational paintings, photography, and video must take care to lead the viewer's attention to the intended visual essence of the message. In Leonardo de Vinci's "The Last Supper" our eyes end up on Jesus rather than the apostles. In his celebrated Sistine Chapel fresco we follow the outstretched arm of Adam as it meets the hand of God.

- *Closure. We fill in what is left out but implied.* The discrete bits of film, television, and digital sampling are completed in a flowing recreation of life. The elemental forms of life such as squares and triangles are seen or violated in the way elements are laid out in the same frame. In art, music, and rhetoric elements that are implied or partly concealed are often completed by their consumers.[28] Photograph a face in partial shadow, and we will fill in features we cannot see. Leave off the last few notes of a well-known tune, and listeners will try to supply them.

To see these elements at work consider the display ad produced by the public service branch of the advertising industry, the Ad Council. The message is a visual evocation of the legacy of Martin Luther King. And like most non-discursive messages, it is meant to communicate its message with an image and just a few words. The ad uses many of the Gestalt values to make its point about the social movement King helped lead. The clear black and white photo helps increase the contrast between the darker "*ground*" of the subway location and the three symbolic phone kiosks that are the key *figures* in this image. The camera's limited depth-of-field also helps put the phones in focus against a slightly out-of-focus background. Any "busier" a background would have created too much visual "noise." And perhaps an even darker and simpler ground would make the ad easier to "read." The principle of *similarity* is observed in the three phones. They are of equal size and placement and framed to create *symmetry* in the visual field. Their proximity to each other and the *continuous line* created by their placement suggests that they are meant to perform the same function in the same place. This line also helps our eye find the racist wording on the phones: an essential process that gives the ad its meaning. The "white only" and "colored only" signs differ and are out of balance: a deliberate subversion of our natural tendency to look for *closure* in this static image. The signs declaring racial restrictions—and parsing out two of the three phones for "whites only"—not only offends our modern sense of social justice but also our visual expectations. We have seen the older images of segregated drinking fountains and building entrances. The short headline on the sign centered under the picture takes away any ambiguity: King made the difference. This would be a different and less just society without his efforts. And for readers who centrally process even advertisements, there is more text to amplify King's role and to invite support for the King National Memorial.

We can only scratch the surface in offering suggestions for the design of messages where time is short and the possibility for distraction is very high. The following is a selective checklist of reasonable expectations and message strategies for nondiscursive persuasion.

Set Modest Goals

In direct one-on-one communication with another person, it may be possible to produce relatively high rates of success. It is far less likely that any brief encounter with a nondiscursive message will have a dramatic effect on attitudes. Our level of involvement in advertising, for example, is less than in most forms of interpersonal contact.[29] To somewhat offset this handicap, audiences must repeatedly be exposed to the same messages. A successful direct-mail campaign in a political contest, for example, may generate a response rate of only three percent.[30] In

order to achieve the final goal of raising money or support for a candidate, it must be duplicated many times.

Keep the Message Simple and Thematically Consistent

With some exceptions, the human attention span is notoriously short and subject to a great deal of distraction. One force that weakens many nondiscursive messages is that they exist among the "clutter" of competing messages in the same context. An hour of commercial television, for example, contains about 40 commercials, "billboards," or public service announcements. Watching anyone peruse a magazine or newspaper can be a sobering experience for an advertiser. A full-page ad may get little more than a glance as it competes for attention with photographs, human interest stories, editorials, attention-grabbing headlines, and other advertising. More within a message designer's control is the problem of noise. Noise refers to elements *within* a message that distract audiences and, hence, weaken its overall impact. Noise may be visual as well as aural, and usually means that there is too much going on in the ground of the message. We can easily imagine such a message: perhaps a 30-second car commercial with a montage of 25 separate shots of different cars and people. Add in an audio track of an announcer reading a lot of copy, background music from a classic popular song, and it all becomes too much.

In order for nondiscursive messages to stand out, they must be simple. Direct, descriptive text and uncluttered visual support can combine to communicate a great deal in a relatively short space. Consider the examples of two single-page ads on the following pages. The Intel "image ad" is thematically unified. It is intended to make us feel better about Intel as a corporate citizen. Everything in the message works to that single persuasive end. It would be enough for a peripheral processor to only see the headline and the sub-head to get the point. Two sentences fulfill the burden of the message. The smaller-point amplifying text and corporate logo at the bottom are useful for central processors, and add to a sense of closure. They do not need to be read to fulfill Intel's persuasive objective. But visually, they complete the page and keep the white ground from swallowing the black text. They essentially "close the sale" by providing details of Intel's philanthropy. There is virtually no noise in the message, and nothing is wasted.

Similarly, the anti-smoking ad from the State of California (p. 394) includes compelling images and text, but nothing more than that is needed. Note the reversal of conventional figure and ground colors. The simple text stands out as white-on-black. The eye is drawn first to the uncomplicated image of the smoker and his limp cigarette, and then to its explanation in the 13-word text. The use of the word "impotence," and the visual pun of the cigarette together provide unambiguous closure to the message, and a potentially powerful "need" appeal. Smoke as a young man, claims the ad, and you risk the loss of sexual function. Again, every element has a reason, and nothing is wasted.

Use Effective Aural and Visual Analogues

The greatest potential for awareness and memorability of ideas, according to John Rossiter and Larry Percy, lies in the use of dynamic pictures (video), static

The Last Time This Many Great Minds Met in Philadelphia There Was a Revolution.

Congratulations to the finalists in the annual Intel International Science and Engineering Fair.

In May, nearly 1200 students from 47 countries gathered in Philadelphia. Not to create a new nation, but to showcase their research projects at the Intel International Science and Engineering Fair. As the world s largest pre-college science competition, the Intel ISEF brings students together to share ideas and interact with some of the world s leading scientists. The fair, celebrating its 50th anniversary, provides over $2 million in scholarships and awards to students, plus the grand prize, a trip to attend the Nobel Prize Ceremonies in Stockholm, Sweden. By recognizing these students, we hope to encourage and inspire their spirit of exploration and discovery. To find out the names of this year s winners, or how to participate in the next Intel International Science and Engineering Fair, visit **www.sciserv.org**. And to learn more about Intel s commitment to science, math, engineering and technology education, visit us at **www.intel.com/education**.

Reproduced by permission of Intel Corporation. © 1999, Intel Corporation.

Courtesy of California Department of Health Services.

concrete pictures (print), and concrete words (audio or print).[31] Aural and visual information create an instant shorthand for feelings and moods that print cannot easily match. Happiness, anger, or fear carry universal cues. We learn what these facial expressions signify in the first years of life, and their symbols (happy faces, poison warnings, and so on) soon after. Unlike learning a foreign language, we do not need to master special access codes to understand many forms of aural and visual information.[32] Concrete pictures take the form of images that have a direct and unambiguous connection to a persuasive message. We know, for example, how we are supposed to "read" images of a family in a commercial for Wendy's or McDonald's. Even if the television satire of *SNL* or the *Daily Show* easily makes fun of them, the visual conventions of selling family products have changed very little. A relentless good cheer and satisfaction must be registered on the faces of the upbeat consumers. Father can be childlike, and mom can be harried before she enters the restaurant. But once inside, no frowns or family tensions are allowed. Every facial cue from staff and customer is registered in close up and reflects complete contentment.

Position Your Message as Entertainment or Information

In U.S. society, the creation of awareness about problems—whether on television, radio, or in the print media—often occurs in the context of entertainment. The lines are increasingly blurred between news, entertainment, information, and advertising. Since we are selective in what we expose ourselves to, any message framed in ways that gratify our insatiable thirst for the unusual or interesting has a decided advantage. Commercials thus pose as mini-dramas featuring character, conflict, and denouement. Or they exist as elaborate visual puns, allowing us to enjoy how its creators play with the materials of popular culture. Print ads and Web pages use elaborate photographic and graphic effects, the latter drawing us in with color, iconic images, and the promise of interactivity.

Use a Sympathetic Figure or Key Icons

The literary device of the synecdoche has a potent counterpart in most short forms of persuasion. A synecdoche is a thing or person that embodies or represents the much larger universe. Kenneth Burke described it as one of four "master tropes," or one of the thought patterns we use to discover and describe basic truths.[33] The statements "Tom Hanks is the perfect 'everyman' in American films" or "Chicago represents the best and worst of American life" speak to our impulse to identify wide swaths of reality in the features of specific people, places, or events.

Imagine, for example, appropriate or inappropriate meanings associated with images of the flag, the World Trade Center in New York, or an ethnic or demographic stereotype. Jokes and humor often play on cultural stereotypes or synecdoches (i.e., How many country singers does it take to change a light bulb? Five . . . one to change it and four to sing about how they miss the old one). Political cartoons frequently get their energy from a simple image that functions as a multiplier of cultural meanings.

Frame the Discussion in the Imagery of Heroes, Villains, and Victims

Storytelling is a universal, familiar method of presenting information and illustrating a point of view. The essence of storytelling is the portrayal of specific characters as they negotiate life's obstacles. We could accurately describe human beings as *homo narrans*, the only living creatures who naturally frame their understanding of the world in terms of narratives and their related characters.[34] In Sharon Lynn Sperry's words, the human is "an incorrigible imagist. To know and give order to the world he lives in, man has always devised and shared stories."[35] We communicate our impressions of events by selectively arranging particular facts and features according to the formulaic requirements of storytelling. There must be action that requires others to respond; the plot must build. Responses should be characterized as appropriate or problematic. Characters must be sorted out as creators of the problem (villains), bystanders who have been harmed (victims), or protagonists who may solve the problem (heroes). There must be a wrapping up—a conclusion that resolves the problem justly. While life is usually messier, we generally want the closure and finality that most storytelling implicitly promises.

In the last few years the authors recall a variety of films where characters were the vessels of persuasive themes. Among them were John Sayles' *Sunshine State:* two women are forced to confront the past when resort developers buy properties on a small Florida island—triggering reflections on the instant disposability inherent in the region's development. Similarly, in *John Q* the hard realities of the health insurance crisis are played out in the life of a factory worker (Denzel Washington) who takes hostages in order to get medical care for his dying son. Using compelling mixtures of fantasy and probability, such narratives use identification to pull us toward characters we feel we already know. Then they draw us even further into their self-contained worlds by inviting us to consider the choices upon which these characters have staked their lives.

SUMMARY
▲

In this chapter, we have explored a number of recommendations for constructing persuasive messages. With a primary emphasis on highly organized discursive messages such as speeches, we reviewed a development sequence of six steps: (1) know the audience; (2) determine your objectives; (3) determine your thesis; (4) develop main points; (5) develop amplification and evidence; and (6) write the introduction. We made two basic claims about persuasive speaking. The first is that it is important to think of a speech as more than a written copy of what you intend to say. Preparing to persuade an audience is as much a process of thinking about the event as it is about writing words on paper. Everything done before the speech should make the contact between you and your listeners as successful and satisfying as possible. And, most importantly, no speech is completed when it is written—only when it is delivered.

The outline contains the basic ideas needed to keep you on track; it should not get in the way of the spontaneous and flexible communication expected when we meet others face-to-face. Our second claim is that the preparation of a speech requires careful attention to detail—how to defend and explain points, how to introduce controversial ideas, and what kind of language will evoke the right response.

We also explored conventional message-building guidelines used by persuaders who have less time or space to develop their views. The shorter, nondiscursive persuasion of advertising, direct mail, and other visual and aural media relies on a kind of symbolic shorthand. These kinds of messages depend heavily on the creation of interesting stories, praise- or blameworthy agents, and familiar iconography to carry their meanings. Because nondiscursive messages must work in confined spaces and grab the attention of distracted audiences, remember these composition rules:

- Use images, fonts, and icons that thematically enhance your message.
- Make every word and image count, with an emphasis on concrete symbols that make your meaning unambiguous.
- Where appropriate, frame persuasion as narratives with heroes who embody the attitudes or behaviors you advocate.

Questions and Projects for Further Study

1. Assess the speech outline entitled "The Advantages of Being a Near Vegetarian." Estimate how a skeptical college-aged audience of nonvegetarians might react to the arguments and the evidence. What are the speeches' flaws and strengths? Given its thesis statement, what would strengthen the speech for that audience?

2. In discussing "one-sided" versus "two-sided" presentations, the authors note that there is no inherent ethical problem in focusing on only one side of an issue. Agree or disagree with the authors, citing real or hypothetical examples to support your point of view.

3. As an exercise in generating good reasons for an assertion, (1) write a thesis statement that presents an attitude with which a partner disagrees and (2) identify two or three good reasons in support of the thesis. These are steps 3 and 4 in the six-step sequence for writing a persuasive message. Working alone, write down the strongest case that you can. Ask your partner about the logical structure you have developed. Your questions may include the following: Do you accept any of the good reasons? If not, where are the flaws? If so, does your acceptance of a good reason make you feel uncomfortable about rejecting the thesis? Is there a major objection that the outline overlooks?

4. Locate and analyze the evidence used (or missing) in the arguments of a newspaper columnist. A sample of nationally syndicated writers may include: Ellen Goodman, Maureen Dowd, and David Broder. Identify the kinds of evidence the writer employs using the categories developed in this chapter and the types of sources cited in chapter 5.

5. Using the standards discussed in the section on preparing nondiscursive messages, assess several pamphlets from your student health center on smoking cessation, HIV, or some other health risk. How effectively is the information organized? How persuasive are the warnings and appeals for safe health practices? What suggestions would you make for improvement? Do the same for a Web site with a persuasive intent (i.e., http://www.drugfreeamerica.org).

6. Considering our comments on "good" and "bad" delivery, analyze and evaluate a persuasive presentation (i.e., at a campus forum, in Congress over cable television's C-SPAN, in church, or in a persuasion class). Some questions to consider: What kind of notes is the speaker using? Are the notes a help or a hindrance in promoting successful communication with the audience? If the speaker were to ask you for suggestion for improvement, what would you say?

7. Working with a partner and using some of the recommendations for constructing nondiscursive forms of persuasion, identify a target audience and design a one-page ad for a social action group that interests you (Greenpeace, Mothers Against Drunk Driving, Christian Coalition, Planned Parenthood, etc.). Consider the role of photos, headlines, key symbols, and additional persuasive copy.

Additional Reading

Amy Arntson, *Graphic Design Basics* (New York: Holt, Rinehart, Winston, 1988).

Bruce Gronbeck, "Reconceptualizing the Visual Experience in Media Studies," in *Communication: Views From the Helm for the 21st Century*, ed. by Judith Trent (Boston: Allyn and Bacon, 1998).

Carl I. Hovland, ed., *The Order of Presentation in Persuasion* (New Haven, CT: Yale, 1957).

William J. McGuire, "Attitudes and Attitude Change," in *The Handbook of Social Psychology*, Vol. II, 3rd ed., eds. Gardner Lindzey and Elliot Aronson (New York: Random House, 1985), pp. 233–46.

Michael E. Roloff and Gerald R. Miller, eds. *Persuasion: New Directions in Theory and Research* (Beverly Hills: Sage, 1980).

Edward Tufte, *Visual Explanations* (Cheshire, CT: Graphics Press, 1997).

Otis M. Walter and Robert L. Scott, *Thinking and Speaking*, 5th ed. (New York: Macmillan, 1984).

Notes

[1] Cicero, *De Inventione*, Books I and IV, trans. H. Hubbell (Cambridge: Harvard University Press, 1960), p. 13.

[2] Donald C. Bryant, "Rhetoric: Its Function and Scope," *Quarterly Journal of Speech,* December 1953, p. 401.

[3] Danny Hakim, "Honda Takes Up Case in U.S. for Green Energy," *New York Times*, June 12, 2002, p. C1.

[4] Brian Lamb, *Booknotes* (New York: Times Books, 1997), p. 10.

[5] Ibid., p. 253.

[6] Ibid., pp. 64–65.

[7] Audiences do not always respond to the presence of strong evidence as a basis for accepting claims, but we believe that ethical persuasion requires reasoning from available evidence. For more discussion of research in this area see Michael Burgoon and Erwin P. Bettinghaus, "Persuasive Message Strategies," in *Persuasion: New Directions in Theory and Research*, eds. Michael E. Roloff and Gerald R. Miller (Beverly Hills: Sage, 1980), pp. 146–48.

[8] Thomas Reardon, "Taking Care of Health Care," in *Representative American Speeches, 1999–2000*, eds. Calvin Logue, Lynn Messina, and Jean DeHart (New York: H. W. Wilson, 2001), p. 112.

9 Bill Clinton, "Tearing at the Heart of America," in *Representative American Speeches: 1995–1996*, eds. Calvin Logue and Jean DeHart (New York: W. H. Wilson, 1996), p. 112.

10 Janet Reno, "Participating in the Process," in *Representative American Speeches: 1995–1996*, eds. Calvin Logue and Jean DeHart (New York: W. H. Wilson, 1996), pp. 17–18.

11 Anson Mount, "The *Playboy* Philosophy-Pro," in *Contemporary American Speeches*, 4th ed., eds. Will Linkugel, R. R. Allen, and Richard Johannesen (Dubuque, IA: Kendall-Hunt, 1978), p. 182.

12 Robert Allen, "Information Unbound," in *Representative American Speeches: 1995–1996*, eds. Calvin Logue and Jean DeHart (New York: W. H. Wilson, 1996), p. 159.

13 Elisabeth Bumiller, "White House Letter; President was Comedian in Chief at Press Dinner." *New York Times*, May 6, 2002 (LEXIS/NEXIS).

14 Raymond S. Rodgers, "The Rhetoric of the NRA," *Vital Speeches*, October 1, 1983, p. 759.

15 Larry R. Gerlach, "Sport as Part of Our Society," in *Representative American Speeches, 1983–1984*, ed. by Owen Peterson (New York: H. H. Wilson, 1984), pp. 106–07.

16 Otis M. Walter and Robert L. Scott, *Thinking and Speaking*, 5th ed. (New York: Macmillan, 1984), p. 292–93.

17 For a discussion of this and other argument-order issues and options see William J. McGuire, "Attitudes and Attitude Change," in *The Handbook of Social Psychology*, Vol. II, 3rd ed., eds. Gardner Lindzey and Elliot Aronson (New York: Random House, 1985), pp. 271–74.

18 "Marc Antony's Funeral Oration," in *The Dolphin Book of Speeches,* ed. by George W. Hibbitt (New York: Dolphin, 1965), pp. 10–11.

19 See, for example, James McCroskey, Thomas Young, and Michael Scott, "Special Reports: The Effects of Message Sidedness and Evidence on Inoculation Against Counterpersuasion in Small Group Communication," *Communication Monographs*, August 1972, pp. 205–12; Edward Bodaken and Gerald Miller, "Choice and Prior Audience Attitude as Determinants of Attitude Change following Counterattitudinal Advocacy," *Communication Monographs*, June 1971, pp. 109–12.

20 Carl I. Hovland, Arthur A. Lumsdaine, and Fred D. Sheffield, "The Effects of Presenting 'One Side' Versus 'Both Sides' in Changing Opinions on a Controversial Subject," in *Experiments in Persuasion,* eds. Ralph L. Dosnow and Edward S. Robinson (New York: Academic Press, 1967), pp. 224–25.

21 Ibid., p. 225.

22 Daniel O'Keefe, *Persuasion Theory and Research*, 2nd ed. (Thousand Oaks, CA: Sage, 2002), pp. 144–45.

23 For an interesting discussion of strategies for increasing resistance to persuasion, see Gerald R. Miller and Michael Burgoon, *New Techniques of Persuasion* (New York: Harper and Row, 1973), pp. 18–44.

24 Werner J. Severin and James W. Tankard, Jr., *Communication Theater: Origins, Methods, and Uses in the Mass Media*, 3rd ed. (New York: Longman, 1992), p. 163.

25 Bruce Gronbeck, "Reconceptualizing the Visual Experience in Media Studies," in *Communication: Views from the Helm for the 21st Century*, ed. by Judith Trent (Boston: Allyn and Bacon, 1998), pp. 291–92.

26 For excellent examples of visual presentations of ideas see Edward Tufte, *Visual Explanations* (Cheshire, CT: Graphics Press, 1997).

27 Roy Behrens, *Design in the Visual Arts* (Englewood Cliffs, NJ: Prentice-Hall, 1984), p. 49.

28 See, for example, Amy Arntson, *Graphic Design Basics* (New York: Holt, Rinehart, Winston, 1988), pp. 58–62; Ralph Haber and Maurice Hershenson, *The Psychology of Visual Perception*, 2nd ed. (New York: Holt, Rinehart and Winston, 1980), pp. 315–16.

29 See, for example, Robert E. Burnkrant and Alan Sawyer, "Effects of Involvement and Message Content on Information-Processing Intensity," in *Information Processing Research in Advertising*, ed. by Richard Jackson Harris (Hillsdale, NJ: Lawrence Erlbaum Associates, 1983), pp. 43–64.

30 Larry J. Sabato, *The Rise of Political Consultants* (New York: Basic Books, 1981), p. 228.

31 John Rossiter and Larry Percy, "Visual Communication in Advertising," in *Information Processing Research in Advertising*, ed. by Richard Jackson Harris (Hillsdale, NJ: Lawrence Erlbaum Associates, 1983), pp. 103–09.

32 Joshua Meyrowitz, *No Sense of Place* (New York: Oxford, 1985), pp. 93–99.

33 Kenneth Burke, *A Grammar of Motives* (New York: Prentice Hall, 1954), p. 503.

34 This is Walter R. Fisher's phrase in *Human Communication as Narration: Toward a Philosophy of Reason, Value, and Action* (Columbia: University of South Carolina, 1987), p. 62.

35 Sharon Lynn Sperry, "Television News as Narrative," in *Understanding Television: Essays on Television as a Cultural Force*, ed. by Richard P. Adler (New York: Praeger, 1981), pp. 297–98.

Index

Ability, and credibility, 113
Acceptance, latitude of, 151–152
Accountability in democracy, 341–342
Acquiescence, and authoritarianism, 122–125
Ad hominem reasoning, 97–98
Adams, John, 36, 304
Administrative persuasion, 310–312
Adorno, T. W., 123
Advertising
  advocacy, 245
  appeal to self-esteem, 285–286
  archetypal images in, 281–282
  audience identification and, 177
  behavioral conditioning and, 271
  brand penetration and, 278
  brand personality vs. brand performance, 271
  campaigns, 232–233
  celebrity endorsements, 178, 262, 271, 279–280
  children as targets of, 292–295
  classification methods of, 265
  commercial campaigns, 232–233
  consumer continuum, 274
  contemporary changes in, 280
  control of media through, 42–44
  cost to consumers, 262
  criticisms of, 275, 290–298
  critiquing, 288–289
  cross-promotion, 293–294
  cultural frames for goods, 266–267
  deception in, 290–292
  defined, 264–266
  demand, methods of creating, 275
  as discourse through and about objects, 265
  ethical, on children's programs, 343
  evolution of, 266–270
  Foote, Cone & Belding (FCB) model of, 275–277
  four levels of persuasion in, 274–275
  freedom of speech, impact of, 296–297
  growth of, 262
  guilt and fear appeals in, 286–287
  influence on TV program content, 297
  Internet, 263
  isolation and loneliness, appeal to, 285
  language corruption in, 292
  likability and, 278
  magic in the marketplace, 275
  market research and, 271–273
  media control through, 44
  minimizing the influence of, 298
  models of buyer behavior, 273–274
  music as persuasive tool in, 269
  as myth, 280–283
  norms dictation through, 284–285
  persuasion, reinforcement, and reminder levels of, 275
  planned obsolescence in, 295

political, 317
power appeals in, 283
precipitation level of, 274
private vs. public inter-
ests, 297–298
product positioning in,
263, 270–271
psychoactive, ethics of,
296
psychographics of,
271–273
psychology, role of, in,
270–273
public relations vs., 233
reach and frequency in,
277–278
sales, 216–218
search for meaning and
identity through,
283–284
sexual appeals in, 280,
287–288
slogans and jingles in,
268–269, 274
social effects of, 296
social science theory on,
265, 296
social structure and, 270
stimulus-response moti-
vation in, 144, 271
subliminal messages in,
279
successful, characteris-
tics of, 278
symbolic nature of,
282–283
textual approach to
understanding,
288–289
Advocacy, interaction with
audience and message,
174–175
Affection, need for, 191
Affective dimension of message reception, 141
Affleck, Ben, 108
Agenda setting
campaign communica-
tion and, 236
mediated, 326

political language and,
66–67
public, 311
Aggression, 201
Ajzen, Icek, 156, 158
Alexander, Jan, 351
Alien and Sedition Acts, 36
Alinski, Saul, 204
al-Qaida, 52
Alter, Jonathan, 2
Alter, Stewart, 263
American Association of
Political Consultants,
345
American Association of
Retired Persons
(AARP), 241–242, 244
American Booksellers Foundation for Free Expres-
sion, 40
American Rifleman, The, 141
Anderson, Rolph, 216
Applebaum, Anne, 310
Argumentation. See also
Arguments; Logic; Rea-
soning
claims and, 92
demonstration and, 90
political language and, 68
public interest and, 101,
103
understanding practical,
87–96
Arguments
analytic, and practical
enthymemes, 87–91
circular, 99
defined, 87
evidence in, 87, 91, 93
factual and judgmental
claims in, 91–92
implied and stated com-
ponents of, 92–94
reasoning to discover and
defend, 94
warrants for, 93–94
Aristotle
on character and credi-
bility, 13
on commonplaces, 171

on democracy, 45
on enthymemes, 90
on ethos, pathos and
logos, 110
on persuasion, 3
on practical reasoning, 87
on proofs, 95
on public opinion, 34
Arnett, Ronald, 345
Arnold, Thurman, 121
Aronson, Elliot, 279
Artifactual communication,
193
Astroturf, 242
Attitude change
attribution theory,
145–147
components in, 133–142
consistency theories and,
147–151
credibility and, 115
elaboration likelihood
theory, 153–156
long-term, 152–153
reinforcement theory,
144–145
social judgment theory,
151–152
Attitude-behavior consis-
tency, 139
Attitudes
belief structure of, 136
change in, 133–156
defined, 135–136
ego-defense function of,
141
expectancy-value theory
and, 139
formation of, 136–139,
277
influence of values on,
140–142
knowledge function of,
141
links with subsequent
behavior, 139
measuring techniques
for, 138
research, and pure per-
suasion, 19

sources of, 343–344
strength of, factors determining, 138
testing through interac-
tion, 63
universal commonplaces
of audiences, 171–172
value-expressive func-
tion of, 142
Attribution theory, 145–147
Audience(s)
advertising classification
scheme, 265
advocate and message
interaction with,
174–175
analysis process, 168–174
concept of, 164–167
credibility and accep-
tance by, 115–117
demographic assessment
of, 173–174
establishing goodwill of,
376–377
ethics of adaptation to,
181–182
gaining interest and
attention of, 376
high credibility/high
agreement persua-
sion of, 176–177
high credibility/low
agreement persua-
sion of, 177–178
identification with,
170–171
low credibility/high
agreement persua-
sion of, 178–179
low credibility/low
agreement persua-
sion of, 179–180
market research on,
168–170
measuring persuasive
effects on, 15
persuader sincerity and,
175–176
principle of identifica-
tion and, 170–171

for public communica-
tion, 229
secondary and unin-
tended, 165, 167
sincerity of advocate and,
175–176
speaker familiarity with,
370–371
specific norms of,
172–174
unintended, 180–181
Authenticity, personal,
175–176
*Authoritarian Personality,
The* (Adorno & Frankel-
Brunswick), 122
Authoritarianism, and
acquiescence, 122–125
Authority
excessive dependence on,
100
leadership vs., 208
moral political, 341
multidimensional aspects
of, 109–110
power vs., 195
Ayer, N. W., 264

Bad-faith communication,
176
Balance theories of persuasion, 147, 150
Barnes, Beth, 233
Barron, Jerome, 45
Baskerville, Barnet, 75
Becker, Samuel, 232
Behavior
attitude-consistent, strategies for encourag-
ing, 139
attitudes as predictors of,
139
enforced discrepant, 149
factors affecting, 139
nonverbal, 193–195
reasoned action and,
156–158
Behavioral dimension of
message reception, 141
Behrens, Roy, 389

Beliefs
attitude change and,
133–135
of audience members,
170
unexamined inherit-
ances and, 141
Benoit, William, 108
Berelson, Bernard, 235
Berger, Asa, 56
Bettinghaus, Erwin, 5,
197–198
Bissinger, Buzz, 308–309
Black, Max, 96
Body communication, 193
Bok, Sissela, 343, 347
Bolstering, and inconsis-
tency, 150
Books, banning of, 40
Borchers, Timothy, 203
Borger, Gloria, 2
Bormann, Ernest, 70
Bormann, Nancy, 70
Boucher, Richard, 39
Bradley, Bill, 353
Brainwashing, 17
Branch Davidians, 8, 16
Brand performance/person-
ality, in advertising, 271
Breck, Edward, 282
Brinkley, David, 70, 355
Broadcast journalism, com-
munication ethics of,
353–359
Brokaw, Tom, 52, 113
Brown, Roger, 148
Browning, Iben, 113
Bunzel, John, 304
Bureaucratese, 73
Burke, Kenneth, 20, 56, 63,
68–69, 96, 395
Burnett, Graham, 7–8
Burns, James MacGregor,
313, 338
Burton, Michael, 235
Bush, Barbara, 180
Bush, George H., 76
Bush, George W., 2–3, 52–53,
167, 172, 181, 311, 318
Butler, Judith, 52

Cacioppo, John T., 153, 155–156
Callahan, James, 100
Campaigns, persuasive advertising, 216–218, 232–233, 278
corporate advocacy, 244–248
defined, 232
implementation of, 254–256
issue management, 237, 244–248
persuasive nature of, 315–322
political. *See* Political campaigns
product or commercial, 232–233
public relations, 233
social forces influencing, 231
social movements, 248–254
Campbell, Joseph, 280
Campbell, Karlyn, 357
Campbell, Richard, 233, 280–281
Canary, Daniel, 200
Cappella, Joseph, 321, 355–356
Carter, Steven, 342
Carville, James, 317
Cash, William, 219–220
Cassirer, Ernst, 54, 62
Castellanos, Alex, 317
Causation vs. correlation, 98
Celebrity endorsements, 177, 262, 271, 279–280
Censorship, 30–31, 35, 37, 39–40, 42–44
Change, communication as, 214
Character, political campaign emphasis on, 319
Cheney, George, 214
Children
ethics of advertising to, 343
influence of advertising on, 292–295

Chirac, Jacques, 53
Chow, Joanne, 30
Christensen, Lars, 214
Cialdini, Robert, 142, 149, 153, 167
Cicero
on commonplaces, 171
on metaphor, 57
on persuasion, 3
Cigler, Allan, 254
Circular argument, 99
Citizen action groups, 240, 243
Claims
factual and judgmental, 91–92
finding good reasons for, 94–95
role in argumentation, 87
Clinton, Bill, 76, 97, 231, 306–307, 310–311, 318
Clinton, Hillary, 97, 306
Coalitions, building productive, 311
Coca-Cola
as American cultural icon, 266–267, 269
slogans, 268–269
Cody, Michael, 5, 197–198
Coercive compliance-gaining strategies, 198
Coercive power, 195
Cognition, and beliefs, 134
Cognitive dimension of message reception, 141
Cognitive dissonance theory, 148–149
Cognitive speech, 60
Cohen, Arthur, 115
Comedy, as illogical communication, 86
Commercial campaigns, 232–233
Commercialism, problems of, in democracies, 298
Commercials. *See also* Advertising
attitude-specific behavior and, 140
in Communist China, 28

cost to consumers, 262
sponsor control of programming through sale of, 43
Committee hearings, and political persuasion, 314
Commonplaces, universal, 171–172
Communication
advertising as, 265
conflict management and, 199–204
cooperative nature of, 5
dramatic form in, 69–70
ethics of. *See* Communication ethics
group fantasy and, 70
illogical, 86
intercultural, 207–208
interpersonal. *See* Interpersonal communication
organizational, 210–214
persuasion vs., 20
public. *See* Public communication
as pure expression, 18
as pure information, 18
as pure persuasion, 19–20
technology, and freedom of expression, 37–38
Communication ethics
basic guidelines for, 346–350
broadcast journalism and, 353–359
categories of, 345–346
globally accepted norms of, 349–350
media's role in, 350-353
new technology and, 350–353
persuasion and, 342–343
political, 359–363
public discourse and, 363–364
social interaction and, 340–342

sources of attitudes and values in, 343–344
values and principles of communicators, 340, 349–350
Compliance-gaining techniques, 197–199
Conditioned response, 143
Conflict, interpersonal
aggression and assertiveness in, 201
coping strategies for, 201
corporate issues and, 247
defined, 199
different levels of, 200
four variables in, 203
gender differences in, 207
myths about, 204
negotiation and bargaining in, 201
positive aspects of, 204
productive qualities of, 203
strategies for avoiding, 202
techniques for managing, 202–203
Connotative meanings, 57
Consensus, seeking political, 326–327
Consistency theories of persuasion, 147–151
Constituent pressure, and political persuasion, 314–315
Consumerism
criticism of, 295–296, 298
encouraged by capitalism, 270
models of purchasing behavior, 273–274
Context
of compliance-gaining requests, 199
meaning of symbols in, 57
media-created political, 76
political language and, 68
Contextual ethics, 345

Control
human need for, 191
interpersonal, 195–197
Cook, Dick, 263
Corax, 33
Corcoran, Paul, 64–65
Coriolanus, 326–327
Corporations
advocacy campaigns in, 244–248
corporate culture, 213–214
power over message dissemination, 42–44
Counterpersuasion, 384
Cousino, Kenneth, 245
Creativity, facilitated by language, 58
Credibility
Aristotle on, 13
believability and, 114–117
ethos and good character, 110–112
high personal, 176–178
low personal, 178–180
media and, 115
rational/legal ideal of, 112–114
reinforcement of, 176
speech fluency affecting, 195
strategic dimensions of, 118–125
three perspectives on, 110–118
Web site checklist for, 351
Creighton, J. E., 86
Crisis communication, in public relations, 234
Cronkhite, Gary, 117
Cross, Donna, 262
Cultural diversity, and interpersonal communication, 207–208
Culture of Narcissism, The (Lasch), 295
Culture, corporate, 213–215
Cupach, William, 200
Customer relations, rules of conduct for, 216

Dalton, Diana, 199, 202, 204
Dance, Frank, 60
Daugherty, Emma, 233
Davis, Richard, 77, 353, 356
Day, Louis, 343
Dean, Howard, 77
Debate, public, 38
Deception in advertising, 290–292
Deductive reasoning, 88
DeFleur, Melvin, 228, 325
Degeneres, Ellen, 297
Demand, creating in advertising, 275
Democracy
accountability and, 341–342
American, 34–36
changing meaning of, 45
early debates over, 32–34
ethics of, 345
problems of commercialism in, 297
Demographics, audience, 173–174
Denial, 100–101, 150
Dennis, Everette, 325
Denotative meanings, 57
Denton, Robert, 248, 250
Devil terms, 251
DeVito, Joe, 192, 196, 203
Dial group testing of audiences, 168–170
Dialogue, and conflict management, 203
Dickinson, Peter, 243
Differentiation, and inconsistency, 150
Dines, Gail, 173
Discursive messages
opposing views, whether to recognize, 384
persuasive language in, 384–386
thesis, when to reveal, 383
Dispositional attribution, 145
Diversity, cultural, 207–208
Doublespeak, as political language device, 71–74
Douglass, Frederick, 59

Dowd, Maureen, 97
Drama, in political language, 69–70
Duncan, Hugh D., 2, 69
Durkheim, Émile, 164

Eco, Umberto, 56
Economic models of buyer behavior, 273
Edelman, Murray, 64
Ego conflicts, 200–201
Ego involvement, and social judgment theory, 151
Eisenberg, Eric, 212
Elaboration likelihood theory, 153–156
Electronic communication, 228
Ellerbee, Linda, 324
Ellul, Jacques, 171
Emotion, as complementary process to logic, 96
Emotional appeals, 198
Emotive speech, 60
English, Diane, 297
Entertainment
    messages as, 395
    as political persuasion, 323–325
Enthymemes, and analytic arguments, 87–90
Ethics
    categories of, 345–346
    codes of professional, 346, 354
    decline of, in America, 338–339
    media, 356–357
    new media and, 77
    in persuasive communication, 342–343
    principles and values of, 340
    social function of, 339
    social interaction and, 340–346
    social values and, 343–344
Ethos, and credibility, 110–112

Euphemisms, 72–73
Evidence
    in argumentation, 87, 91–93
    in message development, 374
    negative, 324–325
Exit polling, 230
Expectancy-value theory, 139
Expert power, 195
Expression
    pure, communication as, 18–19
    through political symbols, 69
ExxonMobil op-ed advertising program, 245
Eye contact and trustworthiness, 194

F (Anti-Democratic) Scale questionnaire, 123
Face management skills, 203
Facts vs. judgments, in argumentation, 91–92
Faith, and placebo effect, 122
Fallows, James, 355
False advertising, 275, 290–291
False cause, 98
Faludi, Susan, 173
Falwell, Jerry, 98, 180
Fantasy themes, and political language, 70
Faucheux, Ron, 239
FCUK (French Connection United Kingdom), 280
Fear, as advertising appeal, 286–287
Feminine communication style, 204–207
Feminist norms, 173
Festinger, Leon, 148
Films
    political persuasion in, 324
    product placement in, 263
Fink, Conrad, 340
Firewise Campaign, 237

First Amendment, 39–40, 45, 74, 244, 341
Fishbein, Martin, 134, 156, 158
Followership, characteristics of exemplary, 210
Foote, Shelby, 374
Fox, Roy, 293, 295
Framing, and political campaigns, 321
Frank, Jerome, 122
Frankel-Brunswik, Else, 123
Frasier, social subtext of, 324
Freedom of expression
    corporate controls on, 42–45
    free speech vs. true access, 45
    hate speech and, 74
    individual vs. factions, 34–36
    marketplace theory, 38
    political control/suppression of, 28–32, 38–42.
        See also Censorship
    public opinion and, 32–34
    technological push toward, 37–38
French, John, 195
Friedenberg, Robert, 317
Friedrich, Gustav, 216

Galbraith, Kenneth, 297
Ganesh, Shiv, 214
Garment, Leonard, 97
Gass, Robert, 136, 150, 197
Gaudet, Hazel, 235
Gender differences, in communication, 204
Genetics, and attitude formation, 138
Gerbner, George, 45
Gestalt concepts for visual information processing, 389
Gill, Ann, 58–59
Gingrich, Newt, 71
Gitlin, Todd, 324

Glaser, Milton, 43
Glynn, Carroll, 230
God terms, 63, 251
Goffman, Erving, 12
Goodall, Harold, 212
Goodman, Michael, 211, 214
Gorgias, 33
Government
    communication endeavors of, 239
    controls in open societies, 38–42
    democratic history of, in U.S., 34–36
    freedom of expression, democratic, 28–36
    language, 67. See also Political language
Graber, Doris, 65–66
Grassi, Ernesto, 56
Grassroots lobbying, 239–244
Gray, John, 207
Green, Martin, 282
Greenberg, Stan, 306
Greenfield, Meg, 39
Gronbeck, Bruce, 236
Group fantasy, 70
Guilt, as advertising appeal, 286
Gusfield, Joseph, 322
Guthrie, W. C., 33

Hacker, Kenneth, 69
Hackman, Michael, 195, 201, 208, 210
Haefner, James, 274
Hainsworth, Brad, 247
Handgun Control Inc., 141
Hardship, and perception of greater value, 149
Hart, Roderick, 5, 320, 355
Hate speech, 74–75
Hauser, Gerard A., 228
Havel, Vaclav, 177
Hayakawa, S. I., 59
Health care reform, campaign for, 306–307
Heath, Robert, 245
Heaven's Gate, 8

Hill, Kevin, 78, 351
Hitchens, Christopher, 374
Hitler, Adolf, 96
Hocker, Joyce, 203
Hoffer, Eric, 122
Holmes, Oliver Wendell, 38
hooks, bell, 374
House Un-American Activities Committee, 17
Hovland, Carl, 114, 142
Hughes, John, 78, 351
Humor, as opposition-softening tool, 377
Hyman, Michael, 296–297

Iconology in advertising, 266
Icons and indices, 54
Identification
    principle of, 170–171
    through political language, 68
Identity management, 199
Ideologies, audience-specific, 173
Idolatry frame of advertising, 266
Impression management, 12
Inclusion, social, 191
Inconsistency, strategies for resolving, 150
Inflated language, 74
Information
    dissemination, and political language, 65
    pure, communication as, 18
Ingenium in language, 56
Initiation ceremonies, 149
Inoculation, and political language, 68
Intentions, and attitude, 157
Interaction
    attitude development and, 136
    of attitudes, beliefs, and values, 141
    conditioned response and, 143
    language, and reality, 62–64

organization-employee models of, 212–213
    self and society defined through, 63–64
    social learning and, 167–168
Intercultural communication, 207–208
Internet. See also World Wide Web
    advertising on, 263
    ethical considerations regarding, 350–351
    freedom of expression on, 38
    fundraising on, 317
    inherent democracy of, 31
    marketing on, 278–279
    political campaigning on, 236, 325
    political role of, 77–78
    privacy issues concerning, 352
Interpersonal communication
    affection dimension of, 191
    cognitive/rational dimension of, 191
    compliance-seeking messages in, 197–199
    conflict in, 199–204
    culture and diversity in, 207–208
    gender differences in, 204–207
    leadership and, 208–210
    persuasion in. See Interpersonal persuasion
    planned persuasive strategies in, 191
    pragamatic qualities of, 192
    relationship dimension of, 191
Interpersonal persuasion
    bargaining and negotiation in, 201
    communication in. See Interpersonal communication

in interviews, 219–221
nonverbal characteristics
    of, 193–195
organizational, 210–214
political campaigns and,
    65–66, 68
power and control in,
    195–197
sales-oriented, 216–218
types of, 190
verbal characteristics of,
    192–193
Interviews, interpersonal
    communication in,
    219–221
Isaacson, Walter, 44
Isolation, advertising's play
    on, 285
Issue advocacy activities/
    management cam-
    paigns, 244
Issue campaigns, 237–248
Iyengar, Shanto, 321

Jacobson, Michael, 284, 297
Jakobson, Roman, 60
Jamieson, Kathleen, 76,
    321, 326, 355–357, 364
Jandt, Fred, 207
Janik, Allan, 87, 100
Jargon, 73
Jefferson, Thomas, 35
Jeffords, Jim, 2
Jhally, Sut, 265–266, 275
Johannesen, Richard, 340
Johnson, Craig, 195, 201,
    208, 210
Johnson, Lyndon, 313
Jones, Jim, 9–10, 167
Jones, John, 270, 278
Journalism
    broadcast/news, 353–359
    checkbook, 355
    self-censorship in, 44
    tabloid, 70, 355
Joyce, Timothy, 280
Judgment, claims of, 91
Juhasz, Joseph, 349
Jung, Carl G., 281
Jury selection, 174

Kant, Immanuel, on ethics,
    339
Keillor, Garrison, 179
Kellett, Peter, 199, 202, 204
Kelley, Robert, 210
Kendall, Shari, 206
Kennedy, Ted, 180
Key terms, defining, 378
Key, Wilson Bryan, 279
Kilbourne, Jean, 264, 286,
    296
Kinder, Donald, 321
King, Andrew, 109
King, Larry, 113
King, Martin Luther, 40
Klapp, Orrin, 165
Kline, Stephen, 266, 275
Koresh, David, 9, 16
Kruckeberg, Dean, 233
Krugman, Herbert, 278
Kursk incident, 108

Labeling, as political lan-
    guage device, 70–71
Langer, Susanne, 54
Language
    advertising, and search
        for identity, 284
    classification of func-
        tions of, 60
    common political devices
        of, 71–75
    criteria for, 58
    cultural and societal
        influence of, 58–59
    debased by advertising,
        292
    dishonest and inhumane
        use of, 72–75
    functions of, 58–62
    human action and expres-
        sion through, 53
    human communication
        and, 3
    interaction and reality,
        62–64
    meaning and, 55–58
    nature of, 53–62
    negative relationships
        and, 56

news-media issues on, 53
persuasive, how to use,
    384–386
political uses of, 52–53,
    64–75. *See also* Politi-
    cal language
power in, 69
signs and, 54
as social behavior,
    340–341
symbolic, 53–56
Leach, Christopher, 295
Latitudes, in social judg-
    ment theory, 151
Lawrence, Regina, 321
Lazarsfeld, Paul, 235
Leadership
    authoritarianism and
        acquiescence, 122–123
    interpersonal communi-
        cation and, 208–210
    legislative, 312–313
    in social movements, 253
    styles of, 209–210
    traits of, 208
League of Nations, 11, 16
Learning theory, and persua-
    sion, 143
LeBon, Gustave, 125
Lee, Harper, 112
Legislative persuasion,
    312–315
Legitimate power, 195
Legitimation and credibility,
    118–120
Leiss, William, 266, 275
Lewinsky, Monica, 39–40
Limbaugh, Rush, 145
Linkage, specificity of, 139
Liska, Jo, 117
Littlejohn, Stephen, 148
Lobbying
    grassroots, 239–244
    political persuasive
        power of, 313
Logic. *See also* Reasoning
    as complementary pro-
        cess to emotion, 96
    formal, vs. enthymemes,
        87–90

persuasion vs., 100–103
rationality and, 132–133
Loomis, Burdett, 254
Lowery, Shearon, 228
Lutz, William, 72
Lynd, Helen, 171
Lynd, Robert, 171

Madison, James, 35–36
Mamet, David, 179
Mandela, Nelson, 311
Manipulation, and compliance gaining, 198
Market research
on children, 292–293
psychographics and, 271–272
VALS approach to, 272–273
Marketing, social norms, 168
Marketplace theory, 38
Masculine communication style, 204–207
Mass persuasion, 228–256
Matalin, Mary, 173
Mathematics, and analytic argument, 88
Mazur, Laurie, 284, 297
McChesney, Robert, 38
McLuhan, Marshall, 262
Meaning
creating, in advertising, 288–289
denotative vs. connotative, 57
identity, search for, through advertising, 283–284, 289
nonverbal, 193
relational elements of, 55–56
Media
advertising, growth of, 252
advertising power of, 42, 264
agenda setting by, 326
attitude formation and, 136
audiences for, 165

celebrity spokespersons in, 344
control of information dissemination by, 42–44
credibility reinforcement through, 176
ethical communication considerations involving, 348, 350–353
event coverage, rules for promoting, 247
framing, in political campaigns, 321–322
freedom of expression and, 37–38
influence on political campaigns, 316, 325
language issues in, 53
manipulative advertising in, 275
military censorship of, 42
new vs. traditional, 77
nondiscursive. See Nondiscursive persuasion
persuasive effectiveness of, 15
political campaigns, significant effects on, 325
political coverage/oratory in, 75–77
portrayals of low-credibility/low agreement persuasion, 179
public communication and, 229
right of access to, 45
self-censorship in, 43–44
support for speech presentations, 382
technological adaptation of, in advertising, 265
terrorist use of, 358
Media Sexploitation (Key), 279
Men Are from Mars, Women Are from Venus (Gray), 207
Men, interpersonal communication style of, 204–207

Message processing
attitude change and, 153–156
attribution theory and, 145
consistency theories and, 149
elaboration likelihood theory and, 153–154, 156
logic and rationality in, 133
peripheral and central, 154
reinforcement theory and, 144
social judgment theory and, 151–152
values and, 141
Messages
communication ethics and, 348
compliance-seeking, 197–199
criteria for judging, 151
discursive vs. non discursive, 370
nonverbal, 193
previewing the scope of, in speech preparation, 377–378
simplicity and consistency in, 392
visual imagery in, 388
Metalingual speech, 60
Metaphor, as ingenium in language, 57
Micro-persuasion, 12
Milgram, Stanley, 124
Mill, John Stuart, 28
Miller, Gerald, 204
Mitchell, Arnold, 272
Modeling, and attitude formation, 136
Monaco, James, 324
Moog, Carol, 284, 292
Morris, Dick, 317
Motivation research, 270
Motives, attribution of, 145
Movies. See Films

Ms. Magazine, 44
Muir, Janette, 74
Music, as persuasive advertising tool, 269
Mystification
  credibility and, 121
  placebo effect of, 121–122

Narcissism
  advertising and, 266
  consumerism as, 295
Narrative
  ethics, 345
  fiction, as advertising, 280–281
  message as, 396
National American Woman's Suffrage Association (NAWSA), 305
National Federation of Independent Business (NFIB), 240
National Press Photographers Association, Inc. Code of Ethics, 354
National Rifle Association, 138, 141, 173, 242, 244, 377
Nationalism, and political language, 68
Negative evidence, 324–325
Negotiation, and interpersonal persuasion, 201
Network news reporting, 355, 357
Newman, Dale, 112
Newman, Robert, 112
News journalism, 353–359
Newsom, Doug, 233
Nicomachean Ethics (Aristotle), 338
1984 (Orwell), 37, 289
Non sequitur, 98–99, 171
Noncommitment, latitude of, 152
Nondiscursive persuasion
  defined, 386
  effective aural and visual analogues in, 392–395

as entertainment or information, 395
  framing imagery for, 396
  honoring gestalt values, 389–390
  setting modest goals, 390
  simple and consistent messages in, 392
  synecdoche in, 395
  visual imagery, 388–389
Nonverbal codes, 193–195
Norms
  audience-specific, 172–174
  dictated by advertising, 284–285
  feminist, 173
  social norms marketing, 168
  subjective, 157

O'Hair, Dan, 216
O'Keefe, Daniel, 5–6, 139
O'Toole, John, 279, 295
Obedience to Authority (Milgram), 124
Objectives of message, determining, 371–372
Objectivity, and credibility, 112–114
Ocularcentricity, and nondiscursive persuasion, 386
Odell, Jack, 342
Ogden, C. K., 55
Omar, Mohammed, 39
One Nation, After All (Wolfe), 172
Open societies, characteristics and limitations of, 36–37. *See also* Freedom of expression
Oratory, political, 75–76
Organizations
  corporate culture in, 213–214
  interpersonal communication in, 210–214
Orwell, George, 12, 37, 289
Owen, Diana, 77, 356
Owen, George, 353

Packard, Vance, 266
Paisley, William, 231
Paralanguage, 193
Park, Maud Wood, 305
Parrott, Roxanne, 234
Patterson, Thomas, 355–356
Pattiz, Norman, 39
People's Temple, 9–10
People's Voice, The, 75
Perception checking, and conflict management, 202
Percy, Larry, 392
Perloff, Richard, 152
Persuasion
  acceptance and compliance in, 19
  advertising as, 262–298
  analytic argument and, 89–90
  attitude change and. *See* Attitude change
  behavioral theories of, 142–158
  campaigns and. *See* Persuasive campaigns
  communication as different from, 20
  communication ethics and, 342–343
  defined, 3–6
  differing motives for, 16
  effects of, 15
  ethical considerations of, 338–364. *See also* Communication ethics
  in everyday life, 12–13
  freedom of expression and, 28–45
  governmental suppression of, 28–32
  interpersonal. *See* Interpersonal communication
  in the jury room, 7–8
  logic/rationalization in, 94
  logical argumentation vs., 100–103
  mass, 228–256

message presentation,
370–396
natural resistance to, 201
nondiscursive, strategic
considerations for,
386–396
political language in. *See*
Political language;
Political persuasion
politics of peace and,
10–12
power of, 3
psychology of, 132–158
public and mass,
228–256
pure, communication as,
19–20
reasoning and, 86–103
religious advocacy and,
8–10
response shaping, rein-
forcement and chang-
ing, 140
self-interest and, 101–102
social explanations of,
164–181
subliminal, 17
unpredictable outcomes
of, 17–18
Peters, Charles, 319
Peters, John Durham, 164
Petty, Richard E., 153–156
Pfau, Michael, 234
Phalen, Patricia, 165
Phatic speech, 60
Phillips, Kevin, 75
Phillips, Michael, 287
Photo manipulation, ethics
of, 352–353
Pierce, C. S., 54
Placebo effect of mystification, 121–122
Planned obsolescence, 295
Plato
on democracy and self-
government, 32
on rhetoric, 4
on sophistry, 33
on truth in persuasion, 94
Pluralism, 34

Poetic speech, 60
Polarization
hate speech and, 74
political language and,
68
Political action committees
(PACs), 243
Political campaigns
agenda-setting theory,
236
character emphasis in,
319–320
defined, 234
emphasis on strategy
reporting, 320–321
evolutionary change in,
317–319
features unique to,
234–235
instrumental and con-
summatory functions
of, 236
Internet's role in, 77
limited effects model
and, 235
logistics of, 317–320
media framing and prim-
ing in, 321–322
media influence on, 236
new style vs. old style,
235–236
presented as dramas, 70
public relations profes-
sionals and, 316–317
purposes of, 237
short-term orientation of,
316
uses and gratifications
model, 236
Political communication. *See
also* Political language
ethics of, 359–363
social judgment theory
and, 152
Political correctness, 173
Political discourse, changing nature of, 75–78
Political dissent, government suppression of,
30, 38–39

Political language
action stimulation func-
tion of, 67
agenda-setting function
of, 66, 67
common devices of,
71–75
criteria for, 65
defining, 64
drama in, 69–70
functions of, 65–67
information dissemina-
tion through, 65
inoculation and polariza-
tion in, 68
interpretation and link-
age through, 66
projection through, 67
reinforcing prevailing
views through, 68–69
self-defining, 322
strategic uses of, 68–70
talk vs. action, 64
war rhetoric, 53
Political persuasion
administrative objectives,
selling, 308–309
entertainment as,
323–325
ethics of professional, 346
forms of, 309–325
health care reform cam-
paign, 306–307
interpreting the national
mood, 311–312
limited effects model, 325
party pressure and,
314–315
religious doctrine and,
307–308
significant effects model,
325–326
through symbolic and
status issues, 322
trust and, 326–327
women's suffrage and,
305
Politics, Burkean view of, 69
Polling, 174, 230
Popper, Karl, 36

Power
  advertising emblems of,
    283
  authority vs., 195
  five sources of, 195
  political communication/
    language and, 65, 69
Power plays, 196
Pratkanis, Anthony, 279
Prayer for the City, A (Biss-
  inger), 308
Presentations, preparation
  for, 370–382
Presentations, preparation
  for. *See* Speeches
Press
  freedom of, 39
  negativity of, 355
Preston, Ivan, 291
Priming, and political cam-
  paigns, 321
Privacy
  Internet concerns regard-
    ing, 352
  right to, 39–42
Procedural code ethics, 345
Product campaigns, 232–233
Product placement in films,
  263
Project for Excellence in
  Journalism, 357
Projection, and political lan-
  guage, 67
Proofs, three forms of, 95–96
Propaganda, limitations of,
  17
Protagoras, 34
Proximity, 194, 212
Pseudo-polls, 230
Psychographics and market
  research, 271–272
Psychological models of
  buyer behavior, 273
Psychology, role of, in adver-
  tising, 270–273
Public communication
  characteristics of, 229
  democratic, 342
  entertainment function
    of, 229

history of, 228
persuasive campaigns,
  232
public opinion and. *See*
  Public opinion
social movements,
  248–254
Public discourse, ethical,
  363–364
Public opinion
  democratic value of,
    32–34
  events as crucibles for, 231
  evolving standards of, 231
  importance of, 230–231
  open societies and, 36
  polling, 230
  social forces influencing,
    231
Public relations
  campaigns, 233–234
  crisis communication in,
    234
  professionals, in political
    campaigns, 316–317

Qi Yanchen, 30

Radio, as political medium,
  75
Randazzo, Sal, 281
Rationality
  compliance-seeking mes-
    sages and, 198
  logic and, 132–133
Raven, Bertram, 195
Reagan, Ronald, 76, 311–312
Reality
  created through interac-
    tion, 62–63
  symbolic vs. physical,
    62–63
Reardon, Kathleen, 152,
  190, 212
Reasoned action theory,
  134, 156–158
Reasoning. *See also* Argumentation; Arguments;
  Logic
  defeat by denial, 100–101

defective, common forms
  of, 96–100
to discover and defend,
  94
excessive dependence on
  authority, 100
Redford, Robert, 120
Referent power, 195
Referents, 55
Reinforcement theory,
  144–145
Rejection, latitude of, 152
Relationships
  interpersonal communi-
    cation and, 191
  negative (ingenium in),
    56
  power and interdepen-
    dence in, 196–197
Religion
  cult advocacy, 8–10
  politics of, 307–308
Rendell, Ed, 308–309
Republic, The (Plato), 32, 47
Response reinforcement,
  shaping, and changing,
  140
Responsive listening, and
  conflict management,
  202
Reward power, 195
Rhetoric
  Plato on, 4
  political, changing nature
    of, 75–78
Rhetoric, The (Aristotle), 95,
  110, 165, 228
Rhetorical speech, 60
Richards, I. A., 55, 57
Rieke, Richard, 87, 100
Rodgers, Raymond, 377
Roosevelt, Franklin D., 76,
  310
Rossiter, John, 392
Rothwell, Dan, 57
Rotzoll, Kim, 274
Rove, Karl, 317, 319
Rumors, 99
Rumsfeld, Donald, 310
Rushdie, Salman, 32

Sales, interpersonal communication in, 216–218
Same-sex marriages, 307–308
Sapir, Edward, 58
Sarnoff, David, 100
Saussure, Ferdinand de, 54, 56
Sayles, John, 396
Schemas and stereotypes, 135
Schultz, Don, 233
Schultz, William, 191
Schwartz, Tony, 170–171, 317
Schwarzenegger, Arnold, 120
Scott, Robert, 382
Second Amendment, 173, 242
Segal, Eli, 315
Seiter, John, 136, 150, 197
Self, defined by interaction with others, 63
Self-censorship in journalism, 44
Self-esteem, advertising's influence on, 285–286
Self-interest, and persuasion, 101
Sennett, Richard, 118
Sequential influence techniques, 199
Sethi, Prakash, 245
Severe Acute Respiratory Syndrome (SARS), 31
Sexual appeals in advertising, 280, 287–288
Shaw, Harry, 296
Shea, Daniel, 235
Shepard, Lester, 349
Sherif, Muzafer, 151
Shils, Edward, 120
Signification, process of, 56, 59
Signs, vs. symbols, 54–55
Simons, Herbert, 5, 140, 232
Simpson, O.J., 174, 352
Situational attribution, 145
Sivulka, Juliann, 264

Slanting, 74
Slayden, David, 74
Slogans
    advertising, 268–269
    as cultural symbols, 262
    political language device of, 70
Smell, as a code system, 194
Smith, Craig, 67, 248, 250
Smith, Gerri, 245
Smith, Mary John, 138
Smokey Bear fire prevention campaign, 237
Snider, Stacey, 263
Social identity, and political language, 68
Social interaction. See Interaction
Social judgment theory, 151–152
Social learning, 167–168
Social movements
    characteristics of, 248–250
    common ground and conflict strategies for, 251
    history of, 248
    leadership in, 253
    life cycle of, 252–253
    persuasive functions of, 250–252
    resistance to, 253–254
Social norms marketing, 168
Social proof, 167
Society
    influence of advertising on, 263
    open vs. closed, 36–38
    as product of interaction, 63–64
Sociological models of buyer behavior, 274
Sophists, 33–34
Sources
    believability of, 114–117
    determining the quality of, 112–114
    objectivity vs. willing credibility in, 113

Soviet Union, and government control of technology, 37
Spatial communication, 193
Speech communication, functions of, 60
Speech, freedom of. See Freedom of expression
Speech, powerless types of, 195
Speeches, preparation for
    amplify and support main points, 373–376
    determine objectives, 371–372
    determine thesis, 372
    develop main points, 372–373
    know the audience, 370–371
    prepare the outline, 379
    present the message, 382
    write the introduction, 376–379
Sperry, Sharon Lynn, 396
Starr, Kenneth, 39–40
Status politics, 322
Steinem, Gloria, 44
Stereotypes, 142
    attitude formation and, 139
    political, 326
    social effects of, 296
Stewart, Charles, 219–220, 248, 250
Stimulus-response theory, 142–144
Stout, Roy, 267
Strategy reporting, 320–321
Stuckey, Mary, 312
Style
    conflict-encouraging, 202
    in language and speech, 60, 62
    leadership, 209–210
    masculine vs. feminine communication, 204, 206
    mediated political, 76
Styron, William, 149

Subjective norms, 157
Subliminal Seduction (Key), 279
Suffrage, women's, 305
Suggestion, power of, 122
Syllogistic reasoning, 88
Symbols
    advertising as cultural, 262
    human use of, 3, 56
    meaning and, 55–58
    modification through interaction, 63
    nondiscursive messages and, 370
    nonverbal, 193
    persuasive campaigns and, 232
    political, 65, 69
    signs vs., 54–55
    social sanctions and, 63
Synecdoche, 395

Tabloid journalism, 70, 355
Tactile communication, 193
Tannen, Deborah, 132, 205–206
Tansey, Richard, 296–297
Tate, Marsha, 351
Technology. *See also* Internet
    adaptation of, in advertising, 235, 275
    building public constituencies through, 243
    building volunteer organizations through, 244
    campaign, 236
    circumventing political boundaries through, 37, 77
    computer online filtering programs, 40
    freedom of expression and, 31, 37–38
    manipulating demand through, 275
    new media, 350–353
    political communication and, 77–78
    polling techniques and, 230

role in understanding messages, 265
Television
    children's advertising and, 293, 295
    grassroots lobbying and, 239
    political coverage on, 75–76, 316, 318
    political persuasion in, 324
    presenting political campaigns as dramas, 70
    social and political subtexts in, 324
    sponsor influence on programming content, 297
Thesis of message, determining, 372
Thirteenth Amendment, 253
Thompson, Dennis, 341
Thornburgh, Richard, 311
To Kill a Mockingbird (Lee), 112
Tompkins, Philip, 212
Touching, and compliance reinforcement, 194
Toulmin, Stephen, 87, 100, 339
Transcendence, and inconsistency, 150
Trent, Judith, 317
Triangulation strategy, 311
Trust
    building in sales, 217
    high credibility and, 115
    political persuasion and, 326–327
Truth
    arguments based on, 16
    Plato on, 33
    St. Augustine on, 343
Turk, Judy, 233
Twitchers, James, 263

Universal-humanitarian ethics, 345
USA Patriot Act, 40

Uses and gratifications model of campaign effects, 236

Vaguerie, Richard, 317
Valence, 134
VALS approach to market research, 272–273
Values
    attitude change and, 140
    clarification of, and conflict management, 202
    communication ethics and, 349–350
    corporate/organizational, 214
    ethics vs., 340
    gestalt, 389–390
    as good reasons for claims, 95
    social institutions and, 63, 344
    sources of, 343–344
    unexamined inheritances and, 141
Ventura, Jesse, 178
Verderber, Kathleen, 210
Verderber, Rudolph, 210
Vicarious modeling, and attitude formation, 136
Vision, rhetorical, 70
Visual imagery, 388

Waldman, Steven, 315
Wallace, Karl, 94–95
Walter, Otis, 382
War on terror, 52–53, 66–67, 311
Warrants for arguments, 93–94
Wayne, John, 323
Webster, James, 165
Weiss, Walter, 114
Whatmough, Joshua, 60
Whillock, Rita, 74
Whorf, Benjamin Lee, 58
Wilcox, Dennis, 239
Williamson, Judith, 288
Wills, Garry, 323
Wilmot, William, 203

Wilson, Woodrow, 10–11, 16
Wolf, Naomi, 173
Wolfe, Alan, 172
Women
    advertising's effect on,
        285–286
    feminine communication
        style, 204–207
    feminist norms and, 173
    impact of advertising on,
        286
    interpersonal communi-
        cation style of,
        204–207
    suffrage movement, 305
Wood, Julia T., 190, 196

Words. *See also* Language
    denotative and connota-
        tive meanings of, 57
    symbolic nature of, 54,
        56
Workplace
    ethical considerations
        regarding, 351
    gender communication
        differences in, 206
    organizational communi-
        cation in, 210–214
World Wide Web. *See also*
    Internet
    ethical considerations
        regarding, 350–351

freedom of expression
    and, 37
inherent democracy of,
    31
privacy issues concern-
    ing, 352

Zakaria, Fareed, 11
Zaller, John, 325
Zimbardo, Philip, 150
Zimmerman, Jan, 278
Zorn, Ted, 214